Collectibles
PRICE GUIDE 2005

Collectibles
PRICE GUIDE 2005

Judith Miller
with Mark Hill

DK PUBLISHING

LONDON, NEW YORK,
MELBOURNE, MUNICH, DELHI

A joint production from DORLING KINDERSLEY
and THE PRICE GUIDE COMPANY

THE PRICE GUIDE COMPANY LIMITED

Publisher Judith Miller

Collectibles Specialist Mark Hill

Publishing Manager Julie Brooke

European Consultant Martina Franke, Nicolas Tricaud de Montonnière

Managing Editor Carolyn Madden

Assistant Editors Sara Sturgess, Claire Smith

Editorial Assistants Jessica Bishop, Dan Dunlavey, Sandra Lange

Design and DTP Tim Scrivens, TJ Graphics

Additional Design Jason Hopper

Digital Image Co-ordinator Ellen Spalek

Photographers Graham Rae, Bruce Boyajian, John McKenzie, Byron Slater, Steve Tanner, Heike Löwenstein, Andy Johnson, Adam Gault

Indexer Hilary Bird

Workflow Consultant Bob Bousfield

Business Advisor Nick Croydon

DORLING KINDERSLEY LIMITED

Category Publisher Jackie Douglas

Managing Art Editor Heather McCarry

Managing Editor Julie Oughton

Designer Martin Dieguez

DTP Designer Mike Grigoletti

Production Sarah Dodd

Production Manager Sarah Coltman

While every care has been taken in the compilation of this guide, neither the authors nor the publishers accept any liability for any financial or other loss incurred by reliance placed on the information contained in *Collectibles Price Guide 2005*

First American Edition, 2004
00 01 02 03 04 05 10 9 8 7 6 5 4 3 2 1

Published in the United States by
DK Publishing Inc.
375 Hudson Street
New York, New York 10014

The Price Guide Company Ltd
info@thepriceguidecompany.com

A CIP catalog record for this book is available from the Library of Congress.

ISBN 0-7566-0523-7

Printed and bound in Germany by GGP Media GmbH

Discover more at
www.dk.com

CONTENTS

CONTENTS

INTRODUCTION

Welcome to the third edition of my Collectibles Price Guide, published in association with Dorling Kindersley. Over the thirty years that I have been collecting and writing about collectibles, I have found this market to be one of the most exciting and innovative areas around. Constantly expanding to take in new areas as well as developments in more established subjects, it is not surprising that it has become one of the most popular hobbies in the world.

By publishing our price guides annually and by covering a completely new selection of collectibles in each edition, we are able to reflect this innovation and growth by covering a huge range of subjects – presented this year across more than 65 subject headings. As well as more traditional subject areas, such as potlids and posters, we cover a number of newer areas such as men's clothing, character collectibles, early computers, and contemporary glass. Each image is specially commissioned in full-color and you can learn more about many items from the numerous footnotes and 'Closer Look' features, as well as discovering other useful resources through 'Find out more'. With this much change every year, I'm sure you'll agree with me that our Collectibles Price Guides build up over the years to become an invaluable reference library for experienced and new collectors alike.

Judith Miller.

LIST OF CONSULTANTS

Advertising

Rick & Sharon Corley
Toy Road Antiques, Winchester, OH

Joe & Sharon Happle
Sign of the Tymes, Lafayette, NJ

Books

Abby Schoolman
Bauman Rare Books
New York, NY

Arts & Crafts Ceramics

David Rago
David Rago Modern Auctions
Lambertville, NJ

Costume Jewelry

Roxanne Stuart
Pennsylvania

Bonny Yankauer
New Jersey

Eyeware

Esther Harris
Vintage Eyeware of New York City Inc.
New York, NY

Glass

Dudley Brown
James D. Julia Auctioneers, Inc.
Fairfield, MA

Stephen Saunders
The End of History
New York, NY

Hatpins

Anita & Al De Old
A Touch of Glass
New Jersey

Posters

Robert Chisholm & Lars Larsson
Chisholm Larsson Gallery
New York, NY

Nicolas Lowry
Swann Gallery
New York, NY

Sam Sarowitz
Posteritati
New York, NY

Sewing

Christina Bertrand
New York

Sporting

John Kanuit
Vintage Sports Collector
California

New Collectibles

Mark Block
Block Glass Ltd.
Trumbull, CT

Allan Shanks
American Art Glass Works
New York, NY

We are also very grateful to our friends and experts who gave us so much help – Barbara Blau of South Street Antiques Center, Sasha & Stacey of Neet-O-Rama, Ted & Diane Jones of Atlantique City, Joseph Soucy of Seaside Toy Center, and Christina Bertrand.

HOW TO USE THIS BOOK

Subcategory Heading
Indicates the subcategory of the main category heading and describes the general contents of the page.

Category Heading
Indicates the general category as listed in the table of contents on pp.5–6.

A Closer Look at...
Here, we highlight particularly interesting items or show identifying features, pointing out rare or desirable qualities.

The Source Code
The image is credited to its source with a code. See the "Key to Illustrations" on pp.576-579 for a full listing of dealers and auction houses.

Find out more...
To help you seek further information, these boxes list websites, books, and museums where you can find out more.

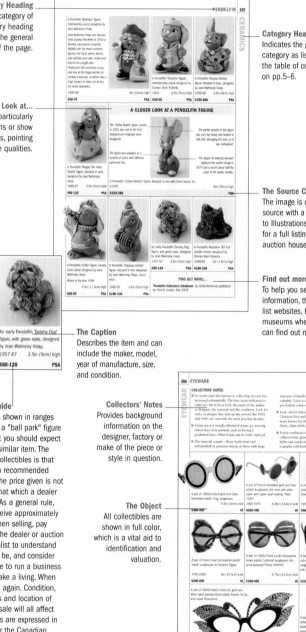

The Caption
Describes the item and can include the maker, model, year of manufacture, size, and condition.

The Price Guide
All prices are shown in ranges and give you a "ball park" figure close to what you should expect to pay for a similar item. The great joy of collectibles is that there is not a recommended retail price. The price given is not necessarily that which a dealer will pay you. As a general rule, expect to receive approximately 30% less. When selling, pay attention to the dealer or auction house specialist to understand why this may be, and consider that they have to run a business as well as make a living. When buying, listen again. Condition, market forces and location of the place of sale will all affect a price. Prices are expressed in US$ (even for the Canadian antiques shown). Canadian readers should refer to latest currency conversion rates at http://finance.yahoo.com/

Collectors' Notes
Provides background information on the designer, factory or make of the piece or style in question.

The Object
All collectibles are shown in full color, which is a vital aid to identification and valuation.

COLLECTORS' NOTES

■ Coca-Cola was developed by Dr John Styth Pemberton of Atlanta in 1886. It was initially marketed as a refreshing 'pick-me-up' and sold by pharmacists. Frank Robinson, Pemberton's bookkeeper, devised the name 'Coca-Cola' and his distinctive script remained in the logo.

■ From 1888-91 Pemberton sold the company to Asa Griggs Candler for around $2,300. Candler was a shrewd businessman who began to expand the company. The first magazine advertisement appeared in 1902 and advertising expanded soon after to many formats and media, in different countries and languages.

■ During the 1920s and 1930s, the Great Depression caused a lull in sales, but Coca-Cola was cleverly

marketed as being able to give a lift when 'at pause', as well as a tonic to be enjoyed in a group such as a family. This latter theme has continued and since then Coca-Cola has always celebrated enjoyment, togetherness and tradition in its advertisements.

■ Any genuine advertising items produced before 1910 are very rare. Visual impact, rare characters, popular artists and the changing face of the brand and how it represents itself are some of the indicators of value. Condition is also important, with worn or damaged goods being less valuable, unless extremely scarce or early. Since the 1970s, 'heritage' products featuring advertisements from previous decades have been produced. Collectors should familiarize themselves with the look and feel of these in order to recognize them.

A 1930s Coca-Cola lithographed tin advertising sign, with thermometer.

16.5in (42cm) high

$300-400 ATA

A Coca-Cola embossed tin advertising door push.

The shape of a Coca-Cola bottle can help to date a piece, as well as the style of the design of the piece itself. Before 1916, bottles were straight-sided and not contoured as the bottle in this example.

c1930   12.25in (31cm) long

$400-600 SOTT

A very rare Coca-Cola calendar for 1946 showing the 'Sprite Boy', in near mint condition.

The perky 'Sprite Boy', developed by legendary Coke artist Haddon Sundblom, is rarer than most advertising characters as he was only used between 1942 and 1958.

21in (53cm) high

$700-1,000 SOTT

A 1950s German Coca-Cola printed and laminated card advertising sign.

13in (33cm) high

$400-600 ATA

A 1950s American Coca-Cola gold-plated illuminated electric advertising wall clock, by Synchron.

11.75in (30cm) high

$180-220 PA

A very rare Coca-Cola printed tin-over-cardboard advertising plaque.

This piece is placed firmly in the 'Roaring Twenties' by the style of the dress and the short, boyish hair of the 'flapper'. This, together with her direct invitation to drink and a clear display of the legendary Coca-Cola logo, make this a desirable piece.

c1925

$1,200-1,800 SOTT

11in (28cm) wide

ADVERTISING

A Coca-Cola lithographed tin advertising tray, with holiday theme.

c1955   13.25in (33.5cm) long

$60-90   DH

A Coca-Cola advertising tin tip tray, with artwork by Hamilton King.

Born in Lewiston, Maine, Hamilton King is ranked amongst the most famous designers for Coca-Cola along with Norman Rockwell and Haddon Sundblom. He is known for his series of ladies with elegant and fashionable hats or hair for Coca-Cola amongst other designs. He died in 1952.

c1920

6in (15cm) long

$500-700   SOTT

A 1950s Coca-Cola 'Picnic Basket' advertising card bottle topper.

8.25in (21cm) wide

$80-120   SOTT

A pack of Coca-Cola advertising 'Service Woman' playing cards.

1943   3.5in (9cm) high

$70-100   SOTT

A pack of Coca-Cola advertising playing cards.

1951   3.5in (9cm) high

$60-90   SOTT

Two 1950s Coca-Cola Thanksgiving advertising carton stuffers.

7.5in (19cm) high

$25-35 set   SOTT

A Coca-Cola 'Toy Town' advertising cut-out.

1927   15in (38cm) wide

$100-150   SOTT

A 1940s Coca-Cola 'Gold Bottle' advertising match book.

1.5in (4cm) wide

$10-15   SOTT

A Coca-Cola paper advertising bottle protector.

1948   6.75in (17cm) wide

$5-7   SOTT

A Budgie No. 228 Karrier Bantam Bottle Lorry advertising Coca-Cola.
1959-64   *5.25in (13.5cm) wide*
$120-180   **SOTT**

A late 1950s Matchbox No. 37 Karrier Bantam Coca-Cola advertising lorry, with 'even' load, boxed.
$80-120   **SOTT**

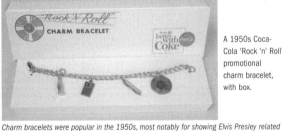

A 1950s Coca-Cola 'Rock 'n' Roll' promotional charm bracelet, with box.

Charm bracelets were popular in the 1950s, most notably for showing Elvis Presley related items.

$60-90   **SOTT**

A 1950s/60s Coca-Cola 15-year service pin, set with three stones.
     0.75in (2cm) wide
$80-120   **SOTT**

A 1950s Coca-Cola bottle novelty lighter.

These lighters were also available in the form of cans.

2.5in (6.5cm) high
$25-35   **SOTT**

A 1950s Coca-Cola advertising plastic music box cooler.
2.75in (7cm) wide
$60-90   **SOTT**

An American 'Vendo 80' Coca-Cola coin-operated vending machine, restored.

Large pieces like this are considered decorative and almost 'architectural' pieces.

c1955   *58in (147cm) high*
$1,200-1,800   **ATK**

A Pepsi Evervess sparkling water advertising tin tip tray.
6in (15cm) wide
$50-70   **SOTT**

A 1950s Coca-Cola advertising celluloid pencil, with bottle-shaped clip.
8.5in (21.5cm) long
$30-40   **SOTT**

A 1950s Pepsi-Cola advertising miniature toy truck, with applied paper label.
2in (5cm) wide
$40-60   **SOTT**

FIND OUT MORE...

'Petretti's Coca-Cola Collectibles Price Guide', *by Allan Petretti, published by Krause Publications, 11th edition, July 2001.*

'Petretti's Soda Pop Collectibles Price Guide', *by Allan Petretti, published by Krause Publications, 3rd edition, March 2003.*

COLLECTORS' NOTES

■ Characters have been used by companies to advertise their products, bringing them a cheerful and personal feel, for decades. They are most often used for products aimed at children, making the product more appealing to them, with the intention of increasing customer loyalty.

■ Always look for those that are immediately recognizable to as many people as possible – nostalgia is a key driver for the market. As generations come and go, characters are introduced and retired – and even updated. Those that have the greatest appeal to the most people are likely to hold higher values.

■ The best known products or brands will usually have a loyal following from collectors of advertising in other forms such as signs or packaging, so these may be more valuable due to increased demand. Characters that have appeared on TV and in advertisements will usually be desirable.

■ Condition is important as materials, particularly plastics, rubbers, and painted surfaces, can degrade. Examine examples carefully as many were played with and may show signs of wear, 'customization' or damage. Those in mint condition will command a premium. Japanese examples can be rare and desirable as are those designed by notable illustrators known for their cartoon of character work.

A late 1960s Campbell's Soup 'Campbell Kid' vinyl mail-out promotional 'Chef' doll, in original card mailing box, mint condition.

Dolls could be obtained by sending in labels from two different Campbell's '4 Beans' cans plus $1.25.

c1966   10.25in (26cm) high

$60-90   **PA**

A pair of Campbell's Soup 'Campbell Kid' mail-out boy and girl dolls, complete with clothes and mailing boxes, in mint condition.

Produced to commemorate the American Bicentennial.

c1976 boy 10in (25.5cm) high

$80-120   **PA**

A 'Mr Peanut' painted and molded papier-mâché advertising container, possibly 1920s.

Ever since the year 1916 'Mr Peanut' has been used in national advertising campaigns as a trademark for Planters Peanuts.

12.25in (31cm) high

$100-150   **PA**

A 1980s Japanese Campbell's Soup handpainted ceramic advertising figurine.

'Campbell Kids', sketched by Philadelphia illustrator Grace Wiederseim in 1904, were invented for a series of streetcar advertisements. Originally posed as little boys and girls, they matured over time and began performing more adult tasks such as cooking.

7.75in (19.5cm) high

$180-220   **PA**

A pair of Eugene Campbell's Soup 'Campbell Kids' vinyl collectible dolls, mint condition, boxed.

1984   boxes 10.25in (26cm) high

$60-90   **PA**

A 1930s 'Mr Peanut' painted carved wooden string-jointed advertising figure.

9in (23cm) high

$100-150   **PA**

A 1960s 'Mr Peanut' black and tan painted plastic money bank, molded "MADE IN USA".

8.25in (21cm) high

$60-90   **PA**

A 'Mr Peanut' handpainted bisque nodder doll.

Unusual for 'Mr Peanut', this figure does not have the typical cane in his hand.

6.5in (16.5cm) high

$180-220 PA

A 'Count Chocula' vinyl cereal advertising figure, by General Mills Inc.

c1975   8in (20.5cm) high

$40-60 PA

A mid-1970s Quaker Oats 'Captain Crunch' vinyl advertising money bank, back stamped "Captain Crunch".

6.75in (17.5cm) high

$30-40 PA

A mid-1970s 'Fruit Brute' vinyl advertising figure, by General Mills Inc.

'Fruit Brute' was the fourth 'monster' advertised cereal produced by General Mills, but also the least popular, not enjoying as long a shelf-life as 'Count Chocula' and his friends.

c1975   7.5in (19cm) high

$60-90 PA

A 1970s 'Marky Maypo' vinyl cereal advertising figure.

Marky Maypo was developed by leading illustrator John Hubley, who worked on many of Disney's 1930s films including Pinocchio, Dumbo, and Bambi. He was laid off by Disney due to his involvement in industrial action against the company and his possible Communist leanings. He then designed Marky to advertise the maple syrup flavored cereal and brought about a rebirth in popularity for the ailing brand. Hubley was also responsible for developing Mr Magoo, based on his uncle, for UPA.

9in (23cm) high

$30-50 PA

A Kellogg's 'Friction Powered Mover' parrot, by Talbot Toys, carded and in mint condition.

1984   card 8.5in (21.5cm) high

$12-18 PA

A 1960s 'Captain D's Seafood' plastic advertising figure.

8in (20.5cm) high

$50-70 PA

A 1960s 'Teddy Snow Crop Frozen Foods' vinyl squeaky advertising toy.

8.75in (22cm) high

$250-350 PA

An Applause 'Chocolate Mousse' handpainted ceramic advertising figurine, with wording to base.

1984   5.25in (13.5cm) high

$80-120 PA

A rare 'Elsie' rubber advertising figurine cow, made by The Oak Rubber Co., with stopper to base.

One of the US best known advertising characters, Elsie was introduced in the late 1930s by the Borden Dairy to advertise their dairy-based products. She appeared at the 1939 New York World's Fair, on the radio, in print and on TV.

A 1970s Japanese 'Colonel Sanders' K.F.C. painted plastic advertising figurine money bank, with applied paper label, moves at waist.

A Green Giant Co. 'Sprout Touch Lamp' advertising table lamp, with plastic figurine.

c1985   14.25in (36cm) high

$70-100   PA

5in (13cm) high

$120-180   PA

8in (20.5cm) high

$180-220   PA

A CLOSER LOOK AT AN ADVERTISING FIGURE

This character was designed by Jim Henson, creator of the Muppets, and is one of the first Muppets collectibles.

Wontkins was one of two characters used in the extremely popular Wilkins coffee advertisements from 1957.

A pair of 1950s Hamm's Beer ceramics salt and pepper shakers, feet stamped "JAPAN".

4.25in (10.5cm) high

$120-180   PA

He was part of a mail-in promotion from 1958 where Wilkins coffee buyers sent in tokens to receive Wilkins dolls. He is in mint condition.

Wontkins was grumpy and sad and refused to drink Wilkins coffee, despite advice from his cheerful sidekick Wilkins.

A very rare Wilkins Coffee 'Wontkins' vinyl advertising figural puppet, in clean condition.

1958   *7in (17.5cm) high*

$250-300   PA

A 'Speedy' Alka Seltzer vinyl advertising figure, for Miles Inc.

'Speedy' was first called 'Sparky' when he was developed by artist Bob Watkins and made his debut under his new name in 1952. He featured in over 200 TV commercials between 1953 and the mid-1960s but was shelved shortly after, making a return during the 1980s. He is now seen from time to time wearing a Hawaiian shirt!

A Sprite 'Lucky Lemon' soft plastic/vinyl talking advertising figure, holding a plastic can of Sprite, push button to operate the battery powered mechanism inside.

c1985   7in (17.5cm) high

$25-35   PA

1963   8in (20cm) high

$300-400   PA

A 1930s/40s 'Peppy Dog Food' cast and handpainted plaster advertising money box.

8in (20.5cm) high

$120-180   PA

A 1950s National Radio sewn fabric and card advertising figure.

6in (15cm) high

$80-120   **PA**

A French 'Achille' Sparkplugs painted rubber advertising figurine, foot molded "MODELE DEPOSE", grip molded "General Motors France".

5.5in (14cm) high

$100-150   **PA**

A rare 1940s 'Big Aggie' cast and handpainted plaster advertising figurine, the tractor with WNAX lettering.

WNAX was established in 1922 and was one of the first commercial radio stations set up in South Dakota. It is aimed at the agricultural community.

7.25in (18.5cm) high

$300-400   **PA**

A 1960s rare Semco Ltd Hoover 'FLUFF' vinyl or soft plastic advertising figure, stopper marked "Made in Germany".

'Fluff' is from a range of three characters used to advertise Hoover's vacuum cleaners in the 1960s, the others being 'Dust' and 'Grit'.

6.25in (16cm) high

$600-900   **PA**

A Norge Mighty Midget 'Sealed Rollator Refrigeration Mechanism' handpainted composition advertising figurine.

c1925   *6.5in (16.5cm) high*

$220-280   **PA**

A 1970s Humble Oil plush and vinyl-headed tiger hand puppet.

8.75in (22cm) high

$100-150   **PA**

A KOOL Cigarettes painted cast metal advertising lighter, in the form of a penguin, with partial transfer reading 'Light up a KOOL'.

The penguin was a popular animal in the 1930s and appeared in many forms and motifs.

c1930   *4in (10cm) high*

$120-180   **PA**

A 1960s Nikon 'eyeball' plastic advertising figurine, the back stamped "Nikon".

5.75in (14.5cm) high

$200-300   **PA**

A 'Buddy Lee' molded hard plastic advertising doll, dressed in Lee denims, possibly 1960s.

13in (33cm) high

$250-300   **PA**

ADVERTISING

COLLECTORS' NOTES

■ Sample and pocket-sized tins can make an excellent start to tin collecting. Small and easy to store, they are also usually more affordable than their larger relations. Given away as promotions by shops, most sample tins are simply smaller versions of the larger tin, using the same colors and, where space allows, graphics.

■ Although produced in large numbers, many are rare as they would have been thrown away after use. Condition is important, with many having been damaged from being carried around in pockets or bags. Look for those that bear attractive and appealing designs in the style of period, such as Art Deco and the 1950s. Examples with images that appeal to another collectible market will usually be more sought after, as are those for notable brands or products .

A Colgate & Co. 'Cashmere Bouquet Talc' sample powder tin.

2in (5cm) high

$70-100　　　　　　　　　　**TRA**

A 'Violets of Sicily For The Complexion And Toilet' sample powder tin.

1.5in (4cm) high

$30-50　　　　　　　　**TRA**

A 'Z.B.T. Olive Oil Baby Powder' sample tin.

2.25in (5.5cm) high

$70-100　　　　　　　**TRA**

A 1930s 'Mennen Borated Powder' printed sample tin.

2in (5cm) high

$30-50　　　　　　　**TRA**

A Dr. J.B. Lynas & Son 'Complexion Beautifier' pocket-sized tin, with printed paper label.

1.5in (3.5cm) wide

$30-40　　　　　　**TRA**

A Colgate & Co. 'Florient Flowers of the Orient' sample powder tin.

2.25in (5.5cm) high

$50-70　　　　　　　**TRA**

A 1930s 'Tangee Face Powder' sample tin.

1.5in (4cm) wide

$25-35　　　　　　　**TRA**

An 'Outdoor Girl The Olive Oil Face Powder' sample tin.

1.5in (4cm) wide

$30-40　　　　　　**TRA**

A 1930s Tuxedo Club Pomade transfer-lithographed pocket-sized tin, by Newbro Mfg Co.

1.75in (4.5cm) diam

$18-22　　　　　　**PKA**

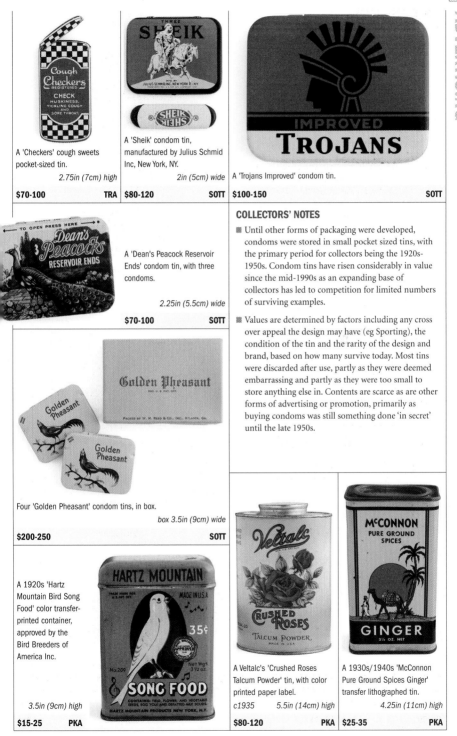

A 'Checkers' cough sweets pocket-sized tin.

2.75in (7cm) high

$70-100   TRA

A 'Sheik' condom tin, manufactured by Julius Schmid Inc, New York, NY.

2in (5cm) wide

$80-120   SOTT

A 'Trojans Improved' condom tin.

$100-150   SOTT

A 'Dean's Peacock Reservoir Ends' condom tin, with three condoms.

2.25in (5.5cm) wide

$70-100   SOTT

COLLECTORS' NOTES

■ Until other forms of packaging were developed, condoms were stored in small pocket sized tins, with the primary period for collectors being the 1920s-1950s. Condom tins have risen considerably in value since the mid-1990s as an expanding base of collectors has led to competition for limited numbers of surviving examples.

■ Values are determined by factors including any cross over appeal the design may have (eg Sporting), the condition of the tin and the rarity of the design and brand, based on how many survive today. Most tins were discarded after use, partly as they were deemed embarrassing and partly as they were too small to store anything else in. Contents are scarce as are other forms of advertising or promotion, primarily as buying condoms was still something done 'in secret' until the late 1950s.

Four 'Golden Pheasant' condom tins, in box.

box 3.5in (9cm) wide

$200-250   SOTT

A 1920s 'Hartz Mountain Bird Song Food' color transfer-printed container, approved by the Bird Breeders of America Inc.

3.5in (9cm) high

$15-25   PKA

A Veltalc's 'Crushed Roses Talcum Powder' tin, with color printed paper label.

c1935   5.5in (14cm) high

$80-120   PKA

A 1930s/1940s 'McConnon Pure Ground Spices Ginger' transfer lithographed tin.

4.25in (11cm) high

$25-35   PKA

A Lambert's 'Death To Lice' tin, by The Klein-Lambert Co., 'For Lice on Poultry, Horses, Cattle etc'.

c1900   *7in (17.5cm) high*

$70-100   **PKA**

An un-opened Canadian dual language Acme Louse Killer tin and card cylindrical carton, by Frasier, Thornton & Co. Limited of Cookshire, Quebec, with color printed paper label.

5.5in (14cm) high

$70-100   **PKA**

A Bobwhite Chemical Corporation 'Kil-Tox' combined insecticide and fungicide tin, with printed paper label.

c1925   *7in (17.5cm) high*

$50-70   **PKA**

A Seibert lithographed tinplate Magic Fly Killer, with five wicks.

c1913-20   4.75in (12cm) diam

$50-70   **PKA**

An Ant Buttons printed card box, manufactured by Harris Products Company Inc. and advertised in Good Housekeeping.

1953

$40-60   **PKA**

A 'Ratmousine' printed card box, containing tube of combined rodent beetle and cockroach killer.

1926   *4.75in (12cm) long*

$40-60   **PKA**

A 1930s 'Sergeant's' antiwormer color lithographed card advertising standee.

15.25in (39cm) high

$300-400   **PKA**

A CLOSER LOOK AT A PESTICIDE TIN

The printed tin bears an attractive design, which would have made it easier to leave out in a room, without being too ugly.

The lithograph is still in excellent condition with bright colors and no serious scratches, wear or rust. It also retains its original paper wrapping, which is rare.

Wetting the yellow pads at the center of the daisies attracts flies who land on them and eat the poison.

The poison is arsenic based, and it bears a label warning the owners of the poison.

A 'Daisy Fly Killer' color lithographed tinplate tin.

1929   *tin 6in (15.5cm) long*

$70-100   **PKA**

A 1920s Wrigley's Chewing Gum gum packet, with five foil-wrapped sticks.

3.25in (8cm) long

$2-3   PKA

A 1960s/1970s Wrigley's Chewing Gum packet, with five sticks.

3.25in (8cm) long

$2-3   PKA

A 1910s Wrigley's Chewing Gum 'Perfumes The Breath', the interior printed with 'Profit Sharing' coupon wording showing that this could be redeemed against items from their catalog.

2.75in (7cm) long

$6-9   PKA

A Fan Tan chewing gum packet, with five foil-wrapped sticks.

This vintage packet, still containing sticks of gum, is much rarer than those produced by market leader Wrigley's at the same time.

c1920   *3in (7.5cm) long*

$40-60   PKA

A 1920s/1930s Gold Tip Tropical Gum card box.

3.25in (8cm) wide

$10-15   PKA

A 1930s Cretors Popcorn card seasoning box.

6.75in (17cm) high

$15-20   SOTT

A 1970s Kellogg's 'Sugar Smacks' cereal packet showing 'Dig 'Em' the frog.

9.25in (23.5cm) high

$22-28   PA

A CLOSER LOOK AT A POPCORN BOX

Popular Ohio amusement park 'Idora Park' was opened in 1895 and closed in 1984 after a fire destroyed its main attraction and ride.

Although thousands of boxes would have been made and sold, the vast majority would have been thrown away after the popcorn had been eaten, making surviving examples rare.

The graphics are typical of the 1960s, when the park enjoyed one of its heydays. The image of the little girl with the balloon was used elsewhere at the park, such as on trash cans and posters.

The condition of the box is excellent, with no tears, stains or crushed areas.

A rare 1960s popcorn box, from Idora Park, outside Youngstown, Ohio, in near mint condition.

6.75in (17cm) high

$40-60   PKA

A Quaker 'Quake' commemorative cereal packet.

An original from the 1970s would cost up to $60-70. It can be distinguished from this commemorative packet by signs of age and original, rather than modern, dates.

1990   10in (25.5cm) high

$12-18   **PA**

A 1940s 'Whistle Soda' advertising match book, with elf logo.

2in (5cm) wide

$10-15   **SOTT**

A CLOSER LOOK AT A STONEWARE CROCK

It retains its original ceramic lid. It is in excellent condition. The lids are often lost or replaced.

This is an early example of Heinz's forms of packaging. Apple Butter was introduced in the 1870s.

Although some of the label has been lost, it is still largely intact and shows an early version of the Heinz logo and brand.

The design is attractive, indicative of the contents and finely lithographed with many colors.

A Heinz 'Apple Butter' stoneware crock, with finely printed label, some missing.

c1910   8.25in (21cm) high

$300-400   **PKA**

A very rare 1950s Nabisco 'Cowboys and Indians Cookies' card box.

This design is extremely rare.

5in (13cm) wide

$70-100   **SOTT**

A 1940s 'Happy Dog Food' cubes cylindrical card and paper carton, from Happy Mills of Memphis, Tenn.

5in (13cm) high

$12-18   **PKA**

A 'What A Treat for Parrakeets' glass jar, with contents.

c1955   4.5in (11.5cm) high

$30-50   **PKA**

A 1930s Giusti's bread shop lithographed tin plate advertising sign.

20in (50.5cm) wide

$250-300 **PKA**

A Grape-Nuts Flakes color lithographed paper and card cereal advertising sign.

c1955 20.5in (52cm) wide

$250-300 **PKA**

A 1930s Art Deco 'The Gift For All Occasions' advertisement for chocolates, reverse transfer on glass.

The color is applied to the reverse of the glass plate so that when it is backlit, the colors light up, but when unlit, the wording is white.

13.75in (35cm) wide

$50-70 **PKA**

A Budweiser 'Say When' lithographed tin advertising plaque, by Beach, with smartly dressed couple cooking with Budweiser.

16in (40cm) diam

$300-500 **SK**

A late 1940s/early 1950s Hires root beer advertising card-over-tin sign.

8.5in (21.5cm) wide

$150-200 **SOTT**

A Ovaltine printed canvas-on-card shop advertising sign.

c1930 16.25in (41cm) high

$200-250 **PKA**

A large 1910s Bank Note Cigars color lithographed card shop advertising standee, with easel back.

21.25in (54cm) high

$250-350 **TRA**

A Picobac tobacco store advertising sign, with tinplate framer and area for writing prices.

10in (25.5cm) high

$30-50 **TRA**

A Mayo's Plug color printed canvas/linen tobacco advertising sign.

30in (76cm) high

$400-600 **TRA**

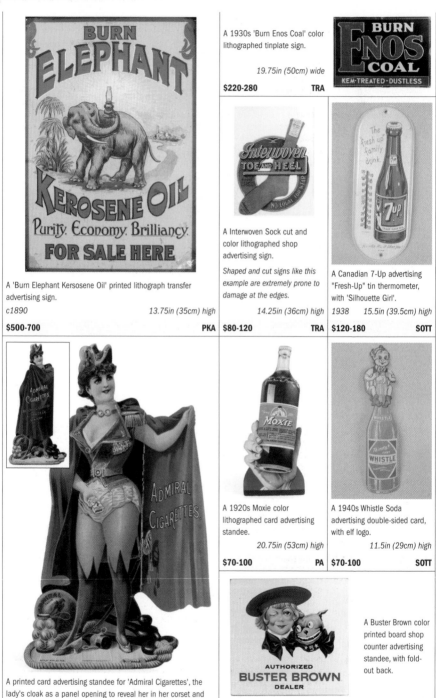

A 'Burn Elephant Kersoene Oil' printed lithograph transfer advertising sign.

c1890   *13.75in (35cm) high*

$500-700   **PKA**

A 1930s 'Burn Enos Coal' color lithographed tinplate sign.

19.75in (50cm) wide

$220-280   **TRA**

A Interwoven Sock cut and color lithographed shop advertising sign.

Shaped and cut signs like this example are extremely prone to damage at the edges.

14.25in (36cm) high

$80-120   **TRA**

A Canadian 7-Up advertising "Fresh-Up" tin thermometer, with 'Silhouette Girl'.

1938   *15.5in (39.5cm) high*

$120-180   **SOTT**

A printed card advertising standee for 'Admiral Cigarettes', the lady's cloak as a panel opening to reveal her in her corset and stockings, with repair to neck.

$80-120   **SOTT**

A 1920s Moxie color lithographed card advertising standee.

20.75in (53cm) high

$70-100   **PA**

A 1940s Whistle Soda advertising double-sided card, with elf logo.

11.5in (29cm) high

$70-100   **SOTT**

A Buster Brown color printed board shop counter advertising standee, with fold-out back.

c1955   *13.5in (34.5cm) high*

$200-250   **TRA**

A CLOSER LOOK AT AN ADVERTISING CALENDAR

An F.J. Offerman Art Works Inc. advertising calendar, with printed color lithograph of 'Bird of A Feather', a lady with a parakeet.

The design, the bold use of color and the style of the lady's haircut are typical of the Art Deco style.

1935   18.75in (47.5cm) high

$80-120   **TRA**

The choice of an elegant and beautiful winged fairy resting by a waterside and the naturalistic branches around the edge are typical of the Art Nouveau style.

The design is well composed. The flowers falling out of the frame add interest and depth.

The chromolithographic image is extremely well printed, with many strong colors and no signs of rubbing or fading.

The flowing skirt and the vines around the borders are further highlighted with gilding and embossed areas.

An extremely fine Larkin Soap Co. color lithographed advertising calendar for 1904.

13in (33cm) high

$600-900   **TRA**

A complete 'Dickinson's Globe Poultry Feeds' color lithographed advertising calendar from 1920.

14.75in (37.5cm) high

$280-320   **PKA**

A Life Savers lithographed tin shop display stand.

c1925   15.25in (38.5cm) long

$700-1,000   **SOTT**

A 1930s 'Colgate Week-End Package', the card box with Art Deco label containing Colgate's Charmis Cold Cream, Cashmere Bouquet Talc, Colgate's Ribbon Dental Cream, and Palmolive Soap.

This bijou box contained all that an elegant lady about town, as seen on the lid of the box, may need for a weekend away from the comforts of Fifth Avenue and her boudoir. As well as being complete and unopened, the extremely attractive artwork that exemplifies the Art Deco movement makes this an attractive piece.

5in (12.5cm) high

$100-150   **TRA**

A rare 'Mr Peanut Blanched Peanuts Roasted in Coconut Oil' card shop display dispenser.

1939   9.25in (23.5cm) wide

$300-500   **PA**

A large Heinz pickle plastic hanging shop display.

The Heinz pickle was introduced in 1893 at the Chicago World's Fair and has grown to become a legendary motif for the company.

c1970   19.25in (49cm) wide

$80-120   **PA**

COLLECTORS' NOTES

■ Pencil clips were made to fit over the shaft of wooden pencils so that they could be safely clipped inside a pocket like more expensive mechanical, propelling pencils. Amongst the many small and functional objects made, advertisers saw that when they were clipped on a pocket, carried and used, the colorful decal would advertise their product in many places for long periods of time.

■ Men and children were primary targets, as they were less likely to use a bag and more likely to use a pencil and carry it around in a jacket. As a result, male– and household–oriented products rather than female interests abound. Those in more unusual shapes, where the clip is more than a small decal applied to a standard clip, are generally more valuable, as are those for recognizable brands that are already collected.

A 'Drink Barg's It's Good' pencil clip.

2in (5cm) long

$25-35   **TRA**

A '45 Dixie Beer' pencil clip.

2in (5cm) long

$15-20   **TRA**

A 'Krueger Beer Ales' pencil clip.

2in (5cm) long

$20-30   **TRA**

A 'Drink Regal Beer' pencil clip.

2in (5cm) long

$15-20   **TRA**

A '7 Up' pencil clip.

2in (5cm) long

$15-20   **TRA**

A 'Buy NBC Bread' pencil clip.

2in (5cm) long

$30-40   **TRA**

A 'The Feeders' Silent Partner' pencil clip.

2in (5cm) long

$25-35   **TRA**

A 'Red Goose Shoes' pencil clip.

2.25in (6cm) long

$40-60   **TRA**

A 'Mascot Crushed Cut Tobacco' advertising hand-held mirror.

2.25in (5.5cm) wide

$70-100   **TRA**

A rare 'Oliver Plow' advertising pocket mirror, showing a portrait of James Oliver.

Manufacturer James Oliver revolutionized the plow industry from his earliest experiments in 1855. His 'chilled' mold plow was less brittle and much sharper due to chilling the edge when it was being molded. By 1906, he held 49 patents and had become extremely wealthy.

2.75in (7cm) high

$250-350　　　　　　　　　　　　　　　　**TRA**

An Angelus Marshmallows advertising mirror, with putto on a box image.

2.75in (7cm) high

$80-120　　　　**TRA**

A Campbell's Soup advertising pocket mirror.

1.75in (4.5cm) wide

$120-180　　　　**TRA**

A 'Cooper Underwear Co. Buy White Cat Union Suits' advertising pocket mirror.

2.75in (7cm) high

$70-100　　　　**TRA**

A 'Carmen Complexion Powder' advertising pocket mirror.

1.75in (4.5cm) wide

$100-150　　　　**TRA**

An 'International Tailoring Co. King of Tailors' printed tin and metal advertising game and pocket mirror.

The addition of a game adds to the value and desirability of this example. The aim of the game is to get the four small white balls into the lion's mouth to give him 'teeth'. As with other examples, the mirror is on the reverse.

1.75in (4.5cm) diam

$180-220　　　　　　　　　　　　　　　　**TRA**

A 'Butterfinger' printed tin advertising whistle.

2.75in (7cm) long

$30-50　　　　**TRA**

A 'Buster Brown Shoes' color lithographed tinplate advertising whistle.

3in (7.5cm) high

$80-120　　　　**TRA**

A 'Red Goose Shoes' printed tin advertising whistle.

2.5in (6.5cm) long

$30-40　　　　**TRA**

A 'Peters Weatherbird Shoes for Girls for Boys' printed tin tubular advertising whistle.

1.25in (3cm) high

$70-100 **TRA**

A 'Poll Parrot Shoes For Boys And Girls Star Brand Shoes Are Better' printed tin advertising whistle toy.

2.25in (6cm) high

$60-90 **TRA**

A 1940s Whistle Soda advertising tin whistle.

2in (5cm) wide

$40-60 **SOTT**

A General Electric Refrigerators celluloid and metal advertising tape measure, the reverse reading "Ahrens Refrigerator company, 504-506 N. Broadway Oklahoma City, Oklahoma".

1.5in (3.5cm) wide

$80-120 **TRA**

A 'Sears Roebuck & Co. David Bradley Plows Cultivators, Planters etc' celluloid and metal advertising tape measure, with guarantee wording to reverse.

1.75in (4.5cm) wide

$200-250 **TRA**

A 'Stromberg New Vis-a-gas Carburettor' celluloid and metal advertising tape measure.

1.5in (3.5cm) wide

$100-150 **TRA**

A 'Eat Purity Ice Cream' printed tin and wood advertising spinning top toy.

1.25in (3cm) high

$40-60 **TRA**

A 'Tasty Kake' printed tin and wood advertising spinning top toy.

1.25in (3cm) high

$25-35 **TRA**

A 'Twinkle Shoes' printed tin and wood advertising spinning top toy.

1.25in (3cm) high

$60-90 **TRA**

A 'McElree's Cardui, The Woman's Tonic' celluloid and metal advertising tape measure reading "...TAKE...CARDUI THE WOMAN'S TONIC", with image of a lady sailor steering a ship.

1.75in (4.5cm) wide

$120-180 **TRA**

A 'Twinkie Shoes' light green lithographed tin advertising clicker.

1.75in (4.5cm) long

$70-100   TRA

A 'Bakers' painted pot metal advertising pencil sharpener, in the shape of a lady serving drinks.

1.75in (4.5cm) high

$50-70   TRA

A 'Peacock Reservoir Ends' condom advertising money clip.

2.25in (5.5cm) high

$70-100   SOTT

A 'Moxie' double-sided color lithographed advertising fan.

1924   8in (20cm) high

$80-120   TRA

An Indian Maiden color lithographed fan, by Hayes Lithog. Co of Buffalo, with wooden handle.

13.25in (33.5cm) high

$50-80   TRA

A 'Bailey's...' advertising fan, the waxed paper leaf with printed cherry blossom pattern, and card sticks.

8in (20cm) high

$60-90   PKA

A 1950s 'Drink Mountain Dew - It'll Tickle Yore Innards' soda jerk hat.

10.75in (27.5cm) long

$30-40   SOTT

A scarce 1960s Mountain Dew 'Yell-A-Phone' megaphone.

7in (18cm) high

$70-100   SOTT

A rare and unusual 'Brunswick Corporation King' plastic coated wood advertising duck pin.

c1955   9.5in (24cm) high

$70-100   TRA

COLLECTORS' NOTES

■ Native Americans have been making baskets for hundreds of years for storage, for serving dishes, for transporting goods, and for ceremonial use.

■ While designs and styles remained static over the years, each of the tribes specialized in their own manufacturing techniques, use of materials and design, which often have specific or ritualistic meanings. All these can help to locate and date an item.

■ It wasn't until the late 19th century arrival of Westerners who began collecting the baskets, that previously unused materials came to be used, such as beads, commercial yarns, and non-native feathers. It also lead to tribes 'borrowing' popular features from other tribes to make their own products more desirable.

■ Many tribes are still making baskets today for domestic use and tourist markets.

An unusual early 20thC Apache weave pinched top basketry olla, for gathering seeds or nuts.

An olla is a bottle-shaped basket and is often used for holding seeds or water.

8.25in (21cm) high

$120-180   **ALL**

A 20thC Apache woven pitch-covered, wide bottom tus, with original braided horsehair handle.

A tus or water jar typically has a narrow neck, is tightly woven and covered in pitch to make it waterproof.

8.5in (21.5cm) high

$150-200   **ALL**

An early 20thC Paiute upright basketry bottle, with upright base and fully covered with basketry in banded design.

12in (30.5cm) high

$150-200   **ALL**

A Paiute-style fully beaded vessel, with bright yellow, red, black, and blue beads, with buckskin base.

c1950   3.5in (9cm) high

$100-150   **ALL**

A rare early 20thC Salish woven upright basketry vessel, with wide base, bulbous center, and three-color imbricated design.

13in (33cm) high

$280-320   **ALL**

An early 20thC Salish hardsided upright bowl, three-color imbricated design, half of the rim loops missing.

6.5in (16.5cm) high

$120-180   **ALL**

A Walapai woven basketry seed jar or tus, with original braided horsehair attachments.

c1950   8in (20cm) high

$70-100   **ALL**

A Havasupai upright basketry vessel, with flared top and encircling bands of dark brown and orange.

c1950   10in (25.5cm) high

$150-200   **ALL**

A Pima miniature basketry olla, with flattened bottom and traditional Pima modified key design.

These tiny baskets are a speciality of the Pima and display the skill of the weaver. They are still being made today.

c1970   1.25in (3cm) high

$120-180   **ALL**

An early 20thC huge Walapai well-woven storage basket, with green bands of color and small black accents.

12.25in (31cm) high

$250-350 ALL

An Apache Jicarilla deep basketry bowl, with weave, banded geometrics and a central reverse star design.

c1940 *14in (35.5cm) high*

$600-900 ALL

A Papago basketry tray, with a checkered blossom in devil's claw pattern.

The Papago are the most prolific of the Native American basket makers today and produce baskets for both the domestic and tourist market.

c1950 *9in (23cm) high*

$100-150 ALL

An early 20thC Tlingit straight-sided basketry bowl, with red and yellow exterior geometrics.

Tlingit baskets are usually decorated with repeating bands of geometric designs using 'false' embroidery that does not show on the inside of the basket.

5in (12.5cm) high

$300-500 ALL

A Havasupai reverse design woven conical basket, with rim and two bands of gold coloring.

c1950 *10.25in (26cm) high*

$60-90 ALL

A Paiute cone-shaped basketry vessel, with three encircling bands of contrasting color.

c1930 *10in (25.5cm) high*

$120-180 ALL

A CLOSER LOOK AT A NAVAJO BASKET

The design is typical with the inner black representing the underworld, the red the earth, and the outer black the upper world.

These baskets were used in a number of ways, including during wedding ceremonies where they held sacred corn meal.

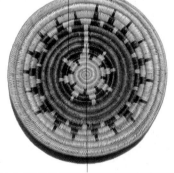

An Apache conical-shaped burden basket, with deer and geometric figures, buckskin and tin cone suspensions.

Burden baskets have a frame or suspension system so that they can be carried comfortably. The tin suspensions are typical of Apache baskets and used to scare away snakes.

c1980 *17in (43cm) high*

$280-320 ALL

The plain line through the rings is called the 'Shipapu' and represents a path of communication between the worlds. The end of the coil of the weaving must end in line with the 'Shipapu' making it easy to align the basket to the east even when dark.

A Navajo polychrome wedding basket, with three red coils, with black radiating stepped inner and outer design and braided rim.

c1950 *13in (33cm) diam*

$180-220 ALL

COLLECTORS' NOTES

■ Native American pottery has been made for nearly 2,000 years, dating back to the Anasazi, whose Pueblo (village) descendants, such as the Hopi and Navajo, still produce pottery today. Many variations exist and the style indicates a specific culture. Within each culture, families also have their own styles.

■ A core foundation reflected in the pottery is that everything is 'from the earth'. Clays are sourced locally and techniques are traditional, using only natural materials. Hopi pottery (produced around North West Arizona) is one of the oldest and most widely collected. The slight variation in colors or 'blush' caused by the traditional firing process is much

admired as is the 'ring' achieved when a Hopi pot is tapped.

■ Pieces are still being made in traditional methods today. Ancient or vintage pots, most notably those made by Nampeyo, (b. c1859) usually command high prices. Equally, the work of notable and more recent and contemporary potters can be valuable. Look for traditional forms and designs, such as geometric patterns, the sun, and eagles, many of which have been revived and reinterpreted by today's artists. Always buy vintage pots from a reputable source.

A late 20thC Mata Ortiz thin-walled, black-on-black Casas Grandes pottery olla.

9.75in (25cm) high

$150-200   **ALL**

A late 20thC Mata Ortiz huge black-on-black Casas Grandes thin-walled pottery olla, signed "Tomas Ozuna".

It is the immense size that makes this olla (or 'pot') so valuable, as well as the fact that it is decorated traditionally.

16.5in (42cm) high

$400-600   **ALL**

A rare late 20thC Mata Ortiz thin-walled, upright polychrome olla, with human, bird, and other geometric designs, signed "Sabino Villalta H".

9in (23cm) high

$120-180   **ALL**

A mid-to late 20thC Hopi pottery vessel, by Joy Navasie, with fine stylized geometrics in polychrome on a cream colored slip, signed.

Navasie uses a frog symbol to sign her work and has thus become known as the 'Frog Woman'.

5.75in (14.5cm) high

$400-600   **ALL**

A CLOSER LOOK AT A MATA ORTIZ OLLA

Mata Ortiz is connected to an ancient tradition of pottery, based on the 'Casas Grandes' culture.

This ancient pottery making tradition was revived in the 1970s, but pots are still made with local materials and traditional methods.

The decoration combines traditional motifs with modern styles.

It is signed by Yolanda Quezada, the niece of revival founder Juan Quezada.

A late 20thC Mata Ortiz handmade fineline pot, by Yolanda Quezada.

12in (30.5cm) high

$300-500   **ALL**

A Hopi pottery olla, by Clinton Polacca Nampeyo, with red top and stylized polychrome bird/feather designs.

c1980   *8.25in (21cm) high*

$120-180   **ALL**

A late 20thC Hopi small tapered pottery jar, by Lawrence Namoki, with fine stylized polychrome parrot designs.

4.5in (11.5cm) high

$150-200   **ALL**

An early 20thC Hopi upright pottery vase, with a stylized polychrome bird and other geometric designs.

7in (18cm) high

$280-320   **ALL**

A Hopi large double-necked vase, with polychrome parrot and other geometric designs, top half reattached with glue but unrestored.

c1900   *14.25in (36cm) high*

$800-1,200   **ALL**

A mid-20thC Pueblo handmade Acoma pottery canteen.

10in (25.5cm) high

$180-220   **ALL**

A late 20thC Acoma style handpainted owl, by M. Chino, with traditional black and red-on-white designs.

This is typical of Acoma pottery, in terms of the design, the colors used, and the white clay body. The Chino family name is also a noted one connected closely to the area.

6.5in (16.5cm) high

$100-150   **ALL**

An Eunice Navasie polychrome pottery wedding vase, with traditional designs, one rim broken and reglued but unrestored.

Eunice 'Fawn' Navasie (1920-1992) is a noted Hopi potter. Her daughter Dolly Joe 'White Swan' Navasie (b.1964) learnt her mother's skills and has become a noted potter in her own right.

c1980   *10in (25.5cm) high*

$150-250   **ALL**

An early Pueblo pottery olla, with orange/red and black-on-white designs, unrestored three-inch triangle reglued near rim.

This olla, or pot, is typical of pottery produced by this culture, in terms of form, color, and pattern. It is interesting to note that the design is similar to rug or carpet designs.

c1910   *11.5in (29cm) high*

$1,800-2,200   **ALL**

A late 20thC painted pot, by M. Chino, in traditional Acoma colors, with man and animal hunters.

5.25in (13.5cm) high

$60-90   **ALL**

COLLECTORS' NOTES

■ Kachina dolls are representations of the 'kachina' – spirits that themselves represent natural objects and forces, such as earth, rain, sun, good health, and long life. They were seen by the South Western tribes such as the Hopi as necessary for a good year and are bound in myth, ceremony, and ritual. The Navajo copied them but their dolls are usually more modern and have no ceremonial or spiritual meaning.

■ In December every year, Hopi men would dress in bright clothes and undertake chants and rituals to bring the spirits down from the hills where they lived. They would then honor them regularly until the end of the growing season in July in the hope that they would be blessed with a good year and harvest. The dolls represented the costumes worn, the dances, the kachina's attributes and their spirit, and were given to children to educate them in spirituality.

■ Traditionally carved from the root of the cottonwood, they would be handcarved and colored using natural stains and dyes, making each unique. All body parts should be handcarved. Dolls wearing colorful detailed costumes tend to be more valuable than the ones wearing plain clothes. Look for good details, the use of natural over synthetic materials and the work of noted artists. There are many modern dolls made simply for the tourist market, so always buy from a reputable source and consider the quality.

A late 20thC handcarved and painted cottonwood root kachina doll, marked "Guard Kachina (Sakwa-hu)".

The Guard Kachina maintains order in the community and ensures respect for the Kachina.

12.75in (32.5cm) high

$100-150   **ALL**

A late 20thC handcarved and painted cottonwood root kachina doll, marked "Suy-ang-e-vif (Left-Handed) 95".

9in (23cm) high

$40-60   **ALL**

A late 20thC handcarved and painted cottonwood root kachina doll, marked "Mountain Lion (Toho) Kachina".

10in (25.5cm) high

$70-100   **ALL**

A rare and large handcarved and painted cottonwood root kachina doll, marked "Hopi Badger Kachina, Stacy Talahytewa".

c1975   16in (40.5cm) high

$70-100   **ALL**

A rare and large handcarved and painted cottonwood root kachina doll, marked "Ogre-Ty Duwyenie".

c1975   17.5in (44.5cm) high

$120-180   **ALL**

A late 20thC handcarved and painted cottonwood root kachina doll, marked "Cross Legged (Huhuwa)".

11in (28cm) high

$400-600   **ALL**

A finely carved and detailed 'Black Ogre' kachina doll, by Tom Hawk.

c1975   13.75in (35cm) high

$70-100   **ALL**

A late 20thC handcarved and painted 'Black Buffalo' kachina doll, by G. Largo.

13.75in (35cm) high

$500-700   **ALL**

A late 20thC handcarved and painted pinewood kachina doll, in the "Mana" style.

13.75in (35cm) high

$60-90 ALL

A late 20thC handcarved cottonwood root 'Revival' kachina doll, decorated with pigment paints.

10.5in (26.5cm) high

$150-200 ALL

A CLOSER LOOK AT A NATIVE AMERICAN DOLL

The form of children clinging to the open-mouthed lady show she is a 'storyteller' doll – tradition leads elders to teach children verbally, or sing to them.

The tradition for making such figurative dolls and storytellers was restarted by potter Helen Cordero in the early 1960s, when this example dates from, making this an early example.

She was made by Persingula Gachupin who, along with her entire family, is very well known for her pottery.

Jemez pottery is popular with collectors, being a reputable name that dates back to the early 18thC. It also has several notable potting families associated with it.

A Jemez polychrome pottery 'Storyteller' doll, by Persingula Gachupin, with four babies, excellent condition.

Persingula's daughter Laura is also a potter and her work is highly regarded by collectors of Native American pottery. She is often credited with having brought about a revival of quality to Jemez pottery.

c1960   6in (15cm) high
$150-200 ALL

A Koshare polychrome pottery 'Storyteller' kachina doll, by Mary Ellen Toya, with three babies eating watermelons, excellent condition.

c1980   6in (15cm) high
$150-200 ALL

A Navajo large kachina doll, with red velvet blouse, satin skirt, sewn cloth body, and seed bead and sequin 'jewelry'.

c1975   17in (43cm) high
$80-120 ALL

A rare Navajo cloth kachina doll, with original long satin skirt, faded purple velvet blouse, and seed bead necklace and earrings.

c1940   25in (63.5cm) high
$250-350 ALL

A Navajo red velvet mother and child kachina doll, stuffed and often used as a pin cushion or jewelry stand.

c1960   13in (33cm) high
$40-60 ALL

A Skookum Indian kachina doll, complete with blanket and hair.

Skookum dolls were made purely as commercial dolls by a company based in Missoula, Montana. Designed in 1914 by Mary McAboy, they were sold until the 1950s, primarily in souvenir shops and trading posts. They came in a variety of designs and sizes, but usually all feature sideways-looking eyes and molded composition faces with long hair.

c1920   11.5in (29cm) high
$180-220 ALL

COLLECTORS' NOTES

■ Beadwork is one of the most familiar arts connected with native American cultures. However, glass beads only arrived in the Americas with the Europeans. They quickly became popular and widely used. Styles of design, construction and technique indicate the area the piece was produced in.

■ The most common form are geometric patterns, created with the 'lazy stitch', where beads are sewn in rows, using different colors and combinations to create a pattern. Unique to the North East are raised designs. Scenes of humans or animals, particularly vintage examples are comparatively scarcer. Ancient bags using shells and seeds instead of beads are

becoming rarer and much more expensive, as are 19thC and even some early 20thC bags.

■ Newer bags can often be discerned by moving a few beads slightly and examining the leather or lining underneath – if it has been dented by the beads it is likely to have some age, but look at other parts of the bag to confirm this – signs of use should be detectable. Bead shapes and colors can also identify a bag's date, but this will only come with experience gained from handling large numbers of new and old bags. Modern and contemporary beadwork is also highly collectible, particularly if pictorial.

A rare Plateau large-sized pictorial beadwork bag, with striking single elk figure.

c1950　　　　　*16.5in (42cm) high*

$280-320　　　　　　　　**ALL**

A Plateau beadwork contour bag, with handle, fringe, and pictorial doe and fawn in the aspen trees.

c1950　　*11in (28cm) high*

$500-700　　　　**ALL**

A Plateau beaded flat bag, depicting a bulldog.

c1950　　*9in (23cm) high*

$300-500　　　　**ALL**

A flat-beaded one-sided bag, with Peyote bird design, done in Plateau-style but most likely Kiowa-made.

c1965　　*12.25in (31cm) high*

$250-350　　　　**ALL**

A Plateau full-beaded flat bag, depicting an Indian woman holding a baby in a cradleboard.

c1940　　*12.75in (32.5cm) high*

$1,200-1,800　　　　**ALL**

A Nez Perce small rectangular twined cornhusk bag, with striking colorful geometric designs.

c1920　　*10in (25.5cm) high*

$300-400　　　　**ALL**

A late 20thC Yakima woven beadwork bag, the front panel with flat beaded tepee and other geometrics.

14in (35.5cm) high

$200-300　　　　**ALL**

A Plateau full-beaded flat rectangular bag, with striking colorful geometric designs.

c1970　　*11.5in (29cm) high*

$300-400　　　　**ALL**

An Iroquois beadwork purse, with foliate designs and seed beads, with signs of use.

c1900　　*13in (33cm) high*

$220-280　　　　**ALL**

COLLECTORS' NOTES

■ As with beading, the creation of jewelry came comparatively very late to Native Americans, dating back to the 1850s when Atsidi Saani learnt how to work metal from the Spanish colonizers. He brought techniques to the tribes who began to make in quantity from the 1870s. The Navajo are perhaps the most prolific makers, with a highly recognizable style using silver and turquoise.

■ 19thC examples are hard to find and valuable, but 20thC designs are much more commonly found. The technique used can help to date and value a piece, as well as any maker's marks, the designs and the materials used. Late 19thC examples may be crudely made with raised designs created using files and chisels, rather than repoussé. Pieces produced up to the 1950s have dull areas, as electric polishing machines were not available at the time.

■ From the late 1890s, the Fred Harvey Company was supplying pre-finished materials for assembly, and even commissioned pieces for sale aimed at the souvenir market. They show machine-made precision in their delicate lines and uniform stamped designs. Techniques, including repoussé, improved from the early 20th century. These areas, as with contemporary examples, do have collectors, with much of the market remaining affordable and varied, offering great scope.

A late 20thC Navajo traditional sterling squash blossom necklace, with ten squashes and naja, all adorned with turquoise stones, hallmarked.

25in (63.5cm) long | *c1975*

$280-320 **ALL**

$280-320

A Navajo all-silver squash blossom necklace, with handmade beads, fancy curled top, stamped blossoms, cast naja, and matching earrings.

26in (66cm) long | *c1985*

ALL

A Pueblo five-strand graduated turquoise bead necklace, with segments and 'corn' accents of spondulus shell.

19in (48.5cm) long

$300-500 **ALL**

A Navajo natural turquoise jaclas, used as necklace drop or earrings.

c1950 *10in (25.5cm) long*

$220-280 **ALL**

A Zuni large ladies' sterling ring, with 16 red coral stones and a large bird inlay shell disc on top.

c1975 *2.25in (5.5cm) diam*

$60-90 **ALL**

A Navajo bracelet, with a large turquoise stone and a natural shaped red coral stone, all on a silver base and band.

c1975 *5.25in (13.5cm) high*

$120-180 **ALL**

A triple-banded sterling cuff bracelet, by Daniel (Sunshine) Reeves, set with 38 light blue turquoise stones and a single purple gem center stone.

c1995 *6.25in (16cm) diam*

$180-220 **ALL**

A Pueblo handrolled three-strand turquoise bead necklace, with spondulus shell pendant overlaid with turquoise, jet and mother-of-pearl and with matching jaclas.

c1985 *24in (61cm) long*

$300-500 **ALL**

A mid-20thC N.W. Coast carved and painted mask, marked "Cedar Bark Mask, Peter Moon, Kingeome Inlet".

14in (35.5cm) high

$400-600   ALL

A late 20thC Kwakiutl native carved and painted beaver mask, with cedar bark hair, from Alert Bay, B.C.

12in (30.5cm) high

$300-500   ALL

An early N.W. Coast carved and painted cedar mask, with beaver trim, signed "Cal Hunt, Wild Woman".

c1970   *9.5in (24cm) high*

$500-700   ALL

An early 20thC Pendleton weave woolen blanket.

64in (162.5cm) long

$60-90   ALL

A Navajo blue ground weaving, with red and white geometric accents.

c1975   *28in (71cm) long*

$70-100   ALL

A late 20thC Kwakiutl handcarved transformation moon mask, Alert Bay, B.C., depicting humans and wolves.

12in (30.5cm) high

$400-600   ALL

A Navajo small weaving, by Lorraine Mark, with single Yei figure.

c1980   *7in (18cm) long*

$70-100   ALL

A Plateau full-beaded hide belt, with unusual geometric design.

c1940   *40in (101.5cm) long*

$120-180   ALL

An early 20thC Nez Perce fully beaded parade tie, in deep red, green, and dirty white beaded diamond designs.

A mid-20thC Yakima fully flat-beaded dance belt, on heavy canvas, with buckskin ties, a few missing beads.

30.5in (77.5cm) long

$30-40   ALL

A Hopi black and green-on-red sash, with braided fringe.

c1975   92in (233.5cm) long

$120-180   ALL

13.5in (34.5cm) long

$150-200   ALL

A Cheyenne lazy-stitch beaded sheath, in black, white, red, and green with chevron and cross designs.

c1935

$220-280   ALL

8in (20cm) long

A pair of Cree puckered toe moosehide moccasins, with floral-beaded vamps trimmed, with fine silk thread piping, mint condition.

c1970   10in (25.5cm) long

$50-70   ALL

A girls' jingle cloth dress, by Gaylynn Running Crane, Heart Butte, MT, decorated with many Copenhagen snuff tin cones.

c1965   36in (91.5cm) long

$80-120   ALL

A Pendleton Beaver State Indian shawl, in Chief Joseph design with fringe on four sides, with alternate colors.

c1980   68in (172.5cm) long

$150-200   ALL

A pair of mid-20thC Cree moosehide mittens, with lining, beaded hunting eagles, and trimmed with sable or similar fur.

16in (40.5cm) long

$220-280   ALL

A pair of mid-20thC Athabascan handmade sealskin boots, with hide uppers, fur trim, and diamond leather tops.

11in (28cm) long

$150-200   ALL

AMERICANA

COLLECTORS' NOTES

■ Similar to the later 1964-65 event, the theme of the 1939 World's Fair was science, technology and the world of tomorrow. Coming at the end of the Great Depression, this theme was especially relevant.

■ The colors of the exhibition were orange and blue, and much memorabilia is based around the custom-built buildings in the exhibition – the 700ft high Trylon 'spike' and the spherical Perisphere.

■ Look for memorabilia that is based around these colors and themes, particularly if it is in the dominant Art Deco style. Fine quality materials, handmade objects and larger pieces, as well as those produced in smaller numbers will usually attract higher prices, with condition being an important consideration.

An American 1939 New York World's Fair button.

1in (3cm) wide

$35-45   BMA

A 1939 New York World's Fair enameled metal badge, showing the Perisphere and Trylon picked out in high relief mother-of-pearl.

1939   1.75in (4.5cm) wide

$70-100   BMA

An American 1939 New York World's Fair painted plastic button, showing buildings including the Trylon and Perisphere, on original card.

1939   Badge 2.25in (6cm) high

$70-100   BMA

An American 1939 New York World's Fair 'Hi Neighbor I'm From Connecticut' button and ribbon.

4.25in (11cm) high

$100-150   BMA

A 1939 New York World's Fair painted composition pin, showing the Trylon & Perisphere, stamped "C NYWF".

1939   1.5in (4cm) wide

$30-50   TM

An American 1939 New York World's Fair painted plastic button, showing buildings including the Trylon and Perisphere, on original card.

1939   Badge 2.25in (6cm) high

$70-100   BMA

An American 1939 New York World's Fair 'Boy Scouts of America' woven fabric badge.

1939   4in (10cm) wide

$60-90   BMA

A 1939 New York World's Fair gilt metal bracelet, with enameled decal, belt buckle-style clip, hinged, rigid, engraved with foliage and flowers, dated.

1940   2.25in (6cm) wide

$70-100   BMA

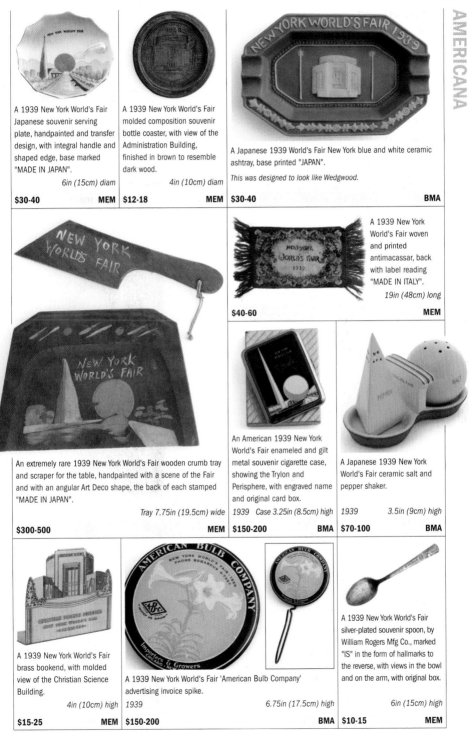

A 1939 New York World's Fair Japanese souvenir serving plate, handpainted and transfer design, with integral handle and shaped edge, base marked "MADE IN JAPAN".

6in (15cm) diam

$30-40   **MEM**

A 1939 New York World's Fair molded composition souvenir bottle coaster, with view of the Administration Building, finished in brown to resemble dark wood.

4in (10cm) diam

$12-18   **MEM**

A Japanese 1939 World's Fair New York blue and white ceramic ashtray, base printed "JAPAN".

This was designed to look like Wedgwood.

$30-40   **BMA**

A 1939 New York World's Fair woven and printed antimacassar, back with label reading "MADE IN ITALY".

19in (48cm) long

$40-60   **MEM**

An extremely rare 1939 New York World's Fair wooden crumb tray and scraper for the table, handpainted with a scene of the Fair and with an angular Art Deco shape, the back of each stamped "MADE IN JAPAN".

Tray 7.75in (19.5cm) wide

$300-500   **MEM**

An American 1939 New York World's Fair enameled and gilt metal souvenir cigarette case, showing the Trylon and Perisphere, with engraved name and original card box.

1939   Case 3.25in (8.5cm) high

$150-200   **BMA**

A Japanese 1939 New York World's Fair ceramic salt and pepper shaker.

1939   3.5in (9cm) high

$70-100   **BMA**

A 1939 New York World's Fair brass bookend, with molded view of the Christian Science Building.

4in (10cm) high

$15-25   **MEM**

A 1939 New York World's Fair 'American Bulb Company' advertising invoice spike.

1939   6.75in (17.5cm) high

$150-200   **BMA**

A 1939 New York World's Fair silver-plated souvenir spoon, by William Rogers Mfg Co., marked "IS" in the form of hallmarks to the reverse, with views in the bowl and on the arm, with original box.

6in (15cm) high

$10-15   **MEM**

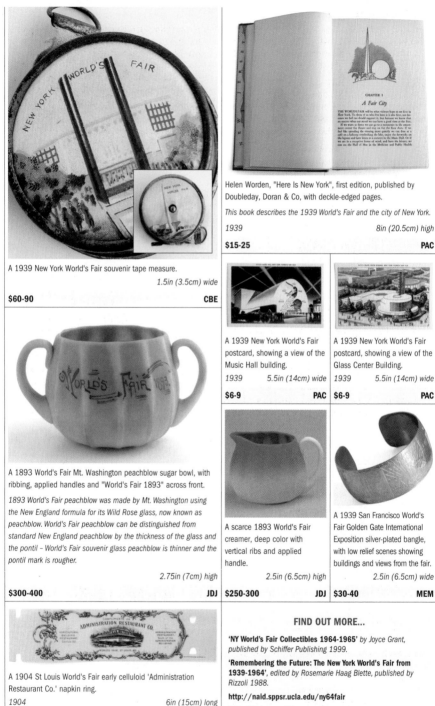

A 1939 New York World's Fair souvenir tape measure.

1.5in (3.5cm) wide

$60-90 CBE

Helen Worden, "Here Is New York", first edition, published by Doubleday, Doran & Co, with deckle-edged pages.

This book describes the 1939 World's Fair and the city of New York.

1939 8in (20.5cm) high

$15-25 PAC

A 1939 New York World's Fair postcard, showing a view of the Music Hall building.

1939 5.5in (14cm) wide

$6-9 PAC

A 1939 New York World's Fair postcard, showing a view of the Glass Center Building.

1939 5.5in (14cm) wide

$6-9 PAC

A 1893 World's Fair Mt. Washington peachblow sugar bowl, with ribbing, applied handles and "World's Fair 1893" across front.

1893 World's Fair peachblow was made by Mt. Washington using the New England formula for its Wild Rose glass, now known as peachblow. World's Fair peachblow can be distinguished from standard New England peachblow by the thickness of the glass and the pontil – World's Fair souvenir glass peachblow is thinner and the pontil mark is rougher.

2.75in (7cm) high

$300-400 JDJ

A scarce 1893 World's Fair creamer, deep color with vertical ribs and applied handle.

2.5in (6.5cm) high

$250-300 JDJ

A 1939 San Francisco World's Fair Golden Gate International Exposition silver-plated bangle, with low relief scenes showing buildings and views from the fair.

2.5in (6.5cm) wide

$30-40 MEM

A 1904 St Louis World's Fair early celluloid 'Administration Restaurant Co.' napkin ring.

1904 6in (15cm) long

$80-120 BMA

FIND OUT MORE...

'NY World's Fair Collectibles 1964-1965' by Joyce Grant, *published by Schiffer Publishing 1999.*

'Remembering the Future: The New York World's Fair from 1939-1964', *edited by Rosemarie Haag Blette, published by Rizzoli 1988.*

http://naid.sppsr.ucla.edu/ny64fair

http://www.nywf64.com

COLLECTORS' NOTES

- The 1964-65 World's Fair was held at Flushing Meadow, Queens, the same location as the 1939 Fair. It was open from April to October in each year. Over 600 acres held 140 pavilions, most of which were American in origin.

- Much of Europe and Russia boycotted the Fair because it was in breach of Bureau of International Expositions (BIE) ruling on two counts. It limited fairs to one-year runs. It also permitted just one US Fair per decade and had already approved an exhibition at Seattle in 1962.

- The modern theme of 'man in a shrinking globe and expanding universe' was based around advances in industry and technology, and of course the start of the space race. More than a billion dollars were invested by participating countries, companies, and states.

- Although over 70 million visitors were expected over the two years, far fewer arrived, despite a last minute peak when over 7 million visited in the final three weeks of the 1965 season. The Fair was not a financial success, but nevertheless attracted 51 million visitors – a new record for international fairs.

- The Fair's official colors were blue and orange, the same as the 1939 Fair, with its official logo being the 'Unisphere'. A vast number of different souvenirs were made and sold and are commonly found. Condition is important, so always buy in the best, original condition you can, as so many items were mass-produced.

A 1964-65 New York World's Fair Jumbo Coloring Book, published by Spertus.

$30-40 MEM

An unused 1964-65 New York World's Fair deluxe coloring book, published by Spertus.

10.5in (27cm) high

$15-25 MEM

"The Official World's Fair Story Book - A Day At The World's Fair with Peter and Wendy", published by Spertus Publishing Co., NY.

The price label on the book shows that it retailed for $1 in or around 1964.

1964   *11.25in (28.5cm) high*

$20-30 MEM

A "Post", May 23 1964, special issue covering the New York World's Fair.

13.5in (34cm) high

$20-30 MEM

"The Official Guide New York World's Fair", by the Editors of Time-Life Books, published by Time Inc.

1964   *8in (20cm) high*

$7-10 MEM

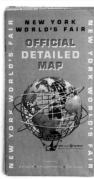

A 1964 New York World's Fair site map.

6in (15cm) high

$10-15 PAC

A 1964 New York World's Fair 'Flashcard' set of color cards.

Each 5.75in (14.5cm) wide

$15-25 PAC

A 1964-65 New York World's Fair transfer-printed glass souvenir ashtray, with night-time view of the 'Unisphere' and 'Fountain of the Continents' amidst fireworks.

This is the standard size found and was available with a wide range of scenes, buildings and views.

4.5in (11.5cm) high

$8-12   **MEM**

A New York World's Fair large transfer-printed glass ashtray, with view of Bell Telephone Systems' display building.

These ashtrays are rarer in this large size. All are very easy to chip, crack, and break. Bell's pavilion presented a history of man's incredible advances in communication, including a 'picture-phone system'.

6.75in (17cm) wide

$8-12   **MEM**

A 1965 New York World's Fair commemorative or souvenir plate, with label reading "Unisphere, presented by United States Steel".

1965   4.5in (11.5cm) diam

$12-18   **PAC**

A 1964-65 New York World's Fair humorous souvenir coffee mug, and applied transfer to base, the base marked "Property of" with an unglazed area for writing a name, the inside marked "BACK TO WORK", with crack to handle and chip.

1964   3.75in (9.5cm) high

$15-25   **MEM**

A 1964-65 New York World's Fair 'Siesta Line' amber glass, brass and wood souvenir mug, with transfer of 'Unisphere'.

5in (12.5cm) high

$10-15   **MEM**

A 1964-65 New York World's Fair 'Unisphere' ceramic ashtray, presented by United States Steel, colored and glazed, but with wear to transfer and finish on base.

c1964   4.5in (11.5cm) high

$20-30   **MEM**

A 1964-65 New York World's Fair 'Unisphere' plastic money bank, in mint condition, with original box.

It is rare to find these comparatively fragile plastic money banks intact with their thin plastic rings. The box is in fine condition and adds to the comparative rarity and desirability of this piece.

c1964   6in (15cm) high

$40-60   **MEM**

A 1964-65 New York World's Fair silver colored and clear plastic butter dish, in rare original card box.

1965   8.25in (21cm) wide

$15-20   **PAC**

A 1964-65 New York World's Fair 'Vatican Pavilion' wood and plastic statue of the Pietà.

This piece celebrates the Vatican pavilion which contained Michaelangelo's masterpiece the Pietà. It was the first time the sculpture had ever left Rome.

5.75in (14.5cm) high

$25-35   **MEM**

A 1964-65 New York World's Fair 'Official World's Fair Coaster and Napkin Set', distributed by ENCO Inc., unopened and sealed.

c1964   Box 8.5in (21.5cm) wide

$30-50   **MEM**

An American 1964-65 New York World's Fair base metal and enamel novelty ring, with molded and enameled decoration.

0.75in (2cm) high

$20-30 **BMA**

An American 1964-65 New York World's Fair silver-finished plastic novelty ring, with dome decal showing the motif of and reading "N.Y. World's Fair 1964-1965".

0.75in (2cm) high

$10-15 **BMA**

A 1964-65 New York World's Fair base metal ring, with 'winking' image.

Turning the ring in the light and viewing it from different angles shows one of two views.

1964 *0.75in (2cm) high*

$18-22 **CVS**

A 1964-65 New York World's Fair clear plastic souvenir 'Rain Bonnet', the hat with printed 'Unisphere' logos, contained in a vinyl packet, the reverse printed with a scene of the Fair.

1964 *Packet 3.75in (9.5cm) long*

$10-15 **MEM**

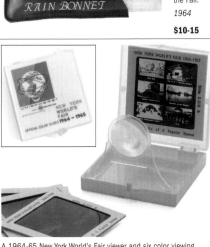

A 1964-65 New York World's Fair viewer and six color viewing slides, the slides of views and buildings, contained in a plastic box.

Box 2.25in (5.5cm) wide

$10-15 **MEM**

A 1964-65 New York World's Fair vinyl inflatable child doll, by Alvimar for the New York World's Fair 1964-65 Corporation, with bell inside.

c1961 *8in (20cm) high*

$18-22 **MEM**

A 1964-65 New York World's Fair printed metal badge/decal, with embossed 'Unisphere' motif and four screw holes.

4in (10cm) wide

$7-10 **MEM**

A 1964-65 New York World's Fair printed card beer mat.

3.5in (9cm) diam

$3-4 **MEM**

A 1964-65 New York World's Fair printed souvenir pennant.

12in (30cm) long

$10-15 **MEM**

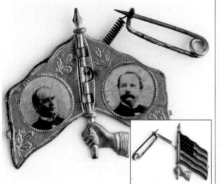

An American McKinley & Hobart gilt metal hinged pin, in the form of a flag, with spring and catch, the reverse with enameled US flag.

Badges showing the Presidential nominee and his vice president are known as 'jugate' badges and are popular with collectors. Those that are complex and well made such as this example will usually be valuable.

c1896   *1in (3cm) high*

$100-150   **LDE**

An American William Howard Taft 'The Safest' campaign button.

Cleverly using the letters in his name, this was his campaign slogan. Many badges, such as this example were made by The Whitehead & Hoag Co. Newark NJ.

c1908   *1in (2.5cm) wide*

$40-60   **LDE**

An American William Jennings Bryan campaign button, with a silver background.

Bryan stood for President four times but never won. This button is on a silver background as he wanted to use silver to back the currency, not gold as his opponent McKinley did. McKinley's campaign button has a gold background. McKinley and gold won the presidency.

1896-1900 1.25in (3cm) wide

$60-90   **LDE**

An American 'Wm. J. Bryan 16 to 1 Free Coinage' campaign badge.

c1900

$60-90   **LDE**

An American Woodrow Wilson campaign button.

0.75in (2cm) wide

$40-60   **LDE**

An American 'Our Leader Franklin D. Roosevelt' campaign button.

c1940   *2.25in (5.5cm) wide*

$100-150   **LDE**

An American Herbert Hoover for President campaign button.

0.75in (2cm) wide

$50-70   **LDE**

A CLOSER LOOK AT A PIN

This pin was made for a single day's event, meaning far less were made than for long-running events.

Surviving examples are extremely scarce, even more so in this condition with bright colors and original gilt printing.

John Llewelyn Lewis was the president of the United Mine Workers, then the largest trade union in the US.

Lewis had supported Roosevelt in the 1932 election and is shown next to him on the pin.

An American Lewis & Roosevelt Labor Day Celebration, Sutersville, PA, Sept 8th 1934 campaign button, made by McMahon Bros., Pittsburgh, PA.

1934   *3.25in (8cm) high*

$800-1,200   **LDE**

WE LIKE DICK

An American Richard Nixon 'We Like Dick' campaign button.

c1960   *2.25in (5.5cm) wide*

$180-220   **BMA**

An American 'Independence Day U.S. - Vietnam 1776-1966' pin.

1966   *1.5in (4cm) wide*

$200-250   **LDE**

A very rare pair of tortoiseshell and silver cufflinks, with an image of 'Machinery Hall', made for the Philadelphia Exposition and Centenary of the American Revolution.

c1876   *1in (3cm) wide*

$200-250   **BMA**

An 'Albany Young Men's Association 65th Anniversary' printed silk bookmark, showing George Washington, with ink inscription reading "R.M. King July 7 1842".

c1842

6.75in (17.5cm) high

$70-100   **BMA**

WIN WITH KENNEDY

A 1960s American 'Win With Kennedy' formica pin.

2.5in (6.5cm) wide

$100-150   **LDE**

An American Packard 'Work To Win Count Me In!' pin.

1in (3cm) wide

$70-100   **LDE**

VOTE FOR WOMAN SUFFRAGE NOV. 6TH

An American 'Vote for Woman Suffrage Nov. 6th' metal pin, with ropetwist border.

1.5in (4cm) wide

$80-120   **LDE**

Two American WWII patriotic pins.

1.25in (3cm) wide

$20-30   **DH**

A CLOSER LOOK AT A COMMEMORATIVE SILK

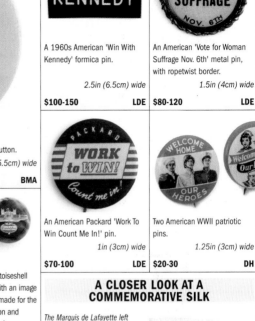

The Marquis de Lafayette left aristocratic France in 1777 to support the Americans in their fight against the British.

These ribbons were usually printed on silk using a metal plate engraved with a design including a portrait of Lafayette.

Many ribbons date from 1824-25 when they were pinned to clothing during parades held when Lafayette visited America for the final time.

After the Americans entered WWII, slogans were themed along 'Lafayette, we're back to help you'.

An American 'Lafayette Ribbon' printed silk bookmark.

c1825   *6.75in (17cm) high*

$60-90   **BMA**

A rare Black Americana Halloween postcard, entitled 'You would laugh too'.

5in (13cm) long

A rare Black Americana Halloween postcard.

5in (13cm) long

A 1930s 'Souvenir Cotton Novelty', in original box, by A. Hirchwitz MFR of N.O. LA.

Box 5.5in (14cm) high

An American hand-colored lithograph of Ulysses S. Grant and family, inscribed "General Grant and His Family", in a period walnut frame with bright colors, waterstains in margins, none affecting image.

Issued in 1866, immediately after the American Civil War, when Grant's popularity as a war hero was at its highest.

A Club Plantation hand fan, reading "Man, Dat Sho Was Good".

13.5in (34.5cm) high   *1866*   *28in (71cm) wide*

An American chromolithographed map of the 'Leadville Mining District', copyright 1901 by Chas. F. Saunders, printed by Denver Litho. Co., detailing claims in color for dozens of mining companies, minor wrinkling of margins from rolling, pinholes.

Leadville was founded as a mining camp 75 miles south-west of Denver, close to Aspen and Copper Mountain. Gold, silver, copper, lead, zinc, bismuth, manganese, and molybdenum were mined in the area. Many fortunes were made in the mines, including those of Carnegie, Guggenheim, and Marshall Field.

An American hand-tinted lithograph, entitled "The Last Call", showing an American Civil War scene of a drummer boy, framed under glass.

An American chromolithographed trade card promoting the 'Grand Festival and Fete Champètre, In aid of a Fund For the Shelter, etc. of the Russian Hebrew Refugees,... June 6, 7 and 8, 1882', featuring Liberty reaching out her hand to welcome the refugees, minor damage to upper left corner, light soil on verso.

14in (35.5cm) high   *6in (15cm) wide*   *1901*   *44in (112cm) high*

A Great Northern railway calendar, with Weinold Reiss' Dancing Boy painting, complete and in mint condition, framed.

c1946   33.25in (84.5cm)

$150-200   ALL

A Great Northern railway calendar, with Weinold Reiss' Lazy Boy painting, complete and in mint condition, framed.

c1947   33.25in (84.5cm)

$120-180   ALL

Con Price, "Trails I Rode", first edition, Trail's End Publishing, illustrated by Charles M. Russell, inscribed by the author.

1947

$300-400   CHAA

A 'decoy' style seagull, carved from wood and finished in white and gray paint with a yellow beak, mounted as if standing on a piece of seashore driftwood.

c1940   28cm (11in) high

$70-100   BCAC

An American painted wood and celluloid souvenir hanging wall plaque for Luna Park, Coney Island, the reverse with painted inscription reading "Luna Park Friday May 27-1904".

This piece comes from the very earliest years of Luna Park which had only been opened on May 16th the previous year. One of Coney Island's most popular attractions during its heyday and built and co-owned by postmodern architect Frederic Thompson, it was gutted by fire in 1944 and closed.

c1904   8in (20.5cm) wide

$400-600   BMA

A cast metal high relief belt buckle with bison motif, for the 1901 Pan-American Exposition.

c1901   3in (7.5cm) wide

$120-180   BMA

A 'Broadway Hotel' hanging sign, painted cartouche-shaped hinged iron sign, with iron hanger, paint with scratches and losses, scattered rust, old lettering on back.

32in (81.5cm) wide

$400-600   BRU

A New York City multicolored vinyl souvenir beenie hat, with silver plastic charms.

7in (17.5cm) wide

$60-90   NOR

A 1950s/60s George Washington card and painted plaster figural candy container.

9.25in (23.5cm) high

$150-200   DAC

ANIMATION ART

COLLECTORS' NOTES

■ The variety of animation art available can seem bewildering and, as the type also dictates the value and desirability, it is important to understand the differences.

■ The most desirable form is a hand-painted original production cel that appears in the final feature. Collectors look for scenes with main characters, particularly from key scenes. Be aware that some original cels are never screened and these are not as desirable.

■ Due to the huge interest in collecting animation art, animation studios are now releasing limited editions in a number of formats.

■ The most sought-after are hand-painted cels. These may be reproductions of original cels or new images; they are unlikely to have been painted by the original artists although they may have signed the piece. Edition runs tend to be quite small and can sell out quickly.

■ Machine-produced serigraphs or sericels are more affordable and easier to obtain as they are produced in greater numbers.

■ Today, very little animation is produced completely by hand, meaning original production cels do not exist for modern films and series such as "Ice Age", "Monsters, Inc." and "The Simpsons". Scenes are drawn by hand and scanned into a computer where they are colored and converted straight to film.

A Walt Disney original production cel from "Mother Goose goes to Hollywood", featuring three men in a wooden tub.

The 'Mother Goose goes to Hollywood' story featured various nursery rhymes. The voices for the men were provided by Charles Laughton, Spencer Tracy, and Freddie Bartholomew, with Kathryn Hepburn as Mother Goose.

1938   11in (28cm) wide

$800-1,200   **AAC**

An MGM original production cel from "Deputy Droopy", featuring Slim Jim.

1955   12in (30.5cm) wide

$1,000-1,500   **AAG**

A 20th Century Fox hand-painted cel from "Futurama", together with the original production drawing, featuring Leela and Fry.

30.5in (77.5cm) wide

$400-600   **AAG**

A limited edition 20th Century Fox giclee 'The Herd' from "Ice Age", from an edition of 750, featuring Sid, Manny, Diego, and Scrat.

A giclee is a high resolution digital scan printed with archival quality inks.

2002   20.5in (52cm) wide

$400-600   **AAG**

A 20th Century Fox 'Simpsons on Sunday' original production cel from "The Simpsons", featuring the family in their Sunday best.

16.5in (42cm) wide

$600-900 AAG

A 20th Century Fox key set-up from "The Simpsons", featuring the family running to the couch in an M.C. Escher-style image.

This scene is used in the opening sequence of the episodes 'The PTA Disbands' and 'Homer the Great'.

c1995 *16.5in (42cm) wide*

$2,200-2,800 AAG

A 20th Century Fox 'Water Pistols at Dawn' original production cel, from "The Simpsons" episode 'Lady Bouvier's Lover', featuring Jackie, Mr Burns, and Bart.

1994 *16.5in (42cm) wide*

$400-600 AAG

A limited edition 20th Century Fox 'Happy Hour' serilitho cel, from "The Simpsons" and an edition of 2,000, taken from original artwork and reference material archived at the studio.

38in (96.5cm) wide

$300-500 AAG

A limited edition Warner Bros. hand-painted cel, from an edition of 50, featuring Sylvester, Tweety Pie, and Spike, signed by Warner Bros. animator Virgil Ross.

17in (43cm) high

$1,200-1,800 AAG

A limited edition Warner Bros. hand-painted cel 'Bacall to Arms', from an edition of 250, taken from original 1946 cartoon of the same name and featuring "Bogey Gocart", "Laurie Becool" and "Wolf".

15.25in (38.5cm) wide

$1,200-1,800 AAG

ANIMATION ART

A Warner Bros. original production cel from Road Runner, featuring "Flying Coyote".

11.5in (29cm) wide

$800-1,200 AAG

An original hand-painted cel, featuring Astérix, Obélix, and Dogmatix.

22.5in (57cm) wide

$12,000-18,000 AAG

A Klasky Csupo original production cel from "Duckman", featuring Eric Duckman.

16.5in (42cm) wide

$600-900 AAG

A Paramount original production cel from the open sequence of "Grease", featuring Danny Zukko.

1978 9.75in (25cm) wide

$400-600 AAG

A Fantasy Films original production cel from "The Lord of the Rings", featuring Frodo Baggins and two other hobbits.

1978 11in (28cm) wide

$300-500 AAG

A Warner Bros. original production cel from the animated sequence of Oliver Stone's "Natural Born Killers".

11.75in (30cm) wide

$1,000-1,500 AAG

An original production cel from "Peanuts", featuring Woodstock and Snoopy, from the Bill Melendez studio.

10in (25.5cm) wide

$800-1,200 AAG

A Don Bluth Productions original production cel from "The Pebble and the Penguin", featuring Hubie and Rocko.

1995 17in (43cm) wide

$400-600 AAG

A Universal Studios original production cel from "Who Framed Roger Rabbit", featuring Jessica Rabbit.

1988 15.5in (39.5cm) w

$1,800-2,200 AAG

A DePatie-Freleng original production cel of the "Pink Panther", from the opening credits of the feature film.

The Pink Panther was created by Friz Freleng for the title sequence of Blake Edward's 1964 comedy farce "The Pink Panther". The character proved so popular that a series of cartoons soon appeared.

10in (25.5cm) wide

$1,200-1,800 AAG

ANIMATION ART

A Klasky Csupo original production cel from "Rugrats", featuring Didi and Tommy Pickles.

12.25in (31cm) wide

$500-700   **AAG**

An Aardman Animations limited edition "Wallace and Gromitt" giclee 'A Grand Day Out', signed by director Nick Park, Peter Sallis (the voice of Wallace), and producer Peter Lord.

23.5in (60cm) wide

$1,000-1,500   **AAG**

An original pen and ink drawing, featuring 'The Cat In The Hat' signed by Dr Seuss, 'The Pink Panther' signed by Friz Freleng and 'Linus Van Pelt' from "Peanuts" signed by Charles M. Schultz.

5.5in (14cm) wide

$5,000-7,000   **AAG**

A set of four Apple Films animation art cels from The Beatles 'Yellow Submarine', featuring three back-views of the Beatles and Ringo driving a car.

1968 each 25in (63cm) wide

$2,800-2,300   **CO**

An Apple Films limited edition reproduction hand-painted cel 'Love, Love, Love' from "Yellow Submarine", from an edition of 175, featuring The Beatles, Jeremy Hilary Boob and the Blue Meeney, signed by George Martin.

20.25in (51.5cm) wide

$1,800-2,200   **AAG**

An Apple Films original production sketch from "Yellow Submarine".

1968   *12in (30.5cm) wide*

$700-1,000   **AAG**

An MGM original production cel from "Pink Floyd The Wall".

1982   *16.25in (41.5cm) wide*

$1,800-2,200   **AAG**

An MGM original production cel from "Pink Floyd The Wall".

15in (38cm) wide

$1,000-1,500   **AAG**

An MGM original production cel from "Pink Floyd The Wall", together with the original production sketch.

1982 image 14in (35.5cm) wide

$1,800-2,200   **AAG**

An MGM original production cel from "Pink Floyd The Wall", featuring the Warlord.

1982   *15.5in (40cm) wide*

$1,000-1,500   **AAG**

A Virgin Films key set-up from "The Great Rock N Roll Swindle", featuring members of the Sex Pistols.

A key set-up is a combination on an original production cel and a background.

1980   *14.25in (36cm) high*

$1,000-1,500   **AAG**

COLLECTORS' NOTES

■ Autograph collecting has been popular for as long as there have been 'famous' people, however, the value depends on more than just the fame of the signer.

■ Signed personal property such as credit cards or checks feature at the high end of the market as they are obviously extremely rare.

■ Handwritten letters are among the most sought-after examples as they provide a glimpse into the author's life with particularly interesting, controversial or historically important content fetching a premium. Typed correspondence and documents are also desirable, though to a slightly lesser degree.

■ When it comes to signed photographs, the bigger the better. An image taken from an actor's most famous film or scene, or a performer in a typical pose, are the most popular. They will be worth more than the same autograph on an image from a less popular film or period of work.

■ Signatures in ink are better than pencil as pencil can fade over time and is usually not as crisp. Look for group signatures on a single image or piece of paper, as they are more desirable than a collection of individually signed examples.

■ Always purchase from a reputable seller, as fakes are common. If in doubt ask for the item's provenance and compare the example to an authentic signature.

■ Good condition is also vital, as tears, rips, and stains will lower the value.

A signed Dirk Bogarde 'The High Bright Sun' video insert.
10in (25.5cm) wide

$100-150   LCA

A signed Michael Caine publicity photograph.
10in (25.5cm) high

$50-80   LCA

A signed Robert De Niro publicity photograph.
10in (25.5cm) high

$80-120   LCA

A Bette Davis American Express credit card, mounted with a signed credit card slip and a signed postcard and engagement contract.
Card 3.25 (8.5cm) wide

$7,000-10,000   LCA

A signed Leonardo DiCaprio 'Titanic' publicity photograph.
10in (25.5cm) high

$60-90   LCA

A signed John Gielguid publicity postcard.
6in (15cm) high

$15-25   LCA

A signed Alec Guiness publicity photograph.
10in (25.5cm) high

$50-70   LCA

A signed Tippi Hedren 'The
Birds' publicity photograph.

10in (25.5cm) high

$50-70   **LCA**

A signed Charlton Heston publicity photograph.

10in (25.5cm) high

$40-60   **LCA**

A signed Harvey Keitel publicity
photograph.

10in (25.5cm) high

$40-60   **LCA**

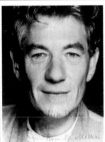

A signed Ian McKellan publicity
postcard.

6in (15cm) high

$15-25   **LCA**

A signed Eric Morcombe and
Ernie Wise publicity photograph.

11.5in (29cm) high

$220-280   **LCA**

A pair of Stan Laurel and Oliver Hardy autographs, mounted with
a publicity photograph.

13.5in (39.5cm) high

$800-1,200   **LCA**

A signed Al Pacino publicity
photograph.

10in (25.5cm) high

$100-150   **LCA**

A signed Arnold Schwarzenegger
'Predator' publicity photograph.

10in (25.5cm) high

$50-70   **LCA**

A signed Sylvester Stallone publicity photograph.

10in (25.5cm) high

$70-100   **LCA**

ERIC CLAPTON

A signed Eric Clapton publicity photograph.

$70-100   **GAZE**

BARRY GIBB
NOW VOYAGER

A signed Barry Gibb "Now Voyager" promotional single.

$40-60   **GAZE**

JANET JACKSON

A signed Janet Jackson publicity photograph.

$18-22   **GAZE**

A signed Mick Jagger photograph, with certificate of authenticity.

$70-100   **GAZE**

A signed Madonna publicity photograph, with certificate of authenticity.

$60-90   **GAZE**

A signed Kylie Minogue publicity photograph, mounted with a 'Je Ne Sais Pas Pourquoi' single, with certificate of authenticity.

$70-100   **GAZE**

A rare signed Prince publicity photograph, mounted with the quote "So tonight I'm gonna party like it's 1999..."

$120-180   **GAZE**

A signed Justin Timberlake photograph.

10in (25.5cm) high

$70-100   **LCA**

A signed Barbara Streisand check, mounted with a publicity photograph.

10in (25.5cm) high

$1,000-1,500   **LCA**

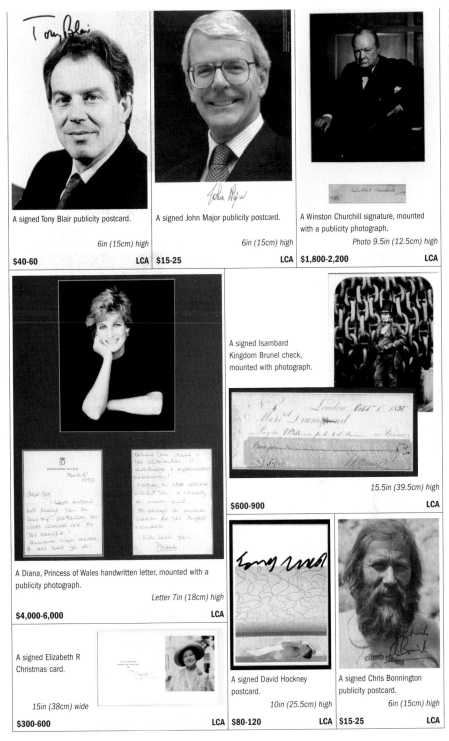

A signed Tony Blair publicity postcard.

6in (15cm) high

$40-60   LCA

A signed John Major publicity postcard.

6in (15cm) high

$15-25   LCA

A Winston Churchill signature, mounted with a publicity photograph.

Photo 9.5in (12.5cm) high

$1,800-2,200   LCA

A signed Isambard Kingdom Brunel check, mounted with photograph.

15.5in (39.5cm) high

$600-900   LCA

A Diana, Princess of Wales handwritten letter, mounted with a publicity photograph.

Letter 7in (18cm) high

$4,000-6,000   LCA

A signed Elizabeth R Christmas card.

15in (38cm) wide

$300-600   LCA

A signed David Hockney postcard.

10in (25.5cm) high

$80-120   LCA

A signed Chris Bonnington publicity postcard.

6in (15cm) high

$15-25   LCA

A Brooklands Society Re-Union pin badge.
1988

$18-22   CARS

A 1980s Brooklands Museum pressed tin
pin badge.

$8-12   CARS

A Brooklands Racing Club annual entry members and guests boxed badges.
1920

$400-600   CARS

A British Racing Drivers' Club
colored enamel lapel pin.

$50-70   CARS

A Riley Motor Club enamel
membership badge.

2.5in (6.5cm) wide

$50-70   CARS

A 1960s Brighton & Hove M.C. Christmas invitation, showing the
club bar interior.

$15-20   CARS

A Brighton & Hove Motor Club Christmas menu, dated 1955.

$18-22   CARS

An unusual bound model book, titled 'The Camelliard-Fullagar
Balanced Marine Internal Combustion Oil Engine', by White and
Pike Ltd, Birmingham.

10.25in (26cm) high

$50-70   F

COLLECTORS' NOTES

- Paper money first appeared in China in the 7th century and was initially issued by merchants in place of large and bulky consignments of copper coins.

- Sweden was the first European country to follow suit in the 1660s and the Bank of England issued its first notes in 1695.

- Examples from collapsed currencies, while worthless in themselves, are popular with collectors, as well as siege notes, and invasion and occupation notes issued during both World Wars.

- Security features such as watermarks, holograms, and guilloche flourishes add interest.

- Condition is crucial and, unlike coins, paper money is more easily damaged. 'Uncirculated' or 'mint state' items are usually the most desirable.

Three English George VI one shilling postal orders, two inscribed with payees' names, all three stamped by issuing office, dated 1943, 1950 and 1953.

5.25in (13.5cm) wide

$10-15   **INT**

A Bank of England ten shilling note, of the last series printed without the Queen's head, brown design featuring Britannia on white ground, watermark, not dated.

This format, using the signature of Leslie K. O'Brien, Governor of the Bank of England (1955-62), was only used for this one year.

c1955   5.5in (14cm) long

$25-30   **INT**

One of five consecutively numbered British Armed Forces second series one pound notes, issued by the Army Council, blue, red, and purple design on white ground, printed by Thomas de la Rue & Co, London.

1948   5.25in (13.5cm) wide

$3-5 set   **INT**

A 1923 German thousand million mark note, overprinted on a thousand mark note from 1922.

During this period of German history inflation peaked at 300 million percent. As printed currency became worthless, higher denominations were stamped onto the faces of existing notes to increase their value.

1923   7in (18cm) wide

$6-9   **INT**

A 500 peso specimen bank note, issued by El Banco Americano de Guatemala, printed with harbor scene with two female figures, ships, and local produce on obverse, four holes punched in base.

6.75in (17cm) wide

$320-380   **INT**

A CLOSER LOOK AT A COMMEMORATIVE BANK NOTE

The contrast between the colors in this metameric window changes under certain lighting conditions.

Text is printed in both vertical and horizontal axis and in varying sizes, making the note more difficult to reproduce.

The transparent panel is a model security feature only possible in polymer substrate bank notes. It is also used on Australian currency.

The colorful design, created by Nicolae Saftoiu, depicts the path of the 1999 solar eclipse through Romania.

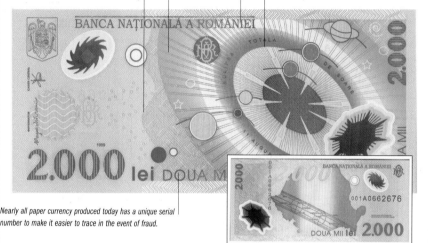

Nearly all paper currency produced today has a unique serial number to make it easier to trace in the event of fraud.

A Romanian 2,000 lei polymer note, issued to commemorate the 1999 total solar eclipse, featuring solar system motif and plan of the path of the eclipse as visible from Romania on reverse, presented in plastic folder, number 001A0662676.

The 2,000 lei denomination was chosen to mark the impending turn of the new millennium.

1999   5.75in (14.5cm) wide

$8-12   **INT**

A Russian 100 rouble note, with very fine portrait of Catherine the Great framed by elaborate decoration of fruits and leaves, watermark of portrait on side panel.

Following the Russian revolution, many of these notes, including 500 rouble denomination notes bearing portraits of Alexander the Great, were brought to the UK by fleeing Russian citizens. The condition of the notes is a crucial factor in determining their value.

1910   10.25in (26cm) wide

$15-20   **INT**

A Thai 60 baht note, issued to commemorate the King of Thailand 60th birthday, depicting the throned King in state dress on obverse, and in audience with Thai women on reverse.

This was the first Thai banknote to include a color-changing security feature.

1987   6.25in (16cm) long

$12-18   **INT**

FIND OUT MORE...

International Bank Note Society (IBNS) *General Secretary, PO Box 1642, Racine, WI 53404 USA*

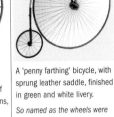

A 'Vélocipède' pedal-driven bicycle, unmarked although probably by Pierre Michaux of Paris, solid iron frame and rims, wooden wheels, excellent working condition.

Michaux, once erroneously credited with inventing the bicycle, did develop the first bicycle pedal and cranks in the early 1860s. He went on to manufacture bicycles, known as 'Michaulina' but nicknamed 'bone shakers'.

c1870

$4,000-6,000 ATK

A 'penny farthing' bicycle, with sprung leather saddle, finished in green and white livery.

So named as the wheels were proportioned like a larger penny is to a smaller farthing, it was realized that the larger the drive wheel, the further one could travel with one rotation.

c1885   57in (145cm) high

$3,000-5,000 LC

A CLOSER LOOK AT A TRICYCLE

The seated rider braces himself with this handle.

It is steered by turning this handle which moves the small wheels.

The Royal Crescent was made for around three years from 1886.

It came in three models: the Lady's, the Roadster and the Racer.

A Daniel Rudge's patent 'Royal Crescent' tricycle, with handle steering mechanism.

c1885   Large wheel 48in (122cm) diam

$12,000-18,000 LC

A Doulton Lambeth stoneware cycling jug, with three white vignettes, inscribed "Military", "Road", and "Path".
c1900   9in (23cm) high

$400-600 TEN

A Crown Devon musical cycling jug, playing 'Daisy Bell'.
8in (20.5cm) high

$320-380 TEN

A cabinet card by A. Huber, Vienna, featuring rider with high-wheel bicycle, dated on reverse, with some soiling on the reverse.

1892

$220-280 AAC

Two 'Aha' bicycle lamps, including headlamp, rear-lamp and dynamo, black-colored metal, in original, unused condition.
c1925

$150-200 ATK

A large scrapbook relating to cycling, containing prints and cuttings.
12.5in (32cm) high

$150-200 TEN

FIND OUT MORE...

The British Cycling Museum, The Old Station, Camelford, Cornwall, England.

The National Cycle Collection, The Automobile Palace, Temple Street, Llandrindod Wells. www.cyclemuseum.org.uk

BONDS & SHARES

COLLECTORS' NOTES

- Bonds, share or stock certificates are issued to investors as proof of capital invested in a company, government or other public body, or an individual.

- The first shares in the modern sense were maritime shares and were traded in the Italian port of Amalfi from around AD1000, although certificates were not issued.

- The first certificates were issued in the late 17th century in England, France, Holland, and Italy. However, the majority of collectible certificates available today are from the 19th and first half of the 20th centuries.

- As this field is so wide, collectors often specialize in one area such as a particular country or period of issue, printing or casting errors, or unusual serial numbers. Shares for automobile, railroad and mining companies are also particularly sought-after.

- Manuscript signatures, especially of famous people, can also have a profound effect on value.

- As with all other paper-based collectibles, condition is crucial in terms of market value.

A certificate for three 500 rupee shares in the private Bank of Bengal, featuring a fine vignette representing the Empire, dated "24th September 1909", complete with the seal of the bank, fine script security device and various manuscript signatures and endorsements.

13.75in (35cm) wide

$22-28   **INT**

A General Motors Corporation common stock certificate.

12in (30.5cm) long

$8-12   **INT**

A Chinese government 5% interest gold loan bond certificate, the first ever issue by the new Republic of China, issued in 1912, GBP100 denomination, green border and background design.

18in (46cm) long

$50-70   **INT**

A Russian 5% interest bond certificate, "Loan of the City of Nikolaef", complete with detachable coupons redeemable for 10 shillings, dated 1912, printed in Russian and English.

15.5in (39cm) long

$15-25   **INT**

A certificate for 100 francs stock in the Société des Cafés de l'Indochine, complete with all 24 redeemable coupons, very attractive red and brown Oriental designs on a green ground, dated "25th August 1926", certificate number 011756.

This certificate is unusual in that it was issued in Saigon rather than the seat of the Colonial government in Vietnam.

14in (36cm) long

$15-25   **INT**

An interest bond certificate issued by Bank Zerubabel, Central Institution of the Palestine Cooperative Movement.

Bank Zerubabel continued operations after the creation of the state of Israel in 1948 – however, pre-1948 bond certificates are worth 4-5 times as much as later examples.

1945   *14in (36cm) wide*

$60-90   **INT**

A "cancelled" certificate for 5% guaranteed preferred shares, in the Waterford, Dungarvan & Lismore Railway Co.

1897   *10.5in (27cm) w*

$12-18   **INT**

A Turkish Ottoman Empire 1/4 livres certificate, printed on one side only with the 'tughra' seal of the Sultan.

1912   *8in (20cm) wide*

$22-28   **INT**

FIND OUT MORE...

'Scripophily: Collecting Bonds and Share Certificates', by Keith Hollender, published by Book Sales, 1985.

www.scripophily.org, the International Bond and Share Society.

COLLECTORS' NOTES

- First edition books are popular as they represent the most original version of the book: the one closest to the author's intent. Later examples can also be sought-after, but only if they contain important additional information.

- Copies signed by the author will add to the value. Even more valuable are early works signed by the author before they became famous because these are usually rare. Inscriptions by other people, unless they are famous themselves, generally decrease the value.

- Classic works by writers such as Agatha Christie and Ian Fleming are always popular but more modern writers, like Margaret Atwood, Vikram Seth, Nick Hornby, Irvine Welsh, and Donna Tartt, are all sought-after. Look out for authors who have won literary prizes as this adds to the desirability of their current and earlier books. The same applies to titles that have been made into films.

- The condition of a book has a huge impact on the value, and mint copies will always command a premium. The presence of a dust jacket is also important, particularly for post-1950 books.

Margaret Atwood, "The Blind Assassin", first edition, published by Bloomsbury, signed by the author.

2000

$22-28   BIB

Margaret Atwood, "Oryx & Crake", first edition, published by Bloomsbury.

2003

$18-22   BIB

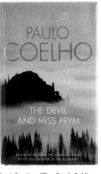

Saul Bellow, "The Victim", first edition, published by The Vanguard Press, New York, signed by the author on the title page.

1947

$2,200-2,800   BRB

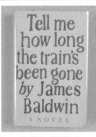

James Baldwin, "Tell Me How Long the Train's Been Gone", first edition, published by Dial Press, New York, signed by the author.

1937

$650-750   BRB

James M. Cain, "Serenade", first edition, published by Alfred A. Knopf, New York.

1937

$600-700   BRB

Ray Bradbury, "Dark Carnival", first edition, published by Arkham House, Sauk City, Wisconsin, signed by the author.

1947

$2,000-2,500   BRB

Paul Coelho, "The Devil & Miss Prym", first English-language edition, published by Harper Collins.

2000

$22-28   BIB

J.M. Coetzee, "Disgrace", first edition, published by Secker & Warburg, signed and dated "25/10/99" by the author.

The date is significant and adds to the value, as it was the day Coetzee was awarded the Booker prize for this book.

1995

$400-600   BIB

Douglas Copeland, "Microserfs", first edition, published by HarperCollins.

1995

$10-15   **BIB**

Stephen Crane, "The Red Badge of Courage", first edition, published by D. Appleton and Company, New York, lacks rare dust jacket.

1895

$2,000-3,000   **BRB**

Pat Conroy, "The Boo", first edition, published by McClure Press, Verona, Virginia.

1970

$3,000-4,000   **BRB**

William Faulkner, "Light in August", first edition, published by Harrison Smith & Robert Haas, New York.

1932

$2,000-3,000   **BRB**

Charles Frazier, "Cold Mountain", first edition, published by Sceptre.

1997

$60-90   **BIB**

William Gibson, "Virtual Light", first edition, published by Bantam.

1993

$80-120   **BIB**

Mark Haddon, "The Curious Incident of the Dog in the Night-Time", first edition, published by Jonathan Cape, with adult's version dust jacket.

This children's book became a popular adult's read, so the publishers re-issued it with an 'adult' cover.

2003

$50-70   **BIB**

Mark Haddon, "The Curious Incident of the Dog in the Night-Time", first edition, published by David Fickling Books, with children's version dust jacket.

2003

$22-28   **BIB**

John Grisham, "The Rainmaker", first edition, published by Century, signed by the author.

1995

$50-70   **BIB**

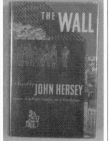

John Hersey, "The Wall", first edition, published by Alfred A. Knopf, New York.

1950

$500-600   **BRB**

Fletcher Knebel and Charles Bailey, "Seven Days in May", first edition, published by Harper & Row, New York and Evanston.

1962

$120-180   **BRB**

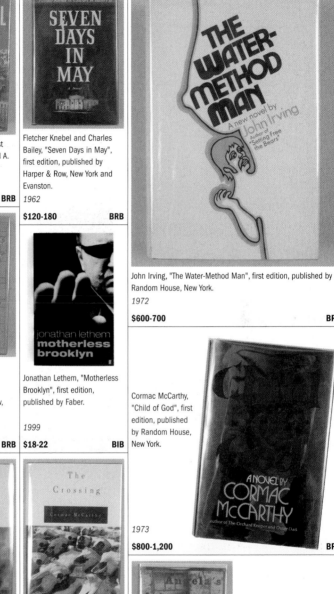

John Irving, "The Water-Method Man", first edition, published by Random House, New York.

1972

$600-700   **BRB**

Milan Kundera, "The Unbearable Lightness of Being", first US edition, published by Harper & Row, New York.

1984

$150-250   **BRB**

Jonathan Lethem, "Motherless Brooklyn", first edition, published by Faber.

1999

$18-22   **BIB**

Cormac McCarthy, "Child of God", first edition, published by Random House, New York.

1973

$800-1,200   **BRB**

Cormac McCarthy, "Cities of the Plain", signed limited first edition of 1,000, published by Alfred A. Knopf, New York.

1998

$500-600   **BRB**

Cormac McCarthy, "The Crossing", first edition, published by Alfred A. Knopf, New York, one of 1,000 copies signed by the author.

1994

$500-700   **BRB**

Frank McCourt, "Angela's Ashes", first edition, published by Scribner, New York.

1996

$450-550   **BRB**

Carson McCullers, "The Heart is a Lonely Hunter", first edition, published by Houghton Mifflin Co.

1940

$1,200-1,800 BRB

Larry McMurty, "The Last Picture Show", first edition, published by The Dial Press, New York, signed by the author.

1966

$1,000-2,000 BRB

Larry McMurty, "Terms of Endearment", first edition, published by Simon and Schuster, New York.

1975

$150-250 BRB

Toni Morrison, "Beloved", first edition, published by Alfred A. Knopf, New York, signed by the author.

1987

$700-800 BRB

Flannery O'Connor, "Everything That Rises Must Converge", first edition, published by Farrar, Straus and Giroux, New York.

1965

$300-400 BRB

Thomas Pynchon, "The Crying of Lot 49", first edition, published by J.B. Lippincott Company, New York.

1966

$800-1,200 BRB

Philip Roth, "The Human Stain", first edition, published by Jonathan Cape.

2000

$18-22 BIB

Tobias Wolff, "Ugly Rumours", first edition, reportedly one of less than 1,000 produced, published by George Allen & Unwin, London.

This novel was never published in the US and the author has refused to list it among his previous publications.

1975

$1,200-1,800 BRB

William Saroyan, "Boys and Girls Together", first edition, published by Charles Scribner's Sons, New York, signed by the author.

1963

$200-300 BRB

Arundhati Roy, "The God of Small Things", first edition, published by Flamingo.

1997

$30-40 BIB

J.D. Salinger, "Raise High The Roof Beam, Carpenters and Seymour: An Introduction", first edition, published by Little, Brown.

1963

$1,200-1,800 BRB

Alice Sebold, "The Lovely Bones", first edition, published by Picador.

2002

$18-22 BIB

Isaac Bashevis Singer, "The Family Moskat", first English-language edition, published by Alfred A. Knopf, New York.

1950

$750-850 BRB

John Steinbeck, "East of Eden", signed limited first edition of 750, published by The Viking Press, New York.

1952

$3,200-3,800 BRB

John Steinbeck, "Of Mice and Men", first edition, published by Covici Friede, New York.

1937

$1,800-2,200 BRB

Amy Tan, "The Joy Luck Club", first edition, published by Heinemann.

1989

$25-35 BIB

Donna Tartt, "The Little Friend", first edition, published by Bloomsbury, signed by the author.

2002

$15-25 BIB

Mark Twain, "Following the Equator: A Journey Around the World", first edition, published by American Published Company, Hartford.

1897

$700-900 BRB

Rev. W. Awdry, "Duck and the Diesel Engine - Railway Series, No. 13", first edition, published by Edmund Ward, London.

1958

$60-90 BIB

Rev. W. Awdry, "The Little Old Engine - Railway Series, No. 14", first edition, published by Edmund Ward, London.

1959

$80-120 BIB

Enid Blyton, "Mr Plod and Little Noddy", first edition, published by Sampson Low, Marston & Co., London.

1961

$40-60 BIB

Rev. W. Awdry, "The Twin Engines - Railway Series, No. 15", first edition, published by Edmund Ward, London.

1960

$100-150 BIB

Enid Blyton, "New Big Noddy Book", first edition, published by Sampson Low, Marston & Co., London.

1950

$80-120 BIB

Enid Blyton, "A Rubbalong Tale, A Werner Laurie Show Book", first edition, published by Werner Laurie, with original hard paper picture boards.

1951

$400-600 BIB

Enid Blyton, "Noddy's Own Nursery Rhymes", first edition, published by Sampson Low, Marston & Co., London.

1958

$100-150 BIB

Enid Blyton, "Tales of Toyland", first edition, published by George Newnes Ltd, London, contains owner's inscription.

1944

$120-180 BIB

Enid Blyton, "Tales About Toys", published by Brockhampton Press, Leicester.

c1950

$25-35 BIB

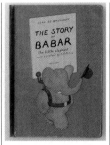

Enid Blyton, "Well Done Noddy", first edition, published by Sampson Low, Marston & Co., London.
1952

$60-90 BIB

Laurent de Brunhoff, "Babar's Visit To Bird Island", first edition, published by Methuen, London, with cloth spine.
1952

$150-200 BIB

Laurent de Brunhoff, "Babar's Fair", first edition, published by Methuen, London.
1969

$40-60 BIB

Laurent de Brunhoff, "The Story of Babar, the Little Elephant", first edition, published by Methuen, London.
1934

$150-200 BIB

Kate Greenaway, "Language of Flowers", published by George Routledge and Sons, illustrations by Kate Greenaway, written inscription, dated "Sept. 20th 1888".

$120-180 BIB

Andrew Lang, "The Brown Fairy", first edition, published by Longmans, Green & Co., London.
1904

$300-500 BIB

A.A. Milne, "The House At Pooh Corner", first edition, published by Methuen, London, illustrated by E.H. Shepard.
1928

$1,000-1,500 BIB

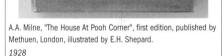

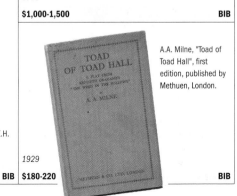

A.A. Milne, "Now We Are Six", first edition with illustration by E.H. Shepard, published by Methuen, London.
1927

$700-1,000 BIB

A.A. Milne, "Toad of Toad Hall", first edition, published by Methuen, London.
1929

$180-220 BIB

A.A. Milne, "Winnie-the-Pooh", first edition, with illustrations by E.H. Shepard, published by Methuen, London.

1926

$150-200   **BIB**

Beatrix Potter, "The Story of Miss Moppet", first edition with panorama, published by Warne and Co., London, retaining its silver tab.

1906

$400-600   **BIB**

Beatrix Potter, "Peter Rabbit and Friends - A Stand Up Story Book", published by F. Warne.

1998

$15-20   **BIB**

Maurice Sendak, "In the Night Kitchen", first edition, published by Harper & Row.

1970

$30-50   **BIB**

Beatrix Potter, "The Story of a Fierce Bad Rabbit", first edition, second issue panorama, published by Warne and Co., London.

1906

$400-600   **BIB**

Beatrix Potter, "The Tale of Mrs. Tittlemouse", first edition, published by F. Warne and Co., London.

1910

$300-400   **BIB**

"Dean's Surprise Model Series No. 1 - Surprise Model Picture Book", published by Dean & Son, London, very scarce.

c1895

$180-220   **BIB**

Beatrix Potter, "The Tale of Pigling Bland", first edition, published by Warne and Co., London.

1913

$400-500   **BIB**

William Shakespeare, "A Midsummer-Night's Dream", published by Heinemann, from a limited edition of 1,000, illustrated by Arthur Rackham with 40 mounted plates, signed and numbered by Rackham, inscription on front inside cover, with dust slip cover.

1908

$3,000-4,000   **BIB**

COLLECTORS' NOTES

■ Known today for its teddy bears, Dean's Rag Book Co. originally made children's cloth story books, illustrated with brightly colored pictures, at its London factory. The company was founded by Henry Samuel Dean in 1903 and made bears from 1917 onwards.

■ For collectors, the most interesting period runs from 1903 until the 1930s, when the company employed popular artists of the day to design the illustrations. These included F.M. Barton, Stanley Berkeley, and John Hasall.

■ As well as English, the books were also produced in French, German, Dutch, and, rarest of all, Russian.

■ The materials used, and the fact that these books were handled by children, means that condition affects value greatly except in the scarcest examples. Look for examples in good, clean condition with no tears or stains.

Gladys Hall and Eugenie Richards, "The Nursery Rhyme Book", Book No. 161, and "Look Here!", Book No. 158, both color-printed illustrated picture books.

1916   *largest 11.25in (28.5cm) high*

$120-180   **BONC**

Yoshio Markino, "Old English Nursery Rhymes", Book No. 188, color-printed illustrated storybook.

1916   *8in (20cm) wide*

$40-60   **BONC**

A. Herouard, "The Playtime Book", Book No. 254, color-printed illustrated picture book.

1927   *11in (28cm) high*

$40-60   **BONC**

"Just Off", a color-printed illustrated picture book.

1905   *9in (23cm) wide*

$60-90   **BONC**

John Hassell, "Ding! Din! Don!", Book No. 9, French language color-printed illustrated storybook, dirty.

1903   *11.5in (29cm) high*

$40-60   **BONC**

John Hassall, "Entrez Dans la Danse", color-printed illustrated storybook.

1913   *10.75in (27.5cm) high*

$120-180   **BONC**

G.H. Dodd, "Le Cirque Pig & Cie", Book No. 81, French language with color-printed illustrations.

1910   *8.75in (22.5cm) high*

$40-60   **BONC**

Stanley Berkeley and Eugenie Richards, "Les Mémoires De Toby Par Lui Même", Book No. 47, French language, color-printed illustrated storybook.

1905   *11.5in (29cm) high*

$70-100   **BONC**

E. Travis, "Le Train Siffle!", Book No. 150, French language, color-printed illustrated train book.

1916   *11.5in (29.5cm) wide*

$100-150   BONC

John Hassall, "Mironton, Mirontaine!", French language color-printed illustrated storybook.

1913   *11.5in (29cm) high*

$120-180   BONC

F. M. Barton, "Puff! Puff!", Book No. 20, French language with color-printed illustrations.

1903   *8.75in (22.5cm) wide*

$40-60   BONC

Left: Chas K. Cook, "Eisenbahnen", Book No. 61, German language color-printed illustrated train book.

1910   *8.5in (21.5cm) high*

$40-60   BONC

Right: Chas K. Cook, "Eins-Zwei-Drei", Book No. 48, German language color-printed illustrated number book.

1905   *8.25in (21cm) high*

$50-70   BONC

A Flip the Frog factory production rag toy sheet, color-printed on orange velvet.

1930   *39.25in (100cm) long*

$180-220   BONC

A Flip the Frog factory production rag toy sheet, color-printed on yellow velvet and a part Flip sheet.

1930   *39.25in (100cm) long*

$280-320   BONC

An Oswald the Lucky Rabbit factory production rag toy sheet, on printed velvet, with various sized heads.

1933   *29in (74cm) long*

$150-200   BONC

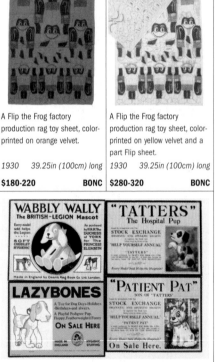

Six Dean's shop display cards, comprising "Lost Dismal Desmond", "Tatters the Hospital Pup", "Patient Pat Son of Tatters", "Lazybones", "Wabbly Wally", and "Gallopin' Gus the Lucky Gee Gee".

c1930   *11.75in (30cm) wide*

$280-320   BONC

Six Dean's shop display cards, comprising "Oswald the Lucky Rabbit", "Bosco and Honey", "Dean's Dancing Dolls", and "Hetty the Help Yourself Girl", together with "Lazybones", and "Ma-Coney".

c1930

$280-320   BONC

FIND OUT MORE...

'Dean's Rag Book Co. - The First 100 Years', *by Neil Miller.*

Enid Blyton, "Enid Blyton's Famous Five Go Adventuring Again" annual.

1978

$15-20 BIB

Mary Tourtel, "Rupert In More Adventures" annual, published by the Daily Express.

1944

$100-150 BIB

Mary Tourtel, "More Adventures of Rupert" annual, published by the Daily Express.

1947

$180-220 BIB

Mary Tourtel, "The Monster Rupert" annual, published by the Daily Express.

1948

$40-60 BIB

Mary Tourtel, "More Adventures of Rupert" annual, published by the Daily Express.

1949

$60-90 BIB

Mary Tourtel, "More Rupert Adventures" annual, published by the Daily Express.

1952

$120-180 BIB

Mary Tourtel, "Rupert" annual, published by the Daily Express.

1949

$150-200 BIB

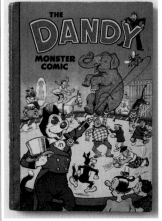

"The Dandy Monster Comic" annual, published by D.C. Thomson, front boards featuring Korky the Cat as ringmaster at a circus.

These annuals are hard to find in such clean condition, making it more desirable.

1951

$150-200 BIB

Mary Tourtel, "Rupert" annual, published by the Daily Express.

1958

$50-80 BIB

"Baedeker's Greece", published by Baedeker.
1894
$100-150 BIB

C.L. Freeston, "The Passes of the Pyrenees", first edition.
1912
$50-70 BIB

J.A.McClymont, "Greece", first edition with illustrations by John Fulleylove, published by A. and C. Black, lacks dust jacket.
1927
$25-35 BIB

Eric Newby, "Departures and Arrivals", first edition, published by Harper Collins.
1999
$25-35 BIB

Geoffrey Moorhouse, "Apples in the Snow – A Journey to Samarkand", first edition, published by Hodder and Stoughton.
1990
$25-35 BIB

John Morris, "Eating the Indian Air", first edition, published by Hamish Hamilton.
1968
$25-35 BIB

Freya Stark, "The Valleys of the Assassins", first edition, published by John Murray.
1934
$300-500 BIB

Freya Stark, "The Journey's Echo", first edition, published by John Murray.
1963
$50-80 BIB

An Ordnance Survey map of Clacton-on-Sea and Harwich.
$15-25 BIB

J. Coutts, "Everyday Gardening", reprint, published by Ward, Lock and Co.

$10-15 BIB

F. Hadfield Farthing, "Saturday In My Garden", third edition, revised by A. Cecil Bartlett, published by McDonald & Co.
1947

$15-20 BIB

L.J.F. Brimble, "Flowers in Britain", published by Macmillan.
1980

$25-35 BIB

A.G.L. Hellyer, "Garden Plants in Colour", first edition, published by W.H. and L. Collingridge Ltd.
1958

$10-15 BIB

Denis Wood, "Practical Garden Design", first edition, published by J.M. Dent and Sons.
1976

$15-25 BIB

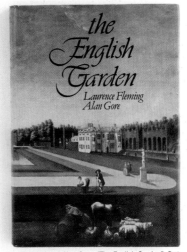

Laurence Fleming and Alan Gore, "The English Garden", first edition, second impression, published by Michael Joseph Ltd.
1980

$25-35 BIB

Edward Step, "Wild Flowers Month by Month", first edition, published by Frederick Warne and Co., two volumes.
1905

$25-35 BIB

Richardson Wright, "The Practical Book of Outdoor Flowers", first edition, published by J.B. Lippincott.
1924

$25-35 BIB

Frank S. Smythe, "The Valley of Flowers", published by Hodder and Stoughton.
1947

$15-25 BIB

COLLECTORS' NOTES

- Before glass bottles became the norm, household liquids were usually stored in tan- or cream-colored stoneware vessels with black lettering, sometimes made by well-known potteries such as Doulton & Co. Blue or green glass bottles, older etched glass versions, and those decorated with pictures are particularly sought-after.

- Glass was increasingly used for storing drinks from the end of the 18thC. Following the invention of a method for carbonating water in the late 18thC, a torpedo-shaped bottle was introduced that prevented bubbles escaping.

- Patented medicines became popular in the early 19thC, and were often attractively packaged, making the bottles appealing to today's collector. Warner's Safe Cure is a popular example and a collecting area in its own right. Standard bottles can be easily picked up.

- Glass and earthenware ink bottles, especially those in unusual shapes such as cottages, birdcages, and figures, are also popular with enthusiasts. Ink bottles made after 1840 are especially common, as more were produced to meet the rising demand caused by improving literacy and the Penny Post.

- Good condition is essential and a crack or chip in the wrong place can make an otherwise valuable bottle almost worthless; a missing stopper can also decrease value. Be wary of the large number of fake colored bottles on the market and look out for photocopied 'original' labels by carefully examining tears and dirt.

An unusual Savory & Moore wooden boxed bottle, clear glass with paper label "The Cordial Stomach Mixture/Savory & Moore/Chemists To The Queen", complete in boxwood case with screw-off top.

c1890   4.5in (11.5cm) high

$120-180   **BBR**

A Hooper & Company bottle, dark olive green glass, rectangular shape with rounded shoulders and beveled corners embossed "Hooper & Compy/55/Grosvenor St/And At/7 Pall Mall East/London Laboratory/Mitcham/Surrey".

c1875   7.5in (19cm) high

$280-320   **BBR**

A rare and early Daffys Elixir bottle, dark olive green glass, rectangular cross section, beveled corners, base cross hinged and pontilled, short neck with crude applied rolled lip, embossed "True Daffys/Elixir" to front and rear, one small patch of iridescence, very good condition.

This early version is identifiable by the lack of lettering on the smaller side panels.

c1835   4.5in (11.5cm) high

$3,000-5,000   **BBR**

A Warners Safe Cure bottle, olive green glass, embossed "Warners/Safe Cure London", with pictorial safe trade mark, good condition.

c1900   7.25in (18.5cm) high

$50-80   **BBR**

A Warners Nervine bottle, olive green glass, weakly embossed "Warners Safe Nervine/London", with the safe pictorial trade mark, misshapen shoulders, top embossing weak, very good condition.

c1905   7.5in (9cm) high

$50-70   **BBR**

A rare Warners Safe Compound bottle, golden amber glass, embossed "Warners/Safe/Compound", with pictorial safe trade mark, a few tiny dings.

c1915   5.5in (14cm) high

$120-180   **BBR**

A Warners Safe Cure bottle, fine deep amber glass, embossed "Warners/Safe/Cure/London", with safe trade mark, very good condition.

c1895   7.5in (19cm) high

$40-60   **BBR**

A CLOSER LOOK AT A WINE BOTTLE

The Nailsea factory is best known today for its tableware produced from 'end of shift' dark bottle glass leftovers. The name became a general term for similar glass made at numerous factories.

The first glass wine bottles date from the 17thC. Early designs tended to be globe- or onion-shaped, by the early 18thC the mallet shape was introduced, followed by the cylinder.

A scarce hair restorer bottle, cobalt blue glass, rectangular shape, embossed "The Maison Benbow/Specialists For The Hair/St Leonards-On-Sea", very good condition.

c1915   *6in (15cm) high*

$30-40   **BBR**

A rare large late 19th/early 20thC Crescent green glass poison bottle, embossed "Not To Be Taken" to center panel with diagonal ribs and dots, "RD NO 461701" to base, together with a small cobalt blue glass example, very good condition.

Poison bottles had to be easily discernable from other bottles and are typically blue or green with ribbed or quilted exteriors and embossed "Not To Be Taken" or "Poison". Clear glass examples are rare and shaped bottles such as skulls are sought-after.

Large 6.75in (17cm) high

$80-120   **BBR**

Small 3.5in (9cm) high

$30-50   **BBR**

This type of glass is often referred to as black glass, when it is actually dark green or brown.

This is possibly the first recorded example of a Nailsea-style bottle with a seal incorporating both a date and pictorial image.

A dated Nailsea-style sealed wine bottle, globular body with longish neck and applied collar, dark olive green with white enameled flecks of varying size, pictorial seal reads "1830/ AC", with a horse pictured.

1830   *9.5in (24cm) high*

$6,000-9,000   **BBR**

A Hyde cobalt blue glass cylinder ink bottle, with pouring lip, embossed "Hyde/London", very good condition.

c1905   *6in (15.5cm) high*

$18-22   **BBR**

An early Hamilton cobalt blue glass bottle, very heavily embossed with large coat of arms, minor neck mark, otherwise extremely good condition.

8.75in (22cm) long

$2,200-2,800   **BBR**

An early Schweppes dark olive green glass Hamilton bottle, with applied rolled lip "J Schweppe & Co./Genuine Superior/Aerated Waters/79 Margaret Street", minor wear.

7.5in (19cm) long

$1,800-2,200   **BBR**

A sealed dark olive green glass wine bottle, applied collar lip and base pontil, seal with the initials "A S", small hairline crack to base.

c1875   *11in (28cm) high*

$280-320   **BBR**

An 1880s sealed dark olive green glass wine bottle, applied heavy double collar lip, seal with wild boar and coronet, deep kick-up pontil base.

11.25in (28.5cm) high

$300-500   **BBR**

A Prices Patent Candle bottle, cobalt blue glass wedge-shaped bottle embossed to front "Prices/ Patent/ Candle/ Company/ Limited", with diamond registration mark, good condition.

7.5in (19cm) high

$120-180   **BBR**

BOTTLES

An unusual small 1880s Weston Super Mare Sykes Macvay patent aqua glass bottle, embossed "Ross & Co./Weston Super Mare" to front, "Sykes Macvay & Co./Patent 1877/Castleford", complete with lead and rubber insert to neck, minor star body crack.

6in (15cm) high

$220-280   **BBR**

A teakettle dark amethyst colored glass ink bottle, fluted sloping octagonal shape with upturned spout, good condition.

c1845   *2in (5cm) high*

$300-500   **BBR**

A very rare 1870s-80s amethyst glass target ball, crisscross embossing, central band embossed "W W Greener St Marys Works Birmm & Haymarket London".

3in (7.5cm) high

$600-900   **BBR**

A Hardens Star fire grenade, cobalt blue glass, vertically ribbed, embossed star to front, central band embossed "Harden Star Hand Grenade Fire Extinguisher", complete sealed with contents and paper label around neck, good condition.

c1890   6.5in (16.5cm) high

$180-220   **BBR**

A Hardens Star fire grenade, cobalt blue glass, vertically ribbed embossed star to front, weakly embossed around central band, sealed with contents, good condition.

c1890   6.5in (16.5cm) high

$80-120   **BBR**

A Mr Punch saltglaze figural ink bottle, formed as a seated Mr Punch, mid-brown saltglaze with touches of dark brown highlights, rear with raised diamond registration mark and particularly well impressed "Gardners Ink Works/Lower White Cross St London", very good condition.

c1845   5in (12.5cm) high

$700-1,000   **BBR**

A Napoleon mid-brown saltglaze ink bottle, probably London, formed as a naturalistically modeled Napoleon's head, impressed to rear "Findleys/Napolion", slight flake to hat front.

This is a previously unrecorded figural Napoleon ink bottle. Napoleon died in 1821 and it is possible this could have commemorated his death, which would make it significantly early.

c1830   2.25in (5.5cm) high

$1,800-2,200   **BBR**

A Bellowing Man light and mid-brown saltglaze ink bottle, formed as a bellowing man's head, quill hole to forehead with elaborate side embossing, minor bottom edge flake.

c1845   3in (7.5cm) wide

$300-400   **BBR**

A Manchester Railway slab seal porter, gray-green glaze, applied seal reads "Midland/B.B." (Midland Hotel Buffet Bar) very crude, very good condition.

The hotel still stands beside Victoria Station in Manchester.

c1865   7in (18cm) high

$320-380   **BBR**

A Sheffield slab seal flask, gray-green glaze, seal reads "Old No. 12", good condition.

Old No. 12 is the name of a public house in Sheffield.

c1855   8in (20cm) high

$120-180   **BBR**

An S.H. Ward & Co. Ltd ginger beer bottle, standard two-tone bottle with "Home Brewed Ginger Beer/S.H. Ward & Co. Ltd Renton Street/Sheffield".

This is the rarest of all the Wards variations.

c1900   7.5in (19cm) high

$50-70   **BBR**

A Firths Darlington ginger beer bottle, standard two-tone Blue transfer "Firths Darlington/Brewed Ginger Beer", locomotive pictorial trade mark Gray Portobello pottery mark, good condition.

c1900   7in (18cm) high

$40-60   **BBR**

An Arliss Robinson & Co. ginger beer bottle, standard blue top "Arliss Robinson & Co./Home Brewed/Ginger Beer/Sutton Surrey", Bourne Denby pottery mark, slight hairline.

c1900   6.75in (17cm) high

$30-40   **BBR**

A scarce Comrie & Co. ginger beer bottle, transfer "Special/Old Scotch Ginger Beer Comrie & Co./Helensburgh", large pictorial of man holding aloft a bottle of ginger beer, Port Dundas Glasgow pottery mark.

c1900   8in (20cm) high

$80-120   **BBR**

A rare late Victorian Tyrconnell whisky jug, off-white glaze, black transfer "Tyrconnell Whisky" depicting Donegal Castle's building ruins, rear handle broken off, Grosvenor Glasgow pottery mark.

9in (23cm) high

$50-70   **BBR**

A Cruiskeen Lawn two-tone whisky jug, handle to rear, black transfer "Cruiskeen Lawn/Mitchells Old/Irish Whisky/Belfast", with cautionary lines to rear, Midland Pottery Melling pottery mark, good condition.

c1900   7.25in (18.5cm) high

$50-70   **BBR**

A Watsons two-tone whisky jug, pouring lip to neck, transfer showing highlander, "Watsons/Dundee/Whisky", Port Dundas pottery mark.

c1900   8.5in (21.5cm) high

$50-70   **BBR**

An unusual Ivanhoe whisky jug, top off-white glaze, base tan, black transfer "Ivanhoe /Old Scotch Whisky", Port Dundas Glasgow pottery mark.

c1905   8in (20cm) high

$150-200   **BBR**

FIND OUT MORE...

'Antique Glass Bottles - Their History and Evolution (1500-1850)', Willy van den Bossche, Antique Collectors Club, 2001.

'Stoneware Bottles: Bellarmines to Ginger Beers', Derek Askey, published by BBR Publishing, 1998.

www.antiquebottles.com

A copper kettle, by Booth & Son of Toronto, patented 1887.

12in (30.5cm) long

$200-250 BP

A Canadian conical metal ice-cream scoop.

c1910   *8.25in (21cm) long*

$70-100 BP

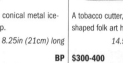

A tobacco cutter, with black shaped folk art horse knife.

14.5in (37cm) long

$300-400 BP

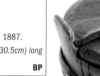

An early 19thC cane-bound butter tub, with swivel action on the cover.

6.5in (16.5cm) diam

$300-400 BP

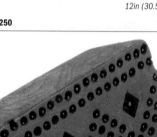

A Canadian decorative border stencil stamp.

6in (15cm) long

$40-60 BP

A rare 19thC Canadian wooden pie crimper.

8in (20.5cm) long

$80-120 BP

A maplewood bobbin, with original green paint.

c1890   *9in (23cm) long*

$15-25 BP

A 19thC six candle mold, from Waterloo county, Ontario.

10.5in (26.5cm) high

$70-100 BP

CANADIANA

A Canadian wooden boot remover, from Waterloo county, Ontario.

19in (48.5cm) long

$70-100   **BP**

A Canadian small quillwork basket, with maple leaf design, native-made from porcupine quills and birch bark.

c1935   *4in (10cm) wide*

$15-20   **TYA**

A 19thC Canadian whimsical green and black painted wooden axe.

15in (38cm) high

$120-180   **BP**

A Canadian patinated metal study of a beaver.

7.5in (19cm) long

$120-180   **WAD**

A children's bowling game, with ten wooden pins and three balls.

c1935   *10in (25.5cm) high*

$220-280   **BP**

A pair of juggling pins, hand-whittled from tiger maple.

c1895   *16.5in (42cm) long*

$70-100   **BP**

A late 19thC Canadian oak-framed school slate.

c1860   *14in (35.5cm) high*

$120-180   **BP**

A CLOSER LOOK AT AN ARGILLITE PENDANT

Argillite is a gray/black slate-like stone found on Graham Island, part of the Queen Charlotte Islands off the West coast of Canada.

It has been used for centuries by the indigenous 'Haida' people to carve sculptures.

Traditional primitive motifs are typical - look out for boxes and large carved poles.

Based in Masset on Graham Island, Douglas White is a collected name - also look out for Robert Davidson, Bill Reid, and Jay Simeon.

A Canadian Douglas White pendant, made from argillite, signed to the back "DOUGLAS WHITE MASSET B.C.".

c1955   *2in (5cm) high*

$80-120   **TSG**

A 1960s Royal Canadian Mounted Police felt hat, with leather band, made by John B. Stetson Co. of Canada, 5/8 size.

The North West Mounted Police was founded in May 1873 by the Canadian Parliament to both preserve order in the West and cement their claim to the region. In alliance with Blackfoot Chief Crowfoot they established order in the plains. In 1885 they helped quash the Northwest Rebellion, and after helped settlers build settlements in the area as well as maintaining order during the Klondike gold rush. King Edward VII officially recognized the force in 1904 and granted them the prefix 'Royal'. In 1920, they merged with the Dominion Police to become the 'Royal Canadian Mounted Police', familiarly called the 'Mounties'. Their red coats, wide brimmed hats and reputation for honesty and probity has led to them becoming a Canadian national symbol the world over, and they have been used in Canadian promotional advertising since the 1880s.

15.5in (39.5cm) long

$220-280   **TAM**

A pair of Royal Canadian Mounted Police leather boots, size 101/2, by Biltrite.

c1975   *18in (45.5cm) high*

$220-280   **TAM**

A pair of North West Mounted Police gauntlets, made from leather and fur.

c1900   *15in (38cm) long*

$120-180   **TAM**

A Royal Canadian Mounted Police officer plastic figure, made by Canadian manufacturer Reliable.

c1965   *7.75in (19.5cm) high*

$40-60   **TAM**

A large 1950s Royal Canadian Mounted Police badge.

4.5in (11.5cm) high

$30-40   **TAM**

A limited edition Royal Canadian Mounted Police officer 'Spirit of The Empire' figure, boxed.

1995   *Box 3.5in (9cm) high*

$25-35   **TAM**

A 'Mounted Policeman, Canadian North West' black and white postcard, of an officer and his horse.

c1915   *5.5in (14cm) wide*

$12-18   **TAM**

A lithographic color postcard of a Mountie, by Kodachrome.

c1955   *5.5in (14cm) high*

$8-12   **TAM**

John Peter Turner, "The North-West Mounted Police", first edition, published in two volumes by King's Printer, Ottawa.

1950   *9.75in (25cm) high*

$200-300   **TAM**

A pearlescent demi-tasse cup and saucer, commemorating the Royal Canadian Mounted Police, made in Japan.

c1965   *Saucer 4.5in (11.5cm) diam*

$15-20   **TAM**

A WWI Royal Flying Corps pilot's hat.

c1915   11.5in (29cm) long

$100-150   TAM

A WWII Royal Canadian Air Force hat.

12in (30.5cm) long

$100-150   TAM

A 1940s Royal Canadian Air Force woollen winter hat.

7in (18cm) high

$80-120   TAM

A WWII Canadian leather pilots helmet and goggles.

c1940   9.5in (24cm) high

$250-300   TAM

A pre-WWI Canadian 'Special Police' hat, with police badge depicting a beaver.

11in (28cm) long

$70-100   TAM

A Canadian Air Force decoration, awarded to Captain P.W. Corns, complete with miniature version and box.

1949   Box 4.5in (11.5cm) high

$100-150   TAM

A Royal Canadian Air Force 1918 pattern insignia badge, consisting of three metal components on dark blue felt.

This pattern was used until 1937.

1918-1937   3in (7.5cm) high

$120-180   TAM

A 1940s Dalton model 'G' dead reckoning computer, by Stanley Manufacturing Co. of Toronto, as used by the Royal Canadian Air Force.

6.5in (16.5cm) long

$180-220   TAM

A Normandy Landing badge.

These badges were worn by the 17th Duke of York's Royal Canadian Hussars of Montreal, who landed in Normandy with the 3rd Canadian infantry division in 1944.

c1945   2in (5cm) wide

$40-60   TAM

A Beaver Soda Water Works bottle, owned by A.W. Burns, at 406 Yonge Street, Toronto.

This bottle was dug up from the site of the Toronto Sky Dome.

c1880   7.5in (19cm) high

$120-180   **BP**

An Ontario Soda Water Mfg Co. bottle, from Welland Ontario, with a Star of David design in relief, designed to appeal to the Jewish immigrant community.

c1915   8in (20.5cm) high

$70-100   **TYA**

A Canadian Verner bottle, with beaver trademark.

The beaver motif helps to make this a desirable piece. A John Verner is known to have made bottles between 1881-97 in Toronto, although a number of Verners are reported to have operated businesses in the area during the 19thC.

7in (18cm) high

$80-120   **BP**

A Hamilton Glass Works 'Beaver' pint jar.

5.5in (14cm) high

$100-150   **BP**

A Canadian light green Chas Wilson bottle, with squirrel trademark.

Charles Wilson originally owned a business in Montreal with W. Farquarhar between 1845-76. After 1876, he moved to Toronto to set up his own business. There are a great many variations to collect in terms of shape, color and decoration, including the way the squirrel faces and mis-spelt names!

c1880   11in (28cm) high

$200-250   **BP**

A half-gallon 'Beaver' fruit jar, made at the Ontario Glass Company in Kingsville Ontario.

c1900   9in (23cm) high

$100-150   **BP**

A 1940s Buckley's Cinnamated Capsules tin, from Toronto, Ontario.

Buckley's are still well-known in Canada for their cough medicines.

2.5in (6.5cm) long

$7-10   **TYA**

A 1940s Nyaloids lozenge tin, with French language text, from Windsor, Ontario.

2.5in (6.5cm) wide

$7-10   **TYA**

A Blake Weaver Canadian honey tin.

c1929   5.25in (13.5cm) diam

$6-9   **TYA**

A Dr. Bishop's Powders package, from Kitchener, Ontario.

c1945   3in (7.5cm) wide

$8-12   **TYA**

A Collegians cedarwood cigar box, the lid depicting University College, University of Toronto.

c1883   8.5in (21.5cm) wide

$40-60   **TYA**

A 1950s Deichmann tall mug, made in New Brunswick.

5.25in (13.5cm) high

$120-180　　　　**TCF**

A 1950s miniature Deichmann jug, made in New Brunswick.

2.5in (6.5cm) diam

$70-100　　　　**TCF**

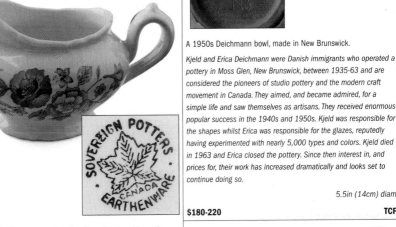

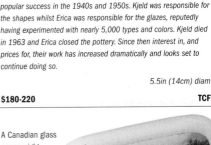

A 1950s Deichmann bowl, made in New Brunswick.

Kjeld and Erica Deichmann were Danish immigrants who operated a pottery in Moss Glen, New Brunswick, between 1935-63 and are considered the pioneers of studio pottery and the modern craft movement in Canada. They aimed, and became admired, for a simple life and saw themselves as artisans. They received enormous popular success in the 1940s and 1950s. Kjeld was responsible for the shapes whilst Erica was responsible for the glazes, reputedly having experimented with nearly 5,000 types and colors. Kjeld died in 1963 and Erica closed the pottery. Since then interest in, and prices for, their work has increased dramatically and looks set to continue doing so.

5.5in (14cm) diam

$180-220　　　　**TCF**

A Sovereign Potters cream jug, Hamilton, Ontario, with purple, blue, green, and yellow floral design, base marked "Sovereign Potters Earthenware Canada", and with maple leaf mark.

Sovereign Potters was founded in 1933 by William Pulkingham, James McMaster and Alfred Etherington with funds from local investors. It specialized in domestic tableware and railway and hotel china (notably for the Kon-Tiki room of the Queen Elizabeth Hotel, Montreal) until it was bought out by British company Johnson Brothers in 1947 and stopped producing dinnerware in 1958. In 1972 its name changed to 'H. & R. Johnson (Canada) Ltd'.

c1945　　　　9in (23cm) diam

$15-25　　　　**TCF**

A Canadian glass paperweight, from Quebec, with lithographic image of an outlet of Lake Memphremagog, dated.

1840　　　　4in (10cm) wide

$25-35　　　　**TYA**

A Callander, Ontario souvenir penant, the town where the celebrated Dionne quintuplets lived.

c1930s　　　　23in (58.5cm) long

$40-60　　　　**TYA**

A 1960s London, Ontario souvenir penant, depicting a Canadian Mounted Police officer.

22in (56cm) long

$12-18　　　　**TAM**

A 1920s Niagara Falls souvenir felt penant, with spectacular five-color Indian design.

28in (71cm) long

$70-100　　　　**TYA**

CANADIANA

A Canadian school cap from St Andrew's College, Aurora, Ontario, dated 1918.

8in (20.5cm) long

$150-200 TYA

A CLOSER LOOK AT A BLANKET COAT

These blankets were introduced by the Hudson's Bay Company in 1780. They were popular with Inuit, indigenous trappers, and mountain men, and were traded almost as a form of 'currency'.

The indigo stripes were known as 'points', each point equaling one fine beaver pelt.

Many blankets were made into protective outerwear and some come with belts, hoods and extending sleeves. This double-breasted coat is more 'fashionably' designed, hinting at a later date.

Differently colored stripes are a typical and traditional feature. They were introduced around 1800, and pastel colors were used from the 1930s. Here the stripes have been used to great decorative effect.

A Canadian sterling silver bracelet, with the badges of the ten provinces of Canada picked out in enamel.

c1940   7.5in (19cm) long

$15-25 TAM

A Canadian jacket fashioned from a Hudson Bay Company blanket.

Although the fur trade has long declined, trade in clothing made in the style of, or from, such blankets is still active, and the blanket and items made from it have become a traditional Canadian style icon. Vintage blankets and clothing are immensely desirable and hotly collected.

c1925

$400-600

36in (91.5cm) high

TYA

A 1940s official Government of Canada leather briefcase.

16in (40.5cm) wide

$70-100 TYA

A photograph of an operation in progress at a Montreal hospital, probably the University of Montreal teaching hospital as indicated by the viewing gallery in the theater, framed.

c1910

$200-250 TYA

A Canadian Berlin and Waterloo Hospital postcard, Berlin, Ontario, renamed 'Kitchener' during WWI, the postcard clearly showing alteration to the name, dated 1917.

5.25in (13.5cm) wide

$8-12 TYA

13in (33cm) wide

RED RIVER EXPEDITION
1870
BY
Colonel G. J. Wolseley
WHO PLANNED & LED IT

Colonel Garnet Wolseley, "Red River Expedition", published by Blackwood Magazine, the author's own copy with several ink annotations, early tree gilt, published December 1870.

9in (23cm) high

$1,000-1,500 BP

COLLECTORS' NOTES

■ Canes first became popular during the 16th century. Their fashionable high point was from the 19th century until WWI and most canes found today date from this period. A gentleman may have had a number of canes for day and evening use. The materials and quality of workmanship indicated a person's status and continue to be important factors for collectors today.

■ Examine the different parts including the handle or rounded pommel, the shaft and the ferrule on the end, as all should be original and not replacements. Missing ferrules are rarely a problem unless it was an intrinsic, decorated part of the cane. Hardwood is used for the shaft, usually Malacca which does not warp or bend.

■ Examples with fine carving, materials such as ivory, gold or inset precious stones are desirable as are 'folk art' canes, which are usually charmingly or naively carved. 'Gadget' canes with hidden or added uses are much sought after, and the more complex, the more valuable a piece usually is.

An erotic walking stick, the ivory handle carved with a reclining naked woman, Malacca shaft with an ivory collar engraved with flowers.
c1850

$2,200-2,800   SEG

A 19thC riding crop, with carved ivory handle of a monkey's head with a long brimmed stylized riding hat, with gilded engraved collar.

$400-600   SEG

A CLOSER LOOK AT A CANE

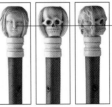

This is a pilgrimage cane used by pilgrims walking to religious towns, they are often called 'bourdons'.

The pommel is carved with a skull and the faces of Christ and Mary, reflecting its religious use and acting as a 'memento mori'.

The carving is extremely fine and realistic, and the good condition and early date makes this exceptionally rare and desirable.

A walking stick with a carved ivory handle, in the form of a reclining mastiff guard dog, with a Malacca shaft, with a gold, engraved collar.
c1870

$800-1,200   SEG

An early 19thC ivory mounted cane, with an ivory skull handled grip, shaft made out of a snake's vertebral column.

The skull has long been identified as a 'momento mori' (remember death). It famously appears in Holbein's 1533 painting 'The Ambassadors'.

$3,000-5,000   SEG

A 19thC 'Seditious' cane, with turned ivory pommel.

Whilst appearing to be an ordinary cane, its shape casts a shadow of a man's profile. These were often used by organizations such as the Freemasons to identify each other. Canes of this type were also used to discreetly demonstrate political allegiances to certain factions or parties.

$2,200-2,800   SEG

An historic walking stick, the figural ivory pommel carved with the head of French King Francis I, with a Malacca shaft, decorated silver collar and brass ferrule.
c1850

$3,000-5,000   SEG

Traces of color can be found on the face of Mary, who was once painted possibly with her traditional colors of blue, red, and white.

A 17th/18thC carved ivory pilgrimage cane, with a Malacca shaft and an ivory pommel mounted on a turned ivory collar, the large brass ferrule with an iron spike for gripping the ground.

$7,000-10,000   SEG

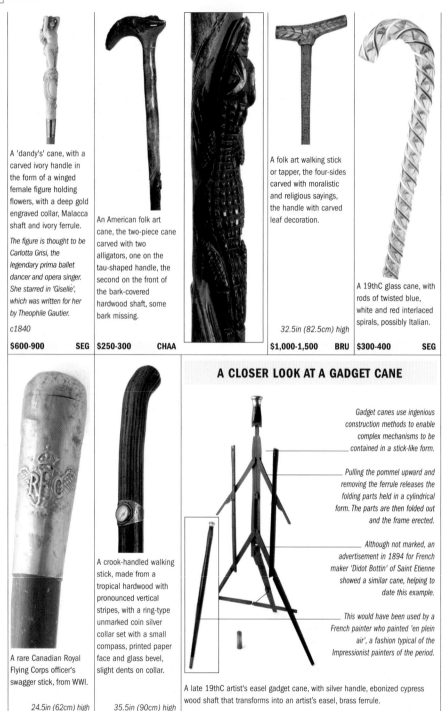

A 'dandy's' cane, with a carved ivory handle in the form of a winged female figure holding flowers, with a deep gold engraved collar, Malacca shaft and ivory ferrule.

The figure is thought to be Carlotta Grisi, the legendary prima ballet dancer and opera singer. She starred in 'Giselle', which was written for her by Theophile Gautier.

c1840

$600-900   **SEG**

An American folk art cane, the two-piece cane carved with two alligators, one on the tau-shaped handle, the second on the front of the bark-covered hardwood shaft, some bark missing.

$250-300   **CHAA**

A folk art walking stick or tapper, the four-sides carved with moralistic and religious sayings, the handle with carved leaf decoration.

32.5in (82.5cm) high

$1,000-1,500   **BRU**

A 19thC glass cane, with rods of twisted blue, white and red interlaced spirals, possibly Italian.

$300-400   **SEG**

A rare Canadian Royal Flying Corps officer's swagger stick, from WWI.

24.5in (62cm) high

$120-180   **TAM**

A crook-handled walking stick, made from a tropical hardwood with pronounced vertical stripes, with a ring-type unmarked coin silver collar set with a small compass, printed paper face and glass bevel, slight dents on collar.

35.5in (90cm) high

$100-150   **CHAA**

A CLOSER LOOK AT A GADGET CANE

Gadget canes use ingenious construction methods to enable complex mechanisms to be contained in a stick-like form.

Pulling the pommel upward and removing the ferrule releases the folding parts held in a cylindrical form. The parts are then folded out and the frame erected.

Although not marked, an advertisement in 1894 for French maker 'Didot Bottin' of Saint Etienne showed a similar cane, helping to date this example.

This would have been used by a French painter who painted 'en plein air', a fashion typical of the Impressionist painters of the period.

A late 19thC artist's easel gadget cane, with silver handle, ebonized cypress wood shaft that transforms into an artist's easel, brass ferrule.

$7,000-10,000   **SEG**

COLLECTORS' NOTES

■ John Beswick founded a pottery at Loughton, Stoke-on-Trent, England, in 1894. Animal figures were added to production in the 1930s and it is this line for which Beswick is renowned.

■ Many collectors focus on a type of animal or bird, and aim to own one in every available color. Cattle are popular and have risen in desirability and value recently, some fetch over $3,000.

■ Certain colors are rarer or more desirable than others, and thus often more valuable. Also look for minor variations in form, such as tails that hang free, or differently positioned legs as this indicates a different version and can also affect value.

■ Models made for short periods of time can also be more desirable and valuable, especially if from the mid-20th century. Condition is important, with protruding horns, thin legs and tails being easily broken, so examine a piece carefully.

■ Interest in Beswick animals has risen over the past two years and so have the values, partly as the factory closed in late 2002. Many prices are now exceeding their 'book' values, so collectors should pay close attention to annual price guides, auctions, and specialist dealers. Rarer models and those in mint condition are the most likely to appreciate in value.

A Beswick 'Jay' gloss figure, MN2417, modeled by Graham Tongue.

1972-82   *5in (12.5cm) high*

$180-220   **PSA**

A Beswick 'Songthrush' gloss figure, MN2308, modeled by Albert Hallam.

The matte version of this model produced 1983-89 is usually worth around 60% of the value of the gloss version.

1970-89   5.75in (14.5cm) high

$150-200   **PSA**

A Beswick 'Large Barn Owl' gloss figure, MN1046a, modeled by Arthur Gredington.

This is the first version with 'split' tail feathers. Produced from 1946, the date of retirement of this version is not known. The second version with a single row of tail feathers is worth around 50% less.

7.25in (18.5cm) high

$80-120   **PSA**

A Beswick 'Kingfisher' gloss figure, MN2371, modeled by Albert Hallam.

1971-91   5in (12.5cm) high

$100-150   **PSA**

A Beswick pottery cock pheasant, modeled by Arthur Gredington, impressed number "1225".

The version without flowers on the base is usually worth around 20% less than the version with flowers.

1951-67   9.75in (25cm) long

$150-200   **CHEF**

A Beswick 'Golden Eagle' matte figure, MN2062, modeled by Graham Tongue.

Look out for the slightly more desirable gloss finish version, produced from 1966-74.

1970-72   9.5in (24cm) high

$80-120   **PSA**

A Beswick 'Parakeet' gloss figure, MN930, modeled by Arthur Gredington.

1941-75   6in (15cm) high

$100-150   **PSA**

CERAMICS

A Beswick 'Friesian Cow Champion Claybury Leegwater' gloss figure, MN1362a, modeled by Arthur Gredington.

The matte version, produced only between 1985 and 1989 is usually more desirable.

1954-97   4.5in (12cm) high

$220-280   **PSA**

A Beswick 'Ayrshire Bull Whitehill Mandate' gloss figure, MN1454b, modeled by Colin Melbourne.

1957-90   5.25in (13.5cm) high

$400-600   **PSA**

A Beswick 'Dairy Shorthorn Bull Champion Gwersylt Lord Oxford 74th' figure, MN1504, modeled by Colin Melbourne.

A Beswick 'Charolais Bull' gloss figure, MN2463a, modeled by Alan Maslankowski in 1973.

This is a desirable model, only produced in this colorway.

1957-90   5.25in (13.5cm) high

$1,200-1,800   **PSA**

     5in (12.5cm) high

$300-500   **PSA**

A Beswick 'Large Hereford Calf' gloss figure, MN854, modeled by Arthur Gredington.

This example is in an unusual light sandy brown color. The gloss, roan colorway is the most sought after.

1940-57   4.25in (12cm) high

$180-220   **PSA**

A Beswick 'Hereford Calf' figure, MN901b, second version with closed mouth.

Look out for the roan colorway of this model, especially if its mouth is open, indicating the first version of the model.

c1940-1957   3.75in (9.5cm) high

$120-180   **PSA**

A Beswick 'Friesian Calf' gloss figure, MN1249c, modeled by Arthur Gredington in 1952.

c1950-97   2.75in (7cm) high

$220-280   **PSA**

CERAMICS

A Beswick 'Large Racehorse' gray gloss figure, MN1564, modeled by Arthur Gredington.

As with many other horses, 'rocking horse gray' is the most desirable and valuable color.

1959-82   11.25in (28.5cm) high

$180-220   **PSA**

A CLOSER LOOK AT A BESWICK HORSE

This piece was modeled by Arthur Gredington, known for his horses and other prolific designs for Beswick.

It is not known how long this color was produced for, but it is likely to have been a very short period.

— *Look out for the black gloss commemorative horse produced in an edition of 135 in 1990 to celebrate 50 years of production of this model.*

This is one of the rarest colorways for this model – other rare colors include blue, palomino, and iron gray.

A rare Beswick 'Shire Mare' piebald gloss figure, MN818, light crazing.

8.5in (21.5cm) high

$1,500-2,000   **PSA**

c1940-62

$800-1,200   **PSA**

A Beswick 'Shire Mare' rocking horse gray gloss figure, MN818, modeled by Arthur Gredington.

A Beswick 'Welsh Mountain Pony Coed Coch Madog' gray gloss figure, MN1643, first version, modeled by Arthur Gredington, introduced in 1961 and retirement date unknown.

6.25in (16cm) high

$220-280   **PSA**

A Beswick 'Arab Xayal' rocking horse gray figure, MN1265, modeled by Arthur Gredington.

This colorway is the most desirable for this model, which is available in a number of different colors.

1953-62   6.25in (16cm) high

$600-900   **PSA**

A Beswick piebald 'Pinto Pony' gloss figure, MN1373, first version modeled by Arthur Gredington, introduced 1972, retirement date unknown.

6.5in (16.5cm) high

$220-280   **PSA**

A Beswick large 'Thoroughbred Stallion' chestnut gloss figure, MN1772, modeled by Arthur Gredington.

One leg of this horse has been restored, lowering his value.

1961-69   8in (20.5cm) high

$300-500   **PSA**

Two Beswick pottery foals, MN836, stretching with splayed forelegs and MN915, reclining, modeled by Arthur Gredington.

c1941-1980   tallest 4.75in (12cm) high

$30-50   **CHEF**

A Beswick pottery 'English Setter' gray gloss figure, probably MN1220, modeled by Arthur Gredington.

1951-73   *8in (20cm) high*

$80-120   **CHEF**

A Beswick 'Solomon of Wendover' golden yellow gloss figure, MN1548, modeled by Arthur Gredington.

1958-94   *5.5in (14.5cm) high*

$40-60   **CHEF**

A Beswick 'Corgi' golden brown gloss figure, probably MN1299B, modeled by Arthur Gredington.

1953-94   *5.5in (14cm) high*

$50-80   **CHEF**

A Beswick 'Lioness' golden gloss figure, facing left, MN1507, modeled by Colin Melbourne.

This colorway is more desirable and valuable than the black one.

1957-67   *4.75in (12cm) high*

$60-90   **CHEF**

A rare Beswick 'Chi Chi The Panda' figure, MN2613, first version with bamboo shoot.

This version of the model, where the bear is eating a bamboo shoot, was produced for The London Natural History Museum for around two years only.

1978-c1980   *3.75in (9.5cm) high*

$180-220   **PSA**

A Beswick 'Atlantic Salmon' figure, MN1233, modeled by Arthur Gredington.

A Beswick 'Loch Ness Monster' gloss full whisky flask for Benegals Whisky, MN2051, modeled by Albert Hallam.

These flasks are also available in eagle, otter, and badger forms. They must be in mint condition, unopened and full to command maximum values.

A Beswick 'Seal' gloss figure, MN1534, modeled by Arthur Gredington.

1952-70   *6.5in (16.5cm) high*

$300-500   **CHEF**

1965-86   *3in (7.5cm) high*

$30-50   **PSA**

1958-66   *5.75in (14.5cm) high*

$80-120   **PSA**

COLLECTORS' NOTES

- Arthur Gredington started a new chapter in the history of John Beswick's pottery when he designed the Jemima Puddle-Duck figurine in 1947. The initial range, consisting of ten characters, was a great success and today over 100 versions of more than 40 different figures are known to exist.

- Beswick was acquired by Royal Doulton in 1969. Over the following six years, the Beatrix Potter line underwent a number of changes, which although designed to standardize the range, in the short term created the myriad variations that continue to fascinate the collecting community today.

- The different types of backstamps that were used attract great interest – the original gold "Beswick England" stamps are generally more sought-after and command higher prices than the later brown stamps which were used after 1972.

- Other changes included the phasing out of lead-based paints and fine details and fragile protrusions on the models. Earlier examples that predate these changes are much harder to find today.

- Look for characters that were discontinued at an early date or were produced in smaller quantities.

- Production of Beatrix Potter figures continues today under Border Fine Art and it will be interesting to see how this will affect the price of original Beswick pieces.

A Beswick Beatrix Potter's 'Anna Maria' figure, BP3, brown backstamp.

1973-83   *3in (7.5cm) high*

$150-200   CHEF

A Beswick Beatrix Potter's 'Appley Dapply' figure, BP3, version two, brown backstamp.

1975-89   *3.25in (8cm) high*

$120-180   CHEF

A Beswick Beatrix Potter's 'Cecily Parsley' figure, BP3, first version with head down, brown backstamp.

1973-85   *4in (10cm) high*

$50-80   CHEF

A Beswick Beatrix Potter's 'Flopsy, Mopsy and Cottontail' figure, BP3, brown backstamp.

1973-89   *2.5in (6.5cm) high*

$50-70   CHEF

A Beswick Beatrix Potter's 'Ginger' figure, BP3b, brown backstamp.

1976-82   *3.75in (9.5cm) high*

$280-320   CHEF

A Beswick Beatrix Potter's 'Fierce Bad Rabbit' figure, BP3b, first version with feet out, brown backstamp.

A later version of this figure with less protruding feet and a lighter coat is worth at least half the value of this earlier version.

1977-80   *4.75in (12cm) high*

$150-200   CHEF

A Beswick Beatrix Potter's 'Foxy Whiskered Gentleman' figure, BP2a, gloss finish, gold oval backstamp.

1955-72   *4.75in (12cm) high*

$120-180   CHEF

A Beswick Beatrix Potter's 'Goody Tiptoes' figure, BP3, with brown backstamp.

1973-89	3.5in (9cm) high
$40-60	**CHEF**

A Beswick Beatrix Potter's 'Jemima Puddleduck' figure, BP2, first version, first variation, gold backstamp.

1955-72	4.75in (12cm) high
$80-120	**CHEF**

A Beswick Beatrix Potter's 'Johnny Town Mouse' figure, BP2, gold oval backstamp.

1955-72	3.5in (9cm) high
$80-120	**CHEF**

A Beswick Beatrix Potter's 'Lady Mouse' figure, BP3, brown backstamp.

1973-89	4in (10cm) high
$60-90	**CHEF**

A Beswick Beatrix Potter's 'Little Black Rabbit', BP3, brown backstamp.

1977-89	4.5in (11.5cm) high
$50-80	**CHEF**

A Beswick Beatrix Potter's 'Little Pig Robinson' figure, BP3, first variation with striped outfit.

The later variation with a checked outfit is less sought-after.

1973-74	4in (10cm) high
$80-120	**CHEF**

A Beswick Beatrix Potter's 'Mrs Flopsy Bunny' figure, BP3, light blue dress, brown backstamp.

1974	4in (10cm) high
$80-120	**CHEF**

A Beswick Beatrix Potter's 'Mr. Jeremy Fisher' figure, BP2, first variation, first version with spotted legs, gold oval backstamp.

1955-72	3in (7.5cm) high
$150-200	**CHEF**

A Beswick Beatrix Potter's 'Mr Alderman Ptolemy' figure, BP3b, brown backstamp.

This brown back stamp was used between 1974 and 1985, it was used on 63 Potter figures as well as 16 variations.

1974-85	3.5in (9cm) high
$50-70	**CHEF**

A Beswick Beatrix Potter's 'Mrs Tittlemouse' figure, BP1, style one, gold backstamp.

1948-54   3.5in (9cm) high

$180-220   **CHEF**

A Beswick Beatrix Potter's 'Mrs Rabbit' figure, BP3, second version with umbrella molded to dress, brown backstamp.

An earlier version of this figure with the umbrella sticking out is worth approximately four times as much.

1975-89   4.25in (11cm) high

$150-200   **CHEF**

A Beswick Beatrix Potter's 'Old Mr Brown' figure, BP3, brown owl and red squirrel, brown backstamp.

1975-89   3.5in (8.5cm) h

$50-80   **CHEF**

A Beswick Beatrix Potter's 'Peter Rabbit' figure, BP2a, first version, first variation, gold oval backstamp.

1955-72   4.5in (11.5cm) high

$80-120   **CHEF**

A Beswick Beatrix Potter's 'Pigling Bland' figure, BP3, first variation with purple jacket, brown backstamp.

Later versions of this figure have a pale lilac jacket which is less desirable and worth less than a third of this version.

1973-74   4.25in (11cm) high

$280-320   **CHEF**

A Beswick Beatrix Potter's 'Pickles' figure, BP3, brown backstamp.

1973-82   4.5in (11.5cm) high

$180-220   **CHEF**

A Beswick Beatrix Potter's 'Poorly Peter Rabbit' figure, BP3, brown back stamp.

1976-89   3.75in (9.5cm) high

$60-90   **CHEF**

A Beswick Beatrix Potter's 'Sally Henny Penny' figure, BP3, brown backstamp.

1974-89   4in (10cm) high

$50-80   **CHEF**

A Beswick Beatrix Potter's 'Pickles' figure, BP2, gold oval backstamp.

Although this figure is identical to later figures, such as the one center left, this earlier figure is worth considerably more as it was only produced with this backstamp for one year.

1971-72   4.5in (11.5cm) high

$300-500   **GORL**

CERAMICS

A Beswick Beatrix Potter's 'Simpkin' figure, BP3b, brown backstamp.

1975-83　　*4in (10cm) high*

$220-280　　　　　**CHEF**

A Beswick Beatrix Potter's 'Sir Isaac Newton' figure, BP3, brown backstamp.

1973-84　　　　　*3.75in (9.5cm) high*

$280-320　　　　　　　　**CHEF**

A Beswick Beatrix Potter's 'Squirrel Nutkin' figure, BP3, first version, second variation, brown backstamp.

1980-89　*3.75in (9.5cm) high*

$60-90　　　　　　**CHEF**

A Beswick Beatrix Potter's 'Tailor of Gloucester' figure, BP2, copyright F. Warne & Co Ltd, gold mark.

1955-72　*3.5in (9cm) high*

$80-120　　　　**CHEF**

A Beswick Beatrix Potter's 'Timmie Willie from Johnny Town Mouse' figure, BP3, brown backstamp.

1973-89　*2.5in (6.5cm) high*

$150-200　　　　**CHEF**

A Beswick Beatrix Potter's 'Timmy Tiptoes' figure, BP2, first variation with brown-gray squirrel in red jacket, gold backstamp.

1955-72　*3.25in (8.5cm) high*

$80-120　　　　**CHEF**

A Beswick Beatrix Potter's 'Tom Kitten' figure, BP3, first version, second variation with light color base and suit, with brown backstamp.

1980-89　*3.5in (9cm) high*

$50-70　　　　**CHEF**

A Beswick Beatrix Potter's 'Tommy Brock' figure, BP3, first version, first variation with spade handle out and small eye patches, brown backstamp.

1973-74　*3.5in (9cm) high*

$150-200　　　　**CHEF**

A Beswick Beatrix Potter's 'The Old Woman Who Lived In A Shoe' figure, BP3, brown backstamp.

1973-89　　　*3.745in (9.5cm) long*

$60-90　　　　　　　**CHEF**

FIND OUT MORE...

'Beswick Quarterly', *Laura Rock-Smith, 10 Holmes Court, Sayville, N.Y. 11782-2408, U.S.A.*

'The Charlton Standard Catalogue of Beswick Animals', *by Diana Callow, The Charlton Press, Toronto, Ontario, 1996.*

'Royal Doulton Beswick Storybook Figurines', *by Jean Dale, (6th edition), published by Charlton International Inc, U.S.A., 2000.*

CERAMICS

COLLECTORS' NOTES

■ Bing & Grøndahl was founded in Copenhagen, Denmark in 1853 by Frederick Grøndahl (1819-56) and brothers Jacob and Meyer Bing. The majority of their pieces are colored under the glaze in white, pale blue or gray. They are marked with a 'three tower' mark based on the city of Copenhagen's coat of arms, over the 'B&G' initials. Seconds are indicated with a horizontal scratch through the towers.

■ Pieces can be dated to a period by the style and color of the printed mark. The 'B&G' initials were blue from 1853-1947 and once again from 1970-83 and black, gray or green at other times. From around 1970, the towers became highly stylized, and much less detailed, being simply tall rectangles with triangular apexes. However, there are many variations so it is best to consult a reference work to date a piece more precisely.

■ Figures were introduced c1895 and proved immensely popular, with their fine modeling and delicacy of color. In 1987, Bing & Grøndahl merged with their rival Royal Copenhagen factory and pieces were then marked with the Royal Copenhagen marks. The numbering system for models changed too. They were numbered from 400 upward and had a prefix of 1020 for animals and 1021 for people.

■ Look for size, complexity, date, designer, and the appeal of the model, as larger, earlier or more complex models will often fetch the higher values, as will those that are no longer in production. Models produced over a long period may be less desirable. Examine a model carefully for variations in terms of form (such as a differently tilted head), pattern, and color. Damage such as cracks and chips will reduce value.

A Bing & Grøndahl porcelain model of a cocker spaniel, No. 2072, by Laurits Jensen.

6in (15cm) long

$220-280 LOB

A Bing & Grøndahl porcelain model of a cocker spaniel, No. 2172, by Svend Jespersen.

4.25in (11cm) long

$100-150 LOB

A Bing & Grøndahl porcelain model of a terrier, No. 2072, by Laurits Jensen.

4.25in (11cm) long

$70-100 LOB

A Bing & Grøndahl porcelain model of a wirehaired terrier, No. 2967, designed by Ingeborg Plockross Irminger.

6.75in (17cm) long

$220-280 LOB

A Bing & Grøndahl 'Pessimist' porcelain model of a titmouse, No. 1635.

This bird was designed by Dahl-Jensen and has remained popular.

c1904 *5in (13cm) long*

$100-150 LOB

A Bing & Grøndahl porcelain model of a sealyham puppy, No. 2027, by Dahl-Jensen.

Jens Peter Dahl-Jensen (1874-1960) was a Danish sculptor who trained at the Copenhagen Academy. He joined Bing & Grøndahl as a designer in 1897, and worked there for 20 years. He is known for his small figurines, especially dogs. In 1925 he set up his own factory.

4in (10cm) long

$120-180 LOB

A Bing & Grøndahl porcelain model of beagle lying, No. 2565.

6.5in (16.5cm) long

$100-150 LOB

CERAMICS

A Bing & Grøndahl 'Optimist' porcelain model of a titmouse, No. 1633, designed by Dahl-Jensen.

5in (13cm) long

$100-150 LOB

A Bing & Grøndahl porcelain model of a parrot, No. 2019, original design by Dahl-Jensen.

c1985 5.5in (14cm) high

$80-120 LOB

A Bing and Grøndahl Copenhagen seagull.

10.75in (27.5cm) wide

$100-150 CHEF

A Bing & Grøndahl porcelain model of a seated guinea pig, no. 2489.

3.25in (8cm) long

$100-150 LOB

A Bing & Grøndahl porcelain model of a deer, No. 1929, designed by Niels Nielsen.

This figure is available in stoneware.

6.75in (17cm) high

$120-180 LOB

A Bing & Grøndahl porcelain model of a seal, designed by Knud Moller.

7.5in (19cm) high

$120-180 LOB

A Bing & Grøndahl porcelain model of a walking bear, No. 2213.

c1950 4in (10cm) long

$150-200 LOB

A CLOSER LOOK AT A BING & GRØNDAHL ANIMAL

This figure is comparatively large. There are also other variations of the polar bear, making it a popular subject to collect.

As it does not have a 400 series number, this example is vintage and was made around 1962.

It was modeled by noted modeler Knud Kyhn (1880-1969) who studied animals in Germany, Lapland, and Greenland, and is well-known for his animal work.

The color and well-modeled form of the bear work well with Bing & Grøndahl's color scheme and style.

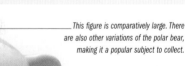

A Bing & Grøndahl large porcelain model of a polar bear, marked 1857.

c1962 *14.5in (37cm) long*

$600-900 LOB

A Bing & Grøndahl 'Who is Calling?' porcelain model, No. 2251, designed by Michaela Ahlman.

6in (15cm) high

$100-150   LOB

A Bing & Grøndahl 'Kaj' porcelain model, No. 1617, designed by Ingeborg Plockross Irminger.

8in (20cm) high

$100-150   LOB

A Bing & Grøndahl 'Flute Player' porcelain model, No. 1897, designed by Ingeborg Plockross Irminger.

11.5in (29cm) high

$180-220   LOB

A Bing & Grøndahl 'Paddling About' porcelain model, No. 1757, designed by Ingeborg Plockross Irminger.

8in (20cm) high

$120-180   LOB

A Bing & Grøndahl 'Love Refused' porcelain model, No. 1614, designed by Ingeborg Plockross Irminger.

6.75in (17cm) high

$180-220   LOB

A Bing & Grøndahl 'Youthful Boldness' porcelain model, No. 2162, designed by Claire Weiss.

8in (20cm) high

$120-180   LOB

A Bing & Grøndahl 'Else' porcelain model, No. 1574.

This model is found in either a blue or white dress and is one of Bing & Grøndahl's (later Royal Copenhagen's) most familiar figurines. It was designed around 1900 by the sculptor Ingeborg Plockross Irminger, who is well known for her designs of children and animals. Irminger had trained at the Royal Academy in Copenhagen between 1893 and 1899. She began work at the Bing & Grøndahl factory in 1898, while also working independently as a sculptor in marble and bronze.

6.75in (17cm) high

$120-180   LOB

A Bing & Grøndahl 'Children Reading' porcelain model, No. 1567, designed by Ingeborg Plockross Irminger.

c1900   4in (10cm) high

$150-200   LOB

A Bing & Grøndahl 'Fish Market' porcelain model, No. 2233, designed by Alex Locher.

8in (20cm) high

$300-500   LOB

A Bing & Grøndahl 'Girl with Calves' porcelain model, No. 2270, by Alex Locher.

8in (20cm) high

$320-380   LOB

FIND OUT MORE...

'Bing & Grøndahl Figurines', by Nick & Caroline Pope, published by Schiffer Books, 2003.

CERAMICS

COLLECTORS' NOTES

■ The Bunnykins series began as a range of nurseryware and was based on the illustrations of Augustinian nun Sister Barbara Vernon, the daughter of Royal Doulton manager Cuthbert Bailey. Early pieces bearing her facsimile signature, produced before 1952, are highly sought-after today.

■ The tableware range was launched in 1934 and was originally fashioned from earthenware or white china. The range proved popular and figures were added in 1939, modeled by Royal Doulton's Art Director Charles Nokes. However, production was soon disrupted by WWII and only six characters were initially available.

■ The original set of six, which bear little resemblance to Sister Barbara Vernon's drawings, are now extremely rare and can fetch up to $1,500-2,500 each.

■ Albert Hallam joined Royal Doulton when the company obtained the Beswick factory in 1969. As he worked on their Beatrix Potter range he was given the task of expanding the line and designed another nine figures.

■ Since the early 1970s, Bunnykins figures have carried identifying 'DB' numbers. So far over 250 have been allocated and many collectors aim to find one of each – no mean feat since figures are frequently retired and replaced by newcomers.

■ Bunnykins is popular all over the world and there are collector's clubs as far afield as Australia and New Zealand. An 'Australian Bunnykins' was specially designed to celebrate the country's bicentenary in 1988.

A Royal Doulton 'Drummer' Bunnykins figure, DB26A, from the Oompah Band Series, version 1.

This figure was released to celebrate the Golden Jubilee of Doulton. A standard version exists and it is worth approximately the same amount. The third version, released in an edition of 250, can be worth around four times as much.

1984   3.5in (9cm) high

$60-90   PSA

A Royal Doulton 'Brownie' Bunnykins figure, DB61.

Examples with unpainted belts have also been found.

1987-93   4in (10cm) high

$100-150   PSA

A Royal Doulton 'William' Bunnykins figure, DB69, boxed.

This figure is based on the 'Tally Ho!' figure released in 1973. A second variation, also called 'Tally Ho!, was released in 1988 and is worth about 30% more.

1988-93   4in (10cm) high

$80-120   PSA

A Royal Doulton 'Paperboy' Bunnykins figure, DB77, boxed.

1989-93   4.5in (11.5cm) high

$100-150   PSA

A Royal Doulton 'Fisherman' Bunnykins figure, DB84.

1990-93   4.25in (12.5cm) high

$70-100   PSA

A Royal Doulton 'Cook' Bunnykins figure, DB85.

1990-94   4.25in (11cm) high

$80-120   PSA

A Royal Doulton 'Aussie Surfer' Bunnykins figure, DB133.

1994-97   4in (10cm) high

$60-90   PSA

A limited edition Royal Doulton 'Out For A Duck' Bunnykins figure, DB160, from the Cricketers Series and an edition of 1,250.

1995   4in (10cm) high

$150-200   **PSA**

A limited edition Royal Doulton 'Clarinet' Bunnykins figure, DB184, from the Jazz Band Collection and an edition of 2,500, boxed with certificate.

1999-2000 4.5in (11.5cm) high

$60-90   **PSA**

A limited edition Royal Doulton 'Double Bass' Bunnykins figure, DB184, from the Jazz Band Collection and an edition of 2,500, boxed with certificate.

1999-2000 4.5in (11.5cm) high

$60-90   **PSA**

A limited edition Royal Doulton 'Saxophone Player' Bunnykins figure, DB184, from the Jazz Band Collection and an edition of 2,500, boxed with certificate.

1999-2000 4.5in (11.5cm) high

$60-90   **PSA**

A limited edition Royal Doulton 'Drummer' Bunnykins figure, DB250, from the Jazz Band Collection and an edition of 2,500, boxed with certificate.

A limited edition Royal Doulton 'Boy Skater' Bunnykins figure, DB187, from a limited edition of 2,500, boxed.

A standard version of this figure was released in 1995 and is of the same value.

1998   4in (10cm) high

$40-60   **PSA**

A limited edition Royal Doulton 'Santa's Helper' Bunnykins figure, DB192, from a limited edition of 2,500, boxed.

This figure is based on 'Christmas Surprise', released between 1994-2000, and worth approximately the same amount.

1999   3.5in (9cm) high

$40-60   **PSA**

2002 4.5in (11.5cm) high

$70-100   **PSA**

A limited edition Royal Doulton 'Easter Surprise' Bunnykins figure, DB225, from a limited edition of 2,500, boxed.

This figure is based on 'Easter Greetings' released between 1995-99 and of approximately the same value.

2000   3.5in (9cm) high

$40-60   **PSA**

A limited edition Royal Doulton 'Trumpeter' Bunnykins figure, DB210, from the Jazz Band Collection and an edition of 2,500, boxed with certificate.

2000   4.5in (11.5cm) high

$60-90   **PSA**

FIND OUT MORE...

'Royal Doulton Bunnykins, A Charlton Standard Catalogue', by Jean Dale & Louise Irvine, published by Charlton Press, 2002.

COLLECTORS' NOTES

■ Carlton Ware is a trade name used from the mid-1890s by Wiltshaw & Robinson Ltd of the Carlton Works, Stoke, England. They became Carlton Ware Ltd. in 1958.

■ In the 1920s and 1930s the company produced a range of richly decorated pieces, many in the Art Deco style, with Oriental or Persian designs and a lustrous finish. The 1930s saw the introduction of mass-produced floral and fruiting designs. These are

not usually as valuable as the luster pieces, but look out for unusual shapes and rare color variations.

■ To attract fashionable postwar buyers, forms in the 1950s became more streamlined and patterns more modern. The 1960s saw many cylindrical forms, echoing the output of other factories.

■ Condition is important. Look out for wear to enameling and gilding on the luster ranges.

A Carlton Ware 'Fish & Seaweed' pattern circular bowl, printed marks.

8in (20cm) diam

$180-220   **L&T**

A Carlton Ware 'Devil's Copse' pattern circular bowl, with printed and painted marks.

This pattern is exactly the same as the background of the pattern known as 'Mephistopheles', although it does not contain the figure of the Devil himself.

7in (17.5cm) diam

$180-220   **L&T**

A CLOSER LOOK AT A CARLTON WARE VASE

The stepped rim and inverted conical form is very Art Deco, and is partly inspired by period architecture.

The 'Bell' pattern can also be found on cream, pale blue, green and dark red glazes.

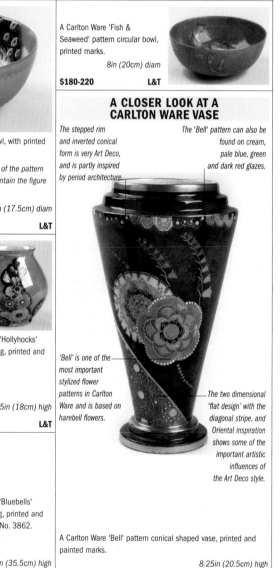

'Bell' is one of the most important stylized flower patterns in Carlton Ware and is based on harebell flowers.

The two dimensional 'flat design' with the diagonal stripe, and Oriental inspiration shows some of the important artistic influences of the Art Deco style.

A Carlton Ware 'Bell' pattern conical shaped vase, printed and painted marks.

8.25in (20.5cm) high

$800-1,200   **L&T**

A Carlton Ware 'Hollyhocks' pattern ovoid jug, printed and painted marks, No. 3973.

'Hollyhocks' is known on a green, black or orange background.

7.5in (19cm) high

$180-220   **L&T**

A Carlton Ware 'Hollyhocks' pattern ovoid jug, printed and painted marks.

10.75in (18cm) high

$80-120   **L&T**

A Carlton Ware 'Bluebells' pattern large jug, printed and painted marks, No. 3862.

14.2in (35.5cm) high

$400-600   **L&T**

A Carlton Ware 'New Mikado' pattern vase, on a pale pink ground, printed marks.

'New Mikado' was made in many colors from the 1920s up until the 1960s, and always features an evergreen tree and a Chinese style house.

6in (15.5cm) high

$220-280   **WW**

A Carlton Ware 'Armand' luster vase, of tapering cylindrical form with canted angles, printed and painted in gilt and colors with exotic moths on a pale blue ground, printed and painted marks 2134/136.

7.75in (19.5cm) high

$180-220   **L&T**

A Carlton Ware 'New Mikado' pattern Bleu Royale tall vase.

11in (28cm) high

$220-280   **PSA**

Two Carlton Ware 'Spangle Tree' and 'New Anemone' Aztec dishes, pattern No. 4626, printed and painted marks.

12.5in (32cm) wide

$200-300   **WW**

A 1930s Carlton Ware 'Blackberry' pattern biscuit barrel.

This barrel is more valuable than most pieces from the floral and fruiting range produced by Carlton Ware during the 1930s as its shape is extremely unusual and typical of the Art Deco style. Most pieces are shaped more like stylized leaves or flowers.

5.5in (14cm) high

$300-400   **BAD**

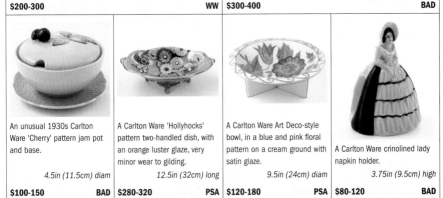

An unusual 1930s Carlton Ware 'Cherry' pattern jam pot and base.

4.5in (11.5cm) diam

$100-150   **BAD**

A Carlton Ware 'Hollyhocks' pattern two-handled dish, with an orange luster glaze, very minor wear to gilding.

12.5in (32cm) long

$280-320   **PSA**

A Carlton Ware Art Deco-style bowl, in a blue and pink floral pattern on a cream ground with satin glaze.

9.5in (24cm) diam

$120-180   **PSA**

A Carlton Ware crinolined lady napkin holder.

3.75in (9.5cm) high

$80-120   **BAD**

CERAMICS

A Carlton Ware 'Walking Ware' egg-cup, with feet in pink shoes, standing, printed mark "Carlton Ware England Lustre Pottery 1978".

2.25in (5.5cm) high

$30-40   **CHS**

A Carlton Ware 'Walking Ware' teacup, with feet in green shoes, walking.

4.25in (11cm) high

$50-70   **CHS**

A Carlton Ware 'Walking Ware' teacup, with feet in brown shoes standing, printed mark "Carlton Ware England Lustre Pottery 1980".

The 'Walking Ware' series was designed by Roger Michell and Danka Napiorkowska of the Lustre Pottery in the 1970s. The first series comprised of feet standing still, but designs became more adventurous with the addition of 'Running', 'Jumping', and 'Big Feet' series. Despite being popular the company was in financial trouble and the series was not produced for long. Pieces usually bear the Lustre Pottery and Carlton Ware marks as can be seen from the thumbnail illustration of the mark on this piece.

4.25in (11cm) high

$30-50   **CHS**

A Carlton Ware 'Walking Ware' egg-cup, with feet in yellow shoes, walking, printed mark "Carlton Ware England Lustre Pottery 1976".

3in (7.5cm) high

$40-60   **CHS**

A Carlton Ware 'Walking Ware' sugar bowl, with feet in blue shoes, crossed, printed marks.

c1973   6.5in (16.5cm) high

$50-70   **CHS**

A scarce Carlton Ware 'French Maid' 'Walking Ware' tea cup.

5in (13cm) high

$100-150   **BAD**

A 1970s Carlton Ware coffee pot, sugar bowl and two mugs.

coffee pot 13in (33cm) high

$80-120   **DTC**

A Carlton Ware egg-cup, the base and handle formed as a tuba-playing man, printed mark "CW England".

2.5in (6.5cm) high

$40-60   **CHS**

A set of three Carlton Ware circular psychedelic dishes.

largest 8.5in (21cm) diam

$70-100   **MTS**

A 1930s Royal Winton 'Sunshine' teacup and saucer.

6in (15cm) diam

$70-100   **BAD**

A 1950s Royal Winton 'Summertime' pattern geometrically shaped dish.

9.5in (24cm) wide

$150-200   **BAD**

A 1950s Royal Winton 'English Rose' pattern cup and saucer.

4.5in (11.5cm) diam

$80-120   **AD**

A 1950s Royal Winton 'Cheadle' pattern butter dish.

Objects as covered in design as possible, even on the handle, are amongst the most sought after by collectors, especially in the more popular, bright colorways.

6.25in (16cm) wide

$280-320   **BAD**

A 1930s Royal Winton 'Welbeck' pattern scalloped edge fruit bowl.

9in (23cm) wide

$100-150   **BAD**

A 1950s Royal Winton 'Julia' pattern ring or candy dish.

6in (15cm) wide

$120-180   **BAD**

A 1930s Royal Winton 'Welbeck' pattern milk jug.

3.25in (8cm) high

$100-150   **BAD**

A Grimwades Royal Winton chintz toast rack, printed in typical bright colors.

6in (15cm) wide

$50-70   **GORL**

A 1930s Royal Winton hand-painted 'Anemone' pattern sugar sifter.

This sifter is unusual as the design is hand-painted, rather than being applied by colored transfer.

6.25in (16cm) high

$100-150   **BAD**

A 1930s Lancasters Ltd 'Pansy' pattern sugar bowl, with chrome-plated lid.

Although it looks as though the lid has been replaced, it has not. Chrome parts are commonly found on chintzware.

3.75in (9.5cm) high

$80-120   **BAD**

CERAMICS

COLLECTORS' NOTES

■ Clarice Cliff was born in 1899 in Tunstall, Stoke-on-Trent, England in the heart of the Potteries. In 1912 she joined Linguard Webster & Co. as an apprentice enameler and, after further study, went to A.J. Wilkinson Ltd of Burslem in 1916.

■ Cliff's colorful designs were influenced by the art of the period, and by flowers and botany. Collectors tend to prefer the patterns that typify her work. The shape and pattern of the vessel is also important – pieces that display the pattern well, such as chargers, plates, Lotus shape jugs, and vases, are all popular.

■ The pottery was impressed with Cliff's skill and in 1927 gave her a studio of her own in the recently acquired Newport Pottery. She was given the opportunity to experiment and produced a range of bright and colorful geometric designs – different from anything previously produced. The range was named 'Bizarre' and launched in 1928. The line proved so successful that the entire pottery was soon devoted to its production.

■ Condition affects the value; any damage or wear will reduce the value on all but the rarest pieces.

■ Due to the popularity of Cliff's work, fakes are on the market. Beware of poor quality painting, smudged designs, washed-out colors and uneven glazes.

A Clarice Cliff Fantasque 'Alton' pattern bowl, with a landscape pattern against green borders.

c1935   8in (20cm) diam

$280-320   **GORL**

A Clarice Cliff Bizarre 'Aurea' pattern planter, of twin-handled oval shape, shape number 450, black printed mark.

c1935   13in (33cm) wide

$400-600   **CHEF**

A Clarice Cliff 'Blue Chintz' pattern octagonal plate, on chromium-plated stand, printed mark, introduced in 1932/3.

The Chintz pattern was also produced in an orange and a scarce green colorway.

8.75in (22cm) diam

$180-220   **L&T**

A Clarice Cliff Fantasque Bizarre 'Blue Chintz' pattern Athens jug, the bellied octagonal shape painted with stylized blue, green, and pink flowers and foliage, printed marks and molded shape number 42.

1932   6in (15cm) high

$300-400   **CHEF**

A Clarice Cliff Bizarre 'Blue Chintz' pattern biscuit barrel, with chrome lid, mounts and swing handle, the ovoid shape supported on three blue edged buttress legs and painted with pink flowers and circular leaves, printed marks.

1932   6in (15cm) high

$400-600   **CHEF**

A Clarice Cliff Bizarre 'Blue Chintz' pattern vase, the barrel shape painted with pink flowers and blue leaves between the flared rim and foot, printed marks and molded shape number 264.

c1930   8in (20cm) high

$320-380   **CHEF**

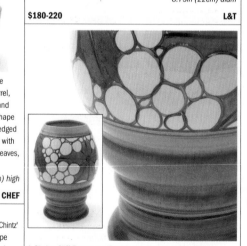

A Clarice Cliff Fantasque 'Broth' pattern vase, the ovoid girth painted with brown bubbles above horizontal rib molding emphasized in orange, blue, and purple, printed marks and impressed shape number 362.

c1930   8in (20.5cm) high

$400-600   **CHEF**

A Clarice Cliff 'Canterbury Bells' pattern sugar bowl.

1932-33   3.5in (9cm) diam

$600-900   **SCG**

A Clarice Cliff 'Crocus' pattern preserve jar and cover, of drum form, painted in colors, the cover with drum finial, on sledge feet, two chips to inner rim, printed Bizarre marks.

Produced in a number of colorways over 35 years, Purple Crocus is the rarest.

c1930   4in (10cm) high

$320-380   **HAMG**

A 1930s/40s Clarice Cliff Bizarre 'Crocus' pattern flower rock, with painted flowers at the base of the pierced shape, and printed marks.

4in (10cm) high

$150-200   **CHEF**

A Clarice Cliff Honeyglaze 'Crocus' pattern sandwich plate, the canted rectangular shape painted with the flowers either side of a brown roundel within a green-lined yellow rim, printed marks and molded shape number 449.

1928-63   12in (30cm) wide

$220-280   **CHEF**

A Clarice Cliff Bizarre 'Forest Glen' pattern bowl, the interior repainted coral red, the horizontally ribbed exterior painted with a cottage in a glen, printed marks and shape number 633.

Produced in a different colorway as 'Newlyn'.

1936-37   9.5in (24cm) diam

$400-600   **CHEF**

A Clarice Cliff Bizarre 'Delecia Pansies' pattern single-handled Lotus jug, printed mark.

The 'Delecia' effect was created by mixing turpentine with color to produce hazy washes of color, with various flowers painted into the design.

1933-34   12in (30cm) high

$1,500-2,000   **WW**

A Clarice Cliff 'Gayday' pattern cylindrical beaker, of tapered outline, printed marks.

1930-34   3.75in (9.5cm) high

$120-180   **L&T**

A Clarice Cliff Bizarre 'Gayday' pattern beehive honey pot and cover, the black-winged orange bee finial above the rope molded sides painted with bright floral border, printed marks.

1930-34   3.75in (9.5cm) high

$400-600   **CHEF**

A Clarice Cliff 'Gayday' pattern single-handled jug, of ovoid form, shape number 634, printed marks.

1930-34   7.25in (18.5cm) high

$400-600   **L&T**

A large Clarice Cliff 'Latona Tree' pattern bowl, painted and glazed.

The Latona range, introduced in 1929, featured a milky-white glaze which formed the base for a number of simple but striking designs.

1929-31   16.25in (40.5cm) diam

$1,800-2,200   **FRE**

A Clarice Cliff 'Lily' pattern ovoid biscuit barrel and cover, with wicker handle, printed marks and retailer's marks.

c1930   5.5in (14cm) high

$300-500   **L&T**

A Clarice Cliff Bizarre Honeyglaze 'Limberlost' pattern plate, painted with two white flowerheads in the foreground and distant trees within target rim bands of greens, coral and brown, printed marks and impressed "6/37".

c1930   9.75in (25cm) diam

$400-600   **CHEF**

A Clarice Cliff Bizarre 'Lydiat' pattern plate, painted to one side with flowerheads and black leaves on a streaky autumnal ground, printed marks and impressed "35".

This is a rare colorway variation of the 'Jonquil' pattern.

c1935   9in (23cm) diam

$220-280   **CHEF**

A Clarice Cliff Bizarre 'Marguerite' pattern beehive honey pot and cover, the latter molded and blue painted with three pink-centered flowerheads about the bud knop, printed marks.

c1930   4in (10cm) high

$300-500   **CHEF**

A Clarice Cliff 'May Blossom' pattern Bonjour shape preserve pot and cover, badly damaged.

1935-36   4in (10cm) high

$70-100   **BAR**

A Clarice Cliff Fantasque 'Melon' or 'Picasso Fruit' pattern jardinière, brightly painted with a band of stylized melons between chocolate brown lines and orange bands, the tapering cylindrical shape rounding to the three strap feet, with printed marks.

1930-32   8.5in (21.5cm) diam

$700-1,000   **CHEF**

A Clarice Cliff 'Nasturtium' pattern Le Bon Dieu bowl, of organic form, printed marks.

c1930   7in (18cm) diam

$220-280   **L&T**

A Clarice Cliff 'My Garden Surprise' pattern circular bowl, with applied foot, molded with lines.

1934-39   6.5in (16.5cm) diam

$120-180   **L&T**

A Clarice Cliff 'Nasturtium' pattern cheese dish and cover, printed marks.

1932   *7.5in (19cm) wide*

$280-320   **L&T**

A pair of Clarice Cliff 'Nasturtium' pattern sugar sifters.

1932   *3in (7.5cm) high*

$280-320   **GORL**

A Clarice Cliff 'Nasturtium' pattern preserve jar and cover, of cylindrical form, printed marks.

1932   *3.5in (9cm) high*

$300-400   **L&T**

A Clarice Cliff Bizarre 'Sunshine' pattern Bonjour biscuit barrel and cover, each of the flat sides of the cylindrical shape painted with hollyhocks, the bamboo handle swinging on yellow-edged knops, printed marks.

c1930   *6in (15.5cm) high*

$300-400   **CHEF**

A Clarice Cliff Bizarre 'Rhodanthe' pattern wall plaque, painted with orange, gray, ocher, and yellow flowers growing from grayish brown mounds, printed marks.

1934   *10.25in (26cm) diam*

$300-500   **CHEF**

A Clarice Cliff galloping horse, the stylized pale mushroom-glazed animal racing with gilt details, blue printed marks.

     6in (15cm) high

$280-320   **CHEF**

A Clarice Cliff 'Rhodanthe' pattern coffee pot and cover, the flared cylindrical sides painted with stylized orange, yellow, and gray flowers growing from brown stems on gray mounds, the handle and spout triangular, printed marks.

1934   *7.5in (19cm) high*

$500-800   **CHEF**

A Clarice Cliff Bizarre 'Viscaria' pattern 'Bonjour' preserve pot and cover, painted with green and blue flowers on the cylindrical body, printed marks.

This is a version of the 'Rhodanthe' design.

1934   *4.25in (11cm) high*

$400-600   **CHEF**

A pair of Clarice Cliff 'Yuan' pattern vases, the cylindrical shapes tapering to spreading feet and horizontally ribbed below a celadon green glaze, printed marks.

1937   *10in (25.5cm) high*

$220-280   **CHEF**

CERAMICS

COLLECTORS' NOTES

■ Susie Cooper was born in 1902. She began work as a paintress in 1922 at A.E. Gray & Co. Ltd, a noted ceramic decorating factory and pottery. She designed a number of floral patterns for Gray's, most marked with a new backstamp including her name. By 1929 she had gained a wealth of experience and left to set up the Susie Cooper Pottery, decorating white 'blanks' made elsewhere.

■ In 1931 she took residence at the now famous 'Crown Works', part of Woods & Sons in Burslem. Woods both supplied blank white wares to be decorated and, from around 1932, started to make Cooper's own shapes. It is this that distinguishes Cooper from her contemporary Clarice Cliff, who did not design her own shapes.

■ As with Clarice Cliff, Susie Cooper's Art Deco style work is the most sought after. Produced up until the 1930s, these wares are handpainted with boldly colored flowers or geometric shapes.

■ Many of her designs were inspired by nature, using floral or foliate motifs. Some pieces were handpainted and others applied by lithographic transfer – examine the pattern closely to spot telltale handpainted brushstrokes.

■ Look for Cooper's classic and very modern shapes, such as 'Kestrel' or 'Rex'. Typical patterns such as 'Dresden Spray' are likely to retain their popularity.

■ In 1950 Cooper acquired a factory and produced bone china, which tends to be less desirable and valuable than her earlier earthenware pieces. In 1966, the factory was acquired by Wedgwood and new bone china designs were produced, many reflecting the styles of the age. As with her other bone china pieces, these tend to be less valuable, but usually offer a more affordable entry point to her designs.

■ Cooper resigned as Director in 1972, and worked solely as a designer. The Crown Works were closed in late 1979 and Cooper worked as a freelance designer from 1986 until her death in 1995.

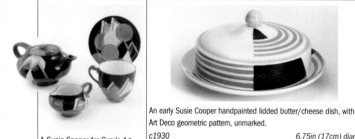

An early Susie Cooper handpainted lidded butter/cheese dish, with Art Deco geometric pattern, unmarked.

c1930   *6.75in (17cm) diam*

$300-500   **BAD**

A Susie Cooper for Gray's Art Deco styled four-piece handpainted 'Moons and Mountains' pattern part teaset, comprising a teapot, teacup, plate, and cream jug, blue enamel worn.

c1930 teapot 3in (7.5cm) high

$1,000-1,500   GORL

A Susie Cooper three handled 'studio ware' earthenware vase, of ovoid form, handpainted with leaves, printed marks.

Demonstrative of Cooper's desire to control both shape and pattern, and in line with studio pottery of the time, this range was made to celebrate handpainting and handthrowing pottery.

c1930   6.25in (16cm) high

$100-150   L&T

A Susie Cooper handpainted dessert plate, with black spiral center.

c1930

$70-100   SCG

A Susie Cooper Art Deco Kestrel shape teapot, with floral pattern.

7.25in (18.5cm) high

$80-120   BAD

A Susie Cooper Kestrel shape teapot, with handpainted green leaf and circle design and pink lid.

7.5in (19cm) high

$120-180   BAD

A Susie Cooper green 'Dresden Spray' pattern Rex shape hot water jug.

7in (17.5cm) high

$120-180   BAD

A Susie Cooper green 'Dresden Spray' pattern Rex shape teapot.

c1960   9.75in (24.5cm) long

$100-150   BAD

A 1950s Susie Cooper bone china 'Romance Pink' pattern Quail shape teapot.

This shape was introduced at the 1951 Festival of Britain. The traditional form appealed to a certain area of the market and draws attention to the elegance of the bone china material.

8in (20cm) long

$100-150   **BAD**

A Susie Cooper for John Lewis blue 'Polka Dot' pattern Kestrel shape teapot.

c1930   5.75in (14.5cm) high

$120-180   **BAD**

A Susie Cooper 'Gardenia' pattern lidded butter dish, crack to lid.

1958   7.25in (18.5cm) diam

$150-200   **BAD**

A Susie Cooper 'Patricia Rose' pattern plate, with broad yellow border.

c1940   8.25in (21cm) diam

$100-150   **BAD**

A Susie Cooper trio set, with handpainted floral pattern surrounded by a green border.

saucer 7in (17.5cm) diam

$100-150   **BAD**

A Susie Cooper Kestrel shape small coffee can, with handpainted green leaf and circle design to exterior and pink interior.

2.25in (6cm) high

$50-80   **BAD**

A Susie Cooper Kestrel shape cup and saucer, the pink ground with leaf and dots decoration, with old repair to handle.

saucer 4.5in (11.5cm) diam

$12-18   **BAD**

A 1970s Wedgwood Susie Cooper Design jade 'Flower Motif' pattern cup and saucer, printed marks.

Part of a set of Wildflower designs, each with different colorways.

saucer 5.5in (14cm) diam

$30-50   **CHS**

A 1960s Wedgwood Susie Cooper Design 'Blue Anenome' pattern cup and saucer, printed marks.

saucer 6in (15cm) diam

$30-50   **CHS**

A Wedgwood Susie Cooper Design 'Diablo' pattern side plate, cup and saucer, printed marks.

c1965   plate 7in (18cm) diam

$50-80   **CHS**

A Wade Heath Cottageware cheese dish.

Wade Heath launched its Cottageware range in 1933 and continued manufacture until 1971.

c1935   6.75in (17.5cm) wide

$300-500   JF

A Royal Winton Cottageware cheese dish and stand.

Of the 1930s Cottageware makers, Royal Winton is known for the quality of its decoration and moldings. The watermill is a popular and desirable shape.

c1935   7.25in (18.5cm) wide

$400-600   JF

A Cantonware 'Cheese Inn' two-piece cheese dish.

     7.5in (19cm) long

$300-400   JF

A Beswick 'Cottage' circular cheese dish.

c1935

$300-400   JF

A Price Bros. three-story coffee pot and cover.

c1945   10in (25.5cm) high

$300-500   JF

An English creamer, probably by Price Bros.

c1935   3in (8cm) high

$400-600   JF

An English creamer, probably by Price Bros.

c1935   3in (8cm) high

$200-300   JF

A Price Bros. Cottageware stovy jug.

c1945   2.5in (6.5cm) high

$200-250   JF

A Kensington Pottery double jam pot.

c1935   8in (20.5cm) wide

$300-500   JF

A Cantonware sugar sifter.

c1935

$200-300   JF

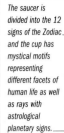

A CLOSER LOOK AT A CUP & SAUCER

The saucer is divided into the 12 signs of the Zodiac and the cup has mystical motifs representing different facets of human life as well as rays with astrological planetary signs.

The registration number 442928 printed on the base dates the design to 1905, but the cup was produced for a number of years after this date.

The outside of the cup reads 'Would'st Learn Thy Future With The Tea, This Magic Cup Will Show It Thee' making the design functional as well as decorative.

The shallow cup is ideal for reading tea-leaves, indicating the drinker's future when read against the design.

An Aynsley 'Japanese Bridge' pattern bone china trio set.

c1920   7in (18cm) diam

$50-80   **JL**

An Aynsley 'The Nelros Cup of Fortune' fortune telling cup and saucer, with transfer-printed design.

c1930   Saucer 5.75in (14.5cm) diam

$70-100   **BEV**

A Carlton china trio set, with hand-painted flowers and gilt details to the rims and foot of the cup.

c1935   Plate 6in (15.5cm) wide

$80-120   **JL**

A 'Chapman' Longton Ltd cup and saucer, with Art Deco styled angular handle and hand-colored transfer-printed design.

c1935

$25-35   **JL**

A 'Chapman' Longton coffee trio set, decorated with a hand-painted and transfer-printed Grecian or Neo-Classical garland design.

c1920   7in (17.5cm) diam

$30-50   **JL**

A 'Chapmans' Longton trio set, with a design of sprays of blue flowers

c1935   Plate 5.75in (14.5cm) wide

$40-60   **JL**

A Copeland Garrett cup and saucer, with transfer-printed design of gray flowers and shaped, gilt rim.

1833-47   Saucer 6in (15cm) wide

$60-90   **JL**

A Crown Derby blue and white transfer-printed cup and two saucers, with Oriental scene similar to the 'Willow' pattern.

c1935   Plate 6.25in (16cm) diam

$60-90   **JL**

A Crown Derby cup and saucer, with cobalt blue and gilt scrolling rococo-style design incorporating a phoenix.

c1935   *6.25in (16cm) diam*

$80-120   **JL**

A Davenport coffee cup and saucer, with cobalt blue, red, and gilt chinoiserie design, slight chip on saucer.

1870-86   *Saucer 4.5in (11.5cm) diam*

$100-150   **JL**

A Duchess China cup and saucer, made by Edwards and Brown, the interior of the cup and saucer decorated with hand-painted flowers.

1910-33   *5.5in (14cm) diam*

$25-35   **JL**

A 'Ye Olde English Grosvenor China' Dulang trio set, with a fuchsia ground and hand-painted flower decoration.

Plate 7in (18cm) diam

$50-70   **JL**

A Habitat 'Scraffito' pattern cup and saucer, printed marks.

This range was named after the decorative technique 'sgraffitto' where a design is created by scoring through a colored layer to reveal the contrasting underlying color.

Saucer 6.5in (16.5cm) diam

$15-25   **CHS**

A Habitat 'Bistro' pattern cup and saucer, printed marks.

Saucer 6in (15cm) diam

$10-15   **CHS**

A Minton cup and saucer, with hand-painted flower motif and gilt rim and handle.

1866   *Saucer 5.25in (13.5cm) diam*

$100-150   **JL**

A 1970s Noritake 'Progression' cup and saucer, printed marks.

Saucer 5.5in (14cm) diam

$10-15   **CHS**

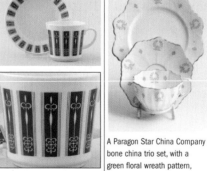

A Paragon Star China Company bone china trio set, with a green floral wreath pattern, molded trellis design in leaf shapes and a scalloped and gilt edge.

Plate 7.25in (18.5cm) diam

$30-50   **JL**

A Paragon China trio set, with citric yellow, orange, and lime floral decoration to the edges and gilt rims, handle and foot.

c1925   5.5in (14cm) diam

$50-70   JL

A Phoenix cup and saucer, with hand-painted floral design, black painted rims and molded and painted handle to the cup.

c1925   Saucer 5.75in (14.5cm) diam

$50-80   JL

A Royal Ascot white bone china trio set, with delicate flower transfer decoration.

Plate 6in (15.5cm) diam

$25-35   JL

A Wileman & Co. trio set, with light blue transfer-printed chrysanthemum design and gilded, scalloped edge.

c1920

Plate 7in (18cm) diam

$50-80   JL

A 1930s Shelley fine bone china trio set, with transfer decoration of pastoral landscape scene.

Plate 6.25in (16cm) diam

$50-80   JL

A Wedgwood mint green trio set, with a gilt edge.

Plate 6in (15cm) diam

$30-50   JL

A cup and saucer, with gilt edging, the interior of the cup painted with two peaches and the saucer with a pear.

c1955   5.5in (14cm) diam

$30-50   JL

A bone china trio, decorated with a transfer-printed design of a hunting scene.

Plate 6.5in (16.5cm) diam

$40-60   JL

A 'Victoria' pattern graduated yellow ground trio set, the molded saucer and plate hand-painted with flowers, with gilt details.

Plate 7in (18cm) diam

$80-120   JL

COLLECTORS' NOTES

■ Denby Pottery was started by William Bourne in 1806 in Denby, Derbyshire, England, after the discovery of a clay seam in the area.

■ It was originally called the Joseph Bourne Pottery after William's son, who ran the business. Production of quality salt-glazed pottery, in particular bottles, began in 1809.

■ By the end of the 19th century the pottery moved away from containers and expanded its kitchenware line, developing the luxurious, colored glazes for which Denby became famous.

■ The 'Danesby Ware' range of the 1920s was a popular range of functional kitchenware, decorative items and giftware. More popular ranges appeared in the 1930s such as 'Electric Blue' with a glossy blue glaze and 'Orient ware' with a matte blue or brown glaze, both

of which are sought-after today. This decade also saw the introduction of kitchenware lines such as 'Cottage Blue', 'Manor Green' and 'Homestead Brown', which remained in vogue into the early 1980s.

■ In the 1950s the Pottery again changed direction. It concentrated on tableware and employed designers such as Glyn Colledge, Gill Pemberton and Kenneth Clark to create patterns like 'Greenwheat' (1956), 'Echo and Ode' (1950s), 'Studio' (1961) and 'Arabesque', known as 'Samarkand' in the US (1964).

■ The pottery continued to move with the times and produced striking tableware, with styles becoming less formal in the 1980s to meet the demand for 'casual dining'. It remains a popular choice for good quality, stylish tableware today.

A Denby Pottery 'Apple Mouse' pattern bowl and spoon, printed marks.
1982 bowl 6.25in (16cm) diam
$30-40   **CHS**

A Denby 'Arabesque' coffee pot, designed by Gill Pemberton.
1964-84   12in (30.5cm) high
$80-120   **DTC**

A Denby Pottery 'Arabesque' pattern salt and pepper shaker and creamer, printed marks.
1964-84 5.75in (14.5cm) high
$15-25 each   **CHS**

A Denby Pottery 'Canterbury' pattern side plate, cup, and saucer, printed marks.
1969-81   6.5in (16.5cm) diam
$22-28   **CHS**

A Denby Pottery 'Biarritz' pattern side plate, cup, and saucer, printed marks.
Produced for the US market at the Langley factory for Denby Tableware. It is uncommon in the UK.
c1975   plate 6.75in (17cm) diam
$25-35   **CHS**

A Denby Pottery 'Chantilly' pattern cup and saucer, printed marks.
c1985   5.5in (14cm) diam
$22-28   **CHS**

A 1920s Denby Danesby Ware plate, printed mark.
9.75in (25cm) diam
$150-200   **WW**

A 1930s Denby Danesby Ware 'Electric Blue' vase, printed mark.
11in (28cm) high
$220-280   **WW**

A Denby Pottery 'Decoy Ducks' pattern side plate, cup, and saucer, printed marks.
1987-89   6.25in (16cm) diam
$40-60   **CHS**

A Denby Pottery 'Dreamweaver' pattern mug, with printed marks.

c1975   3.5in (9cm) high

$15-25   **CHS**

A Denby Pottery 'East Midlands' mug, with printed marks.

Originally commissioned by Cadbury's as a set of 13 'regional' mugs, including Scotland. It appears that the range was eventually produced without any connection to Cadbury's.

c1975

$12-18

4in (10cm) high

CHS

A Denby Pottery 'Green Wheat' pattern side plate, Albert College cup and saucer, printed marks.

c1960   6.5in (16.5cm) diam

$22-28   **CHS**

A Denby Pottery 'Savoy' pattern side plate, cup, and saucer, printed marks.

1982-87   plate 6.5in (16.5cm) diam

$18-22   **CHS**

A late 1950s Denby Pottery 'Gourmet' pattern jug, designed by Kenneth Clark, with lid.

c1955   12.5in (31.75cm) high

$220-280   **GGRT**

A Denby Pottery 'South East' mug, with printed marks.

c1975   4in (10cm) high

$12-18   **CHS**

A 1950s Denby Pottery 'Spring' pattern side plate, cup, and saucer.

6.75in (17cm) diam

$30-40   **CHS**

A 1970s Denby Pottery 'Trees' pattern side plate, cup, and saucer, designed by Diana Woodcock-Beckering, printed marks.

plate 6.5in (16.5cm) diam

$25-35   **CHS**

A mid-1970s Denby Pottery 'Verona' pattern side plate, cup, and saucer, designed by Gill Pemberton, printed marks.

plate 7in (18cm) diam

$30-40   **CHS**

FIND OUT MORE...

'Denby Pottery 1809-1997 Dynasties and Designers', by Irene Gordon Hopwood, published by Richard Dennis Publications, 1997.

'Denby Stonewares: A Collector's Guide', by Graham and Alva Key, published by Ems and Ens Ltd, 1995.

www.denbypottery.co.uk - Official pottery website.

CERAMICS

COLLECTOR'S NOTES

■ Doulton was founded in 1815 at Vauxhall Walk in Lambeth, London by John Doulton, Martha Jones, and John Watts. It became known as Doulton and Co. in 1853. It first produced utilitarian wares, such as pipes and bottles, in stoneware. From around 1871, students of the Lambeth School of Art began to create decorative wares, most notably George Tinworth and Hannah, Florence, and Arthur Barlow.

■ Around 1877-78, the Pindar, Bourne and Co. factory at Burslem in Staffordshire was acquired and its name changed to Doulton and Company Ltd in 1882. It soon became known for fine porcelain. In 1901, the company gained the title 'royal' from Edward VII, and the first new 'Royal Doulton' marks appeared in 1902. Since 1955, it has been known as Doulton Fine China Ltd. The Lambeth factory closed in 1956.

■ Over the past decade there has been a slight decline in demand for all but the finest pieces of Doulton, particularly the stoneware, as the style has become somewhat unfashionable. Now may be a good time to buy as a revival would cause values to rise once again.

■ Look out for work signed by notable artists such as the Barlows – examine bases for their monograms and designs for their typical motifs.

A CLOSER LOOK AT A DOULTON LAMBETH VASE

These vases were decorated by Florence Barlow, part of the notable Barlow family who worked for Doulton.

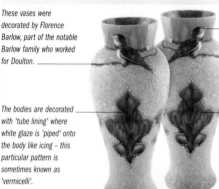

Florence Barlow is especially noted for her birds and flowers, whilst her sister Hannah is known for her horses and other animals.

The bodies are decorated with 'tube lining' where white glaze is 'piped' onto the body like icing – this particular pattern is sometimes known as 'vermicelli'.

Florence Barlow often used the 'pâte-sur-pâte' technique, whereby layers of color are built up to give texture and create a design in low relief.

A Doulton Lambeth stoneware bottle vase, by George Tinworth, incised and applied with scrolling seaweed pattern in shades of blue and brown, impressed mark, incised monogram.

10.5in (27cm) high

$800-1,200   **WW**

An unusual pair of Doulton Lambeth vases, by Florence Barlow, incised in relief with sparrows to the neck, impressed marks.

Many artists at Lambeth practised the pâte-sur-pâte technique, used here on the bird's feathers, particularly between 1878 and 1906.

11.25in (28.5cm) high

$1,200-1,800   **WW**

A Doulton 'Moon' vase, with blue and gilt detailing in the 'Spray' pattern.

The form and pattern of this vase are both Eastern in origin, the 'Moon' name being taken from the Oriental circular doorways known as 'moon gates'.

A Royal Doulton 'Chang' vase, by Charles Noke and Harry Nixon, covered in a running and pitted flambé glaze, signatures.

7in (17.5cm) high

$1,500-2,000   **WW**

A Doulton Lambeth stoneware inkwell, in the form of an old lady, inscribed "Votes For Women".

3.5in (9cm) high

$400-600   **PSA**

A 20thC Doulton Lambeth ring tray, modeled as a large billed bird, impressed mark and numerals 11497 to base.

4.25in (11cm) high

$300-500   **BONS**

c1885   *9.5in (24cm) high*

$100-150   **BAD**

An unusual Royal Doulton ribbed art pottery vase, marked and impressed.

A Doulton vase with blue and gilt detailing, stamped "2055".

c1900   7.25in (18.5cm) high

$150-200   **BAD**

A Royal Doulton two-handled handpainted and gilt transfer vase on stem.

6.5in (16.5cm) high

$150-200   **BAD**

6.5in (16.5cm) high

$300-500   **PSA**

A large Royal Doulton water pitcher, painted with sailboats at sea in dark brown and amber on bottle-green ground, minimal crazing, two small nicks to rim, Royal Doulton ink stamp, and registry mark.

10.5in (26.5cm) high

$280-320   **DRA**

A Royal Doulton Art Deco style 'De Luxe' pattern tea set, each green piece divided by a black and silver arc to leave one third white, comprising a sandwich plate, sugar bowl, milk jug, six teacups, saucers and tea plates, impressed dates.

This tea set was featured in an advertisement for Lipton's Tea in 1933. It's the angular handles, the bright colors and the geometric pattern with simple lines that make this teaset typical of this stylistic movement.

c1933

$500-700 set   **CHEF**

A 1930s Royal Doulton hand-painted hexagonal planter, marked "D4365" on the base.

6in (15.5cm) widest

$80-120   **BAD**

A Royal Doulton "Votes For Women" and "Toil For Men" cruet set, boxed.

3.25in (8.5cm) high

$70-100   **PSA**

A Royal Doulton stoneware figure of the Cheshire Cat.

'The Charlton Standard Catalogue of Royal Doulton Animals' attributes this model to Mark Marshall.

3.5in (9cm) wide

$500-700   **CHEF**

A Royal Doulton 'Shakespeare Jug', produced in a limited edition of 1000, this no.548 depicting Shakespeare characters, complete with certificate of authenticity.

A series of jugs or loving cups with heavily embossed scenes and decoration was designed by Harry Fenton between 1920 and 1938, and once again in 1952. Edition sizes vary between 350 and 1,000 and it is always good to look out for the original certificate bearing the matching limited edition number, which will help make a piece more desirable by 'completing' it.

c1933   10.75in (27cm) high

$600-900   **ROS**

A Royal Doulton 'Sealyham Begging' figure, K3.

1931-77   2.5in (6.5cm) h

$50-70   PSA

A Royal Doulton 'Seated Bulldog' figure.

4.75in (12cm) high

$60-90   PSA

A Royal Doulton 'Dog Licking Plate' figure, HN1158.

5in (12.5cm) wide

$60-90   PSA

A rare Royal Doulton prototype 'Study of an Australian Blue Heeler Dog' figure, in matt finish.

5in (12.5cm) wide

$1,500-2,000   PSA

A mid-20thC Royal Doulton 'Lying St Bernard' figure, K19.

$40-60   PSA

A Royal Doulton 'Tabby Kitten' figure, HN2580, seated licking its paw.

1941-85   2.25in (5.5cm) h

$60-90   CHEF

A limited edition Royal Doulton 'The Walking Cat' figure, DA148, from an edition of 1,000, boxed with certificate.

5.5in (14cm) high

$25-35   PSA

A Royal Doulton 'Butterfly On A Stump' figure, HN141.

2.75in (7cm) high

$280-320   PSA

A 1990s Royal Doulton 'Badger' paperweight.

4in (10cm) wide

$280-320   PSA

COLLECTORS' NOTES

■ Character jugs depict well-known fictional or real-life personalities and have their roots in the early English 'toby' jugs. Whereas toby jugs are modeled on a whole body, character jugs portray just the head, or head and shoulders.

■ The first 20th century character jug is generally thought to be Charles Noke's 1934 John Barleycorn design, although Royal Doulton did produce a Lord Nelson jug as early as the 1820s.

■ Royal Doulton manufacture character jugs in four sizes usually referred to as large, small, miniature, and tiny. Over the years the exact dimensions have varied, although the largest jugs measure around 7.25in (18cm) high and the smallest only 1.25in (3cm).

■ In recent years Royal Doulton have undertaken a great many special commissions, some of which are only released in small quantities, which makes them instantly desirable to collectors.

■ Royal Doulton character jugs will usually carry a mark to help confirm their authenticity. Most jugs made before 1973 will also bear a registration number.

■ Collectors should make themselves familiar with the various color variations that exist on some jugs, many due to shortages during WWII. Examples that were only made for a short period of time and therefore are in short supply are the most sought-after.

A Royal Doulton 'Paddy' small character jug, D5768, with green hat.

1937-60   3.5in (9cm) high

$60-90   **GORL**

A Royal Doulton 'John Peel' small character jug, D5731, with orange riding crop.

1937-60   3.25in (8.5cm) high

$50-70   **PSA**

A Royal Doulton 'John Peel' all white small character jug, D5731.

Apart from three models, all white jugs are factory rejects. White versions of recent or current production are scarce as the factory tries to stop their release.

1937-60   3.25in (8.5cm) high

$220-280   **PSA**

A Royal Doulton 'John Barleycorn' all white miniature character jug, D6041.

1939-60   2in (5cm) high

$80-120   **PSA**

A Royal Doulton 'Old Charley' all white tiny character jug, D6144.
1940-60   1.25in (3cm) high

$400-600   **PSA**

A Royal Doulton 'Samuel Johnson' small character jug. D6296.

1950-60   3.25in (8.5cm) high

$100-150   **PSA**

A Royal Doulton 'Drake' all white small character jug, D6174.
1941-60   3.25in (8.5cm) high

$120-180   **PSA**

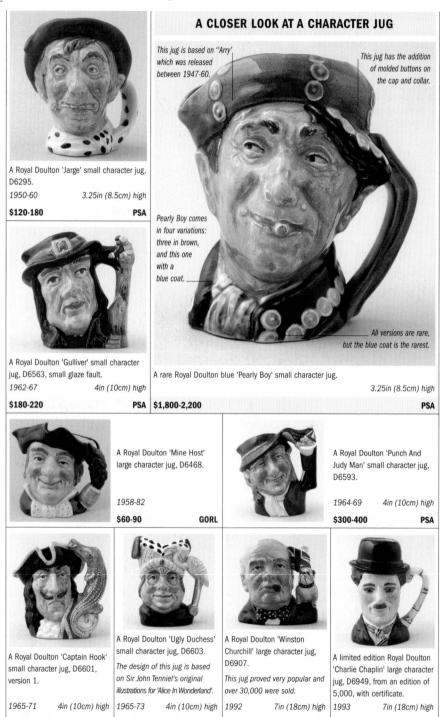

A Royal Doulton 'Jarge' small character jug, D6295.

1950-60   3.25in (8.5cm) high

$120-180   **PSA**

A Royal Doulton 'Gulliver' small character jug, D6563, small glaze fault.

1962-67   4in (10cm) high

$180-220   **PSA**

A CLOSER LOOK AT A CHARACTER JUG

This jug is based on ''Arry'' which was released between 1947-60.

This jug has the addition of molded buttons on the cap and collar.

Pearly Boy comes in four variations: three in brown, and this one with a blue coat.

All versions are rare, but the blue coat is the rarest.

A rare Royal Doulton blue 'Pearly Boy' small character jug.

3.25in (8.5cm) high

$1,800-2,200   **PSA**

A Royal Doulton 'Mine Host' large character jug, D6468.

1958-82

$60-90   **GORL**

A Royal Doulton 'Punch And Judy Man' small character jug, D6593.

1964-69   4in (10cm) high

$300-400   **PSA**

A Royal Doulton 'Captain Hook' small character jug, D6601, version 1.

1965-71   4in (10cm) high

$220-280   **PSA**

A Royal Doulton 'Ugly Duchess' small character jug, D6603.

The design of this jug is based on Sir John Tenniel's original illustrations for 'Alice In Wonderland'.

1965-73   4in (10cm) high

$220-280   **PSA**

A Royal Doulton 'Winston Churchill' large character jug, D6907.

This jug proved very popular and over 30,000 were sold.

1992   7in (18cm) high

$180-220   **PSA**

A limited edition Royal Doulton 'Charlie Chaplin' large character jug, D6949, from an edition of 5,000, with certificate.

1993   7in (18cm) high

$150-200   **PSA**

COLLECTORS' NOTES

- Royal Doulton modeler Charles Noke conceived the idea of reviving the Staffordshire tradition of figurine modeling in the late 19th century. He invited sculptors to submit their design ideas and soon had enough for a collection.

- Since the 1913 launch, most of the figures made in Doulton's Burslem factory have been given 'HN' numbers after Harry Nixon, then manager of the painting department. More than 4,000 of these numbers have been assigned to date.

- One of Doulton's most prolific modelers was Leslie Harradine, a freelancer who submitted a vast number of designs to the factory throughout the 1920s, '30s and '40s. Always popular, many of Harradine's designs are still in production today. Other names to look for include Nada Pedley and Peggy Davies.

- Doulton figures are usually impressed or stamped with the company's lion and crown mark on the base. Some also have date codes, and it is often possible to ascertain the rough age of a figure from the type of stamp used.

- Older, discontinued figures, especially those with fine modeling and in good condition, attract the highest prices. Prewar models are among the most desirable as they were produced in low numbers and seldom come onto the market today.

A Royal Doulton 'Captain Macheath' figure, HN464, designed by Leslie Harradine, from the Beggar's Opera Series, minor restoration.

1921-49   *7in (18cm) high*

$320-380   **PSA**

A Royal Doulton 'Polly Peacham' figure, HN549, designed by Leslie Harradine, style two from the Beggar's Opera Series, light restoration.

1922-49   *4.25in (11cm) high*

$220-280   **PSA**

A Royal Doulton 'Mendicant' figure, HN1365, designed by Leslie Harradine, hand damaged.

1929-69   *8in (20cm) high*

$70-100   **PSA**

A Royal Doulton 'Miss Muffet' figure, HN1936, designed by Leslie Harradine.

1940-67   *5.5in (14cm) high*

$100-150   **PSA**

A Royal Doulton 'The Ermine Coat' figure, HN1981, designed by Leslie Harradine.

1945-67   *7in (18cm) high*

$150-200   **PSA**

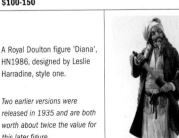

A Royal Doulton figure 'Diana', HN1986, designed by Leslie Harradine, style one.

Two earlier versions were released in 1935 and are both worth about twice the value for this later figure.

1946-75   *6in (15cm) high*

$80-120   **GORL**

A Royal Doulton 'Bluebeard' figure, HN2105, designed by Leslie Harradine.

1953-92   *11in (28cm) high*

$220-280   **PSA**

A limited edition Royal Doulton 'The Mask' figure, HN4141, designed by Leslie Harradine, from an edition of 1,500.

1999   *10in (25.5cm) high*

$220-280   **PSA**

A Royal Doulton 'Christmas Morn' figure, HN1992, designed by Margaret Davies.

1947-96   *7in (18cm) high*

$80-120   **GORL**

A Royal Doulton 'Gentleman from Williamsburg' figure, HN2227, designed by Margaret Davies, from the Figures of Williamsburg Series.

1960-83   6.25in (16cm) high

$100-150   **GORL**

A Royal Doulton 'Lady From Williamsburg' figure, HN2228, designed by Margaret Davies, from the Figures of Williamsburg series.

1960-83   *6in (15cm) high*

$100-150   **PSA**

A limited edition Royal Doulton 'West Indian Dancer' figure, HN2384, designed by Margaret Davies, from the Dancers Of The World series and an edition of 750, boxed with certificate.

1981   9in (23cm) high

$400-600   **PSA**

A Royal Doulton 'Premiere' figure, HN2343, designed by Margaret Davies.

1969-79

7.75in (19.5cm) high

$120-180   **PSA**

A Royal Doulton 'Lorna' figure, HN2311, designed by Margaret Davies.

1965-85   8.5in (21.5cm) high

$70-100   **PSA**

A Royal Doulton 'Good King Wenceslas' miniature figure, HN3262, designed by Margaret Davies, style two.

1989-92   4.25in (11cm) high

$70-100   **PSA**

A Royal Doulton 'The Potter' figure, HN1493, designed by Charles Noke.

A Royal Doulton 'Belle O The Ball' figure, HN1997, designed by R. Asplin.

1949-79   8.5in (21.5cm) wide

$280-320 PSA

A Royal Doulton 'Symphony' figure, HN2287, designed by D.B. Lovegrove.

1961-65   5.25in (13.5cm) high

$150-200 GORL

1932-92   *7in (18cm) high*

$280-320 PSA

A Royal Doulton 'The Moor' figure, HN2082, designed by Charles Noke.

1952-present   *17in (43cm) high*

$1,200-1,800 PSA

A Royal Doulton figure 'Mantilla', HN2712, designed by Eric J. Griffiths, from the Haute Ensemble Series.

1974-79   11.75in (29cm) high

$180-220 L&T

A Royal Doulton 'Harlequin' figure, HN2737, designed by Douglas V. Tootle.

1982-present 13in (33cm) high

$1,200-1,800 PSA

A Royal Doulton 'Samantha' figure, HN2954, designed by Pauline Parsons, style one from the Vanity Fair Ladies Series.

1982-84   7.25in (18.5cm) high

$70-100 PSA

A Royal Doulton 'Columbine' figure, HN2738, designed by Douglas V. Tootle.

1982-present 13in (33cm) high

$1,000-1,500 PSA

A Royal Doulton 'Guy Fawkes' miniature figure, HN3271, originally designed by Charles Noke, style two.

1989-91   4in (10cm) high

$80-120 PSA

A Royal Doulton 'Falstaff' miniature figure, HN3236, originally designed by C. Noke.

1989-90   4in (10cm) high

$50-70   **PSA**

A limited edition Royal Doulton 'Christopher Columbus' figure, HN3392, designed by Alan Maslankowski, from an edition of 1,492, boxed with certificate.

This limited edition, issued in 1992 celebrates the 500th anniversary of Columbus discovering America.

12in (30.5cm) high

$500-700   **PSA**

A limited edition Royal Doulton 'Countess Of Harrington' figure, HN3317, designed by Peter Gee, from the Reynolds Ladies Series and an edition of 5,000.

1992   9.25in (23.5cm) high

$220-280   **PSA**

A Royal Doulton 'Anniversary' figure, HN3625, designed by Valerie Annand.

1994-98   8.5in (21.5cm) high

$180-220   **PSA**

A limited edition Royal Doulton 'Eastern Grace' flambé figure, HN3683, designed by Pauline Parsons, from the Flambé Series and an edition of 2,500.

1995   12.5in (31.5cm) high

$220-280   **PSA**

A Royal Doulton 'Jessica' figure, HN3850, designed by Nada Pedley, style two, Figure of the Year.

Style one (1988-95) is worth slightly less.

1997   8in (20cm) high

$100-150   **PSA**

A Royal Doulton 'Off To School' figure, HN3768, designed by Nada Pedley.

1996-98   5.5in (14cm) high

$150-200   **PSA**

A Royal Doulton 'Wisdom' figure, HN4083, designed by Alan Maslankowski, from the Sentiments Series.

c2000   6in (15cm) high

$50-70   **PSA**

A Royal Doulton 'Bethany' figure, HN4326, designed by Valerie Annard.

c2000   8.5in (21.5cm) high

$60-90   **PSA**

COLLECTORS' NOTES

▣ Devised by Charles Noke in the mid-1890s, seriesware was a range of utilitarian ceramic pieces decorated with scenes by theme. Some sets, such as 'Rip van Winkle' comprise a few pieces whilst others, such as 'Dickens' comprise many hundreds of different pieces. Advertised as "made to adorn, yet serve some useful purpose", the public took to them immediately.

▣ The decoration is applied by transfer, which is then highlighted with a little handcoloring. Many fashionable illustrators were used, such as Cecil Aldin, Kate Greenaway, the humorist Henry Bateman, and poster artist John Hassall. Seriesware was mass-produced for over 50 years until public taste moved on in the 1950s, and new shapes and pattern combinations are often found.

▣ Themes are taken from literature, folklore, plays, and sports. Most collectors focus on a particular series, most notably the extremely varied 'Dickensware'. Sporting series, such as 'Golfing', are often highly valued, primarily as they will be of interest to collectors of sporting memorabilia as well as Doulton seriesware collectors.

▣ Look out for rare shapes from popular series, which will command a premium from collectors keen to add unusual objects to their collections. Cracks, chips, and excessive wear will reduce value as will any damage to the decoration.

A Royal Doulton Dickensware water jug, with 'Old Peggoty' scene.

7in (18cm) high

$150-200   **PSA**

A Royal Doulton Dickensware water jug, with 'Mr Pickwick' scene.

7in (18cm) high

$180-220   **PSA**

A Royal Doulton Dickensware water jug, with 'Poor Joe' scene.

6.25in (16cm) high

$150-200   **PSA**

A Royal Doulton Dickensware two-handled vase, with 'Barnaby Rudge' scene.

6in (15cm) high

$220-280   **PSA**

A Royal Doulton Dickensware tankard, with 'Mr Micawber' scene.

4.75in (12cm) high

$120-180   **PSA**

A Royal Doulton Dickensware teapot, with 'Bill Sykes' scene and an undecorated lid.

6in (15cm) high

$40-60   **PSA**

A Royal Doulton Dickensware two-handled vase, with 'Sgt Buz Fuz' scene.

8.5in (22cm) high

$300-500   **PSA**

A rare Royal Doulton Dickensware match striker, with 'Fagin and the Artful Dodger' scene, slight hairline and nip.

$280-320   **PSA**

CERAMICS

A Royal Doulton 'Bayeux Tapestry' series small water jug, light hairline crack.

5in (12.5cm) high

$22-28   PSA

A Royal Doulton 'Blue Sky' 'Coaching' series hot water jug, with pewter fitting.

6.25in (16cm) high

$280-320   PSA

A Royal Doulton 'Coaching' series plate.

$30-50   CHEF

A Royal Doulton 'Cock A Doodle Do' series beaker.

3.25in (8cm) high

$150-200   PSA

A Royal Doulton 'Dutch' series small water jug.

5in (13cm) high

$60-90   PSA

A Royal Doulton 'Gallant Fishers' series tall water jug.

8in (20cm) high

$100-150   PSA

A Royal Doulton 'Gaffers' series small teapot.

5.5in (14cm) high

$150-200   PSA

A Royal Doulton 'Golfing' series water jug, with the motto "Every Dog Has His Day And Every Man His Hour".

$600-900   PSA

A rare Royal Doulton 'Golfing' series match box holder, light restoration to top.

3.5in (9cm) high

$400-600   PSA

A Royal Doulton 'Historic England' series coffee pot, with 'Shakespeare and Stratford-upon-Avon' scene.

6.25in (16cm) high

$80-120   PSA

A Royal Doulton 'Hunting' series embossed water jug.

10.25in (26cm) high

$220-280   PSA

A rare Royal Doulton 'Motoring' series plate, crazed.

10.5in (27cm) diam

$700-1,000   PSA

A Royal Doulton 'Isaac Walton' series water jug.

5.5in (14cm) high

$70-100   PSA

A Royal Doulton 'The Old Wife' series vase, decorated in low relief with fish under the sea.

1938-55   6.25in (16cm) high

$70-100   PSA

A Royal Doulton 'Plough Horses' series tankard.

5.5in (14cm) high

$100-150   PSA

A Royal Doulton 'Robbie Burns' series water jug.

4.5in (11.5cm) high

$100-150   PSA

A limited edition Royal Doulton seriesware twin-handled vase, molded in relief with 'The Three Musketeers' and other figures, titled 'The Great Romance of Louis XIII's reign', from an edition of 600.

10in (25cm) high

$700-1,000   GORL

A Royal Doulton 'Tutankhamen' series flask, with Titanian glaze, lacks lid.

$100-150   PSA

FIND OUT MORE...

'Royal Doulton Seriesware', Vols 1-4, by Louise Irvine, published by Richard Dennis Publications, 1980-88.

CERAMICS

A Royal Doulton 'Stylish Snowman' figure, DS3.

1985-94   *5in (12.5cm) high*

$150-200   **PSA**

A Royal Doulton 'Cowboy Snowman' figure, DS6.

1986-92   *5in (12.5cm) high*

$180-220   **PSA**

A Royal Doulton 'Highland Snowman' figure, DS7.

1987-93   *5.25in (13.5cm) high*

$180-220   **PSA**

A Royal Doulton 'Snowman Money Bank' figure, DS19, boxed.

1990-94   *8.5in (21.5cm) high*

$180-220   **PSA**

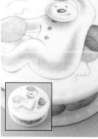

A Royal Doulton 'Snowman Snowballing' figure, DS22, boxed.

1990-94   *5in (12.5cm) high*

$220-280   **PSA**

A Royal Doulton Snowman Gift Collection 'Balloons' pattern lidded box.

       4in (10cm) diam

$60-90   **PSA**

A Royal Doulton 'Skier Snowman' figure, DS21.

1990-92   *5.5in (14cm) high*

$600-900   **PSA**

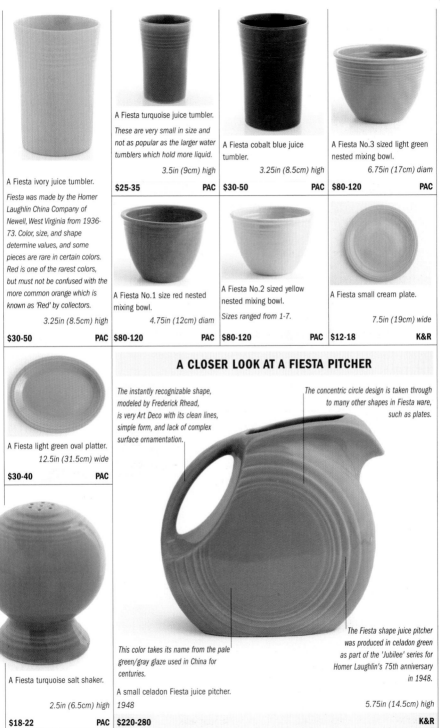

A Fiesta ivory juice tumbler.

Fiesta was made by the Homer Laughlin China Company of Newell, West Virginia from 1936-73. Color, size, and shape determine values, and some pieces are rare in certain colors. Red is one of the rarest colors, but must not be confused with the more common orange which is known as 'Red' by collectors.

3.25in (8.5cm) high

$30-50 PAC

A Fiesta turquoise juice tumbler.

These are very small in size and not as popular as the larger water tumblers which hold more liquid.

3.5in (9cm) high

$25-35 PAC

A Fiesta No.1 size red nested mixing bowl.

4.75in (12cm) diam

$80-120 PAC

A Fiesta cobalt blue juice tumbler.

3.25in (8.5cm) high

$30-50 PAC

A Fiesta No.2 sized yellow nested mixing bowl.

Sizes ranged from 1-7.

$80-120 PAC

A Fiesta No.3 sized light green nested mixing bowl.

6.75in (17cm) diam

$80-120 PAC

A Fiesta small cream plate.

7.5in (19cm) wide

$12-18 K&R

A Fiesta light green oval platter.

12.5in (31.5cm) wide

$30-40 PAC

A CLOSER LOOK AT A FIESTA PITCHER

The instantly recognizable shape, modeled by Frederick Rhead, is very Art Deco with its clean lines, simple form, and lack of complex surface ornamentation.

The concentric circle design is taken through to many other shapes in Fiesta ware, such as plates.

This color takes its name from the pale green/gray glaze used in China for centuries.

A small celadon Fiesta juice pitcher.

1948

A Fiesta turquoise salt shaker.

2.5in (6.5cm) high

$18-22 PAC

$220-280

The Fiesta shape juice pitcher was produced in celadon green as part of the 'Jubilee' series for Homer Laughlin's 75th anniversary in 1948.

5.75in (14.5cm) high

K&R

CERAMICS

COLLECTORS' NOTES

■ Piero Fornasetti was born in Milan in 1913 and studied in Brera and Milan. His love of opulent surface designs set him apart from his Modernist peers who dismissed him. Nevertheless, he was popular with the public during the 1950s.

■ As well as ceramics, he worked as an interior decorator and with Gio Ponti on striking designs for furniture. In the 1980s, his work underwent a renaissance until his death in 1988. The 1990s saw a popular revival of interest in his work including an exhibition at the Victoria & Albert Museum, London.

■ His son Barnaba continues to produce his designs, many with Rosenthal. Look out for pieces that typify his characteristic style featuring Classical motifs in a modern style. Condition is important as the gold surface in particular is prone to wear and scratching, which reduces value.

A Fornasetti Italian Artists plate, featuring Tiziano Veneziano (Titian).

Fornasetti was heavily influenced by Renaissance painters such as Titian and Bellini.

9.5in (24cm) diam

$150-200   **FM**

A Fornasetti Italian Artists plate, featuring Giorgio Barbarelli.

9.5in (24cm) diam

$150-200   **FM**

One of a series of Fornasetti Italian Artists plates, featuring Andrea Mantegna.

10in (25.5cm) diam

$150-200   **FM**

A Fornasetti Italian Artists plate, Antonello da Messina.

9.5in (24cm) diam

$120-180   **FM**

A Fornasetti Opera plate, featuring Pollione from "Norma", by Vincenzo Bellini (1801-1835).

10in (25.5cm) diam

$180-220   **FM**

A Fornasetti Opera plate, featuring Carmen from "Carmen", by George Bizet (1838-1875).

10in (25.5cm) diam

$180-220   **FM**

One of a series of Fornasetti Opera plates, featuring José from "Carmen", by George Bizet (1838-1875).

10in (26cm) diam

$200-250   **FM**

A Fornasetti Astronomer's plate.

1968   *9.5in (24cm) diam*

$150-200   **FM**

A Fornasetti Astronomer's plate.

1969   *9.5in (24cm) diam*

$150-200   **FM**

A limited edition Fornasetti plate, made to celebrate the 45th Annual International Automobile Exhibition in Turin, 3rd-16th December 1967.

7.75in (20cm) diam

$80-120   **FM**

A Fornasetti calendar plate.

1969   *9.5in (24cm) diam*

$120-180   **FM**

A limited edition Fornasetti plate, made to celebrate the 3rd International Exhibition of Industrial Vehicles in Turin, 3rd-11th November 1973.

7.75in (20cm) diam

$80-120   **FM**

A rare Fornasetti dish, with sun motifs.

6.5in (17cm) diam

$180-220   **FM**

A pair of Fornasetti kidney-shaped dishes.

$40-80   **FM**

A pair of Fornasetti dishes.

5.5in (14cm) long

$80-120   **FM**

A Fornasetti plate, created to celebrate 50 years of the company 1925-1975.

9.5in (24cm) diam

$120-180   **FM**

A Fornasetti 'crème de cocu' ashtray.

6in (15cm) diam

$120-180   **FM**

A Fornasetti oval ashtray.

$120-180   **FM**

A set of Fornasetti 'Vini & Legumi' coasters, with original box.

A Fornasetti Balarms ceramic pot.

1958

$100-150   **FM**

Small coasters such as these are also often found in sets, with the complete set forming the shape of a lady or building.

4.25in (10.5cm) wide

$80-120   **FM**

A pair of Fornasetti 'Al Merito' (For Merit) teacups and saucers.

Saucer 5.5in (14cm) diam

$220-280   **FM**

A Fornasetti ceramic biscuit barrel.

24cm (9.5in) high

$800-1,200   **FM**

A CLOSER LOOK AT FORNASETTI CERAMICS

A sun with a face is a typical motif.

Classical motifs such as medals and architecture are frequently found.

A strong, 'flat' gold background is characteristic of his designs.

Black and white are also key colours.

A pair of Fornasetti pen holders.

2.75in (7cm) high

$120-180   **FM**

A Fornasetti ceramic paperweight, with crossed keys motif.

3.5in (9cm) wide

$120-180   **FM**

FIND OUT MORE...

'Fornasetti – Designer of Dreams', *by Patrick Mauries, Thames & Hudson Ltd, 1991.*

www.fornasetti.com

COLLECTORS' NOTES

■ The Fulper Pottery was started by Samuel Hill in 1815 in Flemington New Jersey and produced utilitarian wares from the local heavy clay. Originally named after the founder, the pottery changed name when it was taken over by Abraham Fulper in 1847.

■ In 1909, the company belatedly entered the Art Pottery market with the Vasekraft line, which was influenced by Stangl and had a medieval Germanic style.

■ Rather than hire expenses potters, the majority of the pieces were slip-cast or moulded and attention was instead paid to the glazes, therefore the value rests mainly in the quality and rarity of the finish. Early pieces with flambé, crystalline and mirrored glazes are the most desirable.

■ By the beginning of WWI, pieces displayed a softer Oriental feel but by this point production quality was slipping and a limited range of glazes were used.

■ This decline continued and by 1925 the factory was producing Art Deco influenced lightweight bodies with poor quality glazes.

A Fulper gourd-shaped vase, covered in a 'Leopard Skin' crystalline glaze and 'Elephant's Breath' flambé glaze, vertical mark.

5.5in (14cm) high

$650-750　　　　　　　　**DRA**

A Fulper bullet-shaped bud vase, with a frothy grey, brown and beige glaze dripping over matte mustard, stilt pull chip, bruise to rim, no visible mark.

5.75in (14cm) high

$180-220　　　　　　　　**DRA**

A rare and larger Fulper flaring flower pot, covered in brown, grey and yellow crystalline flambé glaze, grinding chip to base, unmarked.

15.75in (39cm) wide

$600-700　　　　　　　　**DRA**

A Fulper bottle-shaped vase, covered in a fine 'Flemington Green' crystalline flambé glaze, the rectangular Prang mark shows it was made to be sold through the Prang Art Supply Co. catalog.

5.75in (14cm) high

$450-550　　　　　　　　**DRA**

A Fulper 'music' jug, covered in 'Flemington Green' flambé, missing stopper, shallow body line near mold line, Ritz music stamp.

8in (20cm) high

$80-120　　　　　　　　**DRA**

A Fulper hemispherical bowl, covered in frothy mirrored blue glaze, scratches to interior, incised mark.

8.5in (21cm) wide

$180-220　　　　　　　　**DRA**

A Fulper tapered two-handled vase, covered in frothy indigo and periwinkle matte glaze, horizontal mark.

7.5in (19cm) wide

$200-300　　　　　　　　**DRA**

A Fulper squat three-handled vessel, covered in a rich purple and eggplant crystalline glaze, grinding chip, vertical mark.

8in (20cm) wide

$300-400　　　　　　　　**DRA**

A Fulper spherical three-handled vessel, covered in a fine and thick 'Moss-to-Rose' flambé glaze, reglued chip to base, horizontal stamp.

7.5in (19cm) wide

$220-280　　　　　　　　**DRA**

CERAMICS

COLLECTORS' NOTES

- James Taft started the Hampshire Pottery with his uncle James Burnap in 1871. Early production was limited to redware and utilitarian stoneware but the appointment of Taft's brother-in-law, Cadmon Robertson in 1904 saw the company enter the art pottery market.

- The Hampshire Pottery was one of a number of potteries to imitate the Grueby factory, which made some of the most popular art pottery of the day.

- The pottery produced simple, molded vessels cheaply, undercutting Grueby's finer handcrafting, and limited decoration to Robertson's matte glazes, however the quality and variety was sufficient for Hampshire to maintain its own corner of the market.

- In 1916, two years after Robertson had died, Taft sold the pottery to George Morton of the Grueby factory who continued production for a year. The pottery closed in 1923.

A small Hampshire jardinière, with closed-in rim and impressed Greek Key border under a smooth matte green glaze, stamped "HAMPSHIRE POTTERY 76".

5.5in (14cm) wide

$400-600   **DRA**

A Hampshire squat gourd-shaped vessel, in indigo glaze, raised mark.

4.5in (11cm) wide

$250-300   **DRA**

A Hampshire beaker-shaped vase, covered in a thick feathered matte green glaze, marked with numbers in ink.

4.25in (10.5cm) wide

$400-600   **DRA**

A Hampshire spherical vessel, impressed with a geometric pattern under matte green glaze, stamped "Hampshire 152".

5in (12.5cm) wide

$400-600   **DRA**

A Hampshire acorn cabinet vase, embossed with leaves under a fine leathery brown glaze, stamped "Hampshire Pottery".

3.5in (9cm) high

$600-900   **DRA**

An early Hampshire ovoid vase, embossed with leaves and buds under a fine green and blue feathered glaze, stamped mark.

6.75in (17cm) high

$800-1,200   **DRA**

An unusual Hampshire pitcher, embossed with tall trees under a fine, frothy blue and green glaze, stamped mark.

9.5in (24cm) high

$400-600   **DRA**

A Hampshire water pitcher, embossed with large leaves under a fine, mottled matte green glaze, unmarked.

8.25in (20.5cm) high

$400-600   **DRA**

A Hampshire kylix, embossed with leaves and covered in matte green glaze, stamped "HAMPSHIRE POTTERY".

8in (20cm) wide

$400-600   **DRA**

COLLECTORS' NOTES

- Goebel's Hummel figurines were inspired by the charming drawings of children drawn by Sister Berta Hummel, who was born in 1909 in Bavaria, Germany. They were first released in 1935 and since then, over 500 different models have been made, offering great scope to collectors. Examine the base for an impressed mark showing a number as this helps to identify the model and also the name, particularly if there is no transfer showing the model name on the base.

- Always examine the style of the factory mark stamped on the underside of the base as this helps you to date a piece. It is primarily the older pieces from the 1930s and 1940s, followed by the 1950s-1960s, that are the most valuable, along with rare variations in color and form. Larger pieces are also usually more valuable.

- The first mark used was a 'crown' mark from 1934-50, with the name 'Goebel' in script. In 1950, a mark including a bee was introduced and over the following decades the bee became smaller and moved further inside the V mark. In c1960 it became a dot with two simple triangles as wings. In 1964, the entire motif was placed beside three lines of text reading '© by W. Goebel W. Germany' and from 1972, the motif sits in top of the word Goebel and the 'G' becomes larger and almost circular in form.

- Condition is important as the material is fragile and chips, cracks or breaks extremely easily. Always examine protruding parts, heads and the rims of bases for damage or repairs, which devalue a piece. Take care when moving pieces around, especially when on display as if they are too close they can easily get damaged. Hummel figurines are still produced today.

A Hummel 'Little Gardener' figure, stylized bee mark, stamped "74".

This has the stylized bee mark used from 1960-72.

1960-72   4.25in (10.5cm)

$70-100   **EAB**

A Hummel 'Meditation' figure, with stylized bee mark, stamped "13".

c1962   4.5in (11.5cm)

$60-90   **EAB**

A Hummel 'Sister' figure, with full bee mark, restored fringe, stamped "98".

c1950   5.75in (14.5cm)

$100-150   **EAB**

A Hummel 'Forever Yours' special Club Edition figure, with special club edition mark, stamped "793".

Note the difference in form, and the graduated color of the dress which indicate the later Club Edition.

c1996–97   4.25in (10.5cm)

$80-120   **EAB**

A Hummel 'Spring Cheer' figure, late bee mark, stamped "72".

Designed in 1934 by Reinhold Unger, earlier versions than this example have yellow dresses and hold no flowers in the right hand.

c1972–79   5in (13cm)

$100-150   **EAB**

A Hummel 'Weary Wanderer' figurine, stamped "204".

Look out for the very rare variation with blue painted eyes which can fetch up to $1,500 if undamaged.

c1949   5.75in (14.5cm)

$150-200   **GCA**

A Hummel 'Kiss Me' figure, restoration to the doll's neck, three-line mark, stamped "311".

Look out for the early examples that use the 'full' bee mark and inspect pieces carefully for damage as the protruding parts are easy to damage. Later examples, which are less desirable, make the doll look less like a young girl.

c1964–72   6.25in (16cm)

$220-280   **EPO**

A Hummel 'Mother's Darling' figure, stylized bee mark, stamped "175".

Earlier examples with 'pre-bee' crown marks are the most sought after - one of the best ways to check is to look at the color of the bags, which are light pink and yellow-green on older versions.

c1960–72   5.75in (14.5cm)

$150-200   **AGO**

A Hummel 'Signs of Spring' figure, perched bluebird, three-line mark, stamped "203/1".

c1960–72   5in (13cm)

$150-200   **AGO**

A Hummel 'Doll Mother' figure, full bee mark, stamped "67".

c1940–56   4.5in (12.5cm)

$180-220   **EAB**

A Hummel 'Favorite Pet' figure, stylized bee mark, stamped "361".

1964–72   4.25in (11cm)

$120-180   **EAB**

A Hummel 'Good Friends' figure, with full bee mark, stamped "182".

This example has the first of the many 'full' bee marks used from 1940-59.

c1948–59   4in (10cm)

$180-220   **EAB**

A Hummel 'Apple Tree Girl' figure, full bee mark, stamped "141".

c1940–59

6in (15cm)

$180-220   **AGO**

A Hummel 'Chick Girl' figure, incised crown and full bee mark, stamped "57".

c1934-50   3.75in (9.5cm)

$220-280   **AGO**

A Hummel 'Baker' figure, with original "Baker" label, stylized bee mark, stamped "128".

Although there have been a number of variations over the years, unlike many models, the baker does not vary much in value.

A Hummel 'Little Hiker' figure, with full bee mark, restored staff, stamped "16 2/0".

c1956   *4.25in (11cm)*

$60-90   **EAB**

A Hummel 'Soloist' figure, three-line mark, some restoration, stamped "135".

$80-120   **EAB**

c1970–79   *5in (12.5cm)*

$120-180   **EAB**

A Hummel 'Village Boy' figure, stylized bee mark, stamped "51".

This figurine was released in 1936 but withdrawn in the 1960s, to be then reintroduced around 20 years later. Early versions with crown marks and full bee marks are rare, as are those with blue jackets.

c1979   *3.75in (9.5cm)*

$80-120   **EAB**

A Hummel 'Little Drummer' figure, full bee mark, stamped "240".

c1960–63   *4.25in (11cm)*

$60-90   **EAB**

A Hummel 'Let's Sing' figure, no base, full bee mark, stamped "110".

c1938   *3.75in (9.5cm)*

$120-180   **LW**

A Hummel 'Garden Treasures' limited Club Edition figure, base marked "I must keep on digging" and stamped "727".

Designed by Helmut Fischer in 1996, this example was released in the US as a special edition in 1998-99 upon renewing a subscription to the M.I. Hummel Club.

c1998–99   *3.75in (9.5cm)*

$60-90   **EAB**

A Hummel 'Singing Lesson' figure, stylized bee mark, stamped "63".

c1958-72   *3.75in (9.5cm)*

$100-150   **AGO**

CERAMICS

A Hummel 'Skier' figurine, with wooden poles and stylized bee mark, stamped "59".

A Hummel 'She Loves Me, She Loves Me Not' figure, stylized bee mark, stamped "174".

c1958-72   4.25in (11cm)

$120-180   **EAB**

A Hummel 'Barnyard Hero' figure, three-line mark, stamped "195 2/0".

c1964-72   4in (10cm)

$100-150   **AGO**

Older examples have wooden poles, but check the style of the mark as they can easily be replaced.

c1960   5in (13cm)

$280-320   **GCA**

A Hummel 'Joyful' ashtray, full bee mark for December 1984, slight chip on sole of right foot, stamped "33".

This piece was removed from production on 31st December 1984 and is unlikely to be made again. Look out for versions with orange dresses and blue shoes, and faïence painted examples as these are rare and much sought after.

4.5in (11.5cm)

$70-100   **EAB**

A Hummel 'Begging His Share' figure, with Goebel mark with no bee and stamped "9" on the base.

1979-91   5.5in (14cm)

$100-150   **ROX**

A Hummel 'Strolling Along' figure, with Goebel mark with no bee and stamped "5".

1979-89   5in (13cm)

$100-150   **ROX**

A Hummel 'Apple Tree Boy' table lamp figure, with a small, stylized bee, stamped "230".

This piece was modeled by Arthur Moeller in 1953 and uses the standard 'Apple Tree Boy' figure as a base. Older pieces have a proportionately larger figure, although the whole piece is the same size. It was withdrawn from production in 1989.

c1954-89   9.75in (25cm)

$280-320   **AGO**

A Hummel 'Smart Little Sister' figure, three-line/stylized bee mark "No. 346".

c1964-72   4.5in (11.5cm)

$100-150   **EAB**

A Hummel 'Apple Tree Boy' figure, stamped "142 3/0".

Larger versions than this have a bird perched on the branch.

c1958-72   3in (10cm)

$60-90   **EAB**

FIND OUT MORE...

'Luckey's Hummel Figurines & Plates Price Guide – 12th Edition', by Carl F. Luckey and Dean A. Genth, published by Krause Publications, 2003.

'No.1 Price Guide to Hummel Figurines, Plates and More', by Robert L. Miller, published by Portfolio Press, 2003.

COLLECTORS' NOTES

■ The Midwinter Pottery was founded by William Robinson Midwinter in 1910 and was based in Burslem, Stoke-on-Trent, England. Initial production comprised Art Deco-styled tablewares and nurseryware.

■ The company had a fairly small output until 1946 when Roy Midwinter, William's son, joined. He worked his way up through the company and began modernizing the designs and the operating processes.

■ Much of Roy's inspiration came from a trip to the US in 1952 where he saw work by designers such as Eva Meisel and Raymond Loewy.

■ As a result of this trip, the Stylecraft range was launched at the 1953 Blackpool Fair, aimed at younger buyers in the export and domestic market. The job of designing the patterns for this range fell to designer Jessie Tait who had joined the company around the same time as Roy. Some of the first patterns included 'Primavera', 'Fiesta', and the popular 'Zambesi'. Designs could be hand-painted, lithographed or a combination of the two.

■ Roy followed the success of Stylecraft with the Fashion range, first shown at the 1955 British Industries Fair, which featured even more modernized designs with abstract patterns and bright colors.

■ Again, Tait was responsible for most of the designs, but a young Terence Conran and architect Hugh Casson also provided artwork.

■ Shapes, patterns, and colors that typify the period are most popular with collectors. Condition should also be considered, as damage will reduce the value.

A Midwinter Pottery 'Red Domino' pattern hand-painted milk jug, from the Stylecraft range, designed by Jessie Tait.

A blue variation of this pattern was also made and is harder to find.

c1953   2.25in (5.5cm) high

$18-22   **FFM**

A Midwinter Pottery 'Fiesta' pattern charger, from the Stylecraft range, designed by Jessie Tait.

c1954   13.75in (35cm) wide

$150-200   **GGRT**

A Midwinter Pottery 'Tonga' pattern tube-line decorated plate, designed by Jessie Tait.

c1954   12.25in (31cm) diam

$150-200   **GGRT**

A Midwinter Pottery 'Autumn' pattern small plate, designed by Jessie Tait.

c1955   6.75in (15.5cm) diam

$70-100   **GGRT**

A Midwinter Pottery Fashion shape 'Capri' pattern plate, designed by Jessie Tait.

c1955   9.75in (24.5cm) diam

$100-150   **GGRT**

A Midwinter Pottery 'Fashion Check' pattern small plate, designed by Jessie Tait.

c1955   6.75in (15.5cm) diam

$100-150   **GGRT**

A Midwinter Pottery Fashion shape 'Pierrot' pattern small plate, designed by Jessie Tait.

c1955   6.75in (15.5cm) diam

$60-90   **GGRT**

CERAMICS

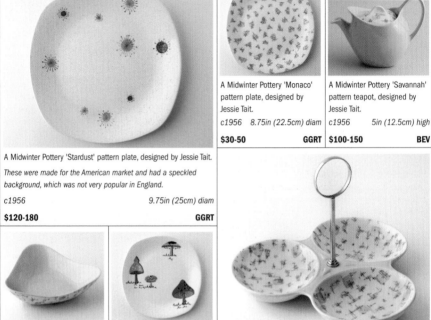

A Midwinter Pottery 'Monaco' pattern plate, designed by Jessie Tait.
c1956   8.75in (22.5cm) diam

$30-50   **GGRT**

A Midwinter Pottery 'Savannah' pattern teapot, designed by Jessie Tait.
c1956   5in (12.5cm) high

$100-150   **BEV**

A Midwinter Pottery 'Stardust' pattern plate, designed by Jessie Tait.

These were made for the American market and had a speckled background, which was not very popular in England.

c1956   9.75in (25cm) diam

$120-180   **GGRT**

A Midwinter Pottery 'Savanna' pattern dish, designed by Jessie Tait.
c1956   8.5in (21.5cm) diam

$120-180   **GGRT**

A Midwinter Pottery 'Toadstool' pattern small plate, designed by Jessie Tait.
c1956   6.75in (15.5cm) diam

$120-180   **GGRT**

A Midwinter Pottery 'Savanna' pattern hors d'oeuvres dish, designed by Jessie Tait.
c1956   6.25in (16cm) diam

$30-50   **GGRT**

A Midwinter Pottery 'Zambezi' pattern hand-painted dish, designed by Jessie Tait.
c1956   7.25in (18.5cm) diam

$40-60   **GGRT**

A Midwinter Pottery 'Zambezi' pattern hand-painted coffee set, designed by Jessie Tait, including six cups and saucers.

This pattern was extremely popular and was copied by other factories at the time.

c1956   coffee pot 7.5in (19cm) high

$800-1,200 set   **GGRT**

A Midwinter Pottery 'Cuban Fantasy' hors d'oeuvres dish, designed by Jessie Tait.
c1957   10.25in (26cm) wide

$150-200   **GGRT**

A Midwinter Pottery 'Flowermist' pattern plate, designed by Jessie Tait.

c1958   *9.75in (25cm) diam*

$100-150   **GGRT**

A 1950s Midwinter Pottery 'Cherokee Variant' pattern mug, designed by Jessie Tait.

This pattern is based on 'Cherokee', designed by Jessie Tait in 1957.

4in (10.5cm) high

$80-120   **GGRT**

A Midwinter Pottery 'Galaxy' pattern coffee pot, designed by Jessie Tait.

c1960   7in (18cm) high

$180-220   **GGRT**

A Midwinter Pottery 'Quite Contrary' pattern vegetable tureen, designed by Jessie Tait.

c1959   9.5in (24cm) diam

$80-120   **GGRT**

A Midwinter Pottery 'Graphic' pattern trio set, designed by Jessie Tait.

c1964 plate 7in (17.5cm) diam

$22-28   **GGRT**

A rare 1950s Midwinter pottery 'Elephant' pattern nursery mug, designed by Jessie Tait.

Midwinter nurseryware is hard to find and is much sought-after.

3.5in (9cm) high

$400-600   **GGRT**

A Midwinter Fine shape 'Sienna' pattern transfer-printed plate, designed by Jessie Tait.

A 1960s Midwinter Pottery 'Homespun' pattern plate, designed by Jessie Tait.

9.75in (25cm) diam

$80-120   **GGRT**

This was one of the most popular designs from the Fine range, which was launched in 1962.

c1962   8in (20.5cm) diam

$5-8   **FFM**

A Midwinter Pottery 'Elstree' pattern small plate, designed by Jessie Tait.

8in (20.5cm) wide

$80-120   **GGRT**

A Midwinter Pottery 'Nature Study' pattern plate, from the Stylecraft range, designed by Terence Conran.

Conran produced designs for Midwinter between 1955-7 as well as re-designing the factory's showrooms. All of his designs proved popular and are sought-after by collectors today.

c1955   8.5in (22cm) diam

$60-90   **GGRT**

A Midwinter Pottery 'Nature Study' plate, from the Stylecraft range, designed by Terence Conran.

c1955   9.5in (24cm) diam

$100-150   **GGRT**

A Midwinter pottery 'Saladware' pattern small plate, designed by Terence Conran.

1955   6.75in (15.5cm) diam

$50-70   **GGRT**

A Midwinter pottery 'Saladware' pattern Boomerang dish, designed by Terence Conran.

1955   8.25in (21cm) wide

$70-100   **GGRT**

A CLOSER LOOK AT A MIDWINTER VASE

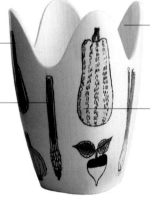

This vase was intended to serve celery, but also doubled as a flower vase.

Unusual shapes such as this will fetch a premium. Plates are the most common pieces available and tend to be less popular with collectors.

The Salad Ware range was hand-painted making it more desirable than lithographed patterns.

This modern design was aimed at the postwar generation who wanted tableware that reflected their modern way of life and less formal dining arrangements.

A Midwinter Pottery 'Salad Ware' pattern hand-painted celery vase, designed by Terence Conran.

7in (18cm) high

$150-200   **BEV**

A Midwinter Pottery 'Saladware' pattern hand-painted dish, from the Stylecraft range, designed by Terence Conran.

c1955   8.5in (21.5cm) wide

$120-180   **GGRT**

A Midwinter Pottery 'Saladware' pattern hand-painted saltshaker and pepper-pot, from the Stylecraft range, designed by Terence Conran.

c1955   5.75in (14.5cm) high

$180-220   **GGRT**

A Midwinter Pottery 'Saladware' pattern hand-painted salad set, including one large bowl and six smaller bowls from the Stylecraft range, designed by Terence Conran.

c1955   large bowl 9in (23cm) w

$700-1,000 set   **GGRT**

A Midwinter Pottery 'Plant Life' pattern plate, designed by Terence Conran.

c1956   *11.75in (30cm) wide*

$150-200   **GGRT**

Three Midwinter Fashion shape 'Transport' pattern transfer-printed dishes or pin trays, designed by Terence Conran, with a bicycle, a train, and a ship.

These dishes come from a series of black and white designs, all featuring forms of transport.

c1955   *3.25in (8.5cm) diam*

$30-50 each   **FFM**

A Midwinter Pottery 'Plant Life' pattern small plate, designed by Terence Conran.

c1956   *6.75in (15.5cm) diam*

$70-100   **GGRT**

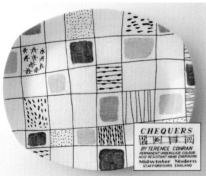

A Midwinter Pottery 'Chequers' pattern charger, designed by Terence Conran.

c1957   *12.25in (31cm) high*

$320-380   **GGRT**

A Midwinter Pottery 'Chequers' pattern cup and saucer, designed by Terence Conran.

c1957   *saucer 6.25in (16cm) diam*

$60-90   **GGRT**

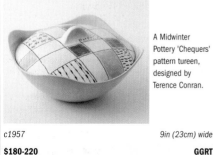

A Midwinter Pottery 'Chequers' pattern tureen, designed by Terence Conran.

c1957   *9in (23cm) wide*

$180-220   **GGRT**

A Midwinter Pottery 'Melody' pattern plate, designed by Terence Conran.

9.75in (24.5cm) diam

$80-120   **GGRT**

A 1950s Midwinter Pottery 'Fishing Boat' pattern plate, designed by Charles Cobelle.

8.75in (22cm) diam

$80-120   **GGRT**

A 1950s Midwinter Pottery 'Fishing Boat' pattern plate, designed by Charles Cobelle.

9.5in (24cm) wide

$100-150   **GGRT**

A 1950s Midwinter Pottery 'Fishing Boat' pattern gravy boat, stand and ladle, designed by Charles Cobelle.

boat 9in (23cm) wide

$180-220   **GGRT**

A Midwinter Pottery 'Riviera' pattern plate, from the Stylecraft range, designed by Hugh Casson.

Casson's inspiration for this pattern came from a holiday in the South of France. Originally issued as part of the Stylecraft range and including a number of different scenes, the pattern was re-issued as 'Cannes' in the Fashion shape in 1960.

c1954   6.25in (16cm) diam

$40-60   **GGRT**

A Midwinter Pottery 'Cannes' pattern chop plate, designed by Hugh Casson.

These were made for the American market, and are larger in size than the standard domestic issue.

c1960   12.25in (31cm) wide

$180-220   **GGRT**

A Midwinter Pottery 'Cannes' pattern celery vase, designed by Hugh Casson.

c1960   6.75in (17cm) high

$400-600   **GGRT**

A Midwinter Pottery 'Cannes' pattern cup and saucer, designed by Hugh Casson.

c1960   saucer 6.25in (16cm) diam

$60-90   **GGRT**

A Midwinter Pottery 'Marguerite' pattern charger, by an unknown designer.

14in (35.5cm) wide

$80-120   **GGRT**

COLLECTORS' NOTES

■ William Moorcroft (1872-1945) joined the James MacIntyre & Company pottery at a time when it was actively trying to move away from utilitarian wares to increasingly popular art pottery. His designs, such as Florian ware, became successful and were one of the building blocks of the Art Nouveau style.

■ He used the 'tube lining' technique where the pattern is drawn onto the surface using liquid clay – like icing, before being colored. Middle and Far Eastern styles influenced many of his patterns, while Classical forms influenced the shapes.

■ Built on the acclaim he had gained at MacIntyre's, he set up on his own with financial backing from Liberty & Co. in 1913. Success followed him. William died in 1945, and his son Walter took over. His exotic floral designs became very popular and a hallmark style for the company.

■ From the 1960s-80, the company did not prosper and in 1984 a controlling stake was sold to the Churchill Group. Production was streamlined, and some patterns were stopped. Sales did not meet the new owners' approval and the pottery was sold to collector

Hugh Edwards and dealer Richard Dennis in 1986.

■ Dennis' wife Sally Tuffin injected new life into the pottery until her departure in 1996. She was replaced by Rachel Bishop, who continues to both be inspired by and develop the stylized, naturalistic style for which Moorcroft has become renowned.

■ William's comparatively more complex early floral and foliate designs, such as Florian ware, are desirable. Look for rare patterns including animals such as fish.

■ Collectors look for uncommon shapes, such as rounded cube biscuit barrels, and unusual colorways. Large pieces such as jardinières on stands, those made for Liberty are also sought after. Those incorporating metal parts, sometimes designed by Archibald Knox can fetch high prices.

■ Modern limited editions by Sally Tuffin and Rachel Bishop can also fetch high prices. This section is arranged alphabetically by pattern name.

A Moorcroft 'Anemones' pattern saltglazed shouldered ovoid vase, impressed mark, signed in blue.

9.5in (24cm) high

$1,000-1,500   **L&T**

A 1990s Moorcroft 'Anemones' pattern baluster vase, impressed marks, initialed in green.

The 'Anemones' range was redrawn by Walter Moorcroft in 1989 and was released in yellow, green, and blue, the first two were withdrawn in 1991.

8.75in (22cm) high

$280-320   **L&T**

A Walter Moorcroft 'African Lily' bowl and cover, decorated in shades of red and yellow and green against a blue-green ground, impressed marks, restored chips to rim of bowl.

c1955   *5.75in (14cm) high*

$280-320   **GORL**

A Moorcroft 'Anna Lily' pattern bowl, designed by Nicola Slaney, of circular shape with tube lined decoration on a cream and cobalt blue ground, printed and painted marks.

c2001   *10.25in (26cm) diam*

$220-280   **CHEF**

A Moorcroft 'Black Tulip' pattern bowl, designed by Sally Tuffin, decorated against a blue-green ground, impressed and painted marks.

1991-2   *6.25in (16cm) high*

$280-320   **GORL**

A Moorcroft 'Buttercup' pattern baluster vase, designed by Sally Tuffin, impressed mark, initialed in green.

c1991   *10.5in (26cm) high*

$400-600   **L&T**

A mid-1990s Moorcroft 'Charles Rennie Mackintosh' pattern ovoid vase, designed by Rachel Bishop, decorated in shades of blue, red, and green, impressed and painted marks.

7in (17.5cm) high

$280-320   **GORL**

CERAMICS

A Moorcroft 'Claremont' pattern tapering vase, with flared rim, impressed marks, signed in blue.

The toadstool design was introduced in 1903 and received its Claremont title from Liberty. However, not all pieces with mushroom decoration are from the 'Claremont' range. Later examples have bold and dark colors.

8.5in (21cm) high

$2,800-3,200 **L&T**

A Moorcroft 'Claremont' pattern circular plate, impressed mark, initialed in blue.

7.5in (18.8cm) diam

$500-700 **L&T**

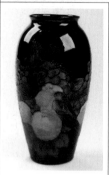

A Moorcroft 'Blue Finches' pattern shouldered tapering vase, designed by Sally Tuffin, impressed mark, initialed in green.

1988   10.25in (25.5cm) high

$300-400 **L&T**

A Moorcroft 'Ocher Finches' pattern shouldered tapering vase, impressed marks, initialed in green.

1989-90   10in (25cm) high

$320-380 **L&T**

A 1930S Moorcroft 'Fish' pattern flambé baluster vase, restored rim, impressed marks, signed in blue.

7.25in (18cm) high

$1,000-1,500 **L&T**

A Moorcroft 'Flamminian' pattern circular twin-handled bowl, with printed Liberty & Co. mark, impressed signature mark.

The red and green pieces from the Flamminian range were produced for Liberty and are from 1906-13, while the blue examples were made at Cobridge in 1914.

1906-13   7.5in (19cm) diam

$400-600 **L&T**

A Moorcroft Florian ware flared vase, printed MacIntyre marks, initialed in green.

8.25in (20.5cm) high

$2,800-3,200 **L&T**

A Moorcroft Florian ware biscuit barrel and cover, with electro-plated mount, decorated with poppies and highlighted with gilt, printed "MacIntyre" mark.

5.25in (13cm) high

$1,200-1,800 **L&T**

A Moorcroft Florian ware circular bowl, with silver mounts, printed "Florian Ware" mark, initialed in green.

5.5in (14cm) high

$1,800-2,200 **L&T**

A Moorcroft Florian ware vase, of tapering cylindrical form, small restoration to rim, printed MacIntyre mark, signed in green.

6in (15cm) high

$1,000-1,500   **L&T**

A Moorcroft 'Hazeldene' pattern ovoid vase, small restoration to rim, printed Liberty & Co. mark, signed in green.

c1915

6.5in (16cm) high

$1,500-2,000   **L&T**

A late 1980s limited edition Moorcroft 'HMS Sirius Bicentenary' ovoid vase, designed by Sally Tuffin, from an edition of 150, decorated in shades of green, brown, cream, and light blue, painted and impressed marks.

Made to commemorate the Australian Bicentenary of 1988.

14.5in (37cm) high

$400-600   **GORL**

A Moorcroft 'Hibiscus' pattern vase, of flattened spherical shape, the design against a green ground, probably 1960s.

4in (10cm) high

$180-220   **GORL**

A limited edition Moorcroft 'Jasmine Carousel' bottle vase, No. 1180, decorated overall in shades of brown and green against a green ground, impressed and painted marks.

1997   9in (22.5cm) high

$180-220   **GORL**

A late 1920s/early 1930s Moorcroft 'Leaf and Berry' pattern baluster vase, impressed marks, initialed in blue.

10in (25cm) high

$600-900   **L&T**

A Moorcroft 'Magnolia' pattern vase, of globe and shaft form, the design against a dark blue ground.

c1976   6in (15cm) high

$100-150   **GORL**

A Moorcroft 'Nasturtium' pattern ginger jar and cover, designed by Sally Tuffin, printed Collectors Club mark, initialed in green.

This jar was made exclusively for the Moorcroft Collectors Club.

1992   7.25in (18cm) high

$100-150   **L&T**

A late 1990s limited edition Moorcroft 'New Swallows' ovoid vase, designed by Rachel Bishop, from an edition of 500, with everted rim, decorated in shades of red, green, purple, and blue against a pale green ground, painted and impressed marks.

10in (25.5cm) high

$800-1,200   **GORL**

A Moorcroft 'Orchid' pattern bowl, painted against a deep blue ground, painted initials mark, cracked.

9in (23cm) diam

$180-220   **GORL**

A Moorcroft 'Oberon' pattern ovoid vase, designed by Rachel Bishop, with everted rim, decorated in shades of pinks, greens, and yellows against a pink and blue ground, impressed marks and painted initials.

1997   *10.75in (27cm) high*

$800-1,200   **GORL**

A late 1990s Moorcroft 'Phoenix' pattern vase, designed by Rachel Bishop, with waisted neck and decorated in shades of blue, green, and orange against a brown-green ground, impressed marks, signed.

11.5in (29cm) high

$700-1,000   **GORL**

A Moorcroft 'Peacock' pattern vase, designed by Sally Tuffin for Liberty, decorated in shades of turquoise, green, and brown against a green ground, impressed and painted marks.

1988-90   *8in (20cm) high*

$300-500   **GORL**

A Moorcroft 'Pomegranate' pattern baluster vase, with flared rim, impressed marks, signed in green, restored rim.

1915-30   *9.5in (24cm) high*

$1,800-2,200   **L&T**

A Moorcroft 'Pomegranate' pattern miniature ovoid vase, impressed mark, initialed in green.

1915-30   *2.5in (6.5cm) high*

$220-280   **L&T**

A Moorcroft 'Pomegranate' pattern miniature ovoid vase, impressed marks.

1915-30   *2.5in (6.5cm) high*

$280-320   **L&T**

A Moorcroft 'Pomegranate' pattern circular bowl, with 'Tudric' beaten pewter foot, stamped mark "Tudric 01306".

1915-30   *7.5in (19cm) diam*

$600-900   **L&T**

A Moorcroft 'Poppies' pattern flambé shouldered tapering vase, restored rim, impressed mark, signed in blue.

8.5in (21cm) high

$700-1,000   **L&T**

An early 1990s Moorcroft 'Rain Forest' baluster vase, designed by Sally Tuffin, decorated with various tropical flowers in shades of yellow, green, and red against a green ground, impressed marks and painted initials.

12.25in (30.5cm) high

$700-1,000   **GORL**

A Moorcroft 'Robin' pattern baluster vase.

1991-92

$100-150   **L&T**

A late 1990s Moorcroft 'Rockpool' pattern squat vase, designed by Wendy Mason, from a numbered edition, decorated in various colored shades against a blue-green ground, impressed marks and painted "Wendy Mason" signature.

6.5in (16cm) high

$300-500   **GORL**

A large Moorcroft 'Spring' pattern shouldered cylindrical vase, impressed marks, initialed in blue.

11.5in (28.5cm) high

$1,200-1,800   **L&T**

A 1930s Moorcroft 'Waving Corn' pattern ovoid vase, impressed signature mark and bearing initials.

6.5in (16cm) high

$400-600   **L&T**

A large 1920s Moorcroft 'Wisteria' pattern jardinière, of deep tapering cylindrical form, decorated with tube lined and painted decoration, restored chip to rim, initialed in green, impressed marks.

16.75in (42cm) diam

$1,500-2,000   **L&T**

A 1980s Moorcroft bottle vase, painted with a mauve plant and green leaves against a cream ground, impressed marks.

6in (15cm) high

$100-150   **GORL**

A 1930s Moorcroft orange luster vase.

7.25in (18.5cm) high

$150-200   **CHEF**

A 1930s William Moorcroft teapot, of circular shape decorated in shades of yellow and red with freesias on a mottled green ground, impressed marks.

c1935   *6in (15cm) high*

$220-280   **CHEF**

FIND OUT MORE...

'Moorcroft, A Guide to Moorcroft Pottery 1897-1993', *by Paul Atterbury, published by Richard Dennis & Hugh Edwards, 1998.*

www.moorcroft.co.uk - *official company website.*

A Keith Murray for Wedgwood moonstone bulbous ribbed vase, with late Etruria "KM" mark.

c1940   7in (18cm) high

$400-600   **PSA**

A Keith Murray for Wedgwood moonstone small hooped bulbous vase, with "KM" mark.

c1935   6.75in (17cm) high

$280-320   **PSA**

A Keith Murray for Wedgwood moonstone vase, decorated with horizontal bands of two widths.

6.5in (16.5cm) h

$800-1,200 BEV

A Keith Murray for Wedgwood moonstone ridged vase.

Murray was born in 1892 and trained as an architect. He was approached by Wedgwood in 1932. His training is clear in his simple, stylish designs, which typify the Art Deco style. His first design was released in 1933 and his work was produced until the late 1960s.

6in (15cm) high

$400-600   **BEV**

A Keith Murray for Wedgwood moonstone stepped bowl.

8in (20cm) diam

$800-1,200   **BEV**

A Keith Murray for Wedgwood large white bowl, with a wide rim.

7.5in (19cm) high

$500-700   **BEV**

A Keith Murray for Wedgwood moonstone hooped cake stand, with signature mark.

c1933   9in (23cm) diam

$80-120   **PSA**

A Keith Murray for Wedgwood moonstone rectangular cigarette box and cover, with signature mark.

Around 1934, Wedgwood introduced a less expensive line of smaller objects, such as this cigarette box (model No. 3871) and an inkstand. They were formed from less expensive and faster to produce slipware. Condition is very important as lids are often chipped or missing.

c1932   7.5in (19cm) long

$320-380   **PSA**

A Keith Murray
for Wedgwood
matte green
vase, the sides
decorated with
horizontal lines.

A Keith Murray for Wedgwood
dark green large tapered ribbed
vase, with signature mark.

c1933   *11.5in (29cm) high*

$400-600   **PSA**

11in (28cm) high

$1,000-1,500   **BAD**

A Keith Murray for Wedgwood
matte green ribbed tapered
vase, with "KM" mark.

c1935   *7.5in (19cm) high*

$180-220   **PSA**

A Keith Murray for Wedgwood
matte green ribbed vase, with
signature mark.

c1933   *6in (15cm) high*

$320-380   **PSA**

A Keith Murray for Wedgwood
matte green bulbous ribbed
vase, with signature mark.

c1933   *9.5in (24cm) high*

$400-600   **PSA**

A Keith Murray for Wedgwood
matte green vase, with an ovoid
body, decorated with horizontal
lines.

6.75in (17cm) high

$400-600   **BEV**

A Keith Murray for Wedgwood
dark green pedestal ribbed
bowl.

10.25in (26cm) diam

$150-200   **PSA**

A Keith Murray for Wedgwood
dark green scalloped fruit bowl,
with signature mark.

c1933   *8.75in (22.5cm) diam*

$120-180   **PSA**

A Keith Murray for Wedgwood
matte green beer mug, model
number 3971.

c1935   *8in (20cm) diam*

$80-120   **BEV**

A Keith Murray for Wedgwood celadon and cream-glazed footed
bowl, with "KM" mark.

c1935   *11in (28cm) diam*

$400-600   **PSA**

A Keith Murray for Wedgwood matte straw vase, with regular line decoration.

7.5in (19cm) high

$600-900   BEV

A Keith Murray for Wedgwood matte straw vase, with an ovoid body and ridged decoration, printed marks and facsimile signature.

9in (23cm) high

$700-1,000   BEV

A Keith Murray for Wedgwood straw water jug, with signature mark.

c1933   8in (20cm) high

$600-900   PSA

A Keith Murray for Wedgwood light blue ribbed tapered vase, with "KM" mark.

c1935   7.5in (19cm) high

$220-280   PSA

A Keith Murray for Wedgwood blue footed bowl, with hooped foot and rim and "KM" mark.

c1935   10in (25.5cm) diam

$400-600   PSA

A Keith Murray for Wedgwood gray vase, with a fluted body and a wide rim.

7.25in (18.5cm) high

$600-900   BEV

A Keith Murray for Wedgwood pale gray-green ribbed cone bowl, with signature mark.

c1933   6.25in (16cm) high

$600-900   PSA

A Keith Murray for Wedgwood black basalt bowl, with signature mark.

Black Basalt pieces are scarcer than other colors and tend to fetch higher prices. They are always signed with a red signature on the base. The technique for the black body was perfected by Josiah Wedgwood in the late 1760s.

c1935   9in (23cm) diam

$400-600   PSA

A rare Keith Murray for Wedgwood commemorative beer mug, the printed puce decoration by Victor Skellern, made to commemorate the opening of a new electrically fired tunnel oven at Barlaston and from the first firing Biscuit & Glost, Summer 1940.

4.75in (12cm) high

$400-600   DN

A set of four Keith Murray for Wedgwood moonstone egg cups, with ribbing to foot, two with minor chips.

$300-400   PSA

COLLECTORS' NOTES

■ Popular during the 1920s and 1930s, wind-up musical mechanisms were fitted to a range of objects. Makers included Royal Winton (known primarily for their chintz pattern ceramics), Fielding's Crown Devon, and Carlton Ware. Jugs and tankards were among the most popular forms, but cigarette boxes can also be found, as can decorative vases.

■ Scenes are often pastoral in theme, ranging from fairs to scenes of people near cottages, or country personalities. Mechanisms should work for a piece to fetch the highest value. Some mechanisms are replaced and this also has a bearing on values. The condition of the piece itself is also important – wear or damage such as crazing or chips will reduce value.

■ Also look for well-decorated or detailed scenes, and notable makers. Musical tunes will often echo the scene on the jug such as 'Daisy Daisy' with a 'Daisy Bell' cycling jug by Crown Devon. Detailed handles will also usually add to desirability, particularly if shaped or very decorative. Certain characters and themes are also popular and be aware that pieces that have a cross-market interest may fetch higher values.

A Royal Winton 'Underneath the Spreading Chestnut Tree' musical tankard, working order, some crazing.

6.25in (16cm) high

$100-150   PSA

A Royal Winton 'Annie Laurie' musical tankard, working order.

6.25in (16cm) high

$150-200   PSA

A Royal Winton 'The Floral Dance' musical tankard, working order, some crazing.

6.25in (16cm) high

$100-150   PSA

A Royal Winton 'Come to the Fair' musical tankard, working order, some crazing.

6in (15cm) high

$50-70   PSA

A Fielding's Crown Devon 'Daisy Bell' musical water jug, working order, some crazing.

8in (20cm) high

$220-280   PSA

A Royal Winton musical tankard, with the handle as a tinker looking over the rim.

8in (20cm) high

$120-180   PSA

A Fielding's Crown Devon 'Widdecombe Fair' musical water jug, working order, some crazing.

7.5in (19cm) high

$150-200   PSA

A Fielding's Crown Devon 'Roamin' in the Gloamin' musical water jug, working order, some crazing.

8in (20cm) high

$300-400   PSA

CERAMICS

A Fielding's Crown Devon 'John Peel' musical tankard, working order, minor roughness to lip and some crazing.

4.75in (12cm) high

$80-120　　　　　**PSA**

A Crown Devon 'Auld Lang Syne' musical tankard, working order.

4.5in (11.5cm) high

$150-200　　　　　**PSA**

A Crown Devon 'Daisy Bell' musical tankard, working order.

6.25in (16cm) high

$100-150　　　　　**PSA**

A Carlton Ware 'John Peel' musical tankard, working order.

5.25in (13.5cm) high

$40-60　　　　　**PSA**

A musical tankard, with a 'John Peel' hunting scene, working order, some crazing.

5in (12.5cm) high

$50-70　　　　　**PSA**

A 'Come Landlord Fill the Flowing Bowl' musical tankard, working order, some crazing.

6in (15cm) high

$100-150　　　　　**PSA**

A Fielding's Crown Devon musical cigarette box, with a hunting scene, working order, minor chip to underside of lid and some crazing.

This box has much cross market appeal, being of interest to collectors of smoking memorabilia and musical ceramics, as well as sporting and hunting collectors. It also has a finely detailed and realistic scene with gilt highlights.

c1930　　　　　*2.75in (7cm) high*

$800-1,200　　　　　**PSA**

A Fielding's Crown Devon 'John Peel' musical footed fruit bowl, in working order, some crazing.

This example, although in a comparatively complex form, has been fitted with a new movement.

9in (23cm) high

$500-700　　　　　**PSA**

A Fielding's Crown Devon musical cigar box, working order, some crazing.

$100-150　　　　　**PSA**

A Pendelfin 'Bellman' figure, membership piece designed by Jean Walmsley Heap.

Jean Walmsley Heap and Jeannie Todd started Pendelfin in 1953 in Burnley, Lancashire, England. Rabbits are the most common figures, but mice, pixies, ducks, and witches were also made and tend to be sought-after. Production still continues today and due to the large number of models produced, condition has a huge impact on value for all but the rarest examples.

1995-96   *4in (10cm) high*

$50-70   **PSA**

A Pendelfin 'Buttons' figure, membership piece designed by Doreen Noel Roberts.

1994   *3.5in (9cm) high*

$60-90   **PSA**

A Pendelfin 'Gussie Rabbit' figure, dressed in blue, designed by Jean Walmsley Heap.

1960-68   *3.5in (9cm) high*

$150-200   **PSA**

A CLOSER LOOK AT A PENDELFIN FIGURE

A Pendelfin 'Megan The Harp Rabbit' figure, dressed in pink, designed by Jean Walmsley Heap.

1960-67   *3.5in (9cm) high*

$80-120   **PSA**

The 'Father Rabbit' figure, issued in 1955, was one of the first designed and originally wore dungarees.

The figure was available in a number of colors with different patterned ties.

The earlier version of this figure was very top heavy and tended to fall over, damaging the ears, so it was redesigned.

This kipper tie-wearing example replaced the earlier design in 1970 and is worth about half the value of the earlier models.

A Pendelfin 'Father Rabbit' figure, dressed in red with floral kipper tie.

c1970   *8in (20cm) high*

$320-380   **PSA**

A Pendelfin 'Puffer' figure, Family Circle piece designed by Jean Walmsley Heap.

Model of the Year 1994.

                          4.5in (11.5cm) high

$60-90   **PSA**

A Pendelfin 'Squeezy Rabbit' figure, dressed in red, designed by Jean Walmsley Heap, minor wear.

1960-70   *3.5in (9cm) high*

$100-150   **PSA**

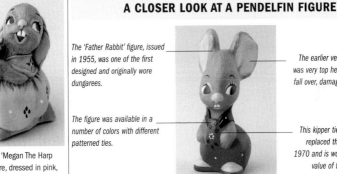

An early Pendelfin 'Tammy Dog' figure, with green eyes, designed by Jean Walmsley Heap.

1957-87   *3.5in (9cm) high*

$80-120   **PSA**

A Pendelfin Metallion 'Elf Tree' candle holder, designed by Doreen Noel Roberts.

1980-85   *3in (7.5cm) high*

$180-220   **PSA**

FIND OUT MORE...

'Pendelfin Collector's Handbook', *by Stella Ashbrook, published by Francis Joseph, May 2004.*

CERAMICS

COLLECTORS' NOTES

■ The Carter & Co. Pottery was started by Jesse Carter in Poole, Dorset in 1873 and produced mainly tiles and architectural products.

■ In 1921, the company formed a subsidiary with designers Harold Stabler and John Adams, called Carter, Stabler and Adams, with the intention of producing decorative wares.

■ John Adams' wife, Truda (later Carter), had a background in embroidery design and became a leading designer at the pottery. She produced a range of designs with Art Deco styled floral, foliate and geometric motifs using bright colors against a white ground. These hand-painted pieces proved extremely popular and the company gained two gold medals at the 1925 Paris Exhibition.

■ After WWII, Ruth Pavely became head of the painting department where traditional designs continued to be made. In an effort to recover from WWII, the pottery employed lamp designer Alfred Burgess Read, who, with senior thrower Guy Sydenham, created the 'Contemporary' range of hand-thrown and hand-painted free-form pieces.

■ Read resigned in 1957 and was replaced by Robert Jefferson in 1958, who designed the 'Delphis' range of studio ware. The 1960s public approved of the pieces' bright colors and individual styling and the 'Aegean' range was added in 1970. It is often difficult to tell which range a piece came from, but the 'Delphis' pieces generally have a finer texture than 'Aegean'.

■ Collectors should look for pieces that exemplify their period, examples by Truda Adams and Ruth Pavely are always popular. As 1930s wares are becoming increasingly rare, pieces from the 1950s and later are gaining more attention.

A small Poole Pottery hand-painted bowl, painted by Phyllis Ryal (1928-37), date code "21".

1925-34   *4.5in (11.5cm) diam*

$70-100   **BEV**

A 1930s small Poole Pottery hand-painted vase, the base indistinctly painted "/EN [G]" and inscribed "968".

4in (10cm) high

$100-150   **BAD**

A 1930s Poole Pottery hand-painted 'Comic Bird' pattern vase.

10.25in (26cm) high

$600-900   **ADE**

A Poole Pottery hand-painted 'Blue Bird' pattern vase.

1934-7   *5.5in (14cm) high*

$100-150   **BEV**

A Poole Pottery red earthenware dish, designed by Truda Carter and painted by Mary Brown, in unusual colors, impressed "Carter Stabler & Adams" mark, painter's mark and "662/BK".

12in (30.5cm) diam

$400-600   **DN**

A Poole Pottery oviform vase, designed by Truda Carter and painted by Marian Heath (De'Ath), impressed "Poole England", marked "596/KD?".

9.25in (23.5cm) high

$320-380   **DN**

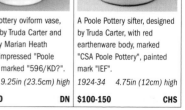

A Poole Pottery sifter, designed by Truda Carter, with red earthenware body, marked "CSA Poole Pottery", painted mark "IEF".

1924-34   *4.75in (12cm) high*

$100-150   **CHS**

A Poole Pottery 'Sugar for the Birds' plate, designed by Olive Bourne and painted by Betty Gooby, with the head of a young woman amid flowers and foliage, marked "Poole England" with a dolphin mark and painter's mark.

10in (25.5cm) diam

$320-380 DN

A Poole Pottery white earthenware tray, molded and pierced in the center with a bird in flight amid highly stylized flowers and foliage, impressed "Poole England".

12.25in (31cm) wide

$80-120 DN

A 1930s Poole Pottery Sylvanware vase.

$220-280 ADE

A pair of Poole Pottery 'Elephant' bookends, designed by Harold Brownsword, covered with a 'café-au-lait' glaze, impressed "Carter Stabler and Adams" mark and hexagonal "trial" mark.

Similar bookends were shown in the exhibition of Industrial and Decorative Art, Monza, Italy, 1930.

6in (15.5cm) high

$600-900 DN

A pair of Poole vases, the waisted cylindrical shapes painted in smoky gray and pink with alternating vertical vines of pink fruits, impressed marks and "E/PH".

c1950   11in (28cm) high

$500-800 CHEF

A Poole Pottery 'Contemporary' style vase.

1952-55   10.5in (27cm) high

$180-220 ADE

A Poole Pottery 'Contemporary' style vase.

1952-55   7.75in (19.5cm) high

$180-220 ADE

A Poole Pottery 'Spiral Leaf' pattern 'Contemporary' style vase, designed by Alfred B. Read.

1952-55   9.75in (25cm) high

$300-500 ADE

A Poole Pottery 'Contemporary' style vase, designed by Alfred B. Read.

1952-55   10in (25.2cm) high

$400-600 ADE

CERAMICS

A Poole Pottery 'Freeform' style bowl, decoration designed by Ruth Pavely.

1955-59   7.25in (18.5cm) high

$180-220   **ADE**

A Poole Pottery 'Freeform' style vase.

1955-59   7.5in (18.5cm) high

$320-380   **ADE**

A Poole Pottery 'Freeform' style vase.

1955-59   12.25in (31cm) wide

$300-500   **ADE**

A 1970s Poole Pottery 'Aegean' plate.

8in (20.5cm) diam

$80-120   **ADE**

A 1970s Poole Pottery 'Aegean' plate.

10.5in (26.5cm) diam

$120-180   **ADE**

A 1970s Poole Pottery 'Aegean' plate, chip to rim, reglued.

10.25in (26cm) diam

$22-28   **GAZE**

A 1960s Poole Pottery 'Delphis' spear-shaped dish, in yellow, greens, and brown glazes.

10.25in (26cm) diam

$100-150   **GAZE**

A Poole Pottery stoneware charger, designed by Guy Sydenham, decorated in slip with a central boss of concentric circles surrounded by a similar band, impressed mark.

13.5in (34cm) high

$300-600   **DN**

A 1970s Poole Pottery charger, marked "Poole Pottery" and "54".

16in (40.5cm) diam

$280-320   **L**

A 1970s Poole Pottery vase, marked "Poole England" and "83" with a dolphin.

6.25in (16cm) high

$70-100   **L**

A 1970s Poole Pottery tall vase, impressed "Poole Pottery" and "93?".

12in (30.5cm) high

$120-180   **L**

A 1970s Poole Pottery vase, marked "Poole England" and "79" with a dolphin.

5.25in (13.5cm) high

$60-90   **L**

A 1970s Poole Pottery tall vase, with printed and painted marks.

15.75in (40cm) high

$300-500   **CHS**

A 1970s Poole Pottery 'Atlantis' hand-thrown vase, decorated by Beatrice Bolton.

7in (18cm) high

$400-600   **ADE**

A 1970s Poole Pottery dish, with printed marks, boxed.

6.5in (16.5cm) wide

$40-60   **CHS**

A 1970s Poole Pottery dish, with printed marks, boxed.

7in (18cm) wide

$25-30   **CHS**

CERAMICS

A 1970s Poole Pottery 'Atlantis' hand-thrown vase, by Jennie Haigh.

8in (20.3cm) high

$300-500 ADE

A 1970s Poole Pottery 'Atlantis' vase, 'A20'5', by Catherine Connett, impressed mark.

8in (20.5cm) high

$280-320 WW

A Poole Pottery vase, by Guy Sydenham, impressed marks.

6.75in (17cm) high

$300-500 WW

A small Poole table lamp base, with glass shade.

11.75in (30cm) high

$30-40 GAZE

A Poole Pottery tankard.

4.5in (11.5cm) high

$50-70 CHS

A Poole Pottery square dish, with "medieval" scene, printed marks.

7in (18cm) wide

$30-40 CHS

A late 1970s Poole Pottery candlestick, from the Aubrey Beardsley collection, designed by Sue Pottinger.

5in (12.5cm) high

$30-50 CHS

Poole
England
436 Scene VI

A Poole Pottery display plate, printed mark "436 Scene VI".

6in (15cm) wide

$12-18 CHS

A Poole Pottery teapot, cup, and saucer, with coffee bean decoration, printed marks.

Teapot 5.5in (14cm) high

$60-90 CHS

FIND OUT MORE...

'Poole Pottery', by Leslie Hayward and Paul Atterbury, published by Richard Dennis Publishing, 1999.

'Collecting Poole Pottery', by Robert Prescott-Walker, published by Kevin Francis Publishing, 2001.

www.poolepottery.co.uk - official company website.

COLLECTORS' NOTES

■ Susan Williams-Ellis is the daughter of Sir Clough Williams-Ellis, creator of the famous Portmeirion village in North Wales. Susan took over the souvenir shop in the village in 1953. She designed patterns for ceramics, which were applied to blank bodies by the famous Gray's Pottery of Stoke-on-Trent.

■ In 1960 she and her husband bought Gray's, and later acquired Kirkhams Pottery in 1961. This enabled her to create shapes as well as decorate them. Portmeirion is best known for the floral and foliate 'Botanic Garden' range of the 1970s onward, however, the 1960s ranges now have a growing base of collectors.

■ Patterns were molded, such as the innovative 'Totem' design, and transfer printed, with printed designs often showing Susan's background in textile design. Inspirations were numerous, including personal memories. Forms tend to be clean lined and cylindrical, reflecting 1960s ceramic design and allowing transfers to be applied and displayed easily and fully.

■ Pattern, color, and condition are the main indicators of value. Early patterns and those produced for short periods such as 'Moss Agate' are sought after and valuable. Some patterns are also more desirable than others, and different colorways can attract different prices. Condition is important, with wear and damage reducing value considerably.

A Portmeirion Pottery 'Talisman' pattern medium storage jar, designed by Susan Williams-Ellis, in yellow and orange.

c1962   6in (15.5cm) high

$70-100   **GGRT**

A Portmeirion Pottery 'Talisman' pattern large storage jar, designed by Susan Williams-Ellis, in blue and green.

c1962   8in (20cm) high

$120-180   **GGRT**

A Portmeirion Pottery 'Talisman' pattern medium storage jar, designed by Susan Williams-Ellis, in blue and plum.

c1962   8in (20cm) high

$80-120   **GGRT**

A Portmeirion Pottery 'Jupiter' pattern 'Serif' shape petrol blue coffee pot, designed by Susan Williams-Ellis, printed marks.

The petrol blue colorway is hard to find in good condition, as the color faded when washed.

12.5in (32cm) high

$70-100   **CHS**

A Portmeirion Pottery 'Phoenix' pattern coffee pot.

Unlike most Portmeirion, this pattern was not designed by Williams-Ellis, but her assistant John Cuffley. A large pattern, it works best on coffee pots.

13in (33cm) high

$25-35   **CHS**

A Portmeirion 'Phoenix' pattern milk jug and sugar bowl.

4in (10cm) high

$8-12   **GAZE**

A Portmeirion 'Tivoli' pattern milk jug.

The Tivoli pattern was inspired by Copenhagen's Tivoli Gardens.

c1964   5.75in (14.5cm) high

$70-100   **ADE**

Two Portmeirion 'Velocipedes' range pieces.

Jug 4in (10cm) high

$15-25   **GAZE**

A Portmeirion 'Dolphin' pattern tea storage jar, designed by Susan Williams-Ellis, printed marks.

3.5in (9cm) high

$50-80　　　　　　　　**CHS**

A Portmeirion 'Dolphin' pattern storage jar, designed by Susan Williams-Ellis, printed marks.

4in (10cm) high

$40-60　　　　　　　　**CHS**

A Grays pottery for Portmeirion 'Moss Agate' pattern jar, designed by Susan Williams-Ellis.

'Moss Agate' was an early design, dating back to the early 1960s. It is extremely desirable today as it was hard and expensive to produce. It was made in limited quantities. Made to resemble the stone moss agate, each gilt disc has a cameo-like shadow pattern, clearly seen here.

3.75in (9.5cm) high

$400-600　　　　　　　　**GGRT**

A Portmeirion 'Dolphin' pattern sugar sifter, designed by Susan Williams-Ellis, printed marks.

5.25in (13.5cm) high

$120-180　　　　　　　　**CHS**

A Portmeirion 'Dolphin' pattern tea storage jar, designed by Susan Williams-Ellis, printed marks.

Designed in 1958, this is one of the earliest patterns and was produced by Gray's. It is an increasingly sought-after pattern due to its early date.

6.5in (16.5cm) wide

$150-200　　　　　　　　**CHS**

A Portmeirion 'Greek Key' pattern 'Cylinder' shape mug, designed by Susan Williams-Ellis, printed marks.

A black 'Greek Key' pattern on any color base is an early design. After 1968, a gold pattern, usually on a black body, was introduced.

5in (12.5cm) high

$25-35　　　　**CHS**

A Portmeirion 'Greek Key' pattern 'Cylinder' shape spice jar, handled, designed by Susan Williams-Ellis, printed marks.

3.75in (9.5cm) high

$18-22　　　　**CHS**

A 1970s Portmeirion white 'Totem' pattern sifter.

6.5in (16.5cm) high

$40-60　　　　　　　　**CHS**

A Portmeirion casserole dish, marked "Portmeirion Pottery 1 Made in England".

10.25in (26cm) wide

$50-80　　　　　　　　**CHS**

A Portmeirion 'Tiger Lily' pattern bowl, designed by Susan Williams-Ellis, with printed marks.

This pattern was designed in 1961 and based on Williams-Ellis' love of painted barge ware.

11in (28cm) diam

$150-200　　　　　　　　**CHS**

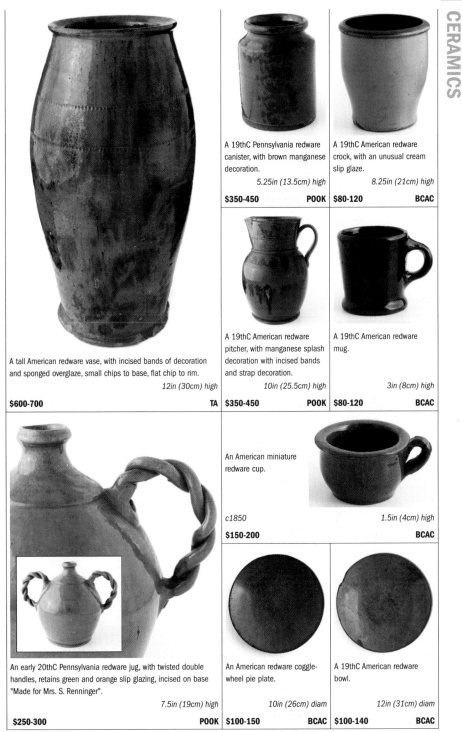

A 19thC Pennsylvania redware canister, with brown manganese decoration.

5.25in (13.5cm) high

$350-450   **POOK**

A 19thC American redware crock, with an unusual cream slip glaze.

8.25in (21cm) high

$80-120   **BCAC**

A tall American redware vase, with incised bands of decoration and sponged overglaze, small chips to base, flat chip to rim.

12in (30cm) high

$600-700   **TA**

A 19thC American redware pitcher, with manganese splash decoration with incised bands and strap decoration.

10in (25.5cm) high

$350-450   **POOK**

A 19thC American redware mug.

3in (8cm) high

$80-120   **BCAC**

An American miniature redware cup.

c1850   1.5in (4cm) high

$150-200   **BCAC**

An early 20thC Pennsylvania redware jug, with twisted double handles, retains green and orange slip glazing, incised on base "Made for Mrs. S. Renninger".

7.5in (19cm) high

$250-300   **POOK**

An American redware coggle-wheel pie plate.

10in (26cm) diam

$100-150   **BCAC**

A 19thC American redware bowl.

12in (31cm) diam

$100-140   **BCAC**

CERAMICS

COLLECTORS' NOTES

■ A member of Cincinnati's high society, Maria Longworth Nichols was one of a number of ladies who decorated ceramics as a hobby. She decided to turn this pastime into a business and founded her own pottery in 1880. The focus on artistic quality rather than quantity, Rookwood's wares soon became popular and well respected.

■ Maria Nichols appointed her friend William Watts Tyler as manager in 1883 and he set about standardizing the pottery's disparate lines. Nichols moved abroad in 1890 and Tyler took control.

■ The pottery was committed to quality and innovation and hired famous artists and pioneering ceramicists accordingly. It won a number of awards including a gold medal at the Paris Exposition in 1900.

■ The Great Depression had a disastrous effect on Rookwood and the pottery never recovered. It closed in 1961. The rights and molds are currently owned by a Michigan-based dentist who releases a small run of tiles each year.

■ Look for polychrome designs by named artists. Pieces with the stylized, molded designs typical of Rookwood are often more valuable than the undecorated forms.

A Rookwood production barrel-shaped vase, covered in a rich mottled purple glossy glaze, a couple of short, shallow scratches, flame mark, dated.

1921   *8in (20cm) high*

$180-220   **DRA**

A Rookwood production tyg, with geometric design under cobalt glaze, flame mark, dated.

1926   *5.75in (14cm) high*

$250-300   **DRA**

A Rookwood production narrow vase, embossed with a band of seahorses under blue glaze, marked, dated.

1923   *6.75in (17cm) high*

$350-400   **DRA**

A Rookwood production baluster vase, covered in crackled curdling blue glaze, flame mark, dated.

1923   *9.5in (24cm) high*

$280-320   **DRA**

A Rookwood production vase, embossed with band of rooks under an indigo glaze, marked, dated.

1919   *7.5in (19cm) high*

$500-600   **DRA**

A Rookwood production tall bulbous vase, deeply embossed with squash blossoms and leaves under blue glaze, stilt pull lines to footring, fired, flame mark, dated.

1927   *13.75in (34cm) high*

$500-600   **DRA**

A Rookwood production cylindrical vase, with three buttresses and a band of embossed rooks under indigo glaze, marked, dated.

1930   *6.5in (16cm) high*

$350-400   **DRA**

A Rookwood production creamer and sugar bowl, embossed with four-square design under shaded blue glaze, flame marks, dated.

1912   *creamer 3in (7.5cm) high*

$300-350   **DRA**

A Rookwood production vase, embossed with mistletoe under a blue and green butterfat ground, flame mark, dated.

1931   *7.5in (19cm) high*

$450-550   **DRA**

A large Rookwood production vase, with a stylized curvilinear design under a matte blue glaze, flame mark, dated.

1928   *10in (25cm) high*

$350-400   **DRA**

A Rookwood production flaring vase, embossed with bamboo stalks under a fine beige and blue matte crystalline glaze, flame mark and dated.

1919   *6.25in (15.5cm) high*

$400-500   **DRA**

A Rookwood production vase, with embossed panels of fish and birds under a flowing green matte glaze, flame mark, dated.

1940   *8.5in (21cm) high*

$400-500   **DRA**

A Rookwood production fan vase, covered in a fine blue and green butterfat glaze, flame mark, dated.

1930   *6.75in (17cm) high*

$150-200   **DRA**

A Rookwood production vase, embossed with four-square design under a good raspberry-to-green matte glaze, flame mark, dated.

1911   *8in (20cm) h*

$550-650   **DRA**

A Rookwood production squat two-handled vase, with a band of Celtic knots under plum-to-turquoise butterfat glaze, horizontal lines inside rim, possibly crazing only, dated.

1915   *5.5in (14cm) wide*

$220-280   **DRA**

A Rookwood production low bowl, impressed with peacock feathers under a fine matte green-to-rose glaze, small chips to feet, dated.

1915   *8in (20cm) diam*

$150-200   **DRA**

A pair of Rookwood production ovoid vases, with embossed peacock feathers under a green-to-pink matte finish, flame mark, dated.

1930   *6in (15cm) high*

$350-450   **DRA**

A Rookwood production vase, embossed with a band of rooks under green-to-pink glaze, marked, dated.

1917   *7.5in (19cm) high*

$350-400   **DRA**

A Rookwood production ovoid vase, with stylized dogwood blossoms, covered in pink glaze, flame mark, dated.

1920   *9in (22.5cm) high*

$200-250   **DRA**

A Rookwood production vase, with buttresses and dogwood blossoms under an unusual purple crystalline matte glaze, dated.

1923   *7.75in (19cm) high*

$500-600   **DRA**

A Rookwood production five-sided vase, embossed with rooks under brown glaze, flame mark, dated.

1930   *4.5in (11cm) high*

$500-600   **DRA**

A Rookwood production trumpet-shaped vase, covered in pink and eggplant crystalline glaze, flame mark, dated.

1924   *7.5in (19cm) high*

$200-250   **DRA**

A 1920s Rookwood production flower frog with two kneeling children covered in matte mustard glaze, several dark firing lines, flame mark.

     6.25in (15.5cm) high

$400-450   **DRA**

A Rookwood production vase, with incised stylized leaves under a green-to-pink Vellum glaze, flame mark and dated.

1912   *9.5in (24cm) high*

$550-650   **DRA**

A Rookwood carved matte squat vessel, by an unidentified artist with a stylized leaf pattern under green glaze, flame mark.

5.5in (14cm) wide

$450-550   DRA

A CLOSER LOOK AT A ROOKWOOD VASE

Rookwood's matte glazes were pioneered by Artus Van Briggle before he left to start his own pottery.

Anna Valentien was one of only a few of Rookwood artists to use the painted matte technique.

Flora and foliage are a common theme in this range.

This method of decoration was highly technical and few survived the firing process.

A small Rookwood carved matte tapering two-handled vase, decorated by C.S. Todd with grapes and leaves on green and brown butterfat ground, restoration to corner of one handle, flame mark, dated and "XII/2018/C.S.T.".

1912   *6.75in (17cm) high*

$500-600   DRA

A Rookwood painted matte baluster vase, decorated by A.M. Valentien with branches of brown leaves and pink berries on a celadon ground, seconded mark for glaze misses, flame mark, dated and "I/3EZ/A.M.V./X.".

1901   *5.75in (14cm) high*

$550-650   DRA

A Rookwood carved matte ovoid vase, by Elizabeth Lincoln with stylized red blossoms and brown leaves on ivory ground, flame mark, dated and "XVIII/30F/LNL".

1918   *6.75in (17cm) high*

$700-800   DRA

A Rookwood wax matte bulbous vase, painted by E.T. Hurley with orange roses and green foliage on ivory ground, uncrazed, dated, flame mark and "XXXIII/S/E.T.H."

1933   *6.25in (15.5cm) high*

$1,000-2,000   DRA

Two Rookwood trivet tiles, with Dutch peasant scenes in pastel matte glazes, small chip and nick to one, flame mark, dated.

1930   *5.75in (14cm) square*

$150-200   DRA

A Rookwood wax matte vase, by Kate Jones, with pink roses and green leaves on a pink ground, flame mark, dated.

1928   *7.5in (19cm) high*

$700-800   DRA

A Rookwood wax matte bullet-shaped vase, by Katherine Jones, with pansies in polychrome on an indigo ground, flame mark, dated and "KJ".

1923   *7.5in (19cm) high*

$650-750   DRA

A Rookwood Standard Glaze squat vessel painted by Irene Bishop with golden primrose blossoms, flame mark and "IV/919E?IB", dated.

1904   *4in (10cm) high*

$350-450   **DRA**

A Rookwood Standard Glaze cylindrical vase painted by Edith Felton with daisies, flame mark, dated and "E.R.F.".

1903   *5.5in (14cm) high*

$500-600   **DRA**

A Rookwood Standard Glaze tall vase, painted by Lenore Asbury, with milk pods, uncrazed, drilled hole to bottom, short scratch to front, flame mark, dated and "L.A.".

1903   *12in (30cm) high*

$350-400   **DRA**

A Rookwood Standard Glaze Light chocolate pot, painted by Jeanette Swing with golden chrysanthemum blossoms, crude touch-up to scrape on base, flame mark, dated and "JS".

1889   *9in (22.5cm) high*

$350-450   **DRA**

A Rookwood Standard Glaze bottle-shaped vase, painted by V.B. Demarest with yellow roses, flame mark, dated and "743C/VBD".

1898   *7in (17.5cm) high*

$350-450   **DRA**

A Rookwood Standard Glaze Light bulbous vase, painted by Sadie Markland with yellow daisies, a few short, shallow scratches, flame mark, dated and "40/W/SM".

1893   *5.25in (13cm) high*

$300-350   **DRA**

A Rookwood Standard Glaze tall tapered pitcher, painted by Mary Nourse with palm fronds, flame mark, dated and "M.N.".

1896   *9.75in (24cm) high*

$450-550   **DRA**

A Rookwood Standard Glaze bottle-shaped vase, painted by Constance Baker with dogwood branches, loss of height on neck and lines to base, flame mark, dated and "CAB".

1894   *8in (20cm) high*

$200-250   **DRA**

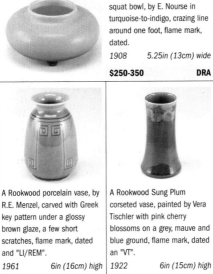

A Rookwood vellum footed squat bowl, by E. Nourse in turquoise-to-indigo, crazing line around one foot, flame mark, dated.

1908   5.25in (13cm) wide

$250-350   DRA

A Rookwood vellum ovoid vase, painted by Elizabeth Lincoln with grey mistletoe on a mauve and mint ground, dated, flame mark and "XII/924E/V/LNL".

1912   4.75in (12cm) high

$700-800   DRA

A Rookwood porcelain vase, by R.E. Menzel, carved with Greek key pattern under a glossy brown glaze, a few short scratches, flame mark, dated and "LI/REM".

1961   6in (16cm) high

$220-280   DRA

A Rookwood Sung Plum corseted vase, painted by Vera Tischler with pink cherry blossoms on a grey, mauve and blue ground, flame mark, dated an "VT".

1922   6in (15cm) high

$650-750   DRA

A Rookwood vellum vase, painted by Vera Tischler with blue cornflowers and green arabesques on cobalt ground, small flake to overglaze near base, hairline from rim, flame mark, dated.

1921   8in (20cm) high

$400-500   DRA

A CLOSER LOOK AT A ROOKWOOD VELLUM VASE

An unusual Rookwood Jewel Porcelain Art Deco four-sided vase, painted by Louise Abel with an abstract design in indigo, pink and grey on ivory, line to one side, flame mark, dated.

1931   7.5in (19cm) high

$500-600   DRA

The glaze produces a hazy effect over the painted decoration.

Vellum ware is usually blue. Cream, pink, yellow or light green examples are rare.

Examples made before 1915 were prone to crazing, uncrazed examples fetch a premium.

Bands or panels of decoration are common in this range, designs covering the whole piece are more desirable.

An early Rookwood pitcher, incised by C.B.F. with a lion, goats, and a bison in black on an ivory ground, stamped "ROOKWOOD 1882/FCE".

1882   8in (20cm) high

$600-800   DRA

A Rookwood vellum tapering vase, painted by Charles J. McLaughlin with ivory dogwood on pink ground, short hairline to rim, flame mark, dated and "CJM".

1914   7.25in (18cm) high

$1,000-1,500   DRA

COLLECTORS' NOTES

■ The Roseville Pottery originally made utilitarian stoneware and painted flowerpots from 1890 and was named after the site of its first pottery in Roseville, Ohio. It moved to Zanesville in 1900.

■ Under the control of art director John Herold, they began manufacturing slip-painted art pottery as part of the Rozane line. Roseville imitated some of its rivals designs, such as Rookwood's Standard Glaze line and many ranges from the Weller Pottery.

■ English potter Frederick Rhead joined Roseville in 1904. He later worked with Frank Ferrell, who joined in 1917, to introduce original ranges including 'Della Robbia', 'Fudji', 'Woodland' and 'Crystallis'. In total, Ferrell was responsible for 96 different designs.

■ Pieces produced during the Depression were made in limited numbers and so are highly sought after by collectors. Later work is readily available and so the values are currently stable.

■ The company closed in 1953 and is now the property of New England Ceramics of Connecticut.

A Roseville gray 'Gardenia' cornucopia vase.

6in (15cm) high

$100-150 **TA**

A Roseville 'Autumn' jardinière, restoration to feet, a few minor scratches.

11.5in (29cm) wide

$600-700 **DRA**

A Roseville 'Carnelian II' urn, with tall stovepipe neck covered in an unusual yellow, blue, green and buff mottled matte glaze, "RV" ink stamp.

10.25in (25.5cm) high

$350-400 **DRA**

A Roseville 'Jonquil' bulbous vase, with good molding and excellent color, minor fleck to one handle, grinding chip at base, unmarked.

10.25in (25.5cm) high

$550-650 **DRA**

A Roseville brown 'Zephyr' lily wall pocket, raised mark.

$200-250 **DRA**

A Roseville brown 'Freesia' wall pocket, bruise to one handle, nick to tip, raised mark.

$150-200 **DRA**

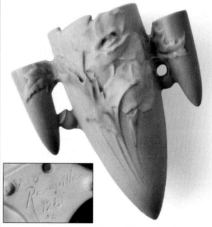

A Roseville green 'Poppy' bullet-shaped triple wall pocket, impressed mark.

8.5in (21cm) high

$650-750 **DRA**

A Roseville green 'Clematis' wall pocket, small burst bubble to tip, raised mark.

$220-280 **DRA**

COLLECTORS' NOTES

■ The Royal Copenhagen Porcelain Manufactory was founded by Franz Heinrich Müller in Copenhagen in 1775. It gained royal patronage in 1779 after running into such severe financial problems that the King of Denmark, Frederick V, had to step in to save the company. Pieces are marked with three wavy lines symbolizing the seas isolating the country.

■ It was known primarily for its fine porcelain, often inspired by Meissen. But from 1885-1916, Danish architect and painter Arnold Krog revived the factory's fortunes with under-glaze designs based on the popular Art Nouveau style, as well as Japanese designs. Look closely at backstamps – a bar above or below a letter in the names 'Royal Copenhagen' or 'Denmark' will identify the year it was made.

■ During the 1950s and 1960s the factory produced a range of stoneware and porcelain 'art ware' designed by a series of notable designers, including Nils Thorsson and Axel Salto. These were often designed in 'modern' styles, which reflected both the fashions of the period and the Scandinavian ceramic tradition.

■ They were handpainted with designs that showed the Scandinavian obsession with nature and the environment, a source of inspiration that was also reflected in period glass design. Pieces can often be dated to a period by noting the painter's number or initials and referring to a reference work. An 'X' implies that it was painted by the person whose initials also appear. Look for the work of notable designers and at larger pieces with handpainted designs. Blue, often seen in the Marselis range, is a popular color.

A 1970s Danish Royal Copenhagen 'Baca' vase, designed by Nils Thorsson.

4.75in (12cm) high

$50-70　　　　**RWA**

A 1960s Danish Royal Copenhagen 'Baca' vase, designed by Nils Thorsson.

7.5in (19cm) high

$70-100　　　　**RWA**

A 1970s Danish Royal Copenhagen 'Baca' vase, by Joanne Gerber.

9in (23cm) high

$120-180　　　　**RWA**

A Danish Royal Copenhagen 'Tenera' vase, by Grete Helland-Hansen, with fruit design.

c1969-74　　7.5in (19cm) high

$120-180　　　　**RWA**

A 1970s Danish Royal Copenhagen 'Tenera' vase, by Bert Jessen.

7.5in (19cm) high

$120-180　　　　**RWA**

A Danish Royal Copenhagen 'Baca' kiln-shaped vase, by Nils Thorsson, with Alumina backstamp.

The Alumina factory was purchased by Royal Copenhagen in 1882. The name continued to appear as a backstamp until 1969.

c1966　　8in (20cm) high

$150-200　　　　**RWA**

$220-280　　　　**RWA**

A 1960s Danish Royal Copenhagen stoneware vase, designed by Jørgen Morgensen, in Sung glaze, with abstract design.

9.5in (24cm) high

RWA

A 1970s Danish Royal Copenhagen 'Tenera' cigarette box, by Marianne Johnson, with stylized design.

4.25in (11cm) high

$60-90   RWA

A 1970s Danish Royal Copenhagen vase, by Ellen Malmer, with abstract design.

6.5in (17cm) high

$120-180   RWA

A Danish Royal Copenhagen vase, by Ellen Malmer, with brown heart-shaped design.

1969-74   3.25in (8cm) high

$50-70   RWA

A 1950s Royal Copenhagen fine porcelain vase, with geometric decoration, printed marks to underside.

5.75in (14.5cm) high

$120-180   MHT

A Danish Royal Copenhagen 'Marselis' vase, by Nils Thorsson, with green glaze and Alumina backstamp.

c1960   4.25in (11cm) high

$120-180   RWA

A Danish Royal Copenhagen 'Marselis' vase, designed by Nils Thorsson, in blue glaze, with diamond pattern.

This vase displays rich and deep Scandinavian blues. It has an excellent detailed pattern and an attractive and classic form based on Oriental shapes while still appearing 'modern' in a particularly Scandinavian style.

c1969

$180-220   RWA

A Danish Royal Copenhagen 'Marselis' vase, by Nils Thorsson, with blue glaze with Alumina backstamp.

c1960   5.5in (14cm) high

$120-180   RWA

A Danish Royal Copenhagen 'Marselis' gourd-shaped vase, designed by Nils Thorsson, with blue striped glaze and Alumina backstamp.

5in (13cm) high

$150-200   RWA

A Danish Royal Copenhagen tall porcelain vase, painted with a white cattleya orchid on a shaded gray ground, stamped "ROYAL COPENHAGEN/Denmark/XL9".

12.5in (30.5cm) high

$600-900   DRA

A CLOSER LOOK AT A ROYAL COPENHAGEN POT

This pot was designed by sculptor Bode Willumsen, (1895-1987) who worked for Royal Copenhagen between 1925 and 1930 and again from 1940-47.

The pot is decorated in the Sung glaze, Royal Copenhagen's most typical and common stoneware glaze. This is a relatively large example in good condition.

Due to the way the glaze changes when painted on and fired, the mottling and streaking on each piece differs, making each piece effectively unique.

The form is complex and is Oriental in inspiration. It also highlights the 'handmade' and 'studio' aspects of Royal Copenhagen stoneware.

A 1960s Danish Royal Copenhagen pot, designed by Bode Willumsen, in Sung glaze, with figural lid and relief design.

8in (20cm) high

$220-280   **RWA**

A unique Royal Copenhagen studio pottery bowl, the flared stoneware vessel covered with a black and streaked milky blue phosphatic glaze which pools on the underside near the turned foot-rim, with a painted wave mark and "Denmark" on base.

7.75in (19.5cm) diam

$220-280   **DN**

A 1960s Danish Royal Copenhagen 'Tenera' bowl, by Marianne Johnson.

4.25in (11cm) diam

$60-90   **RWA**

A 1970s Danish Royal Copenhagen handpainted bowl, by Nils Thorsson, with underwater fish design.

6.75in (17cm) diam

$120-180   **RWA**

A 1960s Danish Royal Copenhagen 'Baca' dish, by Nils Thorsson, abstract design.

6.75in (17cm) wide

$60-90   **RWA**

A 1960s Danish Royal Copenhagen 'Tenera' trinket pot, by Kari Christensen.

4in (10cm) high

$50-80   **RWA**

A 1960s Danish Royal Copenhagen 'Baca' egg vase, by Nils Thorsson.

3in (7.5cm) high

$70-100   **RWA**

A pair of Royal Copenhagen porcelain mounted cufflinks, each of circular form inset with gilt squares and silver beaded decoration, with painted marks.

1.25in (3cm) diam

$80-120   **L&T**

A Royal Copenhagen stoneware model of a bear, glazed with Sung glaze, modeled by Knud Kyhn.

Knud Kyhn (1880-1969) is considered one of the most prolific and accomplished modelers in stoneware at Royal Copenhagen. He also worked for Bing and Grøndahl. His observations of animals in zoological gardens as well as natural environments, such as Greenland, can clearly be seen in his understanding of their poses and expressions.

A Royal Copenhagen stoneware model of a bear, by Knud Kyhn.

4in (10cm) high

$50-70   **LOB**

A Royal Copenhagen stoneware model of a bear, by Knud Kyhn.

4in (10cm) high

$50-70   **LOB**

7in (18cm) long

$150-200   **LOB**

A Royal Copenhagen porcelain model of a polar bear, by Carl J. Bonnesen.

7in (18cm) long

$80-120   **LOB**

A Royal Copenhagen porcelain model of a polar bear playing, number 321, by Carl J. Bonnesen.

5.5in (14cm) long

$80-120   **LOB**

A Royal Copenhagen porcelain model of polar bear cubs playing, number 1107, by Knud Kyhn.

9.5in (24cm) high

$120-180   **LOB**

A Royal Copenhagen porcelain model of a cock, number 1126, designed by Chr. Thomsen.

4.75in (12cm) long

$100-150   **LOB**

A Royal Copenhagen porcelain model of a pheasant, number 862, designed by Jais Nielsen.

Jais Nielsen worked at Royal Copenhagen from 1920 until his death in 1961. He trained under Patrick Nordstrom and is known for his religious models. This complex and well-painted model is also a sought-after example of his work.

6.75in (17cm) high

$320-380   **LOB**

A Royal Copenhagen porcelain model of a kingfisher, number 1769, designed by Peter Herold.

4.25in (11cm) high

$150-200   **LOB**

A Royal Copenhagen 'Penguins Pair' porcelain model, number 1190, designed by Anna Trap.

4in (10cm) high

$100-150   **LOB**

A Royal Copenhagen figure of a sparrow, number 1081.

3.25in (8cm) high

$25-35   **CLV**

A Royal Copenhagen porcelain model of a dachshund, number 1408, by Olaf Mathiensen.

c1969   *4.25in (11cm) long*

$100-150   **LOB**

A Royal Copenhagen porcelain model of a dachshund, number 1407, designed by Olaf Mathiensen.

4.25in (11cm) long

$100-150   **LOB**

A Royal Copenhagen 'Setter with Pheasant' porcelain model, number 1533, designed by Knud Moller.

c1968   *3.25in (8cm) long*

$100-150   **LOB**

A Royal Copenhagen stoneware model of a deer.

4in (10cm) high

$40-60   **LOB**

A 1990s Royal Copenhagen porcelain figure of a kid.

4in (10cm) high

$50-70   **CLV**

A Royal Copenhagen 'Mouse on Corn Cob' porcelain model, number 512, designed by Svend Jespersen.

5.5in (14cm) long

$70-100   **LOB**

A Royal Copenhagen porcelain dish with a lobster, number 3277.

6.25in (16cm) diam

$100-150   **LOB**

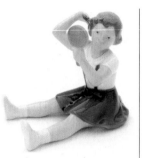

A Royal Copenhagen 'Vanity' porcelain model, number 2318, designed by Svend Jespersen.

5.5in (14cm) high

$100-150   **LOB**

A Royal Copenhagen 'Girl with Cat' porcelain model, number 4631, designed by John Calster.

6in (15cm) high

$180-220   **LOB**

A Royal Copenhagen porcelain model of children with a dog, number 707, designed by Chris Thomsen.

c1986   6in (15cm) high

$300-500   **LOB**

A 1990s Royal Copenhagen 'The Little Mermaid' porcelain model, number 4431, designed by Edvard Eriksen.

A Royal Copenhagen porcelain figure of a girl with a goose, number 528.

7.25in (18.5cm) high

$60-90   **CLV**

A Royal Copenhagen 'Boy Cutting Stick' porcelain model, designed by Chris Thomsen.

c1969   7.5in (19cm) high

$150-200   **LOB**

The original famous 'Little Mermaid' bronze sculpture found in Copenhagen's harbor was designed by Eriksen and was erected in August 1913. She was sponsored by brewer Carl Jacobsen, owner of the Carlsberg brewery.

8.75in (22cm) high

$500-700   **LOB**

A Royal Copenhagen porcelain model of a boy with a calf, No. 772.

c1975   6.75in (17cm) high

$220-280   **LOB**

A Royal Copenhagen 'Boy Naked on a Tray' porcelain model, number 1660.

8.75in (22cm) diam

$120-180   **LOB**

A Royal Copenhagen porcelain group, designed by Christian Thomsen, marked "Royal Copenhagen" and "1012 498".

5in (13cm) high

$180-220   **DN**

A Royal Copenhagen 'Mermaid in Water' porcelain figure, factory marks and numbered "1212".

7.75in (19.5cm) long

$180-220   **DN**

A Royal Crown Derby 'Owl' paperweight, with gold-colored stopper.

Although not realistic, the form is derived from a terracotta model found in Corinth dating back to the 7thC BC.

1981-92

$220-280 PSA

A Royal Crown Derby 'Pheasant' paperweight, with gold-colored stopper.

1983-98

$70-100 PSA

A Royal Crown Derby 'Snake' paperweight, with gold-colored stopper.

1989-92

$220-280 PSA

A Royal Crown Derby 'Dragon' paperweight, with gold-colored stopper.

This paperweight was released in 1988 to commemorate the Chinese year of the Dragon. In 1890 Crown Derby was given the Royal Warrant by Queen Victoria.

1988-92

$300-400 PSA

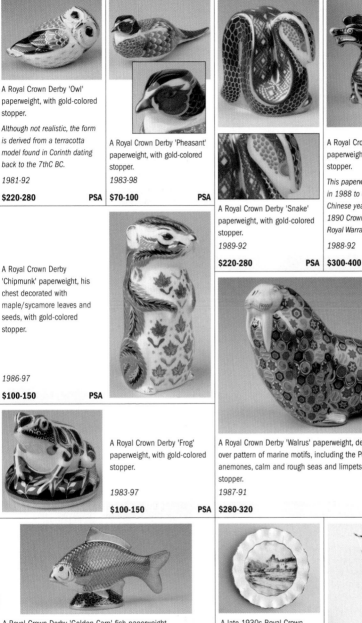

A Royal Crown Derby 'Chipmunk' paperweight, his chest decorated with maple/sycamore leaves and seeds, with gold-colored stopper.

1986-97

$100-150 PSA

A Royal Crown Derby 'Frog' paperweight, with gold-colored stopper.

1983-97

$100-150 PSA

A Royal Crown Derby 'Walrus' paperweight, decorated with an all-over pattern of marine motifs, including the Pole star, sea anemones, calm and rough seas and limpets, with gold-colored stopper.

1987-91

$280-320 PSA

A Royal Crown Derby 'Golden Carp' fish paperweight.

This was the first of the fish shaped models to be released by Royal Crown Derby and heralded the introduction of the 'Tropical Fish' range of models. The decoration on the base of this model represents a pebbly stream bed.

1986-91

$180-220 PSA

A late 1930s Royal Crown Derby plate, by W. E. J. Dean, titled 'Haddon Hall', with grape molded frill border, factory marks printed in green.

8.75in (22.5cm) diam

$400-600 CHEF

A Royal Crown Derby 'Posies' pattern vase, boxed.

7in (18cm) high

$30-50 PSA

CERAMICS

COLLECTORS' NOTES

■ Bjørn Wiinblad was born in 1918 in Copenhagen, Denmark. He studied at Copenhagen's Technical High School and Royal Academy of Arts and worked at the Lars Syberg Studio in Taastrup. He had his first exhibition in 1945 and soon grew to prominence alongside noted Swedish designer Stig Lindberg.

■ Wiinblad has worked in many different media, from poster design and book illustrations to ceramics and glass and has also designed theatrical sets. His style and designs are instantly recognizable and highly personal. They are popular worldwide, but particularly in his home country and the US.

■ He worked at Nymølle from 1946-56 and then at Rosenthal from 1957 until the late 1970s when he took ownership of Nymølle, which had run into problems and was facing closure. He continued at Nymølle until the 1990s when the factory finally closed.

■ He also runs his own successful studio where many of his most recognizable and collected designs are made in brightly decorated, glazed clay. Look out for large figures, figurative candlesticks and bowls, as these tend to be the most popular.

■ His pieces are available at many different price levels, from under $30 for more commonly found transfer-printed mugs produced by Rosenthal or Nymølle to many hundreds of dollars for one of his handpainted Studio figures.

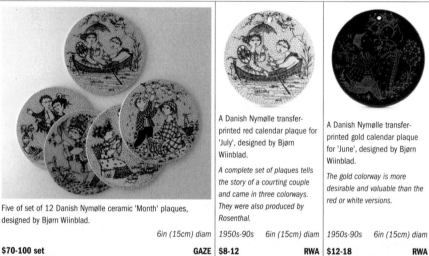

Five of set of 12 Danish Nymølle ceramic 'Month' plaques, designed by Bjørn Wiinblad.

6in (15cm) diam

$70-100 set   **GAZE**

A Danish Nymølle transfer-printed red calendar plaque for 'July', designed by Bjørn Wiinblad.

A complete set of plaques tells the story of a courting couple and came in three colorways. They were also produced by Rosenthal.

1950s-90s   6in (15cm) diam

$8-12   **RWA**

A Danish Nymølle transfer-printed gold calendar plaque for 'June', designed by Bjørn Wiinblad.

The gold colorway is more desirable and valuable than the red or white versions.

1950s-90s   6in (15cm) diam

$12-18   **RWA**

A pair of limited edition Danish Nymølle wall plaques, designed by Bjørn Wiinblad, in original box.

Although a standard pattern, these plaques were produced in an edition of 600 to celebrate the opening of the new Inspirations shop in Herning, Denmark and bear special wording to the back. It is unusual to find the box.

1978

$60-90   **RWA**

A 1980s Danish Nymølle wall plate, designed by Bjørn Wiinblad, decorated with a girl, with flower border.

12in (30cm) diam

$70-100   **RWA**

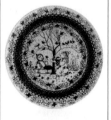

A Danish Nymølle 'Four Seasons' plate for 'Winter', designed by Bjørn Wiinblad.

These sets of four plates were made in four different sizes from 6in to 14in diam, each with a different design.

c1960s-90s 11in (28cm) diam

$50-70 each   **RWA**

A Danish Nymølle transfer-printed candle wall sconce, designed by Bjørn Wiinblad.

10in (25.5cm) high

$80-120   **CHS**

A 1980s Danish Nymølle calendar mug for 'October', designed by Bjørn Wiinblad.

A complete set of calendar mugs tells the story of a courting couple.

3.5in (9cm) high

$22-28 RWA

A 1980s German Rosenthal 'Weihnachten' handpainted porcelain postcard, in original box, designed by Bjørn Wiinblad.

These were produced to be bought, dedicated on the blank reverse and sent through the post in the box as gifts. They can be found in a number of different colorways and designs.

Box 8in (20.5cm) wide

$60-90 RWA

A German Rosenthal '1001 Nights' cylindrical vase, designed by Bjørn Wiinblad, with a vaguely erotic pattern, marked "Rosenthal Studio-Linie" to base.

$150-200 RWA

A 1970s German Rosenthal '1001 Nights' vase, designed by Bjørn Wiinblad.

7in (17cm) high

$180-220 RWA

A 1970s German Rosenthal '1001 Nights' vase, designed by Bjørn Wiinblad.

This pattern was one of Wiinblad's most popular for Rosenthal. This large vase was expensive at the time, costing 832 Krona in 1975, which roughly equates to $120.

8.5in (22cm) high

$280-320 RWA

A Danish Wiinblad Studio handpainted 'Hat Lady' figure, signed and dated on the base, designed by Bjørn Wiinblad.

Examples larger than this are very rare and valuable. The earlier the piece, the more colors it tends to include, later examples tend to be in blue only. This is a typical mark as found on the bases of Studio produced pieces. The 'L13' relates to the model number, the '70' to the year of production and the 'BW' monogram to the Bjørn Wiinblad Studio.

1970   19.75in (50cm) high

$700-1,000 RWA

A Danish Wiinblad Studio 'Four Seasons' figure for 'Autumn', model No. M22, designed by Bjørn Wiinblad, signed and dated on the base.

These figures are top heavy and prone to damage, so examine carefully to ensure that they have not been broken and re-glued. They are still in production today, costing around $500, and can be found in blue or green, rarely in other colors. Examples from the 1970s are the most collectible.

1974   14in (35.5cm) high

$400-600 RWA

A Danish Wiinblad Studio lidded dish, model J115, designed by Bjørn Wiinblad, with unusual brown glaze, the lid formed as a hat, signed "BW" and dated.

1968

$280-320 RWA

A CLOSER LOOK AT A BJØRN WIINBLAD BOWL

This bowl is very large and impressive and the image is typical of his designs. The imperfect circular shape shows that it was hand-thrown.

As well as being produced unusually early in his career, it is a unique design.

The signature on the base includes a 'character' face, the personal signature used by Wiinblad to indicate his own handiwork.

Rather than being painted by his decorators, this piece was handpainted by Wiinblad himself.

An early and unique Danish Bjørn Wiinblad large bowl, decorated with a lady and bird sitting amidst foliage and grass, dated. 1956

18.5in (47cm) diam

$1,000-1,500   **RWA**

A Swedish Gustavsberg wall plaque, by Lisa Larson, with stylized bird design.

11in (28cm) wide

$320-380   **RWA**

A 1950s Swedish Gustavsberg Studio 'Karnavel' dish, by Stig Lindberg.

6.25in (16cm) wide

$120-180   **RWA**

A 1940s/50s Swedish Gustavsberg dish, designed by Stig Lindberg.

Founded in Sweden in 1825, Gustavsberg was the most important of the Scandinavian factories.

Designs were dominated by Wilhelm Kage and Stig Lindberg, his successor. Lindberg's designs are much sought after today for their clean shapes and brightly colored, modern, and abstract designs.

10in (25.5cm) wide

$300-500   **GGRT**

A Swedish Gustavsberg 'Sunflower' wall tile, by Lisa Larson.

From the Unik series of nine different design tiles produced between 1967-86.

9in (23cm) wide

$120-180   **RWA**

A Swedish Gustavsberg 'Sunflower' wall plaque, by Lisa Larson, in production 1967-72.

10.75in (27.5cm) high

$180-220   **RWA**

A 1950s/60s Swedish Gustavsberg 'Domino' conical-shaped vase, by Stig Lindberg, with brown glaze with herringbone design.

5.25in (13.5cm) high

$150-200   **RWA**

A 1950s Swedish Gustavsberg 'Endiv' vase, by Stig Lindberg, in gray-ish glaze.

7in (18cm) high

$180-220   **RWA**

COLLECTORS' NOTES

■ Danish studio potter Arne Bang was born in 1901, the brother of internationally famous architect Jacob Bang. In 1926 he set up a studio with Carl Halier (1873-1948), who had been working as technical manager at Royal Copenhagen.

■ Bang opened his own studio in 1932 and was extremely successful, winning many prizes for his designs. His work also had a great impact on Scandinavian ceramic design in the 1960s and 1970s. Bang's designs often combine Bauhaus elements with a Neoclassical feel. His glazes are rich in color and texture when examined closely. The forms are simple, often featuring vertical ribbing or wide, deep incisions. Arne Bang died in 1983.

A 1930s/40s Danish Arne Bang beige stoneware vase, with ribbed, cog design.

2.25in (5.5cm) high

$60-90   **RWA**

A 1930s/40s Danish Arne Bang stoneware vase, with ribbed, cog design.

3.25in (8cm) high

$80-120   **RWA**

A rare 1920s Danish Arne Bang bowl, produced at Holmegaard Glassworks, with Alumina backstamp.

7.5in (19cm) diam

$180-220   **RWA**

A 1930s/40s Danish Arne Bang green stoneware vase, with ribbed, cog design.

4.5in (11.5cm) high

$120-180   **RWA**

A Danish Arne Bang vase, of ribbed gourd form, with speckled blue and brown running glaze.

5in (13cm) high

$150-200   **RWA**

A 1930s/40s Danish Arne Bang studio bowl, in speckled blue glaze, with ribbed decoration.

7.5in (19cm) diam

$180-220   **RWA**

A 1930s/40s Danish Arne Bang studio vase, in beige matte glaze.

5.5in (14cm) high

$120-180   **RWA**

A 1930s Danish Arne Bang ice bucket, with wicker handle and brown and tan glaze, incised studio mark.

5.25in (13.5cm) high

$220-280   **RWA**

A 1930s/40s Danish Arne Bang jug, with lizard design cane handle mount, in a mottled blue glaze.

5.5in (14cm) high

$220-280   **RWA**

A pair of Finnish Arabia oil bottles, designed by Kaj Frank, with dark brown glaze.

5.5in (14cm) high

$50-70   GAZE

A set of six Swedish Ganiopta small storage jars, with rosewood tops.

3in (7.5cm) high

$30-40   GAZE

A Finnish Arabia hand-decorated stoneware vase, with decorators and potters marks.

9.25in (23.5cm) high

$70-100   GAZE

A Finnish Arabia studio made vase.

10.25in (26cm) high

$60-90   GAZE

A Finnish Arabia handpainted bowl, by Hikkla-Liisa Ahola, with blue and green glazes giving an almost iridescent appearance.

13.75in (25cm) diam

$220-280   RWA

A 1970s large Finnish Arabia tile, with stylized flower design, signed on the front "RU/".

Arabia was founded in 1873 and grew to be the most prominent factory in Finland, with designs being led by Kaj Franck, who is also known for his Scandinavian glass designs for Nuutajarvi Nosjo.

18in (46cm) wide

$300-400   RWA

A 1950s Danish Nymølle vase, by Gunnar Nylund.

10.75in (27.5cm) high

$220-280   ADE

A Danish Nymølle vase, designed by Axel Brüel.

9in (23cm) high

$180-220   RWA

A 1950s Danish Palshus 'Torpedo' vase, by Per Linnermann-Schmidt, in blue haresfur glaze.

Scandinavian ceramics finished in blue glazes are popular and desirable, particularly if the glaze is richly and deeply colored as with this example.

8.5in (22cm) high

$280-320   RWA

A 1950s Danish Palshus 'Torpedo' vase, by Per Linnermann-Schmidt, with olive haresfur glaze.

5in (12.5cm) high

$150-200   RWA

CERAMICS

A 1950s Danish Palshus cylinder vase, designed by Per Linnermann-Schmidt, in caramel haresfur glaze.

9.25in (23.5cm) high

$300-400   **RWA**

A Swedish Rorstrand tall and narrow porcelain vase, by Carl-Harry Stalhane, covered in ocher, apricot, and gunmetal microcrystalline glaze, incised "R" with "crowns/Sweden/CHS/SYT".

11.5in (29cm) high

$400-600   **DRA**

A Swedish Rorstrand vase, by Carl Harry Stalhane, with speckled black glaze.

6.25in (16cm) high

$220-280   **RWA**

A Swedish Rorstrand ovoid porcelain bowl, by Gunnar Nyland, with brown and black mottled matte glaze, incised "R" with "crowns/GN/Sweden/AXK".

6in (15cm) high

$180-220   **DRA**

A 1950s Danish Saxbo vase, designed by Edith Sonne Brunn, with brown mottled glaze.

Founded in 1930, Saxbo grew to be the most important and influential independent Danish pottery. Its look is characterized by Oriental style glazes and simple, clean lined shapes. Saxbo closed in 1968.

8.5in (21.5cm) high

$300-400   **RWA**

A Swedish Upsala Ekeby vase, with sgraffito decoration.

9.75in (24.5cm) high

$70-100   **GAZE**

A Danish Saxbo bowl, unknown designer.

9in (23cm) diam

$150-200   **RWA**

A 1950s Swedish Upsala Ekeby dish, by Mari Simmulson.

7.75in (20cm) wide

$100-150   **ADE**

A Norwegian Stavangerflint bowl, with handpainted decoration, printed and painted marks and two labels including retail sticker from Steen & Strøm A/S Oslo.

Founded in 1949 in Stavanger, Stavangerflint employed the design services of Kari Nyquist and Kaare Fjeldsaa during the 1950s and 1960s. After a merger in 1968, it closed in 1979.

1957   4.5in (11.5cm) high

$60-90   **CHS**

A mid-20thC Shelley vase, the cone shape with recess above the foot streaked with horizontal bands of gray, orange, and yellow, printed marks.

9.5in (24cm) high

$180-220   **CHEF**

A 1930s Shelley 'Melody' pattern chintz and yellow ribbed vase.

4.5in (11.5cm) high

$70-100   **BAD**

A 1930s Shelley 'Kingfisher' vase.

$40-60   **BAD**

A Shelley 'Intarsio' vase, of gourd form with twin handles, painted with sinuous plant forms in bright enamels, pattern 3573, neck repaired.

7.25in (18.5cm) high

$120-180   **GORL**

A 1930s Shelley double eggcup, with gilt rim.

This double-ended eggcup could hold either a hen's egg or a smaller duck's egg.

3.75in (9.5cm) high

$100-150   **BAD**

A 1930s Shelley Mabel Lucie Attwell 'To Fairy Town' mug, with motto reading "Fairies love motoring all about, two wouldn't keep still, so they fell out".

3in (7.5cm) high

$70-100   **BAD**

A Shelley late Foley Oriental-style octagonal jug.

c1910   *6in (15cm) high*

$220-280   **BAD**

A small shaped Shelley teapot, with floral motifs and blue detailing.

7.75in (19.5cm) long

$150-200   **BAD**

A 1930s Shelley trio set, painted marks "12072 F".

7in (17.5cm) wide

$150-200   **BAD**

A Shelley Art Deco trio set.

Saucer 6.25in (16cm) diam

$120-180 **GCL**

A 1930s Shelley Art Deco tea set, each piece decorated with the 11755 pattern of an orange, comprising milk jug, sugar bowl, sandwich plate, four cups, five saucers and six tea plates.

$1,200-1,800 set **CHEF**

A 1930s Shelley Art Deco tea set, the Vogue shapes printed in black and overpainted in orange with the 11792 pattern of interlocking rectangles within rim bands of the same colors, comprising milk jug, sugar bowl, two sandwich plates, 12 cups, saucers, and tea plates.

$4,000-6,000 set **CHEF**

A Shelley 'Boo Boo' nursery figure, designed by Mabel Lucie Attwell, modeled watering flowers, printed mark "LA29".

3in (7.5cm) high

$600-900 **WW**

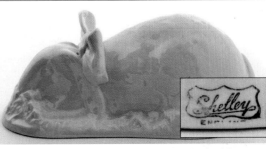

A Shelley white jelly mold, in the form of a crouching rabbit, printed mark in green.

10in (25.5cm) long

$320-380 **LFA**

A Shelley 'Diddums' figure, designed by Mabel Lucie Attwell, painted in colors, printed and painted marks "LA18".

Illustrator Mabel Lucie Attwell's designs for Shelley are much sought after – particularly the rare nursery figurines. 'Diddums' was one of her most popular and famous drawings. Fakes are known so check the marks and quality of the paintwork carefully.

6.25in (16cm) high

$2,800-3,200 **WW**

A Shelley 'Howm'l Doin' figure, designed by Mabel Lucie Attwell, LA16, painted in colors, printed marks.

6.75in (17cm) high

$2,200-2,800 **WW**

A Shelley 'Our Pets' figure, designed by Mabel Lucie Attwell, painted in colors, printed green mark.

8.25in (21cm) high

$2,800-3,200 **WW**

CERAMICS

COLLECTORS' NOTES

■ Studio pottery is characterized by hand-thrown and hand-decorated wares made in small 'personal' studios. It was produced from the 1930s, but primarily after WWII. Although pioneering and notable names such as Bernard Leach and Lucie Rie usually fetch very high sums, more affordable pieces can be found that are typical of their styles, particularly smaller examples. Also look at other, currently less sought-after names and try to buy pieces that represent their style the best.

■ The market is lively, constantly innovative and provides great scope for the collector. Those interested in collecting should also consider looking away from individual personalities towards some of the currently less notable but often prolific potteries such as Troika, Newlyn, and Briglin. Many of these, particularly Troika, have become more sought-after and collectible recently and their importance may continue to grow.

An Ian Auld square ashtray, with slightly nibbled corners.

3.5in (9cm) wide

$50-70   **GROB**

A Richard Batterham stoneware charger, pale celadon glaze, unmarked.

Batterham was born in 1936 and has become one of Britain's finest living studio potters. His forms and glazes are typically minimal.

15.75in (40cm) diam

$280-320   **WW**

An Aldermaston Pottery punch or large tea pot, by Alan Caiger-Smith, painted with brown scrolls.

The Aldermaston Pottery was founded in 1955 by Caiger-Smith and continues to produce today. It has employed many fine potters, with only a few working there at any one time. Caiger-Smith and his pottery are particularly known for their tinglazes.

10.25in (26cm) high

$500-700   **CHEF**

An Aldermaston Pottery oviform vase, by Alan Caiger-Smith, painted in manganese, olive green and muted red in broad brushstrokes with bands of linear decoration against white, painted pottery mark on base.

10.75in (27.5cm) high

$280-320   **DN**

A Winchcombe Pottery vase, by Michael Cardew.

Michael Cardew (1901-1983) was a noted, inspirational potter who studied under Bernard Leach. He set up the Winchcombe Pottery in 1926 but sold it in 1939 to set up a pottery at Wenford Bridge, Cornwall. He also traveled, most notably to Africa, where he founded a third pottery and taught.

c1930

$500-700   **ADE**

A Michael Cardew 'Kingwood' slipware jug, the red pottery partially covered in white slip and having combed and banded decoration, impressed 'K' in circle seal mark.

8.75in (22.5cm) high

$180-220   **DN**

An unusual Chelsea Pottery flared circular bowl, decorated by Joyce Morgan, with a pair of cockerels with extending tail feathers, in autumnal colors, signed "JEM" and "Chelsea P England" on back.

1952-97   12in (30.5cm) diam

$150-200   **DN**

A cruet set, made by Harry Davis at the Crowan Pottery, Cornwall, with iridescent cream and green glaze.

mustard 2.25in (6cm) high

1945-62

$30-50   GROB

A Janet Leach wheel-shaped vase, in cream with a brown stripe.

c1970   7.75in (20cm) high

$400-600   ADE

A Janet Leach stoneware vase, simple temmoku cross brushstrokes over mottled ocher ground, impressed "JL" monogram and St Ives mark.

5.75in (14.5cm) high

$280-320   WW

A Janet Leach pitted stoneware vase, the everted rim covered in an olive green glaze, impressed "JL" with St Ives mark.

5.5in (14cm) high

$300-500   WW

A Janet Leach stoneware dish, square section, painted with temokku cross motif, impressed "JL" and St Ives mark.

6in (15cm) wide

$220-280   WW

A David Leach teapot, from Lowerdown Pottery.

c1960   5.75in (14.5cm) high

$300-400   ADE

A David Leach jug, with temmoku glazed rim and oatmeal body, "L" mark.

7.75in (19.5cm) high

$120-180   CHEF

A small David Leach ramekin dish, with green glazed interior and handle.

5in (12.5cm) long

$15-25   GROB

An ovoid jug, decorated by Katie Muir, painted with foliate panels in shades of green, painted monogram.

5in (12.5cm) high

$25-35   L&T

A CLOSER LOOK AT A STUDIO VASE

Coldstone was founded during the 1950s by Chris Harries who built his own kiln at Ascott-under-Wychwood, Oxfordshire, England. His work typifies the studio pottery movement.

The faces resemble the drawings of Italian artist Modigliani, who was influenced by African tribal and Oceanic art.

This vase was thrown and decorated by Dieter Kunzemann, the chief thrower at Coldstone. It is a unique piece, probably having been made as a 'Christmas Special' between 1960-63.

The style departs from Coldstone's typical designs, which are characterized by crossed wheat-ear and matchstick like decoration. Kunzemann is known for developing his own individual style.

A William Staite Murray bowl, covered in a crackled pale blue glaze, impresséd seal mark.

3.75in (9.5cm) diam

$150-200 | **WW**

A 'Coldstone' pottery oviform vase, decorated with incisions to the beige clay and heightened with dark staining rubbed in to the incisions, impressed on base "Coldstone".

c1960 | *8in (20.5cm) high*

$300-500 | **DN**

A Katherine Pleydell-Bouverie stoneware bowl, impressed seal mark, incised "280".

Pleydell-Bouverie (1895-1985) studied under Bernard Leach. She became known for her work on ash glazes, which is much sought-after.

5.75in (14.5cm) diam

$280-320 | **WW**

A Katherine Pleydell-Bouverie vase, impressed seal mark.

3in (7.5cm) high

$180-220 | **WW**

A Katherine Pleydell-Bouverie vase, impressed seal mark.

3.5in (9cm) high

$180-220 | **WW**

A Bernard Rooke studio pottery vase, with leaves and birds.

7.5in (19cm) high

$40-60 | **GAZE**

A Bernard Rooke Studio pottery vase.

$60-90 | **GAZE**

A Bernard Rooke Studio pottery table lamp base.

$60-90 | **GAZE**

A Bernard Rooke pottery wall pocket.

Born in 1938, Bernard Rooke produces pottery that is eminently saleable and simple to produce. Lamp bases have become a mainstay of his production.

8.25in (21cm) long

$30-50   GAZE

A pair of Bernard Rooke pottery tankards.

4in (10.5cm) high

$30-50   GAZE

A small terracotta planter, by Marianne de Trey, with applied glazed bosses.

2.75in (7cm) high

$25-35   GROB

A Robin Welch pottery bowl, with green mottled glazed interior.

Born in 1936, Welch worked part-time at the Leach Pottery from 1953-59, before opening his own pottery in London which ran from 1960-62. He then set up the Stadbroke Pottery in Eye, Suffolk. He has worked for leading companies including Midwinter and Wedgwood.

c1960   4.75in (12cm) diam

$50-70   GROB

A large studio pottery vase, with impressed decoration, signature to base.

13.75in (35cm) high

$25-35   GAZE

A studio pottery bottle vase.

10.5in (26.5cm) high

$25-35   GAZE

A St. Ives celadon vase, cracked.

9.5in (24cm) high

$60-90   CHEF

A studio pottery bowl, on pedestal foot, white glazed, marks to base.

4.25in (11cm) high

$25-35   GAZE

A studio pottery vase, glazed in brown, olive, and ocher, the interior white, incised marks.

3.5in (9cm) high

$18-22   CHEF

A 1950s Adderley teapot, with transfer decoration of sprigs of hazel.

The streamlined handle of the lid and the simplified form is typically 1950s.

6.75in (17cm) wide

$30-50 JL

A 1950s Crown Dorset teapot, with rose transfer.

10.25in (26cm) wide

$40-60 JL

A Dunmore teapot and cover, of ovoid form with molded band and applied loop handle, covered in mottled green blue and rust glazes, impressed mark.

A 1930s T.G. Green and Co. yellow and beige teapot, with band of transfer decoration showing boats on a lake.

T.G. Green of Church Gresley, Derbyshire, are well-known for their range of 'Cornishware' with its recognizable thick colored bands, produced from the 1920s.

8in (20cm) wide

$60-90 JL

The Dunmore Pottery of Stirlingshire, Scotland made domestic and utilitarian pieces. From 1866 until around 1902 it produced decorative wares under Peter Gardner. In 1917 the pottery was closed and sold off.

8.5in (22cm) high

$120-180 L&T

A 1950s Jackson & Gosling china teapot, with bird transfer.

8.5in (21.5cm) wide

$70-100 JL

A Johnson Bros. coffee pot, decorated with a flock of Canada geese in flight, printed marks.

7in (18cm) high

$60-90 CHS

A Johnson Bros 'Mill Stream' blue and white transfer decorated earthenware teapot.

9in (23cm) wide

$40-60 JL

A Minton 'Mirabeau' hand-painted bone china teapot, with floral and gilt detailing.

10.5in (27cm) high

$60-90 JL

A Royal Winton Grimwades beehive shaped teapot, with bee knop on lid.

Royal Winton, owned by the Grimwade brothers, is better known for its prolifically produced chintzware. Beehive objects such as these and honey pots are also popular.

c1935 *6in (15cm) high*

$320-380 BAD

A Royal Worcester cream fireproof teapot, with obtusely placed handle.

5.75in (14.5cm) high

$30-50 P&I

A 1950s Royal Worcester 'Fiesta' coffee pot, stamped "Shape 3 Size 6".

7in (18cm) high

$60-90   **BAD**

A 1980s Strangeways 'Teddy Boy' ceramic teapot.

7.5in (19.5cm) wide

$50-70   **MA**

A Wade Heath 'Donald Duck' hand-painted novelty teapot, his beak as a spout, in typical colors, printed mark, restored cover.

4in (10cm) high

$400-600   **WW**

A 1930s Wade Art Deco style hand-painted octagonal coffee pot, with jolly floral pattern and printed marks to base.

8in (20cm) high

$100-150   **JL**

A 1940s Wood and Sons 'Yuan' Oriental style pattern blue and white transfer printed teapot, the base with printed marks and Registered No. 656368 for 1916.

8.5in (22cm) wide

$60-90   **JL**

An Enoch Wood's blue and white transfer printed teapot, with design of English scenery.

c1960   9in (23cm) wide

$60-90   **JL**

A novelty automobile teapot, in yellow-glazed earthenware, cover with drivers head handle, registration "OK T42".

Available in an range of colors, the silvered areas are prone to wear, particularly on the corners and the driver's helmet and handle, which reduces value considerably.

c1930   9in (22.5cm) wide

$100-150   **GORL**

A 1950s Bavarian octagonal transfer printed souvenir teapot, from and with dedication for Canvey Island.

8.25in (21cm) wide

$30-50   **JL**

A Victorian chocolate brown teapot, with hand-painted marguerite decoration.

c1895   8.25in (21cm) wide

$60-90   **JL**

A 1950s West German teapot, with lotus bud-shaped handle to lid, flower transfers and gilt detailing.

10.25in (26cm) wide

$60-90   **JL**

CERAMICS

COLLECTORS' NOTES

■ William Day Gates, a lawyer, founded the Terra Cotta Tile Works in Illinois, in 1881 and produced terracotta bricks, drain tiles and pottery.

■ While attending the World's Columbian Exposition in Chicago in 1893, Gates became interested in the matte glazes being shown by the French potters and was inspired to produce his own range, launching the Teco line in 1902.

■ The shapes owe much to the Prairie School of Design, an offshoot of the Arts and Crafts movement, exemplified by Frank Lloyd Wright. This can be seen most clearly in the organically styled pieces, which feature leafy tendrils and whiplash handles. The geometric range includes more traditional Arts and Crafts elements with angular lines and buttressed handles, which are popular features with collectors.

■ Teco pottery was produced in a number of colors but green is by far the most common, and the most sought-after by collectors.

A small Teco floriform bowl or ashtray, covered in matte green glaze, stamped "Teco".

4.5in (11cm) diam

$350-400   **DRA**

A Teco low bowl, with ridged exterior, covered in matte green glaze, several minute flecks inside rim.

10in (25cm) wide

$280-320   **DRA**

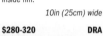

A Teco squat four-sided vessel, covered in smooth matte green glaze, with charcoaling around base and rim, restoration to several corners at rim, missing lid, stamped "Teco 384".

4.5in (11cm) wide

$220-280   **DRA**

A Teco bulbous vase, with undulating rim, covered in matte green glaze, stamped "Teco".

5in (12.5cm) high

$800-1,000   **DRA**

A Teco spherical vase, with small opening, covered in matte green glaze, stamped "Teco", remnant of paper label.

4.5in (11cm) high

$650-750   **DRA**

A Teco ovoid vase, covered in smooth matte green glaze, charcoaling around the base, stamped "Teco".

6.25in (15.5cm) high

$600-700   **DRA**

A Teco corseted vase, with flat top under a smooth matte green glaze with charcoaling on top, stamped "Teco 347".

7in (17.5cm) high

$800-1,000   **DRA**

A Teco cabinet vase, with squat base, stovepipe neck and two buttressed handles, covered in matte green glaze, small chip to corner of handle, stamped "Teco".

3.75in (9cm) high

$1,500-2,000   **DRA**

COLLECTORS' NOTES

■ Tiles have been used in decorative architectural designs for centuries, notably in Turkey and the Middle East. The collector has great scope to choose from: look out for Grueby and Claycraft from the US, William de Morgan and Minton from the UK and Dutch Delft tiles.

■ Condition is important, with cracks and losses devaluing a piece, unless very old and rare. Many tiles are handpainted, but from the mid-19th century onward they tend to be transfer-printed. Beware of modern reproductions, which tend to be lighter and thinner. Look for tiles that are decorated in a style typical of the factory, designer or period.

■ De Porceleyne Fles literally means 'the porcelain jar', which relates to the jar-shaped mark used by this Dutch, Delft-based factory. Established c1635, it is said to be the longest lived and most famous of the 32 earthenware factories founded there.

■ Joost Thooft, an engineer, bought the company in 1876 and revolutionized materials and processes. To restore the fame of Delft, the name was added to the mark, along with Thooft's monogram. The company received Royal designation in 1919. Although better known for its blue and white wares, the company also produced Arts and Crafts and Art Nouveau stylized designs around the turn of the century.

A De Porceleyne Fles large horizontal tile, with peacock, minute flecks to walls, stamped bottle "TL, Delft" mark.

17in (42.5cm) wide

$600-900   **DRA**

A De Porceleyne Fles tall tile, with a peacock in polychrome on a brick wall, stamped bottle "TL, Delft" mark.

13in (32.5cm) high

$400-600   **DRA**

A pair of De Porceleyne Fles tall vertical tiles, with a pair of ibises at an oasis in front of pyramids, surrounded by green-glazed border tiles, mount hiding marks.

13.5in (34cm) high

$600-900   **DRA**

A De Porceleyne Fles vertical tile, with a goose landing in a marsh with fishing boat, stamped bottle "J, Delft" mark.

8.75in (22cm) high

$280-320   **DRA**

A De Porceleyne Fles horizontal tile, depicting a deer hunt in the snow, restoration to one edge and top back, stamped bottle "TL, Delft" mark.

17.25in (43cm) wide

$500-700   **DRA**

A De Porceleyne Fles tile, decorated in cuenca with a hare leaping below branches, two small nicks to upper right edge, stamped bottle with "TL" and "Delft" mark.

8.25in (20.5cm) wide

$500-700   **DRA**

A De Porceleyne Fles large tile, decorated in cuenca with a Viking ship with seahorse prow, a few small nicks to cuenca walls, framed.

8in (20cm) wide

$400-600   **DRA**

A De Porceleyne Fles horizontal tile, with Viking ship, stamped bottle "TL, Delft" mark.

8.75in (22cm) wide

$320-380   **DRA**

A De Porceleyne Fles horizontal tile, with a regatta of tall ships, small nicks to corners, stamped bottle "TL, Delft" mark.

8.25in (20.5cm) wide

$120-180   **DRA**

CERAMICS

Six unusual Californian tiles, depicting a desert scene, unmarked.

28.5in (70cm) wide

$2,200-2,800 DRA

A Claycraft tile, decorated in cuenca with a bowl of flowers in brilliant polychrome on a black ground, several minute flecks to high points, stamped "CLAYCRAFT".

7.75in (19cm) square

$600-900 DRA

A CLOSER LOOK AT TILES

Groups of tiles that form a picture are more scarce than standard tiles, particularly if complete and undamaged.

At 24in (60cm) wide, the image is easier to display in modern houses than larger scenes, but makes much more of a visual impression than a single tile.

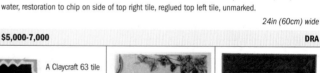

Although not by a notable factory, the colors and modern style of the image with its flat planes of color are strongly in the Arts & Crafts tradition.

The decoration is tube-lined, where the design is hand-applied by trailing liquid clay onto the tiles though a pipe before adding the colors.

An Arts and Crafts twelve-tile panel, decorated with an autumnal landscape with trees, hills, and water, restoration to chip on side of top right tile, reglued top left tile, unmarked.

24in (60cm) wide

$5,000-7,000 DRA

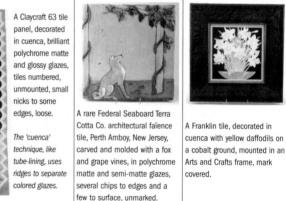

A Claycraft 63 tile panel, decorated in cuenca, brilliant polychrome matte and glossy glazes, tiles numbered, unmounted, small nicks to some edges, loose.

The 'cuenca' technique, like tube-lining, uses ridges to separate colored glazes.

34.5in (86cm) high

$3,000-5,000 DRA

A rare Federal Seaboard Terra Cotta Co. architectural faïence tile, Perth Amboy, New Jersey, carved and molded with a fox and grape vines, in polychrome matte and semi-matte glazes, several chips to edges and a few to surface, unmarked.

14in (35cm) wide

$1,800-2,200 DRA

A Franklin tile, decorated in cuenca with yellow daffodils on a cobalt ground, mounted in an Arts and Crafts frame, mark covered.

9in (23cm) wide

$320-380 DRA

A rare Georgia Tech Ceramics tile, of partly unglazed clay impressed with the college spire against green foliage and blue sky, above "GA TECH CERAMICS '40".

1940 *4.75in (12cm) wide*

$300-500 DRA

A Muresque horizontal panel, molded with a medieval village scene with a woman with basket in front of thatched roof cottages, mounted in an Arts and Crafts frame, stamped "MURESQUE TILES OAKLAND".

12in (30cm) wide

$700-1,000 DRA

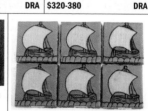

Six Mosaic tiles, decorated in cuerda seca with a sailboat in brown and beige on a blue ground, each stamped "MTC".

3in (75cm) wide

$700-1,000 DRA

COLLECTORS' NOTES

■ Toby jugs probably take their name from the old French word 'tope' meaning 'to drink or toast'. The first Toby jug was given the name 'Toby Fillpot', after the heavy-drinking subject of a popular ballad.

■ Royal Doulton are generally recognized as one of the largest manufacturers of Tobies, although a number of other companies have also made them, including Wood & Sons, Spode, and Kevin Francis.

■ The standard Toby jug, sometimes called the 'ordinary Toby', depicts a seated figure in a tricorn hat holding a tankard and a pipe. Toby jugs also portray literary creations, folk characters and popular statesmen.

■ Value is determined by a combination of age, scarcity, and quality. Jugs that have been withdrawn from production, especially those only made in small quantities, will be more expensive.

■ A number of companies, particularly brewers and distillers, have commissioned promotional Toby jugs. These are often released in limited editions and are very collectible.

■ Toby jugs are available in various sizes, ranging from large 9in (23cm) high examples to small sized jugs, measuring around 4in (10cm) high.

■ The range of small 'Doultonville Tobies', created by William Harper, is accompanied by a series of stories based on the characters.

A Royal Doulton 'The Best Is Not Too Good' Toby jug, D6107.

1939-60   4.25in (11cm) high

$150-200   PSA

A Royal Doulton 'Sir John Falstaff' small Toby jug, D6063.

1939-91   5.5in (14cm) high

$50-70   PSA

A Royal Doulton 'Old Charley' small Toby jug, D6069.

1939-60   5.5in (14cm) high

$180-220   PSA

A Royal Doulton 'Sherlock Holmes' large Toby jug, D6661.

1981-91   8.75in (22cm) high

$70-10   PSA

A Royal Doulton 'Cliff Cornell' large Toby jug, in blue jacket.

A variety of color combinations exist for this Toby jug. This medium size was also produced with a brown jacket and a beige jacket.

c1955   *9.5in (24cm) high*

$280-320   PSA

A Royal Doulton 'Winston Churchill' medium Toby jug, D6172.

5.5in (14cm) high

$60-90   PSA

A limited edition Royal Doulton 'Charles Dickens' Toby jug, D6997, from an edition of 2,500.

1995   5.25in (13.5cm) high

$100-150   PSA

CERAMICS

COLLECTORS' NOTES

■ Ohio-born Artus Van Briggle was employed as an artist by the Rookwood Pottery in 1887, after studying at the Cincinnati Art School.

■ The pottery was impressed by the young man's skill and sent him to further his studies in Paris. This was to be a fortuitous event as he met his future wife while studying and was also exposed to the lost art of the Ming Dynasty's dead matte glazes that were to become his signature.

■ Upon his return to Cincinnati he began experimenting with matte glazes and began creating his own pieces, while still working part-time at Rookwood. Artus moved to Colorado Springs in 1899 due to a bout of tuberculosis, but he was able to exhibit his matte glazes at the 1900 Paris Exposition Universelle as part of the Rookwood display.

■ With his own pottery established in Colorado Springs in 1900, Artus began to produce slip-cast and moulded pieces but output was slow due to the amount of detailing done by hand. Four years after his pottery opened, Artus died and his wife took over the running of the company. It is the only art pottery still surviving today.

■ The most desirable pieces are those that were produced during Artus' lifetime.

A Van Briggle commemorative mug, embossed with an owl over coat of arms under matte purple glaze, minute nick to rim, "AA 1916".

1916   *4.5in (11cm) high*

$350-400   **DRA**

A Van Briggle bulbous vase, embossed with broad spade-shaped leaves under 'Persian Rose' glaze, tight line from rim, "AA 1917".

1917   *7.5in (19cm) high*

$350-450   **DRA**

A rare Van Briggle copper-clad cabinet vase, embossed and incised with trefoils and swirling stems, opposing hairlines from rim, possibly from manufacture, "AA Van Briggle Colo. Springs 657".

c1910   *3in (7.5cm) high*

$800-1,000   **DRA**

A Van Briggle vase, with sloping shoulder, embossed and incised with a stylized pattern under purple and grey glaze, the clay showing through, mark partly obscured by glaze.

c1910   *4in (10cm) wide*

$600-700   **DRA**

A Van Briggle mug, covered in blue and green curdled matte glaze, marked.

1906   *4.5in (11.5cm) high*

$450-550   **DRA**

An early Van Briggle vase, embossed with daisies under a blue-green glaze, shaved base.

7.5in (19cm) high

$220-280   **DRA**

A Van Briggle figure, molded to depict a seated woman holding a large shell in her lap, covered in a turquoise glaze, signed faintly on back.

7in (18cm) high

$400-600   **S&K**

A late Van Briggle center bowl, with crouching maiden figure and flower frog, frog covered in turquoise and blue glaze, incised "AA Van Briggle Colo Spgs".

15in (37.5cm) wide

$350-450   **DRA**

A Van Briggle vase, embossed with crocus blossoms under a sheer turquoise glaze, the clay showing through, mark partly covered by glaze "Van Briggle Colo Spgs 629".

c1910   *5.75in (14cm) wide*

$800-1,000   **DRA**

COLLECTORS' NOTES

■ Robert Methven Heron inherited his father's business, Fife Pottery in Kirkcaldy, Scotland in 1833. Together with Bohemian artist Karel Nekola, who had been hired by Heron Snr., they introduced Wemyss ware in 1882. The range included cat or pig-shaped items, jug-and-basin sets, doorstops, tablewares, candlesticks, and inkstands, which were handpainted with bright and bold designs including roses, fruit, birds, and bees.

■ By Nekola's death in 1915, the style of pottery was less popular with the public and the company was sold to the Devon-based Bovey Tracey Pottery in 1930, when pieces were marked "Plinchta" "Wemyss". Nekola's son Joseph worked there until his death in 1942.

A small Wemyss 'Jazzy' Lady Eva vase, painted in bright colors, brown painted mark "Wemyss 213".

6in (15cm) high

$180-220　　　　　**L&T**

An early 20thC Wemyss honey pot and cover, retailed by T. Goode & Co., painted with a hive in fenced landscape on the cylindrical sides and with large bees flying about, painted mark.

$300-500　　　　**CHEF**

A Wemyss 'Cock and Hen' Low Kintore candlestick, painted with a frieze of a cockerel and three hens, impressed mark "Wemyss Ware".

4.5in (11cm) high

$500-700　　　　　**L&T**

A Wemyss 'Roses' pattern cylindrical jug, with applied handle, impressed and painted marks, "Wemyss".

7in (17.5cm) high

$320-380　　　　**L&T**

A Wemyss ware tankard, decorated with thistles, with an applied handle.

5.5in (14cm) high

$300-500　　　　**L&T**

A Wemyss 'Dog Roses' pattern teapot and cover, of ovoid form painted with sprigs of dog roses, unmarked.

5.5in (14cm) high

$280-320　　　　　**L&T**

A Wemyss 'Daffodils' pattern basket, with frilled rim and applied rope-twist handle, restored handle terminals, impressed "RH&S" mark, printed retailer's mark.

12in (30cm) wide

$700-1,000　　　　**L&T**

A Plinchta figure of a cat, painted with cabbage roses, printed marks.

6in (15cm) high

$220-280　　　　**L&T**

A Royal Worcester flatback jug, decorated with flowers on an ivory ground, puce mark.

1892   7in (17.5cm) high

$280-320   **WW**

A Royal Worcester leaf-molded vase, shape No. 1947, with three leaf handles, decorated in green, orange, and yellow.

c1900   6.25in (16cm) wide

$180-220   **WW**

A Royal Worcester squat vase, painted with blackberries by Micky Miller.

1953   3in (7.5cm) high

$220-280   **GORL**

A Royal Worcester flat back jug, signed "C. Baldwin".

1902   5.25in (13cm) high

$2,200-2,800   **AL**

A Royal Worcester flat back jug.

1901   5.5in (14cm) high

$300-500   **GCL**

A Royal Worcester flat back jug.

1901   5.25in (13.5cm) high

$300-500   **GCL**

A Royal Worcester yellow ground coffee set, each piece printed and painted with floral reserves, comprising six coffee cups and saucers, milk, sugar, coffee pot, and cover, with date code.

1938

$120-180 set   **CHEF**

A Royal Worcester hand-painted demi-tasse cup and saucer.

c1925   3.75in (9.5cm) diam

$300-500   **GCL**

A Royal Worcester plate, painted by John Stinton Jnr after Corot, with a hillside view and two children, against primrose and deep blue borders elaborately gilded with acanthus scrolls and paterae, with date code.

1929   10.5in (26.5cm) diam

$400-600   **GORL**

A Royal Worcester nautilus shell vase, raised on a rocky base with tree stump and molded with shells, printed mark.

1898   7in (17.5cm) high

$220-280   **WW**

A Royal Worcester 'January' figure, modeled by F.G. Doughty, as a little boy in the snow, base stamped "3452".

6.25in (16cm) high

$60-90   **BAD**

A Royal Worcester 'February' figure, base stamped "3453".

6.25in (16cm) high

$280-320   **GORL**

A Royal Worcester 'Grandmother's Dress' bone china figure, designed by Freda Doughty, with date code.

1939   6in (15cm) high

$180-220   **GORL**

A Royal Worcester 'Cook' candle extinguisher, blue with white apron.

1912   2.5in (6.5cm) high

$280-320   **GCL**

A Royal Worcester 'Nun' candle extinguisher.

1903   3.75in (9.5cm) high

$300-400   **GCL**

A Royal Worcester 'Yankee' figure.

c1890   6.75in (17cm) high

$400-600   **GHA**

A pair of Royal Worcester 'Miniature Cairo Water Carriers' models, painted with bronzed colors, green printed marks, one with date code, shape number "1250", man has restored rim to jar.

1901   10in (25cm) high

$700-1,000   **DN**

A pair of Royal Worcester 'Paul' and 'Virginia' lusterware figures, each standing on a rocky base and decorated with enamel details, impressed marks to Virginia.

c1865   13in (33cm) high

$700-1,000   **WW**

A Bauer bulbous vase, by Russel Wright, with teardrop-shaped opening, covered in mottled apricot glaze, with black interior, stamped "Russel Wright/Bauer".

8.75in (22cm) high

$1,000-1,500 DRA

A Clifton Indian ware gourd-shaped vessel, after the Middle Mississippi tribe, painted with petal forms in two tones of terracotta on a darker terracotta ground, incised "Clifton/231".

12.25in (30.5cm) high

$500-700 DRA

A Clifton Indian ware gourd-shaped vase, after the Arkansas tribe, with geometric steps in ivory on red ground, several glaze flakes, marked "Clifton/205".

6.5in (16cm) wide

$280-320 DRA

A Clifton Indian squat vessel, after the Homolobi tribe, incised and painted with brown stylized animals on terracotta ground, incised "Clifton/Homolobi/234".

8.5in (21cm) wide

$220-280 DRA

A large Clifton Indian jardinière, after the Four Mile Ruin, Az tribe, incised and painted with abstracted waves in black and beige on a terracotta ground, short and tight line from rim, incised "Clifton" with tribe, and "248".

12.5in (31cm) wide

$550-650 DRA

A Clifton Indian squat vessel, after the Homolobi tribe, painted and incised with geometric wave pattern in red and brown on terracotta ground, marked "Clifton/Homolobi".

10in (25cm) wide

$500-700 DRA

A large Carl Culbreth modern totemic ceramic sculpture, 'Monolith #25', comprised of three stacking geometric forms with fabric texture in ivory, brown and green, signed, titled and dated on base.

1980   72in (183cm) high

$400-500 DRA

A Denbac tapering vase, modeled with dragonflies under a russet and olive green flambé glaze and copperdust crystalline base, incised "Denbac/35".

9in (23cm) high

$450-550 DRA

A Denbac Arts & Crafts high-fired vase, with four buttressed handles and embossed in a woven pattern under a cream and brown crystalline flambé vase, stamped mark.

9.25in (23.5cm) high

$500-600 DRA

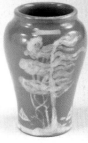

A rare large Dedham Crackleware 'Rabbit' pattern center bowl, with indented rim, the exterior with a large freeform floral pattern, pitting along rim, ink stamp.

11.75in (29cm) wide

$4,000-5,000   **DRA**

A Dedham Crackleware 'Rabbit' pattern pitcher, two firing lines to base, blue ink stamp.

9in (22.5cm) high

$800-1,000   **DRA**

A rare Denver White baluster vase, painted in an opaque white glaze with windblown trees and sailboats on a blue-gray ground, incised "Denver W".

5.25in (13cm) high

$500-600   **DRA**

A David Gilhooly ceramic sculpture, 'Frogs in Beans', of three frogs frolicking around in a cast-iron pot full of black eye peas, incised "Gilhooly/89/Exp.".

c1970   *5.75in (14.5cm) wide*

$650-750   **DRA**

A Maija Grotell porcelain bulbous vessel, with wax-resist organic decoration in brown over an aqua ground, with cobalt rings, firing crack to base, incised "MG".

Finnish Maija Grotell (1899-1973) emigrated to the US in 1927 after studying ceramics in Finland for six years. While teaching art at a number of institutes she worked extensively on glazes. Grotell won twenty five major exhibition awards for her work.

9in (23cm) diam

$4,000-5,000   **DRA**

A Maija Grotell stoneware footed bowl, with sheer flowing umber luster glaze to the exterior, with white crackled interior, small shallow glaze chip to rim, incised "MG".

9in (23cm) diam

$800-1,200   **DRA**

A Maija Grotell stoneware charger, with squeezebag cross-hatched decoration on a glossy blue ground, incised "MG".

13in (33cm) diam

$1,000-1,500   **DRA**

A Grueby floor tile, with a cornucopia-bearing putto in red clay against thick curdled matte mustard glaze, mounted in Arts and Crafts frame, unmarked.

6in (15cm) wide

$350-400 **DRA**

A Vivika & Otto Heino stoneware bowl, with lobed panels alternating with calligraphic signs in white over brown, its interior covered in oatmeal matte glaze, incised "Vivika + Otto".

4.5in (11.5cm) high

$350-400 **DRA**

A Carl Larsen hemispherical hand-built vessel, Mug Shop, Berkeley, CA, of bisque, white and brown clays, with irregular rim, the interior covered in robin's egg blue glaze, paper label.

3.75in (9.5cm) wide

$180-220 **DRA**

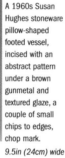

A 1960s Susan Hughes stoneware pillow-shaped footed vessel, incised with an abstract pattern under a brown gunmetal and textured glaze, a couple of small chips to edges, chop mark.

9.5in (24cm) wide

$250-300 **DRA**

A pair of 'Aesthetic Movement' pottery ewers, unmarked but attributed to Linthorpe Pottery and Christopher Dresser, of near globular form with a 'humped' middle, a flared neck and exaggerated loop handles, the red clay body is streaked beige beneath a clear glaze.

c1880 *7.25in (18.5cm) high*

$280-320 **DN**

A small Linthorpe Pottery vase, designed by Christopher Dresser, of double-gourd form with a flat base, covered with a pale greeny-blue glaze with random specks of deeper blue, the interior has amber tones, impressed "Linthorpe" and with designer's facsimile signature, also "HT" for Henry Tooth and numbered "618".

2.5in (6cm) high

$300-400 **DN**

A Linthorpe Pottery vase, designed by Christopher Dresser, decorated with two spiraling bands, one stippled and the other with incised vertical lines, impressed "Linthorpe" and designer's facsimile signature, with "HT" monogram for Henry Tooth and numbered "175".

6in (15.5cm) high

$600-700 **DN**

A Linthorpe dimpled and collapsed jug, designed by Christopher Dresser, covered in an ivory and green mottled glaze over a sheer brown ground, stamped "Linthorpe/Chr Dresser".

5.75in (14.5cm) high

$500-600 **DRA**

A Manbeck covered jar, with sgraffito decoration, re-glued lid, incised signature.

11.25in (28.5cm) high

$350-450 **DRA**

A Manger stoneware kiln-shaped floor vase, with applied 'portholes', also incised and coiled, covered in gray, ocher and gunmetal matte glaze, a few small nicks, incised "Manger".

28in (71cm) high

$350-400   DRA

A Marblehead ovoid vase, covered in a fine speckled matte green glaze, with stamped ship mark.

The pottery was originally designed to provide a therapeutic pastime for patients at the Marblehead sanatorium, Massachusetts. Arthur Baggs joined as manager in 1904 and turned it into a commercial enterprise. The hand-thrown pieces are usually of simple form with satin matte glazes.

5in (12.5cm) high

$600-700   DRA

A Marblehead squat vessel, the exterior in matte lavender, the interior in semi-matte blue-gray, hairline from rim, stamped ship mark.

6.5in (16cm) wide

$200-250   DRA

A Marblehead flaring bud vase, covered in smooth matte gray glaze, restoration to rim chip, stamped ship mark.

4.25in (10.5cm) high

$120-180   DRA

A Marblehead squat vessel, incised with stylized Glasgow roses in blue and green on lavender ground, cracked, stamped ship mark.

5in (12.5cm) wide

$280-320   DRA

A Newcomb College ridged vase, covered in thick yellow-green glaze dripping over smooth matte green ground, glaze flaking and right line at rim, probably from firing, stamped "NC, JM".

6.25in (15.5cm) high

$550-650   DRA

A Marblehead tea tile, decorated with a basket of fruit and flowers in bright polychrome on a pink ground, light abrasion to surface, ship mark.

4.5in (11cm) wide

$350-400   DRA

A Marblehead ovoid vase, covered in smooth lavender matte glaze, minute fleck to rim, stamped ship mark.

5.25in (13cm) high

$450-550   DRA

A Marblehead corseted bud vase, covered in smooth matte speckled brown glaze, stamped ship mark.

4.25in (10.5cm) high

$400-500   DRA

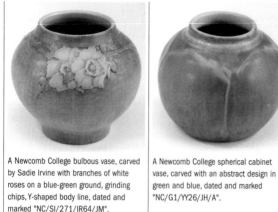

A Newcomb College bulbous vase, carved by Sadie Irvine with branches of white roses on a blue-green ground, grinding chips, Y-shaped body line, dated and marked "NC/SI/271/IR64/JM".

1917   5.75in (14cm) wide

$1,000-1,500   DRA

A Newcomb College spherical cabinet vase, carved with an abstract design in green and blue, dated and marked "NC/G1/YY26/JH/A".

1932   3in (7.5cm) wide

$1,000-1,500   DRA

A Newcomb College barrel-shaped ribbed vase, covered in celadon and black glossy feathered glaze, stamped "NC, L".

7.5in (19cm) high

$500-600   DRA

A Newcomb College bulbous cabinet vase, carved by Sadie Irvine with stylized rose leaves in pink, purple and blue-green, dated and marked "NC/SI/U030/F".

Newcomb College's pottery was established in 1895 to teach young women a suitable career. The male students hand threw the vessels, which were then decorated by the women to their own designs. Early pieces with a high gloss finish are the most sought-after.

1933   3.75in (9cm) wide

$1,200-1,800   DRA

A 1960s Win Ng squat vessel, California, with small opening, covered in brown, indigo and gray volcanic glaze, marked "Ng".

6.5in (16.5cm) wide

$280-320   DRA

A North Dakota School of Mines vessel, covered in indigo-to-oxblood glossy glaze, a few shallow scratches, blue ink circular stamp "AV 1933".

1933   6in (15cm) wide

$180-220   DRA

A North Dakota School of Mines squat vessel, carved by Flora Huckfield with branches of flowers under a good mottled matte green glaze, blue ink circular stamp, "Ericson-Huck".

5in (12.5cm) wide

$450-550   DRA

A North Dakota School of Mines footed bowl, decorated by R. Schnell with ivory leaves on dark brown ground, glossy turquoise interior, circular stamp and "Schnell".

7.25in (18cm) wide

$450-550   DRA

A large North Dakota School of Mines baluster vase, carved by Julia Mattson with stylized oak leaves on a semi-matte blue-gray ground, blue ink circular stamp "J. Mattson".

7.25in (18cm) high

$500-600   DRA

A North Dakota School of Mines ovoid vase, incised with a wreath of purple prairie roses with green leaves on a shaded gray-to-pink ground, blue ink circular stamp "MHS 1934".

1934   *5in (12.5cm) high*

$350-400   **DRA**

A North Dakota School of Mines vessel, the sloping shoulder embossed with a wreath of stylized flowers under matte amber glaze, insignificant burst bubbles and nick to shoulder, blue ink circular stamp "CA Sorbo 196".

6.25in (15.5cm) wide

$350-400   **DRA**

A George Ohr 'Burnt Baby' spherical footed vessel, with remnant of sponged green glaze, damaged in pottery fire, October 1893, stamped "GEO. E. OHR, BILOXI".

George Ohr (1857-1918) lived and worked in Biloxi, Mississippi. His early works are thinly potted with distorted shapes and dark iridescent glazes. From 1903 he made only unglazed bisque pieces claiming: "God put no color in souls, and I'll put no color on my vases".

3.25in (8cm) high

$800-900   **DRA**

A large George Ohr bird-feeder, of bisque clay, gash to body, several chips, stamped "G.E. OHR, Biloxi, Miss".

10in (25cm) high

$800-1,000   **DRA**

A George Ohr 'Burnt Baby' bulbous vase, with torn rim, covered in shards, survived pottery fire, October 1893, no visible mark.

4.5in (11cm) high

$450-550   **DRA**

Two Overbeck figurines of a gentleman and lady in antebellum dress, small nick to base of man, incised "OBK".

4in (10cm) high

$600-700   **DRA**

A 20thC Ben Owen studio pottery saltglaze bowl, with radiating panels of incised lines, splashed in blue and moss green, signed "Ben Owen III 1994".

15in (38cm) diam

$250-300   **S&K**

Two Overbeck figurines of George and Martha Washington, restoration to her fan, incised "OBK".

4.25in (10.5cm) high

$1,200-1,800   **DRA**

A large 20thC Ben Owen studio pottery vase, with short flaring neck, four strap handles and undulating band of molded rope, in turquoise, brick and green faux bronze flambé glaze, signed "Ben Owen III 1994".

18.25in (46.5cm) high

$700-800   **S&K**

A Henry Varnum Poor shallow bowl, decorated in sgraffito with a woman's head in green, yellow, brown and blue on an ivory ground, hairline and restoration, glaze scaling to rim, signed "HVP/33" on front and back.

1933   8.25in (21cm) diam

$400-500   **DRA**

A Richard Riemerschmid spherical mustard pot, with pewter mount and band of excised bubbles in cobalt and gray glazes, minor nick to shoulder, unmarked.

c1905   3.75in (9.5cm) high

$250-350   **DRA**

A 1950s Myrton Purkiss bowl, decorated with "FLW" and squares of flowers and faux-marble on a faux-stoneware ground, signed "M. Purkiss".

Canadian-born Purkiss was educated at the University of Southern California and Chouinard Art Institute.

10.25in (26cm) diam

$500-700   **DRA**

A large Vernon Kilns charger, 'Our America', by Rockwell Kent, with stars around rim and bald eagle above a map of the US dotted with symbols of industry from each state, covered in burgundy and white glazes, red ink stamp, with title.

16.25in (41.5cm) diam

$180-220   **DRA**

A Scheier bulbous vessel, incised in black with a band of figures inside fish, and covered in blue-green and cobalt matte glaze, small glaze chip to footring, incised "Scheier/90", and "3".

1990   7in (18cm) wide

$400-450   **DRA**

A salt-glazed stoneware jug with handle, painted blue flowers, impressed "A. P. Butler, New Brunswick, NJ. 13 1/2".

$280-320   **TA**

A 19thC American half-gallon stoneware jar, with blue flower decoration.

11.5in (28.5cm) high

$150-200   **BCAC**

A 1940s Scheier water pitcher, covered in mottled amber microcrystalline glaze, firing line inside handle, incised "Scheier".

9.75in (25cm) high

$450-550   **DRA**

CHARACTER COLLECTIBLES

COLLECTORS' NOTES

■ Howdy Doody lived in Doodyville with his friends including Buffalo Bob and Clarabell the Clown. He began life known as 'Elmer' on a radio show but gained this name from his regularly used catchphrase, which is a derivation of 'How do you do?'

■ His first TV show, 'Puppet Playhouse', began in December 1947, becoming 'The Howdy Doody Show' in 1949. Highly popular during the 1950s and 1960s, it was amongst the first color TV programs and was the first TV show to complete 1,000 broadcasts.

■ His immense popularity led to a large amount of promotional merchandize, which is hotly sought after today. Copyrights belonged to Buffalo Bob Smith from 1948-51, the Kagran Corporation from 1951-59 and to NBC from 1960, with 1950 seeing the patent office allotting patent No. 156,687 to him.

■ Condition affects value, with wear to card items, restringing of dolls and damage to ceramics reducing value considerably. Look out for memorabilia relating to his friends such as Flub-A-Dub and Clarabell as they are often scarce.

A 1950s 'Howdy Doody' articulated printed card hand puppet.

13in (33cm) high

$70-100   **SOTT**

A 'Howdy Doody' plastic take-apart keychain puzzle, with NBC microphone.

2.25in (6cm) high

$30-50   **SOTT**

A 'Howdy Doody' cookie jar, with winking face and molded 'Howdy Doody' name around neck.

The lids of this rare jar are notorious for having been dropped and broken as they are hard to handle. Values are reduced considerably as it is extremely hard to find a replacement.

c1955   *9.75in (24.5cm) high*

$400-600   **NF**

An American 'Howdy Doody' pin.

1in (2.5cm) wide

$40-60   **LDE**

A 'Howdy Doody' lithographed tin spinning top, made in West Germany.

5.5in (14cm) diam

$100-150   **SOTT**

A Parker Bros. 'Howdy Doody's Own Game'.

box 15.25in (38.5cm) wide

$100-150   **SOTT**

A pair of 'Howdy Doody' celluloid and metal ear muffs, in near mint condition.

3.75in (9.5cm) high

$180-220   **SOTT**

A 'Howdy Doody's Electric Doodler' game.

13.25in (33.5cm) wide

$30-50   **SOTT**

A 'Howdy Doody' red plastic Sunray camera, with molded Howdy Doody faces and original blue plastic straps.

4.25in (11cm) wide

$40-60   **SOTT**

A 1950s Gund 'Popeye' vinyl and stuffed plush roly-poly toy, with bell inside, and original tag.

Popeye the Sailorman, the world's most famous spinach eater, first appeared in January 1929 in a comic strip drawn by Elzie Segar called 'Thimble Theater'. Originally about Olive Oyl (later to become Popeye's leading lady) and her family, Popeye soon took over and a whole new series of characters such as Swee'Pea the 'infink' and Brutus appeared. Over 600 cartoons were made by the Fleischer Studios, the first airing in 1933. Early memorabilia from the 1930s to the 1950s is usually highly sought after but condition is very important.

9in (23cm) high

$40-60   **WAC**

A Gund Mfg. Co. 'Popeye' hand puppet, with soft vinyl head.

9.5in (24cm) high

$40-60   **SOTT**

An 'Olive Oyl' push button puppet, by Kohner Bros. Hong Kong.

These puppets have become a collecting field in their own right.

4.25in (10.5cm) high

$30-50   **SOTT**

An early 'Popeye' cast and painted metal lamp.

This lamp would originally have come with a Popeye shade, but these were easily damaged and are hard to find.

11in (28cm) high

$180-220   **SOTT**

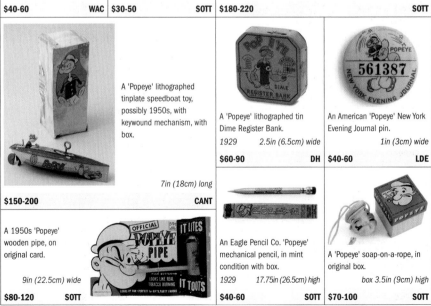

A 'Popeye' lithographed tinplate speedboat toy, possibly 1950s, with keywound mechanism, with box.

7in (18cm) long

$150-200   **CANT**

A 'Popeye' lithographed tin Dime Register Bank.

1929   2.5in (6.5cm) wide

$60-90   **DH**

An American 'Popeye' New York Evening Journal pin.

1in (3cm) wide

$40-60   **LDE**

A 1950s 'Popeye' wooden pipe, on original card.

9in (22.5cm) wide

$80-120   **SOTT**

An Eagle Pencil Co. 'Popeye' mechanical pencil, in mint condition with box.

1929   17.75in (26.5cm) high

$40-60   **SOTT**

A 'Popeye' soap-on-a-rope, in original box.

box 3.5in (9cm) high

$70-100   **SOTT**

A 'Superman' plastic 'Spinball' pinball game, complete and with original colored stickers.

A 'Superman' model SP-19 child's record player, by Dejay Corp, marked "©DC Comics 1978".

c1978   *11.75in (30cm) wide*

$280-320   **NOR**

Superman was originally devised in 1933 by high school students Joe Shuster and Jerry Siegel and first appeared in their fanzine 'Science Fiction' as a villain in 'The Reign of The Superman' series. By 1934, he had become a hero and began to be redesigned, but it was not until June 1938 and the publication of the first issue of 'Action Comics' that he appeared publicly in print and began his superhuman rise to prominence and worldwide fame. Today this comic could fetch as much as $400,000 in near mint condition! Interestingly, many claim that period styles for male bathing suits is the reason why the 'man of steel' wears his shorts as he does - many swimming trunks of the period were 'Speedo' like in shape and belted.

1967   *21.75in (55.5cm) long*

$180-220   **NOR**

A 'Superman' radio, lacks battery cover.

1973   *6in (15cm) wide*

$30-50   **NOR**

An American 'Superman-Tim Club' pin, reverse reading "MEMBER IN GOOD STANDING".

      1in (2.5cm) wide

$30-40   **LDE**

A 'Superman' hairbrush, by Avon, in original box, both mint condition.

      8.5in (21.5cm) high

$25-35   **NOR**

A 'Superman' soft vinyl and cloth handpuppet, by Ideal Toy Corp.

c1965   *11in (27.5cm) high*

$100-150   **NOR**

A 'Mighty Mouse' die-cut card figure.

'Mighty Mouse' first appeared in 1942 and was originally devised as a fly until one of the Terrytoons studio moguls came up with the idea of a mouse instead. The idea was to combine Superman-like powers with a small, insignificant animal. His initial name of 'Supermouse' was changed to Mighty Mouse in 1943 and from then he went on to star in comics from 1945 until the 1990s, and in numerous TV cartoon series in the 1970s and 1980s.

A 1960s 'Supermen of America' pin, by National Periodical Publications Inc.

1961   *1in (3cm) wide*

$50-70   **LDE**

c1960   *11.5in (29cm) high*

$50-70   **SOTT**

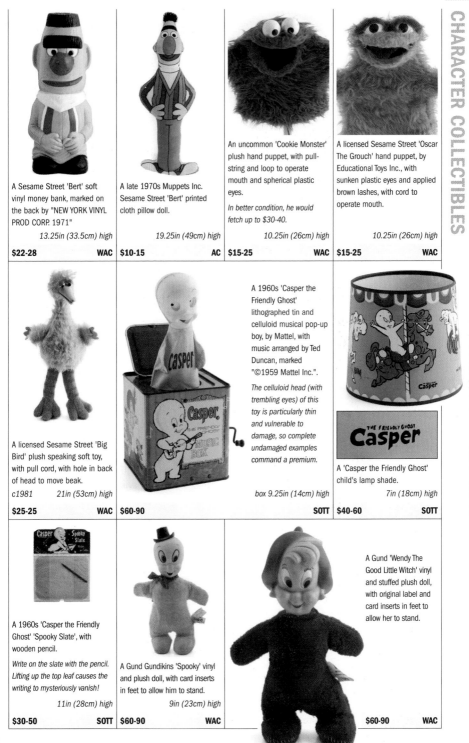

A Sesame Street 'Bert' soft vinyl money bank, marked on the back by "NEW YORK VINYL PROD CORP. 1971"

13.25in (33.5cm) high

$22-28   **WAC**

A late 1970s Muppets Inc. Sesame Street 'Bert' printed cloth pillow doll.

19.25in (49cm) high

$10-15   **AC**

An uncommon 'Cookie Monster' plush hand puppet, with pull-string and loop to operate mouth and spherical plastic eyes.

In better condition, he would fetch up to $30-40.

10.25in (26cm) high

$15-25   **WAC**

A licensed Sesame Street 'Oscar The Grouch' hand puppet, by Educational Toys Inc., with sunken plastic eyes and applied brown lashes, with cord to operate mouth.

10.25in (26cm) high

$15-25   **WAC**

A licensed Sesame Street 'Big Bird' plush speaking soft toy, with pull cord, with hole in back of head to move beak.

c1981   21in (53cm) high

$25-25   **WAC**

A 1960s 'Casper the Friendly Ghost' lithographed tin and celluloid musical pop-up boy, by Mattel, with music arranged by Ted Duncan, marked "©1959 Mattel Inc.".

The celluloid head (with trembling eyes) of this toy is particularly thin and vulnerable to damage, so complete undamaged examples command a premium.

box 9.25in (14cm) high

$60-90   **SOTT**

A 'Casper the Friendly Ghost' child's lamp shade.

7in (18cm) high

$40-60   **SOTT**

A 1960s 'Casper the Friendly Ghost' 'Spooky Slate', with wooden pencil.

Write on the slate with the pencil. Lifting up the top leaf causes the writing to mysteriously vanish!

11in (28cm) high

$30-50   **SOTT**

A Gund Gundikins 'Spooky' vinyl and plush doll, with card inserts in feet to allow him to stand.

9in (23cm) high

$60-90   **WAC**

A Gund 'Wendy The Good Little Witch' vinyl and stuffed plush doll, with original label and card inserts in feet to allow her to stand.

$60-90   **WAC**

A licensed Warner Bros Bugs Bunny hard plastic doll, by M&H Novelty Corp, with original clothes and tag, metal bars in his arms to pose, original baseball and hard foam white painted ball and felt carrot.

The fact that he is complete, clean and a very early make, makes this valuable.

A 1970s licensed Jim Henson's The Muppet Show 'Kermit The Frog' soft toy, by Fisher Price Toys, with Velcro pads on his hands and feet.

19.75in (50cm) high

$18-22   **WAC**

A licensed Jim Henson's The Muppet Show 'Scooter' hugging doll, by Fisher Price Toys, with Velcro patches on his felt hands and hard plastic molded feet.

c1975   16.25in (41.5cm) high

$15-20   **WAC**

c1945

$100-150   **WAC**

14.5in (37cm) high

WAC

A 'Dopey' molded and painted fabric-headed cloth-bodied doll, possibly by Ideal, in original felt clothes.

1938   11.5in (29cm) high

$100-150   **WAC**

A Hanna Barbera's Yogi Bear 'Boo-Boo' vinyl and plush sitting toy, by Knickerbocker Toy Co., possibly 1960s, with original label.

9in (23cm) high

$40-60   **WAC**

A large 'Fred Flintstone' soft vinyl and fabric doll, by Knickerbocker Toy Co., with plush and felt clothing, card inserts in his feet to make him stand and original tag.

c1961   17in (43cm) high

$70-100   **WAC**

A Bendy Toys 'Pink Panther' poseable toy.

The value of these toys is related to their condition as they can degrade very quickly, with the surface and eventually the material itself cracking and even fragmenting. This one has not yet degraded.

A Warner Bros 'Tweety Pie' fabric and hard plastic headed finger puppet.

c1978   4in (10cm) high

$10-15   **WAC**

$40-60   **WAC**

A Chipmunks 'Simon' soft vinyl musical doll, by Knickerbocker, with tag.

c1961   13in (33cm) high

$60-90   **WAC**

A 1960s Ideal 'Mr Magoo' soft vinyl and stuffed fabric seated toy, with felt clothes, plush scarf and corduroy legs.

This toy was re-issued around 1988-89 and is usually worth under $20.

c1962   11.75in (30cm) seated

$80-120   **WAC**

COLLECTORS' NOTES

- Coin collecting is the oldest of the numismatic fields and the sheer range of types available can seem daunting to a new collector.

- It is generally advisable to concentrate on one area such as the ancient world, commemoratives, error coins, or simply examples from one specific period and place.

- When buying commemorative issues look at the edition number, those released in large numbers will appreciate less than more limited issues.

- Beware of facsimile collectors coins, which are common. Although not necessarily made to deceive, it can be hard to tell them from the genuine article.

- Coins should be handled as little as possible as condition is very important, invest in a good quality album and mounts to display and store your collection.

A silver facsimile Chinese coin with a military bust of Yuan Shih-Kai.

Original coins with this design can fetch $300, although the large number of facsimiles now in circulation has reduced the value of the originals.

1914   1.5in (4cm) diam

$3-5   **INT**

A Victorian crown, featuring the 'Old Head' portrait of Queen Victoria on the obverse and a representation of George slaying the dragon on the reverse, dated 1898.

1.5in (4cm) diam

$15-20   **INT**

A five pound coin, struck to commemorate Elizabeth II's Jubilee in 2002, featuring a portrait of the monarch on the obverse and an equestrian portrait of Elizabeth II on the reverse, surrounded by Latin script.

1.5in (4cm) diam

$7-10   **INT**

A 17thC coin, possibly from Flanders, found in the River Thames, very worn portrait and inscription on obverse, arms on reverse.

0.75in (2cm) wide

$8-12   **INT**

An Indian one rupee coin, struck with a portrait of Edward VII on obverse and Indian flora and script on reverse, dated 1909.

1.25in (3cm) diam

$7-10   **INT**

A Roman coin, featuring a portrait of the Emperor Gaius Caesar Augustus Germanicus on the obverse and three figures on the reverse, worn and discolored.

cAD40   0.75in (2cm) diam

$15-20   **INT**

A J.R. Grundy trader's token, featuring a tobacco plant and inscribed "J.R. Grundy Merchant Ballarat 1861".

1861   1.5in (3.5cm) diam

$8-12   **INT**

A South African Commonwealth five shilling bullion coin, struck in 1952 to commemorate the tri-centennial of the establishment of the first Dutch settlement in South Africa, portrait of George VI on obverse and ship from Van Riebeeck's fleet on reverse.

1.5in (4cm) diam

$10-15   **INT**

FIND OUT MORE...

www.money.org – *American Numismatic Association.*

'Standard Catalog of World Coins', *by Chester L. Krause & Clifford Mishler, published by Krause Publications.*

COMICS

COLLECTORS' NOTES

■ Collecting comics first became popular during the 1960s when conventions were first organised and, by the 1970s, it was an established field. Since then the market has grown steadily although, while mainstay characters such as Superman and Spiderman have always been desirable, lesser-known characters are not as stable.

■ The first issue of any comic is usually the most sought-after with values decreasing with later issues. Early comics were printed on poor quality paper so few survive in good condition, which has a major effect on value. Comics are often given a condition grade, sometimes by a third-party company such as Comic Guaranty (CGC) so new collectors should familiarise themselves with their grading.

■ Comics are divided into 'ages', comprising 'Golden Age' (1938-c1955), 'Silver Age' (c1956-c1969) and 'Bronze Age' (c1970-c1979) and collectors often have a favourite period as characters can change quite dramatically between these 'ages'.

■ The comic book collection market is continuing to grow with Superhero titles as popular as ever, aided by Hollywood's continuing trend to turn comic books into films. The anticipated arrival of films featuring established characters such as Spider-Man 2, Batman Beyond, Fantastic Four and The Phantom, as well as relative newcomers like Constantine (Hellblazer) and Hellboy will increase the popularity of the original comics.

■ As well as early examples, look for key story lines such as the death of Superman, the first appearance of characters and artwork by popular artists like Bob Kane (Batman), Jack Kirby (Captain America/The Hulk) and Steve Ditko (Spider-Man).

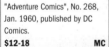

"Adventure Comics", No. 268, Jan. 1960, published by DC Comics.
$12-18   **MC**

"Adventure Comics", No. 294, Mar. 1962, published by DC Comics.
$8-12   **MC**

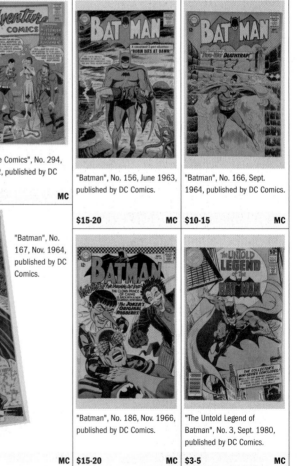

"Batman", No. 156, June 1963, published by DC Comics.

$15-20   **MC**

"Batman", No. 166, Sept. 1964, published by DC Comics.

$10-15   **MC**

"Batman", No. 167, Nov. 1964, published by DC Comics.

"Batman", No. 186, Nov. 1966, published by DC Comics.

"The Untold Legend of Batman", No. 3, Sept. 1980, published by DC Comics.

$6-8   **MC**   **$15-20**   **MC**   **$3-5**   **MC**

"Detective Comics", No. 276, Feb. 1960, published by DC Comics.

$18-22   MC

"Green Lantern", No. 23, Nov. 1959, published by DC Comics.

$5-8   MC

"Justice League of America", No. 23, Nov. 1963, published by DC Comics.

$8-12   MC

"Superman", No. 150, Jan. 1962, published by DC Comics.

$6-8   MC

"Superman vs Kobra", No. 327, Sept. 1978, published by DC Comics.

"Superman", No. 156, Oct. 1962, published by DC Comics.

$8-12   MC

"Action Comics", No. 286, Mar. 1962, published by DC Comics.

$2-3   MC

$2-3   MC

"Wonder Woman", No. 97, Apr. 1958, published by DC Comics.

$15-20   MC

"Giant Superman Annual", No. 2, published by DC Comics.

$3-5   MC

"World's Finest ", No. 144, Sept. 1964, published by DC Comics.

$3-5   MC

"World's Finest", No. 137, Nov. 1963, published by DC Comics.

$5-8   MC

"Walt Disney's Mickey Mouse and His Sky Adventure", No. 105, Feb. 1966, published by Gold Key.

$2-3   MC

"Walt Disney's Comics and Stories", No. 2, Vol. 25, 1964, published by Gold Key.

$3-5   MC

"Woody Woodpecker", No. 59, Mar. 1960, published by Dell.

$2-3   MC

"Tom and Jerry", No. 136, Nov. 1955, published by DC Comics.

$3-5   MC

"Walt Disney's Uncle Scrooge", No. 25, May 1959, published by Dell.

$10-15   MC

"Fightin' Army", No. 57, Mar. 1964, published by Charlton.

$2-3   MC

"Our Fighting Forces", No. 67, May 1963, published by Charlton.

$5-6   MC

"Army War Heroes", No. 15, Aug. 1966, published by Charlton.

$2-3   MC

"Fightin' Marines", No. 63, May 1965, published by Charlton.

$2-3   MC

"The Lone Ranger", No. 41, Nov. 1951, published by Dell.

$6-8   MC

"Turok, Son of Stone", No. 29, Nov. 1962, published by Dell.

$6-8   MC

"Western Outlaws", No. 21, Aug. 1957, published by Atlas.

$5-8   MC

"Wyatt Earp", No. 13, Aug. 1957, published by Atlas.

$8-12   MC

"Strange Tales", No. 148, Sept. 1966, published by Marvel.

$3-5   MC

"G-Men and the Missing Clues" storybook, by K.H. Eisen, published by Whitman Publishing Co.

1938   3.5in (9cm) high

$15-20   BCAC

"Dan Dunn Plays A Lone Hand" story book, by Norman Marsh. published by Whitman Publishing Co.

1938   3.5in (9cm) high

$15-20   BCAC

FIND OUT MORE...

'The Official Overstreet Comic Book Price Guide', by Robert M. Overstreet, published by Gemstone Publishing, 33rd edition, 2003.

A Shawnee 'Smiley Pig' bank-headed pig cookie jar, the base impressed "Patented Smiley 60 Shawnee USA", the head as a lid with a slot to the top for use as a money bank.

Examine the body and the lid carefully as the lid is heavy and often caused damage if it was not put back on with care.

17.25in (26cm) high

$400-600   **NF**

A CLOSER LOOK AT A COOKIE JAR

Light green is a rare color for a neckerchief.

Smiley Pig was one of the most popular and prolific figural cookie jars produced by Shawnee. It has been made in many different solid and decorated colors since 1942.

He has gilt highlights and trim, which is another rare feature.

The strawberry decals on his body are rare, flowers are much more common.

A rare Shawnee 'Smiley Pig' cookie jar, marked "U.S.A.". c1955

11.5in (29cm) high

$1,000-1,500   **NF**

A rare 1950s McCoy turkey-shaped cookie jar, the base molded "McCoy USA".

9in (23cm) high

$200-300   **NF**

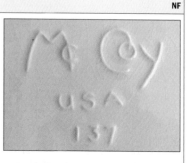

A 1950s McCoy Native American handpainted teepee-shaped cookie jar, base molded "McCoy USA 137".

11.5in (29cm) high

$400-600   **NF**

A Cardinal Chef cookie jar, with transfer for Petits Gateaux (Cookies), impressed "CARDINAL USA", on the back of the neck.

8.75in (22cm) high

$300-500   **NF**

A Cumberley Ware 'Oliver Hardy' ceramic handpainted cookie jar, with gloss glazed bowler, base molded "WC USA".

8.75in (22cm) high

$200-300   **NF**

A 1950s Walt Disney Productions 'Pinocchio' cookie jar.

9.5in (24cm) high

$700-1,000   **NF**

COSTUME & ACCESSORIES

COLLECTORS' NOTES

■ Clothes by globally renowned labels still tend to fetch the highest values when it comes to mid-late 20th century vintage clothes. Look for classic names such as Dior, Chanel, Pucci, and Rhodes. Vivienne Westwood is currently a hot name, but pieces can be very hard to find. Some designer pieces that are only a few years old can be found at far less than their original retail price and may make a good investment if they are typical or from a noted collection.

■ Aim to buy pieces that represent the designer and their signature styles or that reflect the style of the period in terms of look, fit, color, and material. Examine designer labels to ensure that they have not been added to a piece later on – the quality should speak for the name. It's not all about labels however – great pieces indicative of a look or period can be found by lesser names or bearing no name at all, but again look for quality in terms of material, design, fit, and cut.

■ Along with the ever-popular 1960s names of Biba, Quant, and Carnaby Street, 'street' fashion has long been sought after. Values for these clothes, from the more common vintage denims to unusual 'one-off' pieces that give the wearer individuality, have risen. Original vintage sneakers have become hotly sought after, a trend led by the US and Japan, and have spurred a revival for yesterday's styles in 'new' ranges.

■ Fashions come and go, especially in vintage terms, but investing in high quality classics in any given notable 'look' is likely to be the best option. After the popularity of the '60s and '70s, the '80s is touted as the next target for revival. Always look for signs of damage such as excessive wear, tears (unless intended!), sweat marks and stains, as this reduces desirability and value – many pieces are still bought to be worn.

A 1970s Hardy Amies silk dress.

Sir Hardy Amies is known for his classically tailored suits and tweed and wool dresses. In 1955 he was appointed dressmaker to H.M. Queen Elizabeth II.

55in (139.5cm) long

$120-180   **JV**

A 1980s Amor ready-to-wear blue dress.

Born in 1949 in Tangiers, Faycal Amor made use of a new dying process and innovative structures. He created his own label, 'Plein Sud', in 1986.

44in (112cm) long

$280-320   **RR**

A 1960s Christian Dior military-style wool dress.

After Dior's death in 1957, Marc Bohan took over designing for the label. This dress echoes the feminine 'New Look' of the 1950s.

37.5in (95cm) long

$300-400   **HP**

A Chanel sleeveless tunic dress, with square mother-of-pearl buttons.

2000   31in (118cm) long

$300-500   **RR**

A Robert Dorland lime green silk dress.

54in (137cm) long

$120-180   **JV**

A green evening dress and bolero, by Vernier Franka, London.

60in (152.5cm) long

$220-280   **JV**

A 1980s Christian Dior wool dress and jacket.

The striking colors and shoulder pads are typical of the 1980s 'power dressing' trend. The style was adopted by young and upwardly mobile professionals (yuppies) to whom labels, and moreover display of labels, became of immense importance to status.

Size 0

$400-600   **RR**

A 1950s Hartnell dress.

40in (101.5cm) long

$150-200   **RR**

A 1970s Hartnell dress.

Size 12

$120-180   **RR**

A Guy Laroche black lace evening dress.

Laroche once said "It is my intention to try and adapt haute couture to modern requirements: to make dresses that are simple and chic". As well as re-introducing bright colors to collections, his evening dresses are known for a touch of the extravagant, including lace, beading and sequins.

35.5in (90cm) long

$300-400   **HP**

A Lilian eau de nil silk evening dress, with hand-beaded decoration.

55in (139.5cm) long

$150-200   **JV**

A 1980s Bruce Oldfield pink and green silk dress.

St Martin's School of Art graduate Oldfield launched his own label in 1978. He designed for Jerry Hall and Diana Ross and is famous for his evening wear. The puffed sleeves typify the 1980s.

55in (139.5cm) long

$280-320   **RR**

A CLOSER LOOK AT A ZANDRA RHODES GOWN

The neckline is hand-beaded, a motif repeated around the collar which has been cut to allow the printed design to form a garland pattern.

Rhodes is still a popular name and her designs are hotly collected – especially if vintage and typical. When worn, the collar, fitted waist and full, flowing silk skirt would create a look indicative of her style.

Rhodes' style is highly idiosyncratic and fanciful and often inspired by romantic themes – here the design harks back to Victorian and Edwardian styles.

Although the form is reminiscent of a bygone age, the bright colors and style of the printed pattern is highly evocative of the psychedelic 1960s and 1970s.

A 1960s Oscar de la Renta dress.

Oscar de la Renta was born in 1932. He has become known for his opulent and romantic designs, often with ornate and extravagant patterning or detailing. Cinched waists are a particular hallmark of his designs.

38.5in (98cm) long

$220-280   **RR**

A Laura Phillips black hand-beaded dress.

50.5in (128.5cm) long

$120-180   **JV**

A 1970s Zandra Rhodes silk dress, with hand-beaded collar.

51in (129.5cm) long

$700-1,000   **RR**

COSTUME & ACCESSORIES

A 1980s Zandra Rhodes dress.

45in (114.5cm) long

$150-200 RR

A black polyester cocktail dress, by Rino Ross, with beaded bow detail.

$22-28 BR

A 1980s Salvatori silk dress.

38in (96.5cm) long

$220-280 RR

A 1980s Yves Saint Laurent printed cotton dress.

When buying famous names it pays to 'learn your labels'. A brand such as Yves Saint Laurent, as well as Versace and Ralph Lauren, will have many different ranges from the top-of-the-tree couture pieces down to the more commonly found high street ranges. Labels belonging to the different ranges will vary in wording, look and color and often change over time.

57in (145cm) long

$220-280 RR

A 1970s Jean Varon dress.

54in (137cm) long

$120-180 JV

A 1960s Jean Varon printed dress.

Jean Varon was the label used by designer John Bates, who achieved popular success in the 1960s. Varon became costume designer for TV series 'The Avengers' in the 1960s, dressing popular characters such as Emma Peel (Diana Rigg) and Tara King (Linda Thorson). It is said that a design seen on screen one evening could be bought by 1960s fashionistas from his store the next day! Fabrics printed with strong graphics and dramatic designs were typical – look out for catsuits and black and white pieces like those worn by Mrs Peel.

56in (142cm) long

$150-200 JV

A chiffon dress, with matching cummerbund.

c1960 52in (132cm) long

$280-320 HP

A black polyester long dress, by Fashion III by Style Rite, with floral decoration.

$12-18 BR

A 1960s Miss Magninn printed silk dress.

56in (142cm) long

$100-150 JV

A violet crêpe silk dress.
57in (145cm) long

$180-220   **JV**

An unworn 1960s Italian dress.
50in (127cm) long

$100-150   **HP**

A 1960s chiffon dress, with sequin detail.

The contrast of the black top with its scarf-like neck and the psychedelically colored, pleated and patterned skirt makes this piece not only extravagant, but also firmly rooted in the 1960s.

$320-380   **HP**

A red and white shirt dress.

$60-90   **BR**

A copper knitted polyester long dress, by George's Factory, California.

$15-25   **BR**

A 1950s brown patterned day dress.

$60-90   **BR**

A black lace cocktail dress, with beaded detail.

$50-70   **BR**

A 1930s terracotta crepe silk dress.

$60-90   **BR**

A turquoise short dress, with a diamanté belt buckle.

$40-60   **BR**

COSTUME & ACCESSORIES

A 1950s pink cocktail dress.

43.5in (110.5cm) long

$150-200 RR

A 1960s Saks Fifth Avenue silk dress.

Saks moved to its current home on New York's most prestigious shopping street in 1924. Saks' couture and high-end ready-to-wear department has stocked designs by Chanel, Madame Vionnet, Schiaparelli and, in the 1970s, Emilio Pucci. The couture department was closed during the 1970s.

40in (101.5cm) long

$150-200 RR

A 1950s Youth Guild of NY silk plaid dress.

Production from the late 1940s was dominated by clothes for teenagers, with a younger take on the influential 'New Look'. Much of the range was designed by Anne Fogarty who remained with the company until 1950. From 1960 to the mid-1970s, Liz Claiborne designed for the label.

42in (106.5cm) long

$100-150 RR

A Shearing Grecian-style dress.

c1960   52in (132cm) long

$180-220 HP

A copper sequinned short cocktail dress, with brown chiffon cape.

$40-60 BR

A 1950s London Town Model embroidered dress.

This dress is in the 'New Look' style, developed by Christian Dior in 1947, with its elegantly full skirt, cinched waist and fitted bodice. The dress is also valuable and desirable because of the level of hand-embroidered (still strikingly brightly colored) decoration on the bodice and skirt.

45in (114.5cm) long

$400-600 HP

An orange and purple paisley dress and top, by Mister D, the top hand-beaded.

$40-60 BR

A cream long dress, with pink and gold bodice.

$25-35 BR

A silver and gold metallic quilted short dress.

$25-35 BR

A studded red leather short dress.

$30-50   **BR**

A yellow cotton sleeveless blouse, with lace trim and pin tuck front.

$15-25   **CCL**

A cream top, by Isla Engel, decorated with applied flowers and diamanté.

$30-40   **CCL**

A 1960s white ribbon Jackie O-style jacket.

$80-120   **CCL**

A 1950s paper nylon slip, with cream colored ribbon.

$30-40   **CCL**

A red gingham full circle skirt, with lace trim.

$50-70   **CCL**

A handpainted Mexican skirt, with Aztec motifs painted in gold-colored paint, marked "S".

$80-120   **CCL**

A 1960s double-breasted horse hair coat, with a wide collar.

$280-320   **BR**

A striped fun fur coat, with leather trim.

$40-60   **BR**

A fur trimmed black coat, by Evans Furs exclusively at Crowleys.

$30-50   **BR**

COSTUME & ACCESSORIES

COLLECTORS' NOTES

■ Over the past decade men have considered both grooming and fashionable clothing more closely, and as a result there has been a resurgence in interest in vintage styles. However, values for vintage men's clothing are often low compared to women's clothing. Consequently, famous name or well-made bargains still abound as the market has yet to reach its maturity. Many of the same rules apply here as to women's clothing.

A brown satin Western-style shirt, with cream cuffs and shoulders, with hand-stitched decoration.

$30-50 BR

A beige Western-style shirt, decorated with rural scenes, with brown cuffs and shoulders and black tassel trim.

$15-25 BR

An olive Western-style shirt, by Levi's, with hand-stitched mushroom decoration.

$25-35 BR

A blue printed Western-style shirt, from the Kenny Rogers Western Collection by Caravan, with navy piping.

$25-35 BR

A blue and silver Western-style shirt, by Caravan, with ruffle front.

$25-35 BR

A cream satin Western-style shirt, with hand-stitched floral decoration.

Look for western-style shirts produced in the 1940s and 1950s, the most popular decades for collectors and aficionados. Styles like this are still made today, so check the material and any decoration to date a shirt. Gabardine and heavier satins were frequently used for early shirts and the embroidery was hand-stitched, using a triple stitch, rather than machine-stitched. Embroidered pictures such as scenery or cowboy boots command a premium. Brands, such as 'H Bar C', are important and can also help to date examples.

c1955

$60-90 BR

A checked Western-style shirt, by Ron Rigo CA, with light blue cuffs and shoulders.

$15-25 BR

A cream Western-style shirt, by Mid Western Garment Co., with brown sleeves and collar.

$10-15 BR

A WWII embroidered black velvet souvenir jacket, decorated with a tiger and "Japan".

$120-180 BR

A Vietnam War embroidered nylon souvenir jacket, embroidered with Snoopy.

$150-200 BR

A US Navy woolen tunic, with white piping.

$70-100 BR

A 1960s Levi's 'Big E' denim jacket.

The 'e' in the Levi name on the red pocket tag is large, enabling it to be dated to a specific vintage period and making it very popular with collectors.

23in (58.5cm) long

$80-120 BR

A WWII embroidered silk souvenir jacket, decorated with a dragon and "Shanghai China 1948".

Wartime souvenir jackets are still being made today, but it is the period pieces made up to the early 1950s that are sought after and valuable. It can be extremely hard to tell modern from vintage examples and the best way is to handle as many authentic pieces as possible. Areas to examine closely include the zip, which should be old, and any embroidery which must be hand sewn, rather than machined. Older examples also often have the date embroidered on them, but period dates can appear on modern examples too. Older examples from the 1940s also tend to have satin/silk on both sides, with examples from the 1950s being made from satin/silk and velvet.

$600-900 BR

A pair of 1960s Levi denim jeans, without a big 'E' on label.

By introducing the 'Engineered' and 'Anti-Fit' ranges, Levi has retained a top spot for jeans, despite seeing a slight low during the 1990s with their classic 501 brand. The most expensive vintage Levi's found to date are also the oldest known and are owned by Levi Strauss and Co., who bought them in an online auction on eBay. They date from 1880-1885, roughly a decade after denims were introduced by Levi Strauss in 1873 as the original hard wearing 'work wear' for manual workers. They were found in mud in a mining town in Nevada and fetched a staggering $46,532!

38in (96.5cm) long

$150-200 BR

A CLOSER LOOK AT A PUCCI TIE

Pucci is usually associated with women's clothing, with men's ties still being affordable. Look out for Pucci menswear, such as shirts and suits, as it was purportedly only made for five years.

Now that Pucci has been re-launched (including a range of ties!), with the backing of luxury goods conglomerate LVMH, it is likely that original pieces will be even more sought-after.

Art Nouveau-style flowers updated with 1960s psychedelic colors – purples, blues, hot pinks, and yellows – are typical of Pucci, as are geometrical designs.

Genuine Pucci products bear the name 'Emilio' as part of the printed design. Check carefully for original labels and silk linings woven with the 'Emilio' signature.

A 1960s/70s Pucci black, blue and turquoise silk men's tie, with label marked "Italy" and "Emilio Pucci".

3.25in (8cm) widest

$50-70   **NOR**

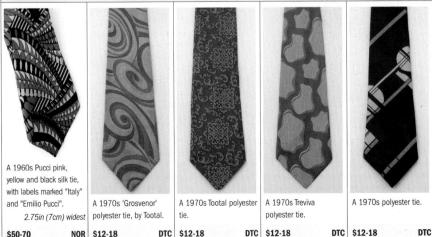

A 1960s Pucci pink, yellow and black silk tie, with labels marked "Italy" and "Emilio Pucci".

2.75in (7cm) widest

$50-70 NOR	A 1970s 'Grosvenor' polyester tie, by Tootal.	A 1970s Tootal polyester tie.	A 1970s Treviva polyester tie.	A 1970s polyester tie.
	$12-18 DTC	**$12-18** DTC	**$12-18** DTC	**$12-18** DTC

A Govan Crusaders team jacket, red with cream trim.

$70-100 BR

A NBCHS Vikings team jacket, by Hunters Manf. Co., blue wool with cream shoulders and trim.

$30-50 BR

A St Anthony's college jacket, by Marv Holland, burgundy wool with cream shoulders and trim.

These jackets are still being made today, although modern examples usually have company brand names instead of college names. Look out for examples from the 1950s especially, but also up to the 1970s, as these tend to be the most popular. The years the original owner attended the particular college are often found on patches on authentic period examples.

A Fort Edmonton yellow nylon college jacket, by Marv Holland.

A green nylon track top, by 'Boar', with white trim.

$15-25 BR **$15-25** BR **$50-70** BR

A 1980s nylon Patagonia jacket.

The Patagonia brand is particularly popular in Japan, perhaps due to the company's concern for the environment. Early examples from the 1980s have a larger label than those made throughout the 1990s.

$50-70 BR

A red and blue 'Sun & Surf' nylon jacket.

$10-15 BR

A Brooks ladies' nylon jacket.

$15-25 BR

A yellow ladies nylon short coat.

$10-15 BR

A red Patagonia children's waterproof jacket.

$10-15 BR

A pale green Patagonia fleece jacket.

$100-150 BR

An Adidas navy sweat shirt, with light blue, green, and white transfer decoration.

$25-35 BR

A Champion black sweat shirt.

$12-18 BR

A "Bears Cheerleader" navy sweat shirt, with orange transfer decoration.

$12-18 BR

A Nike green sweat shirt, with white and yellow transfer decoration.

Graphic design student Carolyn Davidson was originally paid just $35 for her now legendary 'Swoosh' design in 1971, at the birth of what was then a small company. Rough dates can be found by looking at the style and color of the tick and the word 'Nike'. Look out for currently popular orange ticks where the word Nike is in blocky capital letters, indicating a date from 1978 to the mid-1980s.

$30-50 BR

An Adidas burgundy two-piece tracksuit.

Adidas, Champion, and Nike are amongst the most popular names for vintage sportswear. It was not until the 1950s that most working men had enough spare time to play sports. During the 1980s, with the meteoric rise of celebrity sports stars, what was previously a form of 'workwear' became the height of fashion.

$50-70 BR

A pink toweling two-piece tracksuit, by Baycrest.

$15-25 BR

A black sweat shirt, with Mickey Mouse transfer decoration to front.

The mid-to late 1980s saw a fad for sweat shirts featuring popular cartoon characters. Look for authentic period examples which use a printed, rather than woven, label.

$25-35 BR

A knitted cotton one-piece playsuit, by Dominique.

$12-18 BR

A yellow bowling shirt, by Swingter, with brown trim, with "Victory Five" applied to the back.

$80-120 BR

A ladies teal blue bowling shirt, by Air Flow, with pin-shaped buttons, with "Barton Construction Bozeman" stitched on the back.

$60-90 BR

A pink bowling shirt, Hill & Dale Sports Ware, by Gilman, with black trim and marlin detail.

Look out for added details such as differently colored trims, colorful embroidery, people's, teams or sponsor's names and pictorial logos, especially if related to bowling. Men's versions tend to be more popular than ladies' examples, but both are highly collectible – and wearable – particularly if from the most popular decades of the 1950s and 1960s.

$120-180 BR

A blue bowling shirt, by Master Bowler, with "Schrader Bros. Super Mkt." stitched on back.

$30-50 BR

A Dodgers red V-neck T-shirt, with navy and red trim and white transfer decoration.

$10-15 BR

A Nike navy vest, with light blue trim and yellow, white, and navy transfer decoration.

$12-18 BR

A Ralph Lauren blue polo shirt.

Ralph Lauren once said "I'm not just selling clothes, I'm offering a world, a philosophy of life". This is certainly true of his ever-expanding empire, which includes homeware as well as ranges of men's and ladies' clothing. His first designs were launched in 1967 (his first menswear in 1968) and were based around the polo player that later became his logo. The polo shirt is typical of his elitist, 'Ivy league' look as worn by East Coast 'W.A.S.Ps'. Vintage examples are often made in better quality cottons and are available in colors that are no longer produced today.

$7-10 BR

COSTUME & ACCESSORIES

A pair of 1980s Adidas 'Montreal' white ladies' sneakers, with lavender trim.

$10-15   BR

A pair of Adidas 'Lady Boston' lavender ladies' sneakers.

$30-50   BR

A pair of Champion Air white and blue sneakers.

$25-35   BR

A pair of Asics Tiger sneakers.

The famous stripes on Onitsuka Tiger's Asics brand sneakers were first seen on their 1966 'Mexico' training shoe, worn by the Japanese team in the 1968 Olympic Games.

$15-25   BR

A CLOSER LOOK AT A PAIR OF SNEAKERS

John Boyd Dunlop developed the world's first commercial pneumatic tire. He used his invention of bonding canvas to rubber to produce basic footwear in the 1830s.

Although it has remained constant for over 70 years with its Dunlopillo sole and distinctive styling, the design has changed slightly and no longer includes the curving 'S' flash.

A pair of Nike Air white & black sneakers.

$18-22   BR

Green Flash sports shoes were introduced in 1933. They were worn by legendary tennis player Fred Perry when he won the 1934, 1935, and 1936 Wimbledon men's singles championships which stood as a record for 40 years.

A much-remembered favorite of grown-up schoolboys the world over, the Green Flash has recently enjoyed renewed popularity with the revival of vintage sneaker styles and continues to be a style icon.

A pair of original Dunlop 'Green Flash' 1555 tennis shoes.

$25-35   BR

A pair of Reebok white ladies' sneakers.

$10-15   BR

A pair of Nike Air Force Delta Hi-Top sneakers.

Considered a classic, the Air Force was released in 1982 and was the first basketball shoe to have a full length 'air' sole. Look out for earlier examples of the many designs, especially in rare gray.

c1988   10.5in (27cm) long

$60-90   BR

A pair of black cowboy boots, with stitched decoration.

$40-60 **BR**

A pair of plain black cowboy boots, with simple stitched decoration.

$25-35 **BR**

A pair of gray leather cowboy boots, with snakeskin toes.

$40-60 **BR**

A pair of gray cowboy boots, with cream eagle head detail.

$30-50 **BR**

A pair black cowboy boots, with cream and turquoise details.

The condition, color, and quality of the detail, from patterning to accented decoration, are the usual indicators of value for cowboy boots.

$40-60 **BR**

A pair of light gray cowboy boots, with gray snakeskin detail.

$40-60 **BR**

A pair of terracotta cowboy boots, by Tony Lama.

$50-70 **BR**

A pair of three-colored ladies cowboy boots.

$25-35 **BR**

A pair of bronze colored ladies cowboy boots, with cut-out detail.

$30-50 **BR**

A pair of 1940s black leather utility wear peep-toe shoes, with 'diamond' pattern.

8.5in (22cm) long

$30-50 PC

A pair of 1940s black leather utility wear peep-toe shoes, with cross-over decoration.

9.5in (24cm) long

$30-50 PC

A pair of black vinyl and wood clogs.

c1960   9.5in (24cm) long

$8-12 AAC

A pair of 1920s men's speed skates by Canada Cycle and Motor.

11.5in (29cm) long

$50-70 TYA

A pair of 1940s gray suede utility wear shoes, by Oral, with bow decoration and in original box.

9in (23cm) long

$50-70 PC

A CLOSER LOOK AT A PAIR OF SHOES & PURSE

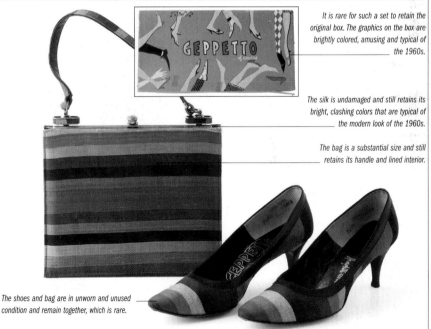

It is rare for such a set to retain the original box. The graphics on the box are brightly colored, amusing and typical of the 1960s.

The silk is undamaged and still retains its bright, clashing colors that are typical of the modern look of the 1960s.

The bag is a substantial size and still retains its handle and lined interior.

The shoes and bag are in unworn and unused condition and remain together, which is rare.

A rare 1960s multi-colored bag and matching shoes, by Hemphill Wells Geppetto, in Geppetto box.

bag 9in (23cm) wide

$60-90 NOR

COLLECTORS' NOTES

- Beaded purses have been fashionable since the early 19thC, and are the most collectible form of vintage bag. They can also be the most valuable – a reflection of the hours of work that went into them, and their fragile nature.

- The bright colors and intricate workmanship often mean they are more for display than use, but that does not diminish their appeal.

- From 1910-1930 designs were inspired by flowers, chinoiserie, Eastern carpets and romantic medieval castles and Venetian scenes.

- In the 1910s and 1920s, manufacturers used Venetian or Bohemian beads. Venetian beads are very small, slightly iridescent and with a pure color that does not fade. Bohemian beads tend to be larger, coarser and fade over time.

- High quality examples were made in France and Belgium during the late 1950s and early 1960s using fine beadwork, with attention to detail and elegant designs.

- Clasps and handles are usually metal and often inset with glass or semi-precious stones. Purses were often lined with silk, which may have deteriorated far more than the exterior. A sympathetic replacement can enhance the value of a bag.

- When buying beaded purses, consider whether the design suits the beads it is made from.

A CLOSER LOOK AT A BEADED PURSE

A 1940s purse, by Caron of Texas, with hand-decorated front.

9in (23cm) wide

$60-90 FAN

A beaded purse, by Caron of Texas, hand-decorated with butterflies and jewels.

11.5in (29cm) high

$60-90 FAN

The black fabric has been hand decorated with gold braid along the top.

A design of scattered leaves dominates the center of the purse.

A tapestry purse, by Caron of Texas, with applied leaves and sequins.

The rear of the bag is made of a contrasting tapestry fabric.

Sequins and gold and copper tone leaves have been used to embellish the surface.

11.75in (30cm) wide

$70-100 FAN

A 1950s hand-decorated purse, by Caron of Texas, with original sales tag.

11in (28cm) wide

$70-100 FAN

A 1950s hand-decorated purse, by Caron of Texas.

14.5in (37cm) wide

$50-80 FAN

A hand-decorated purse, by Caron of Texas, with butterflies and jewels.

11.5in (29cm) wide

$60-90 FAN

A 1950s plastic-coated linen purse, by Souré NY, with applied gold threading, studs and porcelain plaques featuring pastoral vignettes, leather interior.

11.75in (30cm) wide

$50-70   **FAN**

A 1950s black and pale green embroidered purse, probably by Souré NY, with applied beads, glass and leaves.

12.5in (32cm) wide

$100-150   **FAN**

A 1950s hand-decorated purse, by Souré NY, with a Bakelite handle.

13.75in (35cm) wide

$100-150   **FAN**

A 1950s black felt purse, by Souré NY, with applied paste.

11in (28cm) wide

$70-100   **FAN**

A 19thC scenic beaded purse, with metal frame.

7.25in (18.5cm) high

$220-280   **GMC**

A 1920s beaded purse, with Bakelite frame decorated with leaves.

8in (20.5cm) high

$400-600   **GMC**

A 1920s beaded evening purse, with a floral beaded motif, the gold metal embossed frame decorated with red and green semi-precious stone inclusions and a pendant with a colored rhinestone, a beaded fringe and chain handle.

9in (23cm) long

$300-500   **AHL**

A 1920s beaded purse.

6.75in (18.5cm) wide

$60-90   **GMC**

A 1930s white beadwork and woven gilt thread purse, with acorn-shaped ball clasps, with original hand mirror and pocket, with label reading "Bags by Josef HAND BEADED IN FRANCE".

9.75in (25cm) wide

$100-150   **ROX**

A 1920s silver sequin evening purse.

8.5in (21.5cm) wide

$70-100   **GMC**

A green glass beadwork purse, the cylindrical body with tucked 'loose' covering, lid with mirror to inside and lined throughout with brown silk lining.

c1920   *5in (12.5cm) high*

$180-220   **BY**

A 1930s French hand-beaded evening purse, with beaded and enamel frame and clasp marked "The French Bag Shop, 1116 Lincoln Road, Miami Beach, Florida."

9in (23cm) wide

$300-500   **RG**

A 1940s French gold and colored bead clutch bag, with an enameled clasp, decorated with micro-beading.

10in (25cm) wide

$600-900   **AHL**

A 1940s French hand-beaded evening purse, with tambour (tiny chain stitch) embroidery flowers, with gilt snake chain handles, black satin-lined with matching satin coin purse, marked "Made in France Pierre Marot Paris", unused.

10.25in (26cm) wide

$300-500   **RG**

A 1940s Dubinette gunmetal colored glass bead box purse.

6in (15cm) wide

$100-150   **FAN**

A 1940s blue carnival bead purse.

7.75in (19.5cm) wide

$100-150   **FAN**

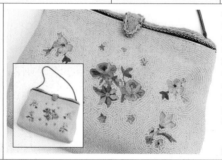

A 1950s mother-of-pearl sequin evening purse.

8in (20.5cm) wide

$50-70   **FAN**

A 1950s French hand-beaded evening purse, made for the American market, embroidered with hand-beaded frame set with two porcelain, Limoges plaques depicting on 18thC courting couple, cream satin-lined with matching coin purse and snake chain handle, marked "Made in France by Hand, Walborg".

8in (20cm) wide

$300-400   **RG**

A 1950s French metal bead evening purse, the bag and handle in silver and gold beads, yellow satin lined, tagged "Hand Made in France", the clasp with rhinestones in an acorn shape.

9.5in (24cm) wide

$220-280   **RG**

A cream and white beadwork purse, with circular catch lifting to open, interior lined with cream silk and with woven label reading "K&G Charlet Bag", with metal frame and gilt metal chain.

8.5in (21.5cm) wide

$180-220   **BY**

A 1950s Belgian white and gold-colored glass beadwork purse, the ball catches inset with faceted rhinestones/glass jewels, lined with cream silk, with label reading "Jorelle Bags MADE IN BELGIUM".

9.75in (24.5cm) wide

$120-180   ROX

A rare flexible plastic and painted wood poodle purse, possibly 1950s American, inlaid with gold thread and decorated with shell and bead, with wood support and gold-plated handle.

11.75in (30cm) wide

$400-600   SM

An early 1950s French black evening purse, decorated with rhinestone decoration, with a silver filigree frame, with a chain handle and cream satin lining.

8in (20cm) wide

$180-220   AHL

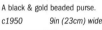

A 1950s three-way convertible purse, with a detachable reversible cover, cream and gold to one side and black to the other.

9in (23cm) wide

$50-70   FAN

A 1950s small evening purse, made in Hong Kong, decorated with faux pearl oval beads, small yellow and green glass beads, green bugle beads and rhinestones, with an embossed metal frame, chain strap and green satin lining.

6.75in (17cm) wide

$300-400   AHL

A black & gold beaded purse.

c1950   9in (23cm) wide

$60-90   GMC

An unmarked 1950s beaded purse, with gold flowers.

8.5in (21.5cm) wide

$120-180   FAN

A large 1950s black fabric purse, with gold and black metal frame, a painted banjo motif and plastic gold flowers with gem insets and a leather handle.

14in (36cm) wide

$300-400   AHL

A 1950s hand-decorated purse, by Veldore of Texas.

9.25in (23.5cm) high

$60-90   FAN

A 1970s brocade purse, by La Jeunesse, studded with faux gems with gold metal surrounds, some with gold foil sparkles, the bead chain strap with multi-colored diamantés interspersed.

8.75in (22cm) wide

$400-600   AHL

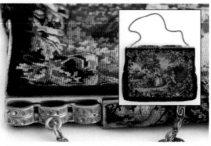

A floral tapestry purse, the gilt metal frame with applied enameled metal Indian scrolling motifs and orange hardstone, the catch with hardstone cabochon, interior lined with cream silk, with suede-covered hand mirror.

c1910   *6.25in (16cm) wide*

$100-150   **ROX**

A 1920s woven tapestry purse, showing an 18thC Watteau-style pastoral scene, with gilt metal frame with applied semi-circles with pink painted dots, and padded tapestry strips, gilt metal chain, lined with cream silk.

9in (23cm) wide

$220-280   **ROX**

A 1930s pink woven wool tapestry purse, showing fish swimming over coral, with gilt metal frame inlaid with orange glass cabochons, lined with fawn silk.

9.25in (23.5cm) wide

$220-280   **ROX**

A 1960s tapestry gilt metal and vinyl bag, with brown vinyl handle, and metal button clasp, lined throughout with beige vinyl.

15in (38cm) long

$70-100   **ROX**

A 1950s white and brown woven and plush figural purse, showing a seated lute player with lady seated at a table, with gilt metal frame and button clasp in the form of an opening rose, lined with white silk and with gilt stamping to interior pocket reading 'Delill', pocket with original hand mirror in envelope, with chain handle and original shop gilt card tag reading 'A Delill Creation'.

12.25in (31cm) high

$70-100   **ROX**

A 1950s woven wool purse, with two donkeys eating daisies, with faux tortoiseshell plastic clasp and handle, with similar catch, lined with green fabric, with original purse in matching green fabric and hand mirror.

9.75in (25cm) wide

$220-280   **ROX**

A CLOSER LOOK AT A TELEPHONE PURSE

This telephone purse was a cult object in the 1950s and 1960s. It was still being made in the 1970s.

The telephone could be plugged into a telephone socket so that calls could actually be made from them.

It was also made in white and red patent leather.

This example is in full working order.

A 1960s American 'Telephone' purse, in patent leather with an embossed design.

15in (38cm) wide

$600-900   **AHL**

A 1990s painted composition box purse, in the shape of a dalmatian's head, with black fabric interior, with label reading "TIMMY WOODS Beverley Hills Collection Handmade in THE PHILIPPINES", with elasticated catch.

A 1950s Californian brown alligator purse, by 'Sydney' - stamped "Sydney California".

10.5in (27cm) wide

$220-280   **RG**

A small, early 1950s red leather bucket purse, with two handles, polka dot lining, and a mirror on the inside of the lid.

8.75in (22cm) wide

$100-150   **AHL**

Former ballet dancer Timmy Woods started designing and manufacturing purses in 1985. Her eye-catching designs were immediately snapped up by stores such as Bergdorf, Bendel's, and Bloomingdales. She took a break from purse design to work for Ken Done for the U. S. A. and B. J. Designs. Then, following serious injury in a car accident, Timmy's father, a real estate developer, suggested she join his lucrative business and include her design skills into real estate marketing. Although her new career proved lucrative it didn't hold the same appeal as the design world. In 1992, inspired by primitive carved wooden boxes she found at a market in the Philippines, Timmy launched Timmy Woods Beverly Hills. Timmy's purses are carried and collected by celebrities including Liz Taylor, Diana Ross, Jody Fisher, Melanie Griffith, and Hillary Clinton.

4.5in (11.5cm) high

$150-200   **ROX**

A CLOSER LOOK AT A BELLESTONE PURSE

Bellestone is one of the most popular names with collectors of vintage bags because the company used high quality skins which are flexible and durable and so have withstood the test of time.

The interiors of Bellestone purses usually feature pockets and are signed Bellestone. Condition affects value – especially interiors: linings can be suede and include change purses and mirrors.

The simple style of the bag is clean and classic.

This bag is in a roomy yet compact size making it a perfect everyday purse.

A 1950s American black alligator skin purse by Bellestone, un-used.

10in (25cm) wide

$300-400   **RG**

A 1960s black crocodile skin purse, with black enamel frame, marked "Genuine Crocodile".

13in (33cm) wide

$300-400   **RG**

A 1960s-70s Coronado leather purse, made in Spain, with stitched detailing, with a brass frame and feet.

15.75in (40cm) wide

$600-900   **AHL**

A 1960s orange plastic clutch bag, with metal frame, lined with fawn fabric, with gilt metal clasp.

16.75in (42.5cm) wide

$40-60   **ROX**

A 1970s Fendi brown leather purse with faux tortoiseshell closure, removable leather strap, and embossed central logo, with change purse.

Fendi was founded in Rome in 1925 by Edoardo and Adele Fendi and is famous for its luxury leather goods.

10.5in (26cm) wide

$180-220   **TA**

A 1960s American pink faux snakeskin vinyl purse, with printed paisley fabric lining and clear polythene internal purse stamped 'Ethan Bags' on gilt metal chain, with silver finished plastic catch.

14.25in (36.5cm) wide

$40-60   **ROX**

A mid-to late 1960s poodle sequin purse.

Sold as a craft kit, this type of bag would be hand-decorated by the purchaser. Although many designs were available, poodles are among the most popular and command higher prices.

10.5in (26.5cm) high

$120-180   **FAN**

A 1950s classic black velvet purse, by Garay, with attached coin purse.

9.5in (24cm) high

$60-90   **FAN**

A CLOSER LOOK AT A GUILD CREATIONS PURSE

The bag is stamped on the inside with the company's logo.

The clasp is made from filigree metal decorated with rhinestones. This is a typical Guild Creations touch.

The felt is pleated at the top on both sides.

The bag is lined with satin and two small internal compartments.

A 1950s Guild Creations black felt purse with cathedral type frame, in used condition.

11in (28cm) wide

$100-150   **FAN**

A 1950s/60s leopard print felt Ingber purse.

12in (30.5cm) wide

$100-150   **FAN**

A 1970s woven cotton psychedelic pattern tote bag.

13in (33cm) high

$30-50   **MTS**

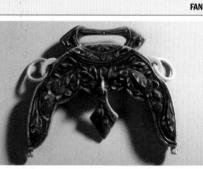

A 1920s fruits and greenery plastic purse frame.

Many collectors buy vintage bag frames and make new bags to fit them.

4.5in (11.5cm) wide

$150-200   **GMC**

A 1950s Antler faux leopard skin vanity case.

11.5in (29.5cm) high

$70-100   **MA**

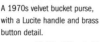

A 1970s velvet bucket purse, with a Lucite handle and brass button detail.

10.25in (26cm) wide

$180-220   **AHL**

A 1940s amber bucket purse, with a Bakelite lid, bronze beading to the body and handle, mirror fixed to the inside lid.

8in (20cm) wide

$280-320   **AHL**

A 1950s translucent purse, by JR USA, with gold vein decoration.

8.25in (21cm) high

$50-70 **FAN**

A CLOSER LOOK AT A LUCITE PURSE

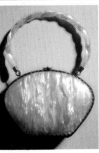

The purse is fully lined in gold satin and has one interior pocket.

The clear Lucite handle is hinged.

This cylindrical bag is made from Lucite and embossed, basketweave, gold-tone metal. The design was patented in 1945.

The purse has all four spherical brass feet.

A 1950s silver Lucite purse, by Dorset-Rex, 5th Avenue, with gold metal panel and gold effect ball feet, with a clear Lucite handle.

7in (18cm) wide

$300-400 **AHL**

A 1950s resin-effect fitted purse.

6.5in (16.5cm) wide

$100-150 **GMC**

A 1950s gray mottled Lucite box purse, with circular handle, the moiré silk lining with pockets.

9.5in (24cm) high

$300-500 **ROX**

A 1950s Lucite vanity purse, with fitted interior.

6.5in (16.5cm) wide

$120-180 **GMC**

An American gold mesh purse.

Metal mesh purses were first made from precious metals in the 1820s, and by the end of the century mesh coin and finger purses, inspired by the trend for Medieval fashion, were in vogue. However, they were handmade and therefore expensive. In 1908 A.C. Pratt patented a mesh machine which meant affordable, mass produced bags could be made. In the 1920s designs started to be screen printed onto the mesh. The style was also a hit during the disco craze of the 1970s.

Mesh purses should be stored flat to prevent the mesh from buckling. Companies such as US firm Whiting and Davis – probably the biggest and most famous mesh bag maker – continue to make mesh bags today.

A marbleized silver Lucite purse, with carved leaf design, double handles and scrolling initials "RJG" to the lid, and clear Lucite feet.

6.75in (17cm) wide

$300-400 **AHL**

A cut-steel beaded purse.

c1910 9in (22.5cm) high

$70-100 **GMC**

c1920

6.5in (16.5cm) high

$100-150 **GMC**

An Art Deco bakelite compact, decorated with a lady's head.	An Art Deco compact, in green and silver, some damage to enamel on base.	A powder compact by Coty, Paris, with printed powder puff decoration in peach and gold.	A 1950s compact, with clear, purple and black paste decoration.
c1930 3.25in (8.5cm) d	c1930 3in (7.5cm) diam	c1930 2in (5cm) diam	3in (7.5cm) diam
$150-200 TDG	**$80-120** TDG	**$60-90** TDG	**$100-150** TDG

A CLOSER LOOK AT A COMPACT

The bright orange color and the design of the two stylized ladies is typically 1950s, with hairstyles that speak of the period and are derived from the 1930s.

American company Richard Hudnut is a known and collected name and produced a number of compacts and vanity cases.

Based in New York, they also owned the well-known DuBarry name.

The transfer of the ladies is unscratched and intact and the materials used are still in very good condition.

A 1940s/1950s 'Three Flowers' powder compact by Richard Hudnut, in paper.

2.75in (7cm) diam

$40-60   TDG

A Coty face powder compact, in original box, with orange and gilt decoration.

The noted maker, brightly colored and complex design of the compact and the fact that it retains its original pictorial box make this a desirable example.

c1930

box 3.75in (9.5cm) wide

$180-220   TDG

A French Art Deco compact, with lovebirds.

c1925   3in (7.5cm) wide

$150-200   TDG

A rare 1920s/1930s Bourgois 'Evening in Paris' compact.

3.25in (8.5cm) wide

$120-180   TDG

A CLOSER LOOK AT A FAN

The scenes of courting lovers are delicately and skillfully handpainted on silk – a more desirable and valuable feature than printed scenes on paper.

The leaf has much additional decoration. Panels have been cut out and lined with gauze, which is still intact. Gold-colored threads have been woven into patterns incorporating sequins.

The overall condition is excellent, with bright colors and no tears, stains or losses to the silk leaf or sticks.

The sticks and guards are made from mother-of-pearl, a luxury material, and have been cut and painted with delicate, typically late-19thC designs.

A delicate French folding fan, with mother-of-pearl monture, the silk and mesh leaf with three cartouches boldly painted with couples, enclosed within ornate sequins.

c1880   9.5in (24.5cm) long

$1,500-2,000   **HD**

A 19thC fan, paper leaf painted in body color with a lady and her suitor in a country setting, with ornately carved and pierced bone sticks and silver and gilt decoration, unusual guards with sea horse heads, some damage.

10.75 (27cm) high

$150-200   **BONM**

A mid-19thC Cantonese export fan, paper leaf painted with courtiers with applied ivory faces and silk robes, pierced and carved ivory sticks and fretwork guards, gilt metal rivets and silk tassels, some damage, in original lacquered box.

11in (28cm) long

$120-180   **BONM**

An 1880s sterling lipstick holder on chain, engraved with foliate designs.

2in (5cm) high

$12-18   **TAB**

A late 19thC to early 20thC fan, with a point de gaze leaf and mother-of-pearl sticks and guards, in a silk covered box.

11in (28cm) high

$400-600   **BONM**

An early 20thC point de gaze fan, with silk insertion, painted in body color, simulated amber sticks, damage.

9.75in (25cm) high

$180-220   **BONM**

An Art Deco hatstand, possibly from Hamilton in Ontario.

c1930   19in (48.5cm) high

$60-90   **TYA**

A selection of Pochoir hand-stenciled prints, from 'Très Parisien'.

c1925   11in (28cm) wide

$70-100 each   **TDG**

COLLECTORS' NOTES

- Founded by 28-year old David McConnell from New York in 1886, Avon started life as the Californian Perfume Company. In 1929, the first products were offered under the Avon brand, a name supposedly inspired by William Shakespeare's birthplace, Stratford-upon-Avon. It was not until 1939 that the company itself became known as Avon.

- In 1906, Avon printed its first color brochure and began to run advertisements in Good Housekeeping magazine. By this time there were 10,000 sales representatives selling Avon products to women throughout America.

- After expanding to Quebec, Canada, in 1914, the company continued to grow, and by 1928 the number of sales staff had more than doubled.

- Avon successfully introduced a line of jewelry in the late 1920s. The reasonable prices and high quality of the pieces made the range immediately popular with American housewives. Today, the jewelry is not particularly valuable to costume jewelry collectors, but does appeal to collectors of Avon memorabilia.

- Values are currently comparatively low, with many pieces being found for under $50, so a collection can be built on a budget. Look out for Christmas Tree pins produced by Avon as this is a popular and collectible type.

A pair of 1990s Avon Christmas present earrings, of goldwashed metal casting with clear rhinestone highlights.

0.5in (1.25cm) long

$22-28   **MILLB**

A pair of 1980s Avon Paisley motif earrings, of goldtone metal casting with three shades of pink enameling.

1.5in (3.75cm) long

$18-22   **MILLB**

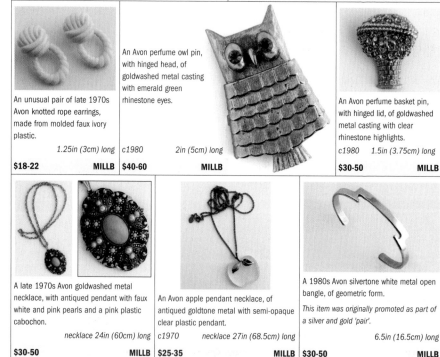

A pair of 1980s Avon earrings, with faux pearls, ruby rhinestones and green enameling, on goldwashed metal castings.

The festive enameled colors of these earrings show that these were made for sale around Christmas time.

1.5in (3.75cm) long

$30-50   **MILLB**

An unusual pair of late 1970s Avon knotted rope earrings, made from molded faux ivory plastic.

1.25in (3cm) long

$18-22   **MILLB**

An Avon perfume owl pin, with hinged head, of goldwashed metal casting with emerald green rhinestone eyes.

c1980   2in (5cm) long

$40-60   **MILLB**

An Avon perfume basket pin, with hinged lid, of goldwashed metal casting with clear rhinestone highlights.

c1980   1.5in (3.75cm) long

$30-50   **MILLB**

A late 1970s Avon goldwashed metal necklace, with antiqued pendant with faux white and pink pearls and a pink plastic cabochon.

necklace 24in (60cm) long

$30-50   **MILLB**

An Avon apple pendant necklace, of antiqued goldtone metal with semi-opaque clear plastic pendant.

c1970   necklace 27in (68.5cm) long

$25-35   **MILLB**

A 1980s Avon silvertone white metal open bangle, of geometric form.

This item was originally promoted as part of a silver and gold 'pair'.

6.5in (16.5cm) long

$30-50   **MILLB**

A pair of late 1990s Dinny Hall pendant earrings, with gold fishhooks and pendant caps with semi-translucent white resin drops.

1.5in (4cm) long

$70-100 PC

A pair of Dinny Hall gold-plated silver earrings, in the form of elongated, stylized leaves.

c2001   1.5in (3.5cm) long

$120-180 PC

COLLECTORS' NOTES

■ Dinny Hall is considered one of Britain's leading jewelry designers and opened her first boutique in West London in 1992. In 1989 she was voted Accessory Designer of the Year by the British Fashion Council. In 1996 she was named 'Jewelry Designer of the year' following a vote by the readers of Marie Claire magazine. She counts Madonna, Liz Hurley, and Uma Thurman amongst her clients.

■ Many of her designs are inspired by natural forms, such as leaves, icicles, droplets, and starfish. Her style is understated and simple, with pared down settings, transcending passing fashions and fads.

■ Typical Dinny Hall pieces are simple and classic in style, showing a global influence and an attention to detail. Many pieces use high colored resinous or precious or semi-precious stones against a simple setting and are created using traditional techniques. Hearts, crosses, and floral designs are common features of her pieces. Each piece is handcrafted using fine quality materials, such as sterling silver and gold, and traditional jewelry making techniques.

A pair of Dinny Hall large circular hoop silver earrings.

This piece was also produced in vermeil. This version can be worth 20 percent more.

c2001   1.5in (3.5cm) long

$80-120 PC

A pair of Dinny Hall earrings, with hand-crafted silver, Classical scrolling forms with with three icicle-form pendants of mauvish-blue resin.

c1992   2.5in (6.5cm) long

$80-120 PC

A late 1990s Dinny Hall 'Diffusion Line' necklace and earrings, with silver chain, fishhooks and pendant caps and semi-translucent white resin drops.

necklace 18in (46cm) long

$120-180 PC

A mid-1990s Dinny Hall 'Diffusion Line' necklace and earrings, with gold chain, fish hooks and scrolling hoops, with baroque pearl drops.

necklace 15.5in (40cm) long

$120-180 PC

A Dinny Hall pendant necklace, with silver chain and pendant cap with semi-translucent violet resin drop.

c1992   necklace 18in (46cm) l

$120-180 PC

A 1960s-1970s Accessocraft necklace, with beads of pearlized brown plastic and clear Lucite with white inclusions, and clear rhinestone roundels.

16in (40.5cm) long

$70-100 **ABIJ**

A 1960s ART snake bracelet, pin and earrings, gilt metal with turquoise-colored stones.

bracelet 7in (18cm) diam

$70-100 **JJ**

A 1940s Beaujewels floral pin and earrings, with fuchsia pink and pink aurora borealis rhinestones set in goldtone metal.

pin 2in (5cm) long

$70-100 **JJ**

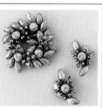

A 1950s-1960s Beaujewels floral wreath pin and earrings, with faux baroque pearls and aurora borealis rhinestones set in goldtone metal.

pin 2.5in (6.25cm) diam

$70-100 **JJ**

A 1980s Butler and Wilson charm bracelet, of goldtone metal with pendant crowns and fleur-de-lis, and faux pearl drops.

7in (18cm) long

$60-90 **PC**

A 1980s Butler and Wilson three-strand, champagne-colored faux pearl necklace, with gilt metal clasp.

16.25in (42cm) long

$50-80 **PC**

A Bettina von Walhof floral pin, with hand-wired yellow, green, and clear poured glass leaves and flowers, the latter with clear and jonquil crystal rhinestone centers, above a carved red and black medallion.

Flowers, leaves, fruit, and animals are motifs commonly found in Von Walhof jewelry, which is all handmade, usually from vintage glass beads and 'poured glass' leaves and flowers.

c1980 *3.25in (8.5cm) high*

$600-900 **SUM**

A 1970s-1980s Carolee bracelet, with round-cut clear crystal rhinestones set in white metal castings.

7in (18cm) long

$180-220 **JJ**

A 1950s Carolee star pin, of asymmetrical design in gold-plated base metal with embossed studs.

3in (8cm) wide

$80-120 **MILLB**

A 1980s-1990s Carolee necklace, with a chain of antiqued goldtone metal and a single strand of faux pearls.

16in (40.5cm) long

$30-50 **MILLB**

A late 1950s pair of Castlecliff floral motif earrings, set with bands and rings of ruby red crystal rhinestones.

$80-120 LB

A 1940s Danecraft bracelet, of sterling silver and vermeil sterling silver links and medallions, the latter with large, faceted purple pastes.

7in (18cm) long

$120-180 JJ

A late 1940s Castlecliff pendant necklace and earrings, with gold-plated Meso-american heads and motifs and semi-precious stone beads and drops.

pendant 4.75in (12cm) long

$300-400 RTZ

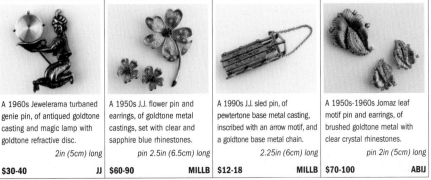

A 1970s Givenchy necklace, with goldtone metal chain clasp and link, the latter threaded through a circular faux onyx ornament.

necklace 17in (43cm) long

$30-50 MILLB

A 1930s German DRGM necklace, with rhodium-plated alloy chain and bib, the latter with clear crystal rhinestones and a cluster of rhinestones configured in a floral motif.

necklace 14.5in (37cm) long

$400-600 LB

A 1960s Jewelerama turbaned genie pin, of antiqued goldtone casting and magic lamp with goldtone refractive disc.

2in (5cm) long

$30-40 JJ

A 1950s J.J. flower pin and earrings, of goldtone metal castings, set with clear and sapphire blue rhinestones.

pin 2.5in (6.5cm) long

$60-90 MILLB

A 1990s J.J. sled pin, of pewtertone base metal casting, inscribed with an arrow motif, and a goldtone base metal chain.

2.25in (6cm) long

$12-18 MILLB

A 1950s-1960s Jomaz leaf motif pin and earrings, of brushed goldtone metal with clear crystal rhinestones.

pin 2in (5cm) long

$70-100 ABIJ

A pair of 1970s Kenneth Jay Lane earrings, of gilt metal with prong-set faux jade and diamond cabochons, above rows of clear rhinestone baguettes.

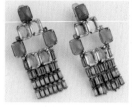

Lane's bright and bold designs designs are typified by creative reworkings of traditional styles, such as Egyptian designs, and unusual combinations of different materials.

2.5in (6.25cm) long

$70-100　　　　　　　　　**ABIJ**

A 1980s pair of Les Bernard interlaced scroll-form pendant earrings, of marcasite and clear and pale green rectangular and pear-cut rhinestones.

3.25in (8.5cm) long

$150-200　　　　　　　　　**JJ**

A pair of 1980s Moschino antiqued goldtone metal earrings, the clips with central faux pearl cabochons encircled by stamped "Moschino Bijoux" branding, and chained to peace symbol pendants.

3in (7.5cm) long

$30-40　　　　　　　　　**MILLB**

A pair of 1980s Richlieu earrings, of geometric form and highly polished, goldtone metal castings, the hinged pendants with three sections of pavé-set, round-cut, crystal clear rhinestones.

1.25in (3cm) long

$30-40　　　　　　　　　**MILLB**

A 1950s Robert figural pin, of an oriental man of gilt metal casting with bands of red and blue enamel.

Robert was founded in New York in 1942. Colors are usually strong, using rhinestones or enameling. Pieces are marked 'Original by Robert'. The company closed in 1979.

2in (5cm) high

$200-300　　　　　　　　　**JJ**

A pair of 1950s Robert floral motif earrings, with gilt wired clusters of faux pearls and faceted clear crystal beads.

1.5in (3.75cm) long

$50-70　　　　　　　　　**JJ**

A pair of Sarah Coventry floral motif silvertone metal earrings, the latticework with faceted cabochon centers.

c1980　2.25in (5.75cm) diam

$30-40　　　　　　　　　**MILLB**

A late 1950s Trifari shoal-of-fishes pin, of gold-plated casting with small ruby red cabochons for the eyes.

Trifari was founded in New York in 1918, becoming immensely successful with its range of Art Deco jewelry in the 1930s. In 1952, President Eisenhower's wife commissioned a parure for the presidential inauguration ceremony, sealing the firm's enduring success and popularity.

2.25in (6.5cm) high

$100-150　　　　　　　　　**ROX**

A 1950s Trifari necklace.

drop 3.5in (7cm) long

$60-90　　　　　　　　　**TR**

A pair of Trifari earrings, with original price tag.

1in (3cm) diam

$25-35　　　　　　　　　**TR**

A late 1970s Yves St Laurent bar pin, of gold tone metal set with square- and rectangular-cut fuchsia and pale amber glass stones.

2.5in (6.5cm) long

$70-100　　　　　　　　　**MILLB**

A pair of Yves St Laurent gold-plated earrings, of oval form with suspended lozenge-shaped centers set with faceted sapphire blue glass stones.

c1980　　　1.5in (4cm) long

$40-60　　　　　　　　　**LB**

A rare, large, 1990s 'catwalk' butterfly pin of French jet, with pale blue glass beads and variegated agate stones, unsigned.

Jet is a black stone, mostly from Yorkshire, England. It was popular during the late Victorian period, particularly for mourning jewelry. The unusual use of this material, the size, shape, and level of carving make this a valuable piece. This piece would have been used as an accessory during a catwalk fashion show.

7.5in (19cm) wide

$400-600   **CRIS**

A 1980s Butler and Wilson dancing couple pin, with prong-set clear paste heads, the black-tie suit and dress of black and clear rhinestones.

This is typical of Butler & Wilson's production during the 1980s, which was very glitzy and studded with diamanté. Look out for their lizard and spider-shaped pins which are considered classics.

4.75in (12cm) long

$60-90   **PC**

A 1950s Florenza floral bow pin, of antiqued silver tone metal, set with rows of small turquoise glass cabochons.

2.5in (6.5cm) long

$60-90   **ABIJ**

A Barry Parman 1920s 'Flapper' pin, in shades of gray, black and white resin with clear crystal rhinestone highlights.

c1975   3.5in (9cm) high

$150-200   **LB**

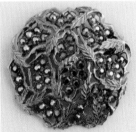

A 1960s Sarah Coventry leaves and berries medallion pin, of antiqued brushed goldtone metal with aurora borealis rhinestones.

2.5in (6.5cm) diam

$50-70   **ABIJ**

A 1970s-'80s Swoboda dragonfly pin, of gilt metal wire and casting with green and ruby glass stones, and channel-set coral and dark and pale brown glass stones.

Pins with colored semi-precious or glass stones set in gold-plated settings typify Swoboda's production.

3in (7.5cm) long

$100-150   **JJ**

COSTUME JEWELRY

An unsigned 1920s-30s necklace, with gilt metal links and oval hoops of mottled amber-colored glass.

15.25in (39cm) long

$60-90   **ECLEC**

An unsigned 1930s necklace, with silver links and hemispheres, roundels and baguettes of clear glass.

13.75in (35cm) long

$80-120   **ECLEC**

An unsigned 1950s triple-strand faux pearl necklace, with a pendant of gilt metal, clear crystal rhinestones and multiple faux pearl drops.

necklace 14in (36cm) long

$180-220   **CRIS**

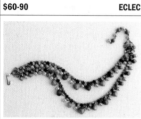

An unsigned 1950s necklace, with fruit and berry motifs, in yellow and green frosted glass interspersed with faux pearls and clear and aqua rhinestones.

22.5in (58cm) long

$120-180   **CRIS**

An unsigned 1950s-60s necklace, with green Murano glass leaves and yellow and orange-red Murano glass bead fruits.

16in (41cm) long

$100-150   **LB**

An unsigned 1960s necklace, with twin strands of faceted gray-blue glass beads and a floral motif of gilt metal with pink glass petals and faux pearls.

necklace 17in (44cm) long

$220-280   **CRIS**

An unsigned 1960s necklace, with discs or rosettes in gilt metal with bead molding encircling turquoise glass cabochons.

necklace 18.25in (47cm) long

$80-120   **CRIS**

An unsigned 1940s floral motif necklace and earrings, of sterling silver vermeil set with faux pearls.

necklace 14in (36cm) long

$80-120   **RG**

An unsigned mid-1950s necklace and bracelet, of gilt metal with peridot green rhinestones and glass cabochons and drops.

necklace 14.75in (38cm) long

$120-180 CRIS

An unsigned 1930s bracelet, with rhodium-plated links and peridot green glass bead berry motifs.

6.75in (17cm) long

$220-280 CRIS

An unsigned 1950s bracelet, of gilt metal with 'butterfly wing' glass cabochons showing a tropical shoreline.

7in (18cm) long

$60-90 ECLEC

An unsigned 1950s bracelet, of solid silver with repeating interlaced diamond motif of square-cut, sapphire blue crystal rhinestones.

7in (17.75cm) long

$300-400 CRIS

An unsigned, late 1950s bracelet, with textured goldtone metal links alternated with links of pavé-set clear crystal rhinestones.

7.5in (19cm) long

$80-120 CRIS

An unsigned 1940s wristwatch bracelet, in gold-plated metal, the watch face encircled by clear crystal rhinestones.

face 1.4in (3.5cm) diam

$150-200 CRIS

An unsigned pin, of organic shape in gilt metal with a turquoise and gold ceramic cabochon and three similar ceramic drops.

c1910 1.25in (3cm) wide

$120-180 CGC

An unsigned 1950s wristwatch, with bracelet and mounting of gilt metal set with polychrome glass beads, faux pearls and round- and baguette-cut rhinestones.

6.75in (17cm) long

$120-180 CRIS

An unsigned 1940s zebra pin-pendant, of sterling silver vermeil with black enameling, clear crystal rhinestones and an emerald glass cabochon.

2in (5cm) long

$150-200 ABIJ

An unsigned 1940s tropical fishes pin, possibly by Mazer Bros., of gilt metal casting with black and ivory enameling, clear crystal rhinestones and 'metallic' faux pearls.

2.75in (7cm) wide

$180-220   **CRIS**

An unsigned 1940s triple flowerhead pin, of white metal casting set with clear crystal rhinestones.

2in (5cm) diam

$100-150   **JJ**

An unsigned 1950s floral pin, possibly by Schreiner, with clear, lime green and diamond-cut white crystal rhinestones, and a lime green glass cabochon.

3.25in (8.5cm) long

$180-220   **CRIS**

An unsigned 1950s floral pin, possibly by Schreiner, with prong-set ruby red and clear crystal rhinestones on a gilt metal back.

2in (5cm) diam

$150-200   **CRIS**

An unsigned 1950s butterfly pin, with gilt wire frame set with pink, mauve, ruby red, and green rhinestones.

2.25in (5.75cm) wide

$100-150   **CRIS**

An unsigned 1950s floral motif pin and earrings, with aquamarine crystal rhinestones and dark blue glass cabochons prong-set in gilt wire backs.

pin 2.75in (7cm) long

$100-150   **CRIS**

An unsigned 1940s pair of earrings, with prong-set aquamarine crystal rhinestones and prong-set amber and red glass cabochons.

1.25in (3.25cm) long

$120-180   **PC**

An unsigned 1950s pair of earrings, with gilt metal castings and prong-set orange-red glass cabochons and aurora borealis rhinestones.

1.5in (4cm) long

$50-70   **CRIS**

An unsigned 1930s pair of ruthenium-plated bow and pendant hoop earrings, with round and baguette-cut clear crystal rhinestones.

2.5in (6.5cm) long

$220-280   CRIS

An unsigned 1950s pair of earrings, with gilt wire frames, prong-set with topaz, olivine, and aurora borealis rhinestones.

1.5in (3.75cm) long

$50-70   CRIS

An unsigned 1950s pair of oval earrings, in textured goldtone metal with a trellis pattern with turquoise glass cabochon centers.

1in (2.5cm) long

$30-40   CRIS

An unsigned 1950s pair of floral motif earrings, with textured gilt metal castings, rings of faux pearls and larger faux pearl centers.

1in (2.5cm) diam

$50-70   CRIS

An unsigned 1960s pair of silvered metal casting earrings, with emerald green, turquoise and coral glass cabochons and faux baroque pearls.

1.25in (3.25cm) diam

$40-60   CRIS

An unsigned pair of Pop Art earrings comprising pendants of goldtone metal coins.

The form of these earrings hints at Antique Roman or Egyptian designs.

c1970   4in (10cm) long

$18-22   MILLB

FIND OUT MORE...

'**Collector's Guide: Costume Jewelry**' *by Judith Miller, published by Dorling Kindersley, 2003.*
www.dinnyhall.com

A 1980s Stanley Hagler Christmas tree pin, gold-plated metal filigree backing set with frosted white glass flowers, hand-wired red crystal rhinestones and red glass beads.

2.25in (6cm) high

$80-120 CRIS

A CLOSER LOOK AT A CHRISTMAS PIN

Christmas Tree pins became popular in 1950, when American mothers and sweethearts wore and sent pins to their sons and lovers serving in the Korean War.

Hagler learnt to hand-wire beads while working for Miriam Haskell. It became a mainstay of his work.

The inclusion of a partridge is an unusual and festive addition.

The three-dimensional design of this pin is typical of Hagler.

A 1980s Stanley Hagler Christmas wreath pin, gold-plated metal filigree backing set with a central intaglio-carved panel of a partridge in a flowering wreath, mother-of-pearl, red, and green glass flowers, frosted clear glass leaves, green bell flowers, red and green crystal rhinestones, hand-wired red glass beads, simulated pearl cabochons, and rose montées.

Rose montées are flat-backed crystal rhinestones.

3.75in (9.5cm) high

$180-220 CRIS

A 1980s Stanley Hagler Christmas tree pin, gold-plated metal filigree backing set with mother-of-pearl flowers, red and green glass beads, and red crystal rhinestones.

2.75in (7cm) high

$80-120 CRIS

A 1950s Art Christmas wreath pin, yellow-tone textured metal set with green and red enamel and multi-colored crystal rhinestones.

1.75in (4.5cm) high

$50-70 CRIS

A 1980s Stanley Hagler Christmas tree pin, gold-plated metal filigree backing set with molded red glass flowers, opaque white glass and jadeite beads and red crystal rhinestones.

$80-120 CRIS

A 1980s Bijoux Stern Christmas tree pin, textured gold-tone metal set with green and red enamel and multi-colored crystal rhinestones.

2in (5cm) high

$30-50 CRIS

A 1980s Stanley Hagler Christmas tree pin, gold-plated metal filigree backing set with blue and white molded frosted glass flowers and leaves, blue glass beads with exposed silver foil cores and blue crystal rhinestones.

Most Christmas tree pins are green, red, and gold, but wintry silver and blue examples such as this can also be found.

2.25in (6cm) high

$80-120 CRIS

COLLECTORS' NOTES

■ Bakelite jewelry saw its golden age from the 1920s-30s and provided an inexpensive splash of color and style for ladies during the Great Depression and wartime. Pieces can attract prices usually paid for jewelry made with precious metals and stones.

■ Look for bright, cheerful colors, such as cherry red. Combinations of colors also tend to be popular. Pieces showing intricate or deeply carved designs will usually attract higher prices, especially if they are large. Chips, cracks, and burns reduce value.

■ Although Bakelite was originally a trademark name, 'bakelite' has become a generic term for jewelry made from a range of plastics.

■ Figurative, novelty-shaped and Art Deco styled pieces are often the most popular. Modern reproductions do exist, but these are usually lighter in weight, slightly shinier and have slightly different colors to period pieces – handle as many authentic pieces as possible to learn how to tell them apart.

An Art Deco chrome and bakelite Chinese design brooch.

c1930   2.25in (5.5cm) diam

$30-50   **GKA**

An Art Deco design bakelite brooch.

c1930   1.75in (4.5cm) diam

$40-60   **GKA**

A 1940s carved faux tortoiseshell circular bakelite brooch, carved with flowers.

2.25in (6cm) wide

$150-200   **BB**

A 1930s reverse carved brooch, the painted and filled ring of 'Apple Juice' bakelite.

2in (5cm) wide

$180-220   **BB**

A 1960s luminous pink and gray checkerboard brooch, possibly homemade.

2in (5cm) wide

$120-180   **BB**

A 1930s laminated cream and cherry red bakelite 'zig-zag' brooch.

2in (5cm) wide

$280-320   **PAC**

A rare 1930s laminated and handcarved 'butterscotch' and 'creamed corn' bakelite triple-flower brooch.

3.25in (8.5cm) wide

$220-280   **PAC**

A 1930s multi-colored bakelite fruit and leaf pendant brooch.

This example has many different types and colors of fruit making it desirable. Those with less fruit or less variety of colors are worth less.

3.25in (8cm) high

$700-1,000   **PAC**

A 1930s/40s well-carved orange bakelite hanging brooch, with inverted teardrop-shaped drop.

3.5in (9cm) long

$120-180   **BB**

A CLOSER LOOK AT A BAKELITE BRACELET

The 'chartreuse' green Lucite is a desirable color. The piece is also handcarved.

The metal is aluminum, a very unusual metal for jewelry, and an innovative one at the time.

The aluminum is embossed with an Art Nouveau-style floral motif and is also used for the chain links.

The bracelet is very light in weight. It is extremely rare.

A carved chartreuse green and aluminum bracelet, the panels carved with flowers, the aluminum parts with hammered and low relief foliate decoration.

c1930   *8in (20cm) long*

$500-700   **BB**

A 1940s carved and painted Lucite cicada bug brooch.

2in (5cm) long

$120-180   **BB**

A 1930s multi-colored injected 'creamed corn' and chartreuse bakelite 'six dot' bangle.

3.25in (8.5cm) diam

$300-500   **PAC**

A 1930s multi-colored injected 'creamed corn' bakelite 'six dot' bangle.

These rare and desirable bangles came with dots in a range of different colors. Those with more than one color are the most desirable.

3.25in (8.5cm) diam

$600-900   **PAC**

A 1930s carved 'creamed corn' bakelite flamingo brooch, with black bakelite beak and inlaid green rhinestone eye.

The flamingo is a popular bird shape to collect.

7.25in (11cm) high

$400-600   **PAC**

A 1930s deeply and intricately handcarved and drilled 'creamed corn' bakelite bangle.

3.25in (8cm) diam

$300-500   **PAC**

A 1930s carved 'creamed corn' bakelite bangle.

2.75in (7cm) diam

$120-180   **PAC**

A 1930s carved 'Apple Juice' bakelite pendant, with inset rhinestones and original matching necklace.

Pendant 2.25in (5.5cm) high

$150-200   **PAC**

COLLECTORS' NOTES

■ Dress clips were popular from the 1920s to the 1950s. They were worn at the neckline of a dress to highlight an outfit, particularly in the evening. They could also be used singly to grip or join the ends of scarves or fur stoles, or worn on hats or as collar or breast-pocket pins.

■ Although examples in precious metals using diamonds and fine gems can be found, they are usually expensive. More affordable pieces from the 1920s and 1930s are made from rhinestones, glass, silver, and plated base metals.

■ Look for the 'glitter' factor, and those with bright, well-cut 'stones'. Geometric Art Deco styles are particularly desirable and those produced in imitation of gems such as sapphires and rubies are popular. Look out for examples by known costume jewelry makers such as Trifari.

■ Bakelite examples are also highly collectible, with bright colors such as cherry red being the most desirable. Deep, intricate hand carving always adds value. Beware of chipped examples.

A 1930s Trifari pink glass and rhinestone dress clip, the back stamped "KTF".

The mark indicates this was made after 1925, when Trifari, Krussman and Fishel was formed.

2in (5cm) high

$60-90   **PAC**

A 1930s lead and rhinestone dress clip.

2.5in (6.5cm) high

$80-120   **PAC**

An Art Deco black Bakelite and red and clear rhinestone dress clip.

c1930   3in (7.5cm) high

$120-180   **PAC**

A large 1930s blue rhinestone dress clip, with pendant.

3.5in (9cm) high

$150-200   **PAC**

A 1930s rhinestone inlaid dress clip, with black glass cabochon.

2.5in (6.5cm) high

$50-90   **PAC**

A scarce mirrored and rhinestone inlaid dress clip.

Mirrored dress clips are scarce, especially those with beveled edges.

1.5in (4cm) high

$60-90   **PAC**

A pair of 1930s Trifari colored glass and rhinestone dress clips, with faceted clear glass bars, the backs marked "KTF".

1.5in (4cm) high

$80-120   **PAC**

A pair of red and rhinestone inlaid dress clips.

1.5in (3.5cm) high

$70-100   **PAC**

A pair of rare Art Deco 'Shooting Star' rhinestone dress clips.

1.5in (3.5cm) high

$100-150   **PAC**

A 1930s carved and polished wood and laminated Bakelite dress clip.

2.5in (6cm) high

$70-100   **PAC**

A CLOSER LOOK AT A DRESS CLIP

This plastic is a form of Lucite known as 'Apple Juice Bakelite' due to its color.

Flowers are typical motifs and the color is hand-applied.

The design is hand-carved onto the flat reverse side of the piece – look for intricate and detailed designs.

Look for large pieces such as bangles and pins as this material and style is much sought after.

A reverse painted 'Apple Juice Bakelite' tear drop-shaped dress clip.

2.25in (5.5cm) high

$60-90   **PAC**

A 1930s red and yellow laminated and carved Bakelite curved dress clip.

2in (5cm) long

$50-80   **PAC**

A carved yellow Bakelite triangular dress clip, with inlaid mosaic of flowers made from glass tesserae.

2.5in (6cm) high

$30-50   **PAC**

A pair of laminated and carved red translucent Bakelite and wood dress clips.

2.5in (6cm) high

$60-90   **PAC**

A pair of 1930s deeply carved yellow Bakelite dress clips.

The intricate and deep hand carving makes this pair desirable.

2in (5cm) high

$60-90   **PAC**

A pair of 1930s carved green Catalin or cast-phenolic leaf-shaped dress clips.

1.5in (4cm) long

$30-40   **PAC**

A leaf-shaped green Bakelite dress clip, inlaid with diamanté.

2in (5cm) high

$30-40   **PAC**

A carved green Lucite dress clip.

3.25in (8cm) high

$40-60   **PAC**

COLLECTORS' NOTES

- Walter Elias Disney (1901-66) started his own studio in Hollywood in 1923 with his partner and brother Roy, and developed the character of Mickey Mouse in 1928.

- Disney was a pioneer in animation, constantly pushing his staff to new artistic heights and technological advances.

- Licensing rights were first granted to George Borgfeldt of New York in 1930 and from 1932 'Kay' Kaymen also represented the characters, expanding the range of merchandize.

- Collectors tend to prefer licensed pieces, however, very early unlicensed examples can be desirable – many were produced in Japan. Officially licensed items made in the US or Germany before 1938 should be marked with "Walt Disney Enterprises" or "Walter E. Disney". Those made in the UK should be marked

"Walt Disney Mickey Mouse Ltd". Post-1939 all items are marked "Walt Disney Productions".

- The better known characters tend to be the most sought after, but are not necessarily the rarest. Date and condition are two of the most important indicators to value. The most popular period with collectors is the 1930s and includes soft toys, tinplate figures, and games.

- Mickey Mouse figures from this period can be identified by their rat-like bodies, a tail and "pie-cut" eyes. By the 1950s, the figures are plumper, often lacking a tail. Materials used and quality of production will also help in dating a piece.

- As pieces from the 1930s become scarcer and more expensive, demand has grown for previously ignored pieces from the 1950s to the 1970s.

A Deans Rag Book Mickey Mouse crushed velvet soft toy, some repairs to feet, hands and shorts replaced.

Deans, together with Steiff, were awarded the first licenses to produced Disney soft toys in Europe.

c1930   12in (30cm) high

$150-200   **BONC**

A 1930s Deans Rag Book Mickey Mouse velveteen soft toy, with Deans Ragbook Co. button, missing one eye, tail and shorts, dirty and well played with.

9in (23cm) high

$70-100   **W&W**

A CLOSER LOOK AT A STEIFF MICKEY MOUSE DOLL

Steiff made Mickey Mouse dolls from 1931 to 1936.

Steiff soft toys are sought after in their own right making this toy doubly collectible.

The large size, together with original tags and stamping on the foot make this a desirable example.

This example is wearing blue pants, the rarest color variation.

Five rare Britains Disney Characters, comprising a 16H Mickey Mouse, minor paint chips to face and body; a 18H Pluto, minor paint loss; a 19H Donald Duck, minor paint loss to beak, a 20H Clarabelle Cow; repaired arm, head support broken and a 21H Goofy, paint chips, small hole to back, all with detachable heads.

1939

$2,800-3,200 set   **VEC**

A 1930s large Steiff Mickey Mouse soft toy, with applied felt 'pie-crust' eyes, original whiskers and tail, retains rubber stamping on foot, chest tag, ear tag, and button, shows some very light darkening, excellent condition, front of pants somewhat faded, face shows some very slight darkening.

18in (45.5cm) high

$12,000-18,000   **NB**

An unusual composition clockwork Pinocchio figure, with rocking action to feet and loose mounted head shakes, some cleaning required.

c1950   *8in (20.5cm) high*

$400-600   **W&W**

A limited edition Royal Doulton Disney Showcase 'Pinocchio' figure, style two designed by Shane Ridge, from an edition of 1,500, boxed with certificate.

1999   *5.5in (14cm) high*

$80-120   **PSA**

An American Ideal Pinocchio wood and composition figure.

As Pinocchio was less popular than other Disney characters at the time, fewer examples were produced, making this figure very collectible.

c1930   *20in (51cm) high*

$800-1,200   **BEJ**

A Britains Snow White Series, comprising Snow White and the Seven Dwarfs, all very good condition.

$300-500   **VEC**

A set of Chad Valley Seven Dwarfs, the cloth dolls with felt faces and painted features, paper labels, in original boxes.

'Snow White and the Seven Dwarfs' was the first feature length cartoon. It was considered madness at the time, but it proved a massive hit with the public and received a Special Academy Award (one full-sized Oscar and seven small ones) from the Motion Picture Academy in 1938.

1937   *6in (15cm) high*

$1,000-1,500   **BONC**

A 1970s Walt Disney Productions Donald Duck painted bisque figurine.

    2.75in (7cm) high

$10-15   **TSIS**

A Cinderella painted china figurine, stamped "DISNEY JAPAN" on the base.

c1980   *5.5in (14cm) high*

$15-25   **TSIS**

A Royal Doulton 'Cruella De Vil' figure, DM1, designed by Martyn Alcock, from the Disney's 101 Dalmatians Collection.

1997-2001   *6in (15cm) high*

$60-90   **PSA**

A limited edition Royal Doulton Disney Showcase 'Thumper' figure, designed by Martyn Alcock, from an edition of 1,500, boxed with certificate.

1999   *3.25in (8.5cm) high*

$50-80   **PSA**

A 1930s Swiss Mickey Mouse lithographed biscuit tin, by Disch Ltd, marked "Par Aut. de Walt Disney Mickey-Mouse S.A. Concessionnaire Disch Othmarsingen".

8.5in (21.5cm) wide

$400-600 **DH**

A large 1930s Swiss Mickey Mouse lithographed biscuit tin, by Disch Ltd, marked "Par Aut. de Walt Disney Mickey-Mouse S.A. Concessionnaire Disch Othmarsingen".

10in (25.5cm) wide

$400-600 **DH**

A late 1930s English Mickey Mouse biscuit tin.

6in (15cm) high

$120-180 **DH**

A rare 1940s Australian Minnie Mouse triangular lithographed sweet tin, marked "W.D. Ent".

This tin was also made with an image of Mickey Mouse, Popeye, and Donald Duck.

5.75in (14.5cm) wide

$150-200 **DH**

1939

$100-150 **DH**

A Belgian 'Snow White' lithographed sweet tin, marked "Par Aut. Walt. Disney - Mickey Mouse S.A." and "Etabl. J. Schuybroek S.A. Hoboken-Anvers".

Another tin with a different scene from the film was also made and is worth a similar amount.

13in (33cm) wide

DH

A mid-20thC Disney Snow White biscuit tin, the cottage-shaped tin printed with the Princess and dwarfs about their thatched half-timbered residence.

6.25in (16cm) wide

$80-120 **CHEF**

A 1930s Walt Disney Enterprises lithographed tin sand pail, with Minnie Mouse in a car, Mickey Mouse and Donald Duck.

8in (20cm) high

$150-200 **SOTT**

A Disney lithographed tin sand pail, by Happynak.

c1940 *6in (15cm) high*

$120-180 **DH**

A 1940s Disney lithographed tin sand pail, by Happynak, marked "by Permission Walt Disney Mickey Mouse".

5in (12.5cm) high

$100-150 **DH**

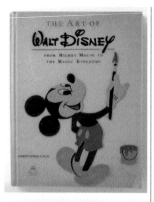

Christopher Finch, "The Art of Walt Disney, From Mickey Mouse To the Magic Kingdoms", published by Abrams.

"Walt Disney's Pinocchio", with illustrations from the film, very scarce.

1940

$100-150   **BIB**

"Walt Disney's Version of Pinocchio", with illustrations from the film, published by Collins, London.

1955

$60-90   **BIB**

1973

$60-90   **BIB**

An original pen, ink, and dotted celluloid cartoon strip artwork, by Floyd Gottfredson, with Goofy, and Mickey, and signed "Walt Disney", dated 8th August.

Gottfredson (1905-86) joined Disney as an apprentice animator in 1929. In 1930 he took over the production of the newly launched Mickey Mouse comic strip which he continued to run for 45 years until he retired in 1975. These strips originally appeared in daily newspapers and were later compiled into picture-books or comic books.

1962   *17.75in (45cm) wide*

$300-500   **MUW**

'Walt Disney's The Jungle Book', US title card.

This was issued for the 1980s re-release of the 1967 film.

14in (35.5cm) wide

$60-90   **ATM**

An original pen, ink, and spotted celluloid cartoon strip artwork, by Floyd Gottfredson, showing Mickey and Minnie gardening, dated 8th September.

1962   *17.75in (45cm) long*

$300-500   **MUW**

An original pen and ink and blue wash cartoon strip artwork, by Floyd Gottfredson, showing Mickey Mouse and Mickey's son painting, signed "Walt Disney, 15th January".

1966   *18in (45.5cm) long*

$220-280   **MUW**

A 1940s Walt Disney Productions molded card Multiplane Painting No. 13, 'Bambi Meets Little Flower, The Skunk', from Walt Disney's "Bambi", produced by Courvoisier, San Francisco.

1939-46   *8.75in (22cm) wide*

$100-150   **TM**

A 'Mickey Mouse Library of Games' card set, by Russell Mfg. Co, Leicester Mass.

c1946   *6in (15cm) long*

$60-90   **TM**

A Japanese Mickey Mouse Acrobat toy, celluloid figure on wire armature, cut-action.

Figure 6in (15cm) high

$280-320 **NB**

A clockwork Marx Donald Duck Duet, embossed lithographed tin, Goofy missing one ear.

10.5in (26.5cm) high

$400-600 **NB**

A 1930s Walt Disney Enterprises lithographed tin child's wash set toy, comprising washbasin, washboard, washing line, and wooden pegs.

Bowl 9in (13.5cm) wide

$400-600 **SOTT**

Three 1980s Disney themed 'Viewmaster 3-D' reels, comprising "Peter Pan", "Cinderella" and "The Little Mermaid".

Cards 8.25in (21cm) high

$10-15 each **TSIS**

A Multiple Toymakers Walt Disney's Donald Duck Express, mint condition, in near mint condition window box.

1968

$300-400 **VEC**

A Multiple Toymakers Walt Disney's Donald Duck's Whirlybird, mint condition, in near mint condition box.

1968

$300-400 **VEC**

A Multiple Toymakers Walt Disney's Mickey Mouse's Tin Lizzy, mint condition, in excellent condition window box.

1967

$220-280 **VEC**

An unusual Happynak English tea set, each of the 15 pieces with printed Walt Disney character decorations, in original box.

Box 16in (40.5cm) wide

$400-600 **F**

A 1950s Walt Disney Productions 'Minnie Mouse' painted candle.

3.5in (9cm) high

$4-6   **TSIS**

A 1930s Mores Snow White tooth brush holder.

6in (15cm) high

$150-200   **BEV**

A 1930s Mores Dopey tooth brush holder.

3.75in (9.5cm) high

$150-200   **BEV**

A 1930s Mores Sleepy tooth brush holder.

3.75in (9.5cm) high

$150-200   **BEV**

A pair of 1930s Japanese Mickey and Minnie Mouse painted bisque toothbrush holders, with large heads and string tails, stamped "WALT DISNEY JAPAN", Minnie's head re-glued.

5in (12.5cm) high

$400-600   **SOTT**

A pair of 1980s Walt Disney 'Mickey Mouse The Cook' salt and pepper shakers.

2.75in (7cm) high

$7-10   **TSIS**

A 1930s American Mickey Mouse pin, marked "Copyright Walt Disney Enterprises".

1in (3cm) wide

$100-150   **LDE**

A Walt Disney Productions 'Mary Poppins' silver-plated metal souvenir spoon, sealed in polythene bag.

c1964   *6in (15.5cm) long*

$25-35   **TSIS**

A Walt Disney World blue and clear iridescent glass souvenir bell, by Crystal Arts, with faceted glass clapper and acid-etched Mickey Mouse motif, dated 1986.

5.25in (13.5cm) high

$8-12   **TSIS**

A 'Ponytail' Barbie number 4 doll, by Mattel, in original black and white bathing suit.

Released in 1959, most collectors look for Barbies and outfits from before 1972 and date dolls by their face and hair.

c1960   11in (28cm) high

$200-300   NOR

A titian 'Bubble Cut' Barbie doll, by Mattel, in red swimsuit, with original box lacking ends.

Although the first 'Bubble Cut' Barbie was released in 1961, she originally wore a black and white striped bathing suit.

1962-67   11.5in (29cm) high

$180-220   NOR

A 'Ponytail' Barbie No. 4 doll, in 'Enchanted Evening' outfit.

This outfit is set No. 983 and dates from 1960-63. It is complete except for her pearl necklace and earrings. The name was re-used for a similar outfit in 1986. The exact gown was re-released in 1996 on a collector's edition doll.

1960-63   11.5in (29cm) high

$300-500   NOR

A CLOSER LOOK AT A BARBIE DOLL

This outfit is No. 982 from the 'Fashion Set' series and is worn by a correct, period 'Bubble Cut' doll.

The outfit was sold from 1960-64, but re-released in 1989 on a porcelain doll and again in 1995.

She retains her floor-standing microphone, which was prone to breaking.

Her 'diva-like' outfit is nearly complete with pink scarf, black mules, and long black gloves. She is only lacking her pearl necklace.

A brunette 'Bubble Cut' Barbie doll, by Mattel, in a 'Solo in Spotlight' outfit.

1962-63   11.75in (30cm) high

$220-280   NOR

A 'Twist 'N' Turn' Barbie doll, by Mattel, in floral skirt and red top.

1969-70   11.5in (29cm) high

$100-150   NOR

A 'Twist 'N' Turn' 'Sweet Sixteen' Barbie doll, by Mattel, in short floral skirt, white sleeves.

'Twist 'N' Turn', often shortened to 'TNT', was a waist feature that was introduced in 1966.

c1973   11.5in (29cm) high

$100-150   NOR

A 'Twist 'N' Turn' 'Olympic Skater' Barbie doll, in red, white, and blue outfit.

c1976-77   11.5in (29cm) high

$60-90   NOR

A limited edition 'Gay Parisienne Porcelain Treasures' porcelain Barbie doll, in correct outfit.

The original 1960s version of Barbie in this dress can fetch up to $500.

1991

$100-150   NOR

A Mattel 35th Anniversary Barbie doll, the replica doll with original 1959 shape, hair, clothes, box, complete with sunglasses, booklets, and box, all in mint condition.

1994   box 12.5in (32cm) high

$30-50   **MEM**

A flock-haired Ken No. 1 doll, by Mattel, in later football uniform.

This version was originally sold with a pair of red swimming trunks and red sandals.

c1961   12.25in (31cm) high

$100-150   **NOR**

An Allan doll, by Mattel, with bendable leg.

The straight leg version of Allan is less desirable and worth around $150.

c1965   12.5in (31.5cm) high

$180-220   **NOR**

A Skooter doll, by Mattel, in a yellow dress, bendable leg.

Skooter was first released in 1965 with a straight leg and is worth 50% of this later version.

1966   9in (23cm) high

$60-90   **NOR**

A blonde-haired Midge doll, by Mattel, with bendable legs and original and correct light and mid-blue two-piece bathing suit.

Midge was introduced in 1963. She has an identical body to Barbie, with a different head. She was only sold for a few years before vanishing (despite apparently being Barbie's best friend!) and returning in 1987 as 'California Midge'. Midge dolls with bendable legs or without freckles are usually worth more than straight leg versions. The clothing colors varied depending on hair color.

1963-66   11.25in (28.5cm) high

$100-150   **NOR**

A CLOSER LOOK AT BARBIE'S FRIENDS

Ricky was Skipper's first male friend, later joined by Scott in 1979 and Kevin in 1990.

He is wearing his original outfit of blue shorts and a typically 1960s stripey beach jacket with terry collar, which are both in excellent condition.

He still retains his original tag, which is extremely rare as it was usually torn off or worn away with play.

He still has his original box and brochure and is in unworn and clean condition with no wear to his red-painted freckled face or hair.

A Ricky doll, by Mattel, in original box.
c1965

$120-180

10in (25.5cm) high

NOR

A 'Red Flare' Barbie outfit, by Mattel.

1962-65

$40-60   **DE**

A Mattel Barbie pink plastic purse.

2.25in (5.5cm) wide

$6-9   **DE**

A Mattel Ken vinyl doll case, dated 1961.

12.75in (32.5cm) high

$50-70   **MA**

COLLECTORS' NOTES

■ Beatrice Alexander Behrman, later styling herself 'Madame Alexander,' was born in 1895 in New York. She opened her own business in 1923, making fabric dolls, which became very successful. Dolls were subsequently made in composition during the 1930s, plastic from 1948 and vinyl from the late 1950s. She died in 1990 at the age of 95, but the company continues today.

■ Madame Alexander dolls are noted and collected for their highly detailed and well-made costumes (rather than for the doll itself) which were made in over 6,500 variations. They were made to be displayed on a shelf rather than to be played with. Both the doll, and particularly the clothes, must be in clean, bright, mint and original condition complete with the original label and preferably with the box, to be of interest to most collectors. Values tumble if there are signs of wear or missing pieces.

■ The 'Storyland', 'Little Women', and 'International Series' are popular with collectors, the latter having been introduced in 1961 with each doll dressed in national costume from some 64 countries around the world. This series used the Wendy-kin/Alexander-kin 8in bent-knee walker doll until 1964. From then until 1972, a bent-knee, non-walking doll was used which was then replaced by the non-walking model still used today which had straight legs.

■ Each year the costumes of the International dolls were changed in some way, giving great scope to collectors who can collect either an entire year's variations across the countries, or one country across the years. Most collectors prefer the earlier (and usually more valuable) bent-knee versions, so examine a doll carefully before buying. Certain dolls made for short periods are rare – look out for the scarce Amish boy and Ecuador and Morocco dolls.

A Madame Alexander 'Brazil' doll, style 0773, with original tag, clothes, and box, in mint condition.

9in (23cm) high

$70-100 MEM

A Madame Alexander 'China' doll, style 0772, from the 'International Dolls' series, with tag, original clothes, in mint condition with original box.

7.5in (19cm) high

$50-70 MEM

A Madame Alexander 'German' girl doll, style 563, with original tag, clothes, and box, mint condition.

7.5in (19cm) high

$50-70 MEM

A Madame Alexander 'Indonesia' doll, from the 'International Dolls' series, with tag and original clothes, booklet and box.

8.25in (21cm) high

$50-70 MEM

A Madame Alexander 'Netherlands' girl doll, style 591, complete with original clothes and tag, in mint condition with original box.

7.75in (19.5cm) high

$50-70 MEM

A Madame Alexander 'Netherlands' boy doll, style 577, with original clothes and accessories, mint and boxed.

8in (20cm) high

$50-70 MEM

A Madame Alexander 'Turkey' doll, style 587, complete with original tag, clothes, and box, in mint condition.

7.5in (19cm) high

$50-70 MEM

DOLLS

COLLECTORS' NOTES

■ When buying plastic dolls, consider condition as being of primary importance, as many dolls were mass-produced and played with. The plastic should be clean and blemish free. Any 'make-up' should not be rubbed off or worn and hair in particular should be in its original style and not cut, dyed or restyled. Costume is important, and clothes should be original, still brightly colored and undamaged. Dolls made for display in particular should retain their boxes.

A later Madame Alexander 'Artiste' Wendy doll, style 31250, with original clothes, tag, and box, in mint condition, including brush and paints.

The paints and brushes were to be used by the child to paint their own picture.

8.25in (21cm) high

$60-90   **MEM**

A Vogue Ginny strung doll, with painted eyelashes, original outfit and box.

The Ginny doll was released in composition in 1948 and made in hard plastic later that year. She was given sleeping eyes and painted lashes in 1950.

7.25in (18.5cm) high

$180-220   **SOTT**

A Madame Alexander plastic 'Bride' doll, from the 'Storyland' series, in mint condition with tag, original clothes and in original card box.

The Storyland series represents different groups and cultures that make up the United States.

1972   Doll 8.25in (21cm) high

$70-100   **MEM**

A Madame Alexander '8in Matthew' doll, style 26424, from the Storyland series, with original clothes, tag, and box, in mint condition.

8.25in (21cm) high

$40-60   **MEM**

A Ginny doll, by Vogue, with molded marks to her back, in original clothes, with shoes, her head moves as she walks and her legs bend at the knee, ruffled hair.

1957-62   7.5in (19cm) high

$70-100   **MEM**

A Ginny 'Majorette' doll, by Vogue, with molded marks to her head, head moves from side to side as her legs are moved, complete in original uniform.

9.5in (24.5cm) high

$100-150   **MEM**

A Madame Alexander 'Mary Cassatt Baby' doll, style 3360, with 'Mary Cassatt Baby' tag, original clothes and box, in mint condition.

Mary Cassatt (1844-1926) was an American painter who both supported the Impressionists and painted in their style. Her pictures are much loved and portray intimate domestic scenes, many featuring children or babies. This doll is based on one of her portrayals of a baby.

Doll 14.25in (36cm) high

$150-200   **MEM**

A Steiff 'Ginny's Pup' soft toy dog, with ball and tag, marked "US ZONE GERMANY", no coat.

Steiff made this for the Ginny range but it was also released as a standard production line.

3.25in (8cm) high

$100-150   **SOTT**

A 1970s Ginny doll, by Vogue, with clothes, molded marks to her back, mint condition, in original box.

Box 9in (23cm) high

$25-35   **MEM**

An Ideal 'Shirley Temple' vinyl doll, with original tagged clothes and hair slide.

The Shirley Temple doll was designed by Bernard Lipfert and first made in the 1930s in composition. It helped propel Ideal to one of the highest positions in the doll industry. This large 15in (38cm) size is more unusual and valuable than the standard sizes.

1957   15in (38cm) high

$180-220   MEM

An Ideal 'Shirley Temple' doll, with original clothes, under clothes, socks, shoes, pearl necklace, hair slide, and hat.

1957   12in (30.5cm) high

$180-220   MEM

An Ideal 'Shirley Temple' 'Stowaway' doll, with original clothes, mint condition, with bright clothes and box.

This character was taken from the 1936 film of the same name where Temple plays stowaway 'Ching-Ching' who ends up in America.

1983   11.5in (29.5cm) high

$30-50   MEM

An Ideal 'Shirley Temple' doll, with original clothes including underpants, with curled hair, jewelry, shoes, box, mint with original net covering hair.

1982   11.5in (29.5cm) high

$50-70   MEM

An Ideal 'Saucy Walker' hard plastic doll, with original clothes and short hair, the back of the head molded "IDEAL DOLL", plaits lost.

1951-55   22in (56cm) high

$80-120   MEM

An Ideal 'Saucy Walker' hard plastic doll, with original clothes and hair, with characteristic plaits.

1951-55   22in (56cm) high

$70-100   MEM

A rare Ideal 'Posie Walker' doll, with bent legs.

1954-56   24.5in (62cm) high

$120-180   MEM

A CLOSER LOOK AT AN IDEAL DOLL

An Ideal Revlon hard plastic bodied doll, with soft plastic head, original clothes, tights, shoes, underclothes, and tag, hair with fragments of hair net and in very good condition.

1955-59   18in (46cm) high

$120-180   MEM

This Ideal doll is in mint condition, with a clean face with original make-up – her hair has also not been cut or restyled.

She retains her original booklet wrist tag.

She retains her box, which has attractive and charming artwork in the style of the period.

Her clothes are still brightly colored, original and complete with shoes and underclothes – she even retains her jewelry.

A 1950s Ideal Revlon doll, with original clothes, underclothes, shoes, hair, jewelry, together with paperwork and booklet, in mint condition and boxed, box with sellotaped edges.

1955-59   17.75in (45cm) high

$600-900   MEM

A 1950s 'Tiny Terrilee' doll, with rare platinum hair, original clothes, socks, and shoes, her head turns as she walks, with rouged cheeks and knees.

This doll has rare 'platinum' blonde colored hair, echoing the hairstyles of famous models and personalities of the day such as Marilyn Monroe. It is the hardest color to find and must not be confused with blonde, which is yellower in tone. Red is the next rarest color. The value of this example is further heightened as the hair is in original condition with curls and ringlets.

10in (25.5cm) high

$150-200   **MEM**

A 1950s Richmond 'Sandra Sue' hard plastic doll, with painted slippers, original clothes, hair, and underwear.

7.75in (19.5cm) high

$100-150   **MEM**

An 1950s unmarked hard plastic doll, with brunette hair, in original green taffeta dress.

18in (45.5cm) high

$150-200   **SOTT**

A 1960s large Chiltern blown vinyl doll, with a blonde hair wig, in original box.

20in (51cm) high

$50-80   **F**

A large Roddy blown vinyl doll, with a platinum hair wig, in original box.

20in (51cm) high

$40-60   **F**

An Alice's Adventures In Wonderland doll, by Palitoy, with a battery operated walking mechanism and fitted miniature record player, with three double-sided discs playing the voice of Alice and songs from the Disney film, in original box.

23in (58cm) high

$150-200   **CO**

An English Sasha 'Cora' plastic doll, No. 118, modeled as a black girl in a floral dress and original box.

$180-220   **F**

A CLOSER LOOK AT A CRISSY DOLL

Her hair can be extended by pushing a button and pulling – then be wound back with a knob on her back. Hair on the earliest versions extended to her feet, but this was abandoned as it tangled easily.

Crissy was made between 1969 and 1975 and was mass-marketed and popular – later versions had moving hips and could 'talk'.

Her dress is in the style of the period, but her brown hair and dark eyes go against the blonde haired, blue eyed stereotype of the day.

A Crissy doll by Ideal, with 'hair that grows and grows and grows', original dress, shoes, 'Letter to Mother' care instructions and box with early wool handle.

In mint condition, she would command over $100.

1969

18in (46cm) high

$60-90   **MEM**

A Hasbro 'The World of Love' 'Flower' doll, that turns, twists, and bends, in original box.

1971   10.5in (26.5cm) high

$70-100   **NOR**

A Hasbro 'The World of Love' 'Love' vinyl doll, in original box.

1970-71 Box 11in (28cm) high

$50-80   **NOR**

An Lyn 'Suntan Brooke Shields' poseable doll, with 'Year Round Funtan', original clothes and box.

This doll was released after Brooke Shields shot to fame as Emmele in the 1980 feature film 'The Blue Lagoon', in which two children were marooned and grew up on a desert island. The Brooke doll was available in many different costumes, or 'High Fashion Designs' as they were known.

c1982

$30-50   **MEM**

A Topper 'Dawn' doll, with bendable legs and dressed in a yellow, gold and blue short-skirted dress.

'Dawn', the 6.5in (16.5cm) fashion doll, was released in 1970 as a smaller rival to Barbie. She clearly did not catch on as Barbie did and was withdrawn from production around 1973. She was produced in a number of ethnicities and variations, each now worth approximately the same. She also had a wardrobe of her own.

c1970   6.5in (16.5cm) high

$15-25   **NOR**

An American 'Cuddly Cathy' blown vinyl doll, in original box.

Box 15.5in (39.5cm) high

$60-90   **F**

A Mego Corp 'Diana Ross' poseable doll, in original box, complete, in mint condition with clothing.

The price label on the box shows that a little girl could own Diana for "$12.39".

1977 13in (33cm) high

$120-180   **MEM**

A Pedigree hard plastic bent leg black doll, in original box.

14in (35.5cm) high

$120-180   **F**

An early Palitoy painted celluloid doll, modeled as young black girl.

6in (15cm) high

$50-80   **F**

A late 1960s 'Heidi Pocketbook' doll, in a hard plastic carrying case, with clothes, missing one shoe, hair with damage.

If her hair was in perfect and original condition, the box was undamaged and her wardrobe was complete, the set would be worth around $60.

Doll 5.5in (14cm) high

$25-35   **MEM**

COLLECTORS' NOTES

■ Barbara Annalee Davies began making dolls as a hobby when she was a child. When she left school in 1933, she began selling her dolls and puppets through the League of New Hampshire Craftsmen and to local shops in Boston.

■ When her husband Charles 'Chip' Thorndike's poultry egg business began to fail in the early 1950s, the couple decided to try and make a living from Annalee's dolls. The dolls were made at the kitchen table and Chip designed the internal metal frame that makes the 'Mobilitee' dolls poseable.

■ The dolls proved popular and before long a small staff were employed, working with Annalee and from their own homes. The first catalog was printed around 1954 and seasonal characters begin to be produced, starting with Santa.

■ The company expanded further in the 1960s and 1970s with the first factory opening in 1964 and Annalee's Workshop in Meredith, New Hampshire, in 1971.

■ In the 1980s holiday-themed dolls were consolidated into series such as 'Harvest Days', 'Halloween' and 'Thanksgiving' and the museum and collector's society were founded. In 1989 Annalee and Chip were invited to the White House for the first time to present a specially-made doll.

■ Annalee died in 2002, however production still continues. The characterful dolls are often based on animals, with mice being one of the most popular. These are usually made to a limited edition, the size of which can affect the value.

■ Look for early dolls from the 1950s, '60s and '70s, those from a small edition or one-of-a-kind examples, as well as dolls signed by Annalee herself.

■ Dolls should be stored out of direct sunlight as the brightly colored fabrics fade. They should also be protected from pest damage, as this will affect the value.

A pair of Annalee 'Hershey's Kiss Mice' dolls, from the 'St Valentine's Day' series.
1996   *3in (7.5cm) high*
$50-70   **MSC**

A pair of 1990s Annalee 'Easter Parade Bunny' dolls, from the 'Easter' series.
                    7in (18cm) high
$40-60   **MSC**

Three Annalee 'Patriotic Elf' dolls, from an edition of 425.
1999   *10in (25.5cm) high*
$40-60 each   **MSC**

An Annalee 'St Patrick's Day Mouse' doll, from an edition of 4,746.
1994   *7in (18cm) high*
$25-35   **MSC**

An Annalee 'Shauna's Scarecrow' doll, from the 'Harvest Days' series.
2000   *7in (18cm) high*
$30-50   **MSC**

An Annalee 'Steve Raking Leaves' doll, from the 'Harvest Days' series.
2000   *7in (18cm) high*
$30-50   **MSC**

An Annalee 'Jeff & Jack o'Lantern' doll, from the 'Harvest Days' series.
2000
$30-50   **MSC**

A 1990s Annalee 'Mouse on Pumpkin' doll.

                    3in (7.5cm) high
$20-30   **MSC**

A 1990s Annalee 'Cornucopia Mouse' doll.

                    3in (7.5cm) high
$15-25   **MSC**

DOLLS

A pair of Annalee 'Harvest Boy Bear' and 'Harvest Girl Bear' dolls, from the 'Harvest Days' series.

2000   *8in (20cm) high*

$70-100   **MSC**

An Annalee 'Autumn Elf' doll, from the 'Halloween' series.

2001   14in (35.5cm) high

$25-35   MSC

An Annalee 'Nurse Kid' doll, from the 'Trick or Treaters' series.

c1999   7in (17.5cm) high

$30-40   MSC

A one-of-a-kind Annalee 'Swarmiboy' doll, from the 'Halloween' series.

2000

$250-350   MSC

An Annalee doll 'Alien Kid' doll, from the 'Trick or Treaters' series.

c1999   7in (17.5cm) high

$30-40   MSC

A pair of Annalee 'Mr & Mrs Tuckered' dolls, with baby doll, from an edition of 4,600.

1983   larger (5in (12.5cm) high

$150-200   MSC

An Annalee 'Clown' doll.

1969   18in (45.5cm) high

$250-350   MSC

Left: An Annalee 'Clown' doll, from an edition of 247.

1971   18in (45.5cm) high

$200-300   MSC

Right: An Annalee 'Clown' doll, from an edition of 708.

1971   10in (25.5cm) high

$150-200   MSC

Left: An Annalee 'Clown' doll, from an edition of 166.

1975   18in (45.5cm) high

$200-300   MSC

Right: An Annalee 'Clown' doll, from an edition of 233.

1975   10in (25.5cm) high

$100-150   MSC

A CLOSER LOOK AT AN ANNALEE DOLL

Dolls such as these with closed eyes were not popular with the general public and were discontinued in 2000 and are now becoming more valuable.

The lively faces are hand-painted with great character and are still in excellent, bright condition, as are the clothes.

At 18in high, they are large examples.

As well as dating 1970s, they are from a limited edition.

An Annalee 'Clown' doll, from an edition of 166.

1975   18in (45.5cm) high

$200-250   **MSC**

Two Annalee 'Clown' dolls, from an edition of 4,784.

1977   10in (25.5cm) high

$100-150   **MSC**

Two Annalee 'Clown' dolls, from a limited edition of 2,343.

1977   18in (45.5cm) high

$250-300 each   **MSC**

Back: An Annalee 'Clown' doll, from an edition of 770.

1986   18in (45.5cm) high

$100-150   **MSC**

Front: An Annalee 'Clown' doll, from an edition of 3,369.

1986   3in (7.5cm) high

$45-55   **MSC**

A 1990s Annalee 'Indian' boy doll.

12in (30.5cm) high

$80-100   **MSC**

A pair of 1990s Annalee 'Indian Couple' dolls.

10in (25.5cm) high

$70-100   **MSC**

A pair of Annalee 'Indian Boy' and 'Indian Girl' dolls.

1996   3in (7.5cm) high

$30-40   **MSC**

An Annalee 'Indian' boy doll, from an edition of 2,700 and 'Indian' girl doll, from an edition of 3,000, each on a tan felt base.

1987   7in (18cm) h

$70-100 pair   **MSC**

Left: A 1990s Annalee 'Indian' doll.

$50-70   **MSC**

Right: A 1960s Annalee 'Indian' doll.

$600-700   **MSC**

A pair of Annalee 'Native Boy Bear' and 'Native Girl Bear' dolls, from the 'Harvest Days' series.

2000

$80-100   **MSC**

An Annalee 'Indian Girl Mouse' doll, from an edition of 2,206 and an 'Indian Boy Mouse' doll, from an edition of 1,495.

1986   *12in (30.5cm) high*

$100-150 pair   **MSC**

Left: An Annalee 'Cowgirl Mouse' doll, from an edition of 1599.

1982   *7in (18cm) high*

$100-150   **MSC**

Right: An Annalee 'Cowboy Mouse' doll, from an edition of 1982.

1982   *7in (18cm) high*

$100-150   **MSC**

A 1990s Annalee 'Buffalo' doll, from the 'Harvest Days' series.

12in (30.5cm) high

$50-70   **MSC**

Two 1960s Annalee 'Yum Yum Bunny' dolls.

7in (18cm) high

$300-400 each   **MSC**

Left: An Annalee 'Dragon with Bushbeater' doll, from an edition of 1257.

1981

14in (35.5cm) high

$350-450   **MSC**

Middle: An Annalee 'Dragon with Bushboy' doll.

1981   *Dragon 29in (73.5cm) high*

$700-800   **MSC**

Right: A miniature Annalee 'Dragon with Boy' doll, edition of 1036.

1982   *5in (12.5cm) high*

$150-200   **MSC**

An Annalee 'Bunny Boy' doll, from an edition of 2,783 and a 'Bunny Girl' doll, from an edition of 1,346.

1978   *18in (45.5cm) high*

$150-250   **MSC**

A 1960s Annalee 'Yum Yum Bunny' doll.

12in (30.5cm) high

$650-750   **MSC**

Left: A small Annalee 'Lamb' doll.

1989   *5in (12.5cm) high*

$20-30   **MSC**

Right: A large Annalee 'Lamb' doll.

1989   *8in (20cm) high*

$30-40   **MSC**

FIND OUT MORE...

'The Annalee Doll Museum', *Reservoir Road, Meredith, New Hampshire, U.S.A.*

www.annalee.com - *the home of Annalee Dolls online, with guidance for researching retired and vintage dolls.*

A pair of Dean's Joan and Peter 'Dancing Dolls', in cloth with painted features, together with trade card, catalog, and instructions.

1928

$180-220   **BONC**

Two Dean's Rag Book 'The Lambeth Walk' cloth dolls, with molded faces, together with sheet music and catalog.

These dolls are based on the popular music hall star of the time, Lupino Lane, who popularized the song 'The Lambeth Walk' from the musical 'Me and My Girl'.

1939   *largest 11.75in (30cm) high*

$180-220   **BONC**

A 1930s Dean's Rag Book doll, modeled as young girl, with molded painted face and wearing a blue velvet winter suit with hand muff.

21in (53.5cm) high

$150-200   **F**

A Dean's Dutch Boy and Girl dolls, designed by Richard E. Ellett, with painted cloth heads, blonde hair on cloth bodies each wearing traditional Dutch costume, boy's right cheek dented and slight lose of paint.

1949   *33in (84cm) high*

$280-320   **BONC**

Seven Dean's 'Dolls of the World', designed by Richard E. Ellett, with handpainted molded rubber heads on cloth bodies, each wearing a traditional costume, Chinese boy, Irish boy, English girl, Dutch boy, Norwegian girl, Russian girl and Native American girl.

1949   *12.25in (31cm) high*

$280-320   **BONC**

Two Peggie and Teddie printed cotton cloth dolls.

1911   *15.75in (40cm) high*

$60-90   **BONC**

A Chad Valley cloth boy doll.

c1930   *24.75in (63cm) high*

$70-100   **HB**

An early 20thC Norah Wellings cloth doll, with molded velvet upper body and felt lower body, modeled as an Native American Chief, in original box.

Norah Wellings dolls are hotly collected, particularly if in good condition with brightly colored fabric and if an unusual or highly detailed character. Beware that there were many copies made at the same time and later and these look very much like Wellings dolls, particularly the sailors. Always look for the Norah Wellings label.

box 12in (30.5cm) high

$280-320   **F**

A CLOSER LOOK AT RAGGEDY ANN & ANDY

The Volland company suggested illustrator and author John Gruelle made dolls to help sales of his stories. Early versions were made by Gruelle's family and are extremely rare, but from 1920 until 1934 the Volland company took over and these professionally produced dolls are valuable and sought-after.

Raggedy Andy was not developed until 1920. Although Volland was still responsible for sales, Gruelle chose another company, Beers, Keeler & Bowman, to make this character. Therefore they were not produced as a pair.

A Pedigree felt doll, designed by Nora P. Hill, with original label, in original box.

12in (30.5cm) high

$120-180   **F**

Fabric does not generally wear well over time, but these dolls are in excellent condition – they have no tears or major stains and retain their clothes which still have their bright colors.

This is the smallest size made by Volland – a larger 29in (73cm) high version can fetch up to 50-70% more than this size if in similar condition.

An early 20thC velvet doll, the molded painted face with inset glass eyes, modeled as a South Seas maiden, dressed in a grass skirt, possibly Chad Valley.

12in (30.5cm) high

$60-90   **F**

An American cloth Volland 'Raggedy Ann' doll.

Raggedy Ann was a rag doll owned by the daughter of American illustrator John Gruelle who told his daughter stories of her 'adventures' when she was ill in 1915. She had been owned by Gruelle's mother and, as her face had faded, he drew one on, resulting in her rudimentary features. His daughter died in late 1915 and he wrote 'Raggedy Ann Stories' in 1918 in her memory.

c1920-1934   16.5in (42cm) high

$1,500-2,000   **HGS**

An American cloth Volland 'Raggedy Andy' doll.

c1930   15.75in (40cm) high

$1,200-1,800   **HGS**

An American 'Beloved Belindy' cloth doll, made by Georgene Novelties.

'Beloved Belindy' was another character from the hand of illustrator and author John Gruelle who also created the Raggedy Ann and Andy stories. The first cloth dolls were made by P.F. Volland from 1926, just before the book was published. Georgene Novelties Co. took over production from 1938. This example dates from the first years of production – later versions from the 1940s onward had forward, not sideways, facing feet. Georgene continued to produce 'Beloved Belindy' until the early 1960s and as well as being early, this doll is valuable as it is larger than the standard 15in (38cm) version.

1938   18.5in (47cm) high

$1,200-1,800   **HGS**

A Käthe Kruse doll, the painted molded head modeled as a young child, on a fabric body, manufacturer's mark applied to the foot.

16in (41cm) high

$1,000-1,500   **F**

A cloth 'Brownie' doll, by an unknown maker, seated on a carved and painted toadstool.

A brownie is a mythical elf-like figure in Britain. It is said to help with domestic tasks, usually at night, in exchange for small gifts and food.

c1930   33in (84cm) high

$280-320   **BONC**

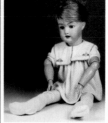

An Armand Marseille doll, bisque head with blue glass eyes, open mouth with row of teeth, brown wig, wooden body, restored, new dress.	An Armand Marseille doll, bisque head, blue sleeping eyes, open mouth with row of teeth, short-hair wig, wooden joint body, marked, restored.	An Ernst Heubach doll, bisque head, blue glass eyes, open mouth with teeth, wooden joint body, damaged, restored, new clothes, marked.	A Kestner bisque socket head doll, human hair wig, sleeping eyes, remnants of plaster pate, jointed composition body, red stamp "Excelsior", impressed "Made in Germany 171".
c1905 24.75in (63cm) high	c1912 21in (53cm) high	c1915 23.5in (60cm) high	19in (48cm) high
$300-500 BMN	**$180-220** BMN	**$280-320** BMN	**$300-500** WHA

A CLOSER LOOK AT A BISQUE DOLL

The bisque is undamaged, smooth and clean with no flaws and she has a desirable fully jointed body.

She has a row of teeth in her open mouth – Kammer & Reinhardt claimed to be the first company to introduce this feature on bisque-headed dolls.

The back of her head bears K*R markings for Kammer & Reinhardt. The heads were actually made by Simon & Halbig, another German doll maker whose marks are often found.

She is very large in size and still retains her original clothes and shoes – all desirable for collectors.

A Kammer & Reinhardt bisque headed doll, with blue sleeping eyes, open mouth with teeth, long dark blonde wig, jointed limbs on a composition body, original clothes with white leather shoes.

29.5in (75cm) high

$600-900   BMN

An early 20thC German bisque-headed doll, numbered "39", with auburn hair, lateral moving sleeping eyes, open mouth and jointed composition body.	A Gebrüder Heubach 'Piano Baby', in tinted bisque with molded hair and intaglio eyes, impressed sunburst mark.	A German all-bisque doll, with articulated arms, in later knitted dress.	A glazed porcelain shoulder head black baby, with well matched five-piece body, dressed in Pierrot outfit, unmarked.
15.75in (40cm) high	15.75in (40cm) high	c1920 4.5in (11.5cm) high	c1930 19in (48.5cm) high
$300-500 CHEF	**$300-500** CHEF	**$220-280** BEJ	**$800-1,200** BEJ

A porcelain half doll, modeled as a lady wearing a wide-brimmed pink hat and pink dress, clasping a rose in her hands, incised marks.

A porcelain half doll, modeled as a lady, her hands placed upon her head, wearing a flower decoration in her hair, incised marks "12756".

4.5in (11.5cm) high

$40-60   F

A porcelain half doll, modeled as a naked lady with her hands placed upon her chest.

4.5in (11.5cm) high

$40-60   F

An Art Deco painted wax half doll, modeled as a naked head and shoulder bust of an attractive young female, together with a pair of molded bisque arms, in original box.

5.5in (14cm) high

$100-150   F

Half dolls were popular from the late 19thC until the 1940s. Values depends on how well the doll is modeled and painted. Simple examples made from one mold are the least expensive, whilst those made from more than one mold with attached outstretched arms or extra details such as flowers or wide-brimmed hats will be the most valuable. Other positive features to look for include fine painting, notable makers (such as Kestner, Goebel or Dressel & Kister) or popular fashions or styles of the day.

5in (12.5cm) high

$40-60   F

A porcelain half doll, modeled as a young lady with painted facial features, her hands placed upon her head, now dressed in a gold silk dress.

Many half dolls retain their original 'clothing' which was originally added to cover a cosmetic box, jewelry box, hairbrush or other object. Those in original period clothes in fine condition will command a premium, particularly if the doll itself is well-modeled and painted.

16.5in (42cm) high

$40-60   F

A bisque porcelain half doll, modeled as a pretty young lady with painted facial features, applied wig and jointed arms, now dressed in a black fabric dress.

20in (51cm) high

$50-70   F

A 'factory-made' tea cosy doll, with a bisque head and articulated arms, in Dutch costume.

c1920   11in (28cm) high

$300-400   BEJ

A Scottish novelty papier-mâché boy pin cushion, on a needle store base.

c1920   5in (12.5cm) high

$100-150   BEJ

A composition boy doll, with rigid limbs jointed at the shoulders and hips and with a molded and painted head.

12.25in (31cm) high

$30-50   HB

A 1940s red and white unused doll's outfit, on original blue retail card, comprising underclothes, dress, hat, and booties.

c1945

$150-200   BEJ

EARLY COMPUTERS

COLLECTORS' NOTES

■ Many have cited early computers as being the 'next big thing' in collecting circles, with good reason as many are important examples of how technology has developed over the past two to three decades.

■ It will be interesting to see if interest in this market actually does widen, as many models lack instant 'eye-appeal' and are bulky to store and largely unusable or 'useless' today.

■ Look for complete examples in as close to mint condition as possible, as wear and missing parts reduce value considerably. Examples must also still work and preferably be useable for hobbies such as gaming.

■ Try to buy the most important, landmark models from the mid-1970s through to the mid-1990s. Look for those that captured the public imagination and were popular, as nostalgia is also an important factor.

■ Handhelds, calculators, and personal organizers may offer a more attractive proposition due to their comparative size and near-usability. Look for names such as Amstrad, Apple, and Sinclair: the latter is already highly collectible.

■ Models that offered innovative systems, or the very first PDAs, may be the most likely to rise in popularity, but always consider condition as many were seriously worn when carried around.

A BBC Micro Computer with monitor and disk drive.

This reliable and expandable machine was promoted by the BBC as part of its Computer Literacy Project, and was the stalwart of most school computer rooms for many years. Acorn originally expected to produce about 12,000, but over a million were eventually sold throughout the 1980s.

c1982

$50-80   **PC**

An Acorn Atom home computer, the forerunner of the BBC microcomputer.

1980-83   15in (38cm) wide

$70-100   **PC**

An Amiga A600 home computer, by Commodore.

c1992   13.5in (34.5cm) wide

$30-50   **PC**

An Acorn Electron home computer, with Advanced Plus 1 expansion unit.

This was effectively a cut-down version of the BBC Acorn Micro and was released in 1983.

$40-60   **PC**

An Amstrad CPC 6128 home computer. with built-in three inch disc drive and with monitor and manual.

1985-90   20in (51cm) wide

$40-60   **PC**

A Dragon 32 home computer.

This was made in Port Talbot, South Wales, UK.

1982

$50-70   **PC**

A Commodore C64 home computer, with Commodore tape drive, 'Terminator T2' games and user manual.

One of the most popular home computers from the company that later went on to produce the Amiga with sales in excess of $25 million! It had very good sound and graphics, as it was originally designed to work inside an arcade machine.

1982-93

$30-50   **PC**

An ORIC Atmos 48K home computer, with manual, 'Introduction To...' book and cover.

The 48K Atmos offered buyers more available, usable memory than equivalent competitors' products, even when programs and peripherals were running – quite a bonus at the time. A 16K version was also marketed, but it could not be upgraded and was thus not successful.

1984-86   11in (28cm) wide

$80-120   **PC**

A Sinclair QL home computer, with microdrive cartridges and manual.

Continuing Sinclair's reputation for innovation at affordable prices, the company released the 'Quantum Leap' in 1984 which was one of the first 32-bit home computers at under $600, placing it well ahead of its time. It also came with an innovative 'microdrive', but due to internal quality control and poor delivery, it was largely unsuccessful, making it comparatively hard to find today.

1984-86

$60-90   **PC**

A Sinclair ZX Spectrum +2 home computer, with built-in tape drive.

This was actually made by Amstrad who had taken over Spectrum's computer arm in 1986 and is commonly found today due to its popularity at the time.

c1987   17in (43cm) wide

$22-28   **PC**

A Jupiter ACE home computer, made by Jupiter Cantab.

Company owners Richard Altwasser and Steven Vickers previously worked for Sinclair on the Spectrum ZX81, which may explain the similarity this machine has to the Jupiter. This was the first and only computer made by the company and originally retailed for $134.95.

c1982   8.5in (21.5cm) wide

$100-150   **PC**

A Sinclair ZX81 home computer, with original packaging, game and power pack.

The third of Sinclair's home computers, it was the first that could be plugged in and used immediately. Despite offering just 1K of memory and having no sound or color, over 1 million units were sold in the UK and US (via Timex) in the first two years.

c1981   13.5in (34.5cm) wide

$30-50   **PC**

A 'Mark-8' mini-computer, including six 'Mark 8' circuit boards, an Intel 8008 chip, two Signetics 8267 chips, two Signetics 8263 and eight National Semiconductor 1101 memory chips, and with a CD-ROM containing various magazine and newsletter pages regarding the computer.

Designed by Jon Titus, the Mark 8 was bought, assembled and housed by the purchaser. It was one of the very first home computers for computer 'hobbyists' offering an LED bulb-based display and 16 switches. It was marketed by 'Radio Electronics' magazine in July 1974.

c1974 $400-600   **ATK**

A Toshiba MSX HX-10 home computer, 64K.

c1983   14.5in (37cm) wide

$22-28   **PC**

An ORIC MCP-40 home computer, with ORIC color printer, manual and games.

This has the same 6502 microprocessor as the BBC Micro and Acorn Electron.

1983

$40-60   **PC**

EARLY COMPUTERS

A TRS-80 model 100 portable home computer, by Tandy Radio Shack, with manual.

c1983   *11.5in (29cm) wide*

$40-60   **PC**

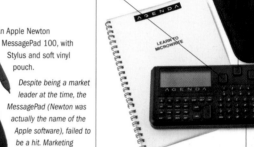

An Apple Newton MessagePad 100, with Stylus and soft vinyl pouch.

Despite being a market leader at the time, the MessagePad (Newton was actually the name of the Apple software), failed to be a hit. Marketing claims over handwriting recognition were arguably somewhat over-blown and it was large and expensive. The Palm system that replaced it was far more successful.

1993-98   *7.25in (18.5cm) high*

$22-28   **PC**

An Apple Macintosh Power Book 180.

The 180 was originally retailed for $4,110 and was the top of the range Powerbook of its time with a faster 33MHZ processor.

1992-94
11.25in (28.5cm) wide

$30-50   **PC**

An HP 22 business calculator, by Hewlett Packard.

Originally sold for $165.

1975-78   5in (12.5cm) high

$30-50   **PC**

A Psion Series 3C organizer.

c1996

$15-25   **PC**

A Datamath TI-2500 II calculator, by Texas Instruments.

c1973   5.5in (14cm) high

$15-25   **PC**

A CLOSER LOOK AT A PDA

The five large keys are placed ergonomically reflecting the natural position of fingertips - this offered comfort and speed to the user and was first seen on the 1980 'Microwriter' writing machine that aimed to replace keyboards.

The innovative system of five buttons, which when pressed in certain sequences (chords) to match the rough shape of a letter, created that letter, was said to be faster than standard typing once learnt.

The main keyboard is arranged alphabetically and has very small buttons, encouraging use of the Microwriter keys. The four-line LCD screen is typically small.

The AgendA won a British Design Award in 1990. Unfortunately it did not cater for left-handed users!

An 'AgendA' Microwriter personal organizer, with 'microwriting' system originally developed by Cy Endfield and Chris Rainey in the 1970s.

c1989   *7in (18cm) wide*

$40-60   **PC**

An Amstrad Pen Pad PDA 600 personal organizer, with touch screen.

This was one of the first PDAs, running on three AA batteries and was offered by Amstrad as a less expensive competitor to the Apple Newton. Values vary depending on the condition of the screen.

c1993

$30-50   **PC**

A 1950s erotic ceramic mug, with moving, wired-on breasts and molded wording reading "Let Them Swing", the base stamped "FOREIGN", and molded "PATENT.T.T".

4.25in (10.5cm) high

$40-60   **CVS**

A 1950s ceramic erotic mug, with girl standing next to a tree trunk, with wired-on, moving ceramic bottom.

4.25in (11cm) high

$50-70   **CVS**

A 'South Carolina' erotic souvenir mug, with a cigarette girl, reading "If you don't see what you want, ask for it!"

The 1950s and 1960s saw a great many erotic novelty souvenir items, such as ashtrays and mugs, being sold in popular resorts such as Florida.

c1960   *4.75in (12cm) high*

$30-50   **CVS**

A 1950s erotic handpainted ceramic small dish or ashtray.

Many of the erotic ceramics of the 1950s were made in Japan and can be identified by their lightweight material. Look for scratches and chips as this affects value.

4in (10cm) diam

$40-60   **SM**

Two English 1950s 'Glamor Girls' bone china gilt scalloped edge dishes, with transfer prints of semi-clad ladies in erotic poses.

4.75in (12cm) wide

$50-70 each   **CVS**

A 1950s Japanese erotic ceramic ashtray, with a semi-clad lady seated by a window and a motto reading "Lady Pull Down Your Shade, I Can't Go To Sleep", based stamped "JAPAN".

Although this was produced decades later, the form, bright colors and use of a motto on the base recalls German fairings – especially as they share the same 'naughty' seaside style humor.

4in (10cm) wide

$70-100   **SM**

A 1950s Japanese erotic ceramic ashtray, with a topless lady standing in front of a doctor and motto reading "But My Dear Young Lady, I'm A Foot Doctor", the back marked "JAPAN".

3.5in (9cm) high

$70-100   **SM**

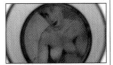

A 1950s erotic Lucite shot glass, with photograph of topless busty seated lady in the base.

2.25in (6cm) high

$25-35   **CVS**

Charles Fay, "Pit of Shame", published by Emerald.

Often known as 'pulp' fiction, erotic paperbacks that peaked in popularity in the mid-1960s have become extremely collectible over the past decade. Condition is important to value as they were not made to last and often fall apart. The cover is one of the most important aspects, partly as the artwork is often so eye-catching, kitsch, and typical of its period – when it would have been considered rather risqué!

1964   6.5in (16.5cm) high

$5-8   **CVS**

Kevin North, "The Golden Girls", published by Playtime Books.

1962   6.25in (16cm) high

$5-8   **CVS**

Clark Davis, "Knights of Lust", published by Spartan Line.

1967   6.5in (16.5cm) high

$5-8   **CVS**

A German tinted erotic photograph of a topless lady, in a towel and heels standing near a decorative log burner, together with two extravagantly designed brochures on the history of customs, one titled 'Forbidden Secret'.

c1960   photo 15in (38cm) high

$150-200   **ATK**

A 1950s American boxed set of plastic-coated erotic playing cards, made by "NOVELTIES MFG & SALES CORP", of St. Louis, MO, each card with a unique image of a posing naked lady protecting her modesty with a different object.

3.5in (9cm) high

$80-120   **CVS**

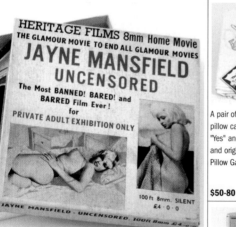

A very rare 1960s Heritage Films 8mm home movie of 'Jayne Mansfield Uncensored', boxed.

box 5.25in (13.5cm) wide

$180-220   **CVS**

A pair of American erotic cotton pillow cases, embroidered with "Yes" and "No" on each side and original paper label for "The Pillow Game".

16.5in (42cm) long

$50-80   **SM**

A 1950s erotic cotton bar towel.

30in (76cm) high

$30-50   **SM**

A 1950s PAC chrome-plated and plastic-sleeved erotic lighter, with photographic images of models posing on a beach.

2in (5cm) high

$60-90   **CVS**

"Playboy" from July 1977.
The label stuck to the cover indicates that pages 169-170 were removed from this issue for legal reasons, possibly due to pornography rules!

11in (28cm) high

$25-35 VM

"Playboy" from October 1978, with Dolly Parton cover.

11in (28cm) high

$30-50 VM

"Playboy" from January 1997, with commemorative Marilyn Monroe cover and containing new James Bond fiction.

11in (28cm) high

$60-90 VM

"Playboy" from May 1998, the cover with Geri Halliwell, 'Ginger Spice' of 'The Spice Girls', in her famous Union Jack dress.

11in (28cm) high

$30-50 VM

A Playboy bunny gold-plated necklace, the eye inset with a diamanté.

pendant 0.75in (2cm) high

$40-60 CVS

A 1960s Playboy bunny gold-plated bracelet, the eye inset with a red diamanté.

bunny 0.75in (2cm) high

$40-60 CVS

A pair of Playboy orange plastic sunglasses, with bunny decal on the arms near hinge and one arm stamped "PLAYBOY".

$100-150 VE

A Playboy Playmate 'Complete Playboy Centerfold' puzzle, complete and contained in a tin with paper label.

c1965   *5.75in (14.5cm) high*

$80-120 P&I

A 1960s Playboy matchbook, from Phoenix.
The Playboy Club in Phoenix, Arizona opened on December 19th 1962.

2in (5cm) high

$4-6 DTC

COLLECTORS' NOTES

■ In recent years the interest in collecting eyewear has increased substantially. The four main indicators to value are: the style or look, the name of the maker or designer, the material and the condition. Look for styles or designs that sum up any period, the 1950s and 1960s are currently the most popular decades.

■ Values are not usually affected if lenses are missing unless they were unusual, such as having a graduated tone. Other lenses can be easily replaced.

■ The material counts – those made from real tortoiseshell or precious metals or those with large amounts of handcrafted work will usually be more valuable. Color is also worth considering with the psychedelic colors of the 1960s much sought after.

■ Look out for famous fashion designers such as Christian Dior and Pierre Cardin, but also those more known for their eyewear designs such as Pierre Marly, Alain Mikli and Emmanuelle Khanh.

■ Frame condition is of vital importance as many collectors buy glasses to wear as well as to display. Splits and cracks reduce value considerably and examples with broken parts are rarely repairable.

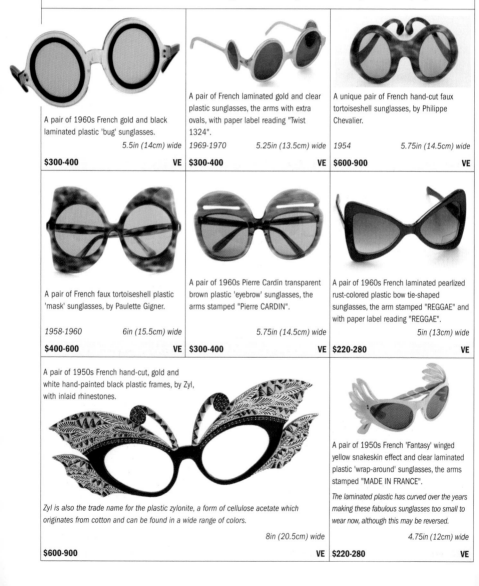

A pair of 1960s French gold and black laminated plastic 'bug' sunglasses.

5.5in (14cm) wide

$300-400 **VE**

A pair of French laminated gold and clear plastic sunglasses, the arms with extra ovals, with paper label reading "Twist 1324".

1969-1970   5.25in (13.5cm) wide

$300-400 **VE**

A unique pair of French hand-cut faux tortoiseshell sunglasses, by Philippe Chevalier.

1954   5.75in (14.5cm) wide

$600-900 **VE**

A pair of French faux tortoiseshell plastic 'mask' sunglasses, by Paulette Gigner.

1958-1960   6in (15.5cm) wide

$400-600 **VE**

A pair of 1960s Pierre Cardin transparent brown plastic 'eyebrow' sunglasses, the arms stamped "Pierre CARDIN".

5.75in (14.5cm) wide

$300-400 **VE**

A pair of 1960s French laminated pearlized rust-colored plastic bow tie-shaped sunglasses, the arm stamped "REGGAE" and with paper label reading "REGGAE".

5in (13cm) wide

$220-280 **VE**

A pair of 1950s French hand-cut, gold and white hand-painted black plastic frames, by Zyl, with inlaid rhinestones.

Zyl is also the trade name for the plastic zylonite, a form of cellulose acetate which originates from cotton and can be found in a wide range of colors.

8in (20.5cm) wide

$600-900 **VE**

A pair of 1950s French 'Fantasy' winged yellow snakeskin effect and clear laminated plastic 'wrap-around' sunglasses, the arms stamped "MADE IN FRANCE".

The laminated plastic has curved over the years making these fabulous sunglasses too small to wear now, although this may be reversed.

4.75in (12cm) wide

$220-280 **VE**

A pair of 1960s hand-painted white plastic sunglasses, with dark neon-colored psychedelic patterns.

6in (15cm) wide

$220-280 VE

A pair of French Op Art black and white checkerboard molded plastic sunglasses, the arm stamped "FRANCE".

c1970   5.5in (14cm) wide

$150-200 VE

A pair of 1960s French white and black striated plastic sunglasses, the arm stamped "FRANCE".

5.75in (14.5cm) wide

$100-150 VE

A pair of 1960s French yellow checkerboard laminated sunglasses, the arm stamped "FRANCE".

5.75in (14.5cm) wide

$100-150 VE

A pair of 1960s Op Art green fabric and laminated plastic frames, the arm stamped "FRANCE".

Op Art or 'Optical Art' describes the work of artists Victor Vasarely and Bridget Riley in the 1960s and is characterized by the use of brightly colored, repeated simple or geometric motifs.

5in (13cm) wide

$220-280 VE

A pair of 1960s French Op Art 'diamond'-shaped black and white laminated plastic sunglasses.

6in (15.5cm) wide

$220-280 VE

A pair of Pierre Cardin brown plastic sunglasses, with hinged arms and nosepiece, in the shape of TV screens.

Dating from a high-point in Cardin's innovative career, these glasses show the sixties' obsession with television.

6in (15cm) wide

$300-500 VE

A pair of laminated reddish wooden 'Woodline' sunglasses, by Jean Lempereur, the arm stamped "JEAN LEMPEREUR".

1979   5.5in (14cm) wide

$220-280 VE

A pair of 1980s French laminated checkered sunglasses, by Alain Mikli.

Alain Mikli has been designing for over twenty years and is renowned for his innovative eyewear. His designs are popular with many stars including Bono of rock band U2.

5.5in (14cm) wide

$300-400 VE

A pair of 1960s laminated and tartan fabric clear plastic sunglasses, the arms stamped "Reminiscence MADE IN FRANCE".

5.75in (14.5cm) wide

$120-180 VE

A pair of Austrian painted black plastic and metal 'Playboy' sunglasses, with the bunny motif by the hinges.

1970   5.5in (14cm) wide

$120-180 VE

A pair of 1970s Italian Yves Saint Laurent laminated blue and white plastic squared 'Aviator' style sunglasses, arms stamped "YSL169 White/Blue/39 140 YVES SAINT LAURENT PARIS MADE IN ITALY".

These glasses benefit from a notable name, retain their original lenses and capture the look of the 1970s, making them highly desirable to collectors.

5.5in (14cm) wide

$300-500 VE

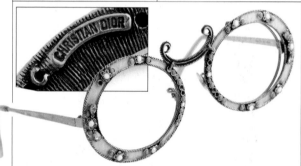

A pair of Christian Dior metal frames, with polychrome enameled decoration, inset green rhinestones.

These revolutionary frames came in six colors.

1967-1970   5.5in (14cm) wide

$300-600 VE

A pair of 1960s 'goggle'-shaped frames, the arm stamped "ITALY".

5.5in (14cm) wide

$100-150 VE

A pair of 1960s French faux tortoiseshell brown and blue 'Cocktail' frames, by Pierre Marly.

Marly was amongst the first to create innovate and exciting designs in the early 1950s and his designs were worn by Sophia Loren and Audrey Hepburn. Peaking in popularity in the 1960s and 1970s, he is known for using unusual materials as well as creating designs that captured the mood and style of the period.

5.25in (13.5cm) wide

$300-400 VE

A pair of 1960s Pierre Cardin smoky gray plastic 'lips' frames, the arms stamped "Pierre CARDIN MADE IN FRANCE", with original, patterned plastic snap case.

5.5in (14cm) wide

$300-400 VE

A pair of 1960s American orange psychedelic fabric laminated frames, by Lumar.

Rather than being surface printed or painted, the fabric is sandwiched between two clear plastic layers.

5.75in (14.5cm) wide

$220-280 VE

A pair of mock tortoiseshell 'bug eye' frames, the arms stamped in gilt "Cabana TS-5078 HEAT TREATED LENSES", the face inlaid with star-shaped decals.

5in (13cm) wide

$40-60 BB

A pair of subsurface metallic silver-finished, black and clear laminated plastic frames, with metal and rhinestone inserts, the arms stamped "U.S.A."

5.5in (14cm) wide

$40-60 **BB**

A pair of American laminated cream and black 'Eskimo' plastic frames, the arm marked "Victory Suntimer Bonetone ZYL".

1957 *6in (15cm) wide*

$300-400 **VE**

A pair of laminated pink and black frames.

5.75in (14.5cm) wide

$40-60 **BB**

A pair of white pearlized frames, the arms marked "BRO 5 1/4 U.S.A."

6in (15cm) wide

$30-50 **BB**

A pair of 1950s French brown plastic laminated frames, with curved, cut away 'eyebrow' rims above the eye, the arms marked "A Paris FRANCE".

Made from many layers of laminated plastic, the frames have been cut away to reveal the different colors.

6in (15cm) wide

$40-60 **BB**

A pair of black and silver striated laminated plastic frames, the arm stamped "POP 360 5 3/4".

The winged area by the hinges is quintessentially 1950s and 1960s.

5.25in (13.5cm) wide

$30-50 **BB**

A pair of pearlized gold plastic and carved black plastic laminated frames, the arms marked "A Paris Frame France".

5in (13cm) wide

$40-60 **BB**

A pair of pink-tinted clear plastic frames, with glitter-like hexagonal silver metal fragments, with diamond-shaped decals.

5.5in (14cm) wide

$40-60 **BB**

A pair of 1950s clear plastic frames, with glitter-like hexagonal silver metal fragments and black thread laminated fabric.

5.5in (14cm) wide

$60-90 **BB**

A pair of laminated pink, gray, and russet frames, with pearlized front face.

5.25in (13.5cm) wide

$30-40 **BB**

A pair of 1940s laminated clear plastic and psychedelic-checkered fabric frames, with metal flower-shaped decals.

5in (13cm) wide

$60-90 BB

A pair of late 1970s American Emmanuelle Khanh plastic frames, covered with real ostrich skin.

Leather and animal skin-covered spectacles have seen a recent revival in popularity. Born in 1935, Khanh began at Cacharel in 1955 before becoming a model and setting up her own design label in the 1960s. She is often known as the 'French Mary Quant'. Her Paris shop has recently closed and there is now increased interest in her designs.

6in (15cm) wide

$300-400 VE

A pair of late 1970s American Emmanuelle Khanh clear plastic frames, covered with lace and lacquered.

6in (15cm) wide

$220-280 VE

A pair of 1950s reverse-carved Lucite frames, with painted and filled floral motifs.

These Lucite frames have been carved from the inside surface and then painted. This is a technique commonly found in clear and 'apple juice' colored plastic jewelry from the 1930s onward.

5.25in (13.5cm) wide

$50-80 BB

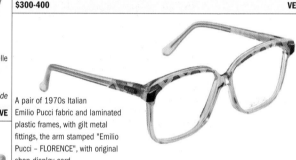

A pair of 1970s Italian Emilio Pucci fabric and laminated plastic frames, with gilt metal fittings, the arm stamped "Emilio Pucci – FLORENCE", with original shop display card.

Legendary Italian fashion designer Emilio Pucci is known for his wild psychedelic, geometric or swirling fabric patterns – original 1960s and 1970s pieces are hotly sought after, particularly as the label has been recently relaunched.

5.5in (14cm) wide

$300-400 VE

A pair of 1960s Italian laminated green and white plastic frames, stamped "MADE IN ITALY" on the arms.

5.25in (13.5cm) wide

$150-200 VE

A pair of Spanish laminated lime green-striped frames, the arms stamped "MAIORCA LOZZA R".

c1970 *5.5in (14cm) wide*

$220-280 VE

A pair of late 1970s French 'Woodline' wooden frames, by Jean Lempereur, with gilt metal decal reading "JEAN LEMPEREUR PARIS" to arm.

6in (15cm) wide

$220-280 VE

A pair of 1950s laminated clear and pearlized plastic round frames.

5.5in (14cm) wide

$30-50 BB

A pair of large black plastic gent's frames, the arm stamped "FRAME BARBADOS 5 1/2".

5.75in (14.5cm) wide

$30-50 BB

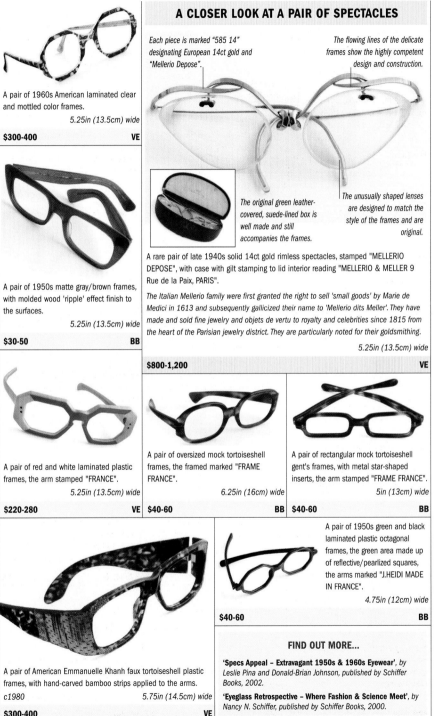

A pair of 1960s American laminated clear and mottled color frames.

5.25in (13.5cm) wide

$300-400 VE

A CLOSER LOOK AT A PAIR OF SPECTACLES

Each piece is marked "585 14" designating European 14ct gold and "Mellerio Depose".

The flowing lines of the delicate frames show the highly competent design and construction.

The original green leather-covered, suede-lined box is well made and still accompanies the frames.

The unusually shaped lenses are designed to match the style of the frames and are original.

A rare pair of late 1940s solid 14ct gold rimless spectacles, stamped "MELLERIO DEPOSE", with case with gilt stamping to lid interior reading "MELLERIO & MELLER 9 Rue de la Paix, PARIS".

The Italian Mellerio family were first granted the right to sell 'small goods' by Marie de Medici in 1613 and subsequently gallicized their name to 'Mellerio dits Meller'. They have made and sold fine jewelry and objets de vertu to royalty and celebrities since 1815 from the heart of the Parisian jewelry district. They are particularly noted for their goldsmithing.

5.25in (13.5cm) wide

$800-1,200 VE

A pair of 1950s matte gray/brown frames, with molded wood 'ripple' effect finish to the surfaces.

5.25in (13.5cm) wide

$30-50 BB

A pair of red and white laminated plastic frames, the arm stamped "FRANCE".

5.25in (13.5cm) wide

$220-280 VE

A pair of oversized mock tortoiseshell frames, the framed marked "FRAME FRANCE".

6.25in (16cm) wide

$40-60 BB

A pair of rectangular mock tortoiseshell gent's frames, with metal star-shaped inserts, the arm stamped "FRAME FRANCE".

5in (13cm) wide

$40-60 BB

A pair of 1950s green and black laminated plastic octagonal frames, the green area made up of reflective/pearlized squares, the arms marked "J.HEIDI MADE IN FRANCE".

4.75in (12cm) wide

$40-60 BB

A pair of American Emmanuelle Khanh faux tortoiseshell plastic frames, with hand-carved bamboo strips applied to the arms.

c1980 *5.75in (14.5cm) wide*

$300-400 VE

FIND OUT MORE...

'Specs Appeal – Extravagant 1950s & 1960s Eyewear', by Leslie Pina and Donald-Brian Johnson, published by Schiffer Books, 2002.

'Eyeglass Retrospective – Where Fashion & Science Meet', by Nancy N. Schiffer, published by Schiffer Books, 2000.

COLLECTORS' NOTES

■ The 1950s are often called 'the new 1930s' in terms of style and collectible potential. The decade certainly saw an optimistic 'New Look' at design as it emerged from the privations of war. This combined with today's vogue for 'retro' styling means that the market looks set to continue to grow.

■ Not all pieces produced during the 1950s meet with the exacting standards of today's collectors, and indeed interior decorators. Consider form and design, material, new technologies, and surface decoration, as all should typify the period. Forms and shapes were often asymmetrically organic, but always clean-lined. They were quintessentially modern in a way linked to, but quite different from, the architectural Art Deco period – from kidney-shaped tables to tulip-like vases.

■ The 1950s saw a great number of new materials come to the fore. Plastic had been popularized in the 1920s and 1930s and developments from the 1950s had a great impact on design. Formica and laminated woods were increasingly used, along with other materials which allowed modern and fashionable forms to be produced efficiently and inexpensively.

■ Surface decoration is diverse, ranging from erotic or glamorous ladies to demure images of fashionable ladies with poodles – signs of a yearning for much desired luxury and prosperity. Polka dots, stars, playing card motifs, 'exotic' zebra prints, and designs based around atomic designs were also common. Colors tend to be cheerfully bright, often taken from a pastel palette and are poles apart from the dominance of dull of the 1940s.

■ Condition is important, as many items were mass-produced. Damage or wear can reduce value dramatically unless the item is extremely rare or desirable. The work of leading designers should continue to be sought after. Do not ignore mass-produced items that cover as many of the above criteria as possible, as eye-appeal and adherence to the style of this key age are very important factors to collectors and style gurus.

A Beswick 'Zebra Fur' vase, the shape designed by Albert Hallam in the late 1950s, marked "1351".

Jesse Tait's zebra-striped 'Zambesi' design, released in 1956, was so popular that it was widely copied. This example is by Jim Hayward for Beswick, who produced this pattern until 1963. The yellow interior is typical of the period.

9.5in (24cm) high

$100-150   **L**

A Sandland 'Zebrette' pattern vase.

6.5in (16.5cm) high

$25-35   **GAZE**

A Vulcanware vase, by Alban, England.

6.25in (16cm) high

$15-25   **L**

A Ridgways 'Barbecue' pattern bowl.

This pattern is much scarcer than the Homemaker pattern.

6.75in (17cm) diam

$30-50   **GAZE**

A Ridgways Homemaker Cadenza coffee pot, with six black coffee cups and six saucers.

The ubiquitous and now legendary Homemaker pattern was designed by Enid Seeney in 1956-57 and was mass-produced, being sold through Woolworths in the UK until c1967. Although plates are common, coffee pots are not and are more valuable.

coffee pot 23.5in (60cm) high

$400-600 set   **GAZE**

A 1950s Burleigh Ware white ground vase, with black and red leaf design.

11in (28cm) high

$25-35   **GAZE**

A 1950s ceramic vase, with handpainted black glazed profile of a lady's head.

Both the 'organic' almost leaf-like form and the black elegant lady are typical of the 1950s.

6.5in (16.5cm) high

$12-18   **MA**

A set of four Old Foley 'Moonglow' pattern dishes, by James Kent, each with handpainted decoration and gilt highlights.

largest 9.75in (25cm) wide

$12-18　　　　　　**MA**

Five Ornamin plastic sandwich plates, and a bread plate.

largest 12.25in (31cm) long

$12-18　　　　　　**GAZE**

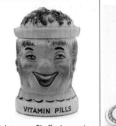

A Japanese Shafford ceramic vitamin box, in the form of a lady's head, stamped on the base "C 1960 THE SHAFFORD CO. 5963Y", with silver label reading "AN ORIGINAL BY SHAFFORD JAPAN".

7.5in (10cm) high

$30-40　　　　　　**DAC**

A 1950s ceramic dressing table set, with transfer of a lady's profile within a pink border.

7in (18cm) high

$80-120　　　　　　**MA**

A Worcester Ware metal tea tray, with transfer decoration of ballerinas posing.

Very few trays have survived in this condition, as the pattern was easily scratched, and then went rusty.

c1955　　　　　　*16.25in (41cm) wide*

$25-35　　　　　　**MA**

A folding laminated wood cocktail tray, with four handpainted cocktail pictures and four cocktail recipes with label reading "FOREIGN".

19in (48cm) long

$100-150　　　　　　**CVS**

A rare, complete American plastic spice rack, with six 'black mamma' plastic spice jars, the lid coming off at the waist to reveal shaker.

c1955　　　　　　*13.5in (34.5cm) long*

$400-600　　　　　　**SOTT**

A set of ten 1950s Australian cast acrylic kitchen canisters, by Nylex, with gilt pictures and descriptions of contents.

largest 10in (25.5cm) high

$100-150　　　　　　**MA**

A 1950s English plastic pineapple ice bucket.

Beware of later Japanese copies which can be identified by a deeper yellow plastic and a lightweight feel.

11in (28cm) high

$30-40　　　　　　**DTC**

A 1950s acrylic Bovril advertising cup.

3.5in (9cm) high

$1-2　　　　　　**MA**

Two from a set of six plastic high ball tumblers, each encasing a lime green felt shark with gold studs and brown string fishing net.

c1955   6in (15.5cm) high

$80-120 set   **CVS**

Two from a set of eight American Federal frosted high ball glass tumblers, with transfer-printed lemons, ice cubes, and cherries.

7in (17.5cm) h

$100-150 set   **CVS**

A 1950s black wire and wicker plant pot holder.

This is the middle height of three sizes of holder made.

7in (18cm) high

$18-22   **DTC**

A 1950s black wire and raffia paper rack.

9.5in (24cm) wide

$30-50   **DTC**

A 1950s black wire and wicker 'Miss Kitty' letter rack.

Letters can be stored in the ribs of her body, and a pen in her curling tail.

$30-50   **DTC**

A 1950s cream acrylic sailboat-shaped alarm clock, made in China.

6.75in (17cm) high

$80-120   **MA**

A CLOSER LOOK AT AN EAMES WALL HANGER

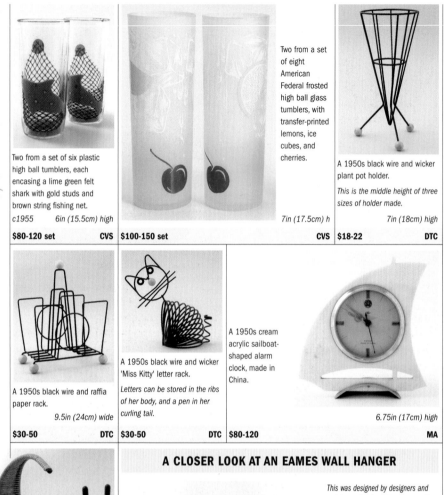

A 1950s black wire and raffia wine pourer.

An example of this wine pourer was included in the influential 'Austerity to Affluence - British Art & Design 1945-1962' exhibition held by the Fine Art Society, London in 1997 and can be seen in their catalog.

$25-35   **DTC**

This was designed by designers and architects Charles & Ray Eames, who aimed to provide good modern design for all.

It was designed in 1952-53 and is still made today by Herman Miller Inc.

Scientific drawings or models of atoms inspired many designers of the period – just as the 'atomic age' was dawning.

It is produced in enameled steel wire with painted maple wood balls in nine different colors.

An Eames 'Hang-It-All', produced by Herman Miller, recent manufacture, with 14-colored wood balls on an enameled metal rack, includes mounting hardware, as new.

$80-120   **FRE**

A Liberty of London alarm clock.

4in (10cm) wide

$30-50 GAZE

A 1950s boxed Taktelli metronome, in gray and red plastic.

6.25in (16cm) high

$18-22 GAZE

A 1950s wooden base and glass sphere money/piggy bank, with color printed card pig on a rainy day, the back with a 'Money Meter' showing the values of different levels.

7in (18cm) high

$22-28 TM

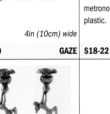

A pair of 1950s chrome candlesticks, with prancing ladies with flowing hair, the bases stamped "REG 873891".

These candleholders and bases can be found on many other designs, which are usually worth much less if in wood – these Art Deco styled chrome ladies are much more desirable.

8.75in (22.5cm) high

$50-70 MA

An early 1950s guitar-shaped wall mirror, with handpainted flower decoration.

Hard to find in such excellent condition, this type of mirror represents the beginning of the modern rock'n'roll movement in its shape, although amusingly not in the painted decoration!

17in (43cm) long

$60-90 MA

A CLOSER LOOK AT A TRETCHIKOFF PRINT

This is typical of the style of Russian-born, South African artist Vladimir Tretchikoff (b1913) in terms of its exotic subject, lighting, color scheme, and female subject gazing out at the viewer.

Look out for the scarcer and more desirable dancing girl pictures, such as 'Balinese Dancer'. Flowers are the least desirable of all subjects.

As well as being one of his most recognizable images, this print has its original, period frame, which is a desirable feature. It is also undamaged – many were stored away badly or thrown away when they fell out of fashion in the 1960s.

The kitsch style typifies the 1950s when many thousands of these highly fashionable, inexpensive reproductions were sold – they have now become highly fashionable again and have risen steeply in value.

A 1950s dressing table 'crinolined lady' lamp, painted plaster with pink net shade over a wired fabric base.

This form derives from the ceramic and wax half dolls popular during the early part of the 20thC. For more information, please see the 'Dolls' section.

15in (38cm) high

$25-35 MA

A 1950s Tretchikoff 'Chinese Girl' print, in period white-painted frame.

frame 25.25in (64cm) high

$60-90 MTS

A 1950s Tretchikoff 'Miss Wong' print, mounted on board and in period gilt frame, with addition retailer's label to rear for Bentalls Picture Department, Kingston.

27.5in (70cm) high

$80-120 MTS

A pair of American 1950s Japanese boy and girl figures, each carrying water buckets, with matte bodies and glazed faces, marked "Foreign".

8.5in (21.5cm) high

$50-70   **MA**

A 1950s long-necked cat ceramic vase, with luster finish.

13.75in (35cm) high

$8-12   **MA**

An unusual 'teacher' guitar playing bottle opener.

Found in a range of characters, including a Mexican, this version is rare. Presumably it would have been less popular than an exotic character at the time.

5.5in (14cm) high

$15-25   **MA**

A 1950s light blue Dansette Popular electric turntable, with built-in speaker.

12.5in (32cm) wide

$60-90   **MA**

A late 1940s Vogue "The House of Charm All-Girl Orchestral Choir" picture disc.

9.75in (25cm)diam

$60-90   **NOR**

A 1950s printed vinyl traveling bag.

13in (33cm) wide

$40-60   **NOR**

"Better Homes and Gardens Decorating Book", published by Meredith Publishing.

1956-61   *10in (25.5cm) high*

$100-150   **DTC**

A set of 1950s American iron-on 'Picture Patches', with portrait of 'Fabian'.

card 7.25in (18.5cm) high

$25-35   **MTS**

A Roland Rainer 'Town Hall' chair, produced by Pollak, Vienna, beech wood and layered wood painted in a greeny brown.

c1950   *34.5in (88cm) high*

$400-600   **QU**

COLLECTORS' NOTES

▪ Many of the rules for collecting 1950s memorabilia apply to 1960s and 1970s memorabilia as well. Look at styling in terms of form, decoration, and material. Try to buy pieces that represent as many of these in the period as possible, preferably by notable makers.

▪ Color is an important aspect of this period, led primarily by the psychedelic 'flower power' movement. Bright, often acid colors dominated in an explosion of color with clashing purples, oranges, lime greens, and yellows. The use of plastics led to innovative designs in furniture and storage solutions.

▪ Interest in all things futuristic, scientific and 'space-aged' continued, supported by movies and the 'space race'. UFO and space helmet shapes are common, formed in futuristic materials such as chrome and plastic. The world of flowers and sinuous plant stems was also popular, with Art Nouveau styling making a reappearance, but with a new makeover in the period palette.

▪ Much of the market is governed by nostalgia and today's 'retro' fashion. Nostalgia becomes even more important with the 1970s, which is still a developing decade for collectors. Always look for brands, names or designs that people will remember, possibly as they owned them once or desired them at the time.

A 1960s J. and G. Meakin Studio 'Cornflower' pattern part coffee service, comprising coffee pot, sugar bowl and two cups and saucers.

The cylinder was a popular and fashionable shape for tableware and other objects during the 1960s, and shows any surface design off very well. The more notable factories of Midwinter and Portmeirion were at the forefront of this style, although Meakin currently offers a more affordable period alternative.

coffee pot 12in (30.5cm) high

$50-70   **DTC**

A 1960s Johnson Bros. coffee pot, in a variation of the 'Focus' pattern originally designed by textile designer Barbara Brown for Midwinter in 1964.

9in (23cm) high

$25-35   MTS

A Midwinter 'Tango' pattern coffee pot, designed by Eve Midwinter.

1969-76   *coffee pot 7.75in (19.5cm) high*

$15-25   **MTS**

A Midwinter 'Tango' pattern cup and saucer, designed by Eve Midwinter.

1969-76   5.5in (14cm) diam

$6-9   MTS

A 1960s Elizabethan English bone china 'Pop' pattern mug and saucer, shape designed by A. Kusmirek.

This came in a number of colors, all roughly of the same value.

saucer 5.75in (14.5cm) diam

$15-25   MTS

A 1960s Staffordshire Potteries storage jar, with psychedelic flower transfer decoration and plastic faux wooden lid.

4.25in (11cm) high

$25-35   MTS

A Lord Nelson Pottery 'Gaytime' flour sifter.

5in (12.5cm) high

$18-22   MTS

An English Ironstone Pottery Ltd 'Beefeater Steak and Grill Set' steak plate.

11in (28cm) wide

$12-18   **MTS**

A 1960s Burleigh 'Orbit' pattern dish, decorated with a psychedelic swirling 'Op Art' design.

7.75in (19.5cm) diam

$15-25   **MTS**

A 1970s Curran of Cardiff enameled metal casserole dish and lid.

9.75in (25cm) wide

$25-35   **MTS**

A 1960s Finel enameled metal saucepan and lid.

5in (13cm) high

$25-35   **MTS**

A set of three 1970s Pyrosil casserole dishes.

As they were inexpensive in their day and much used, it is rare to find a complete and undamaged set of three.

largest 11.75in (30cm) wide

$50-70   **MTS**

A 1960s enameled metal kettle and matching lidded cooking pot, unused.

8.75in (22cm) high

$12-18   **GAZE**

A 1970s enameled metal coffee pot, with remains of label to base.

7in (18cm) high

$15-25   **MTS**

A 1960s tomato red milk glass 'Whisky' decanter, with turned and painted wooden stopper.

9in (23cm) high

$30-40   **MA**

A 1960s lime green milk glass 'Gin' decanter, with turned and painted wooden stopper.

9in (23cm) high

$30-40   **MA**

A set of six 'Babycham' glasses, in original box.

$50-70 set   **GAZE**

FIFTIES, SIXTIES & SEVENTIES

A 1960s/70s German plastic and glass coffee set, comprising glass coffee jug with orange handle and lid, and six matching cups in orange, green, and yellow.

coffee jug 6in (15.5cm) high

$30-40 **MA**

A 1960s American plastic fruit bowl condiment server, with pineapple salt shaker and grapefruit pepper shaker, the whole removing to allow access to the sugar bowl, the base molded "STARKE DESIGN INC, BKLYN N.Y. MADE IN U.S.A.".

4.5in (11.5cm) wide

$30-50 **CVS**

A 1970s Guzzini clear plastic ice bucket, with chrome-plated handle and plastic logo decal.

6.5in (16.5cm) high

$25-35 **DTC**

A late 1970s Crayonne brown plastic ice bucket, retailed by Habitat.

6.75in (17cm) high

$20-30 **DTC**

A psychedelic lithographed string box.

4.75in (12cm) high

$15-25 **MTS**

A psychedelic lithographed biscuit tin, by Baret Ware, the lid with biscuit dryer.

7.75in (19.5cm) high

$25-35 **MTS**

A 1960s Worcester Ware lithographed tin 'flower power' waste paper bin.

7in (18cm) high

$15-25 **MTS**

A 1960s 'flower power' melamine bread board.

13.75in (35cm) long

$15-25 **MTS**

A pair of 1970s psychedelic elephant oven gloves.

6in (15.5cm) long

$12-18 **MTS**

A 1960s melamine four hook key rack.

11.75in (30cm) wide

$15-25 **MTS**

FIFTIES, SIXTIES & SEVENTIES

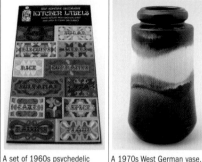

A set of 1960s psychedelic self-adhesive kitchen labels.

11.5in (29.5cm) high

$25-35   **MTS**

A 1970s West German vase, marked "549-21" and "W. German".

8.25in (21cm) high

$40-60   **DTC**

A 1970s West German vase, aqua glazed with abstract lava design, marked "285-18" and "W. German".

7in (18cm) high

$40-50   **DTC**

A 1960s Kilrush Ltd turquoise waisted vase, made in the Republic of Ireland.

7.5in (19cm) high

$15-25   **L**

A 1970s West German Scheurich handled vase, marked "408-40".

A huge number of these molded and glazed ceramic vases were produced during the 1960s and 1970s. Common colors are brown and orange and pieces bore a strong resemblance to Poole Pottery. Nearly all are marked on the base with numbers and a reference to Germany. Little more is known and this may turn out to be a developing market if more information is found. Eye appeal, size, and condition are currently the major concerns for value, which rarely exceeds $120-180.

15.75in (40cm) high

$70-100   **DTC**

A Shelley semi-matte turquoise glazed vase.

10in (25.5cm) high

$30-40   **L**

A 1970s Dialene red plastic party set, boxed.

This party set, often confused as a jewelry box, was made in a range of colors. The purple one is a rare color.

10in (25.5cm) high

$25-35   **DTC**

A 1970s Carousel plastic lazy susan, in the form of a waterlily, with rare original box.

16in (40.5cm) diam

$30-40   **DTC**

An Italian 'Multiplor' red plastic storage box, designed by Rino Pirovano and produced by Rexite of Italy, with swing-out trays and marked "Art 900" and "R".

c1970   5.25in (13.5cm) high

$30-50   DTC

A 1970s green plastic desk tidy, probably Italian, with white plastic drawers.

4.5in (11.5cm) high

$15-25   DTC

A 'Dedalino' orange plastic pen holder, designed by Emma Gismondi-Schweinberger and made by Idarco.

These were designed in five different colored plastics including a chrome-effect finish!

c1966   3.5in (9cm) high

$40-50   DTC

A red and white plastic vanity box.

4.75in (12cm) wide

$15-25   GAZE

A 1970s white desk lamp.

The 'space age' mushroom shaped lamp was a favorite for 1960s homes and was made by a number of companies. Value depends on the maker, designer, size and condition.

16in (41cm) high

$25-35   GAZE

A CLOSER LOOK AT A PAIR OF LAMPS

These lamps demonstrate the formal possibilities of plastic, being molded from a single piece.

The form is also pure, clean lined and modern and almost resembles a space helmet.

They were produced in a range of colors, all bright and typical of the 1970s.

They were designed in 1969 by Italian architect Vico Magistretti (b1920), who began to design plastic furniture in the 1960s.

A pair of 1970s Italian Artemide 'Dalu' red plastic table lamps.

10.5in (26.5cm) high

$150-200   DTC

A Cosmo Designs chromed table lamp, with a four-piece revolving shade.

Different levels of colored light could be created by turning successive leaves of the shade around. The idea is very similar to Danish designer Verner Panton's 'Moon Light' with its curving, revolving strips to alter the strength of the light.

13in (33cm) high

$30-50   GAZE

A 1960s/70s Carlton ware child's lamp base, in the form of a psychedelic cat.

5.5in (14cm) wide

$30-50   **MTS**

A five-tiered ceiling light, of yellow and gray metal bands.

$15-25   **GAZE**

A pair of small green glass ceiling lights.

9.5in (24cm) high

$25-35   **GAZE**

A Shattaline turquoise plastic resin lamp base, with a correct yellow spun fiberglass shade.

These mass-produced lamps were made from 1968 for sale in British Home Stores. They were made of cast resin and came in red, gold, orange, beige or turquoise. This is the middle of three sizes of lamp base.

c1968   *7in (18cm) high*

$50-70   **DTC**

A CLOSER LOOK AT A 1970S LAMP

The light emitted by the half-chromed light bulb at the center is reflected around the room by the gold-plated plastic tentacles, giving a subtle, but sparkling effect.

This lamp design won an award at the 'La Lampada Più' contest of 1975 at the XII Salon of Domestic Arts.

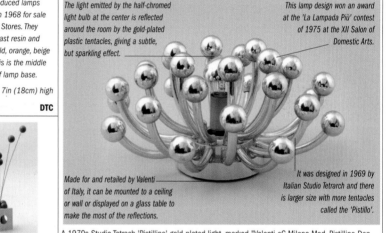

Made for and retailed by Valenti of Italy, it can be mounted to a ceiling or wall or displayed on a glass table to make the most of the reflections.

It was designed in 1969 by Italian Studio Tetrarch and there is larger size with more tentacles called the 'Pistillo'.

A 1970s Studio Tetrarch 'Pistillino' gold-plated light, marked "Valenti eC Milano Mod. Pistillino Dep. Design Studio Tetrarch".

12in (30.5cm) wide

$150-200   **DTC**

A 1970s wire and plastic sculpture.

13.5in (34.5cm) high

$40-60   **DTC**

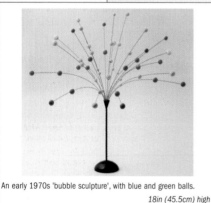

An early 1970s 'bubble sculpture', with blue and green balls.

18in (45.5cm) high

$60-90   **DTC**

A Pifco table fan.

11in (28cm) high

$15-25   **GAZE**

A triangular display piece, with internal decoration, signed on the base "'71" and "J. Walter Thompson Co."

1971   *7.75in (19.5cm) high*

$180-220   **DTC**

A 1960s round wooden Ronson lighter.

4.25in (11cm) wide

$4-6   **GAZE**

A 1980s 4-D quartz clock, by Omni Clock Ltd.

5.5in (14cm) high

$40-60   **DTC**

A 1970s stainless steel and chrome table lighter.

5.5in (14cm) high

$18-22   **DTC**

A 1970s Braun brushed steel table lighter.

3.5in (8.5cm) high

$25-35   **DTC**

A late 1970s Trebors Refreshers oversized advertising money box.

15.5in (39.5cm) long

$25-35   **DTC**

A 1970s Bossons 'Cheyenne' painted plaster wall plaque.

12.5in (32cm) high

$60-90   **BAD**

A BMF 'The Colani' yellow polyethylene chair, made by Top System, organic shape with writing surface.

c1972   26in (65cm) high

$700-1,000   **QU**

A Bossons 'Romany' hanging wall plaque, painted plaster.

Bossons was founded in 1946 by father and son W.H. and W. Ray Bossons, who released their first catalog of handpainted chalk wall plaques in 1948. Wall masks were added in 1959. The factory closed in 1996. Value is largely determined by condition, with mint examples being the most valuable. Those that have been repainted or varnished are worth the least.

9.5in (24cm) high

$60-90   **BAD**

A pair of Günter Beltzig 'Floris' fiberglass chairs, made by Beltzig Design, with artist's signature and number in felt-tip pen.

Designed in 1967, these chairs are from a limited edition of 100 produced in 1992. Made of molded fiberglass resin, they fully explore the fluid nature of the material and have the appearance of an organic, natural form growing upward from the floor. They were made in two parts and had to be handmade.

c1967   42.5in (106cm) high

$1,000-1,500 each   **QU**

A pair of Alexander Begge 'Casalino' red plastic children's chairs, made by Casala Manufacture Lauenau, signed to underside.

c1970   20.75in (52cm) high

$180-220   **QU**

A 'Vicario' chair, with molded ABS plastic body, designed by Vico Magistretti.

c1970

$150-200   **BONBAY**

An American JVC Videosphere, made from 1969 to mid-1970s.

The design of this TV is clearly based on a spaceman's helmet and was influenced by the American lunar landing of 1969. They were made in white and orange in the UK and red, black, and gray in the US. Red is the rarest color. A chain allowed it to be hung from the ceiling. There is a later version with a radio and alarm clock in the base, which is usually more valuable.

13in (33cm) high

$300-500   **DTC**

A 1960s Rexard Creation 'Gabrielle' display doll, designed by Odette Arden, in mint condition with original card tag and box.

12.25in (31cm) high

$25-35   **MTS**

A 1960s Marx Toys of Swansea battery-operated 78rpm 'Kiddi-Tunes' record player, in original box.

box 13in (32.5cm) wide

$70-100   **MA**

A CLOSER LOOK AT A TROLL

This troll was made by Thomas Dam of Denmark, the first and also considered the best and most collectible of toy troll makers, and is marked with his name.

This is one of the most common types of costume – look out for character costumes such as nurses and soldiers, which could also be bought separately.

A 1970s "19" magazine clutch bag.

12in (30.5cm) wide

$40-60   **DTC**

He is in mint condition with clean plastic and original hair, and he retains his clothes and box.

Look out for black and animal trolls, which are rarer and more valuable, especially the legendary alligator troll.

A 1960s troll, by Thomas Dam, with green felt shorts and in original box.

Trolls were an immensely popular fad between the late 1960s and the early 1970s but were first created in the 1950s by Thomas Dam (pronounced Dom).

6in (15cm) high

$40-60   **SOTT**

A 1970s Panasonic "plunger" 8-track player, boxed.

The now obsolete 8-track format was developed in 1965 and was popular until the late 1970s. A great commercial success in its day, it lead to many developments in portable music and was best known for in-car entertainment being available in all Fords in 1966. Although successful, cheaper manufacturing led to use of plastic rollers which caused tape wear and jamming.

9in (23cm) high

$120-180   **DTC**

A 1970s 'Las Vegas' printed paper laminated and plastic magazine purse.

Made for carrying magazines and small items, these were mainly made in Italy and often contained fashion magazines.

11.75in (30cm) wide

$120-180   **NOR**

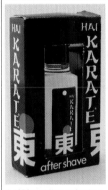

A 'The Pussycats' vinyl lunch box and Thermos flask, by Aladdin Incorporated, the Thermos covered with a paper label.

c1966

$100-150   **NOR**

A 1960s 'Go Go' vinyl lunch box, lacks thermos, by Aladdin Incorporated.

These lunch boxes are very desirable for their funky period artwork that captures the fashions and evokes the music of the period. Splits in the vinyl will devalue them considerably.

c1966   9in (22.5cm) high

$100-150   **NOR**

A pair of 1960s Satellite jumping shoes (to give you a 'spring' in your step!), marked "Model 660", unused and in original box.

10.5in (26.5cm) high

$40-60   **NOR**

A 1970s Hai Karate aftershave and lotion gift set, distributed by Ross of Brighton Ltd.

5.75in (14.5cm) high

$15-25   **DTC**

A 1970s Hai Karate soap-on-a-rope, distributed by Ross of Brighton Ltd.

7.75in (19.5cm) high

$15-25   **DTC**

A 1970s Hai Karate body talc and aftershave gift set, distributed by Ross of Brighton Ltd.

7.25in (18.5cm) high

$25-35   **DTC**

Left: A 1970s Hai Karate musk talc, distributed by Ross of Brighton Ltd.

5.5in (14cm) high

$8-12   **DTC**

Right: A 1970s Hai Karate advertising mug.

3.75in (9.5cm) high

$4-6   **DTC**

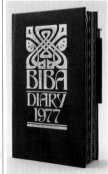

A 1977 Biba diary, unused.

8.25in (21cm) high

$50-70   **DTC**

A pair of yellow 'Smiley' printed canvas shoes, by the Newport Rubber Co.

The ubiquitous smiley face was invented by American artist and inventor Harvey Ball (1922-2001) in 1963 for an insurance company looking for a way to improve company morale. He was paid $45 for sole rights to his creation, which was used on badges. In 1970, two Philadelphia brothers, Bernard and Murray Spain, used the face on a massive range of items with peace themes and the ensuing fad reached its high point over the next two years. The computer smiley face was born later, however, being first used online in late 1982.

c1970   10.25in (26cm) long

$100-150   **NOR**

COLLECTORS' NOTES

■ Born in 1937, Peter Max has grown to become one of America's foremost 'pop' culture artists. His childhood was filled with magic and mystery as he traveled with his family between Shanghai, China, Africa, India, and Israel, where he first developed his love of planets and astronomy.

■ He also drew inspiration from comic books seen as a child and began studying art in Paris before emigrating to the US with his family in 1953. Here he furthered his studies in art and worked in photography. By the 1960s, his photographs gave way to a new quasi-psychedelic style, often called 'Cosmic 60s', for which he is best known. Bright, acid colors and bold, curvaceous forms often inspired by Art Nouveau and the popular cultural movements of the time dominate his work.

■ Look for pieces that typify this style, preferably from the 1960s and 1970s when Max began to shoot to fame. Posters and particularly original artworks fetch high sums but even items produced in great numbers, such as his tin trays, can fetch high prices. Many were disposed of, causing them to be rare today. Ceramics and glass, as well as paper pieces and books, are also popular. Condition is important with such items and scratches, tears and fading reduce the value.

A Peter Max poster, printed by Security Printing, New York, with bright, psychedelic colors and swirling, free-flowing style.

1967   36in (90cm) high

$120-180   **SWA**

An 'Aries' printed card, designed by Peter Max, cut from a book.

$15-20   **NOR**

A Peter Max poster book, published by Crown Publishers Inc.

15.75in (40cm) high

$120-180   **NOR**

A Manhattan 'Yellow Pages' cover for 1970, designed by Peter Max.

This would be worth up to twice as much with the original book.

1970   10.75in (27cm) high

$120-180   **NOR**

A 'Do Not Disturb' hotel door sign, designed by Peter Max.

This was taken from a Manhattan hotel where much of the interior decoration and accessories were designed by Max.

$60-90   **NOR**

An Iroquois China 'Love' ashtray, designed by Peter Max.

5in (12.5cm) diam

$60-90   **NOR**

A Peter Max glass dish, with screen-printed psychedelic flower decoration.

8.25in (21cm) diam

$120-180   **NOR**

A Peter Max 'Happy' tin tray.

12.75in (32.5cm) diam

$40-60   **NOR**

FIND OUT MORE...

'The Art of Peter Max', by Charles A. Riley II and Peter Max, published by Harry N. Abrams, 2002.

COLLECTORS' NOTES

■ Film and TV props are the closest thing an enthusiast can get to being part of their favorite movie or show. Collecting in this industry is continuing to grow.

■ Memorabilia connected to the golden age of Hollywood and its glamorous stars is the pinnacle of this collecting field. As props were not considered desirable at the time, many were discarded after filming, or altered and reused on other productions.

■ Another popular area is cult science fiction and horror movies and shows such as "Star Wars", "Star Trek", "Aliens", and "Dr Who", as well as the perennial spy film favorite "James Bond".

■ Today, major studios sell off props as soon as filming is complete. While this means you may not get a 'bargain', each piece should come with a letter of authenticity from the studio guaranteeing that it is genuine. Provenance is vitally important, so always ask the seller for a history of the piece.

■ Props that appeared in key scenes or had a significant role in a movie are usually the most desirable, but be aware that multiple copies will often be made in case of damage, or to display stages of usage. Examples that are used in the background will often be of poor quality or less detailed, but can be more affordable.

■ Promotional items and crew kit can also be an inexpensive way of entering the film and TV memorabilia market, as they are produced in relatively large amounts but would not have been available to the general market.

A prop 'Floats Like A Butterfly, Stings Like A Bee' badge from "Ali", made to the same design as the original with Will Smith's image replacing Cassius Clay.

The date "Oct. 30th '74" on the badge refers to the day Clay defeated George Foreman in Kinshasa, Zaire. It was the first heavyweight championship fight to be held in Africa.

2001   2.75in (7cm) diam

$50-70   PSL

A floppy disc from "Aliens", with label "AXL/2B.S. VID-CON REET. I. WARRANT OFFICER E. RIPLEY USS NOSTROMO 1128. 9.A. MISSION C.N8V".

Made for the inquest scene at the beginning of the film, when Ripley (Sigourney Weaver) is asked to give her account of events aboard the Nostromo. Despite being mentioned in the script, the disks were never used.

$220-280   PSL

An unworn gray promotional t-shirt for "American Beauty".

1999

$25-35   PSL

An unworn black promotional t-shirt for "Apollo 13".

$25-35   PSL

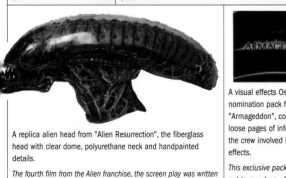

A replica alien head from "Alien Resurrection", the fiberglass head with clear dome, polyurethane neck and handpainted details.

The fourth film from the Alien franchise, the screen play was written by Buffy creator Joss Whedon.

1997   34in (87cm) wide

$400-600   PSL

A visual effects Oscar nomination pack for "Armageddon", containing loose pages of information on the crew involved in the special effects.

This exclusive pack is only sent out to members of the Academy who can vote for the Oscar for best visual effects.

$60-90   PSL

A rubber stunt pistol from the Babylon 5 spin-off TV series "Crusade".

1999   6in (15cm) wide

$220-280   PSL

Two prop 'Joker' $50 bills from "Batman", mounted, framed and glazed.

Seen in the movie when The Joker (Jack Nicholson) parades through the streets, throwing money to the crowds.

21in (53cm) wide

$150-200 PSL

A prop 'Oswald Means Order' metal button from "Batman Returns".

Seen in the movie when The Penguin (Danny DeVito) runs for office.

1995 4in (10cm) wide

$100-150 PSL

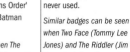

A 'Diamond Exchange Security' sew-on patch from "Batman Forever", made for the film but never used.

Similar badges can be seen when Two Face (Tommy Lee Jones) and The Riddler (Jim Carrey) rob the diamond exchange.

1995 4in (10cm) high

$12-18 PSL

A pair of 'Gotham Observatory' metal security badges from "Batman & Robin", mounted, framed and glazed.

21in (54cm) wide

$600-900 PSL

A prop map from "The Beach", mounted, framed and glazed.

This is the map that Richard (Leonardo DiCaprio) draws on screen to show his new traveling friends the way to 'The Beach'. It is also seen as the other travelers arrive at the adjoining island, as seen through Richard's binoculars.

c2000

$1,200-1,800 PSL

A two-piece Colonial Warrior costume from "Battlestar Galactica", consisting of pants and tunic made of heavy quilted cotton, the tunic shows signs of wear, with embroidered emblem on each arm featuring a series of triangles within a larger circle.

After successfully 're-imagining' the original series, Ronald Moore is producing 13 more episodes for the Sci-Fi Channel, due to air in 2005.

c1978

$600-900 PSL

A sheet of numbers from "A Beautiful Mind", mounted with four stills from the film, framed and glazed.

c2001 24in (60cm) high

$300-500 PSL

A 'Southern City Savings & Loans' blank check from "Big Fish", used by Edward Bloom (Ewan McGregor), mounted framed and glazed.

c2003 15in (38cm) wide

$100-150 PSL

A limited edition reproduction of the original artwork for the 'Machine Pistol' from "Blade 2", by R.T. Ruben, dated November 2000 and titled "Blade's Mach II – Blade Bloodhunt", from an edition of 50, mounted, framed and glazed.

$50-80 PSL

A CLOSER LOOK AT A BUFFY THE VAMPIRE SLAYER PROP

A 'Blair Witch Project Dossier', signed on the cover in silver pen by Daniel Myrick and Eduardo Sanchez, the film's writers and directors.

The Dossier represents a (fictionalized) in-depth investigation into the disappearance of the three students in the Black Hills of Maryland, and also an analysis of the Blair Witch legend itself.

1999

$120-180   **PSL**

This newspaper appeared in the famous season six 'musical' episode 'Once More With Feeling', where the characters uncontrollably burst into song throughout the episode, revealing their inner most fears. It was voted into the top 20 in Channel 4's 100 Greatest Musicals poll.

While not a key prop, the episode is a fan favorite, making it desirable.

2001

$800-1,200

When Buffy finished in 2003, many of the props were auctioned off for charity and on eBay.

Now that the "Buffy" spin-off show "Angel" has been canceled, it is likely that interest in props from these two shows will rise.

A 'Sunnydale Press' prop newspaper from "Buffy The Vampire Slayer", the headline reading 'Mayhem Caused, Monsters Certainly Not Involved, Officials Say', the rest of the front page with unrelated articles copied from a real newspaper, mounted, framed and glazed.

36in (92cm) high

PSL

Three pieces of prop currency from "Buck Rogers In the 25th Century".

1979-81
Largest 2in (5cm) diam

$150-200   **PSL**

An official pictorial moviebook for "Catch Me If You Can", with detailed account of the making of the film, production photographs of locations, props, costumes, and archive photographs from the real life Frank Abagnale's collection.

2003

$15-25   **PSL**

A prop newspaper from "Chicago", from the scene when Roxie (Renee Zellweger) first gets her story in the newspaper, mounted, framed and glazed.

2002   *33in (83cm) high*

$800-1,200   **PSL**

A prop shield from "Clash of the Titans", fiberglass with handpainted detailing.

These shields were used by Jappa's guards, when Perseus asks the Princess to tell her riddle. Also seen when the Princess is about to be sacrificed to the Krackon.

1981   *27.75in (70cm) diam*

$600-900   **PSL**

A cream dress shirt from "The Curse Of The Jade Scorpion", worn by C.W. Briggs (Woody Allen), with labels "Anto, Beverly Hills" and 'W.A. Sept 2000".

Woody Allen wardrobe pieces are scarce.

2001

$300-400   **PSL**

A reproduction 'sonic screwdriver' from "Doctor Who", machined from high-grade aluminum and brass with a red anodized ring, with spring-loaded top section.

The screwdriver was carried by all the Doctors from Patrick Troughton to Peter Davison. This version is synonymous with the fourth Doctor, played by Tom Baker and, while it is a reproduction, it is well made and accurate.

9in (22cm) long

$220-280   **PSL**

A CLOSER LOOK AT A DOCTOR WHO COSTUME

This uniform appears in episode 10 of the Colin Baker story "Trial of a Time Lord – Terror of the Vervoids". The episode is part of a huge 14-story arc revolving around the Doctor's trial for interfering in the affairs of other planets.

This episode is set on board the starliner 'Hyperion III'. The 'Duty Officer' would have been a member of the liner's crew.

Although the fourth Doctor, Tom Baker, is generally considered one of the most popular incarnations of this character, the fifth Doctor Colin Baker and the sixth Peter Davison are gaining in popularity.

The new series of "Doctor Who" is due to air in 2005, staring Christopher Eccleston as the ninth Doctor. This is likely to increase interest in the franchise.

A 'Duty Officer' (Mike Mungarvan) costume from "Doctor Who", the cream-colored pants and tunic with a brown fleck pattern, padded shoulders, a zip-up back and silver colored detailing around the neck and on the sleeves, label reading "Made in BBC Television Workroom" together with the actor's name added in pen.

1986

$700-1,000   **PSL**

A promotional cap for "E.T. the Extra-Terrestrial".
1982

$15-25   **PSL**

An unworn white crew t-shirt from "From Hell", size large.
2001

$50-70   **PSL**

A prop alien knife and sheath from "Galaxy Quest", made of resin in the shape of an alien animal bone, faux alien animal hide grip, the hard plastic scabbard covered with soft scales.

The knife can be seen throughout the film and in particular at the end, as General Sarris (Robert Sachs) attacks the crew as the ship plummets towards Earth.

1999   17in (44cm) long

$300-500   **PSL**

An original pencil and ink storyboard from "Ghostbusters", showing the 'Slimer' ghost scene in the dining room of the 'Sedgewick Hotel', dated 1983 and stamped "Copyright Columbia Pictures Inc", mounted, framed and glazed.

21in (53cm) wide

$600-900   **PSL**

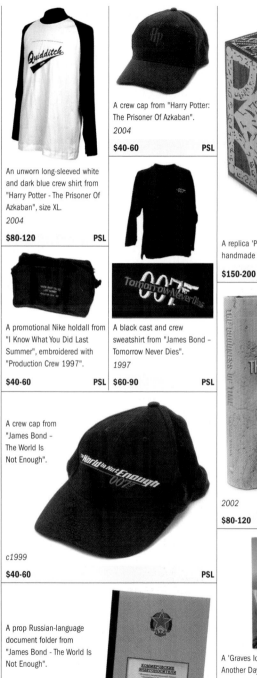

An unworn long-sleeved white and dark blue crew shirt from "Harry Potter - The Prisoner Of Azkaban", size XL.

2004

$80-120 PSL

A crew cap from "Harry Potter: The Prisoner Of Azkaban".

2004

$40-60 PSL

A replica 'Puzzle Cube' from the "Hellraiser" film series, handmade from brass and mahogany.

$150-200 PSL

A promotional Nike holdall from "I Know What You Did Last Summer", embroidered with "Production Crew 1997".

$40-60 PSL

A black cast and crew sweatshirt from "James Bond – Tomorrow Never Dies".

1997

$60-90 PSL

A crew cap from "James Bond – The World Is Not Enough".

c1999

$40-60 PSL

A prop book from "The Hours", the book with facsimile covers for 'The Goodness Of Time' by Richard Brown (Ed Harris).

2002

$80-120 PSL

A prop Russian-language document folder from "James Bond - The World Is Not Enough".

1999

$100-150 PSL

A 'Graves Ice Palace Hotel' postcard from "James Bond – Die Another Day".

This postcard was used as set dressing in the hotel lobby.

2002   6in (15cm) wide

$40-60 PSL

FILM & TV

A premier party menu for "The Lord Of The Rings: The Return Of The King", with 'London Premiere Party December 11 2003' printed at the bottom.

2003   *8in (21cm) high*

$25-35   **PSL**

A visual effects Oscar nomination pack for "Mars Attacks", the card wallet containing loose pages of information on the crew involved with the special effects and details of scenes where the effects came to the fore.

1996

$50-70   **PSL**

A scarce, unworn black crew T-shirt from "Lord Of The Rings", size XL.

$220-280   **PSL**

A US press kit for "The Matrix Reloaded", containing a double CD and a 'digital press kit' with photos, trailers, Quick Time videos, and other information, together with a 56-page color book with dozens of stills and French language text.

2003

$100-150   **PSL**

A press kit for "The Mummy", containing printed production information and a set of five black and white photographs of images from the film.

The kit would have been given to journalists reviewing the premiere or preview of the film.

1999

$25-35   **PSL**

A sweatshirt from "M.A.S.H.", screen used and signed by 'Radar' (Gary Burghoff), with a couple of small holes.

1972-83

$320-380   **PSL**

COPING WITH
VD
AND OTHER
EMBARRASSING
INCIDENTS

JMC
MEDICAL INFO

A 'Coping with VD and Other Embarrassing Incidents' leaflet from "Red Dwarf", the folded paper leaflet with blurred print on the inside, the back page marked "JMC Medical Info".

c1999   *7.5in (19cm) high*

$80-120   **PSL**

A 'Leopard Lager' beer can from "Red Dwarf", with specially printed label with the fictional maker's name, purchased directly from Grant Naylor productions.

c1999   *4.5in (11cm) high*

$80-120   **PSL**

Two costume designs from "The Mighty Morphin Power Rangers", the two copied drawings show multi-colored designs for three spacesuit-type outfits and a green suit with a cape that can be seen in the film.

1995   *12in (30.5cm)*

$40-60   **PSL**

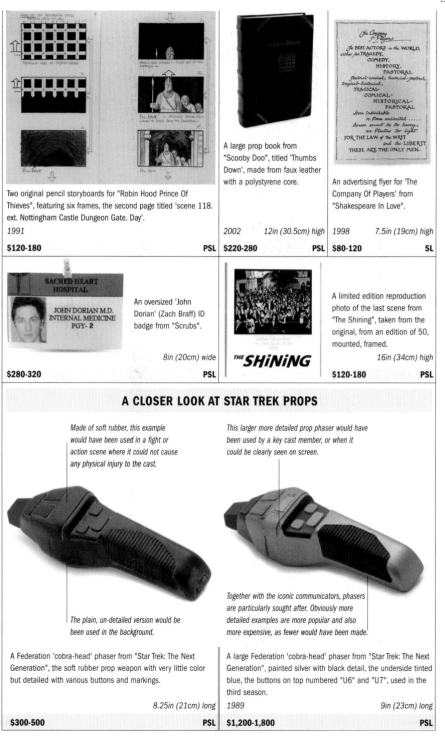

Two original pencil storyboards for "Robin Hood Prince Of Thieves", featuring six frames, the second page titled 'scene 118. ext. Nottingham Castle Dungeon Gate. Day'.

1991

$120-180   **PSL**

A large prop book from "Scooby Doo", titled 'Thumbs Down', made from faux leather with a polystyrene core.

2002   *12in (30.5cm) high*

$220-280   **PSL**

An advertising flyer for 'The Company Of Players' from "Shakespeare In Love".

1998   *7.5in (19cm) high*

$80-120   **SL**

An oversized 'John Dorian' (Zach Braff) ID badge from "Scrubs".

8in (20cm) wide

$280-320   **PSL**

A limited edition reproduction photo of the last scene from "The Shining", taken from the original, from an edition of 50, mounted, framed.

16in (34cm) high

$120-180   **PSL**

A CLOSER LOOK AT STAR TREK PROPS

Made of soft rubber, this example would have been used in a fight or action scene where it could not cause any physical injury to the cast.

This larger more detailed prop phaser would have been used by a key cast member, or when it could be clearly seen on screen.

Together with the iconic communicators, phasers are particularly sought after. Obviously more detailed examples are more popular and also more expensive, as fewer would have been made.

The plain, un-detailed version would be been used in the background.

A Federation 'cobra-head' phaser from "Star Trek: The Next Generation", the soft rubber prop weapon with very little color but detailed with various buttons and markings.

8.25in (21cm) long

$300-500   **PSL**

A large Federation 'cobra-head' phaser from "Star Trek: The Next Generation", painted silver with black detail, the underside tinted blue, the buttons on top numbered "U6" and "U7", used in the third season.

1989   *9in (23cm) long*

$1,200-1,800   **PSL**

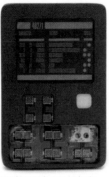

An 'engineering PADD' from "Star Trek: The Next Generation", used by chief engineer 'Geordi LaForge' (Levar Burton), no longer functioning, with a row of buttons missing from the bottom leaving glue marks.

This distinctive red prop can be seen in more than one episode including 'The Masterpiece Society' and 'Realm Of Fear'.

1992   6in (15cm) high

$700-1,000   **PSL**

An 'isolinear chip' from "Star Trek: The Next Generation", with printed paper label and yellow printed circuit board effect on the main body.

3in (8cm) high

$280-320   **PSL**

A plastic bottle from 'Quark's Bar' in "Star Trek: Deep Space Nine", the sports water bottle decorated with gold paint and colored stickers.

This bottle was used in the bar at Quark's casino in the first series.

1993   10in (26cm) high

$120-180   **PSL**

A rare prerelease promotional sticker from "Star Wars", with 'Luke Over Yavin' logo and the title of the movie as "The Star Wars".

This sticker was never taken up by Fox after the 'The' was dropped from the title.

1975   3in (8cm) high

$25-35   **PSL**

A CLOSER LOOK AT A STAR TREK PROP

This prop was used in the 30th anniversary episode 'Trials & Tribble-ations', which reused footage 'The Trouble with Tribbles' episode from the original series.

Call sheets are a vital part of the television-making process and inform members of the cast and crew where and when to be on set.

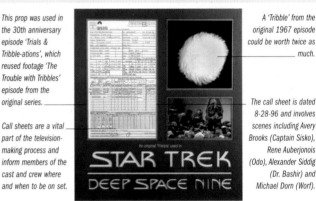

An original 'Tribble' used in

A 'Tribble' from the original 1967 episode could be worth twice as much.

The call sheet is dated 8-28-96 and involves scenes including Avery Brooks (Captain Sisko), Rene Auberjonois (Odo), Alexander Siddig (Dr. Bashir) and Michael Dorn (Worf).

A 'Tribble' and call sheet from "Star Trek - Deep Space 9", the 'Tribble' made from faux white fur, mounted, framed and glazed.

1996   27in (68cm) wide

$800-1,200   **PSL**

A prop 'science award medal' from "Star Trek: Voyager", the gold colored pendant engraved with characters, framed and glazed.

Pendant 2.5in (6cm) long

$600-900   **PSL**

A rare crew sew-on patch from "Star Wars".

This is the first version of the now iconic logo and was designed by Ralph McQuarrie.

c1975   3in (8cm) wide

$150-200   **PSL**

A rare press badge from "Star Wars".

This peel and stick press badge was given to the media for press conferences in 1977. Although very similar to the famous logo, the 'W' is slightly different, this version appears on the first advance posters in Christmas 1976, but was changed by George Lucas in 1977.

4in (10cm) wide

$25-35   **PSL**

A rare crew sew-on patch from "Star Wars - The Empire Strikes Back", unused.

Graphic artist Ralph McQuarrie initially worked at Boeing and later illustrated the Apollo lunar landings. This proved to be the perfect background when he was invited to provide some conceptual drawings for Star Wars. McQuarrie worked on designs for many characters and vehicles including Darth Vader, R2-D2 and the Death Star and went on to work on the rest of the original trilogy. His artwork has also been used in other cult sci-fi classics including "Battlestar Galactica", "Star Trek" and "E.T.".

A rare promotional drink coaster from "Star Wars - The Empire Strikes Back", mint condition.

These were given out to crew members on the set. They are made from uncoated card and virtually all of them were destroyed after just one use.

c1980   4in (10cm) wide

$60-90   **PSL**

A rare original promotional shirt from "Star Wars - The Empire Strikes Back", with Ralph McQuarrie artwork, unworn.

A rare 'Intergalactic Passport' given to cast, crew, and special guests on the set "Star Wars - The Empire Strikes Back", the 18-page book with hard blue cover with unique ID number inside.

These individually stamped and numbered passports were given out to visitors to the soundstages at Elstree Studios in England. The pass allowed guests to visit all areas of the production. There are also fun stamps in the book for 'Moss Eisley', 'Bespin' and 'Tatooine' as well as many others. There is an ID info page and foreign exchange facilities. Only 450 examples were produced and the vast majority are retained by George Lucas' Industrial Light & Magic archives.

c1980   6in (15cm) high   c1980

$400-600   **PSL**

$100-150   **PSL**

c1980

$120-180   **PSL**

A blood analysis device from "Stargate SG-1", the hand-held fishing game sprayed silver, used in season 3 episode 'New Ground', with MGM certificate of authenticity.

1999   6.5in (17cm) long

$400-600   **PSL**

A rare pressbook for "THX 1138", together with an original lobby card.

"THX 1138" was George Lucas' first feature film.

1973   14in (35cm) high

$60-90   **PSL**

A bottle of Moët & Chandon champagne from "Titanic", the label and gold foil with White Star company name on them and a gold foil neck.

1997   12in (30cm) high

$280-320   **PSL**

A visual effects Oscar nomination pack for "Stuart Little", containing information on the crew involved with the special effects, and two glossy color photos of some of the moments from the movie.

1999

$25-35   **PSL**

A pair of 'K White Star Line's' luggage labels from "Titanic", mounted, framed and glazed.

1997

$320-380   **PSL**

9.75in (25cm) wide

An earpiece worn by 'Lara Croft' (Angelina Jolie) in "Tomb Raider".

In much the same way that Nokia linked their 8146 cell phone with "The Matrix", so Ericsson used 'product placement' to increase exposure on their Bluetooth earpiece.

2001   *6in (15cm) long*

$1,200-1,800   **PSL**

A prop check from "Trading Places", used by Lewis Winthorpe III (Dan Ackroyd), mounted, framed and glazed.

1983   *14.5in (37cm) high*

$300-500   **PSL**

A pair of sunglasses from "Waterworld", with pale green plastic lenses, a rough resin frame and wire arms, with a rubber cord at the back and rubber tubing on the bridge of the nose.

c1995

$80-120   **PSL**

A phone used as set dressing in "Waynes World 2".

The Chicago Blackhawks phone can be seen in the Donut shop frequented by Wayne (Mike Myers) and Garth (Dana Carvey).

1993   *8in (20cm) long*

$180-220   **PSL**

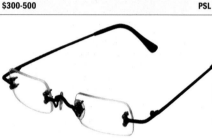

A pair of glasses from "X-Men", worn by the main surgeon during the flashback scene where Wolverine (Hugh Jackman) has adamantium bonded to his skeleton, marked "Hero Doctor".

c2000

$220-280   **PSL**

COLLECTORS' NOTES

■ Increasing nostalgia for the 1970s and 1980s has had a dramatic effect on collecting cult film and TV memorabilia and toys.

■ Science fiction first zoomed across our screens in the 1930s and enjoyed a golden age in the 1950s, but the period gaining in popularity with collectors now is the 1980s. Many shows from that period are re-run on cable TV and also released on DVD and video.

■ British institution Doctor Who is a prime example of the burgeoning popularity of the 1980s. Later incarnations of the Doctor have traditionally been less popular, but interest in Peter Davidson (1981-84) and Colin Baker (1984-86) is growing steadily. With the ninth Doctor set to appear in 2005 in the form of Christopher Eccleston, this series looks set to continue as one of the most popular shows on TV.

■ Memorabilia made at the beginning of a show's run is often the hardest to find as smaller quantities were produced. Condition is very important, as is the original box and any instructions or certificates, particularly for more recent examples.

■ Items produced during a less popular period can be bought at more reasonable prices and may well increase in value if the series gains a new generation of fans.

A handcrafted Doctor Who 'TARDIS' model, by Britannia Miniatures.

c1996   *5.5in (14cm) high*

$30-50   **TP**

A pewter Doctor Who 'Cyberman' bottle stopper, by Scifi Collector.

c2002   *1.5in (4cm) high*

$10-15   **TP**

A Denys Fisher Doctor Who 'Leela' figure, in original box.

A set of pewter Doctor Who 'Dalek' salt and pepper shakers, by Asmortartz Productions.

2001   *3in (7.5cm) high*

$100-150   **TP**

1976   *box 10in (25.5cm) high*

$280-320   **F**

A Doctor Who 'Cyberman Attacking' figure, by Media Collectables.

2002   *figure 2in (5cm) high*

$8-12   **TP**

A Doctor Who 'The Ice Warriors Collection' video box set, by the BBC.

1998   *7.5in (19cm) high*

$50-70   **TP**

A Doctor Who 'Out of the Darkness' audio CD, by the BBC.

1998   *5.5in (14cm) wide*

$30-40   **TP**

Two Doctor Who 'The Secrets of Doctor Who' audio cassettes, tapes one and three.

These cassettes were given away with the 1996 Doctor Who calendar.

1996   *4.25in (11cm) high*

$8-12 each   **TP**

A Doctor Who 'Theme from the BBC TV Series' LP, with hologram sleeve.

1986   12in (30.5cm) wide

$10-15   **TP**

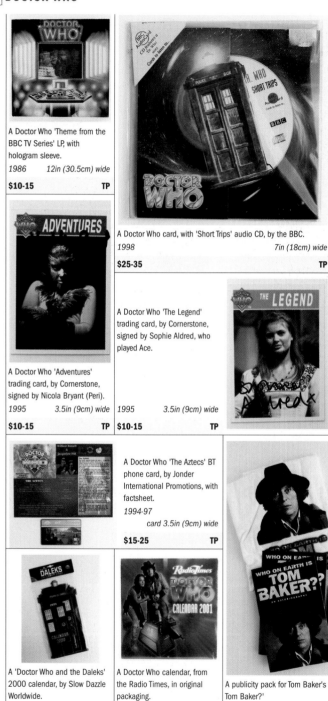

A Doctor Who card, with 'Short Trips' audio CD, by the BBC.

1998   7in (18cm) wide

$25-35   **TP**

A signed Colin Baker Doctor Who publicity postcard, from 'The Two Doctors' episode.

6in (15cm) high

$8-12   **LCA**

A Doctor Who 'Adventures' trading card, by Cornerstone, signed by Nicola Bryant (Peri).

1995   3.5in (9cm) wide

$10-15   **TP**

A Doctor Who 'The Legend' trading card, by Cornerstone, signed by Sophie Aldred, who played Ace.

1995   3.5in (9cm) wide

$10-15   **TP**

A Doctor Who 'The Web Planet' BT phone card, by Jonder International Promotions, with factsheet.

1994-97 card 3.5in (9cm) wide

$15-25   **TP**

A Doctor Who 'The Aztecs' BT phone card, by Jonder International Promotions, with factsheet.

1994-97
card 3.5in (9cm) wide

$15-25   **TP**

A 'Doctor Who and the Daleks' 2000 calendar, by Slow Dazzle Worldwide.

2000   14in (35.5cm) high

$8-12   **TP**

A Doctor Who calendar, from the Radio Times, in original packaging.

2001   12in (30.5cm) wide

$6-9   **TP**

A publicity pack for Tom Baker's autobiography 'Who on Earth is Tom Baker?'

1994

$30-40   **TP**

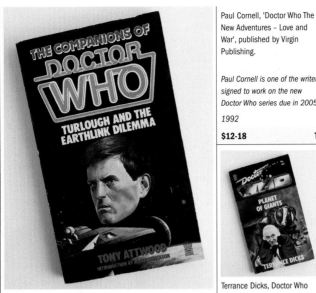

Paul Cornell, 'Doctor Who The New Adventures - Love and War', published by Virgin Publishing.

Paul Cornell is one of the writers signed to work on the new Doctor Who series due in 2005.

1992

$12-18   TP

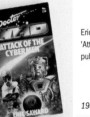

Tony Attwood, 'The Companions of Doctor Who - Turlough and the Earthlink Dilemma', published by Target.

1986   *7in (18cm) high*

$12-18   TP

Terrance Dicks, Doctor Who 'Planet of Giants', published by Target.

1990   *7in (18cm) high*

$10-15   TP

Victor Pemberton, Doctor Who 'The Pescatons', published by Target.

1991   *7in (18cm) high*

$6-9   TP

Eric Saward, Doctor Who 'Attack of the Cybermen', published by Target.

1989   *7in (18cm) high*

$10-15   TP

Justin Richards, Doctor Who 'The Missing Adventures - System Shock', published by Virgin Publishing.

1995

$8-12   TP

Nigel Robinson, Doctor Who 'The Sensorites', published by Target.

1987   *7in (18cm) high*

$5-8   TP

Gary Russell, Doctor Who 'The Missing Adventures - Invasion of the Cat-People', published by Virgin Publishing.

1995

$12-18   TP

Victor Pemberton, Doctor Who 'Fury from the Deep', published by Target.

1986   *7in (18cm) high*

$22-28   TP

A 'The James Bond 007 Secret Service' board game, by Spears, in original box.

box 14.25in (36cm) wide

$40-60   **F**

A James Bond lunch box with Thermos flask, by Aladdin Industries.

1966

$150-200   **TH**

An Airfix 'James Bond's Autogyro' kit, of 'Little Nellie' in 1:24 scale, featured in the film 'You Only Live Twice', with transfers, instructions, and box.

Bond films are well-known for their cool gadgets and vehicles. 'Little Nellie' is a fan favorite and features in a key sequence in this Sean Connery film.

9in (23cm) wide

$120-180   **W&W**

A late 1960s base metal ring, with 'winking' image of James Bond's 'Little Nellie' from 'You Only Live Twice', and flying over an enemy helicopter.

0.75in (2cm) high

$10-15   **CVS**

A 1960s base metal ring, with 'winking' image of James Bond in a white dinner suit and in scuba gear.

0.75in (2cm) high

$12-18   **CVS**

A James Bond 'Moonraker' deluxe figure, by Mego Corp., with helmet and backpack.

A standard version without a helmet or backpack, was also released but is less desirable.

c1979

$300-400   **TH**

A James Bond 'Moonraker' Collegeville costume and mask, by EON Productions.

c1975

$60-90   **TH**

A James Bond 'Moonraker' Collegeville costume and mask of Jaws, by EON Productions.

c1975

$50-80   **TH**

A scarce Lone Star James Bond 'Moonraker' Space Gun, of diecast construction with plastic parts, finished in black and white, with original box, minor wear.

12in (30.5cm) long

$120-180   **W&W**

'Showtime', November 1964, with feature on Sean Connery as James Bond.

11in (28cm) high

$30-40 VM

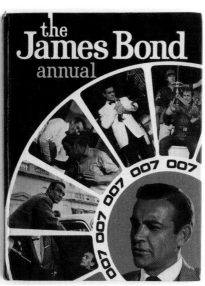

A James Bond annual, including pictures from 'Goldfinger' and 'You Only Live Twice'.

1968 *10.75in (27.5cm) high*

$70-100 VM

'Film Review', August 1977, featuring 'The Spy Who Loved Me'.

10.75in (27.5cm) high

$15-25 VM

A 1960s Arrows 'Goldfinger' jigsaw.

$120-180 VEC

A signed Roger Moore publicity postcard.

6in (15cm) high

$15-25 LCA

A signed Pierce Brosnan publicity photograph.

10in (25.5cm) high

$50-70 LCA

A 1960s Arrows 'Thunderball' jigsaw.

$120-180 VEC

A signed Ursula Andress 'Dr. No' publicity photograph.

The iconic white bikini Andress wears when she emerges from the sea sold at Christies in London for $90,000 in 2001.

10in (25.5cm) high

$60-90 LCA

A signed Honor Blackman 'Goldfinger' publicity photograph.

10in (25.5cm) high

$50-70 LCA

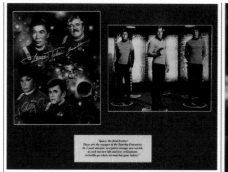

A signed Star Trek publicity photograph, signed by George Takei, James Doohan, Nichelle Nichols and Walter Koenig, mounted with another photograph titled 'Space, the final frontier...'

$100-150   **GAZE**

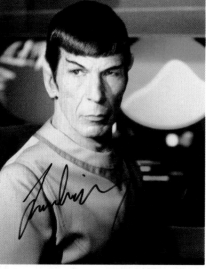

A signed Leonard Nimoy 'Star Trek: The Motion Picture' publicity photograph.

10in (25.5cm) high

$80-120   **LCA**

A Star Trek annual, authorized by the BBC.

1973   *10.5in (27cm) high*

$8-12   **MTS**

A signed George Takei Star Trek publicity photograph.

10in (25.5cm) high

$40-60   **LCA**

A Star Trek 'Champions' Spock pewter figure, by Racing Champions Inc., inspired by 'Star Trek: The Motion Picture', from a limited edition of 9,998.

1998   box 9.25in (23.5cm) high

$60-90   **TP**

A Star Trek 'Champions' Khan pewter figure, by Racing Champions Inc., inspired by 'Star Trek: The Wrath of Khan', from a limited edition of 9,998.

1998   box 9.25in (23.5cm) high

$60-90   **TP**

A Star Trek 'Champions' Kirk pewter figure, by Racing Champions Inc., inspired by 'Star Trek: The Motion Picture', from a limited edition of 9,998.

1998   *box 9.25in (23.5cm) high*

$60-90   **TP**

A signed Patrick Stewart 'Star Trek: The Next Generation' publicity photograph.

10in (25.5cm) high

$50-70   **LCA**

A signed Brent Spiner 'Star Trek: First Contact' publicity photograph.

10in (25.5cm) high

$40-60   **LCA**

'Astounding', July 1940,
science fiction magazine.

9.25in (23.5cm) high

$15-25 VM

A signed Sarah Michelle Gellar
'Buffy the Vampire Slayer'
publicity photograph.

10in (25.5cm) high

$50-70 LCA

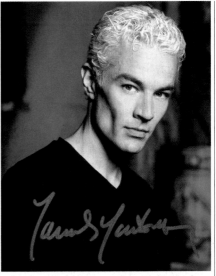

A signed James Masters 'Buffy the Vampire Slayer' publicity
photograph.

10in (25.5cm) high

$60-90 LCA

A signed David Boreanaz 'Angel
the Series' publicity
photograph.

10in (25.5cm) high

$40-60 LCA

A 'Buffy the Vampire Slayer'
action figure, by Moore Action
Collectibles.

2001

$10-15 TP

A 'Buffy the Vampire Slayer'
crucifix corkscrew.

2001

$15-25 TP

A limited edition 'Lorne
the Host' bust from
'Angel the Series',
sculpted by Jeremy Bush
for Moore Creations, from
an edition of 3,000.

2002 6in (15cm) high

$30-50 TP

A limited edition 'Buffy the Vampire Slayer' figurine, by Steve
Varner, from an edition of 4,500.

2000 9in (23cm) high

$80-120 TH

FILM & TV

A 'Countdown' annual, published by Purnell and Sons Ltd, featuring 'UFO', 'Doctor Who', 'Thunderbirds' and 'Captain Scarlet'.

1971   *11in (28cm) high*

$10-15   **MTS**

A 1980s 'Dukes of Hazzard' LCD quartz watch, by Unisonic, boxed.

A big-screen remake of this popular TV series is due in 2005.

10.25in (26cm) wide

$40-60   **DTC**

A 1980s 'Dukes of Hazzard' LCD quartz watch, by Unisonic, in bubble pack.

1981   *9.5in (25cm) high*

$30-50   **DTC**

A King Features number 990 'Flash Gordon' ray gun, on backing card.

1976

$60-90   **VEC**

A signed Daniel Radcliffe, Rupert Grint and Emma Watson 'Harry Potter' publicity photograph.

10in (25.5cm) high

$80-120   **LCA**

An 'Incredible Hulk' bubble bath bottle, by Cliro Perfumeries, with motto reading 'Combat The Evil of Grime With The Hulk's Power', boxed.

c1979   *box 7in (18cm) high*

$10-15   **MTS**

A 1970s Marx 'Lone Ranger' Butch Cavendish fully jointed action figure, in original box.

box 10in (25.5cm) high

$40-60   **F**

A signed Christopher Lee 'Lord of the Rings' publicity photograph.

10in (25.5cm) high

$30-50   **LCA**

A signed Viggo Mortensen 'Lord of the Rings' publicity photograph.

10in (25.5cm) high

$50-70   **LCA**

A signed Elijah Wood 'Lord of the Rings' publicity photograph.

10in (25.5cm) high

$50-70 LCA

A signed Orlando Bloom 'Lord of the Rings' publicity photograph.

10in (25.5cm) high

$40-60 LCA

A 'The Man From U.N.C.L.E.' annual, published by World Distributors.

1968 10.5in (27cm) high

$10-15 MTS

A 1960s base metal ring, with 'winking' image of Illya Kuryakin and Napoleon Solo from 'The Man From U.N.C.L.E.'

0.75in (2cm) high

$12-18 CVS

Nine rare Lone Star 'The Man From U.N.C.L.E.' triangular plastic badges, with the 'U.N.C.L.E.' logo and number 11 in gold with a black background, each with a safety clip fastener, mounted on an associated period backing.

10.5in (26.5cm) high

$280-320 W&W

A 'Masters of the Universe' Modulok figure, by Mattel.

c1985

$25-35 TH

A Bell Records 'The Partridge Family Shopping Bag' album, containing real shopping bag.

1972 12.25in (31cm) wide

$12-18 MTS

'Planet Stories', No. 9, published by Love Romances Publishing Co. Inc.

1953 10in (25.5cm) high

$3-5 MTS

Two 'Super Pops for the Stylophone' sheet music books, with Rolf Harris on the covers, published by EMI.

11in (28cm) high

$10-15 each DTC

FILM & TV

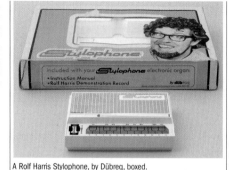

A Rolf Harris Stylophone, by Dübreq, boxed.

c1969-70 box 13in (33cm) wide

$80-120 DTC

A 'The Six Million Dollar Man' annual, published by Stafford Pemberton.

1977 10.5in (27cm) high

$8-12 MTS

A miniature 'Smurf' novelty figure, modeled as a spaceman wearing a clear plastic bubble helmet.

2in (5cm) high

$12-18 F

A bottle of 'Monsieur le Stud' eau de toilette.

This aftershave was released as merchandizing for the 1978 Joan Collins movie. It was advertised on the back of the movie's soundtrack album.

c1978 6in (15cm) high

$15-20 DTC

A 'Starsky and Hutch' annual.

1979 11in (27cm) high

$8-12 MTS

A signed Gerry Anderson 'Stingray' publicity postcard.

6in (15cm) wide

$18-22 LCA

A 'Tarzan' holster, by Lone Star, on original backing.

c1966

$50-70 TH

A 'Terminator 2 Judgement Day' 'Cyberdyne T-800 Endo Skeleton' kit, by Tsukuda.

c1991

$30-40 TH

A 'TV21' annual, published by City Magazines, featuring 'Captain Scarlet', 'Fireball XL5', 'Thunderbirds', 'Stingray' and 'Zero X'.

1969 12in (30.5cm) high

$10-15 MTS

GLASS

COLLECTORS' NOTES

■ Patented by Joseph Locke and Edward Libbey in 1883, Amberina can be recognized from its distinctive coloring which fades from ruby red at the top to amber at the base. The glass contains colloidal gold, which goes red when reheated before letting it cool. Pieces that graduate from red at the base to amber at the top are known as 'reverse Amberina'. It was made by Libbey/New England Glass Co, Hobbs Brockunier & Co and Mount Washington (the latter until 1886) and was very popular. Look out for examples that show a good range of strong tonal colors.

■ Some surface patterns are known under special names by collectors. 'I.T.P.' stands for 'inverted thumbprint' describing an all over pattern that looks like a number of thumb-shaped depressions, and 'D.Q' stands for 'diamond quilted', describing an all over pattern of soft diamond shapes. Look out for the rare and valuable 'plated' Amberina, where the interior is cased in opaque white glass.

An Amberina milk pitcher, with inverted thumbprint design, ruffled top and applied rope handle.

6.25in (15.5cm) high

$200-250　　　**JDJ**

An Amberina pitcher, moiré pattern with tightly crimped top and applied amber reeded handle.

5.75in (14cm) high

$120-180　　　**JDJ**

A small reverse Amberina pitcher, with inverted thumbprint design, applied reeded handle.

4.75in (12cm) high

$40-60　　　**JDJ**

A reverse Amberina pitcher, applied reeded amber handle, four pinched sides, several tool marks to the top edge.

7.5in (19cm) high

$120-180　　　**JDJ**

An Amberina cruet, with inverted thumbprint design, ruffled top and applied amber handle, amber blown stopper, crack in handle.

6.75in (17cm) high

$30-50　　　**JDJ**

An Amberina cruet, with diamond quilted pattern, applied amber handle, and amber stopper, slight damage to stopper.

6in (15cm) high

$120-180　　　**JDJ**

A small Amberina 'Daisy and Button' pattern pitcher, with applied amber handle.

5in (12.5cm) high

$220-280　　　**JDJ**

An Amberina toothpick holder, with diamond quilted pattern, square top, fuchsia shading to amber coloring.

2.75in (7cm) high

$180-220　　　**JDJ**

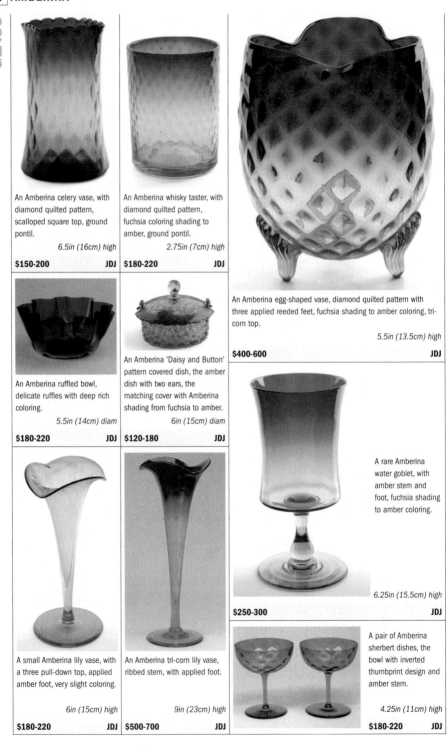

An Amberina celery vase, with diamond quilted pattern, scalloped square top, ground pontil.

6.5in (16cm) high

$150-200 JDJ

An Amberina whisky taster, with diamond quilted pattern, fuchsia coloring shading to amber, ground pontil.

2.75in (7cm) high

$180-220 JDJ

An Amberina egg-shaped vase, diamond quilted pattern with three applied reeded feet, fuchsia shading to amber coloring, tri-corn top.

5.5in (13.5cm) high

$400-600 JDJ

An Amberina ruffled bowl, delicate ruffles with deep rich coloring.

5.5in (14cm) diam

$180-220 JDJ

An Amberina 'Daisy and Button' pattern covered dish, the amber dish with two ears, the matching cover with Amberina shading from fuchsia to amber.

6in (15cm) diam

$120-180 JDJ

A rare Amberina water goblet, with amber stem and foot, fuchsia shading to amber coloring.

6.25in (15.5cm) high

$250-300 JDJ

A small Amberina lily vase, with a three pull-down top, applied amber foot, very slight coloring.

6in (15cm) high

$180-220 JDJ

An Amberina tri-corn lily vase, ribbed stem, with applied foot.

9in (23cm) high

$500-700 JDJ

A pair of Amberina sherbert dishes, the bowl with inverted thumbprint design and amber stem.

4.25in (11cm) high

$180-220 JDJ

GLASS

COLLECTORS' NOTES

■ Blenko was founded in 1922 by John William Blenko and began to produce decorative handblown glassware in the late 1920s when demand for his stained glass fell. This previous experience making strongly colored stained glass influenced the factory's often vibrant designs. Most pieces were produced in one strong color, which can often help to date a piece, and this attribute has become the company's trademark.

■ Although Blenko designed shapes, three other designers were notable, producing designs in styles of their own. Winslow Anderson is known for his Scandinavian styles, Wayne Husted (designer 1952-1963) is know for his decanters, and Joel Myers (designer 1963-1972) is known for his classical, almost geometric vases and decanters. Look out for a combination of strong color and form. The company is still in existence today.

A huge Blenko 'Tangerine' glass bottle with stopper, designed by Joel Philip Myers in 1969, shape number 6955, with vertical optic rib effect to body.

This label was used from the 1930s until the 1960s, dating this bottle to c1969. The shape was produced until 1976.

24in (61cm) high

$1,000-1,500   **EOH**

A Blenko 'Orange' bottle, with slender stopper, designed in 1962 by Wayne Husted, shape number 627L.

1962-67   18in (46cm) high

$250-350   **EOH**

A Blenko 'Turquoise' bottle with stopper, designed by Joel Philip Myers in 1965, shape number 657M.

1965-67 14.25in (36cm) high

$300-500   **EOH**

A Blenko 'Surf green' and clear glass vase, designed by Joel Philip Myers in 1970, shape number 7043L.

1970   10.25in (26cm) high

$700-1,000   **EOH**

A Blenko 'Tangerine' genie shape bottle, with stopper, designed by Wayne Husted in 1958, shape number 5815S.

This sandblasted signature was only used from 1958-61, although this shape was produced until 1964.

1958-61 15.75in (40cm) high

$500-700   **EOH**

A Blenko 'Jonquil' bottle with stopper, designed by Joe Philip Myers in 1964, shape number 649.

1964-66 13.5in (34cm) high

$400-600   **EOH**

A Blenko 'Persian Blue' tall bottle, with crackle effect, designed by Wayne Husted, shape number 6029.

1959   75in (73cm) high

$400-600   **EOH**

A Blenko 'Olive Green' daisy vase, designed by Wayne Husted in 1961, design number 6115L.

1961-67 14.5in (37cm) high

$280-320   **EOH**

COLLECTORS' NOTES

■ Burmese glass was developed by Frederick Shirley in 1881 and patented by Mount Washington in 1885. It is translucent and graduates from salmon pink to lemon yellow and creamy white. As with Amberina, heating a certain part causes the lighter color to become pink. The satin finish is more common than the gloss finish. Production ceased in 1900, but a small range was made again in the 1950s. Fakes and later reproductions are known, but these tend to be garishly colored, often with a gray tint, and are thicker and heavier.

A Burmese finger bowl, with good color separation and ruffled rim.

5.5in (14cm) diam

$150-200   **JDJ**

A Burmese juice glass, light pink fading to yellow coloring.

3in (7.5cm) high

$120-180   **JDJ**

A Burmese large bowl, with thumbprint pattern and slightly scalloped rim, one tiny fleabite to rim.

9in (23cm) diam

$180-220   **JDJ**

A Burmese twist vase, ending in tri-corn ruffled top.

6.25in (15.5cm) high

$150-200   **JDJ**

A Burmese shaped vase, with pink to yellow shading.

8in (20.5cm) high

$120-180   **JDJ**

A Burmese plate, shiny pink to yellow shading.

8in (20.5cm) diam

$120-180   **JDJ**

A Burmese decorated vase, delicate ribbed vase having a handle painted floral and leaf decoration with a ruffled top.

4.5in (11.5cm) high

$600-900   **JDJ**

A CLOSER LOOK AT A BURMESE BOWL

Decorated Burmese bowls are handpainted, rare, and desirable - flowers are a typical motif, but lines of poetry and scenery can also be found.

Examine the style of decoration closely to ensure it fits the style of the period it was made in. Many plain pieces were decorated in the 1950s and 1960s.

The frilled rim and form are typical of Burmese glass and the color is delicately and attractively graduated.

Losses to the decoration reduce value - this example is intact and in excellent condition, including gold highlights.

A Burmese decorated rosebowl, peach shading to off-white with handpainted floral decoration and an inverted ruffled top.

7.5in (19cm) diam

$600-900   **JDJ**

COLLECTORS' NOTES

- Depression glass was mass-produced inexpensively during the 1920s and 1930s when its bright colors and affordability made it immensely popular. Prolific companies include Anchor Hocking, Federal, Jeanette and Hazel Atlas.

- Many collect by patterns, which were named after festive, natural or historical themes. Many patterns can seem alike so examine them carefully and learn how to recognize their differences. As it was produced in such large quantities, try to buy examples in the best condition possible, without chips or cracks.

A 1930s Depression glass clear sugar bowl, with swirled line pattern.

3.25in (8.5cm) high

$2-3　　　　　　　**TAB**

A 1930s Depression glass 'Spiral' pattern clear milk jug, by Hocking Glass Company, with swirled line pattern.

3.5in (9cm) high

$2-3　　　　　　　**TAB**

A 1930s Depression glass clear milk jug, with heavy line design.

4in (10cm) long

$3-4　　　　　　　**TAB**

A 1930s crystal Depression glass clear milk jug.

Crystal Depression glass can be identified by tapping to create a 'ping'. Also, it is heavier than standard Depression glass.

$7-10　　　　　　　**TAB**

A crystal Depression glass 'Early American Prescut' pattern oval dish, by Anchor Hocking Glass Corp.

This pattern occurs in crystal, amber, blue, green, red, and black, sometimes with painted designs.

1960-99　　　　　　　9in (23cm) wide

$6-9　　　　　　　**TAB**

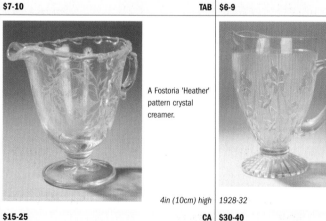

A Fostoria 'Heather' pattern crystal creamer.

4in (10cm) high

$15-25　　　　　　　**CA**

A Jeanette Glass Company 'Iris' pattern crystal pitcher.

This pattern was reproduced between the 1950s and 1970s, particularly on dinner plates and tumblers. The pattern is slightly different and the herringbone rays feel sharper on the reproductions.

1928-32　　　　　　　9in (23cm) high

$30-40　　　　　　　**CA**

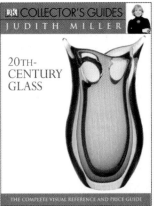

A Hocking 'Block Optic' pattern green footed jar and cover
1929-33

$70-100　　　　　　　　　　**CA**

A very rare late 1920s Hocking Glass Co. 'Standard Floral Edging' lemonade set, with pitcher and six tumblers.

pitcher 8.25in (21cm) high

$150-200 set　　　　　　　　**VGA**

A Hocking Glass Co. 'Block Optic' pattern plate.

6in (15cm) diam

$2-3　　　　　　　　　　　**VGA**

A rare Hocking Glass Co. 'Block Optic' bowl.

5.5in (14cm) diam

$22-28　　　　　　　　　　**VGA**

A 1930s set of four Hocking Glass Co. mixing bowls.

largest 9.5in (24cm) diam

$100-150　　　　　　　　　**VGA**

GLASS

COLLECTORS' NOTES

■ Fenton was founded in Martin's Ferry, Ohio in 1905 by brothers Frank and John Fenton who, after moving to Willamstown, West Virginia, began making their own glass the following year. The company saw great success with its range of pressed and carnival glass and the latter became a mainstay for the company. After WWII their success continued with their popular milk glass ranges introduced in 1952.

■ Since the 1950s they also produced a range of 19thC 'Victorian' styled giftware, usually with frilled edges. Decoration includes hobnail, opalescent finishes, casing and twisted handles. Paper labels were used until 1967, when the name began being stamped into the pieces' base, in an oval. Enameled or gilded pieces date from after 1968, when a decorating department was set up. The company continues to produce today.

A 1950s pair of Fenton sky blue and opalescent hobnail vases, with frilled rims.

25in (11cm) high

$25-35   **MAC**

A 1950s Fenton 'Rose Crest' melon vase.

8.75in (22.5cm) high

$80-120   **PAC**

A 1950s Fenton blue opalescent hobnail jug, with applied clear glass twist handle.

5in (12.5cm) high

$100-150   **PAC**

A Fenton 'Peach Crest Beaded Melon' vase, with double-crimped crystal crest edging.

c1955   *6.25in (16cm) high*

$40-60   **PAC**

A Fenton 'Peach Crest' overlaid vase, with double-crimped gold crest top.

It is very unusual to find a gold crest on a pink body.

c1965   *6.75in (17cm) high*

$70-100   **PAC**

A Fenton light blue 'Coin Dot' double-crimped bowl.

This pattern is named after the circular pattern on the body of the bowl, showing up in lighter blue.

c1955   *10.5in (27cm) diam*

$100-150   **PAC**

A 1970s Fenton milk glass hobnail pedestal cake plate, hand-painted with flowers and butterflies, the base marked "FENTON".

Plain versions of these plates are more common and fetch around $50-80. If marked with Fenton's name, they will date from the 1970s and after.

12.5in (32cm) diam

$80-120   **PAC**

A 1950s Fenton cranberry opalescent double-crimped hobnail squat vase.

This color is more desirable than milk glass, which is the most inexpensive and common.

5.5in (14cm) high

$70-100   **PAC**

COLLECTORS' NOTES

■ Jadeite is the term given to opaque green glass oven-to-table kitchenware produced by Anchor Hocking under their 'Fire-King' brand and also by Jeanette, Fenton, and others. Anchor Hocking Glass Co. introduced Fire-King in 1942 and produced it until 1976. It is found with a molded mark on the base and came in a variety of patterns and colors. Shapes, patterns, and sizes can affect value enormously, so pay attention to forms and details such as spouts, covers, and weight. As it is useable, often affordable, nostalgic and attractive, a large following has developed.

■ Marks on the base differ and can help identify the period when a piece was made with the earliest simply reading 'Fire-King' and dating from 1942-1945. The name 'Anchor Hocking' was used in marks from 1960 onward. Reproductions are becoming increasingly common, especially of Fire-King Jadeite produced in the Far East, so collectors should consult reference works and handle as many pieces as possible. Always examine edges for chips and damage such as scuffs as this reduces value.

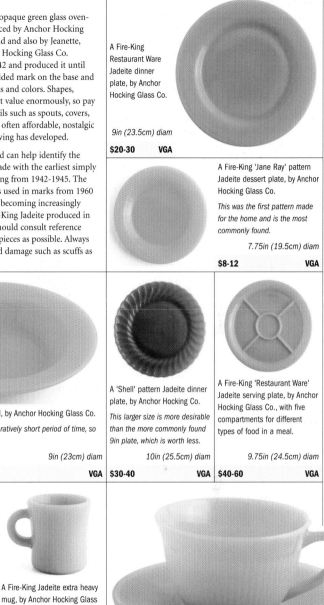

A Fire-King Restaurant Ware Jadeite dinner plate, by Anchor Hocking Glass Co.

9in (23.5cm) diam

$20-30   **VGA**

A Fire-King 'Jane Ray' pattern Jadeite dessert plate, by Anchor Hocking Glass Co.

This was the first pattern made for the home and is the most commonly found.

7.75in (19.5cm) diam

$8-12   **VGA**

A rare Fire-King Jadeite soup bowl, by Anchor Hocking Glass Co.

These were only made for a comparatively short period of time, so are rare and sought after today.

9in (23cm) diam

$100-150   **VGA**

A 'Shell' pattern Jadeite dinner plate, by Anchor Hocking Co.

This larger size is more desirable than the more commonly found 9in plate, which is worth less.

10in (25.5cm) diam

$30-40   **VGA**

A Fire-King 'Restaurant Ware' Jadeite serving plate, by Anchor Hocking Glass Co., with five compartments for different types of food in a meal.

9.75in (24.5cm) diam

$40-60   **VGA**

A Fire-King 'Restaurant Ware' Jadeite heavy mug, by Anchor Hocking Glass Co.

3.25in (8.5cm) high

$30-40   **VGA**

A Fire-King Jadeite extra heavy mug, by Anchor Hocking Glass Co., with 'C' handle.

These thicker and heavier mugs were made so that less coffee could be served, meaning the shop made more money from a pot of coffee.

3.25in (8.5cm) high

$30-50   **VGA**

A Fire-King 'Jane Ray' pattern Jadeite cup and saucer, by Anchor Hocking Glass Co.

saucer 5.75in (14.5cm) diam

$8-12   **VGA**

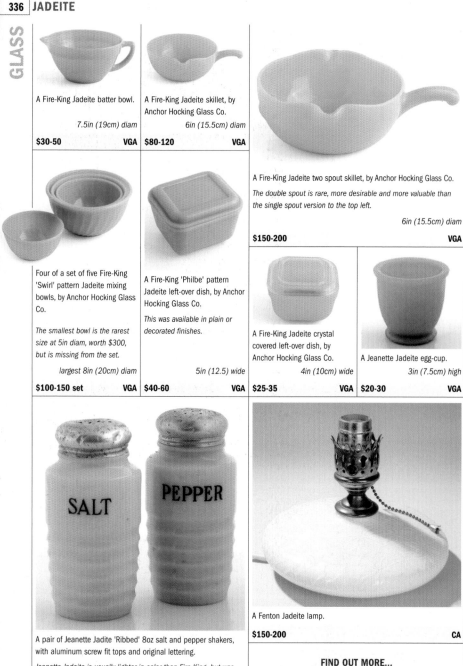

A Fire-King Jadeite batter bowl.

7.5in (19cm) diam

$30-50   **VGA**

A Fire-King Jadeite skillet, by Anchor Hocking Glass Co.

6in (15.5cm) diam

$80-120   **VGA**

A Fire-King Jadeite two spout skillet, by Anchor Hocking Glass Co.

The double spout is rare, more desirable and more valuable than the single spout version to the top left.

6in (15.5cm) diam

$150-200   **VGA**

Four of a set of five Fire-King 'Swirl' pattern Jadeite mixing bowls, by Anchor Hocking Glass Co.

The smallest bowl is the rarest size at 5in diam, worth $300, but is missing from the set.

largest 8in (20cm) diam

$100-150 set   **VGA**

A Fire-King 'Philbe' pattern Jadeite left-over dish, by Anchor Hocking Glass Co.

This was available in plain or decorated finishes.

5in (12.5) wide

$40-60   **VGA**

A Fire-King Jadeite crystal covered left-over dish, by Anchor Hocking Glass Co.

4in (10cm) wide

$25-35   **VGA**

A Jeanette Jadeite egg-cup.

3in (7.5cm) high

$20-30   **VGA**

A pair of Jeanette Jadite 'Ribbed' 8oz salt and pepper shakers, with aluminum screw fit tops and original lettering.

Jeanette Jadeite is usually lighter in color than Fire-King, but was also available in a darker color, although this too, is a different tone to Fire-King. Reproduction Jadeite is usually thinner and lighter in weight than originals.

each 5in (12.5cm) high

$120-180   **VGA**

A Fenton Jadeite lamp.

$150-200   **CA**

FIND OUT MORE...

'Jadite: An Identification and Price Guide', *by Joe Keller and David Ross, published by Schiffer Publishing, 1999.*

'Anchor Hocking's Fire-King and More: Identification and Value Guide Including Early American Prescot and Wexford', *by Gene Florence, published by Collector Books, 2000.*

COLLECTORS' NOTES

■ Although associated with glassmaking since the 14th century, glass design on the island of Murano underwent a rebirth in the 1950s that took them far away from the intricate confections of previous years. Designs became more modern, with clean lines, bright colors and an exuberance quite unlike anything that had been seen before.

■ Key designers leading this movement included Paolo Venini, Fulvio Bianconi, Dino Martens, Gio Ponti, and Carlo Scarpa. Their designs are much sought-after, and as such are often highly priced. The popularity of their pioneering work led to designs and styles being copied and imitated amongst the large number of factories on the island, mainly to fuel the burgeoning tourist market. Many of these generic pieces are eminently affordable today.

■ The 'sommerso' (submerged) technique was popular and large, colored pieces with pulled rims can fetch high prices. Many are not signed, although identifying a known maker or designer will add value. Compare style, technique, form, and color to examples in reference books to help you identify makers or designers. Condition is important, especially for more common, mass-produced pieces, so avoid scratched or chipped glass.

A 1950s Murano glass dish, with colorful millefiori canes in yellow glass and original Seguso label.

4.5in (11.5cm) diam

$50-70 AG

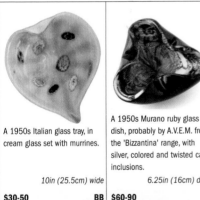

A 1950s Italian glass tray, in cream glass set with murrines.

10in (25.5cm) wide

$30-50 BB

A 1950s Murano ruby glass dish, probably by A.V.E.M. from the 'Bizzantina' range, with silver, colored and twisted cane inclusions.

6.25in (16cm) diam

$60-90 AG

A 1950s Murano emerald green glass bowl, possibly by A.V.E.M., with murrine and aventurine inclusions, two indents.

5.5in (14cm) diam

$40-60 AG

A 1950s Murano glass ashtray, in blue and gold bullicante.

This ashtray was from the Hotel Excelsior Palace, Venice.

4in (10cm) wide

$40-60 AG

A 1950s Murano glass ashtray, by Toso, in blue and clear glass.

4.25in (11cm) wide

$50-70 P&I

A 1950s Murano square glass ashtray, by Toso, in blue, green and clear glass.

4.25in (11cm) wide

$70-100 P&I

A 1950s Murano glass dish, by Cenedese, in red, orange and clear glass.

7in (18cm) wide

$80-120   **P&I**

A 1950s Murano glass ashtray, by Seguso, in yellow, green and turquoise.

6in (15cm) wide

$70-100   **P&I**

A pair of Murano glass ashtrays, pink with gold leaf inclusions, ribbing and folded rims.

4.5in (11.5cm) wide

$80-120   **AG**

A 1950s Murano glass clover leaf bowl, by Seguso.

10in (25.5cm) diam

$120-180   **AG**

A 1960s Murano triple-cased 'Sommerso' glass ashtray with faceted sides.

Such facet-sided vases and ashtrays were popular in the 1960s, and a large number were sold. Always examine the edges and corners for chips as this detracts from the optical, reflective effect created by the facets.

4in (10cm) high

$120-180   **DTC**

A 1960s Murano double-cased glass ashtray with faceted sides.

The shape of the aperture indicates that this ashtray would originally have held a lighter.

4in (10cm) high

$120-180   **DTC**

A late 1960s/early 1970s Murano heavily cased 'Sommerso' glass ashtray.

5.75in (14.5cm) wide

$60-90   **P&I**

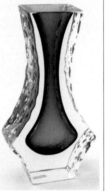

An early 1970s Murano heavily cased glass vase, gray and clear with textured sides.

The combination of the Sommerso and textured techniques used here recalls Scandinavian designs.

5in (12.5cm) high

$60-90   **P&I**

A late 1960s/early 1970s Murano heavily cased tall glass vase, amethyst and clear with textured sides.

7in (18cm) high

$80-120   **P&I**

A 1950s Murano 'Sommerso' glass vase, red and yellow cased in clear glass, with original label.

Although the strong color and technique is typical of Murano, the organic bud-like form echoes the work of Holmegaard designer Per Lütken in the late 1950s and early 1960s.

4.5in (11.5cm) high

$70-100   **AG**

A Murano glass circular pillow vase, with yellow, blue and clear glass in plaid pattern, unmarked but similar to designs by Ludovico Diaz de Santillana for Venini.

c1965   9.5in (24cm) high

$150-200   **TA**

A rare 'cherry' murrine vase, designed and made by Vittorio Ferro at the Fratelli Toso factory.

Showing the skill of Ferro as a glassmaster, these murrines are technically extremely competent and have not been repeated. These murrines can be found used in paperweights, but rarely vases, making this example one of a handful known to collectors.

1950-70   8in (20.5cm) high

$4,000-6,000   **PC**

A Murano teal and red glass vase, with spherical base and collared neck, unmarked but with gilt label for Bucella Cristalli, Murano.

7in (17.5cm) high

$280-320   **TA**

A rare 'flower' murrine vase, designed and made by Vittorio Ferro at the Fratelli Toso factory.

Murrine decoration uses small colored tiles or 'tesserae', made by cutting long glass rods, with internal decoration, into thin sections. These are then laid down in a pattern and 'picked up' by rolling a hot gather of molten glass over the mosaic. This vase uses five different types of murrine. Each acts differently when heated and cooling, contracting or expanding. As a result, distinct open gaps can be felt between the columns of murrines, and sometimes between the murrines themselves.

1950-70   6.25in (16cm) high

$1,800-2,200   **PC**

A Venini 'a canne' glass vase, with alternating broad red and blue vertical stripes with clear glass, unmarked.

9in (22.5cm) high

$320-380   **TA**

A Venini Verticali 'Tasce' carafe, designed by Gio Ponti, with an acid stamp for 'Venini Murano'.

1955   10in (25cm) high

$600-900   **AL**

A CLOSER LOOK AT A MURRINE VASE

The factory, style and design of the murrines reflect the rarity and value of a piece - this was made by Fratelli Toso, renowned for their historic murrine designs.

These murrines were designed for use on a small series of vases made to commemorate the life and work of designer and factory owner Ermanno Toso upon his death in 1973.

As well as being complex, these murrines are extremely rare. Very few vases were made incorporating them.

'San Nicolo' is the patron saint of glassmakers, hence the name of this vase.

An extremely rare Fratelli Toso 'San Nicolo' vase.

1973   7in (18cm) high

$6,000-9,000   **PC**

A CLOSER LOOK AT A MURANO VASE

This vase is typical of the exuberance of many 1950s Muranese glass designs, with bright clashing colors and irregular modern forms.

Dating from c1949, this vase can be considered a forerunner of the revolution in the 1950s which brought Murano worldwide fame in the mid- to late 20thC.

Dino Martens (1894-1970) is particularly renowned for his 'painterly' style. His innovative designs were considered shocking at the time.

This vase retains its original label from the Aureliano Toso factory.

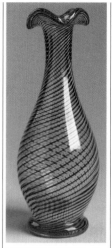

A 1950s Italian glass vase, of baluster form with frilled rim, opaque and blue spiral inclusions and etched marks.

A Murano glass vase, designed by Dino Martens, made by Aureliano Toso, with original label.

c1949   12.25in (30.5cm) high

$2,800-3,200   **FIS**

10in (24cm) high

$100-150   **L&T**

A Murano opaque glass vase, of hour-glass form, maker's label attached.

12in (30.5cm) high

$60-90   **GAZE**

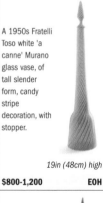

A 1950s Fratelli Toso white 'a canne' Murano glass vase, of tall slender form, candy stripe decoration, with stopper.

19in (48cm) high

$800-1,200   **EOH**

A Fratelli Toso pale blue 'a canne' candy stripe bottle, with stopper.

A Giulio Biancholli heavy clear glass triangular vase, with etched signature and date.

1999   10in (25cm) wide

$600-900   **TA**

A 1960s Murano 'pinnacolo' glass bud vase, designed by Luciano Gaspari for Saluti, in amethyst, turquoise and clear glass.

13.75in (35cm) high

$100-150   **P&I**

Two rare Murano pale blue bottles with stoppers.

Left: 25.5in (65cm) high

$1,800-2,200   **EOH**

Right: 20.5in (52cm) high

$1,200-1,800   **EOH**

1950   14.25in (36cm) high

$700-1,000   **EOH**

A 1950s Barbini footed glass jar with lid, the orange glass with internal gold foil inclusions and trails of spots.

13.75in (35cm) high

$1,200-1,800   **EOH**

A selection of Italian cased wine glasses.

6.75in (17cm) high

$30-50 each   **EOH**

Two Italian cased purple wine glasses.

Left: 9.5in (24cm) high

$40-60

Right: 8.25in (21cm) high

$30-50   **EOH**

One of six Italian caramel cased glasses, with pitcher.

Pitcher 10.25in (26cm) high

$300-500 set   **EOH**

A pair of 1950s Murano 'Sommerso' swans, in cobalt blue with air bubbles encased in clear glass.

Novelty designs such as these swans and the figures on this page have been produced in their millions by a number of factories on Murano, mostly to feed a growing tourist market. Value largely depends on the maker or designer (if known) and the quality of the design and workmanship.

7.5in (19cm) high

$120-180   **AG**

A 1950s Murano glass wild boar figure, by V. Nason and Co., in gray and clear glass, with sticker.

5.25in (13.5cm) wide

$50-70   **P&I**

An early 1960s Cesare Toso molded mauve glass figure of a little girl, in the style of Mabel Lucy Attwell.

4in (10cm) high

$15-25   **AG**

An unusual Seguso free-form glass sculpture, of spiraling serpentine form, signed on edge "Seguso Arte" and "Seguso Murano" on base.

$600-900   **DN**

A pair of 1950s Venetian glass figures, in the form of a Regency couple, some restoration.

Gent 11.5in (29.5cm) high

$180-220   **GMW**

A 1950s Murano glass fish figure, signed "Franco Bottaro, Murano" on the base.

5in (13cm) high

$40-60   **P&I**

FIND OUT MORE...

'DK Collectors Guide: 20th Century Glass', by Judith Miller, published by Dorling Kindersley, 2004.

'Murano Magic', by Carl T. Gable, published by Schiffer Publishing, 2004.

COLLECTORS' NOTES

■ Holmegaard was founded in 1825 on the Danish island of Zealand. Jacob Bang (1899-1965) was the first to bring modern designs to the company when he joined in 1927. In 1941 he was succeeded by Per Lütken (1916-98), whose cool-colored, thick-walled and small vases in grays and blues are often signed on the base with the company name, his initials and a date. Forms tend to be organic with bud-like or teardrop shapes focusing on the plasticity of the material. Avoid scratched or chipped examples as these detract from the purity of color and the form.

■ Lütken was also responsible for the 'Pop' inspired 'Carnaby' range of the 1960s and 1970s, which went to the other pole in terms of colors and form, being bright and largely geometric. The series was mold-blown and opaque with a white interior layer and shares similarities with the 'Palet' range designed by Jacob Bang's son, Michael between 1968 and 1976. First admired by interior decorators, these pieces are now being collected. The Kastrup factory merged with Holmegaard in 1965, enabling production to be expanded to meet demand.

A pair of Danish Holmegaard red cased candlesticks/vases, from the 'Carnaby' range, designed by Per Lütken.

8in (20cm) high

$250-300   **RWA**

A pair of 1960s Danish Holmegaard candlesticks, from the 'Carnaby' range, designed by Per Lütken, one with original paper label.

6in (15.5cm) high

$220-280   **RWA**

A small Danish Holmegaard red cased vase, from the 'Carnaby' range.

6in (15cm) high

$280-320   **EOH**

A small Danish Kastrup & Holmegaard red cased vase, with straight sides, from the 'Palet' line by Michael Bang.

1968-76   *6.25in (16cm) high*

$280-320   **EOH**

A 1970s Danish Holmegaard red cased 'Gulvase', designed by Otto Brauer in 1962, based on a design by Per Lütken from 1958.

This is arguably the most popular color for this shape, with the cased opaque version shown here being more valuable and desirable than the transparent colored versions. Larger sizes command higher values, and were designed to sit on the floor rather than on a table or shelf.

17.75in (45cm) high

$700-1,000   **EOH**

A Danish Holmegaard blue cased 'Gulvase', designed Otto Brauer.

1962   *14.5in (37cm) high*

$600-900   **EOH**

A Danish Holmegaard blue cased spherical vase, with short neck and collar, probably designed by Per Lütken, unmarked.

5in (13cm) high

$100-150   **RWA**

A Danish Holmegaard 'Gulvase' green cased vase, from the 'Palet' range, designed by Michael Bang, unmarked.

$220-280   **RWA**

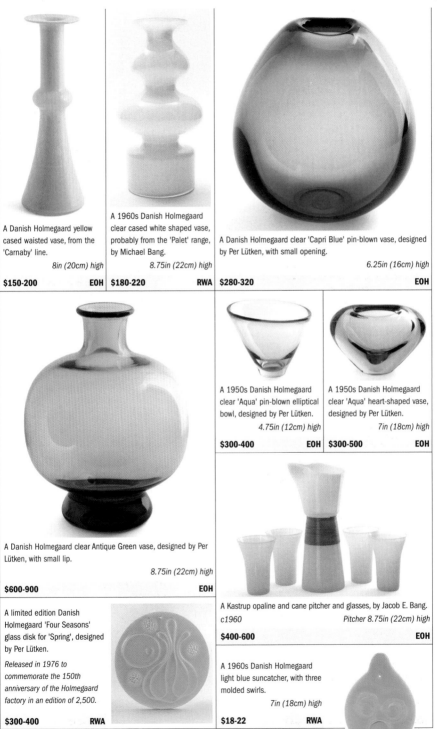

A Danish Holmegaard yellow cased waisted vase, from the 'Carnaby' line.

8in (20cm) high

$150-200   **EOH**

A 1960s Danish Holmegaard clear cased white shaped vase, probably from the 'Palet' range, by Michael Bang.

8.75in (22cm) high

$180-220   **RWA**

A Danish Holmegaard clear 'Capri Blue' pin-blown vase, designed by Per Lütken, with small opening.

6.25in (16cm) high

$280-320   **EOH**

A 1950s Danish Holmegaard clear 'Aqua' pin-blown elliptical bowl, designed by Per Lütken.

4.75in (12cm) high

$300-400   **EOH**

A 1950s Danish Holmegaard clear 'Aqua' heart-shaped vase, designed by Per Lütken.

7in (18cm) high

$300-500   **EOH**

A Danish Holmegaard clear Antique Green vase, designed by Per Lütken, with small lip.

8.75in (22cm) high

$600-900   **EOH**

A Kastrup opaline and cane pitcher and glasses, by Jacob E. Bang.

c1960   Pitcher 8.75in (22cm) high

$400-600   **EOH**

A limited edition Danish Holmegaard 'Four Seasons' glass disk for 'Spring', designed by Per Lütken.

Released in 1976 to commemorate the 150th anniversary of the Holmegaard factory in an edition of 2,500.

$300-400   **RWA**

A 1960s Danish Holmegaard light blue suncatcher, with three molded swirls.

7in (18cm) high

$18-22   **RWA**

A 1960s Finnish Riihimaën Lasi Oy cased red vase.

Founded in 1910 in Finland, the factory became known as Riihimaën Lasi Oy in 1937 and was known for producing domestic and industrial glass. During the late 1930s and 1940s talented new designers joined including Helena Tynell, Nanny Still, Aimo Okkolin and Tamara Aladin. Their designs of the 1950s and 1960s are typically strong in color, cased and mold-blown – often with strongly linear, geometric forms. Pieces appeal to the wide base of those interested in interior or Scandinavian design.

10in (25.5m) high

$50-80 JH

A Finnish Riihimaën Lasi Oy tapering rocket-shaped cased red glass vase, designed by Aimo Okkolin.

c1970 9.25in (23.5cm) high

$50-70 GC

A Finnish Riihimaën Lasi Oy cased red glass vase, designed by Aimo Okkolin.

c1970 9.25in (23.5cm) high

$50-70 GC

A Finnish Riihimaën Lasi Oy cased green waisted glass vase, designed by Aimo Okkolin.

c1970 9.25in (23.5cm) high

$40-60 GC

A Finnish Riihimaën Lasi Oy blue mold-blown vase, designed by Nanny Still, unmarked.

$70-100 RWA

A Finnish Riihimaën Lasi Oy cased blue glass tapering vase, designed by Aimo Okkolin.

c1970 7.25in (18.5cm) high

$40-60 GC

A Finnish Riihimaën Lasi Oy pressed glass sunbottle, designed by Helena Tynell.

This design was produced in four different sizes and in six colors.

c1967-74 5in (13cm) high

$60-90 RWA

A Finnish Riihimaën Lasi Oy mold-blown green cased vase, designed by Tamara Aladin.

10.75in (27.5cm) high

$70-100 RWA

A Flygfors 'Coquille' glass basket, in pink and white, signed to base.

6.25in (16cm) high

$50-70   **GAZE**

A Hyllinge glass vase, of ovoid form, designed by Bengt Orup, decorated with black specks, signed to base, with sticker on side.

$30-50   **GAZE**

A 1960s Boda bottle, designed by Eric Hogland, from the 'People' series, mold-blown green glass, with cork stopper.

Hogland's designs for Boda are known for their 'primitive' feel and appearance and are typically produced in thickly rendered green, orange or red glass.

10.75in (25cm) high

$120-180   **JH**

A 1950s Ekenas green glass vase, designed by John Orwar Lake.

Little is known about the Ekenas factory and its chief designer and art director John Orwar Lake, but vases such as these, with applied molded bands or ribbons, are typical.

5.5in (14cm) high

$60-90   **MHC**

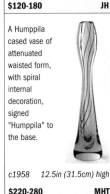

A Humppila cased vase of attenuated waisted form, with spiral internal decoration, signed "Humppila" to the base.

c1958   12.5in (31.5cm) high

$220-280   **MHT**

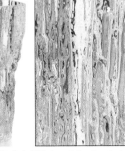

A 1950s Iittala vase, designed by Tapio Wirkkala, with organic form, pulled rim and thickly rendered body, cut with lines.

4in (10cm) high

$150-200   **JH**

An Iittala 'Savoy' green glass vase, designed by Alvar Aalto, of waved organic cylindrical form, with etched marks.

This vase by world-renowned architect and designer Alvar Aalto (1898-1976) has been in continuous production since its introduction in 1937. It was designed for the Savoy Hotel in Helsinki, also designed by Aalto.

$400-600   **L&T**

A CLOSER LOOK AT A SCANDINAVIAN VASE

This vase was designed by Tapio Wirkkala, one of the leading exponents of Finnish glass design, and among the most influential of all 20thC designers.

The form and texture shows Wirkkala's interest in the Scandinavian landscape that surrounded him – he was influenced by the textures and appearances of bark and ice.

It is signed on the base "TAPIO WIRKKALA 3729".

It is in excellent condition with no damage, polished repairs and has a good variation of textures.

An Iittala textured glass 'Iceberg' vase, designed by Tapio Wirkkala and signed on the base.

6.5in (16.5cm) high

$100-150   **GC**

GLASS

A Strombergshyttan brown tinged glass vase, designed by Edvard Stromberg.

c1940   *8.25in (21cm) high*

$100-150   **GC**

A set of four Nuutajärvi Notsjö blue goblets, designed by Kaj Franck, with etched marks.

1962-64   *6.5in (16.5cm) wide*

$180-220   **DRA**

A Skruf hexagonal textured and polished vase, designed by Bengt Edenfalk, with abstract decoration and signed "Skruf Edenfalk".

c1975   *8.25in (21cm) high*

$120-180   **MHT**

An Orrefors heavy glass inkwell.

2.5in (6.5cm) high

$30-50   **AG**

A CLOSER LOOK AT A SWEDISH VASE

This vase was made at the Swedish Strombergshyttan, the company founded by Gerda and Edvard Stromberg after they left the Eda glassworks in 1933.

Stromberg designs are often confused with Orrefors, especially when they are engraved with patterns – however, the rims, heavy walls and bases are different.

A Stromberg elliptical vase.

$300-500

It has a typically thick body and a boldly square-cut and polished rim indicating it was designed by Gerda Stromberg.

The color is austere and cool, recalling ice, and was developed by the Strombergs' son Eric along with similar pale colors that typify the factory.

7in (18cm) high

EOH

A 'Bamboo' mold-blown blue cased white vase, from an unknown factory and designer.

8.5in (21.5cm) high

$50-70   **RWA**

Two Stromberg ice-buckets, with Danish sterling silver handles.

taller: 6in (15cm) high

LEFT: $1,200-1,800 RIGHT: $1,000-1,500   **EOH**

A Stromberg thick walled tapering smoky glass vase, engraved with a fish swimming around pond weed.

6in (15cm) high

$50-80   **GC**

A tall Bischoff red bottle, with tall clear stopper.

Bischoff was founded in 1922 in Huntington, West Virginia and moved to Culloden in the same state in the 1940s. As well as making lighting glass, it is known for its crackle glass produced from 1942-1963. Its vibrant single colors and forms are very similar to those produced by Blenko and Pilgrim. The factories were in the same state and were active at the same time and, like factories in Murano, some influences were bound to be shared and copied. Examine copies of company pattern books and look for labels to identify their shapes.

c1960   23in (58cm) high

$300-500   **EOH**

A Bischoff red urn-style bottle, with tall clear stopper, wide base.

c1960   18.5in (47cm) high

$200-300   **EOH**

A Bischoff orange urn-style bottle, with tall clear stopper.

c1960   16.5in (42cm) high

$220-280   **EOH**

A Bischoff red bottle, with clear stopper.

c1960   13.5in (34cm) high

$200-300   **EOH**

A Bischoff yellow clear bottle with stopper.

c1960   13.75in (35cm) high

$200-300   **EOH**

A huge Bischoff yellow bottle, with stopper.

c1960   36.25in (92cm) high

$1,200-1,800   **EOH**

An orange carnival glass vase.

10.75in (27.5cm) high

$30-40   **BB**

A large 1930s yellow carnival glass tazza table centerpiece, with repeated alternating grape on sycamore leaf and sycamore leaf design.

8.25in (21cm) high

$30-50   **MAC**

A marigold carnival glass 'Leaf Rays' pattern nappy.

6.75in (17cm) long

$40-60   **BA**

An Imperial purple carnival glass 'Diamond Lace' pattern water pitcher and six beakers.

Created by spraying inexpensively press-molded glass with metal oxides to achieve the iridescent effect, carnival glass has become extremely popular. This pattern was first seen in Imperial's 1909 catalog in crystal and this set is desirable due to its completeness and excellent level of iridescence. This pitcher is only known in this color in this pattern.

c1930

One of two Gunderson peachblow cornucopias, raspberry shading to white with applied peachblow foot, ruffled top.

pitcher 8.75in (22cm) high

7in (17.5cm) high

$400-600

MAC

$150-200 pair

JDJ

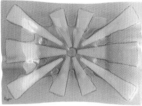

A 1960s Higgins green rectangular dish.

Michael and Frances Higgins met at the Chicago Institute of Design in 1948 and began to work on what has become a highly collectible range of glass designs including plates, dishes, ashtrays, and other tableware. Their technique involves creating a pattern using colored enamels or sections of colored glass upon a sheet of glass already covered with colored enamels. Another sheet of glass covered with colored enamels is laid on top and the 'sandwich' is heated until the layers are fused and the sheets 'sag' into a mold to give them form. Instantly successful, from 1957 they worked at Dearborn Glass in Illinois and pieces from this period can be recognized by an internal gold colored 'signature' in lower case. From 1966, they reverted to producing independently and pieces bear engraved 'signatures'. Michael Higgins died in 1999, but this has not stopped the market in their work expanding making their work one of the most sought after in this sector of the market.

9.75in (25cm) long

$200-250

EOH

A Higgins dish, with bird decoration.

26in (66cm) high

$400-500

EOH

An early millefiori glass vase, signed "Genie Jorgensen and Rolf Wald 1985".

It is extremely unusual for both of them to sign in full, with signatures usually reading 'Genie & Rolf Wald'.

c1985

7.5in (19cm) high

$70-100

BGL

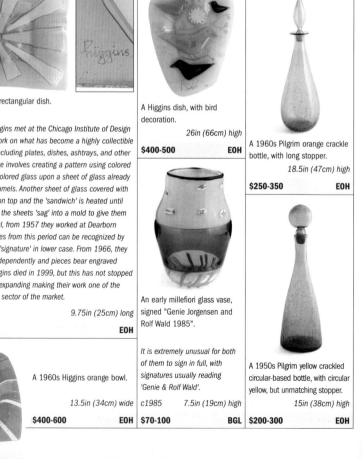

A 1960s Higgins orange bowl.

13.5in (34cm) wide

$400-600

EOH

A 1960s Pilgrim orange crackle bottle, with long stopper.

18.5in (47cm) high

$250-350

EOH

A 1950s Pilgrim yellow crackled circular-based bottle, with circular yellow, but unmatching stopper.

15in (38cm) high

$200-300

EOH

A 1960s Pilgrim textured orange bottle with long stopper.

Pilgrim originated in the Tri-State Glass Manufacturing Company in Huntington, West Virginia in the 1940s. From 1949 until 1970, it was known for producing crackle glass. It can be identified by a strawberry mark on the base or by colored labels. Yellow being used first, followed by black, then white and silver, black and finally black and white. The company closed in 2002.

13.5in (34cm) high

$220-280 EOH

A 1960s Pilgrim orange square bottle with stopper.

9.5in (24cm) high

$100-200 EOH

A Pilgrim purple crackle glass bottle, with tall stopper.

17.75in (45cm) high

$180-220 EOH

A 1960s Rainbow turquoise-blue vase, with disc-like knops.

10.25in (26cm) high

$200-300 EOH

A Rainbow dark turquoise glass bottle, square-based, with circular stopper.

9.75in (25cm) high

$150-200 EOH

A Rainbow red glass rectangular bottle, with stopper.

9.75in (25cm) hight

$120-180 EOH

A Steuben jade green shoulder vase, with swirl ribbing, signed with a Steuben Fleur-de-Lis mark.

6.25in (15.5cm) high

$250-300 JDJ

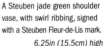

A Viking purple glass bottle, with clear stopper.

Martinsville Glass Company of West Virginia, known for their Depression glass, was renamed Viking Glass Company in 1944 and acquired Rainbow as a subsidiary in the 1970s.

26in (66cm) high

$400-600 EOH

A huge Viking gray glass bottle, with clear stopper.

19.25in (49cm) high

$200-300 EOH

A Steuben gold Aurene on calcite centerbowl, polished pontil, signed on underside "Aurene F. Carder".

12in (30.5cm) diam

$220-280 JDJ

GLASS

Three Viking amber colored glass mushrooms.

largest 5.5in (14cm) wide

LARGE: $100-150 MED: $30-50 SMALL: $25-35   **EOH**

An Italian square-based blue glass bottle, with stopper.

10.75in (27cm) high

$200-300   **EOH**

A satin glass double-gourd shaped vase, pink shading to white with a creamy white lining.

6.25in (15.5cm) high

$60-90   **JDJ**

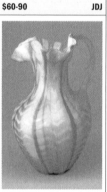

A pink/ruby glass lamp base, with clear glass applied handle.

4.75in (12cm) high

$100-150   **BBR**

A decorated satin glass vase, raspberry shading to white with white cased lining with enamel gold seaweed decoration.

8.25in (20.5cm) high

$180-220   **JDJ**

A mother-of-pearl satin glass vase, decorated with a zig-zag pattern with black amber shading to white, small bruise to side, rim appears to be ground.

7.5in (19cm) high

$80-120   **JDJ**

An Italian rainbow satin glass pitcher, ruffled top, satin pitcher with clear reeded, applied handle in yellow, pink, and blue coloring.

9in (23cm) high

$220-280   **JDJ**

A pair of 1930s Art Deco 'black amethyst' molded glass vases, with heavily stylized geometric design of animals leaping around foliage and bases stamped "MADE IN FRANCE 153".

each 6in (15.5cm) high

$250-300   **PAC**

COLLECTOR'S NOTES

- The 19th century saw ladies' hats and hairstyles grow ever more extravagant and elaborate. In order to hold one successfully to the other, hatpins were developed as an alternative to ribbons. With hats freed of ribbons, they became a functional sign of equality with men, their styles, decoration, and materials showing the wealth and status of the lady who wore them.

- Hatpins saw the beginning of their heyday in 1832, with the invention of the pin-making machine which enabled pins to be produced in larger numbers and more economically than previous handcrafting techniques. They proceeded to peak in popularity from the 1870s until the 1920s, when fashions changed again and women 'bobbed' their hair short, rendering the hatpin obsolete.

- They were made in a wide variety of materials from silver and gold to enameled and painted base metals. Styles varied with the fashions of the day, and Art Nouveau examples are particularly favored today. Some had concealed functions such as compacts – these are rare and valuable. As well as precious materials, look for fine levels of well-executed detail, good representations of a particular style and notable makers.

- Fakes or reproductions are often found – always look at the base of a hatpin 'head' when buying to check that the pin fits well into the head without damaging it. Examples with soldering, gluing or rough and damaged areas should be treated with caution as they may have been converted from earrings or other jewelry. The design should work well visually – think about how it would have been worn and displayed.

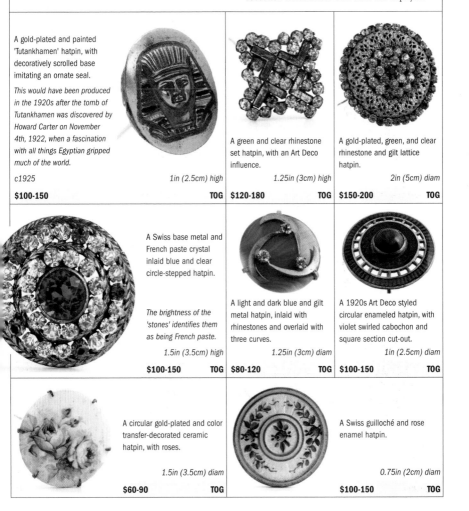

A gold-plated and painted 'Tutankhamen' hatpin, with decoratively scrolled base imitating an ornate seal.

This would have been produced in the 1920s after the tomb of Tutankhamen was discovered by Howard Carter on November 4th, 1922, when a fascination with all things Egyptian gripped much of the world.

c1925   1in (2.5cm) high

$100-150   **TOG**

A green and clear rhinestone set hatpin, with an Art Deco influence.

1.25in (3cm) high

$120-180   **TOG**

A gold-plated, green, and clear rhinestone and gilt lattice hatpin.

2in (5cm) diam

$150-200   **TOG**

A Swiss base metal and French paste crystal inlaid blue and clear circle-stepped hatpin.

The brightness of the 'stones' identifies them as being French paste.

1.5in (3.5cm) high

$100-150   **TOG**

A light and dark blue and gilt metal hatpin, inlaid with rhinestones and overlaid with three curves.

1.25in (3cm) diam

$80-120   **TOG**

A 1920s Art Deco styled circular enameled hatpin, with violet swirled cabochon and square section cut-out.

1in (2.5cm) diam

$100-150   **TOG**

A circular gold-plated and color transfer-decorated ceramic hatpin, with roses.

1.5in (3.5cm) diam

$60-90   **TOG**

A Swiss guilloché and rose enamel hatpin.

0.75in (2cm) diam

$100-150   **TOG**

A silver-plated base metal hatpin, depicting a bird in flight.

2.25in (6cm) wide

$100-150   **TOG**

An English hollow silver hatpin, in the shape of a trumpeting elephant's head, with inlaid ruby-red rhinestone eyes and hallmarks for "A.J.S." of Chester.

1909   1.5in (4cm) long

$100-150   **TOG**

A CLOSER LOOK AT A HATPIN

The back is stamped with an interlaced "UB" mark, showing it was made by the notable Unger Bros of Newark, NJ who flourished between 1895-1907.

Unger Bros were well known for their repoussé work in silver, particularly in the Art Nouveau style, as can be seen with this example.

The level of detail is excellent for such a small object – from the lion's mane to the bent blades of long grass in the background.

This well-composed design is very lifelike.

An American Unger Brothers sterling silver hatpin, molded in the form of a lion's head, the back stamped with Unger Bros "UB" monogram and marked "Sterling".

1in (2.5cm) diam

$220-280   **TOG**

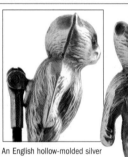

An English hollow-molded silver teddy bear hatpin, on a swiveling joint, with inlaid red rhinestone eyes, with hallmarks for Birmingham.

1909   bear 1in (2.5cm) high

$280-320   **TOG**

A finely detailed hollow repoussé sterling silver 'Indian Chief' hatpin, stamped on the nape of the neck "Sterling".

This desirable hatpin is part of the 'Hiawatha' set which also comprises a similar silver 'Princess Laughing Water' hatpin and a nickel-plated holder decorated with the 'Song of Hiawatha' poem by Henry Wadsworth Longfellow. The 'Princess' is harder to find than the chieftain.

head 1.75in (4.5cm) high

$220-280   **TOG**

An American sterling silver Art Nouveau-styled hatpin, in the form of a lady's head, the back stamped "Sterling".

0.75in (2cm) diam

$60-90   **TOG**

A Scottish white metal 'Irish Harp' shaped hatpin, inset with green hardstone, with three-leaf clover motif and hand-engravings.

1.5in (3.5cm) high

$220-280   **TOG**

An American diamond-shaped hatpin, with polychrome enameled thistle and leaves motif, stamped on the reverse "Sterling".

1in (2.5cm) long

$120-180   **TOG**

A transfer-printed and handpainted ceramic oval hatpin, showing an elegant Georgian lady.

1.5in (3.5cm) high

$180-220   **TOG**

An oval gilt metal and glass shaped tesserae mosaic hatpin, possibly Italian.

1in (2.5cm) long

$120-180   **TOG**

A Japanese white metal and handpainted ceramic 'Geisha Girls' hatpin, with seven Geisha girls, the back stamped with an 'X' in a circle.

1.25in (3cm) diam

$300-500   **TOG**

An English Art Nouveau-style hatpin, with lily and bow motif border and circular iridescent silver foil under glass cabochon, with hallmarks for "PPL" of Birmingham.

1909

$220-280   **TOG**

A gilt metal and ruby red rhinestone set floral bouquet-shaped hatpin.

1.25in (3cm) high

$120-180   **TOG**

A faux amethyst faceted glass hatpin, surmounted with a gilt-metal boss inlaid with rhinestones.

0.75in (2cm) wide

$80-120   **TOG**

An English silver and enamel Art Nouveau-style hollow hatpin, in the form of a flattened flower bud.

c1900   *1.5in (3.5cm) high*

$320-380   **TOG**

An American hardstone and faceted amber glass hatpin, the back stamped "Sterling Silver".

1.75in (4.5cm) long

$280-320   **TOG**

A black glass egg-shaped hatpin, with sterling silver filigree overlay.

c1900   *0.75in (2cm) high*

$120-180   **TOG**

A Day & Clark two-color gold bulbous hatpin, the top inset with a green jade cabochon, maker's mark to base of pin head, lacking gold sleeve on the shaft.

1in (2.5cm) high

$120-180   **TOG**

A CLOSER LOOK AT A HATPIN

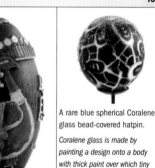

This hatpin is stamped "14K" showing it is made of 14ct gold.

The faceted crystal band is known as a 'rondelle', and imitates diamonds.

There is a small stamp, shaped like a miniature dumbell, on the finding. This shows that the hatpin was made by Day & Clark, who made pieces for jeweler and retailer Tiffany & Co.

The shaft of the pin is also marked, showing it has a solid gold sleeve - this part is often missing.

A Day & Clark 14 carat gold and crystal 'rondelle' hatpin, with faceted crystal band and 'chain link' wire overlay, stamped "14" and with maker's mark to the finding.

0.5in (1cm) high

$100-150   **TOG**

A Day & Clark faceted amethyst and 14 carat gold hatpin, stamped on the finding under the mount with maker's mark and "14k", with gold shaft sleeve stamped "FILLED PIN".

0. 5in (1.5cm) high

$120-180   **TOG**

An inverted teardrop-shaped clear rhinestone hatpin.

1.5in (3.5cm) high

$80-120   **TOG**

A oviform black-finished wood hatpin, probably Japanese, with two applied black-painted and gilt stylized peacocks and Japanese characters.

2in (5cm) high

$280-320   **TOG**

A rare blue spherical Coralene glass bead-covered hatpin.

Coralene glass is made by painting a design onto a body with thick paint over which tiny clear glass beads are sprinkled. As the paint dries, the beads are stuck to the object. The process was developed in Germany in 1883 and was popular into the 1920s. Pieces wear easily, as can be seen here, and examples with complete coats of beads are scarce and valuable.

c1920   *1in (2.5cm) high*

$100-150   **TOG**

A Chinese carved ivory hollow sphere entwined dragon hatpin, with inlaid pearlescent eyes.

sphere 1.25in (3cm) diam

$200-300   **TOG**

A carved ivory bulldog's head hatpin, the head mounted on a disc of ivory.

1in (2.5cm) diam

$150-200   **TOG**

FIND OUT MORE...

'The Collector's Encyclopedia of Hatpins and Hatpin Holders', by Lillian Baker, published by Reflected Images Publishers, 1993.

'Hatpins' by Eve Eckstein & June Firkins, published by Shire Publications, 1992.

COLLECTORS' NOTES

■ Holiday memorabilia is continuing to grow in popularity on both sides of the Atlantic and prices continue to rise. Early German examples from the first few decades of the 20th century are the most sought-after and expensive. Later pieces, generally in plastic, from America, are still very affordable.

■ Santa Claus is the most common figure for Christmas collectibles, and has his roots in European folklore. The jolly, red-suited figure we know today became popular from the 1880s. Other popular Christmas characters include snowmen and snowbabies, elves, and reindeer.

■ Most Halloween memorabilia is connected to confectionery, due to the popularity of the 'trick-or-treat' tradition, where children go from door to door asking for bribes of sweets and chocolate. Pumpkin 'jack-o-lanterns', witches, and black cats are all typical.

■ Early examples are usually made from pulped card or papier-mâché, which is fragile, or from lithographed tin, which is easily scratched. By the 1960s these materials had been replaced by plastic. Condition affects value greatly and pieces should be as complete as possible with no repainting. Look out for rare colors or complex forms with moving parts.

A 1940s German composition Christmas candy container.

3.25in (8cm) wide

$220-280   **SOTT**

A 1950s American Christmas pressed card candy container, by The Pressed Pulp Company, in the form of Santa holding his sack.

10in (25.5cm) high

$100-150   **SOTT**

A 1930s German coated pressed card Christmas candy container, with "Venetian" glass decoration.

4in (10cm) high

$100-150   **SOTT**

A Christmas cake decoration, in the form of Santa's elf.

1in (2.5cm) high

$25-35   **LG**

A German Snowbaby, standing on a sledge.

c1900   *2in (5cm) high*

$120-180   **BEJ**

A seated Snowbaby, with black shoes.

1.5in (3.5cm) high

$30-50   **LG**

A rare Kugel Christmas ornament, in blue with cream and gold decoration.

The term Kugel (German for 'ball') is used to describe early decorative glass balls that were made in Germany from 1848. It became traditional to give Kugels as gifts at Christmas and they can range in size from 1in (2.5cm) to 18in (47cm) in diameter. They arrived in the US in c1880. The larger versions would have been too heavy to hang from a tree so would be suspended from a ceiling.

4in (10.5cm) wide

$220-280   **CA**

A 1950s-60s Santa Claus plastic figure, with rabbit fur trim.

4.75in (12cm) high

$25-35   **SOTT**

A Santa Claus plastic electric light, to display in a window.

7in (18cm) high

$25-35   **SOTT**

A 1960s Santa Claus plastic rattle.

4.75in (12cm) high

$15-25   **SOTT**

A Santa Claus plastic lolly holder, with outstretched arms.

3.75in (9.5cm) long

$15-25   **SOTT**

A Santa Claus in a sled plastic candy container.

5in (12.5cm) long

$15-25   **SOTT**

A Santa Claus in a yellow sled candy container.

5in (13cm) long

$25-35   **SOTT**

A 1950s Santa Claus in a sled plastic lolly holder.

4.75in (12cm) long

$15-25   **SOTT**

A Santa Claus on a bike plastic lolly holder, with yellow wheels.

3.75in (9.5cm) long

$30-50   **SOTT**

A 1960s Santa Claus on green skis plastic lolly holder.

$12-18   **SOTT**

A Santa Claus on a green cart plastic figure, with red wheels.

4.5in (11.5cm) high

$40-60   **SOTT**

A CLOSER LOOK AT A HALLOWEEN CANDY HOLDER

A 1950s press molded card 'cat on a fence' Halloween lantern, with original paper eye insert and wire handle.

To find the original eye insert is very rare.

7.5in (19cm) high

$180-220   **SOTT**

While snowmen are typically connected to Christmas, this one is the pumpkin orange color more usually found on Halloween merchandize. This makes the piece rare.

A snowman in a more traditional color would be worth under $30.

The first few items to come out of the injection-molding machine immediately after the colored plastic was changed, would be in the color of the previous batch. In this case, the snowman has been 'accidentally' made in the orange plastic used for Halloween novelties.

This example retains its removable pipe, making it more desirable.

A Halloween plastic snowman candy holder, with removable pipe.

These candy containers are used to hold 'bribes' for trick or treating children.

5in (13cm) high

$60-90   **SOTT**

A 1960s Halloween plastic pumpkin lolly holder.

$30-50   **SOTT**

A 1940s tin Halloween noisemaker, by Empress, with lithographed decoration of a black cat, wooden handle.

4.25in (10.5cm) wide

5in (12.5cm) long

$50-70   **SOTT**

A Halloween printed tin noisemaker, with wooden handle and two wooden balls inside.

5.5in (14cm) high

$60-90   **DAC**

A Halloween printed tin noisemaker, the handle as a kazoo, the pan with a printed paper face.

9in (23cm) high

$60-90   **DAC**

A 1930s German Halloween card screech owl siren horn.

6.75in (17cm) high

$60-90   **SOTT**

A late 1940s Japanese Halloween paper horn.

6.75in (17cm) long

$12-18   **SOTT**

A Halloween orange and black plastic candy holder.

3.25in (8cm) wide

$25-35   **SOTT**

A 1930s Bonzo salt and pepper set, marked "Foreign".

3in (7.5cm) high

$60-90 **BEV**

A Victorian silver pepper caster, by George John Richards, London.

As well as the material, the attractive and intricate engraving makes this a desirable shaker.

1851 *4in (10cm) high*

$120-180 **CHEF**

A pair of 1970s Homepride Flour 'Fred' salt and pepper shakers, made by Spillers.

'Fred' was designed in 1964 and appeared on Homepride flour bags from 1965. He was so popular that a plastic flour shaker was introduced in 1969, with salt and pepper shakers coming shortly after.

4.25in (11cm) high

$12-18 **L**

A pair of 1970s coated metal salt and pepper shakers, with incised decoration showing the underlying metal.

3.5in (9cm) high

$15-25 **L**

A pair of Japanese hand-painted duck-shaped salt and pepper shakers.

$30-50 **PC**

A rare 1930s Carltonware pepper shaker, in the form of a stylized blue and green toucan.

3in (7.5cm) high

$100-150 **AGO**

A 1930s pair of Kensington cottageware salt and pepper shakers.

2.75in (7cm) high

$30-40 **BAD**

A set of 1930s torpedo-shaped, fluted green and black Catalin salt and pepper shakers.

2.25in (6cm) high

$100-150 **BB**

A pair of Grimwade Royal Winton salt and pepper shakers.

c1940 *6in (15.5cm) high*

$250-300 **JF**

A 1950s Carltonware salt and pepper set, in the shape of fruits.

6.75in (17cm) wide

$40-60 **BAD**

A pair of 1960s Secla salt and pepper shakers on a tray, made in Portugal.

6.5in (16.5cm) wide

$15-25 L

A Susie Cooper bone china cruet set, with dot in a circle design on a green ground.

Mustard 3in (7.5cm) wide

$60-90 BAD

A 1930s Beswick cruet set, in the form of tomatoes on cabbage leaves.

Tray 6in (15.5cm) long

$30-50 BAD

A Japanese ceramic pixie and mushroom cruet set, the mushroom top lifting off to reveal a pot, the pixies as salt and pepper shakers.

c1930   5.5in (14cm) wide

$70-100 BAD

A CLOSER LOOK AT A CRUET SET

The clean-lined form is quintessentially modern but also reminiscent of the Art Deco style.

It is made from solid silver by Gordon Hodgson with the silver contrasting strongly against the lids made of black wood and ivory.

The form is extremely unusual with the shakers fitting neatly around the mustard dish.

It is in excellent condition with no dents or splits which would detract from the form of the pieces by causing irregular reflections.

A silver cruet set, by Gordon Hodgson, comprising a mustard dish of cylindrical form with dished bowl, and a salt and pepper each of crescent form with unstained ivory and black hardwood removable lids with pouring apertures, each fitting around the mustard to form a cylinder, hallmarked London 1969-70.

2.5in (6.5cm) high

$800-1,200 L&T

A 1930s Carlton ware pink 'Lily' pattern cruet set.

This is a rare colorway and is complete, hence its high value. 1930s floral Carltonware is highly collectible.

5.5in (14cm) wide

$150-200 BEV

A 1930s 'cook and housekeeper' cruet set.

3in (7.5cm) high

$60-90 BAD

A 1930s German orange-glazed ceramic cruet set, in the form of three pumpkins, spoon missing.

3.75in (9.5cm) wide

$50-80 BAD

A Goebel ceramic egg timer, in the form of two red rabbits.

The German porcelain factory of Goebel is better known for its Art Deco figurines and ceramics and for Hummel figurines.

c1950   3.5in (9cm) high

$100-150   **DAC**

A painted wooden egg timer, in the form of a cockerel.

c1945   4.5in (11.5cm) high

$25-35   **DAC**

A 1960s painted ceramic egg timer, in the form of a mouse in yellow dress and bonnet.

This bears similarities to the Beatrix Potter range of figurines by Beswick. However, on this piece the colors are brighter and Beswick did not produce egg-timers. She may however have been made to copy the style.

3.5in (9cm) high

$25-35   **DAC**

A 1950s painted ceramic egg timer, in the form of a small girl and dog.

The egg timer of this example is prone to breakage, especially as the ceramic is comparatively delicate. This example is in excellent condition.

3.5in (9cm) high

$100-150   **DAC**

A ceramic blackbird pie bird.

3.75in (9.5cm) high

$70-100   **DAC**

A Josef chick pie bird.

3.25in (8cm) high

$40-60   **DAC**

A ceramic pink and green pie bird.

This pie funnel was given away as a promotion by Pillsbury.

5.25in (13.5cm) high

$70-100   **DAC**

An American Californian Potteries ceramic pie bird.

This example has a rare colorway. They are usually found with pink and green stripes, and are worth around $60.

4.25in (11cm) high

$100-150   **DAC**

A ceramic 'Nutbrown Pie Funnel', in the form of a gray elephant, stamped with "Reg'd No. 800828".

As well as being a well-modeled and unusual shape, gray is very rare, this funnel is more commonly found in white. The white version is worth around $50.

3.25in (8.5cm) high

$220-280   **DAC**

A 1950s ceramic sprinkler, in the form of a Chinese man in a blue robe, with metal and cork sprinkling attachment.

8in (20.5cm) high

$70-100 DAC

A 'The Servex Chef' ceramic pie bird.

4.5in (11.5cm) high

$150-200 DAC

A 1950s ceramic sprinkler, in the form of a Chinese man, with cork stopper and sprinkler attachment.

10.5in (26.5cm) high

$150-200 DAC

A 1950s ceramic cat-shaped sprinkler.

This is an unusual colorway, the more standard lighter brown is worth around $180.

8.25in (21cm) high

$250-300 DAC

A 1950s ceramic wetter-downer, in the form of Dutch girl.

'Wetter-downers' were used for applying water to clothes before ironing, before the development of steam irons.

8in (20.5cm) high

$180-220 DAC

A CLOSER LOOK AT NAPKIN DOLL

A 1960s plastic 'Mr Sprinkle' sprinkler.

9in (22.5cm) high

$20-25 DAC

A 1960s painted pink hard plastic 'Merry Maid' sprinkler.

6.75in (17cm) high

$30-40 DAC

The doll's dress is highlighted with faux rhinestones.

At the back of her head is a candlestick which makes her ideal for use as a table centerpiece.

Napkins are folded and slid into the slots to be pulled out by diners.

Some similar napkin holders came accompanied by salt and pepper shakers.

A 1950s Kreiss & Company ceramic napkin doll and candleholder.

9in (23cm) wide

$70-100 DAC

A late 19thC American cast-iron dog tray and nutcracker, the nutcracker reading "Harper Supply Company No. Chicago".

$350-450 FRE

A Dietz Little Wizard Lantern, inscribed "Prop of Niagara Mohawk Corp", worn red finish.

11in (28cm) high

$15-20 TWC

A pair of H. Picard brass and Rouge Royale marble candlesticks, each slender cast brass stem with a single marble knop, on a circular molded foot, losses.

8.5in (21.5cm) high

$180-220 DAW

A very unusual American 'Toast-O-Later Model J' toaster, with a conveyor belt for passing the bread past the element, with viewing aperture to the side.

c1940

$200-300 ATK

A European brass iron, with turned wooden handle, dated "31 March 1754".

6.25in (16cm) long

$300-400 ATK

A cast iron London Royal Mail horse-drawn carriage doorstop, with red, yellow, and green enamel, minor losses.

12in (30.5cm) long

$80-120 TA

A GEC electric fan, designed in 1946.

7in (18cm) high

$60-90 L

An American coffee grinder, by Enterprise Mfg. of Philadelphia, PA, of red and black enameled cast iron with gilt details, embossed manufacturers mark on the wheel.

12in (30.5cm)

$550-650 TA

A tray-form chocolate mold, produces 48 separate candies, all with hopping bunny theme.

13in (33cm) long

$60-90 TWC

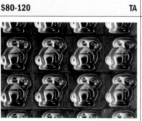

A 1940s Bruton chrome-plated bar heater.

15in (38cm) high

$80-120 L

COLLECTORS' NOTES

■ Lady head vases were originally sold inexpensively as gifts in florists' shops where they were filled with flowers. With styles dominated by fashionably or elegantly dressed ladies, production began in the late 1940s and peaked from the 1950s to the late 1960s. Cute children and teenagers can also be found. The majority were thrown away after the flowers had died.

■ Desirability and values are determined by the complexity of the molding, level of detail and realistic painting, elegance of the form and particularly the 'attitude' or facial expression of the head. Many have been given names by collectors, some related to their theme and form.

■ Look out for good molding, wide-brimmed hats, applied hands, jewelry, complexly curled hair and an elegant, well-painted portrayal of facial features.

■ Learn to recognize the faces of icons of the period – Marilyn Monroe and Jackie Onassis Kennedy examples are particularly sought after and valuable.

■ Makers' names do not necessarily add value. Although some were made in the US, most were made in Japan for export and names include NAPCO (National Potteries Corporation) Enesco, INARCO (International Artware Corporation), Irice and Rubens.

■ Condition is vital – the ceramic is often thin and easily chipped or cracked. Mint condition examples will command a financial premium. Examine examples closely for cracks and chips and look at protruding parts such as fingers, curls, bows, and hat brims to ensure they have not been reglued, as this will lower the value.

A 1950s American lady head vase, by Relpo, Chicago IL, with gloved hand and faux pearl necklace and earrings, stamped on the base "K1633".

6.75in (17cm) high

$150-200   DAC

A small 1950s lady head vase, with molded black eyelashes, base numbered "D-3220".

5in (13cm) high

$100-200   DAC

A very rare lady head vase with earrings and unusual large bow in her hair, with label for 'CAFFCO JAPAN', the base marked "E3287".

5.5in (14cm) high

$150-200   KK

A rare Inarco lady head vase, the base marked "INARCO E5623".

The pleasing expression, jewelry and easily damaged curl on top of her head make this example rare and desirable.

6in (15cm) high

$150-200   KK

A Rubens Originals 'The Teenager' lady head vase, with label to base reading "Rubens Originals Los Angeles MADE IN JAPAN".

From a series of four, this is example is distinguished by its realistic brown 'hair' eyelashes.

4.25in (10.5cm) high

$150-200   KK

A NAPCO 'The Engagement' lady head vase, with diamanté inlaid ring on her finger, marked on base "NAPCOWARE C5037".

This example still retains the original jewelry. These were often given, full of flowers, to recently engaged couples.

5.75in (14.5cm) high

$150-200   KK

A large cold-painted lady head vase, the base marked "T-1647".

This can be identified as cold-painted as the paint is matte and applied to the surface. If washed, the paint is removed, so the dirty cheeks are acceptable and a sign that it is in original condition.

6.75in (17cm) high

$100-150   KK

A Japanese 'Headache Lady' lady head vase, the base marked "Handpainted TILSO JAPAN".

Legend has it that if a wife was not 'fulfiling her obligations', a husband may buy her this vase with flowers!

5.75in (14.5cm) high

$80-120   **KK**

An Irice 'Big Sister' lady head vase, in black with gold-colored eyelashes.

IRICE examples are recognized by their gold eyelashes. A complete series of 'sisters' would comprise four 'big' and four 'little' sisters.

5.75in (14.5cm) high

$100-150   **KK**

An Irice pink and gilt 'Little Sister' lady head vase.

4in (10cm) high

$100-150   **KK**

An Irice lime green 'Little Sister' lady head vase.

4in (10cm) high

$80-120   **KK**

Two Irice 'Little Sister' lady head vases.

4in (10cm) high

$80-120 each   **KK**

A Betty Lou Nichols 'Mary Lou' lady head vase, with painter's signature "J".

Mary Lou is the most commonly found Betty Lou Nichols vase.

5in (12.5cm) high

$300-400   **KK**

A Japanese contemporaneous copy of a Betty Lou Nichols 'Ermintrude' lady head vase, with label and marking to base reading "S 234A".

If this were an original Betty Lou Nichols, she would be worth up to $400-600. The Japanese makers have even copied the style of hair made in a pasta machine. Japanese copies can be recognized by their lighter weight and glossy finishes.

5.5in (14cm) high

$180-220   **KK**

A CLOSER LOOK AT A LADY HEAD VASE

It is hand-made and the hair ruffles are made in a pasta machine.

This example is from the desirable 'Children' series of 'Floradorables'. A smaller series, usually less well painted and detailed, exists known as 'Demidorables'.

The single letter is the signature of the painter.

Reproduction Betty Lou Nichols vases have raised edges on the base, originals are entirely flat.

An American Betty Lou Nichols 'Kathy' lady head vase.

5.5in (14cm) high

$400-600   **KK**

A Japanese contemporaneous copy of a Betty Lou Nichols lady head vase, with removable hat.

Copies of Betty Lou Nichols vases do exist, and are usually Japanese. Those made at the time are collectible, those made after the 1960s are not. This period copy has a removable hat – a desirable and rare feature.

5in (13cm) high

$180-220 KK

A rare Liftons yellowy-green lady head vase, the base marked "MR-4556" and with label reading "Liftons JAPAN".

As well as her pleasing expression, her rare yellowy-green colorway is more desirable and rarer than the more common bluey-green colorway.

5.5in (14cm) high

$120-180 KK

A 'Praying Girl' lady head vase.

There is also a 'Praying Boy' version in blue with brown hair - the two clasped hands is a rare feature, they are more commonly found with one or no hands. The cowl is easily damaged, this example is in mint condition.

5.75in (14.5cm) high

$100-150 KK

An unmarked lady head vase, her unusual eyelashes with white undersides and gray tops.

4.75in (12cm) high

$100-150 KK

A NAPCO 'Southern Belle' lady head vase, with realistic eyelashes, the base marked "C3812B NAPCO 1959".

5.5in (14cm) high

$120-180 KK

$300-400

A 1950s Japanese Rubens lady head vase, with lady in riding clothing and blue top hat, base with label reading "A Rubens Original" and stamped "R 531 JAPAN".

7.75in (19.5cm) high

DAC

An INARCO lady head vase, with unusual feather form, the base marked "INARCO E-191/M/C".

c1961

5.5in (14cm) high

$120-180 KK

An Enesco 'The Secretary' lady head vase, with gilt and red foil Enesco label to base.

5.75in (14.5cm) high

$150-200 KK

A 1950s Japanese lady head vase, with gloss glaze, with molded black eyelashes and applied pink rose on hat.

6.75in (17.5cm) high

$80-120 DAC

A 'Winking Girl' lady head vase, in mint condition.

This model can be found in two sizes, this is the smallest.

5in (13cm) high

$100-150 KK

A rare lady head vase, with black eyelashes, unusual hair and a small bow at the back.

6in (15cm) high

$150-200 KK

A 1950s Japanese NAPCO Christmas lady head vase, with faux pearl earrings and necklace.

7in (18cm) high

$200-300 DAC

An Enesco 'Jackie Kennedy Onassis In Mourning' lady head vase.

This lady head vase was made to commemorate the shooting of John F. Kennedy in 1963. It is also found in white at roughly the same value. Two accompanying figurines of Jon-Jon and Caroline can also be found, but are rare and can be worth up to $1,200.

c1963 6in (15.5cm) high

$600-900 KK

A Japanese 'Umbrella Girl' lady head vase, with original umbrella and with label reading "JAPAN" to base.

Original umbrellas are hard to find as they are precariously balanced on the rod and often fell off and broke.

8.25in (21cm) high

$200-300 KK

A Japanese 'Kissing Couple' lady head vase, with a glossy glaze, the base marked "81708".

This is an unusual colorway - the more muted in tone are more common and less valuable.

5in (13cm) high

$180-220 KK

A 1950s Japanese ceramic NAPCO Christmas theme planter.

5.5in (14cm) high

$40-60 DAC

A hand-painted 'Joan Crawford' lady head vase, signed on the base "Lula Ivomack - 1959".

7.5in (19cm) high

$100-150 KK

A pair of Louis Vuitton stacking automobile trunks, covered in brass-studded black cloth, brass mounts stamped "L.V.", each interior with a detachable tray, paper label.

33.5in (85cm) wide

$800-1,200 CLV

A Louis Vuitton trunk, with removable lid, originally made for the Encyclopedia Britannica, one removable divider missing, with stamped maker's marks to the leather, handle and metalwork, inscribed "Specially made for the Encyclopedia Britannica by Louis Vuitton, 149 New Bond St, London".

Vintage Louis Vuitton trunks are currently enjoying popularity as small pieces of furniture. Those made for specific purposes, such as this example, are also of interest to dedicated collectors of Louis Vuitton luggage.

35.5in (90cm) long

$1,000-1,500 DN

A large American trunk, for long ship passages, with applied stickers including "Norwegian American Line", inscribed with motto "P&S - Trunks That Wear - Everywhere".

38in (97cm) wide

$180-220 ATK

A brown leather suitcase, with two straps, reinforced corners and nickel-plated locks.

c1910   28.75in (73cm) wide

$150-200 TDG

A 1930s Gladstone-type gentleman's toilet case, by Clark of 33 New Bond Street in London, the divided hinged lid opening to reveal an interior fitted with compartments, silver hallmark for London.

1932   15.5in (39cm) wide

$400-600 L&T

A gentleman's traveling toilet set, including cut-glass vessels with hallmarked silver fittings and two ivory brushes, with green leather interior and felt protective cover.

Look closely at maker's marks on both the case and the lids of the contents. Good central London retailers or manufacturers such as Asprey, Leuchars or Mappin and Webb add interest and value, as does fine decoration in lacquer or enamel. A case must be complete with all its original, matching contents to fetch high values.

1935

$500-800 TAG

An Italian alligator briefcase, by Hamilton Hodge for de Vecchi, with fitted interior.

17.5in (44.5cm) wide

$700-1,000 S&K

A maid's traveling nécessaire, the rexine-covered case containing a portable iron and stand and a small plated kettle and stand, both with raffia handles, and a folding pair of wooden-handled curling tongs.

case 8in (20.5cm) wide

$180-220 DN

A black leather briefcase, the flap with the royal cypher of George VI, in mint condition.

1936-52   17in (43cm) wide

$70-100 MHC

LUNCH BOXES

COLLECTORS' NOTES

■ Originally an advertising gimmick by tobacco companies, lunch boxes came into their own when toy manufacturers started to make tin containers specifically to carry lunch in the 1930s. However, the golden age of metal lunch boxes did not begin until the 1950s when manufacturers began to produce licensed examples from popular TV shows and films.

■ Metal lunch boxes continued to be made until Florida mothers, concerned that they could be used as schoolyard weapons, lobbied for their withdrawal. They were phased out between 1972 and 1987 to be replaced with plastic.

■ Collectors look for complete sets of lunch box and matching Thermos bottle as well as those in the best condition possible. Dents, scratches and loss to decals will all reduce the value considerably. Also look out for a marriage of a lunch box and bottle, which will display different degrees of wear.

A 1950s 'Casey Jones' lunch box, with a few scratches and light dents.

8.75in (22.5cm) long

$300-400 **STC**

A 1960s promotional 'Volkswagen Campervan' lunch box and Thermos bottle, manufactured by Omni-Graphics Inc, Yonkers N.Y., with styrofoam-lined plastic Thermos.

$1,000-1,500 **STC**

Two views of an Aladdin Industries Inc 'Voyage To the Bottom Of The Sea' lunch box, with embossed relief details.

c1965 *8in (20.5cm) wide*

$800-1,200 **STC**

A Thermos 'MLB' baseball lunch box and Thermos bottle, with rare magnetic game counters still present, to play game on reverse.

c1970 *8.75in (22cm) wide*

$250-350 **STC**

A Thermos 'Kiss' lunch box and Thermos bottle, near mint.

c1975 8in (20cm) wide

$300-400 **STC**

An Aladdin Industries 'Popeye' lunch box, mint with plastic 'Pop-Top' Thermo flask, tag and instructions.

1980 *8in (20.5cm) wide*

$80-120 **STC**

A rare Ohio Art Car Carry Case PitStop lunch box.

This box could be used as a lunch box or a Matchbox/ Hotwheels carry case, it is rare to find an example that retains its interior. It was only available through Sears department store.

8.75in (22cm) wide

$250-350 **STC**

FIND OUT MORE...

'The Illustrated Encyclopaedia of Metal Lunch Boxes', by Allen Woodall and Sean Brickell, published by Schiffer, 1999.

'The Fifties and Sixties Lunchbox', by Scott Bruce, published by Chronicle Books, 1998.

COLLECTORS' NOTES

■ The three main factors that determine a magazine's value are its cover, content, and condition.

■ Fashion magazines appeal to students and collectors of fashion and fashion history but they are also collected for their decorative covers. Artwork should typify a period, such as the elongated, stylized faces of 1920s Art Deco, the austerity of postwar design or the bright day-glo colors of the 1960s and 70s.

■ Covers featuring celebrities such as Princess Diana or famous models such as Twiggy attract a premium. 'Super Models' of the 1980s and 1990s are also sought after, particularly if this is that model's first appearance. Also look for artwork or photographs by famous names such as Cecil Beaton, Horst P. Horst or Mario Testino.

■ News and current affairs magazines such as "Life" and "Picture Post" that cover major events such as royal events, celebrity weddings or the moon landings are sought-after. However, beware of special editions that were printed in large amounts and were often kept as a memento, making them common today.

■ As with all paper-based collectibles, condition is of upmost importance when it comes to value and desirability. This includes rips and tears as well as doodles, missing pages, and cutout sections.

A CLOSER LOOK AT A VINTAGE MAGAZINE

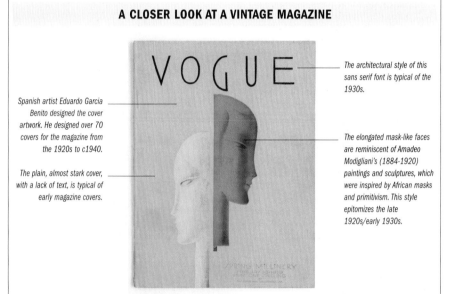

The architectural style of this sans serif font is typical of the 1930s.

Spanish artist Eduardo Garcia Benito designed the cover artwork. He designed over 70 covers for the magazine from the 1920s to c1940.

The plain, almost stark cover, with a lack of text, is typical of early magazine covers.

The elongated mask-like faces are reminiscent of Amadeo Modigliani's (1884-1920) paintings and sculptures, which were inspired by African masks and primitivism. This style epitomizes the late 1920s/early 1930s.

"Vogue", February 20th, 1929, cover artwork by Eduardo Garcia Benito.

12.75in (32.5cm) high

$150-200   **VM**

"Vogue", September 1st, 1937, 21st birthday issue.

Unicorns were a popular motif for Vogue covers.

12.75in (32.5cm) high

$100-150   **VM**

"Vogue Beauty Book", February 22nd, 1939, with cover artwork by Eduardo Garcia Benito.

12.75in (32.5cm) high

$100-150   **VM**

"Vogue", September 1951.

11.5in (29cm) high

$50-80   **VM**

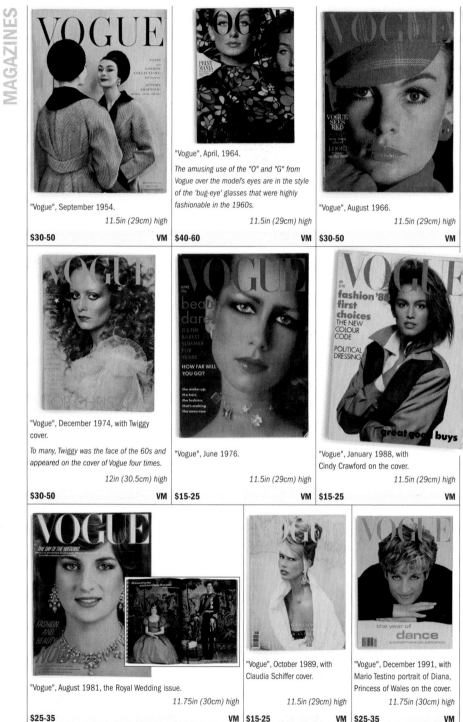

"Vogue", September 1954.

11.5in (29cm) high

$30-50   VM

"Vogue", April, 1964.

The amusing use of the "O" and "G" from Vogue over the model's eyes are in the style of the 'bug-eye' glasses that were highly fashionable in the 1960s.

11.5in (29cm) high

$40-60   VM

"Vogue", August 1966.

11.5in (29cm) high

$30-50   VM

"Vogue", December 1974, with Twiggy cover.

To many, Twiggy was the face of the 60s and appeared on the cover of Vogue four times.

12in (30.5cm) high

$30-50   VM

"Vogue", June 1976.

11.5in (29cm) high

$15-25   VM

"Vogue", January 1988, with Cindy Crawford on the cover.

11.5in (29cm) high

$15-25   VM

"Vogue", August 1981, the Royal Wedding issue.

11.75in (30cm) high

$25-35   VM

"Vogue", October 1989, with Claudia Schiffer cover.

11.5in (29cm) high

$15-25   VM

"Vogue", December 1991, with Mario Testino portrait of Diana, Princess of Wales on the cover.

11.75in (30cm) high

$25-35   VM

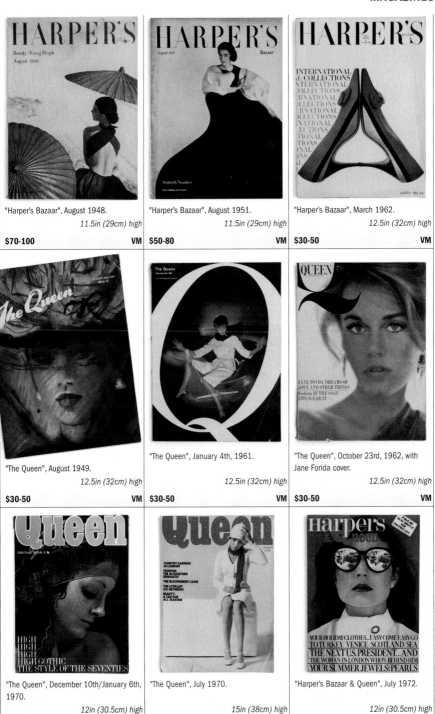

"Harper's Bazaar", August 1948.
11.5in (29cm) high
$70-100 VM

"Harper's Bazaar", August 1951.
11.5in (29cm) high
$50-80 VM

"Harper's Bazaar", March 1962.
12.5in (32cm) high
$30-50 VM

"The Queen", August 1949.
12.5in (32cm) high
$30-50 VM

"The Queen", January 4th, 1961.
12.5in (32cm) high
$30-50 VM

"The Queen", October 23rd, 1962, with Jane Fonda cover.
12.5in (32cm) high
$30-50 VM

"The Queen", December 10th/January 6th, 1970.
12in (30.5cm) high
$15-25 VM

"The Queen", July 1970.
15in (38cm) high
$25-35 VM

"Harper's Bazaar & Queen", July 1972.
12in (30.5cm) high
$10-15 VM

"My Home", November 1929.
11.75in (30cm) high

$30-50 VM

"Good Housekeeping", December 1937.
11.5in (29cm) high

$30-50 VM

"House Beautiful", July 1949.
12.75in (32.5cm) high

$25-35 VM

"Homes & Gardens", January 1972.
11.5in (29cm) high

$30-40 VM

A 1974 "Habitat" catalogue.
11.75in (30cm) high

$30-50 VM

"House & Garden", January 1956.
11.5in (29cm) high

$30-50 VM

"House & Garden", July/August 1976.
12in (30.5cm) high

$15-25 VM

A 1978/9 "Habitat" catalogue.
11.75in (30cm) high

$25-35 VM

A 1980/81 "Habitat" catalogue.
11.75in (30cm) high

$25-35 VM

"Life", July 25th, 1938, with Queen Elizabeth cover.

14in (35.5cm) high

$80-120   VM

"Life", December 6th, 1953, with John F. Kennedy funeral cover.

14in (35.5cm) high

$80-120   VM

"Life", October 23rd, 1961, International edition with Elizabeth Taylor as 'Cleopatra' cover.

14in (35.5cm) high

$80-120   VM

"Life", December 19th, 1969, rare edition with Charles Manson cover.

Charles Manson shocked the world when his 'Family' brutally slaughtered six people including Sharon Tate, the eight-month pregnant wife of film director Roman Polanski, in 1969. The horrific nature of these murders meant that few people kept anything featuring Manson, making this rare today.

14in (35.5cm) high

$220-280   VM

"Life", January 20th, 1969, with Earth seen from Apollo VIII cover.

The Apollo VIII lifted off on December 21st 1968 and returned six days later. It was the first manned lunar orbit mission.

14in (35.5cm) high

$60-90   VM

"Picture Post", December 4th, 1944.

13.25in (33.5cm) high

$25-35   VM

"Picture Post", January 16th, 1954, with Gregory Peck cover.

13in (33cm) high

$25-35   VM

"Picture Post", December 3rd, 1955, with Marlon Brando in "Guys & Dolls" cover.

13in (33cm) high

$50-80   VM

"Picture Post", August 4th, 1956, with James Mason cover.

13in (33cm) high

$25-35   VM

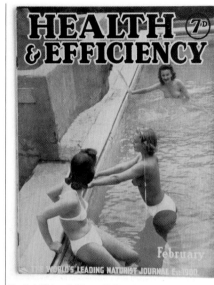

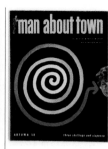

"Health & Efficiency", February 1941.

The world's longest running naturist magazine, Health & Efficiency has been published since 1900.

11in (28cm) high

$30-50 VM

"Man About Town", Winter 1956-7, including a feature on Savile Row suits.

Man About Town was the UK's first glossy magazine for men, and from 1957 was published by Michael Heseltine, later Tory MP.

11in (28cm) high

$30-50 VM

"Man About Town", Autumn '58.

11in (28cm) high

$30-50 VM

"Penthouse", Vol.1 No. 9 1960s, with Nudest Miss World cover.

Published by Bob Guccione in the UK since 1965 and the US since 1969. Guccione resigned in 2003 after the magazines publisher filed for bankruptcy the same year.

11in (28cm) high

$15-25 VM

"Dude", May 1962.

11in (28cm) high

$15-20 VM

"Nova", October 1968, with Twiggy cover and feature on Henry Ford.

Nova was first published in 1965 and became the style bible for the 60s and 70s. As well as fashion, it covered heavy duty issues such as homosexual law reform when the issue was politically controversial. It closed in 1975 and was briefly relaunched in 2000 but closed again a year later.

13.5in (34.5cm) high

$30-50 VM

"Nova", May/June 1969, with Oliver Reed feature.

13.5in (34.5cm) high

$30-50 VM

"Dude", November 1971.

11in (28cm) high

$15-25 VM

FIND OUT MORE...

'Collectible Magazines: Identification and Price Guide' by David K. Henkel, published by HarperCollins 2000.

COLLECTORS' NOTES

■ Marbles are usually divided into three types – German 'handmade' made from c1860-c1920, American 'machine-made' produced from c1905 and contemporary marbles, primarily American in origin.

■ 'Handmade' marbles usually have one or two distinct pontil marks where they were broken off a rod of glass. Look for symmetry and complex designs as well as large examples. Leading US companies include Akro Agate Company and the Peltier Glass Company. 'Eye appeal' is an important aspect – one that appeals to one collector may not to another.

■ Condition is vital with 'machine-made' and contemporary marbles, but less so with 'handmade' examples. However, serious play-wear such as scratching and chipping (especially if it obscures or disturbs the design) will devalue any marble – sometimes by half or more.

A handmade German 'Solid Core Swirl' marble, with an outer swirl of latticinio (white glass) threads.

1860s-1920s 0.75in (2cm)

$30-50 AB

A German handmade English-style swirl marble, with predominately orange, but also white and black strands and a clear pontil mark.

A German handmade English-style 'Latticinio Core Swirl' marble, with a core of orange 'latticinio' strands and an outer layer of colored strands.

A German English-style 'Joseph's Coat' marble, with blue, orange, and white strands and two pontil marks.

Collectors call these 'English-style' as, until the fall of the Berlin Wall revealed an Eastern German factory that primarily exported to Britain, it was thought that they were made in the glass factories of Bristol, England.

1860s-1920 0.625in (1.5cm)

1860s-1920 0.625in (1.5cm)

1860s-1920 0.625in (1.5cm)

$30-50 AB

$70-100 AB

$120-180 AB

A handmade German 'Banded Lutz' marble, with yellow and white bordered Lutz swirls.

Lutz marbles have copper flakes suspended in glass which give the impression of gold.

A handmade German 'Indian' marble, with black base and white banded navy blue swirl and green and yellow strand swirl.

Indian marbles have a black base. The more colors seen in the swirls, the more valuable and desirable it is likely to be.

A handmade German 'Mica' glass marble, with single pontil mark.

Both the single pontil and the fact that the mica does not go all the way through the marble (see detail) show this came from the end of a rod, making this example rarer and more valuable than other mica marbles.

1860s-1920s 0.75in (2cm)

1860s-1920s 0.75in (2cm)

1860s-1920 0.75in (2cm)

$150-200 AB

$120-180 AB

$80-120 AB

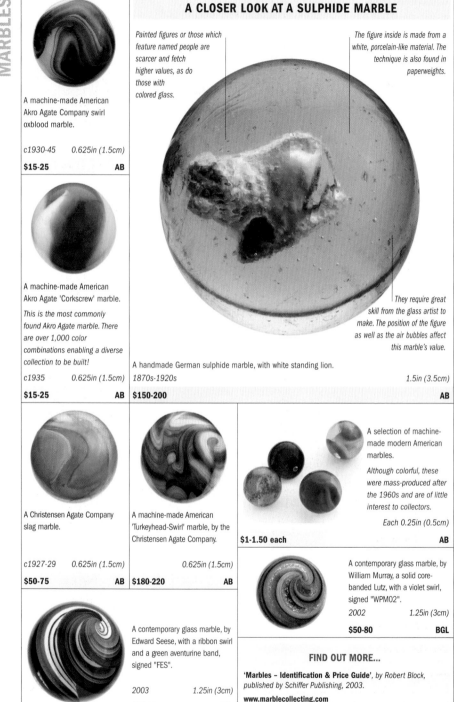

A machine-made American Akro Agate Company swirl oxblood marble.

c1930-45   0.625in (1.5cm)

$15-25   **AB**

A machine-made American Akro Agate 'Corkscrew' marble.

This is the most commonly found Akro Agate marble. There are over 1,000 color combinations enabling a diverse collection to be built!

c1935   0.625in (1.5cm)

$15-25   **AB**

A CLOSER LOOK AT A SULPHIDE MARBLE

Painted figures or those which feature named people are scarcer and fetch higher values, as do those with colored glass.

The figure inside is made from a white, porcelain-like material. The technique is also found in paperweights.

They require great skill from the glass artist to make. The position of the figure as well as the air bubbles affect this marble's value.

A handmade German sulphide marble, with white standing lion.

1870s-1920s   1.5in (3.5cm)

$150-200   **AB**

A Christensen Agate Company slag marble.

c1927-29   0.625in (1.5cm)

$50-75   **AB**

A machine-made American 'Turkeyhead-Swirl' marble, by the Christensen Agate Company.

0.625in (1.5cm)

$180-220   **AB**

A selection of machine-made modern American marbles.

Although colorful, these were mass-produced after the 1960s and are of little interest to collectors.

Each 0.25in (0.5cm)

$1-1.50 each   **AB**

A contemporary glass marble, by William Murray, a solid core-banded Lutz, with a violet swirl, signed "WPM02".

2002   1.25in (3cm)

$50-80   **BGL**

A contemporary glass marble, by Edward Seese, with a ribbon swirl and a green aventurine band, signed "FES".

2003   1.25in (3cm)

$30-50   **BGL**

FIND OUT MORE...

'Marbles – Identification & Price Guide', by Robert Block, published by Schiffer Publishing, 2003.

www.marblecollecting.com

A 1920s Mexican painted wood carnival or festivity mask.

11.75in (30cm) high

$100-150 ANAA

A 1930s Mexican red painted wood mustachioed Devil mask.

11.75in (30cm) high

$80-120 ANAA

A 1930s Dutch painted papier-mâché carnival mask, from Amsterdam.

12.5in (32cm) high

$100-150 ANAA

A 1930s painted fabric mule's head carnival mask.

10.5in (27cm) high

$18-22 ANAA

A Guatemalan carved wooden face tribal mask.

8.75in (22cm) high

$120-180 ANAA

A Mexican painted wooden festival mask, possibly related to the figure of Death, with label reading "MUERTO CUERTZAIA".

c1915   24.5in (62cm) long

$80-120 ANAA

An American painted metal gauze and black horsehair bearded man ceremonial mask, from an Odd Fellows' meeting hall.

The Odd Fellows, originally founded in England in the 18thC, staged their first US meetings in 1819. One of the largest fraternal societies in the US, its key tenets are friendship, love, truth, and support for the needy.

c1910   12.25in (31cm) high

$60-90 ANAA

An American painted metal gauze and gray horsehair bearded man ceremonial mask, from an Odd Fellows meeting hall.

c1910   15.25in (39cm) high

$60-90 ANAA

A 1920s wood, composition, and plaster painted mask of a demon's face.

15in (38cm) high

$300-500 ANAA

COLLECTORS' NOTES

■ The gramophone was developed in 1887 by Emile Berliner and became popular around the turn of the century. It soon took over from other methods of reproducing sound, such as Thomas Edison's phonograph which used wax cylinders, and the 19th century metal cylinder and disc musical boxes.

■ Table-top examples are found with both integral and external horns. Those with original decorative external horns tend to be the most popular, although beware of modern reproductions of HMV examples, with bright yellow brass, dark, pixillated HMV transfers and use of dark, reddish tropical woods for the case.

■ Portable gramophones can make an affordable collection that is easy to display and store. Look out for well-known makers and unusual forms or shapes. Children's tinplate-cased examples can be very desirable and can fetch higher values than those made for the adult market.

A Madison table gramophone, with metal case, minor damage to reproducer.

c1930

$80-120　　　　　　　　　　　　　　**ATK**

A Swiss Maestrophone portable gramophone, by Paillard, with mahogany case and original reproducer.

Paillard is also well known for its fine quality cylinder mechanical music boxes made in the 19thC.

c1930

$320-380　　　**ATK**

An English Cameraphone, small folding portable gramophone, with oak case, spherical imitation tortoiseshell 'Saturn' sound box replaced.

7in (17.5cm) long

$320-380　　　**ATK**

A Swiss portable Thorens folding gramophone, with metal case, complete with one record entitled "Karnevals-Shimmy".

$400-600　　　**ATK**

A portable Belgian Colibri gramophone, with original Swiss soundbox and spring motor.

c1930

$400-600　　　**ATK**

A Czechoslovakian portable Supralion gramophone.

c1930

$60-90　　　**ATK**

A Bing of Nuremburg toy gramophone, lithographed tin case, with one record entitled "Pigmynette", good working condition.

Bing is known for its tinplate toys, recognized by a "GBN" trademark.

$320-380　　　**ATK**

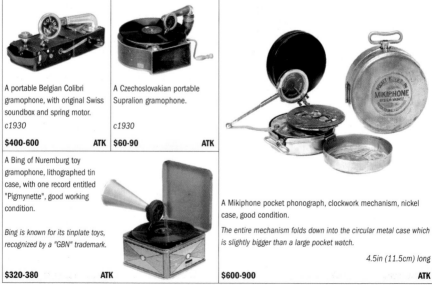

A Mikiphone pocket phonograph, clockwork mechanism, nickel case, good condition.

The entire mechanism folds down into the circular metal case which is slightly bigger than a large pocket watch.

4.5in (11.5cm) long

$600-900　　　**ATK**

A decorative horn gramophone, small oak case with Swedish dealer's label, colored tin horn, 'Veni-Vidi-Vici' soundbox, needs restoration.

12.5in (32cm) long

$300-400 ATK

A 19thC Swiss cylinder musical box, playing 20airs, faux rosewood and stenciled case.

24in (61cm) wide

$1,000-1,500 LC

A CLOSER LOOK AT A GRAMOPHONE

The Xb is the largest standard production gramophone ever made.

The case, mechanism and horn are all handmade and hand assembled.

The enormous horn is made from papier-mâché, and easily damaged. This example is in excellent condition.

Due to the quality of materials and sound, many claim this to be the finest acoustic gramophone ever made.

An English EMG gramophone, model 'Xb', with a large papier-mâché horn.

c1935 *Horn 33.5in (75cm) diam*

$5,000-7,000 ATK

An HMV 'Model 460' gramophone, with special pleated diaphragm by Lumière, mahogany case, brass-plated fittings, automatic stop function.

Rather than using a horn to amplify the sound, a vibrating gilt-finished pleated paper diaphragm was used – values plummet if the paper is torn. This rare model was produced only for the English market between 1924 and 1925.

c1925 *15.5in (39cm) wide*

$2,800-3,200 ATK

An Edison 'Gem Model C' phonograph, two- and four-minute gearing, replaced brass horn, original wooden case, complete with three cylinders.

c1910

$1,000-1,500 ATK

A brass singing bird cage, with a mechanism of small bellows which operates a slide whistle and emits a warbling sound, complete but not working.

c1950

$300-400 ATK

A 'Sewing Lady' musical box, the plastic female figure with full-skirted dress and storage for eight cotton spools and a tape measure, hand-painted features and flowers.

c1960 *7.5in (19.5cm) high*

$120-180 ATK

A ceramic 'Phonograph' plate, by Creil & Montereau, with an illustration of a phonograph and French text.

8.25in (21cm) diam

$120-180 ATK

A Liberty and Co. Tudric pewter vase, the open-work tapering sides with three loop handles and embossed with a band of berries and leaves on a round base, with a green glass liner, stamped beneath "Tudric 0957".

8.75in (22cm) high

$400-600   **DN**

A Liberty and Co. Tudric pewter bowl, stamped "English Pewter, Made by Liberty and Co. 0277", some wear and pitting to inside.

5in (12.5cm) diam

$320-380   **DN**

One of a pair of Liberty and Co. Tudric pewter glass holders, designed by Archibald Knox, each of cylindrical form, the body diagonally pierced and cast with entwined foliage and leaves, stamped marks "0534".

3in (7.5cm) high

$80-120 pair   **L&T**

A pair of Liberty and Co. Tudric pewter vases, each with S-shaped handles, stamped beneath "English Pewter 030, Solkets".

7in (18cm) high

$600-900   **DN**

A pair of Liberty and Co. Tudric pewter candlesticks, each with circular base and cylindrical stem above open-work section, the tops of the stems molded with stylized foliage, detachable sconces, stamped "TUDRIC 022".

5in (12.5cm) high

$400-600   **GORL**

A Liberty and Co. Tudric pewter twin-handled bowl, designed by Archibald Knox, of circular form with pierced sides cast with stylized leaves and tendrils, lacks liner, stamped marks "0320".

9in (23cm) wide

$180-220   **L&T**

A Liberty and Co. Tudric round caddy, designed by Archibald Knox, the cylindrical caddy decorated with stylized flowers, the cover with concave center and horizontal flat handle, stamped beneath "T", "Tudric" and "0193".

4in (10cm) high

$600-900   **DN**

A CLOSER LOOK AT ART NOUVEAU METALWORK

The naturalistic, tapering and curving handles are typical of the Art Nouveau movement.

Stylized floral and foliate decoration was a popular theme of the movement.

The pierced areas draw attention to the shapes and forms and allow the glass inside to be seen, providing contrast.

The Württemberg Metalwork Factory (W.M.F.) became known for its elaborate Art Nouveau styled metalware and its success inspired the design of the Liberty and Co. 'Tudric' range.

A W.M.F. Art Nouveau pewter siphon stand, with two tendril handles, pierced and embossed with leaves, impressed marks.

8in (20cm) high

$220-280   **LFA**

METALWARE

A W.M.F. easel-back dressing table mirror, the beveled heart-shaped plate within a surround of stylized leaves and berries with two flared scroll feet and a crest and shoulders in the form of open work panels of entwined leaves.

15.5in (39cm) high

$1,000-1,500   DN

A W.M.F. octagonal plate, embossed with an Art Nouveau maiden's head and shoulders in profile, her long hair knotted at the back of her neck and trailing over her shoulders, the border with flowers and ribbons.

8.75in (22cm) high

$280-320   DN

A W.M.F. plated metal fruit or sweet dish, with three attached bowls, embellished with a leaf and a curved branch-like handle enclosing the figure of a maiden in diaphanous robes, stamped on handle "WEPCO", "EP", "1\0" and "OX".

7.25in (18.5cm) high

$220-280   DN

An Art Nouveau bronze doorstop, the woman with outstretched arms holding her dress hem.

9in (23cm) high

$400-600   JDJ

A pewter Art Nouveau tray, the nude woman with arms spread and butterfly-type wings, signed on front "H.P."

7.5in (19cm) high

$400-600   JDJ

A German Art Nouveau pewter figurine.

c1905   6.75in (17cm) high

$700-1,000   TO

An Art Nouveau pewter and brass strawberry bowl, molded with fruit, leaves, and flowers on stylized feet, with clear glass liner.

9in (23cm) diam

$400-600   DN

MILITARIA

An Ashmor porcelain figure of a Battle of Britain pilot, 'A Royal Air Force Fighter Pilot of Churchill's Few', from a limited edition of 250.

$300-500   **W&W**

An Ashmor porcelain figure, 'Field Marshal The Viscount Montomery of Alamein, KGB, DSO', from a limited edition of 375.

$300-500   **W&W**

An Ashmor porcelain figure of a Gurkha soldier in the Falklands Campaign, 'A Soldier Representing the 1st Battalion 7th Regiment of The Duke of Edinburgh's Own Gurkha Rifles', from a limited edition of 250.

$280-320   **W&W**

An Ashmor porcelain figure, 'United States 8th Army Air Force Pilot, 1942-1945', from a limited edition of 250.

$280-320   **W&W**

An unframed watercolor '1st Royal Dragoons'.

10in (25.5cm) high

$300-500   **L&T**

A watercolor, signed "E Benassit", depicting a French Revolutionary period reconnaissance party seeking local knowledge from a peasant.

16in (40.5cm) wide

$700-1,000   **W&W**

A silver-colored metal cup, engraved "Presented to Bertie Beresford Hart by his godfather Lord William Beresford 9th Lancers VC Calcutta 30".

8in (20cm) high

$400-600   **W&W**

A brass candlestick, made from the hilt of an Imperial German infantry officer's sword, regulation hilt with crowned eagle in guard, crowned WWII device to wire bound leather-covered grip, brass base and sconce mounted on section of blade.

11in (28cm) long

$70-100   **W&W**

A Scottish oval plated military shooting match trophy shield, on wooden back plate, decorated with an angel holding laurel wreaths above two soldiers with Martini falling block rifles and with St. Giles, Edinburgh Castle and the Scott Monument all framed by thistles.

Known as the Artisan Challenge Shield, it was started in 1891 and competed for until the outbreak of WWII in 1939, there is a gap in the list of named winners from 1913-28, in part due to WWI.

28in (71cm) high

$600-900   **L&T**

A scarce and interesting Georgian officer's campaign knife and fork, two-pronged steel fork, curved knife, the blade unclearly stamped "MIL/...PD", tapered hexagonal agate handles with scalloped edge bands, in velvet-lined, fitted leatherette case, some rust pitting, one band restored, few worn patches to case.

$400-600   **W&W**

COLLECTORS' NOTES

■ The speed at which the technology developed makes this a particularly interesting subject and early examples with their cumbersome and blocky designs are among the most sought-after.

■ Designs that have become iconic through media coverage are also desirable. When the Nokia 8110 had a pivotal role in the sci-fi blockbuster 'The Matrix' it instantly became the must-have handset of the moment. This marketing ploy proved so successful that Samsung specifically designed a handset for the first sequel.

■ Cellular phones are now seen as an indispensable part of everyday life and handsets are regularly upgraded as new designs and technology are released. Look for examples that are complete and in good condition.

■ The market is still in infancy with very little literature available to collectors other than the original catalogs, company literature or magazine reviews, and no standardized structure, so it will be interesting to see how the market develops.

An Alcatel HD1 cellular phone, with blue fascia.

6in (15cm) high

$30-50　　　　　　**GC**

A British Telecom TCR M0600 cellular phone, made by Matsushita, with extending aerial.

6.75in (17cm) high

$30-50　　　　　　**GC**

An Ericsson GA628 GSM cellular phone, with green fascia.

c1995　6.5in (16.5cm) high

$25-35　　　　　　**GC**

An Ericsson GH198 cellular phone, with flip aerial.

5.5in (14cm) high

$30-50　　　　　　**GC**

An Ericsson GA628 GSM cellular phone, with colored fascia, and fixed aerial.

This model came in a variety of color finishes.

c1995　6.5in (16.5cm) long

$30-50　　　　　　**GC**

A Maxon SL500 cellular phone, in the form of a walkie talkie.

8in (20cm) long

$80-120　　　　　　**GC**

A black Motorola 6800X cellular phone and base battery unit, with cord and revolving aerial.

9.5in (24cm) long

$120-180　　　　　　**GC**

A gray Motorola Star-TAC GSM cellular phone.

c1995　3.75in (9.5cm) long

$70-100　　　　　　**GC**

A gray Motorola Independent cellular phone, the fixed aerial unscrews.

7.75in (19.5cm) long

$100-150　　　　GC

A gray NEC Jade P3 ETACS cellular phone, lacks aerial.

c1992　　*6.5in (16.5cm) long*

$25-35　　　　GC

A black Nokia THX-6X cellular phone, with extending aerial, illuminating keys and three lines for speaker.

7.25in (18.5cm) long

$30-50　　　　GC

A Nokia NHK-4RY cellular phone, with black keys and gray panels under screen.

6.75in (17cm) high

$30-50　　　　GC

A Philips Fizz blue and black GSM cellular phone, with extending aerial.

c1995　　*7in (18cm) high*

$30-50　　　　GC

A silver Siemens J7 Digiphone cellular phone, with extending aerial.

6.75in (17cm) high

$30-50　　　　GC

A white Storno 220 cellular phone.

9.75in (19.5cm) high

$120-180　　　　GC

A Technophone PC2215T cellular phone, with extending aerial.

c1995　　*7.75in (19.5cm) long*

$100-150　　　　GC

A Sony CM-R111 ETACS cellular phone, with flip arm microphone.

c1995　　*4.25in (11cm) high*

$120-180　　　　GC

A Faust magic lantern, by Gebrüder Bing, together with 12 3in slides, electrified.

Contained in a fitted box with small glass slides of children's stories, these lanterns were popular toys. Look for complete examples in excellent condition.

c1905   14.5in (37cm) high

$220-280   **ATK**

A 'Lampadophore' magic lantern, by Lapierre, Paris, in original wooden box, with 28 glass slides.

c1880

$800-1,200   **ATK**

A Lanterne Riche magic lantern, by Gebrüder Lapierre, Paris, for 2.5in slides, some patches of rust, lacks burner.

Lapierre are known for their brightly colored, novelty-shaped tin lanterns – condition is important to value with splits, wear, and rust devaluing examples considerably. Look for examples in the shapes of buildings, such as the Eiffel Tower, which are very valuable.

c1880

$400-600

12in (30.5cm) high

ATK

A mahogany and brass 'Lothian' magic lantern by A.H. Baird of Edinburgh, with fabric bellows on a sliding focusing mechanism.

This magic lantern design was illustrated in the 1st November, 1892 edition of 'The Practical Photographer' and was said to be both of good value and excellent design. Baird was a photographic dealer based at 15 Lothian Street, Edinburgh, Scotland.

18.5in (47cm) high

$400-600   **ET**

A mahogany mechanical, hand-painted magic lantern chromotrope slide.

c1890

$150-200   **ET**

A French mahogany stereoviewer, by Unis-France, together with a binocular-type stereoviewer.

$500-700   **ATK**

A walnut table-mounted stereoviewer, probably French, with 50 erotic stereocards.

17.75in (45cm) high

$600-900   **ATK**

An incomplete mahogany-cased Praxinoscope Theater, by Emile Reynaud of Paris.

c1880   9.75in (25cm) wide

$400-600   **F**

An unusual floor-standing Mutoscope, by the International Mutoscope Reel Co. Inc., New York, USA, with Mutoscope reel No. 7698, featuring a semi-naked maiden, holding a harp, dancing in the forest.

Mutoscopes held 'wheels' of single photographic images – turning a handle would rotate the wheel and show a sequence of images in quick succession, giving the impression of movement. Many were found at the seaside and other tourist attractions.

c1900   56in (143cm) high

$2,200-2,800   **ATK**

PAPERWEIGHTS

COLLECTORS' NOTES

■ The 'classic' period of paperweight manufacture was between c1845 and c1860 and was centered in France around the glasshouses of Clichy, Baccarat, and St. Louis. Millefiori canes arranged in different patterns are the most common types, along with 'posy' weights of flowers. Look for complex and densely packed 'set-ups' and large 'magnum' or smaller 'miniature' sizes.

■ America and Scotland in particular led the revival of paperweight art during the 20th century, with names such as Paul Ysart, Charles Kaziun and later Paul Stankard and John Deacons. Natural designs still dominate as does the use of millefiori canes, but lamp or torch worked forms have also become important, further demonstrating the skill of the maker. Unlike 19th century examples, most are signed or contain canes with monograms making identification easy.

An 1850s Baccarat 'Anemone' paperweight.

2.25in (6cm) diam

$1,000-1,500 **BGL**

An 1850s/60s French Baccarat 'Primrose' paperweight, with star-cut base.

2.75in (7cm) diam

$1,000-1,500 **BGL**

An 1850s French Baccarat 'Anemone' paperweight, with red flower on a white latticework ground.

2.5in (6.5cm) diam

$1,000-1,500 **BGL**

An 1850s St Louis 'Double Clematis' paperweight, with amber ground and pink flower.

2.25in (5.5cm) diam

$1,000-1,500 **BGL**

A 19thC St Louis 'Fruit Bouquet' paperweight.

2.75in (7cm) diam

$1,000-1,500 **BGL**

A rare Clichy paperweight, green and white carpet ground with millefiori canes, underneath a Clichy rose.

c1850   2.75in (7cm) diam

$1,000-1,500 **FIS**

A mid-19thC Baccarat paperweight, two stone formations and moss glass imitations of green glass, concave base.

2.5in (6.5cm) diam

$300-500 **WKA**

A mid-to late 19thC Baccarat 'Sand Dune' paperweight.

These almost abstract patterns are made of unmelted sand and fragments of mica and green glass.

2.5in (6.5cm) diam

$100-150 **AB**

A 19thC Bohemian-Czechoslovakian magnum paperweight, with a three-dimensional sulphide of a white rabbit.

4in (10cm) diam

$400-600 **LHS**

PAPERWEIGHTS

An unsigned Perthshire millefiori paperweight.

2.5in (6.5cm) diam

$70-100   **BGL**

A 20thC Perthshire paperweight, on a dark red glass cushion millefiori canes and white strings of glass, in the center a flower, blossom and leaves, concave base.

Perthshire Glass was formed by Stuart Drysdale in 1968. He had worked with the Ysarts at Caithness and continued to make paperweights in that style.

3in (8cm) diam

$400-600   **WKA**

A 20thC Perthshire paperweight, with millefiori canes on a clear glass cushion, overlaid in red, cut through with circular panels and with star-cut base.

3.25in (8cm) diam

$400-600   **WKA**

A 1960s/70s Perthshire paperweight, with blue ground and millefiori rods arranged in a chain link star, with paper label to base for "Perthshire Paperweights Crieff Scotland".

2.25in (6cm) diam

$220-280   **BGL**

A 1970s Ysart paperweight, with bubbles emerging from a multicolored ground, with blue PY sticker to base.

Paul Ysart is considered one of the fathers of 20thC paperweight design and began making paperweights in the 1930s for Monart at the Moncrieff glassworks and then Caithness Glass from 1963. He then set up his own company specializing in paperweight production in 1970 which ran until 1982.

2.25in (5.5cm) high

$200-300   **AB**

A William Manson 'Blue Dahlia' paperweight, signed to the base "William Manson SNR 2001".

2.5in (6.5cm) diam

$120-180   **BGL**

A late 1970s Charles Kaziun 'Pansy with Gold Bee' paperweight, the bee in gold foil resting on a milky pale yellow base, signed with a gold signature "K".

1.75in (4.5cm) diam

$1,500-2,000   **BGL**

A CLOSER LOOK AT A PAPERWEIGHT

Kaziun aimed to revive French paperweight manufacture techniques. Both the ground, known as 'muslin', made up of sections of canes, and the flower, are typical techniques.

The rose is 'lampworked' using a small gas blow torch to manipulate the glass before it is centered and cased in flawless clear glass – all typical features of many 20thC artist-made paperweights.

Kaziun had admired and studied roses made by noted American paperweight and glass designer and maker Emil Larson (1879-unknown).

An American Charles Kaziun 'rose on muslin' paperweight, signed with "K" signature cane.

Kaziun is one of the 20thC's foremost and influential paperweight artists, beginning his work in 1939. He was self-taught and worked from his studio at his home, kick-starting a 'studio artist' movement in paperweight manufacture.

c1955   **$1,200-1,800**

2.25in (5.5cm) diam

BGL

A unique William Manson footed 'Strawberry Patch' paperweight, signed to the base "William Manson SNR 1/1 1999 Joyce Manson", with "William Manson Made in Scotland" paper label to base.

2.75in (7cm) diam

$150-200 **BGL**

A William Manson 'master sample' 'Almond Tree Flowers' type paperweight, with pink, blue, and white cherry flowers on a green ground, signed inside with 'WM' cane, and to base "William Manson 2002 Master Sample".

William Manson founded his factory in Perth, Scotland in 1997 with his family. Each piece bears a signature cane in the design and an inscribed signature, number and date on the base. Many are released in limited editions, with unique examples such as this 'master sample' being highly sought after.

2002 *2.25in (6cm) diam*

$220-280 **BGL**

A John Deacons millefiori paperweight, with label to base, signed with "JD 2004" double hearts and thistle cane.

2004 *2.75in (7cm) diam*

$100-150 **BGL**

A Gordon Smith paperweight, with coral on a gray-blue ground and a red-black frog over a clear glass base, signed with a monogram cane and engraved with the year of production.

1944 *3in (7.5cm) diam*

$320-380 **WKA**

A John Deacons 'Pom Pom' paperweight, signed to the base with "JD 2002 cane".

2.75in (7cm) diam

$320-380 **BGL**

A Lewis and Jennifer Wilson faceted orange frog, snake and flowers paperweight, signed with blue 'CM' cane.

2.75in (7cm) diam

$280-320 **BGL**

A Daniel Salazar cherry blossom and dragonfly paperweight, signed to rim "Daniel Salazar Lundberg Studios 2003 06/927".

In 1974 Salazar and Steven Lundberg launched what has become known as the 'California' style, using complex, 3-D torchworked designs.

2.5in (6.5cm) high

$400-600 **BGL**

A large Steven Lundberg moon and cherry blossom paperweight, the moon made from gold foil, the base signed "Steven Lundberg Lundberg Studios 1995 051128".

3.5in (9cm) diam

$400-600 **BGL**

A Lindsay Art Glass 'New Zealand Coral Reef' dichroic paperweight, signed "Lindsay Art Glass 2002" on base.

3in (7.5cm) diam

$220-280 **BGL**

A crown paperweight, with radiating canes separated by twisted canes.

$100-150 **ROS**

A CLOSER LOOK AT A DUNHILL NAMIKI PEN

The box increases the desirability of this piece. Boxes are rare as they were often lost or damaged and thrown away.

This pen was made under a partnership between British luxury goods retailer Alfred Dunhill Ltd and the Japanese Namiki Mfg Co. Ltd, who were responsible for the lacquerwork decoration.

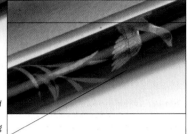

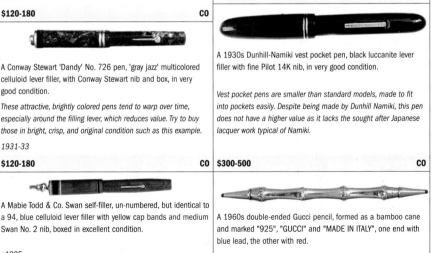

The decoration was painstakingly handpainted by skilled artists over a period of weeks onto a black lacquered background using clear and colored lacquer and gold and silver dust.

The decoration is artistically applied around the entire body of the pen, encouraging it to be turned around to view the entire design. A part of the design is shown however the pen is held.

A 1930s Dunhill Namiki three-quarter size lacquer fountain pen, showing a duck in flight on the barrel, with reeds on the barrel and cap, in original Dunhill Namiki box, artists signature on the barrel.

$2,200-2,800   **GORL**

An American Le Boeuf 'Unbreakable' 40 ringtop, navy blue and ivory striped celluloid, with Le Boeuf Pen nib, in very good condition with light ambering.

The white stripes here tend to discolor, as they do on the Parker 'True Blue', which reduces value.

c1930

$120-180   **CO**

A 1920s Chicago handpainted ringtop, black lever filler decorated with Art Deco stylized flowers in different colors, with fine warranted 14K No.3 nib.

$220-280   **CO**

A Conway Stewart 'Dandy' No. 726 pen, 'gray jazz' multicolored celluloid lever filler, with Conway Stewart nib and box, in very good condition.

These attractive, brightly colored pens tend to warp over time, especially around the filling lever, which reduces value. Try to buy those in bright, crisp, and original condition such as this example.

1931-33

$120-180   **CO**

A 1930s Dunhill-Namiki vest pocket pen, black luccanite lever filler with fine Pilot 14K nib, in very good condition.

Vest pocket pens are smaller than standard models, made to fit into pockets easily. Despite being made by Dunhill Namiki, this pen does not have a higher value as it lacks the sought after Japanese lacquer work typical of Namiki.

$300-500   **CO**

A Mabie Todd & Co. Swan self-filler, un-numbered, but identical to a 94, blue celluloid lever filler with yellow cap bands and medium Swan No. 2 nib, boxed in excellent condition.

c1925

$100-150   **CO**

A 1960s double-ended Gucci pencil, formed as a bamboo cane and marked "925", "GUCCI" and "MADE IN ITALY", one end with blue lead, the other with red.

$150-200   **CO**

A late 1920s Mabie Todd & Co. Swan 172-53, scarlet celluloid ringtop lever filler with black cap bands and fine Swan No.2 nib, in fair to good condition.

$70-100 CO

A late 1920s Mabie Todd & Co 54 ETN pen, pearl and black veined and marbled celluloid lever filling ringtop with fine Swan Eternal 4 nib, in very good condition with mild ambering.

$80-120 CO

A Mabie Todd & Co Swan Eternal E644B, mottled red and black hard rubber lever filling pen with medium Swan Eternal No.6 nib, in good but over-polished condition.

Large sized pens are desirable. The price would have increased by around 30% if it had not been overpolished.

c1920

$100-150 CO

A late 1930s Mabie Todd & Co 'Cygnet' stylo, un-numbered burgundy and black marbled celluloid lever filler with 'PATENT APPLIED FOR' barrel imprint and chrome trim.

Stylos or 'ink pencils' have thin, tubular nibs instead of a standard nib.

$80-120 CO

A late 1920s Mabie Todd & Co. self-filling pen, un-numbered jade green celluloid lever filler with fine Swan No.2 nib, in very good condition with a little brassing to the clip.

$80-120 CO

A 1980s Parker 75 Lacque pen and pencil set, 'thuya' lacquer cartridge/convertor filler with Parker 585 france nib and matching push cap ballpen, in near mint condition.

Although still deemed 'modern', the 75 has become a hot niche collecting market. Pens must be in mint condition or have unusual finishes to be of interest to most collectors.

$80-120 CO

A Wahl Eversharp Skyline, sapphire blue pearl and black striped celluloid cap and barrel, with gold filled cap top and Eversharp nib, in excellent condition.

This is an unusual color for a comparatively common pen.

c1945

$150-200 CO

A Montblanc 14k gold No. 744 pen and No. 772 pencil, stamped "585", fully working, no dents, engraved name.

This set is in excellent condition with crisp engine turned decoration and no dents or engraved names. Not all overlays on fountain pens were made or approved by the maker. Look carefully for authentic maker's marks. Many marks were added later by jewelers or added by unscrupulous collectors to raise the value of the pen.

c1955

$1,500-2,000 ATK

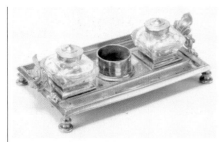

A 19thC brass rectangular inkstand, with leaf-chased handles, two cut-glass wells and a central recess, on round feet.

11.75in (30cm) wide

$400-600   DN

An unusual brass building-shape inkstand, with 'lift-up' roofs revealing inkwells, "Samuel Thompson & Sons/ Midland Maltings/ Smethwick Birmingham" in raised lettering to middle section with lift-off roof to take pens.

10.75in (27.5cm) long

$320-380   BBR

A German 'inky boy' bisque inkwell. c1900   *5in (12.5cm) high*

$150-200   BEJ

A late 19thC brass novelty dog inkwell, after Landseer, in the form of a begging terrier, with glass eyes on circular beaded base.

The finely modeled and comparatively large form is much like the terrier seen in 'Macaw, Love Birds, Terrier, and Spaniel Puppies' painted by Sir Edwin Landseer in 1839. The painting is now owned by H.M. Queen Elizabeth II and is in the Buckingham Palace Collection, London.

7in (17.5cm) high

$600-900   GORL

A white metal stags head inkstand, the base engraved "Ryton Regatta 1894/ Steeplechase & Swimming/ J Geo Joicey", some damage to inkwells.

7in (18cm) wide

$60-90   BBR

A 19th/20thC Louis XV-style gilt-bronze and porcelain inkwell, the lobed porcelain bowl decorated in the Imari style, the dish base with scroll mounts, with scroll cast cover.

7in (17.5cm) high

$180-220   SL

A 1950s Parker green glass pen base, by Whitefriars, with internal bubble decoration, to hold a Parker 51 pen.

Ball 2.75in (7cm) high

$40-60   GC

A European satinwood, ebony, and brass standish, rectangular table-top form supported by turned standard resting on rectangular satinwood plinth with in-curved sides and single drawer.

13.75in (35cm) long

$400-600   SL

A Victorian electroplate inkstand, with pierced gallery and foliate molded feet, mounted centrally with an underglaze blue painted ink reservoir in the Chinese taste, flanked by molded pen trays.

c1870   *9.75in (25cm) wide*

$150-200   BONS

An English Victorian papier-mâché standish, rectangular box with single drawer having central carrying handle and pair of pen trays and pair of clear glass inkwells, decorated with floral mother-of-pearl inlaid design.

14in (35.5cm) long

$220-280   SL

A CLOSER LOOK AT A STAPLER

The chrome-plated body and the green bakelite handle are colorful and typical of the Art Deco period.

The Catalin is still bright and undamaged and the chrome is clean and largely un-pitted.

This model is styled unlike any other stapler made by the ACE Fastner Corp. Their staplers were usually solidly made with large door-knob shaped striking heads and little attention to decorative styling.

The form is typical of the 1930s style, with the clean lines and futuristic streamlining seen in the plastic bar and curving bracket.

An American Ace Model 502 stapler, by Ace Fastner Corp. of Chicago, Illinois, with a chrome-plated body and green Catalin handle.

The Ace Fastner Corp made many staplers during the 1930s, with names such as 'Pilot', 'Scout' and 'Cadet'. Although they never recovered fully after being made to support the war effort during WWII, certain models such as the 'Pilot' are still available today.

c1938

$50-80 ATK

A Victorian silver bookmark, in the form of a trowel, with mother-of-pearl handle, Birmingham hallmark.

1894   2.75in (7cm) long

$60-90 AGO

A 1920s brass bookmark, in the form of a Lincoln pixie standing on one leg.

3in (7.5cm) long

$40-60 AGO

A late 19thC Persian handpainted papier-mâché pen case, with painted flowers and delicate floral patterns in reds and earthy tones.

Condition is important on these, as is the level of decoration. Splits to the body or losses to the finish are highly detrimental to value.

9.5in (24cm) long

$280-320 EPO

A Victorian metal bookmark, possibly Scottish, in the form of a sickle, with striated agate handle.

c1880   3.5in (9cm) long

$40-60 AGO

A cast-iron stamper, with revolving holder for this and other stamps.

$150-200 ATK

An English letter scale, with weights, wooden base with brass weights and official weight divisions.

$300-500 ATK

COLLECTORS' NOTES

- Initially an Austrian peppermint breath-freshener, Pez was introduced into the US in 1952. It was not an immediate success, but when fruit flavors were added and the dispensers redesigned to appeal to children, the product took off.

- The heads cover a range of subjects, though rarely real life personalities, and include Disney, Star Wars, comic book heroes, and holiday-themed characters.

- Feet were added to the base of the dispensers in 1987 and were intended to help keep them upright. Soon these were replaced with a thicker version. As examples with no feet tend to be earlier they are also the most desirable.

- With over 300 different Pez available and more being produced each year, there is something for every pocket. Rare variations in color and design, and full-figural examples tend to be the most desirable, as well as those in mint condition in the original packaging.

An early 1980s 'Petunia Pig' Pez dispenser, no feet.

Petunia Pig is a Warner Bros. cartoon character.

4in (10cm) high

$50-70   ATA

A 1970s 'Santa Claus' Pez dispenser, no feet.

Santa Claus Pez dispensers have been made since the 1950s and come in a variety of formats. This example, without feet and with a flesh-colored face, is the most common. Look for full-body versions which can fetch around $200.

4.25in (10.5cm) high

$7-10   ATA

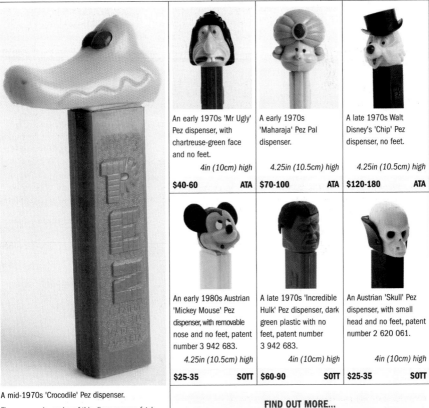

An early 1970s 'Mr Ugly' Pez dispenser, with chartreuse-green face and no feet.

4in (10cm) high

$40-60   ATA

A early 1970s 'Maharaja' Pez Pal dispenser.

4.25in (10.5cm) high

$70-100   ATA

A late 1970s Walt Disney's 'Chip' Pez dispenser, no feet.

4.25in (10.5cm) high

$120-180   ATA

An early 1980s Austrian 'Mickey Mouse' Pez dispenser, with removable nose and no feet, patent number 3 942 683.

4.25in (10.5cm) high

$25-35   SOTT

A late 1970s 'Incredible Hulk' Pez dispenser, dark green plastic with no feet, patent number 3 942 683.

4in (10cm) high

$60-90   SOTT

An Austrian 'Skull' Pez dispenser, with small head and no feet, patent number 2 620 061.

4in (10cm) high

$25-35   SOTT

A mid-1970s 'Crocodile' Pez dispenser.

The rare purple version of this dispenser can fetch twice as much as this green one.

4in (10cm) high

$120-180   ATA

FIND OUT MORE...

'Collector's Guide to PEZ Identification & Price Guide', by Shawn Peterson, published by Krause, 2nd edition.

www.pezcollectors.com

COLLECTORS' NOTES

■ Photography has become an extremely popular and diverse sector of the collecting market in recent years. High prices are paid for early examples and masterpieces by noted, often surrealist, photographers. Away from this higher end, interesting collections can still be built for hundreds of dollars, or under.

■ Always consider the type of photograph that you have, as this will help you identify the time period when it was taken. Also look at the clothes the sitter is wearing, as this will also give information about the date. If the sitter can be identified as a notable person, this can raise value – 'nobodies' are usually not of high value, unless there is another redeeming feature. A photograph of a 'nobody' with an early date, size or one depicting a quirky or unusual subject, such tools of a trade, are of interest.

■ Not all images of famous people are rare and valuable, as some were printed in large quantities or are not sought after by collectors. The photographer also may have a bearing on value – look on the back and corners for a printed or stamped mark. Condition is important, with cut down images, tears, scuffs and fading all reducing value.

An American sixth-plate daguerreotype, anonymous, showing an elder in the 'Odd Fellows', his dark sash and gloves signify his rank, one tiny spot on plate.

Although small, this image is crisp and clear and would be of interest to 'Odd Fellows' collectors as well as to collectors of photography. It will be rarer than other daguerrotypes showing unknown members of the public. For other items relating to and a brief explanation of the 'Odd Fellows', see the 'Masks' section of this book.

$600-900 **CHAA**

A sixth-plate hand-tinted daguerreotype of a young man, in complete leather case.

3.75in (9.5cm) high

$40-60 **ANAA**

A quarter-plate ambrotype of a baby girl, in a partial leather-covered case, the reverse with paper label reading "Edith Harper, Born in San Francisco, California".

4.75in (12cm) high

$60-90 **ANAA**

A sixth-plate daguerreotype of a husband and wife, in complete leather case.

3.5in (9cm) high

$60-90 **ANAA**

An ambrotype of a rather portly and frumpy seated lady, in a bonnet, in a complete leather-covered case.

A sixth-plate daguerreotype, of two men, one with arm on shoulder, case lacks lid.

An American sixth-plate ruby ambrotype, anonymous, of a three-story clapboard building under construction, the scaffolding is visible at the right side of the building, in full pressed paper case.

The inset image shows the case closed. This is a typical case for many such early photographic images.

3.5in (9cm) high

$40-60 **ANAA**

The inset image shows the silvery reflective appearance of daguerreotypes, an effect not found on ambrotypes or tintypes.

3.75in (9.5cm) high

$50-70 **ANAA**

$150-200 **CHAA**

An American Civil War albumen photograph, by the Brady Studio, titled "71st Regiment NY. Navy Yard, Washington, D.C." with an 1861 copyright line, mounted on board.

14.75in (37.5cm) wide

$400-600   **CHAA**

A photograph album with musical movement, black leather-bound album contains historical carte de visites and photographs and incorporates a key-wound music box with two tunes.

10.5in (27cm) high

$300-500   **ATK**

A black and white photograph of Edward Prince of Wales (later King Edward VIII), signed and entitled "H.M.S. Renown Nov 1919", framed and glazed.

Between 1919 and 1925, Edward made four tours on the HMS Renown, then the newest and largest British Royal Navy battleship, including voyages to Canada, the US, New Zealand and over 40 other countries. This image was taken upon his return journey from the US in November 1919.

8in (20cm) high

$220-280   **CLV**

A Japanese photograph of General Pershing and dignitaries, by R. Maruki of Tokyo, showing General Pershing, Ambassador of Knox and eight other dignitaries on front porch of house, mounted on board that exhibits some warping, surface soiling and corner bumps.

10.5in (26.5cm) wide

$180-220   **AAC**

An American carte de visite of Edwin Booth, an actor, by Gurney & Son, New York.

Edwin Booth (1833-93) had noted acting skills, which were described at the time as 'a spell from which you can not escape'.

c1864

$300-400   **AAC**

A CLOSER LOOK AT A CARTE DE VISITE

Cartes de visites (or CdVs) were inexpensive photographs mounted on standard sized cards and given out as gifts and stored in albums - many millions were produced.

This CdV is by Edward Anthony of New York City, a prolific producer throughout the 1860s.

The photograph shows Edwin Perrin, a US expediter. He was sent to New Mexico in 1862 by the Secretary of War to help arm New Mexican troops for conflict in the Southwest. This CdV is more valuable as it shows a known person with a military connection.

It was taken in 1862, at the height of the CdV fashion, which lasted from around 1860 until 1866.

A rare American carte de visite, probably taken in Albuquerque, January 1862, showing Edwin Perrin, seated on a burro, wearing a fringed jacket, armed with a bowie knife, a sword and a carbine, with a tin cup and other utensils, Anthony backmark, lower corners clipped.

1862

$1,500-2,000   **CHAA**

A tortoiseshell photograph album, the cover with a central strapwork cartouche and a wide border in piqué and pose d'or, with purple moiré silk lining.

The condition and quality of materials and decoration affect the value of a Victorian photograph album such as this. Here the gilt tooling and use of tortoiseshell on the cover add to the value.

9.25in (23.5cm) long

$600-900   **HAMG**

COLLECTORS' NOTES

■ Pins are an immensely popular collectible area, due in part to their great variety, colorful designs, feeling of nostalgia, and small size, making them easy to display and wear. As the variety available is so wide, many choose to collect a particular theme such as Disney, comic book heroes, club pins or cowboy pins, the latter popular during the 1950s. Many categories have crossover appeal to other sectors, so can fetch high prices due to increased competition.

■ Condition is important so try to avoid pins in poor condition including fading, scratches, bubbling of the plastic coating, and rusting. Always try to buy licensed versions, rather than imitations and watch out for modern reproductions by examining the type of decoration method used and by checking the backs.

An American Captain Marvel Club 'Shazam' pin.

When Billy Batson shouted the magic word "Shazam" he gained his superhero powers.

1in (2.5cm) wide

$50-70   **LDE**

An American Valley Pride Meats 'Cecil' pin, with copyright for Bob Clampett.

Bob Clampett (1913-1984) worked for the animation section of Warner Bros. Studios and was responsible for their first character, Porky Pig. In 1946 he started his own studio and created the live puppet show 'Time for Beany' featuring the propeller-hatted Beany and his sea serpent friend Cecil.

1in (2.5cm) wide

$250-350   **LDE**

An American 'Some Swell Sweater' Little Orphan Annie pin, design by Harold Grave, marked "Mfrd by Parisian Novelty Co. Chicago, Sole Licensees".

1in (3cm) wide

$70-100   **LDE**

An American 'Andy Gump Funy Frostys Club' member's pin.

Average man Andy Gump and his family were invented by Captain Joseph M. Patterson who hired cartoonist Sidney Smith to draw him for the Chicago Tribune. This popular character first appeared in 1917 and moved to the The New York Daily News in 1919. A vast array of merchandise was produced for the Gump family and it became the first strip to move into radio in 1931. When Smith was killed in a car crash in 1959, he was replaced by sports cartoonist Gus Edson but his style was not as popular and circulation declined with the series being discontinued in 1959.

1in (2.5cm) wide

$50-70   **LDE**

An American Secret Agent X-9 pin.

Launched in 1934, Secret Agent X-9 was so secret he didn't even have a name or an agency, although it was later revealed he worked for the FBI and gained the name Phil Corrigan. The strip was not particularly popular at the time, but is favored by comic book afficionados today. It was scripted by 'Sam Spade' author Dashiell Hammett and Leslie Charteris, creator of 'The Saint', and drawn by Alex Raymond, famous for his Flash Gordon strip.

1.5in (4cm) wide

$120-180   **LDE**

An American Walt Disney's Dumbo DX pin, marked "C Walt Disney Productions".

1in (2.5cm) wide

$30-50   **LDE**

An American 'Dick Tracy Detective' pin.

1in (2.5cm) wide

$40-60   **LDE**

An American 'Looney Tune Club' pin.

0.75in (2cm) wide

$100-150   **LDE**

A Canadian 'I Read Hopalong Cassidy in the Toronto Star' pin, possibly 1950s.

1in (2.5cm) wide

$150-200 LDE

An American 'Dale Evans' pin.

1in (2.5cm) wide

$40-60 LDE

An American 'Wyatt Earp' pin.

"The Life & Legend of Wyatt Earp" debuted on ABC in 1955 and starred Hugh O'Brian in the title role. It ran for six years.

1.75in (4.5cm) wide

$70-100 LDE

An American 'Fort Orange Council - Boy Scout Pow Wow, June 1, 2, 1935' pin.

c1935

$80-120 LDE

An American Horlicks Malted Milk pin.

This design was also made in a pocket mirror.

1in (2.5cm) wide

$25-35 LDE

An American 'Roy Rogers & Trigger' pin.

c1955 *1.75in (4.5cm) wide*

$40-60 LDE

An American 'Roy Rogers King of the Cowboys' pin.

1.75in (4.5cm) wide

$80-120 LDE

An American 'Sugarfoot' pin.

Tom 'Sugarfoot' Brewster, played by Will Hutchins, was a law student who traveled the west in search of his fortune. It ran from 1957 to 1961 and two episodes were directed by famous Hollywood director Robert Altman early in his career.

1.75in (4.5cm) wide

$70-100 LDE

An American 'The Shadow of Fu Manchu' pin.

The villanous character of Dr. Fu Manchu was created by Sax Rohmer (1883-1953). He first appeared in novel form in "The Insidious Dr. Fu Manchu" in 1913 and then featured in over 14 further novels, including a clash with Sherlock Holmes in "Ten Years Beyond Baker Street" by Cay Van Ash. The stories were also adapted for radio and film, and James Bond's "Dr. No" bears close comparison.

1in (2.5cm) wide

$80-120 LDE

COLLECTORS' NOTES

■ Bakelite was developed by Belgian chemist Dr Leo Baekeland in 1907 and was dubbed 'the material of 1,000 uses'. It is usually found in plain and mottled browns and black, with brighter colors such as blue and red being more desirable, and often more valuable.

■ Not all plastics are Bakelite, which can be recognized by rubbing a piece with a finger, which produces a strong carbolic smell. Other desirable plastics include cast phenolic, often known as Catalin. Many pieces were produced for the home, particularly the kitchen.

■ When buying plastics, look for bright color and good period styling – pieces showing the clean lines of the Art Deco style are often the most desirable. Damage such as chips, cracks, and burn marks will always devalue a piece, but if a piece is extremely rare it may still be worth adding to your collection.

A black vulcanite circular box with lid, marked "Stipendum Reg. Greaseproof".

Vulcanite, also sometimes known as 'ebonite' is another name for 'hard rubber', which was patented by Charles Goodyear in 1844. It is recognizable by a strong sulphuric smell when rubbed.

c1910   3.25in (8cm) diam

$15-25   **JBC**

A 1920s green, maroon, and black mottled Bakelite bowl.

5in (13cm) diam

$15-25   **JBC**

A 1940s multicolored speckled urea-formaldehyde bowl.

4in (10cm) diam

$5-8   **MHC**

A 1920s dark green mottled Bakelite lidded pot.

4in (10.5cm) diam

$15-25   **JBC**

A 1930s lidded maroon mottled Bakelite pot.

3.5in (9cm) diam

$15-25   **JBC**

A brown mottled Bakelite tray, the base marked "Made in England MCC122", the center with molded profile of a stylish 1930s lady.

c1930   12in (30.5cm) diam

$40-60   **MHC**

Two 1920s English celluloid simulated tortoiseshell dressing table items.

$5-8 each   **JBC**

A pair of 1930s black Bakelite salt and pepper shakers, with very rare sterling "HJNS" tops.

2.25in (5.5cm) high

$60-90   **BB**

A rare 1930s Catalin salt and pepper shaker set, in the form of the Washington Monument.

4.25in (10.5cm) high

$120-180   **MHC**

A set of three small Art Deco sherry glasses and three wine glasses, made from orange Catalin-type plastic with chromed stems, molded to base "NEWDAWN U.S.A. PAT. APPLD FOR".

$120-180   **BB**

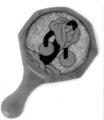

A 1930s fruit knife with a blue and white mottled urea formaldehyde handle, stainless Sheffield steel blade, leather holder.

4.5in (11.5cm) long

$8-12   **JBC**

A celluloid hand mirror, green with painted decoration of a lady and glitter.

c1930   3.75in (9.5cm) l.

$150-200   **TDG**

A General Electric alarm clock, with spherical face and ribbed orange Bakelite housing, marked on face and backplate.

4.5in (11.5cm) high

$280-320   **DRA**

A 1930s green and yellow Catalin mantel clock, by Viking.

Both the combination of colors and the shape make this clock desirable.

3.5in (9cm) high

$180-220   **CBU**

A 1930s tortoiseshell-effect cast phenolic-handled umbrella, the handle carved as a Scottie dog.

24.75in (63cm) long

$180-220   **ROX**

A Diehl 'Ribbonaire' Bakelite table fan, with two speeds and original grosgrain ribbons and wire, in working order.

9.75in (25cm) high

$300-400   **DRA**

A scarce 1940s Carvacraft green blotter, made by Dickinson Products.

The green is considerably scarcer than the amber or yellow.

6in (15.5cm) long

$100-150   **MHC**

A 1930s cherry red cast and carved Catalin magnifying glass, with folding handle.

4.25in (11cm) long

$50-80   **MHC**

A very rare Catalin scarab desk accessory.

Egyptian motifs were popular in the 1920s and 1930s, following the discovery of Tutankhamun's tomb by Howard Carter in 1922.

c1930   3.25in (8.5cm) wide

$120-180   **MHC**

A 1930s French brown mottled Bakelite fountain pen.

4.75in (12cm) long

$30-50   **JBC**

COLLECTORS' NOTES

- As modes of travel expanded in scope and variety from the early to mid-20th century, and people became better able to afford holidays, travel posters increased in popularity. Ocean liner and railway company posters are amongst the earliest and most prolific designs. Today these categories remain the most popular with collectors.

- A notable designer adds value, but it is the image that is often of primary importance – striking designs, bold use of color and adherence to popular styles, such as Art Deco or the 1950s 'modern' style, are important indicators of value.

- Most posters were aimed at luring people away from the 'daily grind' and show seductive or exotic, brightly colored landscapes. Evocative scenes, from the rolling hills of England to the sun soaked shores of Africa, tend to be the most popular.

- Travel posters often have important socio-economic tales to tell. They document changing fashions and lifestyles, and highlight technological change. For example, they show how airlines began to compete commercially with cruise liners from the 1950s.

- Condition is important – before posters became popular collectibles, many were stored folded, so folds are acceptable and often easily removed. Tears that extend into the image, or more seriously, damage to the surface of the image, will reduce value considerably.

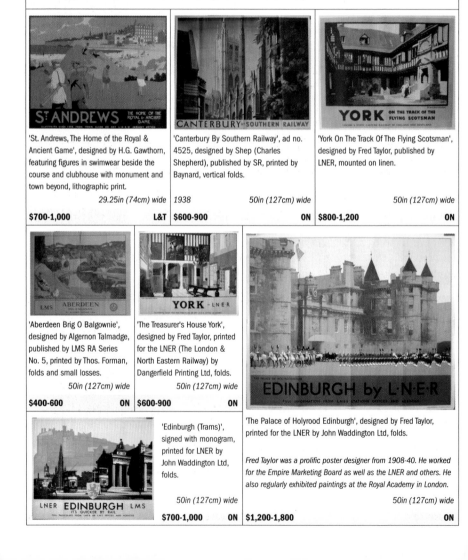

'St. Andrews, The Home of the Royal & Ancient Game', designed by H.G. Gawthorn, featuring figures in swimwear beside the course and clubhouse with monument and town beyond, lithographic print.

29.25in (74cm) wide

$700-1,000   **L&T**

'Canterbury By Southern Railway', ad no. 4525, designed by Shep (Charles Shepherd), published by SR, printed by Baynard, vertical folds.

1938   *50in (127cm) wide*

$600-900   **ON**

'York On The Track Of The Flying Scotsman', designed by Fred Taylor, published by LNER, mounted on linen.

50in (127cm) wide

$800-1,200   **ON**

'Aberdeen Brig O Balgownie', designed by Algernon Talmadge, published by LMS RA Series No. 5, printed by Thos. Forman, folds and small losses.

50in (127cm) wide

$400-600   **ON**

'The Treasurer's House York', designed by Fred Taylor, printed for the LNER (The London & North Eastern Railway) by Dangerfield Printing Ltd, folds.

50in (127cm) wide

$600-900   **ON**

'The Palace of Holyrood Edinburgh', designed by Fred Taylor, printed for the LNER by John Waddington Ltd, folds.

Fred Taylor was a prolific poster designer from 1908-40. He worked for the Empire Marketing Board as well as the LNER and others. He also regularly exhibited paintings at the Royal Academy in London.

50in (127cm) wide

$1,200-1,800   **ON**

'Edinburgh (Trams)', signed with monogram, printed for LNER by John Waddington Ltd, folds.

50in (127cm) wide

$700-1,000   **ON**

'Llandudno for Sun Ray and Sea Spray, Travel in Comfort by LMS', designed by Warren Williams, printed by John Horn Ltd, mounted on linen.

This is typical of the type of railway poster that aimed to attract the public into taking affordable holidays at the many British seaside resorts that sprung up in the early 20thC. Along with the LMS, the notable LNER, the GWR and the SR were the leaders in graphic railway posters. LNWR had begun the trend by commissioning Norman Wilkinson as designer in 1905.

50in (127cm) wide

$1,200-1,800   ON

'Buxton The Mountain Spa', designed by S.J. Lamorna Birch, published by LMS, The Best Way Series No. 37, printed by Thos. Forman, folds with small losses.

Folds such as this are commonly found on railway posters, especially large ones, as they were often stored folded before posters became so sought after. Providing the surface is not damaged, they can usually be made to 'disappear' by a professional.

50in (127cm) wide

$600-900   ON

'Cornwall', designed by Ronald Lampitt, published by GWR, printed by J. Weiner, mounted on linen with minor repairs to bottom margin.

The evocative subject matter, the strong colors suggesting sunshine and the familiar holiday location, make this an extremely desirable poster. The unusual 'mosaic' style is a hallmark of Lampitt's work, used in posters from c1936.

50in (127cm) wide

$1,500-2,000   ON

'The Clyde Coast The Narrows, Kyles of Bute', designed by Alasdair Macfarlane, printed for BRSR by McCorquodale.

50in (127cm) wide

$600-900   ON

'Alnwick Castle Northumberland', designed by Fred Taylor, printed for the LNER by Dangerfield Printing Ltd, folds.

50in (127cm) wide

$800-1,200   ON

'Northern Ireland', designed by Hesketh Hubbard, published by LMS, printed by Jordison.

50in (127cm) wide

$700-1,000   ON

'Huntingdonshire Hemingford Grey', by Edward Wesson, published by BRER, printed by Waterlow.

50in (127cm) wide

$400-600   ON

'The South Downs', ad no. 6657/A3, designed by Jack Merriott, printed for BRSR by Baynard, folds.

50in (127cm) wide

$600-900   ON

'Callander The Trossachs Gateway', LMS Best Way Series No. 52, designed by Archibald Kay, printed by McCorquodale.

50in (127cm) wide

$280-320   ON

'Waterloo Station A Centenary of Uninterrupted Service During Peace and War 1848-1948', ad no. 5416 1946, designed by Helen McKie, published by SR, printed by Baynard, two folds and small tears to margin.

McKie's incredibly detailed and complex watercolor aimed to show how little service at Waterloo had varied in times of peace or war.

c1948   *50in (127cm) wide*

$3,000-5,000   ON

POSTERS

'Another Convoy Is Discharged The Lines Behind The Lines', No. 522, designed by Frank H. Mason, published by BR, printed by Haycock, vertical folds.

50in (127cm) wide

$1,200-1,800   **ON**

'Unceasing Service The Lines Behind The Lines', designed by Frank H. Mason, published by BR, printed by Haycock, folds.

c1945   50in (127cm) high

$1,800-2,200   **ON**

'On Early Shift, Greenwood Signal Box New Barnet', designed by Terence Cuneo, printed for the the Railway Executive by Waterlow Ltd, mounted on linen.

50in (127cm) wide

$2,800-3,200   **ON**

'The Continent', designed by W. Smithson Broadhead, printed for GW, LMS, LNE & Southern Railways by the Haycock press.

W. Smithson Broadhead was also a well-known portrait and horse painter. This finely detailed and painted poster depicting café society was designed for a number of companies to promote travel to Continental Europe.

50in (127cm) wide

$6,000-9,000   **ON**

'Somerset', designed by Jack Merriott, published by REWR, printed by Jordison, small tears to bottom margin.

40.25in (102cm) high

$300-500   **ON**

'Suffolk Codenham', designed by Leonard Squirrell, printed for BRER by Waterlow, mounted on linen.

40.25in (102cm) high

$700-1,000   **ON**

'Worcestershire', designed by Frank Sherwin, published by BRWR, printed by Waterlow, mounted on linen.

40.25in (102cm) high

$300-500   **ON**

'The Dales Of Derbyshire Monsal Dale And The River Wye', designed by S.R. Badmin, published by BRLMR, printed by McCorquodale, small tear to bottom right corner.

40.25in (102cm) high

$600-900   **ON**

'Ullswater The Lake District for Holidays', designed by Clodagh Sparrow, printed for the LMS by Stafford Ltd, mounted on linen.

40.25in (102cm) high

$600-900   **ON**

'North Wales For Holidays Dolbarden Castle Llanberis', designed by John Mace, published by LMS, bottom margin slightly trimmed.

39.5in (100cm) high

$300-500   **ON**

'Guildford Picturesque And Historic', ad no. 1480, designed by Walter E. Spradbery, published by SR, printed by Waterlow.

Guildford's notable Tudor landmark, Abbott's Hospital, was founded in 1619 by Archbishop Abbot as an almshouse. This poster may have more local, rather than tourist, interest from collectors.

1931

$70-100 ON

39.75in (101cm) high

'Shrewsbury Ireland's Mansion', designed by Claude Buckle, published by GWR No. 198, printed by Lowe and Brydone.

40.25in (102cm) high

$600-900 ON

'Tamworth Castle Staffordshire', designed by Ronald A. Maddox, published by BRLMR, printed by Jordison.

40.25in (102cm) high

$180-220 ON

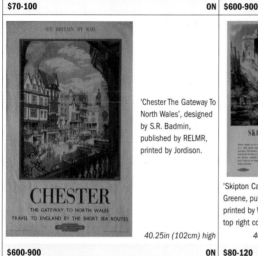

'Chester The Gateway To North Wales', designed by S.R. Badmin, published by RELMR, printed by Jordison.

40.25in (102cm) high

$600-900 ON

'Skipton Castle', designed by Greene, published by BRLMR, printed by Waterlow, staining to top right corner.

40.25in (102cm) high

$80-120 ON

'Loch Derg Ireland for Holidays', designed by Paul Henry, printed for the LMS by Jordison Ltd.

1949   40.25in (102cm) high

$600-900 ON

'Isle of Man', designed by Clive Uptton, published by RELMR, printed by Waterlow.

40.25in (102cm) high

$120-180 ON

'Rothesay Isle of Bute', designed by Frank H. Mason, published by BRLMR, printed by McCorquodale.

40.25in (102cm) high

$180-220 ON

'Montrose', designed by Austin Cooper, published by LNER, printed by McCorquodale, folds.

40.25in (102cm) high

$40-60 ON

'Winter In Warmth at Bournemouth', ad no. 2500, color photographic, printed for SR by Waterlow.

1933   40.25in (102cm) high

$300-500 ON

'Northern Ireland The Amphitheatre Giants Causeway', designed by Eric Lander, published by RELMR, printed by Waterlow.

1952   40.25in (102cm) high

$300-500   ON

'Dolgoch Station On The Talyllyn Railway', designed by Terence Cuneo, published by TR, printed by Waterlow.

40.25in (102cm) high

$180-220   ON

'Essex Coast Oysters', designed by Frank H. Mason, published by LNER, printed by Ben Johnson, mounted on linen.

39.75in (101cm) wide

$400-600   ON

'North East Coast Crabs', designed by Frank H. Mason, published by LNER, printed by Ben Johnson, mounted on linen.

40.25in (102cm) wide

$400-600   ON

'Warrenpoint Co. Down Ireland', designed by Odin Rosenvinge, The Best Way Series No.32, published by LMS, printed by McCorquodale, folds.

Born in Newcastle-upon-Tyne of Danish descent, Rosenvinge (1880-1957) is known for his designs that incorporate a striking use of orange – he used such bright colors with great, eye-catching effect.

40.25in (102cm) high

$1,200-1,800   ON

'Greatstone By The Romney Hythe And Dymchurch Railway', designed by N. Cramer Roberts, printed by Vincent Brooks Day.

40.25in (102cm) wide

$300-400   ON

'East Coast Route To The Lake District', published by North Eastern Railway, printed by McCorquodale, mounted on linen.

40.25in (102cm) high

$400-600   ON

'Take The Family To The Lancashire Coast', designed by Septimus E. Scott, published by LMS, printed by Beck and Inchbold.

40.25in (102cm) high

$320-380   ON

'Butlins For Holidays', designed by Mervyn Scarfe, published by REER, printed by Jarrold, mounted on linen.

Holiday camps were popular tourist destinations, and posters featuring them appeal as much to collectors of camp memorabilia as to railway collectors. They show the changing tastes of the British public.

40.25in (102cm) high

$600-900   ON

'Bath In 1828 By The New Steam Carriage Today By Western Region', designed by Eric Fraser, published by BRWR, printed by Waterlow.

40.25in (102cm) high

$180-220   ON

'Weston-Super-Mare', designed by Tom Purvis, published by the Railway Executive, printed by Jordison.

1949   40.25in (102cm) high

$1,200-1,800   ON

'Ireland The Land of Eternal Youth', designed by R. Breslin, printed for the Great Southern Railways by Alex Thom Ltd Dublin, mounted on linen with restoration.

39.75in (101cm) high

$280-320   ON

'Skegness Is So Bracing, The Jolly Fisherman celebrates his Golden Jubilee', designed by John Hassall, printed for BRER by Baynard Press.

This is the third version of this famous railway poster that first appeared in 1908. The main difference from the earlier LNER version is the addition of the pier, and it can also be found in a landscape format. Skegness was a popular holiday destination – in 1871 Skegness had a population of 500, but by 1907 it attracted some 300,000 tourists per year.

1958   40.25in (102cm) high

$2,800-3,200   ON

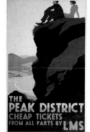

'The Peak District', designed by Ralph Mott, printed for LMS by S.C. Allen, mounted on linen.

40.25in (102cm) high

$800-1,200   ON

'Swanage', designed by Broomfield, published by BRSR, printed by Baynard, folds.

40.25in (102cm) high

$400-600   ON

'Colwyn Bay', designed by Bruce Angrave, published by BRLMR, printed by Baynard.

40.25in (102cm) high

$220-280   ON

'Lovely Llandudno Holds All The Aces!', designed by Amstutz, published by RELMR, printed by McCorquodale, small tear to bottom margin.

1952   40.25in (102cm) high

$220-280   ON

'Southern England', designed by Albert Brenet, printed for BRSR by Waterlow Ltd, mounted on linen.

40.25in (102cm) high

$300-500   ON

'The Lune Valley In England's Enchanting North West', designed by Bradshaw, published by BRLMR, printed by Wood, Rozelaar & Wilkes.

40.25in (102cm) high

$180-220   ON

'Metropolitan Railway, Look on the back of your ticket "It's a pity to puncture the picture"', designed by John Hassall, printed for R.H. Selbie General Manager by David Allen.

42.25in (107cm) high

$800-1,200   **ON**

'When In Doubt Take The Underground', designed by John Hassall, printed by the Hassall Designs Co., mounted on linen with restoration.

40.25in (102cm) high

$800-1,200   **ON**

'Edgware by Tram', designed by E.A. Cox, printed for Electric Railway House by Avenue Press, mounted on linen.

1916   30in (76cm) high

$400-600   **ON**

'Cunard LNER The United States & Canada link with the East Coast and the Continent', printed by Thos. Forman & Sons Ltd, mounted on linen.

The two powerful images of a cruise liner and a steaming train, combined with the Cunard name, make this an evocative and desirable poster depicting typical forms of travel of the era.

39.75in (101cm) high

$4,000-6,000   **ON**

A CLOSER LOOK AT A RAILWAY POSTER

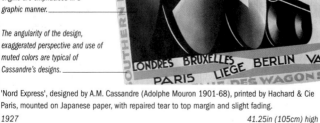

Cassandre is the pseudonym used by Adolphe Mouron, one of the 20th century's most respected poster designers.

The poster sums up the 1930s perfectly - the style is the epitome of Art Deco, with its clean, angular lines.

The power and speed of the steam engine are emphasised in a graphic manner.

The angularity of the design, exaggerated perspective and use of muted colors are typical of Cassandre's designs.

'Vitesse', designed by Hildenbrand.

1934   39.25in (98cm) high

$800-1,200   **SWA**

'Nord Express', designed by A.M. Cassandre (Adolphe Mouron 1901-68), printed by Hachard & Cie Paris, mounted on Japanese paper, with repaired tear to top margin and slight fading.

1927   41.25in (105cm) high

$6,000-9,000   **ON**

'Summer In Germany', designed by E. Frommbold, published by the German Railways.

39.75in (101cm) high

$220-280   **ON**

'Summer days on German Lakes', designed by Von Axster-Heudhab, published by the German Railways.

39.75in (101cm) high

$220-280 ON

'Lucerne Springtime A Delightful Season', designed by O. Landolt, printed for SFR by Fretz Bros Zürich, pin holes and small losses.

35.5in (90cm) high

$70-100 ON

'Bex Solbad Simplon-Linie Klimatischer Kurort-Golf', designed by Nico Heart, printed by Paul Attinger Neuchatel for SBB (Swiss Federal Railways), small losses and pin holes.

37.5in (95cm) high

$220-280 ON

'Giorgio Viola di C Trieste', printed by Modiano Trieste for ENIT and Italian Railways, small loss to top left corner.

40.25in (102cm) high

$100-150 ON

'L'Aquila Degli Abruzzi', designed by Umberto Noni, printed by Besozzi Milano for ENIT and Italian Railways, losses to bottom left margin.

1931   39.75in (101cm) high

$180-220 ON

A CLOSER LOOK AT A RAILWAY POSTER

Canadian designer, Peter Ewart is a noted artist who designed many posters for Canadian Pacific.

The snowy peaks of the Rockies highlighted by the sun and the shadowy forest are evocative of Canada's natural landscape.

'Norway 1931', designed by W. Midelfart, printed for Norwegian Railways by Hagen & Kornmann Oslo, pin holes.

39.75in (101cm) high

$120-180 ON

'Norway Summer Season June-September', designed by Ben Blessum, printed by A. Worner for Norwegian State Railway.

39.75in (101cm) high

$180-220 ON

The perspective, taken from close to the ground, and the dark, black train against the bright colors suggest the power and speed of the train.

The Canadian Pacific united Canada coast to coast and grew to be known as 'The World's Greatest Travel System'. By 1903 it sailed ships across the Pacific and Atlantic.

'Travel Canadian Pacific Across Canada', designed by Peter Ewart.

c1950   35.75in (89cm) high

$1,800-2,200 SWA

'Nelson Line Fast and Regular Service Canary Islands and South America', signed "ABW", mounted on linen.

40.25in (102cm) high

$300-500 ON

'Nelson-Line to South America (Highland Monarch)', signed "ABW", mounted on linen.

40.25in (102cm) high

$600-900 ON

'Nelson-Line The Bridge to South America', signed "ABW", mounted on linen.

40.25in (102cm) high

$300-500 ON

'Canada For Game Birds' designed by Tom Hall.

35.5in (89cm) high

$1,800-2,200 SWA

A CLOSER LOOK AT A CRUISE LINER POSTER

Although by an anonymous artist, this poster design is striking.

The use of the towering ship's bow motif is similar to the famous poster designed by Adolphe Mouron (Cassandre) for the 'Normandie' in 1935.

The simple lines, flat planes of color and type of font are all in the desirable Art Deco style.

At around 3ft 4in (1m) in size, it is a popular size – ideal for display in many homes.

'NSNC' (Nelson Steam Navigation Company), stock poster showing line up of ships, signed "AW", mounted on linen.

40.25in (102cm) high

$800-1,200 SWA

'Canada For Game Fish' designed by Peter Ewart, printed by Exhibits Branch, C.R.R. for Canadian Pacific, a trout fighting the line in its mouth, against a blue background.

35.75in (89cm) high

$1,800-2,200 SWA

'Cruise on the Great Lakes / Canadian Pacific' designed by Peter Ewart, a young woman against a blue background, lettering in khaki and blue.

35in (87.5cm) high

$800-1,200 SWA

'Blue Star Line, Mediterranean Cruises', designed by Maurice Randall, printed by Philip Read London, small losses and folds.

Similar to many railway posters, the colors used in cruise liner posters are often bright and saturated, giving the impression of bright sun. Exotic views of other peoples were a further draw for those stuck in the gray, humdrum life in a town or city.

40.25in (102cm) wide

$300-400   **ON**

'Welsh Norway Luxury Cruises by Blue Star Line', printed by Philip Reid London, small losses and folds.

40.25in (102cm) high

$320-380   **ON**

'Orient Pleasure Cruises by "Orontes" and "Ophir"', designed by John Hassall, mounted on linen.

40.25in (102cm) high

$300-500   **ON**

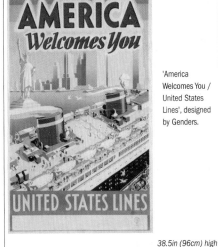

'America Welcomes You / United States Lines', designed by Genders.

38.5in (96cm) high

$1,000-1,500   **SWA**

'Mediterranean Cruises Hamburg–Amerika Linie', designed by Otto Anton, small tears to margins.

40.25in (102cm) high

$280-320   **ON**

'Cruises Around Africa, German African Lines', designed by Otto Anton, printed by Kunst I.M. Druck August 1936.

39.75in (101cm) high

$300-400   **ON**

'Linea Rapida Para Habana Y Veracruz, Com Cie Gle Transatlantique (Liner Espagna)', printed by Champenois, mounted on linen.

40.25in (102cm) high

$300-400   **ON**

'Ellerman's City & Hall Lines to & from Egypt-India-Ceylon, (SS City of Benares)', designed by Frank H. Mason, printed by S. Straker and Sons London, small tears and folds.

40.25in (102cm) high

$500-700   **ON**

'Messageries Maritimes Mediterranean', loss to bottom margin.

The damage greatly reduces the value of this poster.

40.25in (102cm) high

$40-60   **ON**

'Orient-Royal Mail To Australia', designed by John Hassall, Managers F. Green & Co., mounted on linen.

40.25in (102cm) high

$400-600   **ON**

ONSLOWS

THE POSTER PEOPLE

John Hassall Skegness Is So Bracing, printed for the LNER by Waterlow & Sons Ltd.- 102 x 127 cm. Estimate £2000 - 2500

19th & 20th Century Posters
For over 20 years Onslows have been developing the market in Posters which have seen remarkable growth in value.

Areas of particular interest include those published by the pre war railway companies LNER, LMSR, GWR and SR, London Transport, Imperial Airways, BOAC and BEA, Shipping Companies including Cunard White Star, Shell and BP, Motoring and Sporting including Racing, Skiing and the Olympics, The Empire Marketing Board, War Propaganda and Pop Art, European Posters, and any other vintage advertising.

Onslow's Collectors Auctions are held twice yearly. Colour illustrated catalogues are available by post or can be viewed free of charge on our website.

Please contact **Patrick Bogue** for advice on selling and catalogues.
We have an extensive Picture Library of Poster Images available for Media and Publishing purposes.

ONSLOW AUCTIONS LTD. THE COACH HOUSE, STOURPAINE, DORSET. DT11 8TQ
TEL: 01258 488838   enquiries@onslows.co.uk   WWW.ONSLOWS.CO.UK

'Cunard U.S.A. / Etats Unis Et Canada' designer unknown, a French poster showing dramatically-angled view of three towering, red funnels, with colorful, stylized men and women waving farewell from the ships deck.

40.5in (101cm) high

$1,000-1,500   **SWA**

'West Indies and Spanish Main by French Line SS Colombie SS Cuba', designed by E.J. Kealey, printed by Hill Siffken London, small losses and tears to margin.

40.25in (102cm) high

$280-320   **ON**

'Scotland's Wonderland by Macbraynes Steamers', designed by E.C. Le Cadell, printed by McCorquodale, small losses, tears and pinholes to margin, fold.

40.25in (102cm) high

$400-600   **ON**

'Shaw Savill & Albion Line New Zealand Direct, Mt Egmont sighted by Captain Cook 1770', designed E. Walters.

40.25in (102cm) high

$300-400   **ON**

'Aberdeen and Commonwealth Line To Australia', designed by P. H. Yorke, printed by Howard Jones, mounted on linen.

40.25in (102cm) high

$320-380   **ON**

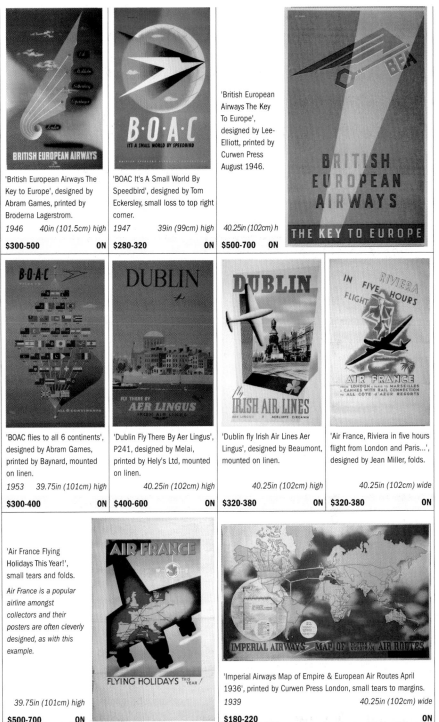

'British European Airways The Key to Europe', designed by Abram Games, printed by Broderna Lagerstrom.

1946   40in (101.5cm) high

$300-500   **ON**

'BOAC It's A Small World By Speedbird', designed by Tom Eckersley, small loss to top right corner.

1947   39in (99cm) high

$280-320   **ON**

'British European Airways The Key To Europe', designed by Lee-Elliott, printed by Curwen Press August 1946.

40.25in (102cm) h

$500-700   **ON**

'BOAC flies to all 6 continents', designed by Abram Games, printed by Baynard, mounted on linen.

1953   39.75in (101cm) high

$300-400   **ON**

'Dublin Fly There By Aer Lingus', P241, designed by Melai, printed by Hely's Ltd, mounted on linen.

40.25in (102cm) high

$400-600   **ON**

'Dublin fly Irish Air Lines Aer Lingus', designed by Beaumont, mounted on linen.

40.25in (102cm) high

$320-380   **ON**

'Air France, Riviera in five hours flight from London and Paris...', designed by Jean Miller, folds.

40.25in (102cm) wide

$320-380   **ON**

'Air France Flying Holidays This Year!', small tears and folds.

Air France is a popular airline amongst collectors and their posters are often cleverly designed, as with this example.

39.75in (101cm) high

$500-700   **ON**

'Imperial Airways Map of Empire & European Air Routes April 1936', printed by Curwen Press London, small tears to margins.

1939   40.25in (102cm) wide

$180-220   **ON**

'Bailie's B.B. Tours to Ulster, Seven Glorious Days', mounted on linen.

30in (76cm) high

$300-400 ON

'Northern Ireland', designed by Griffin, published by British Travel Association, printed by James Upton.

1955 40.25in (102cm) high

$70-100 ON

'Come to Ulster For A Happy Holiday', designed by Bernhard Higham, published by Ulster Tourist and Development Association, printed by S.C. Allen, mounted on linen.

40.25in (102cm) wide

$400-600 ON

'Ireland Invites You', designed by Melai, printed for the National Tourist Organisation by Browne & Nolan Ltd Dublin, mounted on linen.

40.25in (102cm) high

$300-500 ON

'Country Houses And Gardens In Britain', designed by Rowland Hilder, published by British Travel Association, printed by James Upton.

1954 40.25in (102cm) high

$120-180 ON

'London Piccadilly Circus', designed by Leonard Squirrell, published by the British Travel Association, printed by W. Cowell.

30in (76cm) high

$300-500 ON

'Bournemouth Britain's All Season Resort, A Place In The Sun', designed by Eustace Nash, published by the Town Council.

30in (76cm) high

$80-120 ON

'Farming', designed by James Arnold, published by the LT, printed by Curwen Press.

1950 40.25in (102cm) high

$300-500 ON

'Adelboden', designed by W.T., printed by Wolfsberg, Zürich, a partial view of a man mid-tennis game, against a blue and white mountainscape and a green and yellow pasture, text banner in red.

39.75in (99cm) high

$800-1,200 SWA

'National Parks Zetu Zinaleta – Donated by the Frankfurt Zoological Society', designed by Anon, printed by P.R. Wilk.

32.75in (83cm) high

$180-220 ON

'Hungary Hortobagy', designed by Fery Konecsni, printed by G. Klosz Budapest for Hungarian National Office for Tourism.

37in (94cm) high

$280-320 ON

'Jutland Denmark, The Bathing Beach of the Continent', designed by Henrik Hansen, printed by Chr. Olsen, small losses.

39in (99cm) high

$120-180 ON

'Sweden Värmland An Unspoiled Mekka for Tourists', designed by Beckman, printed by J Olsens Stockholm.

39.75in (101cm) high

$70-100 ON

A CLOSER LOOK AT A TRAVEL POSTER

'Davos Switzerland', designed by Otto Glaser, printed by Basler Druck Basel, small tears to margin.

40.5in (103cm) high

$80-120 ON

'Camping', 1950s French sporting poster, artwork by Brocherun.

52in (132cm) high

$150-200 CL

Gert Sellheim (1901-70) was one of the first designers commissioned by the Australian National Travel Association (est. 1929) to design posters to attract tourists to Australia.

Sellheim's most famous design is the leaping kangaroo logo for airline Qantas, designed in 1947.

The flat plane of perspective is typical of much of Sellheim's designs – also look out for his use of Aboriginal motifs in his other travel poster designs.

His hallmark brightly colored and overtly modern designed posters were displayed in ANTA's London, Bombay, and San Francisco travel offices.

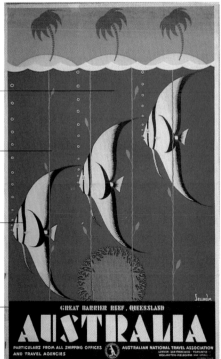

'Australia Great Barrier Reef Queensland', designed by Sellheim, published by Australian National Travel Association, tear top margin.

40.25in (102cm) wide

$1,500-2,000 ON

COLLECTORS' NOTES

■ Indicators to value for skiing posters are the destination, the artist and the design itself. Look for notable resorts and striking, powerful imagery.

■ These posters combine travel, sport, and fashion – as well as modern design. Vibrantly colored and romantic, they also combine many already collected forms of travel from railways to ships and planes.

■ Skiing has long been a fashionable pursuit, with great cachet. As it has become a more accessible pastime in recent decades, the audience has grown, leading to ever healthier prices, with many specialist poster sales devoted to them.

■ Skiing posters can be considered less common than others types, railway posters for example, and comparatively fewer were produced. Look out for Winter Olympic posters as this combines two popular collecting areas.

'Ski New York' designed by H.W., printed by Stecher-Traung, Rochester, a seldom seen image promoting skiing in the Empire State.

Here the typography is angled in opposition to the slope to create a dynamic graphic.

26in (65cm) high

$1,000-1,500   **SWA**

'Austria', designed by Prof. Kirnig (Atelier), printed by Christoph Reisser's Wein for the Austrian Railways, small tear to top margin.

37.5in (95cm) high

$700-1,000   **ON**

'New Hampshire' designed by Hechenberger, an orange haired woman holding a brown pair of skis on her shoulder, against a bright blue background.

36in (90cm) high

$1,500-2,000   **SWA**

'Sun Valley Idaho / Gretchen', color photomontage of local hero Gretchen Fraser.

Gretchen Fraser won the 1948 St. Moritz Winter Olympics Women's Slalom.

1948   38in (95cm) high

$600-900   **SWA**

'Mürren Schweiz', color photographic, designed by Helios, published by Amstutz & Herdeg, small tears to margins.

41in (104cm) wide

$500-700   **ON**

'Villars Chesières Switzerland', color photographic, printed by Brugger SA Meiringen, small tears to margin.

40.25in (102cm) wide

$280-320   **ON**

'Alpes & Jura', designed by Eric De Coulon, printed by Le Novateur, Paris.

1933   39in (97.5cm) high

$700-1,000   **SWA**

'Ski-High Skiing / Lackawanna R. R.' designed by Beverly Towles.

28.5in (71cm) high

$600-900   **SWA**

'Winter In Italy', printed by Pizzi & Pizio Milano for ENIT and Italian Railways.

39.5in (100cm) wide

$400-600   **ON**

COLLECTORS' NOTES

■ Pictorial posters became a popular form of advertising during the early years of the 20th century. Posters from the 1950s are becoming increasingly valuable and collectible. The advent of television effectively saw the end of the golden age of the poster. Look out for oddities produced in small numbers, or those advertising brands that are already popular.

■ Certain long-lived brands are considered 'household names' and are already desirable. They usually fetch high prices, particularly if they exemplify the Art Nouveau or Art Deco movements of the 1900s-30s. However, if the artwork is strong, evocative or by a noted designer, then it is worth considering lesser brands that currently may not be as sought-after.

■ Consider posters advertising products which have become modern-day classics, as many posters from the 1970s onward are not as comparatively highly priced. These may be worth investing in, particularly if nostalgia for a certain product or brand grows in the future.

■ Always look for noted designers, iconic products and striking, colorful and attractive artwork that sums up a period or a style associated with it. Condition is important too, particularly with posters from the 1970s onward, so always aim to buy those in as close to 'mint' condition as possible, avoiding those with tears and damage to the surface.

'Son & Co. BOS Blended Old Scotch Whisky', English advertising poster, artwork by Pease, printed by Walter Scott on three sheets, damp staining and losses to edges.	'Stromness "OO" Old Orkney Whisky, You want a change My Boy I know Sample a bottle of Double "O"', English advertising poster, artwork by John Hassall.	'John Kenyon Ltd Light Dinner Ales & Oatmeal Stout', English advertising poster, artwork by John Hassall, printed by Kingsway Press, repaired tear and small losses to margin.	'Cognac Jacquet', 1920s French advertising poster, artwork by Camille Bouchet.
67in (170cm) high	*25.25in (64cm) high*	*30in (76cm) high*	*63in (160cm) high*
$300-400 ON	**$50-80** ON	**$150-200** ON	**$700-1,000** CL

'Cognac Otard', 1920s French advertising poster.

63in (160cm) high

$1,800-2,200 CL

'Toni-Kola', 1930s French advertising poster, artwork by Roby.

78in (198cm) high

$1,500-2,000 CL

'Aubel & Fils', 1930s French advertising poster.

47in (120cm) high

$1,200-1,800 CL

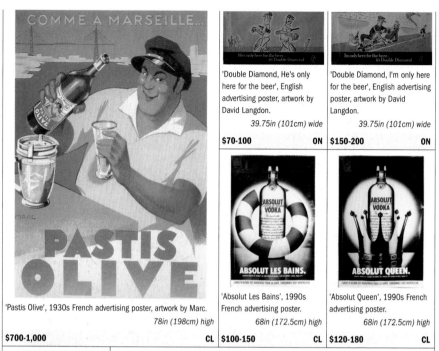

'Double Diamond, He's only here for the beer', English advertising poster, artwork by David Langdon.

39.75in (101cm) wide

$70-100   **ON**

'Double Diamond, I'm only here for the beer', English advertising poster, artwork by David Langdon.

39.75in (101cm) wide

$150-200   **ON**

'Absolut Les Bains', 1990s French advertising poster.

68in (172.5cm) high

$100-150   **CL**

'Absolut Queen', 1990s French advertising poster.

68in (172.5cm) high

$120-180   **CL**

'Pastis Olive', 1930s French advertising poster, artwork by Marc.

78in (198cm) high

$700-1,000   **CL**

'Absolut China Club', 1990s French advertising poster.

68in (172.5cm) high

$100-150   **CL**

'Absolut Vodka', 1990s American advertising poster, artwork by Ellen Steinfeld.

37in (94cm) high

$300-500   **CL**

A CLOSER LOOK AT AN ADVERTISING POSTER

This poster design was produced specially for an appearance in the popular TV series 'Sex and the City', where it was displayed in bus stops.

It was inspired by 1970s' campaigns featuring Burt Reynolds on a rug and Farah Fawcett in a swimsuit.

It was not released generally and features Smith Jared (actor Jason Lewis), a popular character from the hit TV show.

Very limited numbers of the official poster were produced, with the copyright wording showing it is not simply a reproduction of the photograph.

'Absolut Hunk', rare 2000s American faux advertising poster.

36in (91cm) high

$150-200   **CL**

A CLOSER LOOK AT AN ADVERTISING POSTER

The simple lines, minimal decoration and limited use of wording are striking and entirely modern.

The position of the legs and style hints strongly at desirable elegant and romantic night-time dalliances.

'Bally', 1970s French advertising poster, artwork by Jacques Auriac.
22in (56cm) high

$150-200   **CL**

'Bally', 1970s French advertising poster, artwork by Jacques Auriac.
22in (56cm) high

$150-200   **CL**

The use of flat planes of bright color against a black background is eye-catching.

Bernard Villemot is a celebrated poster designer and was the first to use such designs for Bally.

'Bally', French advertising poster, artwork by Bernard Villemot.
c1981   24in (61cm) high

$100-180   **CL**

'Bally - La Chaussure Qui Habille', 1950s French advertising poster, artwork by Hervé Morvan.
63in (160cm) high

$600-900   **CL**

'Bally', 1980s French advertising poster, artwork by Bernard Villemot.
63in (160cm) high

$700-1,000   **CL**

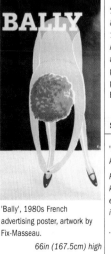

'Bally', French advertising poster, artwork by Bernard Villemot.

The design, style and use of color hark back to paintings by famous modern painter Matisse.

c1975   68in (172.5cm) high

$300-400   **CL**

'Bally', 1980s French advertising poster, artwork by Fix-Masseau.
66in (167.5cm) high

$500-700   **CL**

'Abercrombie & Fitch', 1990s American advertising poster, with photograph by Bruce Weber.
51in (125cm) wide

$120-180   **CL**

'Abercrombie & Fitch', 1990s American advertising poster.

Photographer Bruce Weber is known for his images that emphasize the male body, often in a voyeuristic way.

56in (142cm) high

$150-200   **CL**

'United Colors of Benetton', 1980s Italian advertising poster.

31in (78.5cm) wide

$120-180 CL

'United Colors of Benetton', 1980s Italian advertising poster.

Italian fashion retailer Benetton have long delighted and shocked the world with their high profile, different stance to advertising. Social, political, and economic statements often dominate their campaigns.

36in (91cm) wide

$120-180 CL

'Levi's', 1970s Belgian advertising poster.

37in (94cm) high

$220-280 CL

'Levi's', 1970s Belgian advertising poster.

37in (94cm) high

$220-280 CL

'Chanel No. 5', 1990s French advertising poster, featuring Carole Bouquet.

68in (172.5cm) high

$120-180 CL

'Chanel No. 5', 2000s French advertising poster, featuring Estella Warren.

68in (172.5cm) high

$120-180 CL

'Jean Paul Gaultier, Classique', 1990s French advertising poster.

The perfume bottle illustrated has become a collectible classic. It is said to have been modeled on Madonna and the classic 1930s 'Shocking' perfume bottle by Schiaparelli.

68in (172.5cm) high

$100-150 CLG

'Jean Paul Gaultier, Le Male', 1990s French advertising poster.

The striped 'matelot' (sailor) sweater has become a trademark for fashion designer Jean Paul Gaultier and is echoed by the model's hat.

68in (172.5cm) high

$100-150 CLG

'Dior, Eau Sauvage', 1990s French advertising poster, artwork by René Gruau.

René Gruau was born in 1909 and began his career as a fashion designer, before turning exclusively to advertising from 1949. He worked for some of the greatest names in fashion, including many magazines, such as Marie Claire. His work is characterized by economical use of line and bright color.

63in (160cm) high

$100-150 CL

'Polo Cigaretter', 1920s Scandinavian advertising poster.

30in (76cm) high

$400-600 CL

'Pelican Cigarettes', 1920s French advertising poster.

32in (81.5cm) high

$300-400 CL

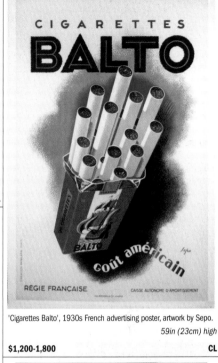

'Cigarettes Balto', 1930s French advertising poster, artwork by Sepo.

59in (23cm) high

$1,200-1,800 CL

'Mildé Radio', 1930s French advertising poster, artwork by F. Nadal Raquin.

47in (120cm) high

$600-900 CL

'4 Gitanes Caporal', 1950s French advertising poster, artwork by Jean Colin.

63in (160cm) high

$600-900 CL

'Marlboro', 1980s American advertising poster.

Despite the tag 'The Marlboro Man', a number of different men have represented him. Underlining the unhealthy aspects of the habit, two of these men, both habitual smokers, died from lung cancer in the 1990s.

81in (205cm) high

$220-280 CL

'Camel Lights', 1990s American advertising poster.

68in (172.5cm) high

$300-400 CL

'Gitanes', 1960s French advertising poster, artwork by Aurion.

58in (147.5cm) high

$600-900 CL

'Oxo For Cup And For Cooking', English advertising poster, published by Oxo Ltd Thames House London, folds.

60in (152cm) wide

$400-600 ON

'Oxo Health And Vigour Thanks To Oxo', English advertising poster, published by Oxo Ltd Thames House London, folds.

60.25in (153cm) wide

$400-600 ON

'Ovaltine', English advertising poster, the central part of a multiple sheet hoarding poster, small tears, together with three other sheets from the poster, folds and small tears.

c1930

$280-320 ON

'Ovaltine', incomplete English advertising sheets from multiple sheet hoarding poster, small tears and folds.

c1930 61in (155cm) high

$30-50 ON

'Perrier', 1960s French advertising poster, artwork by Bernard Villemot.

25in (60cm) high

$100-150 CL

'Orangina', 1980s French advertising poster, artwork by Bernard Villemot.

36in (91.5cm) high

$220-280 CL

'Milk', 2000s American advertising poster, with Pete Sampras.

33in (80cm) high

$100-150 CL

'Olio Radino', 1940s Italian advertising poster, artwork by Boccasile.

55in (140cm) high

$600-900 CL

'Maison Bresilienne, Cafe Sao Paulo', 1900s French advertising poster, artwork by Villefroi.

37in (94cm) high

$800-1,200 CL

'Philips, Prêt Pour Le 2eme Programme', 1960s French advertising poster, artwork by Saint-Genies.

63in (160cm) wide

$400-600 CL

'La Musique C'est Philips', 1960s French advertising poster.

63in (160cm) wide

$300-500 CL

'Cigno', 1950s Italian advertising poster.

28in (71cm) high

$150-200 CL

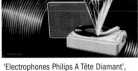

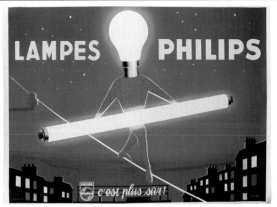

'Electrophones Philips A Tête Diamant', 1950s French advertising poster, artwork by Eric.

63in (160cm) wide

$400-600 CL

'Lampes Philips', 1950s French advertising poster, artwork by Paul Igert.

63in (160cm) wide

$800-1,200 CL

'Disques Radio-Télé', 1950s French advertising poster, artwork by Eric.

63in (160cm) high

$700-1,000 CL

'Join the Olivetti Girls', 1990s Italian advertising poster.

26in (66cm) high

$100-150 CL

'Yum. Think Different', 1990s American advertising poster for Apple iMacs.

Ownership of home computers has increased dramatically since the 1980s and most homes now own one. Apple revolutionized typical designs with the release of the 'Bondi Blue' iMac in August 1998. It made the home computer fashionable, covetable and worthy of display. Unsurprisingly, it has gone on to become a design classic.

36in (91cm) high

$80-120 CL

'Radio la Voix de Son Maitre, Pathe Marconi', 1950s French advertising poster.

63in (160cm) wide

$500-700 CL

'British Vacuum Cleaner Model FF, A Perfect Electric Vacuum Cleaner', English advertising poster, artwork by John Hassall, printed by Hill Siffken, small tears and creases.

15.75in (40cm) wide

$700-1,000   **ON**

'"Dustmo" The Dustless Sweeping Powder, Cleans The Carpet And The Floor And By Jove It Kills The Germs Too!', English advertising poster, artwork by John Hassall, printed by John Hassall Designs Co, small tears.

30in (76cm) high

$300-400   **ON**

'Francisco Tamango Terrot Dijon Cycles Motocycles', French advertising poster, printed by Romanet, mounted on linen.

53.25in (135cm) high

$500-700   **ON**

'Volvo', 1950s Swiss advertising poster.

Here, the famed reliability and durability of Scandinavian-built Volvo cars is alluded to as they give you 'the key to the world'.

51in (125cm) high

$300-500   **CL**

'Cycles de Dion - Bouton', 1920s French advertising poster, artwork by Fournery.

47in (120cm) high

$1,000-1,500   **CL**

'Peugeot', 1930s French advertising poster, artwork by Faure.

47in (120cm) high

$700-1,000   **CL**

'Beeston Tyres Go By Themselves!', artwork by John Hassall, tears and losses.

1896   30in (76cm) wide

$180-220   **ON**

'Fiat Panda', 1970s Italian advertising poster.

The exploration of 'space', links the two disparate vehicles.

55in (140cm) high

$280-320   **CL**

'The Hartford Shock Absorbers "Make Every Road A Good Road" "Any Garage can fit Them"', English advertising poster, artwork by John Hassall, printed by John Waddington.

30in (76cm) high

$220-280   **ON**

'The Weekly Telegraph, On the Road', English advertising poster, artwork by John Hassall, printed by Sir W.C. Leng & Co., London.

25.25in (64cm) high

$180-220 ON

'The Printseller, A Monthly Journal Devoted to Prints & Pictures Ancient & Modern', English advertising poster, artwork by John Hassall.

26.5in (67cm) high

$120-180 ON

A CLOSER LOOK AT AN ADVERTISING POSTER

The design is typically Art Nouveau, a style in vogue at the time pictorial posters began to become popular forms of advertising.

Writing equipment is a popular subject with many collectors.

The wording is shown in an Art Nouveau font and fits seamlessly as part of the design.

The elegant pose and clothing, thoughtful gaze and flowing clouds and locks of hair exemplify the style.

'Encre L. Marquet', French advertising poster, artwork by Eugene Grasset, printed by Malherbe, mounted on old linen with restoration.

1892   45.75in (116cm) high

$1,000-1,500 ON

'Penthouse', 1980s American advertising poster, featuring Jessica Hahn.

Jessica Hahn shot to fame after her affair with religious televangelist Jim Bakker was revealed in 1987. After a brief career in soft pornography, during which she appeared on the front cover of Playboy and Penthouse, she married and now lives in California.

45in (114.5cm) high

$80-120 CL

'"Give 'em all Kodaks", Brownie's message from the Kodak girl', English advertising poster, artwork by John Hassall, small tears to margin.

Kodak is a popular brand to collect. This poster is also desirable because of the bright, colorful depiction of Santa Claus and the festive season.

30in (76cm) high

$600-900 ON

'Tudor by Rolex', 1960s Swiss advertising poster.

Tudor is a sub-brand of Rolex and their watches can generally be found for more affordable prices than similar Rolexes.

51in (125cm) high

$400-600 CL

'Zotos Prevents Sea-Sickness (SS Rol Polley), No. Tips!! "Zotos has done for me!!!"', English advertising poster, artwork by John Hassall.

30in (76cm) wide

$600-900 ON

'Cooper's Dip, The Happy Shepherd', English advertising poster, artwork by John Hassall, printed by William Cooper & Nephews, small tears.

35in (89cm) high

$320-380 ON

COLLECTORS' NOTES

- The value or desirability of a poster depends on a number of factors. The popularity of a film and the actors in it make a poster sought-after. Posters for little-known films, unless they have a cult following, will be less desirable.

- Posters are often re-issued if the film is re-released, or when the video or DVD is released. These are not as desirable and buyers should be careful they are not buying a poster for a re-release instead of an original.

- Posters are produced for each country a film is released in and will tend to have different artwork. The poster from the film's country of origin is usually the most desirable, however posters from other countries such as Czechoslovakia and Poland are

known for their visually stunning artwork. US one sheets or British quads are the standard and most popular sizes.

- Some collectors concentrate on posters by particular artists, such as Saul Bass, Robert Peak, or Giuliano Nistri.

- Early film posters were not made to last and were often thrown away after the film's release. Those that survived were often folded and damaged from being displayed – water stains, tears and fading will all affect the value of a poster. A professional restorer can repair many of these faults, and can also back a poster onto linen to make it more robust and easier to display.

"Alias the Champ", featuring Gorgeous George.

1949

$40-60   **GAZE**

"American Graffiti", UK quad poster.

1973   *40in (101.5cm) wide*

$400-600   **P**

"An American In Paris", US one sheet poster.

1951   *41in (104cm) high*

$1,500-2,000   **P**

"Annie Get Your Gun", US one sheet poster.

1950   *41in (104cm) high*

$400-600   **P**

"Bambi", by Walt Disney, Argentine Spanish language stone lithographed poster.

1942   *43in (109cm) high*

$1,200-1,800   **P**

"Blade Runner", US one sheet poster, with artwork by John Alvin.

1982   *41in (104cm) high*

$600-900   **P**

"For Your Eyes Only", UK quad poster.

1981   *40.25in (102cm) wide*

$40-60   **ON**

"From Russia With Love", Italian language locandino poster, mounted on linen.

1964   *26.75in (68cm) wide*

$300-400   **ON**

"Goldfinger", US one sheet poster.
1965   41in (104cm) high
$1,800-2,200   P

"The Living Daylights", UK quad poster.
1987   40.25in (102cm) wide
$120-180   ON

"Moonraker",
UK quad
poster.
1979   40.25in (102cm) wide
$40-60   ON

"The Spy Who Loved Me", UK quad poster.
1977   40.25in (102cm) wide
$30-50   ON

"Never Say Never Again", UK quad poster.
1983   40.25in (102cm) wide
$18-22   ON

"Never Say Never
Again", German
language one sheet
poster.
1983
$50-70   GAZE

"A View To A Kill", UK quad poster.
1985   40.25in (102cm) wide
$280-320   ON

"You Only Live Twice", UK quad poster.
1967   40.25in (102cm) wide
$180-220   ON

"Bonjour Tristesse", Japanese language
poster, with artwork by Saul Bass.
1958   29in (73.5cm) high
$600-900   P

"Breakfast At Tiffany's/Sabrina", re-release US one sheet double-bill poster.

1965   *41in (104cm) high*

$600-900   **P**

"Carry On England", poster.

$15-20   **GAZE**

"Carry On Round The Bend", poster.

$20-30   **GAZE**

"Casablanca", re-release Italian fotobusta poster.

1961   *27in (76cm) wide*

$600-900   **P**

"Casablanca", 1940s Austrian German language poster.

34in (86.5cm) high

$1,200-1,800   **P**

"Citizen Kane", 1960s re-release Italian locandino poster.

28in (71cm) high

$400-600   **P**

"Clockwork Orange", UK quad poster, folded.

1971

$300-500   **ON**

A CLOSER LOOK AT A HORROR FILM POSTER

"The Creature from the Black Lagoon" is one of the most popular monster movies of all time.

Although this Argentine version is desirable, the US version can be worth around $18,000.

Horror movie posters are the most popular genre with collectors and usually make the most money.

The stone lithography printing process produces a high quality image and can offer a wide range of tones and colors.

"The Creature From The Black Lagoon", Argentine Spanish language stone lithographed poster.

1954   *43in (109cm) high*

$3,000-5,000   **P**

"Dangerous Years", US half-sheet poster.

This was one of Marilyn Monroe's first movies.

1947   *28in (71cm) high*

$180-220   **ATK**

"Death Wish
II", poster.

1982

$15-25   **GAZE**

"The Deer Hunter", UK quad poster.

1978   *40.25in (102cm) wide*

$50-70   **ON**

"Destination Gobi", poster.

1953

$40-60   **GAZE**

"Dirty Harry", Australian daybill
poster.

1971   *30in (76cm) high*

$400-600   **P**

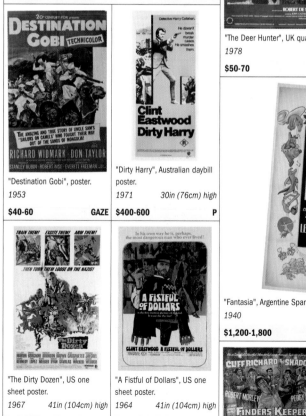

"Fantasia", Argentine Spanish language poster.

1940   *43in (109cm) high*

$1,200-1,800   **P**

"The Dirty Dozen", US one
sheet poster.

1967   *41in (104cm) high*

$400-600   **P**

"A Fistful of Dollars", US one
sheet poster.

1964   *41in (104cm) high*

$1,200-1,800   **P**

"Finder Keepers", UK quad
poster.

1967

$60-90   **GAZE**

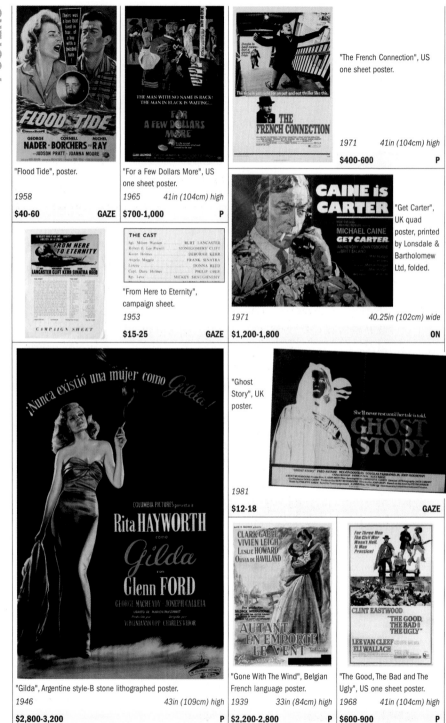

"Flood Tide", poster.

1958

$40-60 GAZE

"For a Few Dollars More", US one sheet poster.

1965 *41in (104cm) high*

$700-1,000 P

"The French Connection", US one sheet poster.

1971 *41in (104cm) high*

$400-600 P

"From Here to Eternity", campaign sheet.

1953

$15-25 GAZE

"Get Carter", UK quad poster, printed by Lonsdale & Bartholomew Ltd, folded.

1971 *40.25in (102cm) wide*

$1,200-1,800 ON

"Ghost Story", UK poster.

1981

$12-18 GAZE

"Gilda", Argentine style-B stone lithographed poster.

1946 *43in (109cm) high*

$2,800-3,200 P

"Gone With The Wind", Belgian French language poster.

1939 *33in (84cm) high*

$2,200-2,800 P

"The Good, The Bad and The Ugly", US one sheet poster.

1968 *41in (104cm) high*

$600-900 P

"The Guns of Navarone", UK quad poster.
1961   *40.25in (102cm) wide*
$70-100   **ON**

"Harry Potter and the Philosopher's Stone", UK quad advance poster, signed by Daniel Radcliffe, who played Harry Potter, together with a sheet of Daniel Radcliffe headed note paper.

This film was released as "Harry Potter and the Sorcerer's Stone" in the US.

23in (58.56cm) high
$180-220   **CO**

"Horror House", US poster.
1970
$15-25   **GAZE**

"Hot Spell", poster.
1958
$40-60   **GAZE**

"Hud", US one sheet poster.
1963   *41in (104cm) high*
$300-500   **P**

"In Prison - Behind Bars", 1950s German poster.
$80-120   **GAZE**

"If....", photo-montage UK quad poster, printed by W.E. Berry Ltd, folded.
1968   *40.25in (102cm) wide*
$400-600   **ON**

"A Jolly Bad Fellow", US one sheet poster.
1964
$15-25   **GAZE**

"Janis: A Film", US one sheet poster.
1974   *41in (102cm) high*
$100-150   **CO**

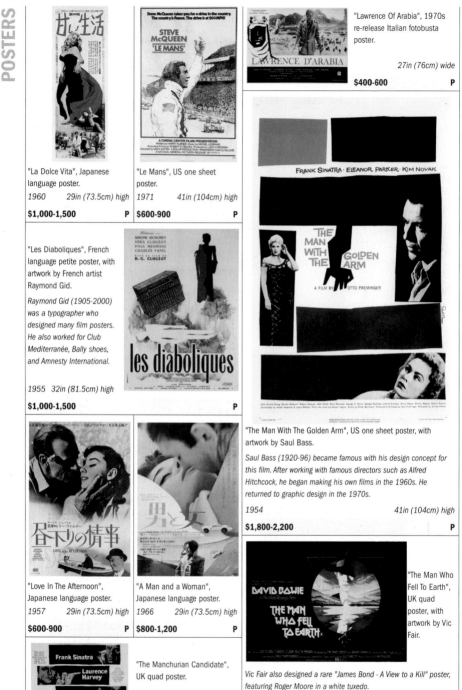

"La Dolce Vita", Japanese language poster.
1960   29in (73.5cm) high
$1,000-1,500   P

"Le Mans", US one sheet poster.
1971   41in (104cm) high
$600-900   P

"Lawrence Of Arabia", 1970s re-release Italian fotobusta poster.
27in (76cm) wide
$400-600   P

"Les Diaboliques", French language petite poster, with artwork by French artist Raymond Gid.

Raymond Gid (1905-2000) was a typographer who designed many film posters. He also worked for Club Mediterranée, Bally shoes, and Amnesty International.

1955   32in (81.5cm) high
$1,000-1,500   P

"The Man With The Golden Arm", US one sheet poster, with artwork by Saul Bass.

Saul Bass (1920-96) became famous with his design concept for this film. After working with famous directors such as Alfred Hitchcock, he began making his own films in the 1960s. He returned to graphic design in the 1970s.

1954   41in (104cm) high
$1,800-2,200   P

"Love In The Afternoon", Japanese language poster.
1957   29in (73.5cm) high
$600-900   P

"A Man and a Woman", Japanese language poster.
1966   29in (73.5cm) high
$800-1,200   P

"The Man Who Fell To Earth", UK quad poster, with artwork by Vic Fair.

Vic Fair also designed a rare "James Bond - A View to a Kill" poster, featuring Roger Moore in a white tuxedo.

1976   40in (101.5cm) wide
$600-900   P

"The Manchurian Candidate", UK quad poster.
1962   40in (101.5cm) wide
$400-600   P

A CLOSER LOOK AT AN ALFRED HITCHCOCK FILM POSTER

"The Man Who Knew Too Much", US one sheet poster.

1956   *41in (104cm) high*

$700-1,000   **P**

This is the original first release, one sheet poster of this film, making it the most desirable example.

Posters from the film's country of origin, such as this one, are usually the most sought-after.

Hitchcock films and posters are very popular and are a collecting area in their own right.

Cary Grant and Ingrid Bergman were Hollywood legends and this film featured one of the most famous screen kisses in cinema history, which is hinted at in the poster image.

"Mean Streets", Italian language fotobusta poster.

1975   *27in (76cm) wide*

$400-600   **P**

"Notorious", US one sheet poster.

1946   *41in (104cm) high*

$6,000-9,000   **P**

"The Outlaw Josey Wales", UK quad poster.

1976   *40.25in (102cm) wide*

$12-18   **ON**

"The Pink Panther Strikes Again", UK quad poster, folded and torn.

1976

$100-150   **ON**

"Walt Disney's One Hundred and One Dalmatians", US one sheet poster.

1961   *41in (104cm) high*

$400-600   **P**

"Psycho II", German language one sheet poster.

1983

$15-25   **GAZE**

"Renaldo and Clara", Spanish language one sheet poster.

1978   *39in (99cm) high*

$120-180   CO

"Repulsion", Japanese language poster.

1965   *29in (73.5cm) high*

$600-900   P

"Rock Show", US one-sheet poster.

1979   *41in (104 cm) high*

$70-100   CO

"Sidewalks Of New York", Australian one sheet stone lithographed poster.

1931   *41in (104cm) high*

$2,800-3,200   P

"The Rocky Horror Picture Show", one sheet poster.

1975

$120-180   GAZE

"Shaft", Italian language locandino poster, with artwork by Giuliano Nistri.

1971   *28in (71cm) high*

$300-500   P

"Singin' In The Rain", Argentine Spanish language stone lithographed poster.

1951   *43in (109cm) high*

$1,000-1,500   P

"Some Like It Hot", rare US soundtrack poster.

1959   *25in (63.5cm) high*

$400-600   P

"Spellbound", re-release US insert poster.

1949   *36in (91.5cm) high*

$400-600   P

THE GREATEST EVENT IN MOTION PICTURE HISTORY!

PARAMOUNT PRESENTS

CECIL B DeMILLE'S
PRODUCTION

THE TEN COMMANDMENTS

CHARLTON · YUL · ANNE · EDWARD G. · YVONNE · DEBRA · JOHN
HESTON · BRYNNER · BAXTER · ROBINSON · DE CARLO · PAGET · DEREK

SIR CEDRIC HARDWICKE · NINA FOCH · MARTHA SCOTT · JUDITH ANDERSON · VINCENT PRICE

TECHNICOLOR

"The Ten Commandments", rare style-B US one sheet poster.
1956 *41in (104cm) high*
$800-1,200 P

PETER SELLERS · GOLDIE HAWN

There's a GIRL IN MY SOUP.

"There's A Girl In My Soup", UK quad poster.
1970 *40.25in (102cm) wide*
$220-280 ON

IRVING BERLIN'S
THERE'S NO BUSINESS LIKE SHOW BUSINESS
CinemaScope

ETHEL · DONALD · MARILYN
MERMAN · O'CONNOR · MONROE
DAN · JOHNNIE · MITZI
DAILEY · RAY · GAYNOR

"There's No Business Like Show Business", US one sheet poster.
1954 *41in (104cm) high*
$800-1,200 P

TINTIN ET LES
ORANGES BLEUES

UN FILM POUR LES JEUNES DE 7 À 77 ANS

"Tintin And The Blue Oranges", French language petite poster.
1963 *32in (81.5cm) high*
$400-600 P

"Come Dance with Me!", French language petite poster, with artwork by Clement Hurel.

1959 32in (81cm) h.
$400-600 P

FRANCIS COSNE
BRIGITTE BARDOT
HENRI VIDAL

voulez vous
danser
avec
moi ?

RICHARD
BURTON
CLINT
EASTWOOD
MARY URE

WHERE
EAGLES
DARE

"Where Eagles Dare" and "Wild Geese", double-bill UK quad poster.

c1980 40in (100cm) wide
$80-120 ON

"Where's Jack?", US one sheet poster.

1969
$15-20 GAZE

Buster
Keaton
in seinem ersten Tonfilm

der Mann, der niemals lacht

in
Wildwest

"Wild West", 1950s one sheet poster.
$70-100 GAZE

ravaged – robbed & busted
from county to county

**THE YOUNG
CYCLE GIRLS**

"The Young Cycle Girls", US poster.
1977
$18-22 GAZE

POSTERS

COLLECTORS' NOTES

■ As part of an overall change in the direction of graphic design during the 1960s, commercial artists in San Francisco began to advertise concerts in a different way. They looked to previous styles such as Art Nouveau and presented it in a new way.

■ They were particularly inspired by poster artists Toulouse Lautrec and Alphonse Mucha. The text often dominates, forming part of the overall design. Colors are usually bright and reflective materials are common.

■ Collectors often concentrate on one artist, many of whom were performing artists themselves, such as Hapsash and the Colored Coat or Rick Griffin.

A Pink Floyd and Jimi Hendrix silkscreen poster, for two concerts at The Saville Theater, The Pink Floyd on 01.10.67 and The Jimi Hendrix Experience 08.10.67., designed by Hapshash and the Colored Coat, published by Osiris Visions.

55in (140cm) high

$800-1,200   CO

A Pink Floyd 'Games For May' concert poster, at the Queen Elizabeth Hall, May 12th, designed by Barry Zaid, featuring three dancing silhouetted fairies, tears to bottom edge but otherwise complete.

1967   *30in (76cm) high*

$6,000-9,000   CO

A Berkeley Bonaparte 'Psychedelic Dream' poster, designed by Rick Griffin.

c1965   *35in (89cm) high*

$220-280   CO

A Colosseum in concert with the New Jazz Orchestra poster, at the Guildhall, Portsmouth, Thursday 28th May at 7.45pm, silkscreened in cerise pink on blue ground, very good condition.

1970   *30in (76cm) high*

$180-220   CO

An Isle of Wight Festival 'Psychedelic Drummer' promotional poster, for August 26th-30th 1970, designed by David Roe.

c1970   *30in (76cm) high*

$280-320   CO

A rare alternative Jimi Hendrix "Open Air, Love & Peace Festival" poster, on the isle of Fehmarn, Germany, 4-6 September 1970.

The festival was Jimi's last official performance, the bassist was sent home due to ill health and the remainder of the tour was canceled. By September 18th Hendrix was dead.

43in (109cm) high

$180-220   CO

A Dr. Strangely Strange silkscreen poster, at Southampton University Students Union Entecom, Saturday 6th March, black on yellow ground, very good condition.

This poster was produced by Southampton Students Union and designed by the then Publicity Officer, John Liverton.

1971   *30in (76cm) high*

$30-50   CO

FIND OUT MORE...

'High Art: A History of The Psychedelic Poster', by *Ted Owen & Denise Dickson, published by Sanctuary Publishing Ltd, 2001.*

FERODO FIRST

DUTCH GRAND PRIX
ZANDVOORT 22-6-75

1st **J. HUNT**
HESKETH-FORD 111.11 m.p.h.

2nd **N. LAUDA**
FERRARI

3rd **C. REGAZZONI**
FERRARI

Who said one disc brake pad is as good as another?

A Ferodo First Dutch Grand Prix poster, for Zandvoort 22nd June, 1975.
1975 *29.5in (75cm) high*
$80-120 **ON**

FERODO FIRST

LE MANS 1975
14th & 15th JUNE

1st **D. BELL / J. ICKX**
GULF-FORD 111.97 m.p.h.

2nd **J. L. LAFFOSE / C. CHASSEUIL**
LIGIER-FORD

3rd **V. SCHUPPAN / J. P. JAUSSAUD**
GULF-FORD

FIT RACE-PROVED **FERODO** DISC AND DRUM BRAKE LININGS

A Ferodo First Le Mans poster, by Dexter Brown.
1975 *29.5in (75cm) high*
$25-35 **ON**

CRYSTAL PALACE
MOTOR RACING

FIRST RACE 2 p.m.

WHIT MONDAY

A 1950s Crystal Palace Motor Racing poster, illustration by Raymond Groves, Whit Monday at 2p.m., small tear to lower right corner.
30in (76cm) high
$400-600 **SAS**

GOODWOOD
MOTOR RACING AT ITS BEST!

EASTER MONDAY 11th APRIL

INTERNATIONAL PROGRAMME
FIRST RACE 1.30 p.m.

6/-

BRITISH AUTOMOBILE RACING CLUB

A 1950s Goodwood Easter Monday International Programme poster, for 11th April 1.30p.m.
30in (76.5cm) high
$300-500 **SAS**

60th BRIGHTON SPEED TRIALS

THE FROSTS BRIGHTON NATIONAL SPEED TRIALS
SATURDAY 14th SEPTEMBER 1996
ON BRIGHTON SEAFRONT 9am – 6pm

A Brighton Speed Trials poster.
1996
$18-22 **CARS**

A CLOSER LOOK AT A MOTOR RACING POSTER

Executed in a modern style, Hans Thoni also designed a version without the forest for the 1936 race.

The Alps and forest add 'romance' and hint at the location of the race.

IIme GRAND PRIX AUTOMOBILE DE SUISSE

BERNE 25 AOUT 1935

The 'streaking' implies speed as does the dizzying perspective.

The bold red car is striking and is in a design of the period.

IIME Grand Prix Automobile De Suisse designed by Thoni.
1935 *38.25in (95.5cm) high*
$3,000-5,000 **SWA**

DIEPPE RETRO
GRAND PRIX DE L'A.C.F.

NOSTALGIE DU CIRCUIT DE DIEPPE
2 et 3 septembre 1995
RASSEMBLEMENT DE VÉHICULES ANCIENS
Dimanche 3 septembre - Pelouse de la Plage - DIEPPE

A Dieppe Retro poster.
1995
$30-50 **CARS**

POSTERS

COLLECTORS' NOTES

■ Both World Wars required participation from every citizen – a theme that can be seen in posters produced at the time, which ranged from call-up posters for the Army, Air Force or ancillary units to posters produced for the home front to encourage careful use of supplies or investing in savings schemes to fund the war effort.

■ All types used encouraging imagery, bolstering the public's morale as much as encouraging them to fulfil the act required. Many designs were striking and employed bold colors – patriotic themes and images were widely used.

■ Look out for modern designs by leading designers of the time such as Abram Games and Norman Wilkinson. Posters with a humorous element by artists such as Fougasse and H.M. Bateman are also popular.

"Bones help to fire the guns... save more ships", by Beverley Pick, printed for HMSO by Fosh & Cross Ltd, folds.

Pick was a member of the Society of Industrial Artists. She designed posters and displays at Charing Cross Underground station for the Ministry of Information during WWII. After the war she worked for airlines B.O.A.C. and B.E.A. Her style is indicative of the 'modern' designs produced by the leading poster artists of the day, but slightly less innovative.

30in (76cm) high

$50-70   **ON**

"Kitchen waste feeds pigs & poultry, kitchen scraps are wanted to produce bacon and eggs, don't waste kitchen scraps the Nation needs them now", by Beverley Pick, printed for HMSO by Fosh & Cross Ltd, folds.

30in (76cm) high

$120-180   **ON**

"Plan before you buy", by Beverley Pick, photo montage printed for HMSO by Fosh and Cross, folds.

30in (76cm) high

$80-120   **ON**

"Miles and miles of silk – a parachute for every airman, no silk for new frocks convert your old...", printed for HMSO by Multi Machine Plates Ltd.

30in (76cm) high

$50-70   **ON**

"The man who wasted power!", by H.M. Bateman, issued by the Ministry of Fuel and Power, printed for HMSO by Chromoworks, folds.

30in (76cm) high

$280-320   **ON**

"The worker who left the lights on! Don't be fuel-ish, wasted electricity means less fuel to make weapons we need for victory", by H.M. Bateman, issued by the Ministry of Fuel and Power, printed for HMSO by J. Weiner, fold.

Bateman had become famous for his cartoons showing the uproar caused by social gaffes - he was the caricaturist for 'The Tatler' and 'Punch' amongst others.

15in (38cm) wide

$50-70   **ON**

"The Hun and the home... back up the men who have saved you", by David Wilson, folds.

30in (76cm) high

$120-180   **ON**

"Electricity, 100 tons of coal to build a Spitfire, electric fires should be used only when absolutely necessary", printed for HMSO by Multi Machines Plates Ltd, folds.

29.5in (75cm) high

$280-320   **ON**

"Lend to defend his right to be free - Buy National Savings Certificates", by Tom Purvis, printed for H.M. Stationery Office by Fosh & Co. Ltd.

This popular and attractive poster appeals to collectors of Meccano as well as wartime poster collectors.

c1940   30in (76cm) high

$300-500   **PC**

"Convoy your country to victory - Buy National Savings Certificates", designed by Rowland Hilder, printed for H.M. Stationery Office by J. Weiner Ltd.

c1940   30in (76cm) high

$150-200   **PC**

"War savings are warships", by Norman Wilkinson, published by National Savings, printed by J. Weiner, folds.

30in (76cm) high

$180-220   **ON**

"Keep mum - she's not so dumb! Careless talk cost lives", by A. Forster, published by HMSO, printed by Lowe & Brydone, folds and small tears.

30in (76cm) high

$280-320   **ON**

A CLOSER LOOK AT A WARTIME POSTER

"Careless talk costs lives" by Fougasse, four of eight posters including the 'Telephone Box'.

Fougasse's small "Careless talk costs lives" posters are perhaps the best known posters of their type - each scene contains a 'hidden' Hitler or Goering eavesdropping on a conversation in a public place.

12.5in (32cm) high

$700-1,000   **ON**

The designer Abram Games is well known for his graphic design work across industrial, commercial, and government sectors from the 1930s-1960s.

He also favored simple graphics, obtaining 'maximum meaning' from 'minimum means' as seen in the patriotically colored, heroic soldier's profile against a camouflage background.

He was designated official war artist in 1942 due to his experience and contacts made at Shell before the war.

Games wanted his wartime posters to be as seductive and striking as commercial art, combining eye-catching imagery and typography.

"Salute the soldier, save more, lend more", by Abram Games, issued by National Savings Committee London, printed by Alf Cooke Ltd.

1944   14.5in (37cm) high

$400-600   **ON**

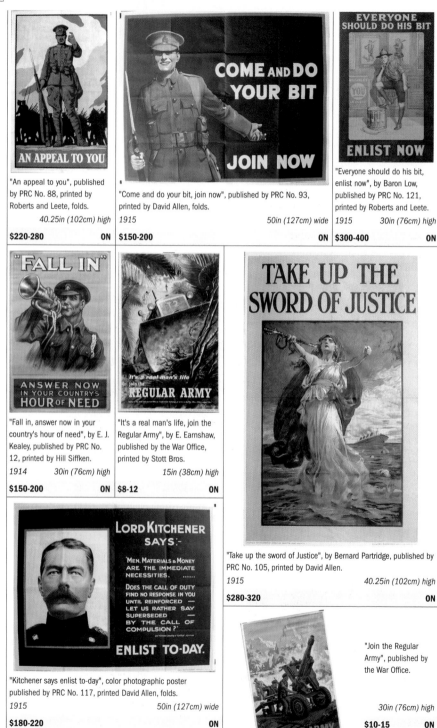

"An appeal to you", published by PRC No. 88, printed by Roberts and Leete, folds.

40.25in (102cm) high

$220-280　　**ON**

"Come and do your bit, join now", published by PRC No. 93, printed by David Allen, folds.

1915　　　　　　　　*50in (127cm) wide*

$150-200　　**ON**

"Everyone should do his bit, enlist now", by Baron Low, published by PRC No. 121, printed by Roberts and Leete.

1915　　　*30in (76cm) high*

$300-400　　**ON**

"Fall in, answer now in your country's hour of need", by E. J. Kealey, published by PRC No. 12, printed by Hill Siffken.

1914　　　*30in (76cm) high*

$150-200　　**ON**

"It's a real man's life, join the Regular Army", by E. Earnshaw, published by the War Office, printed by Stott Bros.

15in (38cm) high

$8-12　　**ON**

"Take up the sword of Justice", by Bernard Partridge, published by PRC No. 105, printed by David Allen.

1915　　　　*40.25in (102cm) high*

$280-320　　**ON**

"Kitchener says enlist to-day", color photographic poster published by PRC No. 117, printed David Allen, folds.

1915　　　　　　*50in (127cm) wide*

$180-220　　**ON**

"Join the Regular Army", published by the War Office.

30in (76cm) high

$10-15　　**ON**

"Serve with the Coldstream Guards", by Charles Wood.

17.75in (45cm) high

$18-22   ON

"Boys, come over here you're wanted", published by PRC No. 82, printed David Allen, folds.

1915   50in (127cm) wide

$150-200   ON

"A message.. to ambitious men.. join the Royal Signals", poster.

15in (38cm) high

$8-12   ON

"There are vacancies in the Intelligence Corps", mono-photographic poster, published by the War Office.

15in (38cm) high

$120-180   ON

"The De Havilland 'Mosquito' light bomber", color cutaway with technical details, copyright of The Aeroplane, folds.

28.75in (73cm) wide

$180-220   ON

"ATS at the wheel", by Beverley Pick, photo montage printed for HMSO by Field Sons & Co Ltd.

The ATS was the Army Transport Service.

29.5in (75cm) high

$400-600   ON

The British Handley Page "Halifax II", color cutaway with technical details, copyright of The Aeroplane, folds.

28.75in (73cm) wide

$180-220   ON

"Aircraft Torpedo Sight, Air Diagram 2385, June 1943", prepared by Ministry of Aircraft Production, printed for HMSO by Alf Cooke Ltd London.

19.75in (50cm) wide

$40-60   ON

FIND OUT MORE...

'Images of War: British Posters 1939-45', by J.D Cantwell 1989.

The Imperial War Museum, Lambeth Road, Kennington, London SE1 6HZ, UK.

COLLECTORS' NOTES

■ Pot lids are currently enjoying a particularly buoyant period, with collectors from the US and Australia in particular showing strong interest in English pot lids.

■ Among the most popular pot lids are those made for bear's grease, which was used in large quantities by barbers for use as a gentlemen's hair styling product. These are followed by toothpaste pot lids with good, detailed pictures. 'Regional' lids are also sought after as they are rare – the majority were made for London-based companies.

■ Condition of the face is important and any damage should not affect the image. The flange and rim underneath the face are often damaged, but this does not have a great impact on the value.

■ There are a number of reproductions on the market at present so buyers should be wary, particularly of internet transactions. Original examples will have the glaze applied over the transfer decoration rather than vice versa, and will have a shiny appearance. Run your finger over the lid – if it is a reproduction you may be able to feel the texture of the transfer. Other copies have paper transfers stuck on plain pot lids, which are then lacquered – check that you cannot feel the edge of the transfer with your nail.

■ Collectors are not interested in the pot base, unless it is also decorated. Complete pots are popular with casual collectors, however, as they are often easier to display.

A 'Bears At School' Pratt pot lid, number 9, from the Pratt factory, in cream-colored wooden frame.

4.75in (12cm) diam

$60-90 BBR

A 'Bear, Lion and Cock' Pratt pot lid, number 19, from the Pratt factory, clearly printed with colors.

c1855   3.25in (8.5cm) diam

$60-90 BBR

An 'Allied Generals' Pratt pot lid, number 168, from the Pratt factory, signed "J. Austin".

The numbers refer to Pratt pattern design numbers, as listed in 'Price Guide to Pot Lids' by A. Ball, published by the Antique Collectors' Club.

c1855

$150-200 BBR

An 'Eastern Repast' Pratt-type pot lid, number 98, from the Mayer Factory.

3in (7.5cm) diam

$40-60 BBR

An 'Eleanor Cross, London' Pratt-type pot lid, number 194, probably by Bates, Brown-Westhead, Moore and Co.

4in (10cm) diam

$80-120 BBR

A 'Volunteers' Pratt-type pot lid, number 214, probably by Bates, Brown-Westhead, Moore and Co., in strong colors.

c1860   3in (7.5cm) diam

$150-200 BBR

A 'Rifle Contest, Wimbledon 1865' Pratt-type pot lid, number 224, titled with blue marbled surround, some minor staining and chips to flange.

4.75in (12cm) diam

$400-600 BBR

A "Dr Ziemer's Alexandra Tooth Paste" pot lid, with a portrait of Princess Alexandra to the center with gold border, some outer edge restoration.

3.5in (9cm) diam

$60-90 BBR

A "Carbolic Tooth Paste" pot lid, with brown print, inner hairline crack to flange.

2.5in (6.5cm) wide

$100-150 BBR

An early "Hindoo Tooth Paste" pot lid, with slight body discoloration.

3in (7.5cm) diam

$180-220 BBR

An "Imperial Coralline Tooth Paste" oblong pot lid, hairline crack at the bottom.

3.75in (9.5cm) wide

$60-90 BBR

A Lewis and Burrows Ltd "Cherry Tooth Paste" oblong pot lid, hairline crack down top side.

3.75in (9.5cm) wide

$60-90 BBR

A Lorimer and Co. "Cherry Tooth Paste" pot lid, with a large bunch of cherries plus an arm holding a globe, flange hairline crack.

2.5in (6.5cm) diam

$100-150 BBR

A "Maw's Indian Betel Nut Or Areca Tooth Paste" pot lid.

2.5in (6.5cm) diam

$25-35 BBR

A "St. Paul's Cherry Tooth Paste" pot lid, with a pictorial trademark of St. Paul's.

2.75in (7cm) diam

$25-35 BBR

A May Roberts "Cherry Tooth Paste" pot lid, the detailed transfer depicting a young bonneted girl, arms folded, leaning on wall, with trade mark below.

2.75in (7cm) diam

$280-320 BBR

A "James Atkinson's Bears Grease" pot lid, with a fine and sharp black transfer of a chained and muzzled bear, restored chip to flange.

2.5in (6.5cm) diam

$70-100   **BBR**

A "Holloway's Ointment" pot lid, flange chips.

3.25in (8.5cm) diam

$30-50   **BBR**

A Knowle's "Esauline or Pomade D'Esau" pot lid, with a portrait of a gentleman with a long mustache, marked "I Used It", some crazing, clear dark transfer.

3in (7.5cm) diam

$320-380   **BBR**

A "Genuine Russian Bear's Grease" pot lid, with a pictorial transfer showing bear with trees in background, flange chips.

2.75in (7cm) diam

$180-220   **BBR**

A "Genuine Russian Bears Grease" pot lid, with a strong black pictorial transfer of two bears, flange chips and hairline crack.

3in (7.5cm) diam

$150-200   **BBR**

A "Savage's Celebrated Peruvian Balm" pot lid, with a large vase of flowers pictured to center.

2.75in (7cm) diam

$120-180   **BBR**

A very rare "Spaks Wonderful" hair restorer pot lid, with St George slaying the dragon pictured to center, small chip under top edge.

3.75in (9.5cm) diam

$400-600   **BBR**

A rare "The Children's Pomade" ceramic domed lidded pot, with a boy and girl pictured either side.

4.25in (11cm) high

$300-500   **BBR**

An early John Bell "Pure Cold Cream of Roses" pot lid, with a large and highly detailed chemists shop front pictured on the flat top.

3in (7.5cm) diam

$600-900 BBR

A "Sharp Brothers Cold Cream" pot lid, with a harp pictorial above banner and decorative outer border, minor crazing.

2.75in (7cm) diam

$280-320 BBR

A "Squire Cold Cream" pot lid, with gold border intact, overall crazing.

3.25in (8.5cm) diam

$60-90 BBR

A French "Icilma Crème" pot lid, with a sharp and stylish pictorial of a girl holding a pot, atop waterfall landscape, flange repair and some crazing.

3.75in (9.5cm) diam

$150-200 BBR

A Buisson Freres "Ambrosial Shaving Cream" pot lid.

3.25in (8.5cm) diam

$50-70 BBR

A "Roussel's Shaving Cream" pot lid, top edge chip repair and damage, repair underneath.

3.25in (8.5cm) diam

$50-70 BBR

A very rare "Isola Bishop's Balm" ointment pot, the black transfer with an image of a bishop with miter in hand, with a swan and a church behind.

1.75in (4.5cm) high

$500-700 BBR

A "Blanchflower" pot lid, the farmyard scene showing a cow, bull, sheep, pigs, and hens, two chips to underside flange.

3.75in (9.5cm) diam

$400-600 BBR

A "Bales Mushroom Savoury" pot lid, with brown transfer decoration of mushrooms.

3.5in (9cm) diam

$100-150 BBR

QUILTS

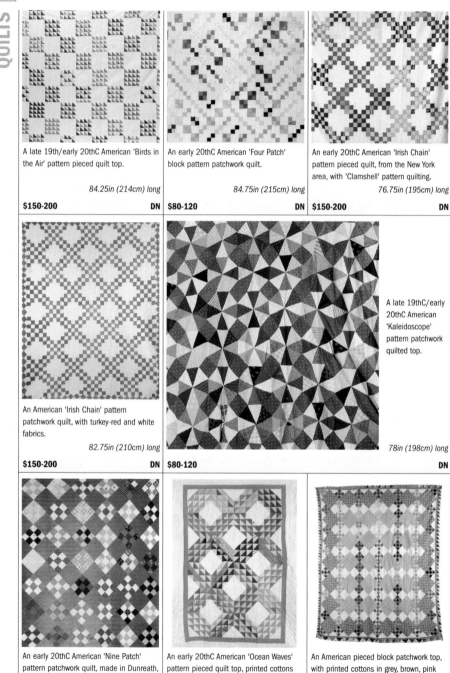

A late 19th/early 20thC American 'Birds in the Air' pattern pieced quilt top.

84.25in (214cm) long

$150-200 DN

An early 20thC American 'Four Patch' block pattern patchwork quilt.

84.75in (215cm) long

$80-120 DN

An early 20thC American 'Irish Chain' pattern pieced quilt, from the New York area, with 'Clamshell' pattern quilting.

76.75in (195cm) long

$150-200 DN

An American 'Irish Chain' pattern patchwork quilt, with turkey-red and white fabrics.

82.75in (210cm) long

$150-200 DN

A late 19thC/early 20thC American 'Kaleidoscope' pattern patchwork quilted top.

78in (198cm) long

$80-120 DN

An early 20thC American 'Nine Patch' pattern patchwork quilt, made in Dunreath, Indiana.

c1900

$120-180 DN

An early 20thC American 'Ocean Waves' pattern pieced quilt top, printed cottons and other fabrics, made into a quilt in 1991 by a quilter in the Quilters' Guild.

77.5in (197cm) long

$140-200 DN

An American pieced block patchwork top, with printed cottons in grey, brown, pink and cream.

80.75in (205cm) long

$100-150 DN

RADIOS

COLLECTORS' NOTES

■ With vintage radios, the case, rather than the quality of the electronics or sound, makes the most difference to value. During the 'golden age' of the radio between the 1920s and 1950s, many were produced in revolutionary 'Bakelite' cases. Although Bakelite was originally a trademark name, 'bakelite' has become a generic term for a range of plastics. When buying vintage radios, do discriminate – look for those in cases that either reflect the style of the period, such as Art Deco, or those in brightly colored cases.

■ Condition is crucial. Bakelite, and its more colorful cousin 'Catalin', was prone to cracking, warping or chipping, all of which affect value. Feel the surface and edges of a radio to discover such faults. Look for classic forms and names such as Fada and Emerson. Many valve radios can be restored to working order, but always seek professional advice before plugging an example in. Many transistor radios from the 1960s and 1970s exhibit the funky styling so beloved today.

A Philips 'Superinductance Type 830 A' radio, five valves, long and medium wave bands, needs new cloth.

Rather than Bakelite, this radio is Arbolite, a material specific to Philips, made from plastic laminated board.

c1930

$280-320 ATK

A German Siemens '23 WL' radio, with bakelite case, original cloth, three valves and single circuit receiver.

1932

$300-500 ATK

A TFK '33 WL' radio, case in very good condition, cloth worn, missing lever on right side.

$150-200 ATK

A German SABA Bakelite radio, with four valves and replaced speaker cloth.

1934

$220-280 ATK

A CLOSER LOOK AT A CATALIN RADIO

It retains both of its knobs, which is desirable. The knobs are smooth and rounded – correct for the period. After WWII ended, ribbed knobs were used.

It is deemed a 'classic' radio and is in excellent condition with no cracks, chips or burn marks from the heat of the valves.

This very rare 'All American' patriotic color combination was produced just before the US entered WWII.

White Catalin oxidizes and changes color to a butterscotch tone over time. Restoring the color takes hours of skilled polishing.

An American Fada Streamliner Model 189 'Bullet' radio in white, blue, and red Catalin, with smooth knobs.

1941 10.25in (26cm) wide

$3,000-5,000 CAT

A Fada 5F60 butterscotch and blue grilled Catalin radio, with ribbed knobs.

This model was one of the first Catalins radio to be designed and produced by Fada. It was also made with a wooden body, which was much less expensive than its Catalin counterpart at the time.

1936 8in (20.5cm) wide

$3,000-5,000 CAT

A 'Telefunken 340W' radio, known as 'Katzenkopf', bakelite case, five valves, straight receiver.

1931

$600-900 ATK

A Fada L-56 lapis lazuli blue and alabaster Catalin radio.

1939 9in (23cm) widest

$2,200-2,800 CAT

A Sentinel Model '284-NR' cherry or ox-blood red and yellow Catalin radio, with later grille cloth.

This radio was prone to cracking that was caused by the Catalin shrinking over the metal chassis, which did not shrink. It was also produced in a rare, but less unappealing, version without a grille.

1945   11in (28cm) wide

$1,200-1,800   **CAT**

A Bendix model '526 C' jade green, white marbled and black Catalin radio.

1946   11in (28cm) wide

$700-1,000   **CAT**

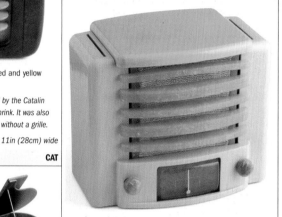

A Kadette Model 'L' Art Deco radio, in cream, with a yellow top and a marbled mustard colored grille.

Along with many Catalin radios, this model came in a range of colors. The metal top and grille can also be found in different colors, including green.

7.75in (20cm) high

$1,500-2,000   **CAT**

A Emerson 'tombstone' Model 'BT245' butterscotch radio, with original turtle transfer to top and other transfers, cream grille and knobs, lacks two knobs.

1937   9.75in (25cm) high

$1,500-2,000   **CAT**

A Swedish radio, in the form of a miniature grand piano, with AGA radio and 78rpm record player, rare construction.

1948

$300-500   **ATK**

A Decca Transistor radio model 'TPW 70', in plastic, with dial and pointer volume controls.

This radio was produced to hang on a wall. It originally cost the equivalent of around $150.

1962

$80-120   **ROS**

A 1970s Weltron '2001' or 'Space Ball' radio cassette recorder, in an ivory plastic case, spherical form on a circular stand.

11.75in (30cm) high

$180-220   **QU**

An early 1970s National Panasonic 'Pana Pet 70' radio, with original box and instructions.

Without the original box, this radio would be worth approximately $50.

box 5.5in (14cm) high

$80-120   **DTC**

A yellow Panasonic 'Tootaloop' bangle transistor radio.

When closed, this radio could be worn around the wrist like a bangle. It was produced in a number of colors. Mauve, lilac, and lime green are the rarest.

c1972   6in (15cm) diam

$70-100   **DTC**

COLLECTORS' NOTES

■ As far as rock and pop memorabilia is concerned, Elvis Presley is still 'The King' and The Beatles still top the popularity charts. Due to the long careers of these acts and the high quantity of merchandize, memorabilia is available for all budgets. Other popular acts include The Rolling Stones, The Doors, Jimi Hendrix, and The Who.

■ Pieces personally owned or used by the artist are the most desirable, but are also the most expensive. Provenance is vital so always ask for a letter of authenticity or details of the item's history.

■ Merchandize was produced in vast amounts, but much was damaged or destroyed over the years. Look for licensed examples in good condition, images of the star's faces on the original packaging are desirable.

■ Posters, programs and tickets are all popular collecting areas. Collectors often concentrate on concerts they attended in person or legendary or notable performances. Always look carefully at the condition of paper-based collectibles as it has a huge effect on value.

■ Anything signed by an artist is desirable, but beware that signatures obtained from fan clubs were often printed or signed by a secretary or assistant and that band members often signed for each other. Look for items with signatures from the whole band, preferably not crossing each other. Beatles signatures are among the most faked so make sure to have them authenticated by a recognized expert.

A 'Meet The Beatles Star Special' No. 12 souvenir program.
1963
$25-35   GAZE

An original program for 'The Beatles Show', with poor condition cover, contents in good condition.
c1963
$60-90   GAZE

A 'The Beatles' Pyx Productions souvenir program.
c1963
$15-25   GAZE

A 'The Beatles by Royal Command' souvenir program.
1963
$15-25   GAZE

A 'The Beatles in America' souvenir program.
1964
$25-35   GAZE

A 'The Beatles at Carnegie Hall' souvenir program, by Ralph Cosham.
c1964
$40-60   GAZE

A 'The Beatles Christmas Show' program, at Finsbury Park Astoria.
1963
$100-150   GAZE

A rare Beatles Australian Tour concert program, June 1964.

$220-280 GAZE

A program for 'Another Beatles Christmas Show' 1964/65 at the Hammersmith Odeon, London, together with an original ticket stub for a second performance on Friday January 8th 1965.

$220-280 GAZE

A 1971 'FAB-208 annual', published by L.P.C. Magazines, featuring an interview with DJ Tony Blackburn at home, The Beatles and Steve McQueen.

1971   10.5in (27cm) high

$15-25 MTS

A 1970 'Teenbeat' annual, compiled by Albert Hand, featuring The Beatles, Status Quo, Jimi Hendrix, The Beach Boys, The Monkees and more.

1969   10in (25.5cm) high

$15-20 MTS

A 'Beatles on Broadway' souvenir booklet, by Sam Leach.

1964

$8-12 GAZE

A rare 'The Beatles' official magazine, No.1 Sept.-Nov. 1964, published by Dell.

First issues of a series are always desirable. This comprehensive magazine also shows the band in their prime.

10.25in (26cm) high

$400-600 NOR

'The Beatles Illustrated Lyrics', published by Gilvrie Misstear and David Hillman, edited by Alan Aldridge.

1969

$80-120 GAZE

A copy of The Daily Mirror, Wednesday December 10th 1980, "John Lennon Shot Dead" special issue.

$30-40 GAZE

A lilac-colored ticket stub for The Beatles / Roy Orbison show at the Gaumont Theatre Ipswich, for the first performance on Wednesday 22nd May 1963.

$120-180 GAZE

A Nems Enterprises Beatles scrap book and contents.

$30-40   **GAZE**

A 'Yellow Submarine' set of eight re-issue lobby cards.
1999

$30-40   **GAZE**

A 1960s set of 20 Beatles 'Yellow Submarine' pop-out art decorations.

15in (38cm) high

$70-100   **NOR**

A Beatles printed ring binder, by Nems Enterprises Limited.
11.5in (29.5cm) high

$300-500   **NOR**

A 'The Beatles Book' issue calendar for 1964, lacks June.

$40-60   **GAZE**

An American The Beatles 'Yellow Submarine' eight-track tape, released by Capitol.
c1967   *5in (13cm) high*

$15-25   **NOR**

An early American 'Introducing The Beatles England's No. 1 Vocal Group' stereophonic LP, on Vee-Jay label, No. SR1062.

$150-250   **B&H**

A Beatles cookie plate, with transfer decoration.

$30-50   **GAZE**

A Parlaphone presentation gold disc for the soundtrack to The Beatles film 'A Hard Days Night', in recognition of sales exceeding 100,000 in the UK.
1964

$120-180   **GAZE**

An 'I Love Ringo' badge.

3.5in (9cm) diam

$15-25   **NOR**

A 'Help Stamp Out "Beetles"' badge.

"Beetles" is mis-spelt as this was not a licensed product. It may also be connected to when John Lennon made anti-Christian comments in 1966 in the San Francisco Chronicle.

3.5in (9cm) diam

$15-25   **NOR**

A 1960s Beatles silver plastic button, showing two people dancing.

0.75in (2cm) diam

$5-8   **CVS**

A rare Beatles signed photograph, featuring Stuart Sutcliffe, at their first ever foreign engagement at the Indra Club, Hamburg in 1960, signed by the original drummer Pete Best, with the group's name and date of the photograph.

$50-70   **GAZE**

A Beatles signed photograph, featuring the group onstage at The Cavern Club in 1961, signed by their original drummer Pete Best who has also added the groups name below his signature, mounted and framed with the heading "The Beatles" and photograph description.

$60-90   **GAZE**

A Beatles signed photograph, featuring the group wearing their first ever stage suits, and signed by their original drummer Pete Best, mounted with a description of the first time they wore the suits in 1962.

$60-90   **GAZE**

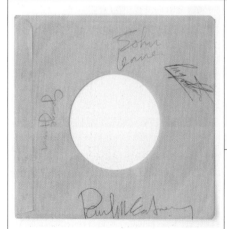

A white single cover sleeve, signed by Paul McCartney, John Lennon, Ringo Starr and George Harrison.

$400-600   **GAZE**

A handwritten letter from John Lennon's aunt, Mimi Smith, to a fan, dated 9th December 1963, plus a typed list of George Harrison's biography with facsimile signature.

John's aunt Mimi famously bought him his first guitar and is quoted as saying "The guitar's all right John, but you'll never make a living with it".

$100-150   **GAZE**

An American United Artists Corp press release, detailing the opening week's figures in Chicago for the second Beatles film "Help".

1965

$6-9   **GAZE**

A set of four Richard Avedon Beatles posters, German issue.

Commissioned by Nems, the Beatles' management company, these images were licensed to US magazine 'Look', UK newspaper 'The Daily Express' and German magazine 'Stern'.

1967

$400-600   **GAZE**

A early 1970's French Beatles "Oldies But Goldies" promo poster for the LP.

$18-22   **GAZE**

"Let It Be", German one sheet poster.

1971

$100-150   **GAZE**

A black and white Elvis Presley photograph.

$10-15   **GAZE**

A 1963 Star Pics Elvis Presley calendar, lacks 'September'.

$6-9   **GAZE**

"Love Me Tender", poster signed by Debra Paget (Cathy Reno) and James Drury (Ray Reno).

1956

$60-90   **GAZE**

A 1950s Elvis Presley necklace, the metal frame with a portrait of Elvis Presley.

Pendant 0.75in (2cm) high

$60-90   **CVS**

A CLOSER LOOK AT A LOCK OF ELVIS PRESLEY'S HAIR

The hair and accompanying letter of authenticity are professionally mounted with a photograph of the famous haircut, making an attractive display.

Locks of Elvis' hair have come up for sale in the past and attract great interest, a clipping the size of a cricket ball sold for $100,000 in 2003.

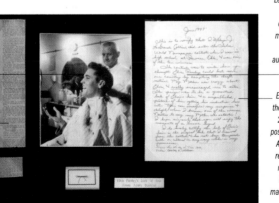

Letters of authenticity are vital when considering celebrity memorabilia - always ask the dealer or auction house how the item was obtained.

Elvis was drafted into the US Army on March 24th, 1958 and was posted to Fort Chaffee, Arkansas. He had his regulation haircut the next day at the local barber shop and his manager made sure no hair was stolen.

A lock of Elvis Presley's hair, mounted with a photograph of Elvis getting his Army hair cut, a letter of provenance from the winner of the lock in a competition and a related newspaper article.

24in (9.5cm) high

$1,500-2,000   **LCA**

An Elvis Presley 'The King of Rock & Roll 1935-77' commemorative badge, by Boxcar Enterprises.

c1977   3in (7.5cm) diam

$4-6   **NOR**

An Elvis Presley 'striking' match book.

                    2in (5cm) high

$2-3   **NOR**

A 1980s box of Elvis Cologne by Elvis Fragrances Inc, licensed by Elvis Presley Enterprises.

                    2.5in (6.5cm) high

$25-35   **CVS**

An Elvis Presley doll, by Eugene Doll Co. Inc., endorsed by Graceland Elvis Presley Enterprises, boxed.

c1984   14.75in (37.5cm) high

$120-180   **NOR**

"The Rolling Stones Book", souvenir booklet of pictures and features.

c1965

$25-35   **GAZE**

An Elvis Presley radio, with dressed figure of Elvis.

c1978   9.75in (25cm) high

$60-90   **NOR**

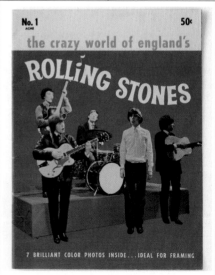

An "On The Scene - The Rolling Stones" souvenir booklet, by June Knight.

1964

$40-60   **GAZE**

A Rolling Stones publicity photograph, issued by the BBC, in original envelope.

1964

$50-70   **GAZE**

An American "The Crazy World of England's Rolling Stones" souvenir program, Summer 1964 Issue No 1.

$60-90   **GAZE**

A program for the Rolling Stones concert at the London Palladium, with the original ticket stub for the second evening performance on Sunday 1st August.

$180-220   **GAZE**

An original program for The Rolling Stones, at Romford ABC cinema, with two original ticket stubs for the second performance on Thursday 18th March, with Compliments of the Manager slip.

1965

$220-280   **GAZE**

An original show souvenir program supplement for a tour featuring The Rolling Stones, Ike and Tina Turner, The Hollies, the Small Faces and others.

A 1960s Rolling Stones transfer sheet, with line drawn busts and facsimile signatures.

c1965

A Rolling Stones 66 souvenir brochure, featuring Ike and Tina Turner, The Yardbirds and others.

$30-50   **GAZE**   **$80-120**   **GAZE**   **$80-120**   **GAZE**

A "Stones In The Park - Full Story behind the TV show" magazine.

c1969

A Rolling Stones concert poster, from a 1973 concert in Frankfurt, Germany.

$80-120   **GAZE**   **$120-180**   **GAZE**

An Animals fan club badge.

3.25in (8.5cm) diam

$15-25   **NOR**

A very rare 1970s boxed bar of 'ABBA The Soap', by J. Grossmith, the bar in the form of a green audio tape.

$30-40   **MTS**

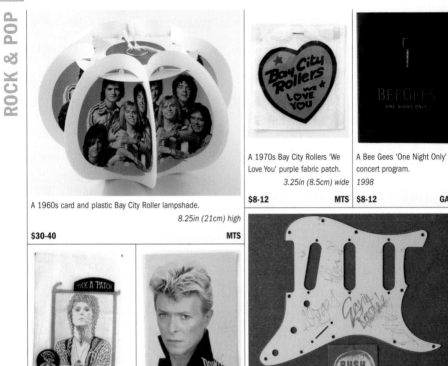

A 1960s card and plastic Bay City Roller lampshade.

8.25in (21cm) high

$30-40   **MTS**

A 1970s Bay City Rollers 'We Love You' purple fabric patch.

3.25in (8.5cm) wide

$8-12   **MTS**

A Bee Gees 'One Night Only' concert program.

1998

$8-12   **GAZE**

A 1970s David Bowie Pick-A-Patch patch, with gold colored details.

3.25in (8.5cm) high

$12-18   **MTS**

A David Bowie 'Serious Moonlight' tour concert program.

1983

$22-28   **GAZE**

A guitar scratch plate signed by all four members of Bush, together with a 'Local Crew' access pass dated "Feb 22 2000".

$30-40   **GAZE**

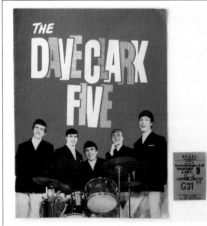

An original program for "The Dave Clark Five Show", with original ticket stub for a second performance on Thursday 9th April.

$60-90   **GAZE**

A guitar scratch plate signed by The Charlatans guitarist Mark Collins, together with two crew access passes, dated 24th/25th April 2000, framed.

$30-40   **GAZE**

A John Denver at the London Victoria Apollo concert program, together with two ticket stubs.

1982

$8-12   **GAZE**

A concert program for The Everly Brothers, with two ticket stubs.

1985

$10-15   **GAZE**

A Bob Dylan at the NEC concert program, together with ticket stub.

1989

$15-20   **GAZE**

A Sophie Ellis-Bextor signed "Murder on the Dance Floor" CD single, annotated with "Don't steal the move!! Be good. Love Sophie", mounted with a photograph.

$30-50   **GAZE**

A pair of Mick Fleetwood signed wooden drum sticks.

$25-35   **GAZE**

An Emerson, Lake & Palmer concert poster, for Germany 28th November 1970 or 71, artwork by Gunter Kieser.

$100-150   **GAZE**

A Fleetwood Mac 'Tango in The Night' tour concert program.

1987

$12-18   **GAZE**

A program and ticket stub for Larry Parnes "Big Star Show", featuring Billy Fury, the ticket stub for the first performance on Sunday 13th October.

$60-90   **GAZE**

An original program and ticket stub for "The Sunday Special" show, featuring Billy Fury at the Britannia Theatre, Great Yarmouth, England.

$40-60   **GAZE**

An original program for the Larry Parnes "Billy Fury Show - Meet The Beat", at the Britannia Theatre, Great Yarmouth.

Pop impresario Larry Parnes (1930-89) managed acts including Tommy Steele, Marty Wilde, and Billy Fury. He turned down the opportunity to manage Cliff Richard and The Beatles on more than one occasion.

1960

$70-100   **GAZE**

An original Arthur Howes and Brian Epstein program, featuring Gerry and the Pacemakers, The Kinks, Gene Pitney and others, together with the ticket stub for Wednesday 25th November.

$50-70   **GAZE**

An original Arthur Howes program, featuring Gerry and the Pacemakers, Del Shannon and others.

$25-35   **GAZE**

A 1970s plastic 'Pink Pop Bag' carrier bag, with facsimile signatures and portraits of Mark Bolan, Michael Jackson.

14.75in (37.5cm) high

$15-25   **MTS**

A KISS printed souvenir mirror.

5in (12.5cm) high

$12-18   **NOR**

A CLOSER LOOK AT A SET OF KISS DOLLS

These dolls were packed in card boxes with cellophane fronts, the backs were printed with cut-out instruments for the band.

These are very rare and sought-after today. A complete set is more desirable than individual dolls – single dolls are worth $100-150 each.

US toy manufacturer Mego Corp. made dolls and action figures from 1970 and held licenses for a large number of franchises. The high quality of their lavish figures makes them popular with collectors today.

Make sure the dolls retain all their original clothing and accessories and that their hair is in good condition.

A set of four KISS dolls, by Mego Corp.
c1977

13.25in (33.5cm) high

$700-1,000   **NOR**

"Kiss – A Marvel Comics Super Special", No. 1 Sept. 1977, published by Marvel Comics.

The comic was printed with ink containing the band's blood.

10.75in (27.5cm) high

$100-150   **NOR**

"TV Guide", Sept. 23-29 1967, 'The Day the Monkees Rebelled'.

19677.25in   (18.5cm) high

$30-50   **NOR**

An 'Official Monkee Puzzle', by E.E. Fairchild, 340-pieces, complete.

c1967   13in (33cm) wide

$80-120   **NOR**

A Gary Moore signed scratch plate, framed with an 'all areas' access pass dated 28rd March 2000.

$50-70   **GAZE**

A reproduction Roy Orbison concert poster.

Reproductions of early 'boxing' style posters such as this differ from the originals in that they contain the year of the event as well as the day and month. As the posters were destined for the rubbish bin as soon as the concert was over, the date was considered unnecessary and is missing from the vast majority of the original examples.

$15-25   **GAZE**

A scarce vinyl Jimmy Osmond pennant, with tassles.

15.75in (40cm) long

$25-35   **MTS**

An American Teen Pin-Ups magazine, June 1974, featuring the Osmonds, the Jackson Five, and others.

This issue originally retailed for 15 pence (25 cent) in the UK.

10.75in (27.5cm) high

$3-5   **MTS**

A 1970s Donny Osmond plastic face mask.

12in (30.5cm) long

$15-25   **MTS**

"Pink Floyd: Live at Pompeii", US one sheet poster.

1973

$280-320   **GAZE**

A The Osmonds' annual for 1976, by Osbro Productions.

10.5in (27cm) high

$8-12   **MTS**

A Pink Floyd World tour concert program.

1987

$25-35   **GAZE**

A 'Paul Revere Interviews The Raiders' picture disc, 33.5rpm, with exclusive interview.

6in (15cm) diam

$40-60   **NOR**

A "Meet Cliff and The Shadows in Wonderful Life" Star Special magazine, together with a Cliff "Life With the Stars" magazine.

$25-35   **GAZE**

A late 1950's Cliff Richard program for "Oh Boy Its Cliff Richard" Cliff and the Drifters, together with Pop Weekly No.1 with Cliff Richard front cover.

$18-22   **GAZE**

A Roxy Music concert poster, from their 1973 tour of Europe, with artwork by Gunter Kieser.

$70-100   **GAZE**

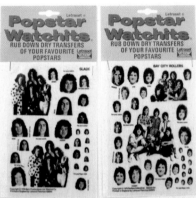

A 1960s set of Popstars Watchits Slade transfers, together with card of Bay City Rollers transfers.

10in (25.5cm) high

$15-20   **MTS**

A 1970s Marc Bolan T-Rex fabric patch, with red flock lettering.

3in (7.5cm) diam

$15-20   **MTS**

A Tina Turner 'Break Every Rule' tour concert program.

1987-8

$12-18   **GAZE**

A Bonnie Tyler 'Bitterblue' five track CD, framed with a signed photograph.

c1991

$10-15   **GAZE**

A Wham 'Club Fantastic' tour concert program.

1983

$7-10   **GAZE**

A 1960s 'Yes' psychedelic reflective belt buckle.

3.25in (8.5cm) wide

$15-25   **NOR**

COLLECTORS' NOTES

- The development of transfer printing in the late 18th century allowed commemorative ceramics to become more widely available. As the technique spread and distribution methods grew during the 19th century, it became more popular.

- As the variety of items available is so vast, many collectors choose to collect pieces related to a single monarch or member of the Royal family, or a single event in a monarch's life. Interest in the young Princes William and Harry is growing.

- The quality of the piece is a key indicator to value, with those by well-known makers made from high quality materials and with fine decoration usually being the most valuable. Condition is also vital as so many of each item were produced – always buy in the best condition you can, as this will help value remain constant or grow.

- As well as ceramics, many other different items have been produced to celebrate events such as coronations and jubilees. Some, such as biscuit tins, were special versions of usual items, whilst some were specially produced for the event itself.

- These 'ephemeral' items, including magazines and card and paper items, can be found regularly at affordable prices and can make a satisfying collection – again try to buy in the best condition you can.

A Tunnicliffe 'Queen's Diamond Jubilee' commemorative match holder and striker, printed mark, small bruise to top rim.

It is thought this match holder was given by William Tunnicliffe to Colonel Harry Johnson, chairman of the Johnson Pottery to celebrate the Jubilee.

1897   3in (7.5cm) high

$60-90   **WW**

A Victorian découpage picture of the Royal family, including Queen Victoria and her children.

Découpage is a decorative technique involving cutting out paper designs. The inked inscription on the back adds desirability as it indicates that the picture was made by Lady Churchill, a Lady-in-waiting to Queen Victoria, on September 20th 1843, an excellent dated attribution close to the Queen.

1843   6.75in (17cm) high

$220-280   **GAZE**

A Queen Victoria Golden Jubilee plate.

1887   8.75in (22cm) diam

$60-90   **GAZE**

A reproduction Parian ware bust of Queen Victoria, in Coronation robes.

16in (40.5cm) high

$80-120   **GAZE**

A limited edition Royal Doulton 'Queen Victoria' large character jug, D6788, from an edition of 3,000.

This was specially commissioned in 1988 in a limited edition of 3,000 by The Guild of Specialist China & Glass retailers.

1988   7in (18cm) high

$80-120   **GAZE**

An edition of the London Illustrated News, commemorating the marriage of Princess Louise of Wales, containing silks.

1889   *16.5in (42cm) high*

$30-50   **GAZE**

A small Edward VII Coronation milk jug, inscribed with the date, "26th June 1902".

The June date shown was the proposed date of the Coronation, but the event did not actually take place until August 9th as the uncrowned King developed appendicitis. Look out for commemorative pieces with both dates or only the August date shown, as these are usually more sought after.

1902   *3.75in (9.5cm) high*

$22-28   **GAZE**

A handkerchief commemorating Queen Victoria's Diamond Jubilee, inscribed "Souvenir of Her Majesty's Reign, The Longest on Record 1837-1897", framed and glazed.

c1897   *19.5in (49.5cm) wide*

$50-70   **GAZE**

An Edward VII and Alexandra monochrome milk jug, dated June 26th 1902.

          4.75in (12cm) high

$40-60   **GAZE**

A horse brass, commemorating Queen Victoria's Diamond Jubilee.

1897   *3.5in (9cm) diam*

$8-12   **GAZE**

A copy of the Daily Mirror, the lead story being the funeral of King Edward VII.

1910   *15in (38cm) high*

$100-150   **GAZE**

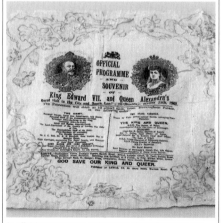

An official paper program and souvenir of King Edward VII and Queen Alexandra's Royal visit to the City and South London, on Saturday October 25th, frayed, torn, and faded.

1902

$30-40   **GAZE**

COMMEMORATIVE

A pair of Royal Doulton George V & Queen Mary commemorative beakers, inscribed "The Silver Jubilee 1910-1935".

c1935   3.25in (8.5cm) high

$30-40   **GAZE**

A pair of George V Silver Jubilee cups and saucers.

1935   saucer 5.75in (14.5cm) diam

$25-35   **GAZE**

A George V Silver Jubilee commemorative beaker.

1935   4.25in (11cm) high

$6-9   **GAZE**

A Doulton plate, commemorating the coronation of George V and Queen Mary.

8in (20.5cm) diam

$50-80   **GAZE**

A signed Royal presentation photograph of Queen Mary, gilt-tooled and embossed crown decoration, signed "Mary R".

1936   photograph 8in (20.5cm) high

$280-320   **GAZE**

A copy of "King Emperor's Jubilee", published by Daily Express Publications commemorating 25 years of rule by King George V, with extensive illustrations.

12in (30.5cm) high

$6-9   **GAZE**

A trio set, commemorating the proposed Coronation of Edward VIII.

1936-37   plate 6in (15cm) diam

$25-35   **GAZE**

A Shelley mug, commemorating the proposed Coronation of Edward VIII.

1936-37   3in (7.5cm) high

$30-40   **GAZE**

An unusual Bretby 'Edward VIII' commemorative musical character jug, covered in a matt white glaze, impressed mark, lacks movement.

8in (20cm) high

$150-200   **WW**

A Poole Pottery 'Edward VIII' plaque, designed by Harold Brownsword, impressed "Poole England", facsimile signature "Harold Brownsword Sc", repaired damage.

11.25in (28.5cm) high

$120-180　　　**WW**

A metal badge of Edward VIII, with Union Jack.

1.25in (3cm) diam

$8-12　　　**LG**

A Tuscan china mug, commemorating the Coronation of George VI and Elizabeth.

1937　　*2.75in (7cm) high*

$40-60　　　**GAZE**

A George VI Coronation trio set.

1937　　*7in (18cm) diam*

$15-25　　　**GAZE**

A souvenir songbook for the Coronation of George VI and Elizabeth entitled "National Airs of the Empire".

1937　　*11.75in (30cm) high*

$12-18　　　**GAZE**

A commemorative mug, made for the Coronation of George VI and Queen Elizabeth.

1937　　*3.5in (9cm) high*

$60-90　　　**GAZE**

A Coronation arrangement pamphlet, with map, for the Coronation of George VI and Elizabeth.

1937　　*6in (15cm) wide*

$6-9　　　**DH**

A 1937 edition of the Radio Times, the cover illustrating the Coronation of King George VI.

11.5in (29cm) high

$8-12　　　**GAZE**

A commemorative fold-out booklet, produced by Ogden's Tobacco, complete with a full collection of George VI's Coronation procession cigarette cards.

1937　　*42.5in (108cm) long*

$8-12　　　**GAZE**

Four album pages mounted with labels, by Harrison, commemorating the Coronation of George VI.

c1937   *6.5in (16.5cm) wide*

$6-9   **GAZE**

A set of 12 First Day covers, commemorating the Coronation of George VI, with stamps from across the Commonwealth.

1937   *largest 6.5in (16.5cm) wide*

$25-35   **GAZE**

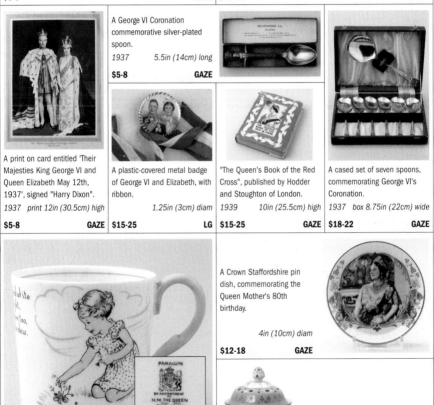

A George VI Coronation commemorative silver-plated spoon.

1937   *5.5in (14cm) long*

$5-8   **GAZE**

A print on card entitled 'Their Majesties King George VI and Queen Elizabeth May 12th, 1937', signed "Harry Dixon".

1937   print 12in (30.5cm) high

$5-8   **GAZE**

A plastic-covered metal badge of George VI and Elizabeth, with ribbon.

                     1.25in (3cm) diam

$15-25   **LG**

"The Queen's Book of the Red Cross", published by Hodder and Stoughton of London.

1939   *10in (25.5cm) high*

$15-25   **GAZE**

A cased set of seven spoons, commemorating George VI's Coronation.

1937 box 8.75in (22cm) wide

$18-22   **GAZE**

A Paragon nursery cup, inscribed "A Christmas Gift from the H.M. The Queen, Christmas 1938".

1938   *3in (7.5cm) diam*

$180-220   **GAZE**

A Crown Staffordshire pin dish, commemorating the Queen Mother's 80th birthday.

                4in (10cm) diam

$12-18   **GAZE**

A Spode bone china pot-pourri, commemorating the 90th birthday of the Queen Mother, from a limited edition of 500.

c1990   *8in (20cm) high*

$280-320   **H&G**

ROYAL MEMORABILIA

A Wedgwood Queen Elizabeth II Coronation mug, designed by Richard Guyatt, of cylindrical form with applied handle, in pink and brown colorway with gilt decoration, printed marks.

1953   *4.75in (12cm) high*

$50-70   **L&T**

A Wedgwood commemorative mug, designed by Eric Ravilious, commemorating the Coronation of Queen Elizabeth II.

1953   *4.25in (11cm) high*

$300-500   **REN**

A Honiton Pottery earthenware mug, commemorating the Coronation of Queen Elizabeth II.

1953   *4in (10cm) high*

$70-100   **H&G**

A Royal Albert Queen Elizabeth II loving cup, damaged.

If in perfect condition, these loving cups can fetch $300 or more.

7.5in (19cm) wide

$150-200   **GAZE**

A Thornton Crown ware trio set, to commemorate the Coronation of Queen Elizabeth II.

1953   *6in (15cm) wide*

$15-25   **GAZE**

A Royal Worcester bone china mask-head jug, commemorating the Coronation of Queen Elizabeth II.

1953   *5.75in (14.5cm) high*

$100-150   **H&G**

A Burleigh hand-painted earthenware jug, commemorating the Coronation of Queen Elizabeth II.

1953   *8.25in (21cm) high*

$220-280   **H&G**

A Minton bone china loving cup and cover, commemorating the Coronation of Queen Elizabeth II, designed by John Wadsworth.

Without the cover, the value of this piece falls to $220-280.

1953   *5.75in (14.5cm)*

$400-600   **H&G**

Two Wade commemorative pin dishes, commemorating the Coronation of Queen Elizabeth II.

1953   *4.75in (12cm) diam*

$15-25   **GAZE**

A CLOSER LOOK AT A COMMEMORATIVE ORB

A costume jewelry brooch, commemorating the Coronation of Queen Elizabeth II, in the form of her crown.

American costume jewelry company Trifari are perhaps the best known maker of crown-shaped pins, made from the 1930s to the late 1950s. In 1953, they released their popular 'Coronation gems' range. In vermeil look out for 1940s designs by Alfred Philippe for Trifari which can fetch around $150-250. These are more sought after than the reissues of the 1980s.

1953   1.5in (4cm) wide

$50-80   **GAZE**

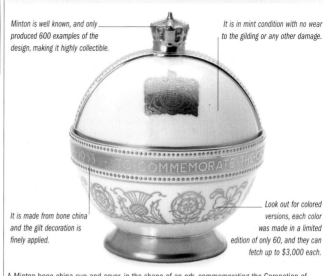

Minton is well known, and only produced 600 examples of the design, making it highly collectible.

It is in mint condition with no wear to the gilding or any other damage.

It is made from bone china and the gilt decoration is finely applied.

Look out for colored versions, each color was made in a limited edition of only 60, and they can fetch up to $3,000 each.

A Minton bone china cup and cover, in the shape of an orb, commemorating the Coronation of Queen Elizabeth II, a limited edition of 600.

1953   6in (15cm) high

$600-900   **H&G**

A scarf commemorating the Coronation of Queen Elizabeth II.

1953   28in (71cm) wide

$30-40   **GAZE**

A limited edition Paragon two-handled loving cup, from an edition of 750, commemorating the silver wedding anniversary of Queen Elizabeth II and Prince Phillip, complete with certificate.

1972   8.75in (22cm) wide

$100-150   **GAZE**

A plastic-covered metal badge, commemorating the Coronation of Queen Elizabeth II.

1953   1in (2.5cm) diam

$15-25   **LG**

A Union Jack card shield, commemorating the Coronation of Queen Elizabeth II.

1953

$40-60   **DH**

A limited edition Crown Staffordshire mug, commemorating the silver wedding anniversary of Queen Elizabeth and Prince Phillip.

1972   4.25in (11cm) high

$12-18   **GAZE**

A limited edition silver presentation plate, designed by Pietro Annigoni, commemorating the silver wedding anniversary of Queen Elizabeth II and Prince Philip.

1972   *plate 9in (23cm) diam*

$30-50   **GAZE**

An earthenware mug, commemorating the Silver Jubilee of Queen Elizabeth II, the back decorated with other 20thC monarchs.

1977   *3.5in (9cm) high*

$15-25   **H&G**

A Kaleidoscope for Liberty & Co. earthenware mug, commemorating the Silver Jubilee of Queen Elizabeth II.

c1977   *3.25in (8.5cm) high*

$40-60   **H&G**

A Sheridan china bowl, commemorating the Silver Jubilee of Queen Elizabeth II.

1977   *6.25in (16cm) diam*

$12-18   **GAZE**

A Wedgwood lidded dish, commemorating the Silver Jubilee of Queen Elizabeth II.

1977   *4.5in (11.5cm) diam*

$15-25   **GAZE**

Two glass goblets, commemorating the Silver Jubilee of Queen Elizabeth II, boxed.

1977   *5in (12.5cm) high*

$12-18   **GAZE**

An earthenware teapot, by Chiswick Ceramics Community, commemorating the Silver Jubilee of Queen Elizabeth II, from a limited edition of 100.

c1977   *8in (20cm) high*

$280-320   **H&G**

A white metal presentation tray, commemorating the Silver Jubilee of Queen Elizabeth II.

1977   *12.5in (31.5cm) diam*

$25-35   **GAZE**

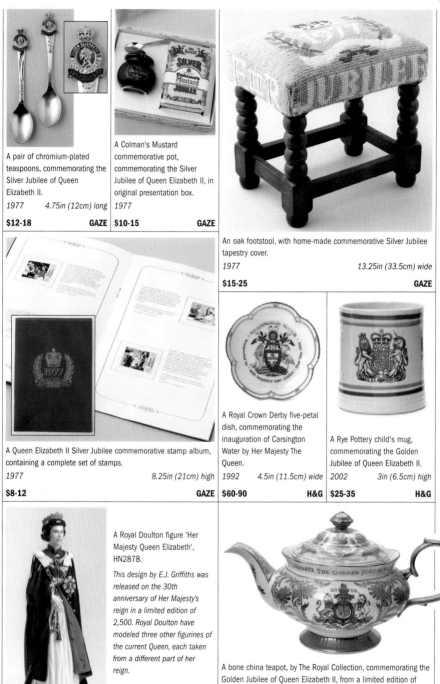

A pair of chromium-plated teaspoons, commemorating the Silver Jubilee of Queen Elizabeth II.

1977   4.75in (12cm) long

$12-18   **GAZE**

A Colman's Mustard commemorative pot, commemorating the Silver Jubilee of Queen Elizabeth II, in original presentation box.

1977

$10-15   **GAZE**

An oak footstool, with home-made commemorative Silver Jubilee tapestry cover.

1977   13.25in (33.5cm) wide

$15-25   **GAZE**

A Queen Elizabeth II Silver Jubilee commemorative stamp album, containing a complete set of stamps.

1977   8.25in (21cm) high

$8-12   **GAZE**

A Royal Crown Derby five-petal dish, commemorating the inauguration of Carsington Water by Her Majesty The Queen.

1992   4.5in (11.5cm) wide

$60-90   **H&G**

A Rye Pottery child's mug, commemorating the Golden Jubilee of Queen Elizabeth II.

2002   3in (6.5cm) high

$25-35   **H&G**

A Royal Doulton figure 'Her Majesty Queen Elizabeth', HN2878.

This design by E.J. Griffiths was released on the 30th anniversary of Her Majesty's reign in a limited edition of 2,500. Royal Doulton have modeled three other figurines of the current Queen, each taken from a different part of her reign.

1983   10.75in (27cm) high

$150-200   **L&T**

A bone china teapot, by The Royal Collection, commemorating the Golden Jubilee of Queen Elizabeth II, from a limited edition of 750.

2002   11in (28cm) wide

$280-320   **H&G**

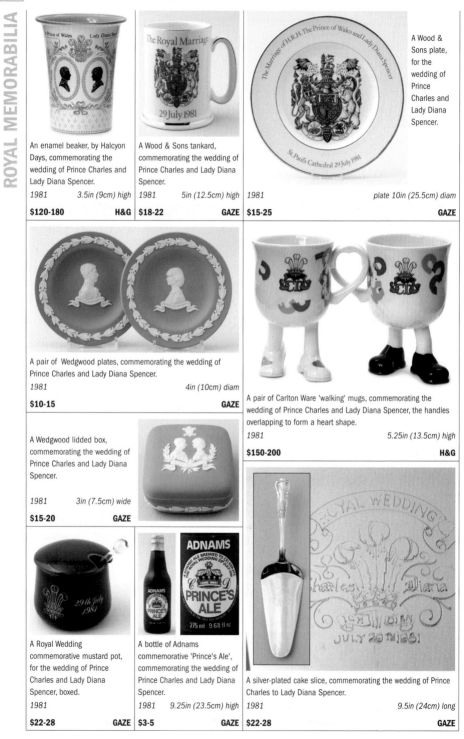

An enamel beaker, by Halcyon Days, commemorating the wedding of Prince Charles and Lady Diana Spencer.

1981   *3.5in (9cm) high*

$120-180   **H&G**

A Wood & Sons tankard, commemorating the wedding of Prince Charles and Lady Diana Spencer.

1981   *5in (12.5cm) high*

$18-22   **GAZE**

A Wood & Sons plate, for the wedding of Prince Charles and Lady Diana Spencer.

1981   *plate 10in (25.5cm) diam*

$15-25   **GAZE**

A pair of Wedgwood plates, commemorating the wedding of Prince Charles and Lady Diana Spencer.

1981   *4in (10cm) diam*

$10-15   **GAZE**

A Wedgwood lidded box, commemorating the wedding of Prince Charles and Lady Diana Spencer.

1981   *3in (7.5cm) wide*

$15-20   **GAZE**

A pair of Carlton Ware 'walking' mugs, commemorating the wedding of Prince Charles and Lady Diana Spencer, the handles overlapping to form a heart shape.

1981   *5.25in (13.5cm) high*

$150-200   **H&G**

A Royal Wedding commemorative mustard pot, for the wedding of Prince Charles and Lady Diana Spencer, boxed.

1981

$22-28   **GAZE**

A bottle of Adnams commemorative 'Prince's Ale', commemorating the wedding of Prince Charles and Lady Diana Spencer.

1981   *9.25in (23.5cm) high*

$3-5   **GAZE**

A silver-plated cake slice, commemorating the wedding of Prince Charles to Lady Diana Spencer.

1981   *9.5in (24cm) long*

$22-28   **GAZE**

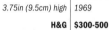

A bone china mug, by Chown, commemorating the divorce of Prince Charles and Diana, Princess of Wales.

1996 3.75in (9.5cm) high

$70-100 **H&G**

A rare Wedgwood basalt mug commemorating the investiture of Prince Charles as the Prince of Wales, designed by Richard Guyatt, a limited edition of 200.

1969 4in (10cm) high

$300-500 **H&G**

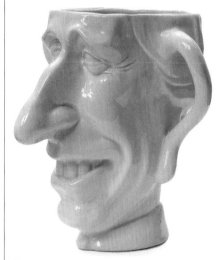

A bone china plate, by Caverswall, commemorating the 30th birthday of H.R.H. The Princess of Wales.

1991 10.25in (26cm) wide

$150-200 **H&G**

A Crown Staffordshire pin dish, commemorating the birth of Prince William.

1982 4in (10cm) diam

$12-18 **GAZE**

A Spitting Image Prince Charles mug, commemorating the marriage of Charles and Diana.

This mug is scarce as very few were made because they were so vulnerable to breakage.

1981 7.5in (19cm) high

$280-320 **H&G**

A Bells scotch whisky decanter, by Wade, commemorating the birth of Prince William.

Had this piece retained its rectangular card box, its value could have been around 50% more.

1982 8in (20.5cm) high

$50-70 **GAZE**

A bone china mug, by Aynsley, commemorating the 18th birthday of Prince Harry, from a limited edition of 5,000.

2002 3.75in (9.5cm) h.

$60-90 **H&G**

A bone china mug, by The Royal Collection, commemorating the 21st birthday of Prince William.

2003 6in (15cm) high

$30-40 **H&G**

ROYAL MEMORABILIA

A bottle of Adnams 'Wedding Ale', commemorating the wedding of Prince Andrew to Sarah Ferguson.

1986   9.25in (23.5cm) high

$3-5   **GAZE**

A Bells 'Old Scotch Whisky' decanter, by Wade, commemorating the birth of Princess Eugenie, unopened and boxed.

1990

bottle 7.75in (19.5cm) high

$50-80   **GAZE**

A commemorative china mug depicting Prince Andrew and Sarah Ferguson, probably commemorating their wedding.

1986   3.5in (9cm) high

$5-8   **GAZE**

A late 1980s Duke and Duchess of York commemorative dish, with certificate, boxed.

4.25in (11cm) diam

$10-15   **GAZE**

A bone china lion-head beaker, by Sutherland Pottery, commemorating the 60th birthday of Princess Margaret, from a limited edition of 750.

1990   4.5in (11.5cm) high

$70-100   **H&G**

A Crown Ducal bone china mug, featuring the young Princess Margaret, commemorating the Coronation of her parents.

A similar mug was made depicting Princess Elizabeth. Commemorative ware depicting the Royal children is particularly popular.

1937   3in (7.5cm) high

$180-220   **H&G**

A bone china mug, by Chown, commemorating Princess Alice, Duchess of Gloucester, the longest lived Royal, from a limited edition of 35.

The previous longest lived Royal was Queen Elizabeth, The Queen Mother.

2003   3.75in (9.5cm) high

$40-60   **H&G**

A saucer in memoriam to Princess Charlotte, with pink luster decoration.

The pink luster makes this saucer appealing to collectors of lusterware as well as of commemorative ware. Princess Charlotte died in child birth at the age of 21.

1817   5.5in (14cm) diam

$120-180   **H&G**

A Parian bust of Princess Mary, by Robinson and Leadbeater, made at the time of her wedding to the Duke of York.

A matching bust of the Duke of York was also produced.

1893   8.5in (21.5cm) high

$400-600   **H&G**

COLLECTORS' NOTES

■ Scent bottles fall into one of two categories: decorative bottles into which perfume is decanted, and commercial bottles that are designed for and sold with a specific perfume. It is the latter that are covered in this section.

■ Commercial scent bottles came into their own when Rene Lalique began designing scent bottles for his friend François Coty in 1907. As well as Coty, he went on to work with Guerlain, Caron, Worth, and Lucien Lelong. Needless to say, his designs are highly sought-after, as are those by rival glass producer Baccarat.

■ The field expanded further in 1921 when Coco Chanel became the first couturier to release a perfume. She intended that women who could not afford her clothes could buy her perfume. Since then virtually every fashion designer releases at least one perfume and continues the trend of employing popular artists and designers of the day to design the bottles.

■ The value of commercial scent bottles can vary greatly, making them popular with collectors at many levels. Many collectors specialize in a particular designer such as Lalique or Dali, a company such as Guerlain or Schiaparelli, or even individual fragrances such as 'An Evening in Paris' by Bourjois.

A set of three Elizabeth Arden miniature scent bottles, comprising My Love (1948), Night & Day (1935), and On Dit (1944).

These bottles were probably part of a miniatures gift set.

2.75in (7cm) high

$22-28 each   **LB**

A Quadrille by Balenciaga, France scent bottle, clear glass bottle with plastic lid and embossed leather slip case.

This is a classic 1950s perfume. This example has a leather slip case to protect the bottle while in the purse.

1956   Bottle 2in (5cm) high

$25-35   **LB**

A Jolie Madame by Balmain scent bottle, introduced in 1957.

Bottle 2.75in (7cm) high

$40-60   **LB**

A 1930s Evening in Paris by Bourjois of Paris, novelty scent bottle, with tassel.

Introduced in 1928, Evening in Paris became one of the best known perfumes in the world. The Christmas novelty bottle, shaped as the Eiffel Tower, is very desirable and worth around $350. The 1930s version of this bottle with a Bakelite stopper is worth approximately $50.

3.25in (8.5cm) long

$100-150   **LB**

A Kobako by Bourjois of Paris scent bottle, the bottle designed by Borsse and in a Chinese red Bakelite box, introduced in 1936.

Bottle 2.75in (7cm) high

$400-600   **LB**

A Le Narcisse Noir by Caron scent bottle, with black glass flower stopper and box, introduced in 1911.

Bottle 3in (7.5cm) diam

$80-120   **LB**

Two Vœu de Noël by Caron of Paris tester scent bottles, one lacks label, etched "Caron", introduced in 1940.

2.5in (6.5cm) high

$25-35 each   **LB**

A limited edition 'Three Gold Pearls' So Pretty by Cartier scent bottle, the crystal bottle containing a pink, white and yellow gold 'pearl', in Harrods box, introduced in 1995.

Bottle 5.75in (14.5cm) high

$300-500   LB

A CLOSER LOOK AT A CHANEL SCENT BOTTLE

Legend has it that Coco Chanel's perfumier presented her with a selection of numbered samples. She chose "No. 5", and it went on to become her lucky number.

The simple, classic design of the bottle and packaging, which was in stark contrast to the elaborate bottles of the time, has changed little over the years. Values for even the earliest examples are relatively low.

Chanel No. 5 is perhaps the most famous perfume in the world and was the first to carry the name of a fashion designer.

A Chanel No. 5 scent bottle, with box, introduced in 1921.

Marilyn Monroe boosted sales when she claimed it was the only thing she wore to bed.

Bottle 3.75in (9.5cm) high

$25-35   LB

A L'Aiment by Coty scent bottle, introduced in 1928.

Established in 1904, Coty was a pioneer in the industry and was considered the world's premier perfumer by 1910.

Bottle 2.5in (6.5cm) high

$50-70   LB

A Dashing by Lily Daché scent bottle, in a padded pink satin box topped with a fabric rose, also in pink, introduced in 1941.

Bottle 5in (12.5cm) high

$400-600   LB

A set of two Celui by Jean Dessès scent bottles, introduced in 1921.

5in (12.5cm) high

$220-280   LB

A 1920s Le Dandy by D'Orsay of Paris black geometric scent bottle and stopper, introduced in 1926.

It is unusual to find these bottles with their original label.

2.5in (6.5cm) high

$100-150   LB

A Fabergé scent bottle, the crystal bottle made exclusively by St Louis Cristalleries, France.

Bottle 6in (15cm) high

$800-1,200   LB

A Fragile by Jean-Paul Gaultier scent bottle introduced in 2001.

Bottle 2.75in (7cm) high

$25-35   LB

A 1990s set of two Parfums Grès scent bottles, comprising Cabochard and Cabotine.

The company was started in 1959 and Cabochard was launched the same year. Cabotine was launched in 1990.

Bottles 2in (5cm) high

$25-35 **LB**

PIERRE-FRANÇOIS GUERLAIN

Pierre-François Guerlain founded Guerlain in Paris in 1828 after studying medicine and chemistry in England. His success was such that he was appointed perfumer to the French Imperial court in 1853. Pierre's sons Aimeé and Gabriel took over in 1890 and were responsible for one of the first uses of synthetic oils in 'Jicky'. Pierre's grandson Jacques was made creative director in the early 20thC and was responsible for some of the company's most popular perfumes such as 'L'Heure Bleu' and 'Shalimar'. The company has now produced over 200 different perfumes and until 1996 was still a family run business.

A No. 90 by Guerlain scent bottle.

When a rival company launched a perfume using the name of an existing Guerlain perfume 'Shalimar', the company temporarily changed the name to its stock number 'No. 90' while copyright issues were dealt with.

5.75in (14.5cm) high

$100-150 **LB**

A Chant de Arômes by Guerlain scent bottle, the frosted and clear glass bottle with rosebud-shaped stopper, introduced in 1962.

Bottle 4.5in (11.5cm) high

$70-100 **LB**

A Guerlinade by Guerlain scent bottle, signed by Jean-Paul Guerlain, introduced in 1989.

This limited edition bottle was released in 1989 and commemorated the bicentenary of the company.

Bottle 4.5in (11.5cm) high

$80-120 **LB**

A Jardins de Bagatelle by Guerlain scent bottle, introduced in 1983.

13.75in (35cm) high

$700-1,000 **LB**

A L'Heure Bleue by Guerlain scent bottle, introduced in 1912.

L'Heure Bleue was created by Jacques Guerlain, grandson of the company founder, Pierre.

12in (30.5cm) high

$80-120 **LB**

An early Liu by Guerlain scent bottle, with clear glass bottle and stopper, paper label to base, introduced in 1926.

This perfume was named after the slave girl in Puccini's opera 'Turandot' and is now discontinued.

2.5in (6.5cm) high

$80-120 **LB**

A Mahora by Guerlain scent bottle, with applied hammered gold-colored disc, in original bag, introduced in the 1980s.

5in (12.5cm) high

$25-35 **LB**

A 1960s Vol de Nuit by Guerlain scent bottle, with zebra-pattern printed box, glass bottle with plastic stopper, introduced in 1933.

3.5in (9cm) high

$120-180 **LB**

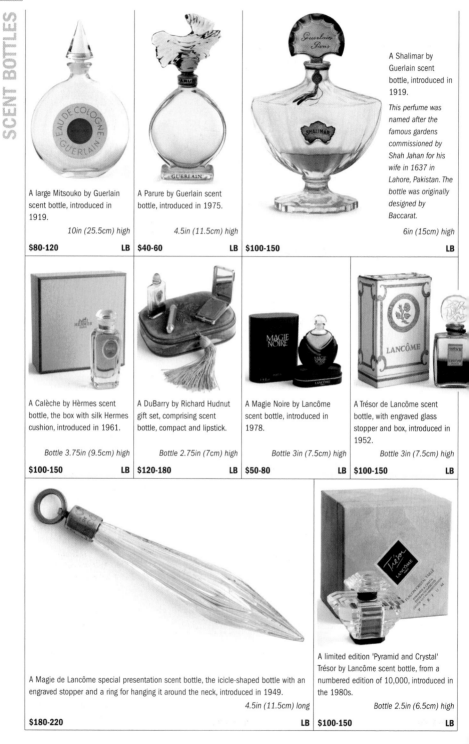

A large Mitsouko by Guerlain scent bottle, introduced in 1919.

10in (25.5cm) high

$80-120   **LB**

A Parure by Guerlain scent bottle, introduced in 1975.

4.5in (11.5cm) high

$40-60   **LB**

A Shalimar by Guerlain scent bottle, introduced in 1919.

This perfume was named after the famous gardens commissioned by Shah Jahan for his wife in 1637 in Lahore, Pakistan. The bottle was originally designed by Baccarat.

6in (15cm) high

$100-150   **LB**

A Calèche by Hèrmes scent bottle, the box with silk Hermes cushion, introduced in 1961.

Bottle 3.75in (9.5cm) high

$100-150   **LB**

A DuBarry by Richard Hudnut gift set, comprising scent bottle, compact and lipstick.

Bottle 2.75in (7cm) high

$120-180   **LB**

A Magie Noire by Lancôme scent bottle, introduced in 1978.

Bottle 3in (7.5cm) high

$50-80   **LB**

A Trésor de Lancôme scent bottle, with engraved glass stopper and box, introduced in 1952.

Bottle 3in (7.5cm) high

$100-150   **LB**

A Magie de Lancôme special presentation scent bottle, the icicle-shaped bottle with an engraved stopper and a ring for hanging it around the neck, introduced in 1949.

4.5in (11.5cm) long

$180-220   **LB**

A limited edition 'Pyramid and Crystal' Trésor by Lancôme scent bottle, from a numbered edition of 10,000, introduced in the 1980s.

Bottle 2.5in (6.5cm) high

$100-150   **LB**

An Arpège by Lanvin dummy scent bottle, introduced in 1929.

Initially launched in 1929, this perfume was relaunched in 1994 in an updated version of the original round bottle.

9in (23cm) high

$700-1,000 **LB**

A My Sin Extrait by Lanvin scent bottle.

Bottle 2.5in (6.5cm) high

$40-60 **LB**

A Gardenia by Lucien Lelong scent bottle.

5.5in (14cm) high

$100-150 **LB**

An Indiscrete by Lucien Lelong of Paris scent bottle, with bow-shaped stopper, introduced in 1935.

Indiscrete was Lelong's best selling perfume.

3.75in (14.5cm) high

$120-180 **LB**

A rare and early Tweed by Lentheric of Paris scent bottle, clear glass bottle and stopper, introduced in 1935.

3in (7.5cm) high

$120-180 **LB**

A Wind Song by Prince Matchabelli scent bottle.

Bottle 2.75in (7cm) high

$120-180 **LB**

A small Prince Matchabelli scent bottle, the crown-shaped bottle decorated with gilt.

Prince Matchabelli was a Russian emigré who fled to New York. He began make perfume for his friends in the 1930s and based the bottle design on his family's crown. Most examples have lost their labels, making it difficult to tell which fragrance they contained.

c1925

2in (5cm) wide

$150-200 **LB**

A glass crown-shaped scent bottle, with label for eau de cologne by Curtis.

6in (15cm) high

$80-120 **LB**

A Crêpe de Chine by F. Millot scent bottle, introduced in 1929.

Bottle 3.25in (8.5cm) high

$100-150 **LB**

A 1930s Le Narcisse Bleu by Mury of Paris scent bottle, clear glass with blue Bakelite top, the bottle with floral decoration.

4.25in (11cm) high

$70-100 LB

A Joy by Jean Patou scent bottle, in box.

Bottle 2in (5cm) wide

$40-60 LB

A Joy by Jean Patou scent bottle, clear glass with gold label, introduced in 1993.

2in (5cm) high

$60-90 LB

A large Joy by Jean Patou display scent bottle, black with red stopper, pictured with a smaller version to show scale.

7.25in (18.5cm) high

$100-150 LB

A small Joy by Jean Patou display scent bottle, black with red stopper.

These bottles are influenced by Oriental fashions and are similar in shape to 19thC snuff bottles.

2.25in (5.5cm) high

$40-60 LB

A Moment Suprême by Jean Patou miniature scent bottle, introduced 1929.

2.25in (5.5cm) high

$60-90 LB

A Replique by Raphael scent bottle, designed by Lalique, in the form of a pine cone with orange ribbon, introduced in 1944.

2in (5cm) high

$220-280 LB

A Chichi by Renoir of Paris, scent bottle, heart-shaped and in clear glass, made in France for the US market, introduced in 1942.

3in (7.5cm) high

$220-280 LB

A Cœur Joie by Nina Ricci scent bottle, designed by Lalique, the clear glass bottle with three heart-shaped motifs and a gold-plated stopper, introduced in 1946.

3.25in (8.5cm) high

$120-180 LB

A Cœur Joie by Nina Ricci of Paris scent bottle, designed by Lalique, introduced in 1946.

This was the first perfume released by Nina Ricci.

2.5in (6.5cm) high

$280-320 LB

A Cœur Joie by Nina Ricci scent bottle, designed by Lalique, lacks label.

4in (10cm) high

$100-150 LB

A set of three Deci Delà by Nina Ricci scent bottles, each with heart-shaped stoppers, introduced in the 1980s.

Bottles 2in (5cm) high

$40-60 LB

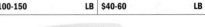

A limited edition L'Air du Temps by Nina Ricci 'The Winged Bottle' scent bottle, designed by Lalique.

Bottle 4.25in (11cm) high

$80-120 LB

A L'Air du Temps by Nina Ricci scent bottle, in yellow satin-covered box.

Bottle 4in (10cm) high

$120-180 LB

A Femme by Rochas scent bottle.

Bottle 3in (7.5cm) high

$40-60 LB

ELSA SCHIAPARELLI

▪ Italian born fashion designer Elsa Schiaparelli (1890-1973) opened her first shop in Paris in 1929.

▪ A passionate advocate of Surrealism, Schiaparelli collaborated with artists such as Salvador Dali and Jean Cocteau, and incorporated the elements of the school into her own designs.

▪ Her first perfume, 'Salut' was launched in 1934, and her most famous 'Shocking' in 1937. The 'Shocking' bottle was in the shape of a lady's torso and is said to be based on the dressmaker's dummy sent to Schiaparelli by Mae West to use for fitting her clothes.

A Violette by Rosine of Paris scent bottle, in clear glass with gilt decoration and large key-shaped stopper, introduced in 1924.

Rosine was owned by couturier Paul Poiret and named after his daughter.

4in (10cm) high

$100-150 LB

A Shocking by Schiaparelli scent bottle, shaped as a tailor's dummy, with frosted stopper.

15.5in (39.5cm) high

$1,200-1,800 LB

A Zut by Schiaparelli scent bottle, formed as the lower half of a lady with her skirt around her ankles, decorated with gilt.

1948-49   5.75in (14.5cm) high

$400-600   LB

A CLOSER LOOK AT A SCENT BOTTLE

Bottles with their hair and labels, like these, are more desirable.

These designs, which today are considered 'politically incorrect', are based on the character created by Florence K. Upton in 1895.

Vigny also produced a perfume pin in the form of a Golliwogg head and a rare trio set of bottles called 'Jack-Junior-Jill'.

Golliwogs are collectible in their own right, which makes these scent bottles very sought-after.

Two Le Golliwogg by Vigny of Paris scent bottles, with seal fur hair, introduced in 1918.

Largest 3.5in (9cm) high

LARGE: $400-600 SMALL: $320-380   LB

A miniature Schiaparelli sample scent bottle, in the form a female torso.

                    2in (5cm) high

$150-200   LB

A Head Over Heels by Ultima II scent bottle, the stopper in the form of a pair of lady's legs, boxed, introduced in the 1980s.

Bottle 7in (18cm) high

$100-150   LB

A limited First by Van Cleef and Arpels scent bottle, introduced in the 1990s.

Bottle 4in (10cm) high

$100-150   LB

A Je Reviens by Worth of Paris, scent bottle, designed by Lalique and decorated with stars, introduced in 1932.

Bottle 4in (10cm) high

$70-100   LB

A Dans la Nuit by Worth of Paris scent bottle, designed by Lalique, in round, blue glass.

This perfume and style of bottle was first introduced in the 1920s and relaunched in 1985.

c1985   Bottle 3.5in (9cm) high

$50-80   LB

A Vers Le Jour by Worth of Paris scent bottle, with square clear glass bottle, introduced in 1926.

                    2in (5cm) high

$25-35   LB

A microscope by W. Watson & Sons of London, with original wooden box.

c1890　　*13.5in (34cm) high*

$400-600　　　　　　**ATK**

A microscope by E. Leitz of Wetzlar, with original wooden box.

c1890　　*14in (36cm) high*

$700-1,000　　　　　　**ATK**

A Culpeper-type brass microscope, with shuttered objective lens over four-division calibrated focus and circular stage supported within two tiers of S-scroll supports with mirror mounted below, on circular molded mahogany base, in pyramid-shaped mahogany case with drawer containing accessories to interior and brass loop handle to top.

This type was first made from card and wood in the 1720s, and then in brass until the mid-19thC. Many are unsigned, but look for names such as Adams. Beware of reproductions and examine cases, which are being reproduced today.

c1800　　　　　　*13.75in (35cm) high*

$1,500-2,000　　　　　　**BAR**

A Burkhardt Arithometer, in oak case, damage to 'tens' transfer.

The Arithometer was invented by Charles Xavier Thomas de Colmar c1820 and was used up until the first decades of the 20thC. It could calculate all four arithmetic functions (addition, multiplication, subtraction, and division). The Burkhardt was the first German calculating machine of this type.

1878

$1,200-1,800　　　　　　**ATK**

A Curta 'Type 1' miniature calculation device, with original plastic box, shipping carton and two manuals.

$700-1,000　　**ATK**

An early hour-glass in a tin frame, marked with four symbols including "CB" monogram.

c1850　　*5in (12.5cm) high*

$300-500　　**ATK**

An American WWII compass.

2in (5cm) diam

$50-80　　**COB**

A 19thC 'Admiral Fitzroy's Barometer', with thermometer.

Named after Admiral Robert Fitzroy who reorganized the Meteorological Office from 1854, the more complex and decorative the example, the more valuable it is likely to be. Damage to the printed card backing reduces value dramatically.

c1870　　*41in (104cm) high*

$150-200　　**ATK**

A German orbit tellurium, by Columbus of Berlin, made for the Scandinavian market, electrified later.

Telluriums show the daily and annual movements of the Earth around the sun, with a candle/lightbulb and curved mirror acting as the sun.

c1920　　*20in (50cm) long*

$700-1,000　　**ATK**

COLLECTORS' NOTES

■ Most surviving sewing tools found today date from the late 18th century and the 19th century, when sewing was a fashionable and virtuous hobby for a lady. Many were made to fill comprehensive work or sewing boxes, which have since been broken up. Whilst many were manufactured, some charming items were made at home, often with parts bought from a shop and assembled at home.

■ Materials vary, and value largely depends on this, as well as age and the quality of design and decoration. Wood, metals such as pressed brass, bone, and ivory are common. 19th century and earlier silver and gold tools are usually much sought after and valuable, particularly if finely crafted. The quality of any carving is also worth considering.

■ Many items were sold as souvenirs, the most frequently found being Tunbridgeware from Kent, Mauchlineware from Scotland and carved wooden items from Switzerland. During the early decades of the 20th century, sewing machines became inexpensive, better quality factory needlework developed and sewing became less necessary and fell from fashion, resulting in a steady decline in the production of sewing tools.

■ Thimbles began to be machine-made from the mid-18th century, with Germany and England being notable producers. Early silver thimbles are often not marked as they were too small to be covered by the hallmarking laws. Look for intricately decorated thimbles, those in precious metals, or those by notable makers such as Charles Horner or Iles.

A French abalone shell-covered souvenir pin case, with red silk interiors and loops to hold a stiletto.

c1890   *2.25in (5.5cm) high*

$100-150   **JSC**

A French carved ivory pin case, covers with carved foliate design, with silk and material interior.

          2.5in (6.5cm) high

$180-220   **JSC**

A Tunbridgeware needle case, the cover with stickwork and central mahogany panel, the paper-lined interior with material pages.

Tunbridgeware is made from tiny, thin tiles or 'tesserae' of differently colored woods glued to the surface.

          2.25in (5.5cm) high

$120-180   **JSC**

An amboyna wood needle case, lined with ebony and with ivory bands.

c1820   *3in (8cm) long*

$180-220   **JSC**

A glass needle case and packet holder, showing Old Court, St Peter's College, Cambridge, with silver and gilt highlights and mirror as back cover.

Made from glass and painted with a scene from the reverse, these can be found with a series of notable buildings such as Osborne House.

          3.5in (8.5cm) high

$280-320   **JSC**

An early 19thC beadwork needle case, over a bone body.

          3.5in (9cm) long

$180-220   **JSC**

A rare Tunbridgeware stickwork parasol-shaped needle case, with turned mahogany handle pulling off to reveal storage in interior.

Both the form and the use of the woods in this manner are rare for Tunbridgeware.

c1840   *4in (10cm) long*

$220-280   **JSC**

A straw work needle case, with fine mosaic-like pattern.

Straw work is made from flattened colored strands of straw and is often associated with objects handmade by French prisoners of war during the Napoleonic wars of the early 19thC.

c1850   4.25in (11.cm) long

$100-150   **JSC**

A mid-19thC English milk glass needle case, with painted flowers, gilt bands and paper lined interior.

3.75in (9.5cm) long

$220-280   **JSC**

A Tartanware needle case, with label reading "Prince Charlie".

3.5in (8.5cm) long

$120-180   **JSC**

A Transferware torpedo-shaped needle case, with color transfer reading "A Happy Christmas" amidst holly.

3.75in (9.5cm) long

$80-120   **JSC**

A late 19thC black lacquerware needle case, with transfer of flowers, a dove and an envelope.

3.25in (8cm) long

$100-150   **JSC**

An early 19thC French ivory needle case, in the form of a pea pod.

Both the material and the realistic carving of this piece makes it valuable and desirable.

4in (10cm) long

$280-320   **JSC**

An English vegetable ivory needle case, with pineapple-shaped ends.

Vegetable ivory is not derived from animals as with other ivory, but is rather made from the 'coroso' or 'tagua' nut, the fruit of a tropical palm. When fresh it is a creamy white, but it yellows over time. Large pieces such as this are made from more than one nut.

c1860   3in (7.5cm) long

$100-150   **JSC**

A pressed brass 'Britannia Needle case', by W. Avery & Son, Redditch, with repoussé dolphin to center, knob on reverse pushing to reveal 6/7 or 8/9 needles.

2.25in (5.5cm) high

$150-200   **CBE**

A 'Beatrice Case' accordion-style needle packet case, with different leaves unfolding, each holding a needle packet, with fitted case.

Patented on 3rd April 1867 by Lewis & Archibald, this case was made to commemorate the birthday of Princess Beatrice.

2in (5cm) high

$300-500   **JSC**

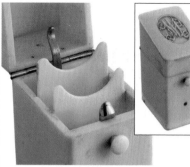

A leather pocket for needle packets, contained in a card case, the front with chromolithographic portrait of Jenny Lind, 'The Swedish Songbird'.

c1870   *3.5in (9cm) high*

$100-150   **JSC**

A 19thC ivory needle packet holder, with deeply engraved initials to top of hinged lid, with ivory dividers to interior.

2.75in (7cm) high

$300-500   **CBE**

A color printed and embossed card needle packet holder box, interior with concertina holding different needle packets, the lid with inset mirror.

Box 2.25in (6cm) wide

$40-60   **CBE**

A late 19thC English velvet-covered and color lithographed card needle packet holder box, the interior with concertina of panels holding different needle packets.

Box 2.75in (7cm) long

$60-90   **CBE**

A late 19thC card needle box, with Baxter color lithograph print of Prince Frederick of Prussia, from the 'Queen Mary' set.

2.25in (6cm) high

$40-60   **CBE**

A late 19thC card needle box, with Baxter color lithograph print of The Princess Royal, Princess F.W. of Prussia, from the 'Queen Mary' set.

2.25in (6cm) high

$40-60   **CBE**

A card 'Synoptical Needle case', patented on 14th November 1867, with applied embossed chromolithographic panel.

c1865 3.75in (9.5cm) high

$80-120   **JSC**

A German metal needle-holder, with blue fabric ribbon to hold needles, the finials as winders.

c1890   *4in (10cm) long*

$40-60   **JSC**

A French silver thimble, commemorating WW1, stamped "PAX" and "LABOR" and marked "F.P. Lasserie".

These commemorative thimbles were sold as souvenirs to people who visited battlefields in France and are of interest to collectors. The use of silver and the sympathetic, comparatively intricate, low relief design also make this example desirable.

c1919

$300-500 CBE

A French silver commemorative thimble, for the "Exposition 1889", with French control marks.

$150-200 CBE

A cupro-nickel thimble, commemorating Queen Victoria's Golden Jubilee.

This thimble was also made in silver and brass.

c1885

$70-100 CBE

An early 20thC French silver thimble, with an applied band of leaves and flowers and punched dot design.

$60-90 CBE

An early 20thC German silver thimble, with applied scrolling band inset with coral cabochons, stamped "800".

0.75in (2cm) high

$80-120 CBE

A silver Queen Elizabeth II Coronation thimble, by James Swann & Son, with low relief scene of coronation carriage, Westminster Abbey, Birmingham hallmark.

The same scenes are found on the George and Mary commemorative thimble.

1953

$150-200 CBE

A sterling Irish-themed thimble, by James Fenton, with a band of clovers and a harp, Rd No. 202536 for 1892.

James Fenton of Birmingham was a very prolific thimble maker c1850-1900, the last use of his mark was 1923. Many of his thimbles are highly desirable today.

$120-180 CBE

An early 20thC European brass thimble, with repeated 'star' design and milled band.

0.75in (2cm) high

$22-28 CBE

An American 'Patriotic' brass thimble, with an applied painted plaque of the 'Stars & Stripes'.

Probably produced to commemorate the American participation in WWI.

c1917 *0.75in (2cm) high*

$40-60 CBE

A French sewing set, comprising a pair of scissors and thimble in a plush-lined fitted case marked "Languedoc Rue du Septembre 18", the scissors with applied miniature gold coronet and cross motifs.

Avoid buying sets where one or more pieces are missing as it can be extremely difficult to find an exact replacement.

c1870

$150-200   JSC

A Tartanware barrel-shaped thimble-case, containing a silver thimble.

Tartanware thimble-cases are hard to find.

3in (4.5cm) high

$150-200   JSC

An Edwardian silver novelty pin cushion, by Levi & Salaman, Birmingham, in the form of an old boot, with Reg No.

1907   2in (5cm) long

$150-200   WW

A handmade card, silk, and beadwork pin holder.

c1800   1.5in (4cm) diam

$40-60   JSC

A scarce green plush-covered Iles thimble shop counter display case, with beveled glass lid.

c1895

$70-100   CBE

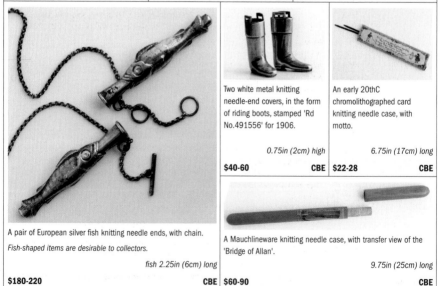

A pair of European silver fish knitting needle ends, with chain.

Fish-shaped items are desirable to collectors.

fish 2.25in (6cm) long

$180-220   CBE

Two white metal knitting needle-end covers, in the form of riding boots, stamped 'Rd No.491556' for 1906.

0.75in (2cm) high

$40-60   CBE

An early 20thC chromolithographed card knitting needle case, with motto.

6.75in (17cm) long

$22-28   CBE

A Mauchlineware knitting needle case, with transfer view of the 'Bridge of Allan'.

9.75in (25cm) long

$60-90   CBE

COLLECTORS' NOTES

■ Although patents exist from the turn of the 19th century, the first functional sewing machine was developed by French tailor Barthelemy Thimonnier in 1830. Sewing machines did not go into commercial production until the 1850s when Isaac Singer and Elias Howe founded their companies.

■ Although an interesting collection can be built comparatively inexpensively, collectors tend to seek out early or scarce machines from the 1850s-1870s, often from companies that were short-lived.

■ Commonly found names include Willcox & Gibbs and Singer. Most Singer machines fetch under $50 unless early or scarce. Condition is important, look for machines which are complete and retain their bright, gilt transfers and, if applicable, their cases.

A Canadian domestic sewing machine, made by Wanzer, retailed in London.

Manufacturer R.M. Wanzer of Buffalo, NY ran the first Canadian sewing machine factory in Hamilton, Ontario between 1860 and 1886. In 1878, they bought the Canada Sewing Machine Company and also distributed their machines in London.

c1885

$220-280   **ATK**

A German 'Saxonia' lock-stitch sewing machine, probably made by Gustav Winselmann GmbH.

c1895

$120-180   **ATK**

A domestic sewing machine, probably German, retailed in London by 'American Sewing Machine Co.'

c1900

$150-200   **ATK**

An extremely rare German 'Mignon' sewing machine, made by Schröder of Darmstadt, complete with original wooden box.

Only a very few examples of this comparatively early machine are known to exist, with this example retaining many of its bright, gilt transfers.

c1865

$3,000-5,000   **ATK**

An English sewing machine, by Jones, inscribed "As supplied to HRH the Princess of Wales".

c1890

$300-400   **ATK**

An American sewing machine, by Willcox & Gibbs, popular early version with wooden base and glass tension bar, inscribed with patent date "22nd March 1864".

c1870

$300-400   **ATK**

A rare miniature 'Moldacot' lock-stitch sewing machine, with handcrank and shuttle.

The pocket-sized Moldacot was patented by S.A. Rosenthal of Berlin in 1885 and was made in both England and Germany from the late 1880s.

c1890

$400-600   **ATK**

An English domestic sewing machine, by Taylor, previously bronzed, an unusual and desirable early example.

During the 1870s, this attractive 'Art Nouveau' styled machine was offered by S. Smith & Sons of Soho Bazaar, London for £4 4s ($6).

c1870

$500-700   **ATK**

FIND OUT MORE...

'Antique Needlework Tools and Embroideries', by Nerylla Taunton, published by Antique Collectors Club, 1997.

The Textile Museum, Vadianstrasse 2, 9000 St. Gallen, Switzerland, www.textilemuseum.ch

COLLECTORS' NOTES

■ Sheet music is collected as much for its decorative cover as for its musical content and is popular due to the quantities available and affordable prices.

■ Demand for sheet music grew during the 19thC and, as color printing became cheaper, so the designs became more detailed.

■ Hand-illustrated covers reached their peak during the late 19thC but had been replaced by pictures or

photographs of the performers by the 1930s and 1940s as their public images eclipsed that of the composers.

■ Due to the vast quantities produced, very few examples of sheet music are rare. However, the quality of the paper was often poor so condition is still important. Look for complete copies with crisp colors and no tears or rips.

A Grieg's "Holberg-Suite" sheet music book.

12in (30.5cm) wide

$2-4   **CANT**

A "Sunset Trail" sheet music book.

1936   *12.25in (31cm) wide*

$2-4   **CANT**

An "Oh, What a Beautiful Mornin'" sheet music book, from "Oklahoma".

1943   *11in (28cm) wide*

$3-5   **CANT**

An "I Got The Sun in the Morning" sheet music book, from "Annie Get Your Gun".

1946   *11in (28cm) wide*

$3-5   **CANT**

An "Easter Parade" sheet music book.

1947   *11in (28cm) wide*

$5-7   **CANT**

A Mario Lanza "Because You're Mine" sheet music book.

1952   *11in (28cm) wide*

$5-7   **CANT**

A Frank Sinatra "I'm Walking Behind You" sheet music book.

1953   *11in (28cm) wide*

$6-9   **CANT**

A "(How Much Is) That Doggie In The Window?" sheet music book.

1953   *11in (28cm) wide*

$2-4   **CANT**

A Johnny Mathis "Misty" sheet music book.
1954   11in (28cm) wide
$2-4   **CANT**

A "My Fair Lady" sheet music book.
1956   11in (28cm) wide
$3-5   **CANT**

A "The Sound of Music" sheet music book.
1959   11in (28cm) wide
$6-9   **CANT**

A Carpenters "(They Long to be) Close to
You" sheet music book.
1963   11in (28cm) wide
$6-9   **CANT**

An "If I Were a Rich Man" sheet music
book, from "Fiddler on the Roof".
1964   11in (28cm) wide
$3-5   **CANT**

A Tom Jones "The Green Green Grass of
Home" sheet music book.
1965   11in (28cm) wide
$3-5   **CANT**

A "Day by Day" sheet music book, from
"Godspell".
1971   11in (28cm) wide
$2-4   **CANT**

A Roberta Flack "Killing Me Softly With His
Song" sheet music book.
1972   11in (28cm) wide
$4-6   **CANT**

A Brotherhood of Man "Save Your Kisses
for Me" sheet music book.
*This song won the Eurovision Song Contest
for England in 1976.*
1976   11in (28cm) wide
$3-6   **CANT**

SMOKING ACCESSORIES

COLLECTORS' NOTES

■ Unlike other smoking-related collectibles, many non-smokers collect ashtrays. Ashtrays became a popular collectible at the beginning of the 20thC when tire manufacturers in the US started to produce them as advertising gimmicks. These form the base of many collections today.

■ Production of promotional ashtrays stopped during WWII but began again in earnest in the 1950s. Those made prior to WWII are highly sought-after, particularly ceramic ashtrays from the 1930s.

■ As well as advertising products, many examples are connected to travel and come from hotels, airlines, and cruise liners. Look for designs that are typical of the period, and those made by companies that no longer exist such as BOAC and TWA.

■ Many ashtrays cross over to other collectible areas and this can help to push the price up. Examples that belonged to or are associated with famous smokers, such as Orson Welles, are also desirable.

■ Ashtrays are generally mass-produced and in everyday use, so condition is vital. Check carefully for chips and cracks.

A 1930s S.S. Santa Paula cast bronze ashtray, in the shape of a seahorse.

5.5in (14cm) long

$220-280 — **CW**

A French ceramic ashtray, in the form of a ship's funnel.

3.25in (8cm) high

$120-180 — **CW**

A 1930s Linea C ship's funnel ashtray.

3.5in (9cm) high

$50-70 — **CW**

A T.G. Green Gresley ware Orient Line ceramic ashtray.

7.25in (18.5cm) wide

$80-120 — **CW**

A 1930s French 'jadeite' glass French Line ashtray.

3.25in (8cm) wide

$80-120 — **CW**

A Swedish-American Line ceramic ashtray, by Lagun of Gustavsberg, with ship-shaped silver inlay.

6in (15.5cm) wide

$180-220 — **CW**

$280-320 — **CW**

A pair of Royal Worcester presentation ashtrays, showing the 'Orestes' and 'Agamemnon' for the Blue Funnel Line Ltd, in original gift box.

Box 8.5in (21.5cm) wide

CW

A 1930s Art Deco Mobil Oil cast bronze ashtray, with Pegasus model.

5.75in (14.5cm) high

$280-320 CW

A 1950s German ceramic "Gebr. Vermeulen" advertising ashtray.

4.25in (11cm) wide

$50-80 CW

A 1940s Rookwood Pottery ashtray, showing a Woodburn 7895, the back stamped "Walter E. Schott Willy's Distributor Cash for Cars. 2320 Gilbert Ave. Cincinnati Ohio".

6.75in (17cm) wide

$400-600 CW

A 1950s square glass Vespa ashtray.

3.5in (9cm) wide

$100-150 CW

A 1960s glass Travette camper coach advertising ashtray.

6.75in (17.5cm) wide

$100-150 CW

A 1960s ceramic "Pontiac Fine Car" ashtray, the base stamped "Pontiac Fleet Sales".

6in (15cm) high

$100-150 CW

A 1960s Rose Cutri Pontiac enameled tin advertising ashtray.

6in (15cm) wide

$100-150 CW

A 1970s Canadian Georgian China Ferrari 410 ceramic ashtray.

8.75in (22cm) wide

$80-120 CW

A "Try The Thunderbird" metal ashtray.

Despite this being an American car, the steering wheel is shown here on the right-hand side.

c1990 *5.5in (14cm) wide*

$10-15 CW

A brass "MCMXX ANVERS" Olympics commemorative ashtray.

The 1920 Olympics were held in Antwerp, Belgium. It was the first time that the Olympic oath was recited and also the first time the Olympic flag, with its famous five colored rings, was flown.

1920   4in (10cm) high

$220-280   **CW**

A 1924 Paris Olympics commemorative pressed brass ashtray.

1924   5in (13cm) wide

$180-220   **CW**

A 1924 Paris Olympics metal ashtray, showing a boxer.

1924   5.5in (14cm) long

$220-280   **CW**

A 1936 Berlin Olympics commemorative clear glass ashtray.

1936   4.5in (11.5cm) wide

$280-320   **CW**

A rare 1950s Cleveland Indians milk glass ashtray, one of only 100 made.

7.25in (18.5cm) long

$220-280   **CW**

A German ceramic soccer stadium-shaped advertising ashtray.

Bild am Sonntag is a popular German Sunday paper. This ashtray advertises their coverage of the previous day's soccer.

7.5in (19.5cm) long

$70-100   **CW**

A rare Washington Pottery Football Association "World Cup Willie 1966" ashtray.

1966   4.75in (12cm) wide

$400-600   **CW**

A "Mexico 70" plastic football ashtray.

1970   4.25in (11cm) wide

$80-120   **CW**

A Faenza "Italia 90" ceramic ashtray.

1990   4.75in (12cm) wide

$60-90   **CW**

A 1920s Players advertising ashtray.

5in (12.5cm) wide

$100-150   BS

A 1920s Gilbeys advertising ashtray.

5in (12.5cm) wide

$40-60   BS

A 1920s Johnnie Walker advertising copper ashtray.

5in (12.5cm) wide

$80-120   BS

A 1920s Chester Northgate Ales brass ashtray.

4.5in (11.5cm) diam

$10-15   DH

A 1950s "Players Finest Virginia Weights" ceramic ashtray.

4.75in (12cm) diam

$8-12   DH

A 1950s ceramic Electrolux advertising ashtray, made by Sculptural Promotions Inc. of New York.

6.5in (16.5cm) wide

$60-90   BB

A 1950s "Black & White Scotch Whisky" ceramic advertising ashtray, by James Green & Nephew Ltd.

5.25in (13.5cm) wide

$80-120   CW

A 1930s Michelin Bakelite advertising ashtray.

5in (12.5cm) high

$120-180   DH

A 1950s German Ornamin Presswerk melamine advertising ashtray for Pepsi Cola.

4.25in (11cm) wide

$100-150   CW

A 1950s Bass ceramic ashtray.

5.25in (13cm) wide

$7-10   DH

SMOKING ACCESSORIES

COLLECTORS' NOTES

■ Smoking accessories are hotly sought after, even though smoking is becoming rapidly more and more unfashionable. Lighters are perhaps the largest and most popular area and are divided into pocket and table lighters. Although many have already reached high values, they may yet have some way to go, particularly good quality table and integral compact case lighters. Other items, such as cases, tobacco jars, and cigar cutters are also collectible. Look for quality in terms of material and form, and notable makers.

■ Dunhill lighters are the most desirable, due to the high quality of their manufacture and materials, and the range available. Collectors tend to prefer the liquid filled lighters of the 1920s-50s, but certain later examples in fine quality materials or with hidden features such as watches are also popular. Also look for Zippo lighters which are generally more affordable.

A Zippo 'Bahamas' souvenir pocket lighter.

c1970   2.25in (5.5cm) high

$30-50   **ML**

A Dunhill 'Tinder Pistol' table lighter, with wood handle and liquid-fueled mechanism, marked beneath "Prov.Pat 19273/34, Regd. No.794093".

There is also a 1960s gas-filled version which is rare.

c1940

$220-280   **DN**

A Dunhill 'Aquarium' table lighter, the perspex body of shaped-oblong outline and decorated in reverse with fish amidst aquatic foliage and enclosing the liquid-fueled plated-brass mechanism, the hinged wick cover signed "Dunhill".

The quasi-kitsch 'Aquarium' lighter has become an immensely collectible model in recent years, partly due to the large number of variations available in terms of size and type of wildlife. Fish are the most common, but rarer birds and even an ultra-rare racehorse have been depicted in the reverse carved and painted perspex panels.

c1955   4in (10cm) long

$1,500-2,000   **DN**

A 1960s Swank table lighter, in the form of a television.

4in (10cm) wide

$25-35   **GAZE**

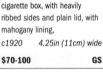

A small Swedish silver cigar or cigarette box, with heavily ribbed sides and plain lid, with mahogany lining,

c1920   4.25in (11cm) wide

$70-100   **GS**

A half-size or small Zippo lighter, with plain sterling case, the base simply marked "ZIPPO STERLING".

Zippo were founded in 1932 in Brandford, Pennsylvania and have produced millions of their reliable and simply operated pocket lighters. They have become immensely collectible and most can be dated by the patent number and dot and slash markings on the base.

1960   2.25in (5.5cm) high

$120-180   **ML**

An Arts & Crafts style copper cigarette box, with rivet decoration to the fish tail hinges and bracket feet.

7.5in (19cm) wide

$60-90   **CLV**

A Dunhill 'Bumper' or tankard table lighter, with engraved initials, with a thumb-piece activating liquid mechanism, marked "Reg. Des. Appl. No. 861972".

c1950   3.5in (9cm) high

$80-120   **DN**

A CLOSER LOOK AT A TOBACCO JAR

This jar was made by Royal Winton, a notable British factory well-known for their transfer-decorated chintzwares and quality ceramics.

The lid is held on with a sprung arm mechanism that seals the jar making it airtight to preserve the tobacco – as such many can still be used today.

It was made for high quality historic pipe maker and retailer Comoy's of London, founded in 1879 by Henry Comoy.

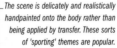

The scene is delicately and realistically handpainted onto the body rather than being applied by transfer. These sorts of 'sporting' themes are popular.

A Royal Winton handpainted tobacco jar, for Comoy's of London, decorated with a scene of woodcocks in a field.

1920-1930   5in (13cm) high

$280-320   **BAD**

An elegant porcelain smoke dispeller, in the form of a kneeling female figure.

After being plugged into an electric supply, an element inside the dish heated perfumed liquid and dispersed pleasantly smelling vapors around the room. The unusual form of a semi-clad 1920s flapper girl is well modeled, well painted and would have appealed greatly to gentlemen smokers of the day.

c1950   8.5in (22cm) high

$80-120   **ATK**

A meerschaum type pipe, carved with a dog chasing a monkey, in fitted case, with retailer name "Ludwig Hartmann Wien", losses.

$180-220   **ROS**

A Japanese Bonzo dog pottery matchbox holder, the blue and milky white glazed cartoon character seated beside a floral molded rectangular trough.

4in (10cm) wide

$120-180   **CHEF**

A European majolica match holder, in the form of a recumbent goat with panniers on its back, raised on a rockwork base.

4.75in (12cm) long

$80-120   **ROS**

An American Unger Bros. sterling fob cigar cutter, with grotesque mask.

For more information about Unger Brothers, see the first page of the 'Hatpins' section in this book.

1.75in (4.5cm) long

$150-200   **CAC**

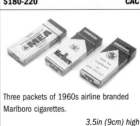

A 14ct gold cigar cutter, with inset cabochons.

1.5in (3.5cm) long

$180-220   **CAC**

Three packets of 1960s airline branded Marlboro cigarettes.

3.5in (9cm) high

$15-25 each   **DH**

SNOWDOMES

COLLECTORS' NOTES

■ Snowdomes have been made since the late 19thC, although specific dates and manufacturers are unknown. Examples from this period can be identified by their materials, such as glass, ceramic, and marble and, as a consequence, their heavy weight.

■ Production grew during the 1920s, with religious themes becoming the most common. The explosion of cheap plastic production methods after this time led to a wider range of designs and themes.

■ Snowdome collecting became popular in the late 1940s, and as workers became used to paid vacations and cheaper travel costs, the demand for holiday souvenirs grew.

■ Europe and the US were the main manufacturers until the 1970s, when a number of Asian countries started to produce snowdomes. These often copy existing designs with small changes to details to avoid copyright laws, and in the main are of a lesser quality.

■ Collecting became popular again in the 1980s, and in response manufacturers began making high quality pieces in traditional materials such as glass and wood, as well as novelty items like snowdome watches and T-shirts.

■ Look for early pieces in good condition and unusual shapes from any period, especially those with a surround or moving parts inside. Advertising snowdomes are always popular as they often have a crossover appeal.

A late 1990s South Park advertising snowdome, for the Comedy Channel.

This snowdome was made exclusively for executives at the Comedy Channel and was not available for retail.

5in (12.5cm) high

$40-60　　　　　　　　　　　　　　　　　**NWC**

Three 1970s Mr Men snowdomes.

2.25in (5.5cm) high

$20-30 each　　　　　　　　　　　　**NWC**

A 1990s Nickelodeon advertising snowdome.

3in (7.5cm) high

$20-30　　　　**NWC**

A "Die Hard 2" advertising snowdome.

c1990　　2.25in (5.5cm) high

$30-50　　　　**NWC**

A late 1970s/early 1980s Jerry glass snowdome, by Rosarium.

4in (10cm) high

$15-20　　　　**NWC**

A Media Markt advertising snowdome, made in Germany.

2.5in (6.5cm) high

$30-50　　　　**NWC**

An HBO Couch Potatoes advertising snowdome.

3in (7.5cm) high

$20-30　　　　**NWC**

A 1960s Welsh souvenir snowdome.

6in (15cm) high

$15-25 NWC

A 1970s/80s London Bridge souvenir calendar snowdome.

4in (10cm) high

$20-30 NWC

A 1980s souvenir World Trade Center, New York City snowdome.

3.25in (8.5cm) high

$15-25 NWC

An early 1990s Lyon souvenir snowdome, with 'Lyon' upside down.

2in (5cm) high

$25-35 NWC

A 1990s Salzburg souvenir snowdome, made in Germany.

Snowdomes made in Germany can be identified by their fine snow flakes.

2in (5cm) high

$8-12 NWC

A 1990s Washington DC souvenir snowdome.

2in (5cm) high

$8-12 NWC

A 1990s Taronga Zoo, New South Wales souvenir snowdome.

2in (5cm) high

$12-18 NWC

A 1990s Brussels souvenir snowdome.

3in (7.5cm) high

$8-12 NWC

A 1990s London Bridge souvenir snowdome, produced missing the bridge.

These 'rejects' can make an amusing collecting area of their own.

2.25in (5.5cm) high

$25-35 NWC

FIND OUT MORE...

'Collector's Guide to Snowdomes: Identification & Values', *Helene Guarnaccia, Collector Books 1993.*

'Collectible Snowdomes', *Lélie Carnot, Flammarion, 2002.*

SPORTING MEMORABILIA

COLLECTORS' NOTES

■ Away from balls, bats, uniforms, and cards, other items of baseball memorabilia remain popular, either forming or complimenting many collections. Paper ephemera, publications, and advertisements can be inexpensive and are often colorful, with attractive visuals that also reflect the design styles of the day. Many show interesting period details such as players, uniforms, and equipment – those with notable players or teams will usually fetch more, especially if signed.

■ Condition is important so look for clean, bright, and undamaged examples, especially from the first few decades of the 20thC. If the product or brand promoted on certain advertising pieces is also collectible, then competition and thus values are likely to increase. Yearbooks, kit catalogs and souvenir books can make excellent reference resources as well as displaying excellent artwork. As many were used and became worn, they can be rare today, especially early examples from the 1900s-1920s.

■ Gloves are a highly collectible area. The maker, player's name, date, and especially the condition are important indicators to value. The condition of the palm stamping and the leather as a whole should be considered and gloves should ideally retain their manufacturer's label. Older gloves are hard to find in near mint condition. Prewar gloves can be recognized by their shape and often, in the case of fielder's gloves, by their laced fingers.

A World Series Beech Nut tobacco tri-fold advertising display, cardboard fold-out display picturing Yankee Stadium during the 1926 World Series between the Yankees and Cardinals, retaining very strong overall color and surface with some minor wear mostly along the edges, joint lines have been reinforced.

As well as the very large size, appealing panoramic scene, World Series connections and bright condition, tobacco advertising is a popular collecting area.

1926   61in (155cm) long

$5,000-6,000   **HA**

A Chew Honest Scrap baseball tobacco advertising sign, cardboard color lithograph sign with comical baseball scene on front advertising five cent scrap tobacco, has some wear to top edge and damage.

c1905   13in (33cm) high

$200-300   **HA**

A 1940s/50s Walter Johnson Carstairs Whiskey cardboard advertising sign, die-cut cardboard sign features photographic image of Johnson pitching in center, retaining original unused adhesive strips on back, very clean for this issue.

19in (48.5cm) high

$400-500   **HA**

A Pittsburgh Pirates Iron City Beer advertising display, large paper on board sign depicting the World Champion Pirates including Roberto Clemente, Bill Mazeroski, and Danny Murtaugh, has some areas of damage.

1960   34in (86.5cm) long

$180-220   **HA**

A 'Safe at Home' lobby card, featuring Mickey Mantle, Roger Maris, and Casey Stengel, color card pictures batting tips being given by the three Yankee Stars, edge wear.

1962   11in (28cm) long

$120-180   **HA**

A 'Safe at Home' lobby card, featuring Mickey Mantle, Roger Maris, and Casey Stengel, color card pictures in batting stance at center, Yankee manager in cameo at right.

1962   14in (35.5cm) long

$120-180   **HA**

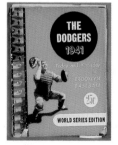

A "The Dodgers" souvenir book, yearbook style book with player photos, spine is separated.

1941

$25-35   **HA**

A CLOSER LOOK AT PRESS GUIDE

This was the first guide issued by the team and was created by their publicity director Larry Shenk in response to other teams who had produced guides of their own.

This is one of only a handful known to exist and is in excellent, original condition with all its 58 pages.

The Phillies experienced a legendary collapse in this season making this a must for collectors of the team's history.

Only 300 examples were ever produced, each having a cover hand-colored by Shenk's wife Julie – following this all guides were mass-produced.

A scarce 1964 Philadelphia Phillies press guide.
1964

$2,500-3,500 HA

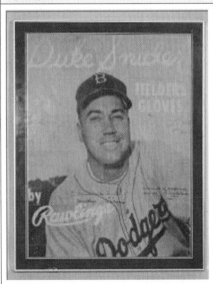

A 1950s Duke Snider autographed Rawlings glove advertising poster, featuring image of Snider in Brooklyn uniform endorsing Rawlings fielder's gloves, signed at bottom, "Edwin "Duke" Snider #4 Brooklyn Dodgers" and "The Duke of Flatbush 407 HR's 11 World Series HOF 1980", some damage, matted and framed.

36in (91.5cm) long

$220-280 HA

A New York Mets Official Yearbook.
1971 *11in (28cm) high*

$40-50 VSC

A rare New York National League Baseball Club official program and score card.

The following year saw the 1964-65 New York World's Fair which interestingly used the same colors seen on this program. These were also the colors used for the 1939 event.

1963 *9.25in (23.5cm) high*

$55-65 VSC

A 'Big Mitt' child's school composition book, some of the ruled pages with scraps.

10in (25.5cm) high

$100-150 VSC

A Babe Ruth composition, early children's notebook with image of Ruth batting on front cover, dated 1921 inside along with period notations.

1921

$550-650 HA

A Brooklyn Dodgers yearbook.
1955

$60-90 HA

An "Open Road Magazine", with Ted Williams on the cover, rare vintage publication with mailing label.

1950

$25-35 HA

SPORTING MEMORABILIA

A P. Goldsmith & Sons 'Goldsmith Official League Ball' baseball scorecard.

6.25in (16cm) high

$55-65   **VSC**

A St Louis Sticker Co. baseball sticker.

c1920   *6in (15cm) high*

$120-180   **VSC**

A 'Lucky Dog Score Card', with views of the Draper Maynard Building to the reverse.

6.5in (16.5cm) high

$35-45   **VSC**

A 1908 Chicago Cubs pocket schedule, patriotic-themed cover with photo of Frank Chance.

1908

$280-320   **HA**

A rare Redless baseball color-lithographed postcard.

c1920   *5.5in (14cm) wide*

$70-100   **VSC**

A Reach celluloid scorer, with eight dials, labeled "Reach Scoring tablet" on the front and with the Reach logo on the reverse.

4in (10cm) long

$40-60   **HA**

A scarce Ebbets Field celluloid mirror, picturing image of the crown jewel of Brooklyn, celluloid has some typical surface scratching retaining a very strong image and clean overall toning, original mirror remains intact with only some light foxing spots.

c1920   *2.75in (7cm) long*

$3,000-5,000   **HA**

An early 'Take Your Base' color lithographed baseball postcard with embossed cherub and hearts.

5.5in (14cm) high

$60-90   **VSC**

A 1914 color lithographed baseball calendar, mounted on card, with gilt embossing.

6in (15cm) high

$180-220   **VSC**

A 1920s Kiki Cuyler brown and beige leather buckle-back catcher's mitt.

9.5in (24cm) high

$150-250 VSC

A GSW 'MD' of Philadelphia dark brown leather baseball glove, with stamped marks to palm.

c1920   9.25in (23.5cm) high

$220-280 VSC

A late 1940s tan leather hand-formed baseball glove, with palm stampings for Elmer Riddle.

8.25in (21cm) high

$80-120 VSC

A Victor, Wright & Ditson 'Amateur' white leather baseball glove.

The fact that it is in white leather and good condition makes this glove more valuable.

c1915   8.75in (22cm) high

$300-400 VSC

A CLOSER LOOK AT A BASEBALL GLOVE

Spalding is a renowned and much sought-after name.

It has full webbing between the thumb and finger.

Compared to other gloves, it has a vertically elongated form, showing an early date and making it rarer.

It retains its button and Spalding label and is generally in excellent game worn condition.

An early Spalding leather baseball glove.

c1900   9.25in (23.5cm) high

$800-1,200 VSC

A Goldsmith brown leather baseball glove, with label and stamping.

c1915   9in (23cm) high

$200-300 VSC

A Tryon Co. of Philadelphia black leather Reach basemitt.

c1905   8.25in (21cm) high

$100-150 VSC

A baseball cigar box, lidded mahogany box with baseball decor on lid and interior, label featuring crossed bat and ball decor surrounded by a baseball belt, retains majority of tax stamp and has some general age wear.

c1885

$350-450 HA

A 1940s J. DeBeer & Son of Albany NY baseball in box, with color printed graphics, unopened.

3in (7.5cm) high

$60-70 VSC

A Yankee Stadium seat, blue painted cast iron and wood single chair, includes Winston Cigarettes premium envelope with brass commemorative plaque.

$2,000-3,000 HA

A Mickey Mantle's Backyard baseball stick, by L.C. Toy Distribution, in mint condition with original packaging.

22.5in (57cm) high

$220-280 SOTT

A Bob Lemon baseball pin.

1.75in (4.5cm) diam

$12-18 HA

A Ted Williams baseball pin.

c1940 1in (3cm) diam

$80-120 BCAC

A woven straw hat, with rare plastic Mets player sewn on.

These hats were worn at the opening games for the Mets. It is rare to find one complete with the plastic figure.

10.75in (27cm) wide

$70-100 SOTT

A rare Winchester 'goggle eye' baseball catcher's mask or cage.

Collectible firearm manufacturer Winchester made sporting goods for only a very short period during the 1920s so this would also appeal to a Winchester collector. If this mask was not made by Winchester and did not have its label, the value would be around $500.

c1925 10.25in (26cm) high

$850-950 VSC

A very rare 1960s Lady Mets painted ceramic baseball head figure.

6in (15cm) high

$250-350 SOTT

A 'Ken-Wel Fall & Winter 1924' athletic equipment catalog, with American footballer image to front cover.

1924   *9in (23cm) high*

$100-150   **VSC**

A Wilson Athletic Equipment Fall and Winter 1927-28 catalog, with color lithographed cover.

1927   *7.75in (19.5cm) high*

$70-100   **VSC**

A 1930s American Football Valentine's card, the arm giving a kicking action and moving the boy's body.

9.75in (24.5cm) high

$25-35   **VSC**

A University of Pennsylvania Football Team color lithographed photographic 'scorecard' postcard for 1908.

1908   *5.5in (14cm) wide*

$150-200   **VSC**

A 'The Ellery Arms Company' of San Francisco athletic equipment catalog, with football player on the color lithographed cover.

1925   *7.75in (19.5cm) high*

$80-120   **VSC**

NEW YORK JETS vs. HOUSTON OILERS
Shea Stadium   October 20, 1969   Official Program 75¢

A New York Jets vs Houston Oilers official program, at Shea Stadium, Oct 20, 1969.

11.25in (28.5cm) high

$20-30   **VSC**

A Thanksgiving football-themed color lithographed and gilt postcard.

5.5in (14cm) high

$70-100   **VSC**

Two Army vs. Navy football tickets for Franklin Field, University of Pennsylvania, for 1932 and 1933.

Largest 4.5in (11.5cm) wide

$70-100   **VSC**

A 'Goldsmith Fall & Winter Sports' athletic equipment catalog for the 1926-27 season, with child American football players to the cover.

1926   *8.75in (22.5cm) high*

$100-150   **VSC**

COLLECTORS' NOTES

- Golf originated in Scotland and developed slowly between the 15th and 17th centuries. By the late 19th century, it had become very popular.

- Pieces prior to this period are rarely found and most equipment dates from the late 19th century onward.

- Golf clubs and balls tend to form the upper end of the market, but a wide range of merchandize and memorabilia with a golfing theme is available, including ceramics, prints and paintings, books and photographs.

- Collectors tend to focus on the historical aspect of the game, looking for pieces that depict old equipment, courses or clothing as well as famous players.

A long nose putter, indistinctly stamped, some later whipping and later grip, re-shafted.

$500-700   **L&T**

A center shafted putter, possibly with later head.

$180-220   **L&T**

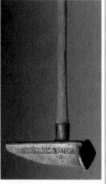

A Hardinghams patent putter, the face scored with 20 vertical lines, "C - V" markings to the back of the plate, later shaft, grip lacking, some damage.

$6,000-9,000   **L&T**

An early and rare sand iron, with large concave face, hosel with deep nicking.

c1830

$6,000-9,000   **L&T**

An 18thC blacksmith-forged iron, with nicked face and replacement grip.

c1750

$12,000-18,000   **L&T**

A Spalding Gold Medal No. 4 Jigger, with hammer stamp and "Patented Jan 1914" and "Patented Aug 29, 1916", with perforated 'Lard' shaft and hand-punched dot face.

c1920

$2,200-2,800   **L&T**

A Banner spade mashie, with 'brick pattern face'.

$220-280   **L&T**

A rut niblick, stamped "Harrods Ltd., London", with good original leather grip and under listing.

$80-120   **MM**

A Muhammad Ali photograph.

$15-25   GAZE

A signed Frank Bruno HP Sauce publicity postcard.

6in (15cm) wide

$15-25   LCA

A World Heavyweight Championship Joe Frazier v Muhammad Ali souvenir edition program, 8th March 1971, together with a scarce large lapel badge for the fight.

$100-150   MM

A World Heavyweight Championship Joe Frazier v Muhammad Ali program, 8th March 1971.

$320-380   MM

A Muhammad Ali v Joe Bugner ticket, 14th February 1973, for a $100 ringside seat.

$220-280   MM

A 'Bang - Boxing's Weekly Wallop' magazine, with Joe Louis on the cover, for week ending January 23rd 1937.

9in (23cm) high

$40-60   VSC

A signed Stirling Moss publicity postcard.

6in (15cm) high

$25-35   LCA

A signed Damon Hill publicity photograph, in Arrows-Yamaha Formula 1 racing car.

10in (25.5cm) wide

$60-90   LCA

A signed Jonah Lomu publicity photograph, in New Zealand All Blacks strip.

10in (25.5cm) high

$50-70   LCA

STANHOPES

COLLECTORS' NOTES

■ Stanhopes are small, often utilitarian, objects set with a tiny lens, when held to light and close to the eye, the lens reveals a tiny photograph. The microphotograph itself is no bigger than the size of a full stop, but is magnified when viewed through the lens.

■ Three people contributed to the development of Stanhopes – J.B. Dancer, inventor of microphotography, Lord Stanhope, inventor of the lens and René Dagron, who first combined the two and set the result into novelty objects, thereby popularising the technique.

■ Mass-produced on a rapidly increasing scale from the early 1860s onwards, most were sold as inexpensive souvenirs of places or as commemorative objects for events and exhibitions.

■ From the mid-1860s, Dagron exported thousands of lenses from his factory in Gex, France. People could send him photographs, which he would miniaturize and mount on a lens making them ready for insertion into any object. Exported lenses were marked 'Made in France' or with Dagron's company name.

■ The objects into which the lens was inserted are usually made from inexpensive materials such as bone, vegetable ivory bog oak or pot metals. Plastic was used after the 1920s. Sewing items, charms and penholders worn on a chain predominate.

■ Scenic views are more common than dated historical personalities and events, which tend to have a higher value. Erotic subjects fetch higher prices still.

■ The 20th century saw a decline in inventiveness and range, but Stanhope novelties were still produced for commemorative events, such as the accession of Queen Elizabeth II in 1953, and for advertising purposes. Demand and production declined in the 1960s and ceased completely in 1972.

■ Condition is important. Primarily, the lens must be present and the novelty should not be damaged. The image should be visible and sharp – crazing, bubbling of the gum or scratches reduce value. Never immerse examples in water as this can destroy the adhesive between the image and lens. Also avoid sharp knocks, which can also separate the image from the lens.

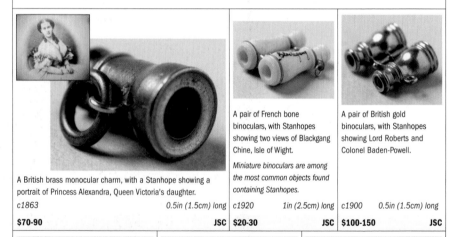

A British brass monocular charm, with a Stanhope showing a portrait of Princess Alexandra, Queen Victoria's daughter.

c1863   0.5in (1.5cm) long

$70-90   **JSC**

A pair of French bone binoculars, with Stanhopes showing two views of Blackgang Chine, Isle of Wight.

Miniature binoculars are among the most common objects found containing Stanhopes.

c1920   1in (2.5cm) long

$20-30   **JSC**

A pair of British gold binoculars, with Stanhopes showing Lord Roberts and Colonel Baden-Powell.

c1900   0.5in (1.5cm) long

$100-150   **JSC**

A pair of British mother-of-pearl and brass binoculars, with Stanhopes showing twelve views of Scarborough, Yorkshire.

c1890   0.75in (2cm) long

$80-120   **JSC**

A British metal and peach stone fob pencil, the pull set with Stanhope with six views of Olney, Buckinghamshire.

c1890   1.75in (4.5cm) high

$100-150   **JSC**

A British wooden fob pencil in the form of a bellows, with Stanhope showing six views of the Isles of Scilly.

c1920   2in (5cm) long

$60-90   **JSC**

A British metal fob pencil in the form of an axe, with a Stanhope showing six views of the Isle of Wight.

c1900   2.25in (5.5cm) long

$70-100   **JSC**

A French red-stained bone crucifix, with a Stanhope showing five views of Rome and Pope Pius XI.

Most crosses, such as this one, are parts of larger necklaces or rosaries which have now been broken or lost.

c1930   2in (5cm) high

$40-60   **JSC**

A French silver religious pendant, with a Stanhope showing eight views of Paris.

c1890   1in (2.5cm) high

$50-80   **JSC**

An Irish bog oak Celtic cross charm, with a Stanhope showing four views of Killarney.

Bog oak, or 'Irish ebony', is made from trees that fell into peat bogs in prehistoric times and were darkened.

c1890   1.5in (3.5cm) high

$70-100   **JSC**

A British silver lantern charm, with a Stanhope showing four views of Exeter, Devon.

Although the piece is only 0.75in (2cm) high, the close-up shot shows the even tinier set of images in the middle of the lens.

c1900   0.75in (2cm) high

$50-80   **JSC**

An American gilt metal lady's boot charm, with a Stanhope showing a view of the Bunker Hill Monument.

c1890   0.75in (2cm) high

$70-100   **JSC**

A British agate 'book', with a Stanhope showing a view of Shanklin Chine, Isle of Wight.

c1890   1in (2.5cm) long

$70-100   **JSC**

A British silver metal articulated fish charm, with a Stanhope showing extracts from the Torah.

c1900   1.5in (3.5cm) long

$70-100   **JSC**

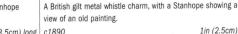

A British gilt metal whistle charm, with a Stanhope showing a view of an old painting.

c1890   1in (2.5cm) long

$70-100   **JSC**

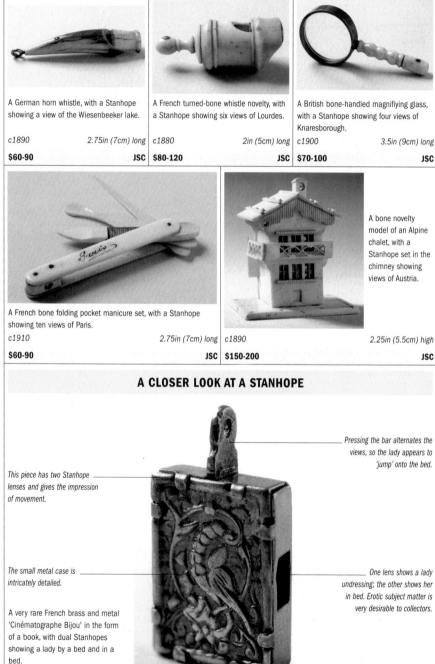

A German horn whistle, with a Stanhope showing a view of the Wiesenbeeker lake.

c1890   2.75in (7cm) long

$60-90   JSC

A French turned-bone whistle novelty, with a Stanhope showing six views of Lourdes.

c1880   2in (5cm) long

$80-120   JSC

A British bone-handled magnifiying glass, with a Stanhope showing four views of Knaresborough.

c1900   3.5in (9cm) long

$70-100   JSC

A French bone folding pocket manicure set, with a Stanhope showing ten views of Paris.

c1910   2.75in (7cm) long

$60-90   JSC

A bone novelty model of an Alpine chalet, with a Stanhope set in the chimney showing views of Austria.

c1890   2.25in (5.5cm) high

$150-200   JSC

A CLOSER LOOK AT A STANHOPE

This piece has two Stanhope lenses and gives the impression of movement.

Pressing the bar alternates the views, so the lady appears to 'jump' onto the bed.

The small metal case is intricately detailed.

One lens shows a lady undressing; the other shows her in bed. Erotic subject matter is very desirable to collectors.

A very rare French brass and metal 'Cinématographe Bijou' in the form of a book, with dual Stanhopes showing a lady by a bed and in a bed.

c1890   1in (2.5cm) high

$300-400   JSC

A French stamped brass perfume flagon, with a Stanhope in the stopper showing four views of Napoleon's tomb.

c1890   3.5in (9cm) high

$120-180   **JSC**

A British stamped brass oval perfume bottle, with a Stanhope in the stopper showing seven views of Ayr.

c1890   2.25in (6cm) high

$120-180   **JSC**

A British engraved metal vesta case with inset compass, and a Stanhope showing six views of the Giants' Causeway.

c1900   1.75in (4.5cm) high

$100-150   **JSC**

A French carved bone combined measuring tape and pin cushion, with a Stanhope showing a religious scene.

c1870   2.25in (6cm) high

$120-180   **JSC**

A French bone measuring tape, with a Stanhope showing a view of Mont St. Michel.

c1900   1.5in (4cm) high

$80-120   **JSC**

An Alpine carved wood thimble or needle case, with a Stanhope showing a view of Fueller.

c1890   2in (5cm) high

$100-150   **JSC**

A French vegetable ivory thimble and case, the case with a Stanhope showing four views of Ireland.

Vegetable ivory is carved from the coroso or tagua nut, which is the fruit of a tropical palm.

c1880   2in (5cm) long

$120-180   **JSC**

A French mother-of-pearl and velvet pin holder, with a Stanhope showing a view of Paris.

The Stanhope lens is inset into the center of the embroidered roundel.

c1870   1.5in (4cm) high

$150-200   **JSC**

A pair of German 'Universal Pocket Scissors', with a Stanhope showing German views.

These ingenious scissors have eighteen separate functions. The lens is mounted on one arm.

c1900   4.5in (11.5cm) long

$120-180   **JSC**

COLLECTORS' NOTES

■ Teddy bears have grown to be as important to the collecting world as they were to the children who owned them. Steiff are still the most recognized and valuable maker but others, such as the German firm Bing, British makers Farnell and Merrythought and American maker Ideal, can fetch similarly large sums. Try to buy examples in good condition, or those by noted makers, but also look for those with 'eye-appeal'.

■ As prewar teddies become increasingly scarce and valuable, fine quality postwar bears and modern limited edition bears by makers such as Steiff have begun to interest collectors, although the market for modern bears has perhaps yet to reach its peak.

■ To help identify bears, study images and books, but preferably the bears themselves as the shape of the head, limbs, wear, and type of materials used will help you work out who made your bear and when. As with all high value markets, reproductions and fakes do exist, so learn to spot signs of intended wear. Always smell a bear as the smell of years of love cannot yet be faked!

A Bing tumbler bear, with stitched woolen nose and claws, boot button eyes.

German maker Bing were very well-known for their mechanical bears, which are rare today. Their tumbler bears have typically extra long arms to allow them to tumble. Some did not have paw pads, others were dressed following a typical Bing fashion, but intact clothes are rarely found today.

1909-10   *11.5in (29cm) high*

$3,000-4,000   **HGS**

A Wendy Boston brown woolen teddy bear, with white woolen snout and pads.

Although this appears like many modern unjointed bears, Wendy Boston was a pioneering maker founded in Wales and active between 1954 and 1976. The majority of their bears were machine-washable and used synthetic fabrics.

15in (38cm) high

$25-35   **F**

MERRYTHOUGHT
IRONBRIDGE SHROPS.
MADE IN ENGLAND
REGᴰ DESIGN

A Merrythought 'Cheeky' bear, the ears fitted with bells, amber eyes and vertical stitched pointed Draylon snout, stitched white felt pads and makers label.

Merrythought's 'Cheeky' bear was introduced in 1957 and is still made today. He always has bells in his ears.

11in (28cm) high

$400-600   **F**

A 1950s Chad Valley teddy bear, with wide pricked ears, amber eyes, stitched snout and brown velvet pads.

19in (48.5cm) high

$180-220   **F**

A Chad Valley golden plush teddy bear, with wide pricked ears, amber eyes, stitched snout and brown velvet pads.

14in (35.5cm) high

$180-220   **F**

A Merrythought beige art silk 'Cheeky' bear, with fitted bells to the ears, amber eyes and stitched velvet snout.

10.5in (27cm) high

$150-200   **F**

A 1930s Chad Valley golden plush teddy bear, the bear with wide pricked ears, amber eyes and vertical stitched snout, jointed limbs and leatherette pads.

14.5in (37cm) high

$300-500   **F**

An unidentified American brown mohair bear, with boot button eyes, black wool stitched nose and fabric pads.

Although it is hard to specify a maker, he may be by Ideal due to his long and slender body, widely spaced ears and arms placed lower down on the body.

1906-08   12.5in (32cm) high

$1,000-1,500   HGS

A Tara Toys gold plush teddy bear, with wide pricked ears, amber eyes and stitched pointed snout.

This bear was made in Elly Bay, County Mayo, Ireland after 1953 when the name Erris Toys changed to Tara Toys. His form is also typical of postwar bears from the 1950s and 1960s.

23in (58.5cm) high

$120-180   F

A Steiff 'Amelia' Collector's edition teddy bear, the dusty pink bear with recorded voice and ruffled red/white collar.

The form of this bear is based on the 'Teddy Clown' produced in a limited number of 30,000 between 1926 and 1928, but without the clown's hat.

1993   12.5in (32cm) high

$220-280   RP

A 1950s Steiff small blonde bear, with original peach ribbon, paper chest tag and ear stud with raised "Steiff" logo.

7.5in (19cm) high

$700-1,000   HGS

A limited edition Steiff brown mohair muzzled bear.

13.5in (35.5cm) high

$120-180   F

An early Steiff miniature bear, with boot bead eyes and stitched woolen nose, metal ear stud with "Steiff" logo.

c1909   3.5in (9cm) high

$800-1,200   HGS

A 1950s English golden plush bear, with rexine pads, the head detached.

$80-120   ROS

A CLOSER LOOK AT A TEDDY BEAR

Long, thin limbs, a firm body and ears set widely apart are typical features of early American bears produced around 1910 after the re-election of Teddy Roosevelt in 1906.

The triangular shape of his head and pointy feet suggest the most popular American maker Ideal, although his down-turned paws also hint at Bruin. He is probably by an unknown maker who produced bears at this time when they were highly popular with the public.

At over two feet high, he is a very large size and has early 'boot button' eyes and a woven cotton nose.

He is well proportioned and his mohair is in superbly furry condition with his feet and paws retaining their original felt pads, woven claws and card inserts.

A scarce and early American golden mohair teddy bear, with black boot button eyes, woven nose and claws.

c1905   24.5in (62cm) high

$2,800-3,200   SOTT

A CLOSER LOOK AT A STEIFF SNAIL

Nelly the snail is typical of Steiff's creation of unusual, not normally cuddly, animals and is rare and sought after today.

Of typically fine Steiff quality, she was made in two colorways for a comparatively short period of time between 1961 and 1963.

She has a vinyl and velvet body and should not be confused with the furry plush version known as 'Cosili', which is still available today.

She is in excellent, bright condition and complete with her tentacles, shell fabric and paper tags, all in excellent condition.

A Steiff 'Nelly' snail vinyl and cotton soft toy, with original paper chest tag, ear stud with raised "Steiff" logo, and yellow "Made in Germany" tag.

1961-63

6in (15cm) long

$400-600   **TCT**

A 1930s Steiff finch soft toy, with wire feet and plastic beak, boot bead eyes, ear stud with raised "Steiff" logo and yellow label.

This example is larger than the less valuable miniature 'Pom-Pom' toys made from the 1930s until the 1950s. Prewar examples have a wire internal body and feet, whilst postwar examples have plastic feet.

5in (12.5cm) high

$180-220   **TCT**

A Steiff giraffe soft toy, with dappled body markings, date unknown.

9.25in (23.5cm) high

$30-50   **RP**

A Steiff kangaroo soft toy, with original tag.

2.25in (6cm) high

$25-35   **RP**

A 1950s Steiff Airedale terrier, in brown and black.

Famous German teddy bear maker Steiff, founded in 1877, are also well known for their stuffed or soft animals. Indeed, founder Margerete Steiff made these (initially as gifts) before introducing teddy bears. Prewar animals can be expensive, but some of the more unusual postwar examples can fetch higher prices too. As with all stuffed toys, try to buy in as clean and undamaged condition as possible, preferably with labels. However, also always consider the personal 'Aaah' factor which makes so many of them instantly appealing.

8in (20cm) long

$70-100   **RP**

A 1960s Steiff cocker spaniel soft toy, in sitting position, with glass eyes.

10.25in (26cm) high

$70-100   **RP**

A miniature Steiff chimpanzee soft toy, with silver button and yellow label to ear.

4.5in (11.5cm) high

$40-60   **F**

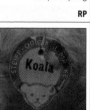

A Steiff koala bear, with pad feet and nose, glass eyes, paper chest tag and ear stud with raised "Steiff" logo.

5in (12.5cm) high

$300-400   **TCT**

A Merrythought buffalo brown plush soft toy.

This label was used by Merrythought from 1957 until 1991.

20in (51cm) wide

$30-50   F

An amusing Merrythought camel soft toy.

14.5in (39cm) high

$30-50   F

A 1950s American Agnes Brush Heffalump soft toy.

The 'never seen' Heffalump in A.A. Milne's short stories is as rare in reality as in the books, as indicated by its high value! This is possibly as it was less popular than the main characters, such as Winnie the Pooh, at the time.

13.75in (35cm) high

$1,000-1,500   HGS

Four Dean's printed cloth sitting cat soft toys.

c1906   8.25in (21cm) high

$120-180   BONC

A Schuco blond mohair cat, with faceted green glass eyes and pink stitched woolen nose and mouth, head movement controlled by tail.

German maker Schreyer & Co, known as Schuco, are renowned for their moving and miniature toys, but these are usually monkeys or teddy bears, with cats being less common. Postwar examples tend to have shorter, plumper limbs and fatter, more rounded bodies.

c1930   8.5in (21.5cm) high

$400-600   TCT

A Merrythought chimpanzee soft toy, in seated pose.

13in (33cm) high

$30-50   F

A Chad Valley dog soft toy, with two-tone fur.

11.5in (29cm) high

$25-35   F

A Deans Childs Play chimpanzee fabric glove puppet, with tag and label.

10in (25.5cm) high

$25-35   F

A 1950s Chiltern 'Twurly Toys' cat plush soft toy, with poseable limbs, tag and label.

11in (28cm) high

$80-120   DE

A 1930s Farnell nightdress case, modeled as a monkey in recumbent pose.

British company J.K. Farnell are better known for their high quality 'Alpha' range of teddy bears which can fetch high prices today. This embroidered label was used on toys made from 1925 until c1945.

23in (58.5cm) long

$50-70   F

TOYS & GAMES

COLLECTORS' NOTES

■ Welsh toy company Mettoy, founded in the 1930s, released Corgi toys in 1956 as a competitor to Dinky's highly successful range of model vehicles. As well as having realistically glazed windows (leading to the slogan 'The Ones With The Windows'), from 1959 they often had extra features such as opening doors and hoods, suspension and 'jeweled' headlights – exciting features for young boys!

■ Corgi are very well known for their large range of models produced during the 1960s and 1970s to tie-in with popular TV shows and films. These models were highly popular at the time and stole the lead from Dinky. They continue to be popular with fans of the series or film as well as with Corgi collectors today, which can leads to higher values due to increased competition, especially for some of the Bond cars.

■ As with other die-cast models, condition and unusual variations are key indicators to value. Collectors grade examples from 'poor' through 'good' and 'very good' to 'excellent' and 'mint', with the top prices being paid for mint condition examples. Original boxes add a substantial amount to the value and the condition of the box is also important.

■ Unusual variations produced in small numbers or for short periods of time can also fetch high values and can add excitement to collecting and diversity to a collection. Look out for nonstandard colors, different wheels, transfers or decoration that are unusual and consult a reference book to learn how to spot them.

■ Look out for models produced with 'Whizzwheels' as many are still comparatively affordable – but always buy in the best condition possible with boxes. Many tip these to be a good investment for the future. Some 1970s bubble-packed and carded examples from the 'Rockets' and 'Juniors' range are also worth looking out for and may even still be found in independent local toyshops.

A Corgi No. 408 "AA Road Service" Bedford Van, yellow, black, spun hubs, near mint condition, apart from very minor marks, in a good condition blue and yellow carded box.

1959-63

$180-220   VEC

A Corgi No. 403 "Daily Express" Bedford Van, blue, flat spun hubs, near mint condition, in a fair condition all-carded blue box.

1956-60

$70-100   VEC

A Corgi No. 421 "Evening Standard" Bedford Van, black, silver, flat spun hubs, excellent condition, in good condition blue and yellow carded box.

The variation with an 'AVRO BODE' logo in place of the Evening Standard logo and with a blue body can fetch up to twice the value of this variation.

1960-63

$150-200   VEC

A Corgi No. 354 Commer Military Ambulance, green, dark tinted glass and roof light, near mint condition, very slight discoloration marks, in good condition blue and yellow carded box.

1964-66

$80-120   VEC

A Corgi No. 483 Dodge Kew Fargo Tipper, white, blue, graphite gray chassis, cast wheels, excellent condition, in good condition blue and yellow window box.

1968-72

$60-90   VEC

A Corgi No. 454 Commer Platform Lorry, lemon, silver, flat spun hubs and a No. 101 Platform Trailer, yellow, silver, flat spun hubs, in incorrect No. 100, box, both in good to excellent condition, in good condition blue and yellow carded boxes.

The trailer is worth under a quarter of the value of the lorry.

1957-63

$150-200   VEC

A Corgi No. 441 VW "Toblerone" Van, blue, lemon interior, spun hubs, mint condition, in slightly crushed, blue and yellow carded good condition box.

1963-67

$150-200   VEC

A Corgi No. 246 Chrysler Imperial, red, pale blue interior, cast wheels, excellent condition, in a fair condition, blue and yellow carded box.

The version of this model in metallic kingfisher blue is the most sought after and can fetch more than twice the value of this color variation.

1965-68

$70-100   **VEC**

A Corgi No. 313 "Graham Hill" Ford Cortina GXL, metallic bronze, black roof, white interior, Whizzwheels, mint condition, in a good condition although crushed orange and yellow window box, complete with figure.

A variation with a tan body, black roof and number plate reading 'CORTINA' was released as a promotional model and can fetch up to double the value of this version.

1970-73

$120-180   **VEC**

A Corgi No. 238 Jaguar Mark 10, mid-blue, lemon interior, spun hubs, slightly Superdetailed, excellent condition, in a good condition carded box.

1962-67

$80-120   **VEC**

A Corgi No. 307 Jaguar E-type, graphite gray, red hood, spun hubs, mint condition, in a good condition blue and yellow plain carded box.

1962-64

$220-280   **VEC**

A Corgi No. 318 "I've Got a Tiger in My Tank" Lotus Elan, blue, black interior, spun hubs, figure, with small racing No. 20 decals, excellent condition, in a good condition blue and yellow carded box.

1965-67

$60-90   **VEC**

A Corgi No. 388 Mercedes C111, orange, black, Whizzwheels, near mint condition, orange and yellow window box.

1970-74

$30-40   **VEC**

A Corgi No. 230 Mercedes Benz SE Coupe, cream, red interior, spun hubs, excellent condition, in a good condition blue and yellow carded box.

1962-64

$100-150   **VEC**

A Corgi No. 330 Porsche Carrera 6, white, red, blue, cast wheels, racing number "60", excellent condition, slight surface corrosion to rear wheels, in a good condition blue and yellow carded box.

1967-69

$30-50   **VEC**

A Corgi No. 485 "Surfing" Mini Countryman, turquoise, a figure, two surf boards, excellent condition, in a good condition blue and yellow picture box.

It is essential that the surfer and boards are present with the box and model for examples to fetch this value.

1965-69

$220-280   **VEC**

A Corgi No. 389 Reliant Bond BUG, lime green, Whizzwheels, mint condition, in an excellent condition window box.

1971-74

$70-100 VEC

A Corgi Juniors No. E2529 "James Bond - The Spy Who Loved Me" twin-pack, comprising Lotus and Helicopter, mint condition, in an excellent condition film-strip picture card.

1977

$220-280 VEC

A Corgi Juniors No. E3019 "James Bond - Octopussy" gift set, comprising Land Rover, Trailer and small Jet Aircraft, mint condition, on a good condition blister card.

1983

$150-200 VEC

A Corgi No. 267 "Batman" Batmobile, black, clear screens, instruction pack containing folded leaflet and some missiles still attached to sprue, mint condition, in a good condition striped window box.

1967-72

$150-200 VEC

A Corgi Juniors No. 2601 "Batman" three-piece gift set, comprising Batmobile, Batboat on Trailer and Batcopter, mint condition, on an excellent condition blister card.

1975-91

$280-320 VEC

A Corgi No. 497 "The Man From U.N.C.L.E." Thrush-buster, blue, plastic lamps, cast wheels, Waverley ring, near mint condition, in a good condition inner pictorial stand and outer blue and yellow picture box.

1966

$220-280 VEC

A Corgi No. 290 "Kojak" Buick, gold, two figures and red roof light, near mint condition, in an excellent condition inner pictorial stand and a good condition outer window box, slight tear to front and grubby around corners, missing badge.

1976-77

$180-220 VEC

A Corgi No. 808 "Basil Brush" car, yellow, red including plastic hubs, missing sound box, otherwise mint condition, in a good condition box.

1971-73

$70-100 VEC

A Corgi No. 2 gift set, comprising Land Rover, beige, cream complete with trailer of same color but with silver base, excellent condition, in a fair condition blue and yellow picture box.

1958-68

$220-280   **VEC**

A Corgi No. 7 "Daktari" Land Rover gift set, with figures and animals, good condition, box damaged.

1968-76

$60-90   **CHEF**

A Corgi No. 14 Hydraulic Tower Wagon gift set, with lamp standard, fair to good condition, box damaged.

1961-64

$30-40   **CHEF**

A Corgi No. 11 London Transport gift set, comprising Austin Taxi, Routemaster Bus and Mini Minor, all mint condition, including inner polystyrene packing and Policeman on dome, in a good condition outer with striped window.

The later No. 11 London Transport gift set, produced between 1980-82, does not include a Mini and is usually worth under a quarter of the value of this set.

1971-72

$150-200   **VEC**

A Corgi No. 13 Tour de France gift set, comprising Renault 16 "Paramount" Car, white, black, cast wheels, near mint condition, apart from slightly worn decal to front hood, excellent condition inner polystyrene tray, good condition outer blue and yellow window box.

1968-72

$180-220   **VEC**

A Corgi No. 31 Buick Riviera Gift Set, with No.245 Buick, red trailer, and Dolphin Cabin Cruiser towing lady water skier, fair to good condition, box rather misshapen and lacking two flaps.

1964-68

$120-180   **CHEF**

A Corgi No. 14 "Daktari" gift set, comprising Bedford Giraffe Transporter, beige, brown; Land Rover, green, black; and Cattle Truck, blue, brown, plus various figures, near mint to mint condition, mint condition inner polystyrene packing, good condition outer blue and yellow picture box, excellent condition picture header card.

As well as being complete with all its packaging and models, the superb condition of the packaging, including the picture card, helped this example to reach this value.

1969-73

$600-900   **VEC**

A Corgi No. 36 "Tarzan" gift set, in excellent condition window box, although grubby around corners.

1976-78

$300-400   **VEC**

A Corgi No. 8101 Wings Flying School gift set comprising Land Rover, Trailer with Plane and Helicopter, all finished in silver, mint condition, excellent condition outer blue window box.

This gift set was produced by Corgi exclusively for Marks & Spencer.

1978

$220-280   **VEC**

A Corgi No. 503 "Chipperfields Circus" Bedford Giraffe Transporter, red, blue, spun hubs, mint condition including inner carded packing, excellent condition outer blue and yellow box, apart from slight tear to end flap.

1964-70

$180-220 VEC

A Corgi No. 23 "Chipperfields Circus" gift set, comprising Land Rover, six-wheeled Crane, Bedford Giraffe Transporter, Elephant Cage on Trailer and two Animal Cages, excellent to near mint condition, in a good condition inner polystyrene tray and fair condition but complete outer picture box.

This set was released in two variations. On the earlier, and usually more valuable, set produced between 1962-66, the giraffe transporter was replaced with a booking office.

1964

$400-600 VEC

A Corgi No. 1121 "Chipperfields Circus", red, yellow, blue, silver jib and hook, excellent condition, in a good condition blue and yellow picture box.

1963-69

$180-220 VEC

A Corgi No. 1139 "Chipperfields Circus" Scammell with Menagerie Trailer, red, blue, three animal cages, good condition, in a good condition, although grubby blue and yellow window box.

1968-72

$220-280 VEC

A Corgi No. 1123 "Chipperfields Circus" Animal Cage, red, blue, yellow, spun hubs, excellent condition, in a good condition all-carded blue and yellow picture box.

1963-68

$120-180 VEC

A Corgi No. 1111 Massey Ferguson 780 Combine Harvester, red including front and rear plastic hubs, yellow plastic tines, excellent condition, apart from a couple of very minor marks, in a good condition box.

1961-64

$220-280 VEC

A Corgi No. 66 Massey Ferguson 165 Tractor, red, gray, white, mint condition, in an excellent condition blue and yellow carded box, apart from one side where price label has been removed.

1966-72

$220-280 VEC

A Corgi No. 412 Bedford "Ambulance", cream, flat spun hubs, excellent condition, in a good condition all-carded blue box.

A very small number of this model were produced with labels reading 'HOME SERVICES'. These are extremely scarce with none having been found recently, making values difficult to predict.

1957-60

$180-220 VEC

Front: A Corgi No. 437 Cadillac Superior Ambulance, good condition, surface corrosion in places, in a good condition but grubby blue and yellow carded box.
1962-65

$40-60 VEC

A Corgi No. 448 BMC Mini "Police", one rear door hinge broken, in a good condition inner pictorial stand, including tracker dog and policeman.
1964-69

$100-150 VEC

A Corgi No. 468 "Natural Corgi Toys" London Transport Routemaster Bus, with Corgi Classics side decals, red, spun hubs, excellent condition, in a good condition although grubby blue and yellow carded box.

Of the first casting series, the rarest of the Routemaster buses is the green, cream, and brown example produced for the Australian market with a transfer reading 'NEW SOUTH WALES'.

1964-66

$100-150 VEC

A Corgi No. 1120 "Midland Red Birmingham to London" Motorway Express Coach, red, flat spun hubs, excellent condition, in a good condition box.

$150-200 VEC

Two Corgi Rockets, a No. 902 Jaguar XJ6, metallic green, near mint condition, and a No. 907 Cadillac Eldorado, gold, cream interior, mint condition, both on good condition blister cards.

The 'Rocket' series was produced to compete with Mattel's 'Hotwheels' series and was advertised as being stronger than other die-cast series. In general they are hard to find carded and in mint condition, which explains their comparatively high values for such modern die-cast toys.

1970-72

$80-120 VEC

A Corgi No. 486 Chevrolet Impala Kennel Club Van, white over red, cast wheels, mint condition, very minor marks, in an excellent condition carded box.
1967-69

$180-220 VEC

A Corgi No. 436 "Wildlife Preservation" Citroen Safari, missing rear window otherwise good condition, in a good condition blue and yellow carded box.
1963-65

$60-90 VEC

A Corgi No. 653 "Air Canada" Concorde, white, red, blue, near mint condition, in an excellent condition correct issue blue and yellow carded box.

Although not uncommon, interest in these models has increased due to Concorde being 'retired' by British Airways and Air France in 2003. The Japan Airlines and Air Canada versions are usually the most valuable.

1973-81

$400-600 VEC

A Corgi No. 438 Land Rover, metallic green, dark green plastic canopy, cast wheels, near mint condition, apart from slight marks to roof, in a good condition blue and yellow window box.

$60-90 VEC

A Corgi No. 1106 Decca Mobile Airfield Radar, beige, five orange stripes, flat spun hubs, good condition although one side showing slight discoloration in color, in a good condition box.
1959-61

$100-150 VEC

FIND OUT MORE...

'Ramsay's British Die-cast Model Toys Catalogue', by John Ramsay, 9th edition, published Swapmeet Publications, 2001.

'The Great Book of Corgi Toys', by Marcel van Cleemput, published by New Cavendish Books, 2001.

COLLECTORS' NOTES

■ Dinky toys were first launched in 1931 as 'Meccano's Model Miniatures' – a range of accessories to Hornby train sets in die-cast and tinplate materials. Known under the 'Dinky' brand a year later, cars were first introduced in 1934.

■ The 1930s were one of Dinky's most successful decades with over 200 models to choose from by 1935. These prewar toys are usually the most desirable and valuable.

■ 'Supertoys' were introduced in 1947 and 'Speedwheels' in the 1970s, to compete against the growing strength of competitors. Dinky's English factory closed in 1979 and since 2001, the name has been dormant.

■ Condition and variations in color are two key indicators to value. Collectors prefer to buy examples in the best condition possible, using terms such as poor, fair, good, very good and mint to describe the models.

■ An original box can add 40% or more to the value, and the condition of the box is important too. Models without their boxes offer a more affordable option, but always try to buy in the best condition.

■ Variations in color or detailing (such as an unusual transfer advertising a certain product) can have a major impact on value. National variations such as models made in France or models made for specific foreign markets such as South Africa are particularly noteworthy. Examine paintwork closely to ensure that the model has not been repainted.

■ In this section, where prices for variations of a particular model are given in the footnotes, they are for pieces in a similar condition to the piece shown.

A Dinky No. 342 Austin Mini Moke, light metallic green, grayish brown hood, spun hubs, near mint condition, in good condition box, slight repair to one end.
1966-72

$180-220　　　　　　　　　**VEC**

A Dinky No. 282 Austin 1800 Taxi, blue, white bonnet and boot, red interior, roof box, spun hubs, excellent condition, in good condition box.
1967-69

$80-120　　　　　　　　　**VEC**

A Dinky No. 152 Austin A40 Devon, deep yellow lower body, mid-blue upper and ridged wheels, excellent condition, in fair condition box, some sellotape repairs.

The rarest and most valuable color variation of this model has an all-over tan body and green hubs and can fetch over three times the value of this variation.
1956-59

$280-320　　　　　　　　　**VEC**

Two Dinky No. 155 Ford Anglias, one pale green, red interior, spun hubs, excellent condition, in good condition box, slight tear to end flap, and one turquoise blue, good condition, in good condition box.

In 1966 only, Dinky released a cream version and a light blue version for the South African market. These are much rarer and can fetch over three times the value of the versions shown here.
1961-66

$220-280　　　　　　　　　**VEC**

A Dinky No. 154 Hillman Minx, lime green lower body, cream upper body and ridged wheels, near mint condition, small chip marks to rear of roof, in excellent condition box, small amount of graffiti to side.
1955

$300-500　　　　　　　　　**VEC**

A Dinky No. 38f Jaguar SS100, mid-blue, gray interior, black ridged wheels, treaded tires, good condition.
1947-50

$80-120　　　　　　　　　**VEC**

A Dinky No. 157 Jaguar XK120, in original box.

1954-57

$120-180 **F**

A Dinky No. 172 Studebaker Land Cruiser, mid-blue, fawn ridged hubs, in good condition box, tear to end flap.

Look out for two-tone examples with a cream lower body as these can fetch up to 25% more.

1954-56

$100-150 **VEC**

A French Dinky No. 559 Ford Taunus 17M, light metallic gold, red interior, dished hubs, white tires, good condition, including box, tear mark to one end.

$80-120 **VEC**

A French Dinky No. 542 Simca Arianne Taxi, black, red roof, meter and roof light, chromed hubs, white tires, good condition, slight corrosion to hubs, in good condition box.

$120-180 **VEC**

A Dinky No. 108 MG Competition Midget, red, light tan interior, driver, racing number "24", red ridged wheels, good condition, including box.

The version produced for the US market is numbered '129' rather than '108'.

1955-59

$100-150 **VEC**

A French Dinky No. 1409 Chrysler 180, metallic sea-green, black roof, light beige interior, excellent condition, in good condition box.

$150-200 **VEC**

A French Dinky No. 531 Fiat Grande Vue, metallic bronze, off-white roof, chromed hubs, replacement front tires, good condition, including box.

$80-120 **VEC**

A rare South African issue French Dinky No. 552 Chevrolet Corvair, pale blue, cream interior, concave chromed hubs, white tires, excellent condition, in excellent condition dual language box, small tear mark to one end.

Production of Dinky toys in France began in 1934, at the Paris Meccano factory. Many were English models assembled in France but finished in different colors. Production recommenced after ceasing during the war, with a series of typical French family cars such as the Peugeot 203. During the 1950s a new series of cars and trucks was produced. In 1970 the factory moved to Calais but by 1971 increased competition led to a downturn in production and 1971 saw the last French catalog.

$800-1,200 **VEC**

A South African issue French Dinky No. 555 Ford Thunderbird, metallic blue, red interior, driver, white tires, slight corrosion to hubs and damage to windscreen, good condition, including box, slight marks to end flap.

1962-65

$400-600 **VEC**

A Dinky No. 501 Foden Diesel 8-wheel Wagon, first type cab, light gray, black chassis, red side flash and ridged wheels, herringbone tires, no hook, good condition, in good condition box, space to side and split to one end.

The variation produced for only the US market is much sought after and can be identified by its red cab, back and hubs, black chassis, silver cab flash and no hook. It can fetch three to five times as much as some other variations.

1947-48

$300-400 VEC

A Dinky No. 501 Foden Diesel 8-wheel Wagon, first type cab, dark blue, black chassis, silver flash, dark blue ridged hubs, no hook, fair condition including box.

1947-48

$120-180 VEC

A Dinky No. 501 Foden 8-wheeled Wagon, first type cab, light gray cab and back, black chassis and wings, red side flash, red ridged wheels, herringbone tires, no hook, good condition, some minor detailing to rear, in good condition buff box.

1947-48

$300-500 VEC

A scarce Dinky No. 935 Leyland Octopus Flat Truck with chains, dark blue cab and chassis, pale gray back, yellow band around cab, pale gray plastic hubs, rivetted back, fair condition, in poor condition box.

Although scarce, the rarest variation of this model has a blue cab and chassis, a yellow flash on the cab and a light gray flatbed and can fetch up to three times more than this version.

1964-66

$700-1,000 VEC

A Dinky No. 503 Foden Flat Truck with tailboard, first type cab, violet blue cab and chassis, burnt orange back and side flash, mid-blue ridged hubs, excellent condition, minor chip to right-hand side screen post and a few minor chips to edge of tailboard, in good condition box.

1948-52

$600-900 VEC

A Dinky No. 902 Foden Flat Truck, second type cab, orange cab and chassis, mid-green back and Supertoy wheels, excellent condition, some minor retouching to mudguards and cab roof, in good condition box.

1954-57

$220-280 VEC

A Dinky No. 438 Ford D800 Tipper Truck, metallic red cab, white interior, silver chassis, yellow back, yellow plastic hubs, near mint condition, in good condition box, dymo tape stuck over end flaps.

1970-77

$80-120 VEC

A Dinky No. 433 Guy Flat Truck with tailboard, first type cab, dark green cab and chassis, mid-green back and Supertoy wheels, good condition, in good condition yellow lift-off lid box, incorrect color spot.

1956-57

$120-180 VEC

A Dinky No. 410 Bedford End Tipper, red cab and chassis, cream back, glazing to cab, red ridged hubs, excellent condition, small chip to roof, in good condition box, label applied to one end flap and puncture hole to one side.

Look closely at the hubs of this model. Die-cast hubs are earlier dating from 1954-61. Models with die-cast hubs are usually worth around 20-25% less than examples like this with plastic hubs.

1962-63

$220-280 VEC

A Dinky No. 25b Covered Wagon, type two, light green chassis, orange body, cream tin tilt, black smooth hubs, good condition, damage to rear hook and slight damage to chassis.

1936-40

$280-320 VEC

A Dinky No. 30v Job's Dairy Electric Milk Float, cream, red, red ridged wheels, excellent condition, unboxed.

1949-54

$150-200 VEC

A Dinky No. 436 Atlas Copco Compressor Lorry, very good condition, boxed.

1963-69

$60-90 CHEF

A Dinky No. 981 British Railways Horsebox, maroon, red Supertoy wheels, excellent condition, in good condition box.

1954-60

$180-220 VEC

A Dinky No. 29b Streamlined Bus, two-tone green, black ridged wheels, good condition.

If the rear window of the bus is open rather than filled in, the bus dates to between 1936-46, although values remain similar.

1947-50

$80-120 VEC

A Dinky No. 949 Wayne School Bus, deep yellow, red interior, red side flash and red plastic hubs, excellent condition, minor chips to protruding edges, in good condition box.

1961-66

$300-500 VEC

A Dinky No. 952 Vega Major Luxury Coach, pale gray, metallic maroon side flash, cream interior, silver cast hubs, flashing indicators, good condition, in good condition box.

1964-71

$60-90 VEC

A Dinky No. 886 Richier Road Grader, yellow, driver, red hubs, excellent condition, including box complete with inner packing.

$150-200 VEC

A Dinky No. 60y Shell Aviation Service Thompson Pressure Refueller, red, white solid rubber wheels, black base, good condition, no visible signs of fatigue.

1938-40

$320-380 VEC

A Dinky No. 60r Caledonia Empire Flying Boat, silver, orange, plastic roller, red propellers, G-A DHM, gliding hook, fair condition, no visible signs of fatigue.

1937-40

$100-150   **VEC**

A Dinky No. 62y Giant Highspeed Monoplane, gray, dark green wing edges, red propellers, G-A TBK, good condition.

The postwar version, produced between 1945-49, has wing lettering reading 'G-ZBK'.

1939-40

$100-150   **VEC**

A Dinky No. 60w Clipper III Flying Boat, silver, red propellers, red plastic roller, USA NC16736, gliding pin and hole, nose of aircraft and engine cowls fatigued, repaired damage to one wing, good condition, in good condition box, slightly sunfaded.

The similarly valued US issue of this model is identical except for missing out the letters 'USA' on the left wing, retaining only the numbers.

1938-40

$100-150   **VEC**

A Dinky No. 62d Blenheim Bomber, camouflage, with two roundels to wings, black and white to underneath, red propellers, excellent condition, no signs of fatigue.

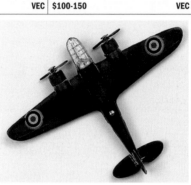

Many early and prewar die-cast toys used a metal compound known as 'mazac' or 'zamac' comprising aluminum and zinc. If the metals were poorly combined, the cast metal began to 'fatigue' over time, crumbling and warping. This reduces value considerably and is often found on airplane wings and fittings. Handle models showing fatigue as little as possible and keep them at room temperature to stave off further damage.

1940-41

$280-320   **VEC**

A Dinky No. 62w Imperial Airways Liner, Frobisher class, Falcon, silver, red propellers, gliding pin and hole, G-A FDJ, good condition, slight distortion to one wing, in good condition but sunfaded box.

1939-41

$220-280   **VEC**

A Dinky No. 998 Bristol Britannia Canadian Pacific Airliner, white, silver, blue, red propellers, excellent condition, in good condition blue and white striped box, split to one corner, complete with inner packing.

1959-64

$300-500   **VEC**

A Dinky No. 998 Bristol Britannia 'Canadian Pacific' Airliner, silver-gray, white, red, red propellers, CF-CZA, excellent condition, in yellow picture lift-off lid box.

1964-65

$280-320   **VEC**

A French Dinky No. 804 Noratlas, silver-gray, silver propellers, French rosettes to wings, near mint condition, in good condition box, puncture hole to one side, complete with inner packing.

$300-500   **VEC**

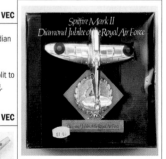

A Dinky No. 700 Spitfire Mark II Diamond Jubilee of the Royal Air Force, chrome-plated, on marble effect plinth, near mint condition, in excellent condition box.

This model, which could be mounted on a plinth, was released to celebrate the Diamond Jubilee of the Royal Air Force and was sold in a special presentation box.

1979

$180-220   **VEC**

A Dinky No. 353 Shado 2 Mobile, in original box.

1971-79

$80-120 F

A Dinky No. 353 UFO Shado 2 Mobile, blue, black base, rollers and tracks, white interior, near mint condition, with mint condition inner polystyrene packing, in good condition outer window box.

The version with the blue finish is usually more desirable and more valuable than the version with the green finish, also shown on this page. However, green-finished examples with a smooth, flat roof can fetch similar values to the blue variation.

1971-79

$400-600 VEC

A Dinky No. 351 UFO Shado Interceptor, green, red legs, blue tinted glass, excellent condition, in good condition inner pictorial stand and outer picture box.

1971-79

$320-380 VEC

A Dinky No. 101 Thunderbirds 2 and 4, metallic bluish-green, yellow legs, red thrusters, good condition, in mint condition bubble pack.

1973

$300-400 VEC

A Dinky No. 100 Thunderbirds Lady Penelope's FAB 1, pink, clear roof slides, cast wheels, excellent condition, base badly pitted and screen discolored in places, in excellent condition bubble pack.

1970-75

$120-180 VEC

A Dinky No. 477 The Adventures of Parsley, Parsley's Car, with un-cut inner card in original box, excellent condition, in good condition box.

1970-72

$100-150 SAS

A Dinky No. 360 Space 1999, Eagle Freighter, white, blue, unapplied decal sheet, near mint condition including inner polystyrene moon display.

1975-79

$220-280 VEC

A Dinky No. 358, Star Trek U.S.S. Enterprise, in original box.

1976-80

$80-120 F

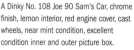

A Dinky No. 108 Joe 90 Sam's Car, chrome finish, lemon interior, red engine cover, cast wheels, near mint condition, excellent condition inner and outer picture box.

1969-71

$150-200 VEC

FIND OUT MORE...

'Ramsay's British Die-cast Model Toys Catalogue', by John Ramsay, 9th edition, published Swapmeet Publications, 2001.

'The Great Book of Dinky Toys', by Mike & Sue Richardson, published by New Cavendish Books, 2000.

COLLECTORS' NOTES

■ Tri-ang launched the 'Spot-On' range in 1959 in direct competition with rivals Dinky Toys and the newly established Corgi Toys.

■ To differentiate their toys from other companies, Tri-ang modeled all the vehicles to an exact 1:42 scale – slightly larger than the competition – making them closer to models than toys.

■ Over 100 different models were produced at a new factory in Belfast. The range was expanded to include building and road signs, all to 1:42 scale.

■ Production ceased when Tri-ang bought Dinky in 1967, however some variations continued to be made in New Zealand for a couple of years.

■ Each model came in a variety of rich colors and all variations are collectible today, particularly commercial vehicles and sets. Boxes are particularly fragile and boxed examples will fetch a premium.

A Tri-ang Spot-On No. 100 Ford Zodiac, lilac, cream interior, excellent condition, in fair condition box complete with leaflet.
1959

$180-220   **VEC**

A Tri-ang Spot-On No. 115 Bristol 406, metallic blue, cream interior, excellent condition, including box.
1960

$220-280   **VEC**

A Tri-ang Spot-On No. 101 Armstrong-Siddeley Sapphire, light green, black roof, cream interior, good condition, in fair condition box.

This is one of the most valuable colorways for this model.

1959

$150-200   **VEC**

A Tri-ang Spot-On No. 118 BMW Isetta, pale turquoise-green, cream interior, excellent condition, in good condition box with sellotape repair to end and slightly crushed.

1960

$150-200   **VEC**

A Tri-ang Spot-On No. 119 Meadows Frisky, pale gray, black roof, blue interior, excellent condition, in excellent condition box with light tear mark.
1960

$100-150   **VEC**

A Tri-ang Spot-On No. 120 Fiat Multipla, very pale blue, cream interior, good condition, in poor condition box.
1960

$70-100   **VEC**

A Tri-ang Spot-On No. 157SL Rover 3 liter, with lights, slightly darker shade of gray, light beige interior, slight chrome loss to plastic parts, good condition, in fair condition box.

This model was also released without lights and is worth approximately the same.

1963

$120-180   **VEC**

A Tri-ang Spot-On No. 154 Austin A40, red, cream interior, excellent condition, in good condition box.
1961

$120-180   **VEC**

A Tri-ang Spot-On No. 131 Goggomobile, pale yellow, black roof, cream interior, good condition, in good condition box, some sellotape repairs.
1960

$100-150   **VEC**

A Tri-ang Spot-On No. 165 Vauxhall Cresta, light beige, white interior, good condition, front suspension has dropped, in poor condition box.

The version of this car with a roof rack is worth approximately the same amount.

1961

$80-120 VEC

A Tri-ang Spot-On No. 166 Renault Floride, metallic green, cream interior, excellent condition, in fair condition box.

1962

$120-180 VEC

A Tri-ang Spot-On No. 184 Austin A60 Cambridge, with skis, bright pale blue, white interior, roof rack, skis and pole, near mint condition, in good condition box with slight tear mark to one side.

1963

$150-200 VEC

A Tri-ang Spot-On No. 185 Fiat 500, pale blue, cream interior, good condition, in excellent condition box.

The yellow and dark blue versions of this car are worth about 30% more than other colors.

1963

$100-150 VEC

A Tri-ang Spot-On No. 191/1 Sunbeam Alpine, with hard top, lilac, black roof, cream interior, excellent condition, in good condition box.

This and the yellow version are the most desirable for this model.

1963

$150-200 VEC

A Tri-ang Spot-On No. 193 NSU Prinz 4, red, cream interior, driver, excellent condition, in good condition box.

1963

$100-150 VEC

A Tri-ang Spot-On No. 215 Daimler SP250, light beige, cream interior, good condition, in poor condition box complete with leaflet.

1961

$80-120 VEC

A Tri-ang Spot-On No. 213 Ford Anglia, red, cream interior, near mint condition, in fair condition box.

1963

$280-320 VEC

A Tri-ang Spot-On No. 217 Jaguar E-type, beige, white interior, excellent condition, in fair condition box.

1963

$150-200 VEC

A Chad Valley RMS Queen Mary, excellent condition, in good condition box.

$30-50 VEC

A CIJ Douglas "UAT", silver, yellow, blue, white, F-B GTX, excellent condition, some discoloration, in excellent condition box.

$220-280 VEC

A CIJ Boeing 707, white, red, blue, excellent condition including box.

$80-120 VEC

A J.R.D. articulated Berliet truck No. 120, in red and white Kronenbourg livery, complete and boxed, some wear, minor chips.

$180-220 W&W

A Lone Star Viscount "Aer Lingus", silver, green, white, four propellers, excellent condition, in fair condition box, complete with leaflet and a Bristol Britannia "British and Commonwealth", silver, blue, four propellers, good condition.

$220-280 VEC

A Mercury Models No. 416 Convair, silver, silver propellers, US decals to one wing and fuselage, good condition.

$150-200 VEC

A Mercury No. 402 Fiat G212, silver, Italian rosette decals to wings and fuselage, three propellers, good condition, in excellent condition box.

$70-100 VEC

A rare Matchbox series MB17 Bedford removals van, with "Matchbox Removals Service" with silver trim and metal wheels, minor rusting to axles.

$60-90 W&W

A scarce Mettoy Metair Hangar, finished in powder blue and red tinplate hangar with airsock and retractable doors, complete with two Vickers Viscounts and DeHavilland Comet plastic friction-drive aircraft and one Tudor Rose plastic aircraft, excellent condition, in good condition box.

$400-600 VEC

A Mettoy Luxury Motor Coach, blue, gray, clear roof, tinplate base, missing figures and luggage, good condition, in fair condition box.

$60-90   **VEC**

An Indian Milton Models, Double-Decker Bus, light blue lower body, white upper, white interior, excellent condition, in good condition box, some sellotape repairs.

$80-120   **VEC**

A Morestone No. 4 Express Delivery wagon, yellow cab and chassis, gray back, yellow wheels, near mint condition, in excellent condition box.

1955-57

$150-200   **VEC**

A Morestone No. 1 Foden Petrol Tanker "ESSO", red, red wheels, excellent condition, slight nick marks to decals to sides, in good condition box.

1955-57

$300-500   **VEC**

A Nickytoys, Calcutta, No. 999 DeHavilland Comet, silver, blue, white, good condition, in fair condition box.

$150-200   **VEC**

A Tekno No. 419 Ford Taunus Van "Solgryn", red, white, excellent condition, in good condition box, labels stuck to one end.

$320-380   **VEC**

A Tekno No. 787 Super Saber, silver, FW-761, US decals to front nosecone and wing, near mint condition, in good condition box.

$180-220   **VEC**

A Tekno No. 834r Mustang Rally Car, white, dark blue, black roof, red interior, racing number "169", excellent condition, box in excellent condition, label on one end flap.

$80-120   **VEC**

A Tri-ang Minic No. 2 clockwork Jeep, khaki, complete with key and petrol can, good condition, including box.

$150-200   **VEC**

A CLOSER LOOK AT A LOCOMOTIVE

This is a rare shape for a model train and is based on the real-life 'Schienenzeppelin' that set a railway speed record on June 21st 1931 – this toy was released shortly after this event.

It is made of tinplate and is handpainted, showing the quality of Märklin's toys – early versions of this model have a two-bladed, rather than four-bladed propeller.

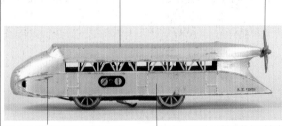

A 1920s Hornby O-gauge 4-4-0 and six-wheel tender LMA No. 2711, a clockwork locomotive, finished in black with gold, red lining to splashers and LMS shadow lettering, crest to cab sides and "RN" to tender, minor damage and wear.

15.25in (38.5cm) long

$320-380　　　　　　**W&W**

This is the electric version, as indicated by the red flash on the nose, electric pick-up bar and two screw marks on the side – a clockwork version (No SZ970) with a keyhole was also available.

It is in very good condition with its original light gold finish and no serious dents or splits, but it would have sold for more if areas of the finish were not worn and it retained its window transfers.

A Märklin O-gauge 'Schienenzeppelin' (track zeppelin) SZ 12970 locomotive, in working order.

This and the real-life 'Schienenzeppelin' are based on the form of a Zeppelin airship, a popular and novel form of transport in the 1930s. The actual locomotive was designed by Franz Kruckenberg and only one example was ever made.

c1932

$700-1,000　　　　　　　　**LAN**

A Märklin 1-gauge train set 'R 981/72/3', with a B-movement locomotive 981, a tender, two carriages 1872, eight curved and ten straight tracks, chromolithographed in green, sheet metal wheels, original box with old cover painting.

8in (20cm) wide

$1,200-1,800　　　　　　**LAN**

A Märklin O-gauge steam locomotive, two parts, with tender, handpainted in black, movement in working order, some wear.

$700-1,000　　　　　　**LAN**

A Hornby O-gauge 4-4-2 tank locomotive, a clockwork No. 2 special tank locomotive finished in Southern 2091 green and black, paint chips, some sympathetic restoration.

$280-320　　　　　　**W&W**

A Hornby O-gauge 0-4-0 locomotive and tender, a well restored clockwork No. 1 special finished in Southern B343 black livery, coal load missing.

$150-200　　　　　　**W&W**

A fine scale O-gauge electric motored 2-6-2 tank locomotive, finished in LMS maroon, lettering to tank sided and RN2 to bunker and smoke box door, brass and diecast construction sprung buffers, with a fully detailed cab and fireman figure.

11in (28cm) long

$280-320　　　　　　**W&W**

A GCR 0-8-4 kit built O-gauge electric tank locomotive, finely detailed with black livery and red line details.

12.25in (31cm) long

$280-320　　　　　　**ROS**

A Mamod live steam model SC1 steam locomotive, with railway carriage, open wagon and track.

8in (20cm) wide

$220-280　　　　　　**F**

TOYS & GAMES

COLLECTORS' NOTES

■ Since their introduction as toys in the mid-19th century, trains have generally become more finely modeled, more realistic and smaller in size. The widths between the wheels, known as a 'gauge' (such as 'I', 'II', and 'III'), were standardized in 1891. The 'OO' gauge was introduced by Märklin and Bing in 1935 and by Hornby as 'Dublo' in 1938. Märklin introduced the 'HO' gauge in 1948. Plastic was introduced in the mid-1950s and became prevalent in the 1960s.

■ Collectors look for the most popular names in the industry and also often ones remembered nostalgically from childhood. Hornby, Märklin, Wrenn, and Bassett-Lowke are popular, especially if early, large or of high quality. Condition is important unless the train is extremely rare. Wear through play, missing pieces or broken mechanisms reduce value dramatically, particularly for later sets from the 1950s onward. Look out for boxes where possible, which should also be in good condition.

An Issmayer scenery train station, chromolithographed tinplate, marquee missing, wear.

7.25in (18cm) wide

$300-500   **LAN**

A Hornby 00-gauge Class A4 4-6-2 Mallard locomotive, in original box.

box 13in (33cm) long

$60-90   **F**

A Wren 00-gauge 4-6-2 Class A4 Mallard, in LNER blue, with original box, "RN 4468" to cab sides, "LNER" lettering to tender, minor wear.

11in (28cm) long

$180-220   **W&W**

A Wren 00-gauge 2-6-0 and tender 'Windsor Castle', in original box, finished in BR blue, splasher name plate RN 4082 to cab sides, BR symbol to tender, with paperwork, minor wear.

10.5in (26.5cm) long

$180-220   **W&W**

A Lima 00-gauge 'Vale of York' electric locomotive, in original box.

box 14in (35.5cm) wide

$60-90   **F**

A Märklin signal hut with signal, backrest of chair broken off, base with some color damage.

4in (10cm) wide

$280-320   **LAN**

A lithographed tinplate train station, including a waiting hall and little shop, imitation of clock and telegraph, electrified.

20in (50cm) wide

$180-220   **LAN**

A Märklin 0-gauge locomotive TWE 12930, handpainted in red and cream, two electrified headlights, roof restored, some wear.

13.25in (33cm) wide

$300-500   **LAN**

A CLOSER LOOK AT A TCO HIGHWAY COURIER

This car is marked "TCO" showing it was made by the notable maker Tipp and Co. of Nuremburg in Germany, founded in 1912.

At 14in (35cm) in length, this is a comparatively large example of a tinplate car.

This is a very rare prewar model and is styled extremely attractively. It is also typical of the 1930s when Tipp and Co. made some of their best cars.

Although this model has signs of rust that devalue it, it is in relatively good condition for such a rare piece. It still works and has no serious damage to the bodywork or transfers.

A TCO chromolithographed tinplate highway courier, in light green and brown, with driver, movement in working order, slightly rusty.

14in (35cm) long

$6,000-9,000   **LAN**

A Märklin handpainted tinplate torpedo boat 'Granatiere', no engine, partly overpainted.

In this condition this model is ideal for restoration, which would increase its value.

22.5in (56cm) long

$1,500-2,000   **LAN**

A Fleischmann single-funneled tinplate clockwork model ocean liner, with cream and blue hull, brown decking and detailed superstructure.

20.5in (52cm) long

$800-1,200   **F**

A Lehmann chromolithographed tinplate taxi 755, with driver and taximeter, movement in working order, some wear.

7.25in (18cm) wide

$1,200-1,800   **LAN**

A Japanese T.N. trademark tinplate model Benz, battery-powered, boxed, in good condition.

11in (28cm) wide

$180-220   **CHEF**

A painted tinplate and wooden model veteran car, scratch-built, with four-seater open body.

13.75in (35cm) long

$15-25   **CHEF**

A Märklin green painted sheet metal steam boat, lacks burner, old finish, shows some wear.

15.25in (38cm) wide

$400-600   **LAN**

TOYS & GAMES

A CLOSER LOOK AT A TINPLATE CAT

A Köhler polychrome chromolithographed turkey, movement in good order, slight wear.

4in (10cm) high

$80-120   LAN

The whimsical form may suggest this is by a Japanese maker of the 1950s or 1960s. It is in fact made by well-known German maker Günthermann, operational from 1877 to 1965.

This simple and 'naïve' toy is made purely of tinplate. An examination of the finish reveals that it is handpainted which means that it is an early tinplate toy dating from around the turn of the century.

Günthermann are well known for their humor and vitality of design as seen in this and the other examples on this page.

This figure is in good condition, with bright colors and a working moving and musical mechanism – if the base had not been restored it would have been worth $800-1,200.

A Günthermann handpainted tinplate figure of a cat, with double bass, base restored.

c1908   9.5in (24cm) high

$600-900   LAN

An EBO 'Trili' chromolithographed tinplate jumping bird, with original box, slightly damaged.

7.25in (18cm) long

$400-600   LAN

A Günthermann handpainted tinplate moving figure of a man on a bicycle, with hat and drum, movement in working order.

3.5in (9cm) w.

$400-600   LAN

A Günthermann tinplate man riding on a pig toy, movement in working order, slight wear.

5.25in (13cm) long

$300-500   LAN

A Japanese Yonezawa tinplate battery-operated 'Sleeping Baby Bear' novelty toy, in part original box.

9.75in (25cm) wide

$100-150   F

A 'Funny Tiger' lithographed tinplate wind-up toy, by Marx Toys.

6.5in (16.5cm) high

$100-150   NOR

A 19thC painted tinplate toy engine, tender, and passenger coach, painted red, green, orange, and black, paint loss, some breaks to wheel spokes.

9in (22.5cm) long

$150-200   FRE

A Japanese T.P.S. tinplate clockwork 'Clown on Roller Skates' novelty toy, in original box.

box 6.5in (16.5cm) wide

$300-500   F

COLLECTORS' NOTES

- Japan is considered the most important producer of toy robots, and the 1950s and 1960s are deemed the 'golden age'. Robots and space toys fascinated the public at this time when the 'space race' and Cold War dominated news, and cinemas showed endless science fiction movies.

- Forms vary and are rarely based on real spacecraft, instead focusing on fantasy and fiction. The majority in this period were made of tinplate decorated with brightly colored transfers. Plastic began to dominate more and more from the 1960s onward, eventually taking over completely as it was less expensive to produce. Pieces made before the mid-1950s are usually marked 'Made in Occupied Japan', changing to 'Made in Japan' after this period.

- Identifying the maker can be difficult as not all have their full names printed on them. Popular makers include Alps, who usually print their full name, Yonezawa, identified by a mark of a 'Y' in a flower and Masudaya, identified by the letters 'TM'. As there were so many makers of robots, many have fallen into obscurity and are simply known by their letters, such as 'SY'.

- Condition is an important indicator to value, with scratches to the lithographic transfers and dents or splits to the metal reducing value, especially if rust has taken hold. Rare, large and early robots and those that have complex functions, as well as those made by the major manufacturers, will usually hold the most appeal to robot collectors. The addition of an original box will also add to desirability and value – many of them have amusing and appealing graphics.

A 1960s Japanese Atomic Robot tinplate and plastic wind-up toy, with original printed card box.

robot 6in (15cm) high

$600-900   **RSJ**

A 1970s Japanese Rotate-O-Matic Super Astronaut robot, by SJM, in tinplate and plastic, with battery powered automatic 'stop 'n' go' action, blinking and shooting guns, firing noise and rotating body, in original box.

12in (30.5cm) high

$120-180   **W&W**

A Japanese Taiyo Blink-A-Gear tinplate and plastic toy robot, with walking action, panel to chest containing multi-colored plastic gears, eyes with lights, swinging arms, damage to foot.

14in (35.5cm) high

$280-320   **W&W**

A late 1960s Japanese Laser 008 tinplate toy robot, by Daiya, with plastic arms, clockwork mechanism.

This style of arms, body, and legs can also be found on Daiya's X20 Astronaut, which has a different head but similarly bright paintwork.

6.5in (16.5cm) high

$500-700   **RSJ**

A 1950s Japanese Revolving Flashing Robot remote control toy, by Alps, in original box.

The exact design and transfers of this robot is unique. It has a door that allows a view of part of the mechanism. The head is like the famous Robby the Robot, even though it has no precise face. Two pins in the feet allow it to waddle along. The rubber hands are prone to perishing, but are in good condition here. The excellent condition, original box and noted maker help account for the high value.

10in (25.5cm) high

$2,200-2,800   **RSJ**

A Super Space Explorer plastic battery operated toy robot, by HK, Hong Kong, with automatic 'stop 'n' go' action, rotating antenna and a large screen depicting the Apollo spacecraft, in original multi-colored box.

11in (28cm) high

$150-200   **W&W**

A Japanese Engine Robot battery operated toy, by JH, with clear plastic box containing gear mechanism, blinking lights and swinging arms.

9in (23cm) high

$400-600   **RSJ**

A CLOSER LOOK AT A ROBOT

His head can be inverted to make a watering can, with the handle modeled as an ear. His body can be converted into a sand pail, which can be used with the spade that forms the carrying handle.

The lid of the pail can be used as a sieve and the legs make excellent sand molds.

Sand or earth would have scratched the lithographs and water rusted the tin plated material, but as he is in incredible condition with no dents, he must have rarely or never been played with!

This rather unusual, comparatively simple looking robot has no mechanized parts but comes apart to make further toys to be played with.

An American Wolverine tinplate 'Mr Sandman Robot', with wooden arms and fragment of original box with instructions on his use.

c1955   11in (28cm) high

$600-900   **RSJ**

A 1960s Japanese 'Super Robot' mechanical wind-up toy, by Noguchi, with flashing lights and rotating arms, marked "N", complete with original box.

This unusual robot is wound by turning the yellow plastic arms. Once in motion, his arms hit the floor and move him in other directions.

5.5in (14cm) high

$220-280   **RSJ**

A Japanese Naito Shoten Deep Sea Robot, the tinplate wind-up toy marked "AN JAPAN", on the back.

Modern reproductions of this robot are known – they are taller than this authentic example and have plain, undecorated backpacks. They are also typically marked with a ToM logo.

7.75in (19.5cm) high

$700-1,000   **RSJ**

A Japanese mechanical toy spaceman, by SY, with spinning antenna and flapping feet, with 'NASA' insignia on shoulder, complete with original box.

6.5in (16.5cm) high

$400-600   **RSJ**

A Japanese tinplate clockwork toy robot, modeled as a spaceman.

5.5in (14cm) high

$60-90   **F**

A Japanese Yoshiya 'Mr Chief' smoking toy robot, by KO.

This is the hardest to find of the Yoshiya 'skirt' bodied robots, hence his high value. A small tube projecting from his domed head emits smoke which is puffed out by small bellows in the mechanism, hence his rather odd name. On the box he is called 'Chief Smokey', but the chest is marked 'Mr Chief'.

A Japanese 'Moon Creature' mechanical toy, made by Louis Marx, box bears legend "Moves forward with mouth movement and sound".

A variation with the uniform depicted on the box is also known.

c1968   6in (15cm) high

$120-180   **RSJ**

c1965   11.75in (30cm) high

$1,000-1,500   **RSJ**

A 1960s Japanese Space Radar Pilot battery powered tinplate and plastic toy, made by Asakusa Toy Co., for Asahi Trading Co., with handlebar controls, automatic stop action and mystery movement, with three discs that eject from launch point to the front of the craft, the plastic pilot with moveable arms, with original box.

8.25in (21cm) wide

$150-200   **W&W**

A Japanese Masudaya tinplate and plastic Space Capsule 3481, with battery powered mystery action, flashing lights and sound, two astronauts in nose cone, a landing ring for the floating astronaut, marked "TM, Japan", in original picture box and packing.

10in (25.5cm) wide

$180-220   **W&W**

A 1950s 'Friendship No. 7' battery operated tinplate spaceship, with spaceman dangling from rotating arm and driver with moving hands, complete with original box.

7.5in (19cm) wide

$400-600   **RSJ**

A Japanese tinplate wind-up robotic dog, with flapping ears and opening mouth.

7.25in (18.5cm) wide

$150-200   **RSJ**

A scarce Planet Explorer tinplate toy vehicle, by Alps of Japan, in silver litho blue tinplate, with mystery action, printed tracks, light to turret and moving twin guns, battery powered, on four small rubber wheels, with original box.

11.25in (28.5cm) wide

$180-220   **W&W**

A scarce Eagle Comic Dan Dare pocket watch, by Ingersoll, the face with a compass in unusual hand position rotates with movement, an engraved Eagle Comic logo on the reverse.

c1965   *2.75in (7cm) diam*

$220-280   **W&W**

A 1960s Japanese Nomura tinplate and plastic Lunar Bulldozer, battery operated mystery movement, with orange tinplate body, rotating action, with flashing lights, blue plastic half tracks and rear wheels, side handle for yellow dozer blade, "NASA" symbol to body, marked "TN, Japan", in original box.

10in (25.5cm) wide

$180-220   **W&W**

A Japanese SH model of an American space capsule, battery powered, in tinplate and plastic, a blue lithographed finish to the capsule body, the cockpit window showing an astronaut figure, a rotating beacon and two spring aerials, "United States NASA" to sides, some damage to canopy.

10.75in (27.5cm) wide

$100-150   **W&W**

A Japanese Masudaya X07 Space Surveillant tinplate and plastic toy craft, with battery powered mechanism, marked "TM, Japan", in original box.

c1965   *9in (23cm) wide*

$220-280   **W&W**

A scarce Dan Dare space control station, by Merit, comprising multi-color plastic radio station, two remote handsets, an operating morse code key for hand set and a flashlight, with log book pad and instruction booklet, in original box.

box 13.75in (35cm) wide

$300-500   **W&W**

COLLECTORS' NOTES

■ Lead figures and in particular soldiers, have been collected since the 19th century. William Britain, established in 1845, revolutionized the industry in 1893 when he developed a hollow-cast process using less materials, thus enabling him to undercut his competitors. To this day, Britains are one of the most sought-after manufacturers primarily due to their quality and accuracy and many collectors focus on this maker.

■ Other manufacturers of note include Mignot (1825-), Charbens (1920-55), John Hill (1898-1960), and Pixyland (c1920-33). Manufacturers often marked their names on the bases, so look here if you are unsure.

■ After WWI, the popularity of soldiers waned and domestic themes such as farming, gardening, and zoo became more popular. Interest grew at the time of Queen Elizabeth's Coronation and figures based on characters from the new children's television programs helped maintain this for a short while but by the beginning of the 1960s lead had been replaced by cheaper plastic figures.

■ Collectors look for good quality figures with fine detailing that retain their original paintwork as well as unusual characters or variations. Repainted and replaced or missing parts will detract from the value, so examine pieces closely. Boxes add value, particularly if in good condition or from a smaller manufacturer.

A 1960s scarce Britains set of 10 Hommes De Corvee (fatigue party), by C.B.G. Mignot, comprising 10 figures each with a wheelbarrow, broom, pick, shovel, bucket, two water cans, sack, billie can, set of four billie cans or a wood bale, all dressed in gloss white fatigue smock, red pants and black cap.

2.75in (7cm) high

$300-500 **W&W**

A Britains British Infantry active service dress with helmets and gas masks set 258, comprising eight figures matching at the trail, in original Whisstock box.

c1925 2.25in (5.5cm) high

$100-150 **W&W**

A 1930s Britains Royal Engineers General Service wagon set 1331, comprising of a two horse limbered wagon, in peaked cap service dress at the gallop.

8.25in (21cm) long

$320-380 **W&W**

A Britains Belgian Infantry set 1389, comprising eight Ors marching rifles at the slope, in khaki service dress greatcoats with packs and steel helmets, in original box.

1935 2.75in (7cm) high

$220-280 **W&W**

A Britains set No.1611 gas mask men, comprising of seven men with rifles and fixed bayonets and an officer with a sword and pistol to hand, in original box.

3in (7.5cm) high

$120-180 **W&W**

A Britains RA regiment Gunners with shells set 1730, comprising four kneeling and three standing figures, all in khaki paint with moving arms, shells and steel helmets, all banded to original box, with Whisstock label.

c1940 Tallest 2.25in (5.5cm) high

$120-180 **W&W**

A scarce Britains Danish Guard Hussar regiment set 2018, comprising of six men with swords and an officer, all on brown horses, and a trumpeter on a gray horse, in original box.

3.25in (8.5cm) high

$400-600 **W&W**

A rare Britains King George VI figure, in the uniform of Colonel-in-Chief of the Welsh Guards, produced to commemorate the Royal visit to South Africa, with unusual flat base.

c1945 3in (7.5cm) high

$800-1,200 **W&W**

TOYS & GAMES

A Britains Farm Series 5F Farm Wagon, dark green wagon, red wheels, non-matching brown horses, wagon floor has paint loss, carter with whip, very good condition, contained in a poor faded box, old tears, marks and repairs.

$100-150 VEC

A Britains Set 161 Boy Scouts 1925 version, comprising scout master together with eight various scouts marching, two missing arms, with poles, very good condition, contained in a good condition box with illustrated label, lid paper lifting.

$280-320 VEC

A Britains Hunt Series Set 1447 Full Cry, comprising galloping huntsman and huntswoman, side saddle, a fox and seven hounds, all very good condition.

$150-200 VEC

A Britains Knights of Agincourt No. 1662 Mounted Knight with standard, excellent condition, in very good condition 'stone' type box, no insert.

$150-200 VEC

A Britains Set 1664, Knights of Agincourt, five Foot Knights in various poses, excellent condition, in good condition box with Historical Series Label, small lid edge missing, no insert.

$180-220 VEC

A Britains The Aga Khan Racing Colours, excellent condition, in very good condition box name label missing.

$320-380 VEC

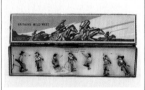

Seven Britains Cowboys on foot, various poses, excellent condition, in very good condition box with illustrated label, end label missing, lid edge has two tears.

$280-320 VEC

A Britains 'Sunderland' Famous Football Teams Series, comprising ten footballers, goalkeeper, and referee, goalpost, three corner flags, one base missing, excellent condition, with only minor chipping and paint loss unstrung and contained in a very good condition green box with illustrated label, three lid corners torn, one box base side partially crushed.

$1,500-2,000 VEC

A Britains Circus Series Merry-go-round, six children on horses, cardboard ring and canopy with original hollowcast central organ.

This rare toy, first issued in 1936, is of an unusual subject and is in good condition, making it desirable.

$5,000-7,000 VEC

A Charbens Costermonger's Cart, with man, donkey and two baskets of produce, good condition.

$50-70 CHEF

A Charbens, No.817 Tip Cart, yellow cart, red wheels and shafts, brown horse, excellent condition, in very good condition box.

$100-150 VEC

A Charbens Horse-Drawn Baker's Delivery Van, with horse and baker carrying basket, damage to van shaft, fair condition, in fair condition box.

$280-320 CHEF

A Charbens The Farm Wagon, green cart, red wheels, shafts and racks, brown horse, carter in yellow smock, very good condition, in good illustrated box.

$120-180 VEC

A Charbens Horse Drawn Tar Boiler from the Roadmenders set, together with watchman's hut, brazier, 'No Road' sign, two hurdles, also workmen with pickaxe, pneumatic drill, standing with shovel, digging with shovel, broken end.

$300-500 VEC

A Charbens Horse Roller from the Roadmenders set, together with a nightwatchman, watchman's hut and brazier, 'No Road' sign, three barrier supports, and two poles, all very good condition.

$180-220 VEC

Twenty Charbens Animals, including a crocodile, three monkeys, two lion cubs, pelican, tiger cub, polar bear, two moose, two walrus, a rhinoceros, bison, ostrich, goat, and zebra.

$150-200 VEC

A Charbens No.500 Gypsy Caravan, comprising a blue caravan, tan wheels and shafts, brown horse, gypsy wife with baby, stool and washing line, mainly good condition, caravan roof has paint loss, contained in a fair/good condition box, end of lid and label missing.

$400-600 VEC

A Charbens Circus Figures set, comprising ringmaster, clown with hands in pockets, strongman with barbells, unicyclist, clown on stilts, clown with hoop and dog, acrobat on chair and policeman with truncheon.

$400-600 VEC

A John Hill Wedding Party, comprising two brides in white, one with hand broken, one bride in blue, no painted detail, hand broken, and one bridesmaid in green, good condition.

$70-100   **VEC**

A John Hill Tennis Players, two male players with rackets across their body, one male with overhead racket, also female player with racket to side, all good/very good condition.

$150-200   **VEC**

A John Hill Millers Series, corn bin, miller, man carrying sack, four various sacks, sack barrow, rare rat, pigsty, all very good condition.

$180-220   **VEC**

A John Hill Pirates Series, Captain Hook, pirate with eye patch, cutlass and pistol, Long John Silver with bottle, with hook hand and sitting on a barrel with accordion, all good/very good condition, except Captain Hook which is fair, hole to back and paint loss.

$280-320   **VEC**

A John Hill Police Issues series, motorcycle with sidecar, rider and cast in observer, together with a patrolman on motorcycle, both excellent condition.

$280-320   **VEC**

A John Hill Street Gas Lamp Set, comprising lamp, ladder and lighter, all very good condition, in very good condition box with illustrated label.

$220-280   **VEC**

A John Hill Blacksmith's Set, comprising a forge, blacksmith, anvil, horse, latter with broken hoof.

$100-150   **VEC**

A John Hill Stage Coach, brown coach, red wheels, pair of brown horses, driver and guard, all excellent condition, in very good condition box with illustrated label.

$220-280   **VEC**

A John Hill Stage Coach display set, comprising a standard stage coach, two horse team, driver and guard together with small scale figures, three standing cowboys firing rifles, two kneeling firing pistols, three Indians standing firing, two kneeling with bows and arrows, with box and illustrated label, end missing, lid end missing, old marks.

$300-400   **VEC**

A Pixyland Kew Father Christmas, together with a rare Town Crier, both in very good condition.

$80-120 each   **VEC**

A Pixyland Kew Lyons 'Nippy' Waitress, a rare promotional item, very good condition.

$150-200   **VEC**

A rare 1930s Kew Chicks on a Log, very good condition, together with a Gardener bending over to flower, fair/good condition.

$80-120   **VEC**

A Pixyland Kew Farmer with pitchfork, together with a scarecrow, tramp, landgirl with bucket and a dog, all good/very good condition.

$100-150   **VEC**

A rare Pixyland Kew figure of Monk, together with two girls in red coats, a small scale postman with sack, man carrying can, chimney sweep and a painted figure of man with cudgel.

$120-180   **VEC**

A large scale Pixyland Kew Man with hands in his pockets, together with a postman with sack, hand broken, postman with moveable arm, butcher with side of beef, another with knife, repainted man in trilby hat and a Huntswoman, side-saddle.

$120-180   **VEC**

Ten Pixyland Kew Animals, comprising a camel, zebra, two hippopotami, a tiger, gorilla, ibis, mule, two peacocks, one with open plumage.

$150-200   **VEC**

Twenty six Pixyland Kew Farm Animals, including three cows, three bulls, swan, large cockerel, sheep dog, three ducks, begging dog, spitting cat, goose, rabbit and ten further animals and birds.

$70-100   **VEC**

A Crescent Bullfighter, in full Spanish ceremonial dress including red cape, together with a charging bull, one bull's horn broken.

$70-100 VEC

A Crescent Highwayman on horse and foot, together with a civilian stretcher party with stretcher and patient, and a Dan Dare figure marching in green uniform, all good/very good condition.

$120-180 VEC

An Elastolin Wild West Covered Wagon, brown tin wagon, blue tin wheels, cotton tilt, driver with whip, two horses on wooden bases which also have four tin wheels, wagon driver, good, horses poor to fair condition.

$50-70 VEC

A rare Elastolin 2-D Wild West covered wagon, appearing flat to one side, broken shaft, very good condition, together with an Indian totem pole, man tied to tree, tomahawk missing, Indian tepee, camp fire with hanging meat and rock formation, all very good condition, minor damages.

$60-90 VEC

A F.G. Taylor Blacksmith set, comprising forge, horse, blacksmith, anvil, horseshoe, all very good condition, in fair/good condition illustrated box.

$150-200 VEC

A Taylor and Barrett Elephant Ride, elephant, keeper, keeper with fish, plastic elephant keeper and two children, all very good condition.

$120-180 VEC

A Timpo Station Passengers, porter carrying luggage, signalman with flag and whistle, railwayman with lamps, Mr. Brown, Mr. & Mrs Smith and soldier with kitbag, mainly very good condition.

$120-180 VEC

A Timpo Arctic Series Sledge with Dog Team, together with an Eskimo with whip, shooting rifle and walking, polar bear, two penguins, all very good condition.

$70-100 VEC

A rare and unusual 18-piece set comprising mounted and foot Cowboys and Indians, by an unknown maker, depicting models by Timpo, Benbros etc, all very good condition and contained in a fair condition plain cardboard box, insert dirty and a little creased.

$300-400 VEC

COLLECTORS' NOTES

■ The market for Star Wars toys is as strong as ever, as a pensioner in Flintshire, England discovered in 2003. In the late 1970s, this lady bought two sets of 20 action figures, one set for her grandson to play with and one to put in storage to replace any lost figures.

■ When put up for auction 20 years later, the Palitoy figures which remained in mint condition on their backing cards, made over $15,000. The top sellers were 'Luke Skywalker' and 'Chewbacca' who each made $1,500. In contrast, a standard loose Skywalker action figure would only be worth about $30.

■ The figures were originally issued in a set of 12 in 1978. The card backing featured a picture of all the characters and these, known as '12-backs', are the most desirable. The range was soon expanded to sets of 20 and to sets of 21 with 'Boba Fett'. These '20/21-backs' are also highly sought-after, particularly Boba sets.

■ Eventually, around 100 different figures were released, with a number of variations of each the figure.

■ In 1995, after a gap of nearly a decade, Kenner started making Star Wars toys again. These were called "The Power of the Force", reusing the name from the rare 1985 line. The action figure market had changed in those 10 years so the figures were remodeled to be more muscular. At first these models were poorly received but interest from collectors grows slowly and the market continues to expand. Look for characters with lightsabers that have the reissued short weapon in the original long tray in the packaging – it can be a valuable variation.

■ Condition and packaging also affect value when considering other toys such as vehicles or playsets. Look for complete examples and rare variations; invest in a specialist price guide, which lists the variations and their comparative values.

A Star Wars 'Princess Leia Organa' large action figure, by Kenner, lacks shoes, comb, brush, and booklet.
1979-80
12in (30.5cm) high
$40-60 **W&W**

A Star Wars 'Darth Vader' large action figure, by General Mills Fun Group, lacks lightsaber.
1979-80
15in (38cm) high
$40-60 **W&W**

A Star Wars 'C-3PO' large size action figure, by General Mills Fun Group.
c1978
12.5in (31.5cm) high
$30-50 **W&W**

A Star Wars 'Luke Skywalker' large action figure, by Kenner, complete with lightsaber, grappling hook, boots and utility belt.
Kenner made 12 different large size figures between 1979 and 1980. The last was 'IG-88', issued in an 'Empire Strikes Back' box, and is the hardest to find.
1979-80
12in (30.5cm) high
$60-90 **W&W**

A Star Wars 'R2-D2' large size action figure, by General Mills Fun Group, plastic yellowed.
c1979
7.5in (19cm) high
$22-28 **W&W**

A Star Wars 'Boba Fett' large action figure, by Kenner, lacks equipment.
1979-80
13in (33cm) high
$22-28 **W&W**

A Star Wars 'Stormtrooper' large action figure, by General Mills Fun Group, with laser rifle, some age mottling to plastic.
1979-80
12in (30.5cm) high
$30-50 **W&W**

A Star Wars 'Power Droid' action figure.

A Star Wars 'Death Star Droid' action figure.
c1979   *3.75in (9.5cm) high*
$15-20   **KF**

A Star Wars 'Hammerhead' action figure.
c1979   *4in (10cm) high*
$8-12   **KF**

c1979   *2.5in (6.5cm) high*
$15-20   **KF**

A Star Wars - The Empire Strikes Back 'Lobot' action figure.

c1981   *3.75in (9.5cm) high*
$6-9   **KF**

A Star Wars 'R5-D4' action figure.
c1979   *2.5in (6.5cm) high*
$15-20   **KF**

A Star Wars 'Snaggletooth' action figure.
c1979   *3in (7.5cm) high*
$12-18   **KF**

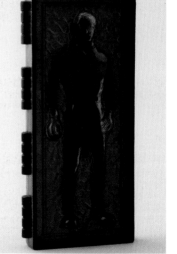

A Star Wars - The Empire Strikes Back 'Bossk (Bounty Hunter)' action figure.
c1980   *3.75in (9.5cm) high*
$8-12   **KF**

A Star Wars - Return of the Jedi 'Bib Fortuna' action figure.
c1983   *4in (10cm) high*
$7-10   **KF**

A Star Wars - Return of the Jedi 'Han Solo in Carbonite Chamber' action figure with chamber.
c1985   *4.75in (12cm) high*
$60-90   **KF**

A Star Wars 'Patrol Dewback' figure, by Kenner, from the reissued Collector Series, complete with saddle and reins, boxed.

The original version from 1979, identical except for the red 'sunburst' decal in the corner of the box is worth half as much again as this reissue.

c1983   box 11in (28cm) wide

$30-50   **W&W**

A Star Wars - Return of the Jedi tri-logo 'Sy Snootles and the Rebo Band' figures multi-pack, boxed.

c1984 box 9.25in (23.5cm) wide

$30-50   **W&W**

A Star Wars - Power of the Force (II) 'Wampa with Luke Skywalker' figures, by Kenner, in green box.

c1998 box 11in (28cm) wide

$15-20   **W&W**

A Star Wars - Power of the Force (II) 'Luke Skywalker and Tauntaun' figures, by Kenner, in green box.

c1998 box 11in (28cm) wide

$12-18   **W&W**

A Star Wars 'Jawa' action figure, by Meccano, with cloth cape, on 20-back card.

Originally issued with a vinyl cape, it was quickly replaced with a cloth version as it was deemed 'cheap' looking. Vinyl examples are considerably more valuable, but fakes with other capes exist.

c1978

$60-90   **W&W**

c1980   9in (22.5cm) high

$60-90   **W&W**

A Star Wars - The Empire Strikes Back 'Han Solo (Hoth Outfit)' action figure, by Palitoy, on 30-back card.

A Star Wars - Return of the Jedi 'Ree-Yees' action figure, by Kenner, on 65-back card.

c1983   9in (22.5cm) high

$15-20   **W&W**

A Star Wars - The Empire Strikes Back 'Luke Skywalker (Hoth Battle Gear)' action figure, by Palitoy, in opened bubble pack.

c1982   9in (22.5cm) high

$40-60   **W&W**

A Star Wars - Return of the Jedi 'General Madine' action figure, by Kenner.

c1983   9in (22.5cm) high

$12-18   **W&W**

A Star Wars - Return of the Jedi tri-logo 'Death Star Droid' action figure, by Palitoy, bubble pack opened.

This multi-lingual packaging was intended to save money on a range losing public interest. These figures often have variations not found on standard US or UK figures.

1984-86   9in (22.5cm) high

$40-60   **W&W**

A Star Wars - Return of the Jedi tri-logo 'Luke Skywalker (in Battle Poncho)' action figure, by Palitoy.

1984-86   9in (22.5cm) high

$70-100   **W&W**

A Star Wars - Return of the Jedi tri-logo 'Weequay' action figure, by Kenner, on 70-back card.

1984-86   9in (22.5cm) high

$18-22   **W&W**

A Star Wars - Return of the Jedi tri-logo 'Weequay' action figure, by Kenner, on 70-back card.

9in (22.5cm) high

W&W

A Star Wars - Shadows of the Empire 'Chewbacca' action figure, by Kenner, in 'Bounty Hunter Disguise', on multi-language red header card.

The Shadows of the Empire range of figures are based on the book and computer game of the same name that takes place between 'The Empire Strikes Back' and 'Return of the Jedi'.

c1996   9in (22.5cm) high

$5-7   **W&W**

A Star Wars - The Power of the Force 'Barada' action figure, by Kenner, on 92-back card, with special collectors coin.

Two years after 'Return of the Jedi' had been released, Kenner reissued 22 existing and 15 new figures in new packaging with a collectors coin. The ploy failed and few were bought. Today they are some of the rarest figures, particularly those only released outside the US.

c1985   9in (22.5cm) high

$80-120   **W&W**

An Italian Star Wars - Shadows of the Empire 'Luke Skywalker' action figure, by GIG under license to Kenner, in 'Imperial Guard Disguise', on red header card.

c1996   9in (22.5cm) high

$8-12   **W&W**

A Star Wars - The Power of the Force (II) 'Han Solo in Hoth Gear' action figure, by Kenner, on multi-language red header card.

c1996   9in (22.5cm) high

$8-12   **W&W**

A Star Wars - The Power of the Force (II) 'Luke Skywalker Jedi Knight' Theater Edition action figure, by Kenner, on green header card, with Special Edition trilogy logo.

c1997   9in (22.5cm) high

$8-12   **W&W**

A Star Wars - The Power of the Force (II) 'Princess Leia' action figure, by Kenner, from Collection 1, on green Freeze Frame header card.

c1997   9in (22.5cm) high

$4-6   **W&W**

A Star Wars 'Landspeeder' vehicle, by Palitoy, mint condition in slightly worn box.

c1978

$80-120   **W&W**

A Star Wars - Return of the Jedi 'Scout Walker' vehicle, by Kenner.

c1982 box 11.5in (29cm) high

$18-22   **W&W**

A Star Wars - The Empire Strikes Back 'Millennium Falcon Spaceship' vehicle, by Palitoy, lacks lightsaber and radar screen, labels used, boxed.

c1977

$100-150   **W&W**

A Star Wars - Return of the Jedi 'Imperial Shuttle' vehicle, by Palitoy, boxed.

c1983   *18in (45.5cm) high*

$320-380   **W&W**

A Star Wars - Return of the Jedi 'Millennium Falcon' vehicle, by Palitoy, lacks ramp, boxed.

c1983

$80-120   **W&W**

A French Star Wars - Return of the Jedi 'Rebel Armoured Snowspeeder' vehicle, by Meccano.

c1983   *12.5in (32cm) wide*

$18-22   **W&W**

A Star Wars - The Power of the Force (II) 'TIE Fighter', by Kenner, with ejecting solar panel wings, in red box.

c1995 box 11.5in (29cm) wide

$10-15   **W&W**

A Star Wars - The Power of the Force (II) 'Cruisemissile Trooper' vehicle, by Kenner, in green box.

c1997 box 10.5in (26.5cm) wide

$7-10   **W&W**

A Star Wars - The Power of the Force (II) 'Darth Vader's TIE Fighter' vehicle, by Kenner, with multi-language green box.

c1997 box 12in (30.5cm) wide

$15-20   **W&W**

A Star Wars - The Empire Strikes Back 'Radar Laser Cannon' accessory, by Kenner, boxed.

c1983

$10-15 W&W

A Star Wars - Return of the Jedi 'Vehicle Maintenance Energizer' accessory, by Kenner, sealed in box.

c1983 *box 6in (15cm) high*

$10-15 W&W

A Star Wars - Return of the Jedi 'Ewok Assault Catapult', by Kenner, complete in box.

c1984 *box 6in (15cm) high*

$10-15 W&W

A Star Wars - Return of the Jedi 'Ewok Combat Glider' accessory, by Kenner.

c1984 *box 6in (15cm) high*

$10-15 W&W

A Star Wars - Return of the Jedi 'ISP-6 (Imperial Shuttle Pod)' mini-rig, by Kenner.

c1983 *box 6in (15cm) high*

$8-12 W&W

A Star Wars - Return of the Jedi tri-logo 'Endor Forest Ranger' mini rig, by Palitoy, boxed.

c1984 *box 9in (23cm) wide*

$15-20 W&W

A Star Wars 'Cantina' playset, by Palitoy, complete and boxed.

c1979 *18in (45.5cm) wide*

$150-200 W&W

A Star Wars - Return of the Jedi 'Jabba The Hut Dungeon' action playset, by Kenner, version two, complete and including 'EV-9D9', 'Amanaman' and 'Barada' action figures, in red box with instructions.

Version two was exclusive to Sears department store. Version one included with 'Klaatu', 'Nikto' and '8D8' is worth less than half of this version.

c1984 *13.25in (33.5cm) wide*

$120-180 W&W

A Star Wars - Return of the Jedi tri-logo 'One-Man Sail Skiff' mini-rig.

Also seen as 'Desert Sail Skiff' on standard boxes.

c1984 *box 5.5in (14cm) high*

$8-12 W&W

A Star Wars 'Escape from the Death Star' board game, by Kenner.
c1979   box 18.25in (46.5cm) wide
$8-12   **W&W**

A Star Wars 'Adventures of R2-D2' board game, by Parker.
c1977   box 17in (43cm) wide
$8-12   **W&W**

A Star Wars 140-piece jigsaw puzzle, by Kenner, with a picture of Luke and Han in the Death Star trash compacter.

This puzzle is worth slightly more with a blue box.

1977-79
$4-6   **W&W**

A Star Wars 'Authentic R2-D2 (Artoo Detoo)' model kit, by Denys Fisher, complete and unmade.
c1977   10in (25.5cm) high
$12-18   **W&W**

A Star Wars - The Empire Strikes Back 'Slave I' model kit, by Airfix, complete and unmade.

c1980   box 14in (35.5cm) wide
$15-20   **W&W**

A Star Wars 'Authentic C-3PO (See-Threepio)' model kit, by Denys Fisher, complete and unmade.
c1977   10in (25.5cm) high
$12-18   **W&W**

A Star Wars electronic 'Talking R2-D2', by Micro Games of America, carded.
c1995   11in (28cm) high
$6-9   **W&W**

A Star Wars 'Chewbacca' stuffed plush toy, by Kenner, with utility belt and original card tag, in mint condition.

c1977   20.5in (52cm) high
$100-150   **KNK**

A scarce Star Wars - The Empire Strikes Back 'Yoda' Magic 8-Ball fortune teller figure, by Kenner, the base with transparent plastic window revealing the liquid-filled body, with a white plastic dodecagonal dice with Yoda-style phrases such as 'Ready are you, no' and 'Certain I cannot be'.
c1981   5.25in (13.5cm) high
$25-35   **KNK**

A set of Star Wars - Return of The Jedi bubble gum cards, by Topps, unopened.

c1983   *3.5in (9cm) high*

$3-5   **KNK**

A Star Wars 'Darth Vader' plastic lunch box, by King Seeley-Thermos.

c1978   *10in (25.5cm) wide*

$4-6   **W&W**

A Star Wars - The Empire Strikes Back 'Yoda' thermos flask, by King Seeley-Thermos.

c1980   *6.5in (16.5cm) high*

$3-5   **W&W**

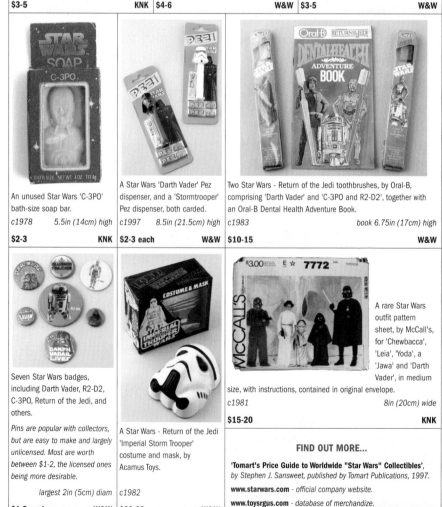

An unused Star Wars 'C-3PO' bath-size soap bar.

c1978   *5.5in (14cm) high*

$2-3   **KNK**

A Star Wars 'Darth Vader' Pez dispenser, and a 'Stormtrooper' Pez dispenser, both carded.

c1997   *8.5in (21.5cm) high*

$2-3 each   **W&W**

Two Star Wars - Return of the Jedi toothbrushes, by Oral-B, comprising 'Darth Vader' and 'C-3PO and R2-D2', together with an Oral-B Dental Health Adventure Book.

c1983   *book 6.75in (17cm) high*

$10-15   **W&W**

Seven Star Wars badges, including Darth Vader, R2-D2, C-3PO, Return of the Jedi, and others.

Pins are popular with collectors, but are easy to make and largely unlicensed. Most are worth between $1-2, the licensed ones being more desirable.

largest 2in (5cm) diam

$1-2 each   **W&W**

A Star Wars - Return of the Jedi 'Imperial Storm Trooper' costume and mask, by Acamus Toys.

c1982

$22-28   **W&W**

A rare Star Wars outfit pattern sheet, by McCall's, for 'Chewbacca', 'Leia', 'Yoda', a 'Jawa' and 'Darth Vader', in medium size, with instructions, contained in original envelope.

c1981   *8in (20cm) wide*

$15-20   **KNK**

FIND OUT MORE...

'Tomart's Price Guide to Worldwide "Star Wars" Collectibles', by Stephen J. Sansweet, published by Tomart Publications, 1997.

www.starwars.com - *official company website.*

www.toysrgus.com - *database of merchandize.*

A CLOSER LOOK AT A WOODEN FIGURE

This popular character was made by one of the leading makers of wooden toys.

The figure is in excellent condition and his clothing is not faded or torn.

He retains all his original clothing and accessories, making him rare and desirable.

Theodore Roosevelt was the 26th President of the United States from 1901 to 1909.

A Schoenhut clown, in 'Sunburst' suit and hat, retaining original leather ears, clothes somewhat dirty.

8in (20cm) high

$250-300   NB

A Schoenhut giraffe, with glass eyes, original ears and tail, some scuffing but bright color.

11in (28cm) high

$500-600   NB

A Schoenhut Bactrian camel, with glass eyes, original ears and tail.

The head and legs are intact, with only slight wear.

7in (18cm) high

$500-600   NB

A Schoenhut 'Mary and her lamb' with desk, the figure with original clothes, the hat possibly replaced, the lamb with glass eyes and bell, some chipping on Mary's hair.

mary 7.5in (19cm) high

$1,500-2,000   NB

A Schoenhut Teddy Roosevelt figure, complete with original helmet and rifle, painted face, some paint flaking on top and back of head, obscured by helmet.

9in (23cm) high

$3,000-4,000   NB

A Liberty seaplane, painted wood and lithographed tin, separate clockwork motors for each prop, original decals, some paint loss on pontoons and along one edge of hull.

This is a large and very scarce Liberty toy.

21in (53.5cm) wide

$2,000-3,000   NB

A Cass roadster, painted wood and boat tail styling, with spare tire, missing steering wheel.

15in (38cm) long

$600-700   NB

A Buddy "L" long distance moving van, painted wood with bright original decals, one side decal flaking.

26in (66cm) long

$500-600   NB

A Bliss Chicago Limited train set, lithographed paper on wood, replaced steam domes, damage to engine roof and one coach roof.

54in (137cm) long

$800-1,000   NB

A Metal Craft Goodrich wrecker truck, painted pressed steel, with rubber tires, over-painted.

12in (30.5cm) long

$120-180 NB

A Kingsbury Divco Borden dairy truck, painted pressed steel wind-up mechanism, over-painted.

9in (23cm) long

$200-250 NB

An American Hubley die-cast road grader, finished in orange and silver paintwork.

13.5in (34.5cm) long

$25-35 F

A Hubley general shovel truck, painted cast iron, rubber tired wheels, nickel plated shovel boom, a nice example, very good condition.

10in (25.5cm) long

$250-350 NB

A Märklin Metall box set 4, black, two layers, including propellers and chains, original box partly damaged.

$180-220 LAN

A Champion police motorcycle, painted cast iron, rubber tired wheels, raised letters on gas tank "Champion", excellent condition.

7in (18cm) long

$350-450 NB

A Märklin Metall polychrome box set 105/2, two layers, including sprockets, brass cogwheels and axle gears, mostly complete, in original box.

Germany's 'Märklin Metall' was a direct competitor to the British Meccano sets. Märklin had a relationship with Meccano as German distributor from 1912, but upon the outbreak of war in 1914, Märklin took over all Meccano's German rights and sold their own sets, which took off when they stopped supporting the war effort in 1919. The trademark was a boy proudly standing next to a crane. The 1930s were the golden age of Märklin sets. Set 105 cost 180DM in 1954 and was typical of the period. After 1947 larger sized boxes contained comparatively less tightly packed components than before. Märklin ceased production in 2000.

c1954

$800-1,200 LAN

A Kilgore "Sea Gull" airplane, painted cast iron with nickel plated wheels and engine, excellent condition.

Kilgore Mfg. Co. was founded in 1925 in Westerville, Ohio, and introduced cast iron trucks and other vehicles in 1928. It moved to Tennessee in 1961 and closed in 1985. Look for large or rare examples with as much of the original paint intact as possible.

8in (20cm) long

$700-1,000 NB

A Märklin Metall box set 101/2, black and red, mostly complete.

Märklin changed the color of their boxes relatively frequently, and at certain points choose red to match Meccano's choice at the time.

$600-900 LAN

A CLOSER LOOK AT A NOAH'S ARK

The Noah's Ark is a traditional toy popular in the 18th and 19thC as both an educational and moral plaything.

The material is china clay powder mixed with sawdust and glue, which was heated and molded around a wire frame.

Elastolin was made from around 1910 and began with animal figures. This set dates from shortly afterwards.

The figures and ark are made from 'Elastolin', the trade name for composition products made by German maker Hausser. Always try to buy examples in as complete condition as possible, although with more modern, mass-produced sets such as these, replacement animals can sometimes be found.

An Elastolin Noah's Ark, the ark modeled as if constructed of logs, with removable roof, opening door, working rudder and wheeled hull, together with a good selection of figures.

Ark 22.5in (57cm) wide

$800-1,200 F

A 'Jolly N' cast iron money box, with top hat and original paint.

Repainting cast iron money boxes devalues them considerably. Collectors look for examples in as close to mint condition as possible, with the highest prices being obtained for those in truly mint condition with no damage or restoration.

$120-180 ROS

A large German miniature theater, by Jos Scholz of Mainz, complete with multiple backgrounds, seven scripts and approximately 150 actor figures.
c1920

$1,000-1,500 ATK

A plush-covered clockwork novelty toy, modeled as a monkey wearing a pointed felt hat and playing a drum.

8.5in (21.5cm) high

$25-35 F

An early 20thC American cast iron model of a French bulldog.
11in (28cm) high

$280-320 ROS

A cast iron 'walking' elephant, with 1878 patent mark.
c1880   *3.5in (9cm) wide*

$80-120 ROS

A late 19th/early 20thC toy theater, with printed decoration around the frame of the stage.
12in (30cm) high

$220-280 GORL

An unusual 1950s German plastic clockwork novelty toy, modeled as two dancing figures on a mirror topped base, marked "Magneto, West Germany".

4.5in (11.5cm) wide

$18-22   **F**

A 1960s Slinky, by James Industries Inc, with box.

Box 3.25in (8cm) wide

$15-20   **SOTT**

A rare 1950s Slinky, by James Industries Inc, with maroon box.

The Slinky was developed in 1945 by naval engineer Richard James, who was experimenting with tension springs to keep ship instruments steady. After dropping it and finding it 'walked', he and his wife decided to make it into an amusing toy. It had its debut in department store Gimbell's in Philadelphia in 1946. Since then, over a quarter of a billion Slinkys have been sold. This example is an early one, dating from the early 1950s and retains its rare box and excellent condition. Note the difference in the design of the box to the later example above.

Box 3.25in (8cm) wide

$22-28   **SOTT**

An American Hubley 'Dagger Deringer' cast metal and plastic toy pistol.

c1960   *7in (17.5cm) long*

$80-120   **BB**

A cast iron toy stove, with moveable parts and scale model kettle, pots and pans.

$100-150   **TA**

An unusual 1970s official Batman plastic battery powered Zoomcycle, with Batman seated on a plastic and chromed motorcycle, separate battery pack which plugs into exhaust pipes, made in Hong Kong and in original window lid box brightly printed, internal packing.

$120-180   **W&W**

A child's miniature white glazed ceramic tea set, with floral transfer decoration, in original box.

8.5in (21.5cm) wide

$18-22   **F**

A large early wooden Pelham puppet, modeled as a skeleton, in original box.

18.5in (47cm) high

$120-180   **F**

An incomplete set of 1870s De La Rue playing cards, with square corners, no indices, double figures, marked with numbers, reverse design of gold and green flora, eight cards missing.

The lack of indices suggests that these cards predate the 20thC, the double figures (two-headed picture cards) indicate that they are from the latter part of the 18thC as earlier cards had single figures.

3.75in (9.5cm) high

$5-8 INT

A set of 50 tarot cards, made by Ferdinand Piatnik & Son, of Vienna.

1908-1928 4.5in (11.5cm) long

$50-70 INT

A 1980s pack of 54 vinyl Ninetendo 'Tactics' playing cards, crosshatch design on reverse with large 'T'.

3.75in (9.5cm) high

$22-28 INT

A set of 55 playing cards issued by the US military, to be distributed among Coalition forces in the aftermath of the 2003 war with Iraq, the cards bear portraits of the 52 most wanted members of the Ba'athist regime, the jokers have explanations of Iraqi military ranks and Arab titles, reverse pattern of army camouflage, in original plastic case.

2003 3.25in (8.5cm) high

$5-8 INT

A set of 54 vinyl playing cards to commemorate the tri-centenary of Bevis Marks Synagogue, ace of spades with photo of Yasha Beresiner, Master of the Worshipful Company of Makers of Playing Cards, reverse with arms of the Company.

A set of cards is commissioned every year for the annual dinner of the Worshipful Company of Makers of Playing Cards and distributed to the Livery only. A mint double pack from 1888 recently sold for $2,400.

2001 3.25in (8.5cm) long

$50-70 INT

A 1930s pack of 52 'Kargo' golf playing cards, made by Castell Brothers of London, complete with instruction booklet in original case.

3.5in (9cm) long

$40-60 INT

A 1930s pack of Walt Disney 'Silly Symphony' snap cards, by Chad Valley.

box 4in (10cm) high

$60-90 DG

A Mickey and the Beanstalk card game, by Pepys, taken from Walt Disney's "Fun and Fancy Free".

c1945 box 3.5in (9cm) high

$50-70 DG

A 1950s Famous Five card game.

box 3.5in (9cm) high

$50-80 DG

A 'L'Attaque - The Game of Military Strategy' board game, by H.P. Gibson & Sons Ltd.

This is a very early version of the game and may well be from the first edition.

c1900   Box 12.5in (31.5cm) wide

$120-180   **DG**

A 1930s 'Hokus-Pokus' magic set, boxed.

Box 15.5in (39.5cm) wide

$120-180   **DG**

A 1930s 'Peter Rabbit's Race Game'.

Box 21in (53.5cm) high

$120-180   **DG**

A 1940s 'Escalado' horse racing game, by Chad Valley.

Box 11in (28cm) wide

$80-120   **DG**

A 'Chasing Charlie' game, by Spears.

c1930   12.5in (31.5cm) wide

$80-120   **DH**

A 'Journey by Air' board game, by Spears Games.

c1935   10in (25.5cm) wide

$50-70   **DH**

A 'Table Quoits' game, by Royal Letters Patent, with bone rings.

Box 7in (9.5cm) wide

$30-50   **DG**

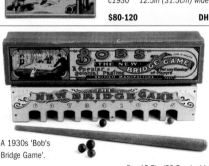

A 1930s 'Bob's Bridge Game'.

Box 15.5in (39.5cm) wide

$70-100   **DG**

A 'Dovecote Puzzle' dexterity game, by R. Journet.

c1900   *4.25in (11cm) high*

$50-70   **DG**

A 1920s/30s 'Ringtail Cat Puzzle' dexterity game, by R. Journet.

4.25in (11cm) high

$60-90   **DG**

A 'Tiddledy Winks' game, by J. Jacques, boxed.

c1895   *Box 4in (10cm) wide*

$40-60   **DG**

A late 19thC wood cube jigsaw, each side making a different picture, in original box with original lithographed picture sheets, lid broken.

14in (35cm) high

$120-180   **GORL**

An early 19thC English jigsaw or dissected puzzle of the British Isles, in a painted wooden box.

7in (17.5cm) wide

$150-200   **PC**

A set of bone alphabet tiles, in upper and lower case.

c1900   *Box 4in (10cm) wide*

$150-200   **DG**

An octagonal carved bone teetotum, for use with board games.

2.25in (5.5cm) high

$60-90   **DG**

A carved ivory spinning top.

c1910   *1in (2.5cm) high*

$25-35   **DG**

A carved ivory spinning top.

c1910   *1in (2.5cm) high*

$25-35   **DG**

COLLECTORS' NOTES

■ Computer games irrevocably redefined children's play during the 1980s and 1990s. They have a growing base of collectors keen to build representative collections and nostalgically revisit the toys of their youth. 'Shoot 'em up' and 'Beat 'em up' games are popular with names such as Nintendo (particularly the Game & Watch series), TOMY and early names such as CGL being sought after.

■ Condition is extremely important and games should be undamaged and complete with their battery covers and preferably boxes and instructions. Games must work and always examine the battery cases for signs of damage from battery leakages.

A Bandai 'Missile Invader' handheld game.

c1980   *3.5in (9cm) wide*

$30-50   **HLJ**

An Entex 'Raise the Devil' handheld game.

c1980   *5in (13cm) wide*

$50-70   **HLJ**

A Nintendo 'Spitball Sparky BU-201' Supercolor game and watch.

This unusual vertically-oriented game used colored screen overlays to give the impression of color – an innovative feature.

c1984   *5.25in (4.5cm) wide*

$150-200   **HLJ**

An Atari 'Asteroids' record and story book.

c1982

$22-28   **HLJ**

A Texas Instruments 'Speak & Spell' electronic game.

c1978   *15.5in (39.5cm) high*

$40-60   **DTC**

A Nintendo monochrome Game Boy.

Already a household name for the 1980s 'Game & Watch' series and the 1981 arcade classic 'Donkey Kong', this was the first in a series of Game Boys and originally cost around $150. Every cartridge driven unit included the now world famous Tetris game (developed by Russian mathematician Alexey Pajitnov) and was able to play the Super Mario games.

c1989   *6in (15cm) high*

$22-28   **PC**

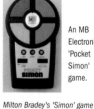

A CGL 'Galaxy Invader' handheld game.

c1980   *5in (12.5cm) wide*

$40-60   **HLJ**

An MB Electronics 'Pocket Simon' game.

Milton Bradey's 'Simon' game debuted at the legendary nightclub 'Studio 54' in 1978 and went on to be a classic 1980s hit.

c1980   *7in (18cm) high*

$22-28   **DTC**

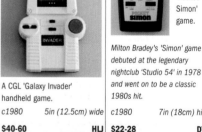

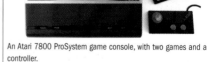

An Atari 7800 ProSystem game console, with two games and a controller.

c1984   *11.25in (29cm) wide*

$22-28   **PC**

COLLECTORS' NOTES

■ From the 1970s onward, wristwatches with traditional mechanisms had to compete against those with newer, electronic technologies. A range of quartz and tuning fork movements, manual and electronic wind timepieces were all vying for market attention.

■ Case designs from this period are typically large and chunky, and were available in many non-traditional shapes. Bezels are often correspondingly heavy and bold.

■ Space travel was a particularly popular theme, inspiring both the design and names of watches. Andre Le Marquand's 'Spaceman Audacieuse', for example, is a much-valued classic of the period.

■ The design of a watch is often as important as its mechanism, those that sum up the style ethics of the period are often the most popular with collectors.

■ While collectors often concentrate on a particular designer or company, the quality of the mechanism and the iconography of the design, are also important factors to consider.

■ Many watches from this period can be found for sale in their original state, sold as 'old new stock'. They are, however, often purchased to be worn and so the amount of 'old new stock' available is diminishing all the time.

■ There is a growing market for all kinds of accessories from this period, fuelled in part by today's post-modern tendency to make sly references to yesterday's styles.

A 1970s Amida wristwatch, faux marble plastic bezel, cream dial, brown plastic strap.

Face 2in (5cm) wide

$40-60   **SEVW**

A Pierre Balmain manual wristwatch, wedge-shaped brushed chrome bezel, signed blue/black dial, on original black leather strap, signed "PB" on the buckle.

Pierre Balmain was a French fashion designer well known for dressing the aristocracy of Europe. Between 1971 and 1973 he designed about 30 watches.

A Pierre Balmain manual wristwatch, wedge-shaped brushed steel bezel, signed silver dial, wine red numerals, on original wine red strap signed "PB" on the buckle.

Face 1.75in (4.5cm) wide

$150-200   **SEVW**

Face 1.5in (4cm) wide

$150-200   **SEVW**

A 1970s Buler Super-Nova wristwatch, brushed chrome bezel, black dial, on black leather strap.

Face 1.75in (4.5cm) wide

$220-280   **SEVW**

A late 1960s Buler manual wristwatch, blue plastic bezel, white dial, blue Arabic numerals, original red plastic strap.

This watch was sold together with an interchangeable blue strap to change the style.

Face 2in (5cm) wide

$50-80   **SEVW**

A 1970s Buler Super-Nova wristwatch, brushed chrome bezel, black dial, on black leather strap.

Face 1.75in (4.5cm) wide

$220-280   **SEVW**

A rare mid-1960s Bulova Accutron Spaceview wristwatch, with tuning fork movement, stainless steel bezel, on black leather strap.

Face 1.5in (3.5cm) wide

$400-600   **SEVW**

A 1960s Clarina Incabloc ladies' manual wristwatch, shaped oval brushed and textured chrome bezel, scarlet dial, on original scarlet strap.

Face 2.25in (5.5cm) wide

$100-150   **SEVW**

A 1970s Elka automatic wristwatch, steel bezel, deep bronze sunburst dial, date function, black strap.

Face 1.5in (4cm) wide

$100-150   **SEVW**

A 1970s Eza automatic wristwatch, brushed steel bezel, blue dial, sweeping second hand, original strap.

Face 1.5in (3.5cm) wide

$80-120   **SEVW**

A 1970s Josmar wristwatch, brushed steel bezel, red and light gold striped dial, red strap.

Face 1.5in (4cm) wide

$120-180   **SEVW**

A 1980s Lip Datolip electronic wristwatch, gold bezel, 'lightning bolt' seconds hand, date function, on original, pierced strap.

This was the first electronic watch to have a date function.

Face 1.5in (4cm) wide

$220-280   **SEVW**

A Lip wristwatch, with dark brown anodized metal body, brown dial, white Arabic numerals and brown leather strap.

This is one of a series of watches designed by French architect Isabelle Hebey for Lip.

1973   *Face 1.25in (3cm) wide*

$320-380   **SEVW**

A 1970s Lip hexagonal ladies' manual wristwatch, steel bezel, silver herringbone dial, extended lugs, on original strap.

Face 1.5in (3.5cm) wide

$100-150   **SEVW**

A 1970s Lordex manual wristwatch, brushed steel bezel, blue dial, on brushed steel bracelet.

Face 1.5in (4cm) wide

$100-150   **SEVW**

A 1970s Lucerne Direct Time wristwatch, heavy chrome bezel, blue dial, on a new oiled black leather strap.

Face 1.75in (4.5cm) wide

$80-120   **SEVW**

A 1970s Lucerne manual wristwatch, brushed steel bezel, blue dial, on steel bracelet.

Face 1.5in (4cm) wide

$100-150 SEVW

A 1970s Lucerne digital wristwatch, brushed steel bezel, blue dial, on pierced ridged steel bracelet.

Face 1.5in (4cm) wide

$180-220 SEVW

A 1970s Nelco manual wristwatch, with black, white, and red dial and yellow second hand, brushed chrome bezel, original strap.

Face 1.5in (4cm) wide

$70-100 SEVW

A 1970s Sicura ladies' wristwatch, 17-jewel movement gold bezel, manual wind, bronze sunburst dial, on a thin black strap.

Face 1.5in (4cm) wide

$100-150 SEVW

An unusual mid-1970s Parger manual wristwatch, stainless steel bezel, black dial, on steel bracelet.

Face 1.5in (3.5cm) wide

$120-180 SEVW

A 1970s Daniel Perret ladies' manual wristwatch, gold-filled bezel, brushed at the front and polished at the sides, gold dial, on tan leather strap.

Face 1in (2.5cm) wide

$120-180 SEVW

A Pronto Automatic wristwatch, with silver and white dial, blue seconds hand and date function, black strap.

Face 1.5in (3.5cm) wide

$100-150 SEVW

A 1970s Ruhla manual wristwatch, green-striped white plastic bezel, white dial, green Arabic numerals, on original plastic strap.

Face 2in (5cm) wide

$60-90 SEVW

A very rare Sicura manual wristwatch, brushed steel bezel, champagne dial, on replaced metal bracelet.

Face 1.5in (4cm) wide

$220-280 SEVW

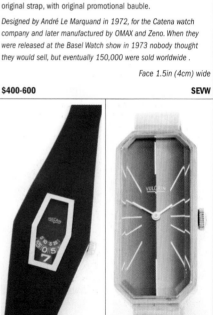

A 1970s Sorna bullhead Chrono World Time wristwatch, black world time bezel, black dial, stopwatch function with two subsidiary dials, on black leather strap.

Face 1.75in (4.5cm) wide

$300-400   SEVW

A 1970s Sorna Direct Time manual wristwatch, 17-jewel movement, brushed chrome bezel, two-tone blue dial, on original wet-look blue plastic strap.

Face 1.5in (3.5cm) wide

$150-200   SEVW

A Spaceman Audacieuse automatic wristwatch, wine red dial and original strap, with original promotional bauble.

Designed by André Le Marquand in 1972, for the Catena watch company and later manufactured by OMAX and Zeno. When they were released at the Basel Watch show in 1973 nobody thought they would sell, but eventually 150,000 were sold worldwide .

Face 1.5in (4cm) wide

$400-600   SEVW

An early 1970s Sorna Chrono World Time wristwatch, blue outer bezel and stainless steel inner bezel, blue dial, two subsidiary dials, date function, on black leather strap.

Face 2in (5cm) wide

$220-280   SEVW

A Spaceman Oval automatic wristwatch, brushed chrome bezel, blue dial with day-glo orange hands and date function, on original blue foam and plastic strap.

This is the other famous watch designed by André le Marquand in the late 1960s. Other colors made include red, white, brown, and green, all worth approximately the same amount.

c1970   Face 2in (5cm) wide

$180-220   SEVW

A Spaceman Audacieuse automatic wristwatch, by O.M.A.X., wedge-shaped steel bezel, black dial, date function, on metal bracelet.

Face 1.5in (4cm) wide

$400-600   SEVW

A Vulcain Direct Time automatic wristwatch, steel surround, with all-in-one strap.

Face 1.5in (3.5cm) wide

$220-280   SEVW

A 1970s Vulcain ladies' manual wristwatch, hexagonal gold-plated bezel, brown dial, on ridged gold-plated bracelet, with original tag.

Face 0.75in (2cm) wide

$80-120   SEVW

COLLECTORS' NOTES

■ The first digital watch was designed by Hamilton in 1970. The earliest examples had light emitting diode (LED) displays that consumed a lot of power, and so the screens only lit up at the push of a button. It wasn't until the introduction of the liquid crystal display (LCD) that the numbers were permanently visible.

■ The earliest Pulsar watches were very expensive when they were first sold. Various models were produced, some of them in solid gold. In Europe, the technology was repackaged by Omega in cases of their own design.

■ Most digital watches keep time by sending an electric current through quartz crystals. Japanese-made quartz watches are both inexpensive and accurate, and have dominated the market for years.

■ From the late 1970s, digital timepieces were sometimes combined with other features, such as calculators. These multi-function watches are particularly evocative of the period and eagerly collected by many.

■ Condition is vital: ideally, a watch from this period should still have its original packaging. Many examples are marketed as 'new old stock', having never been worn. Replaced components and other signs of wear will have a detrimental effect on the value of a watch.

■ It can be hard to locate original batteries to fit vintage digital watches today, although modern equivalents are usually available.

A Bulova Computron gold-plated LED watch, with Drivers-style shaped case and with hours, minutes, seconds, and day and date displays on the side window.

c1975   Face 1.5in (4cm) wide

$300-400   **PC**

A 1970s Bulova LCD wristwatch, stainless steel bezel, on matching steel bracelet.

Face 1.25in (3cm) wide

$100-150   **SEVW**

A 1970s Bulova Accuquartz LCD wristwatch, textured gold-filled bezel, on matching bracelet.

Face 1.5in (4cm) wide

$300-400   **SEVW**

A 1980s Casio CA-505 LCD calculator/wristwatch, calculator, alarm, dual time, stopwatch, lap counter, time and date functions, on original metal bracelet.

Face 1.5in (3.5cm) wide

$60-90   **SEVW**

A rare early 1980s Casio 52 LCD wristwatch, time, day/date, stopwatch and chronograph function, on steel bracelet.

Face 1.5in (4cm) wide

$60-90   **SEVW**

A 1980s Commodore Time Master stainless steel bracelet LED watch, by Commodore Computers, with time and date functions.

Face 1.5in (4cm) wide

$220-280   **PC**

A Junghans Mega LCD wristwatch, hexagonal steel bezel, on original black leather strap.

This is the British version of the first watch to have the time radio-controlled by the Atomic Clock - it was designed by Frog Designs and synchronizes itself at 2pm every day.

1991   Face 1.75in (4.5cm) wide

$220-280   **SEVW**

WRISTWATCHES

A Nivada CompuChron stainless steel bracelet LED watch, with time and date functions.

c1975   *Face 1.75in (4.5cm) wide*

$150-200   **PC**

A 1970s Novus LED wristwatch, gold-plated bezel, on gold-plated bracelet.

Face 1.5in (4cm) wide

$220-280   **SEVW**

A 1970s Novus LCD wristwatch, gold-plated bezel, on gold-plated bracelet.

Novus is the brand name for watches made by National Semiconductors, who made many of the early LCD watch modules.

Face 1.5in (4cm) wide

$220-280   **SEVW**

An Omega Time Computer stainless steel integral bracelet LED watch, with time and date functions.

c1975   *Face 1.5in (4cm) wide*

$300-400   **PC**

A 1980s Phasar LCD chronograph, made for retail by Sears, on metal bracelet.

Face 1.5in (4cm) wide

$60-90   **SEVW**

A Pulsar Calculator stainless steel integral bracelet LED watch, with time, date, and calculator functions.

c1975   *Face 1.5in (4cm) wide*

$400-600   **PC**

A scarce 1980s Pulsar Sport Timer LCD wristwatch, on original black plastic strap.

This watch is unusual as it can time four people at once due to four combined stopwatch settings.

Face 1.5in (4cm) wide

$80-120   **SEVW**

A CLOSER LOOK AT A DIGITAL WATCH

Its calendar is programed until 2100, hence its name.

The gold and black ceramic-coated versions are rare and can be worth in excess of $3,000.

The two solar panels on top of the watch power it for up to a year when charged.

The unusual side mounting of the display made it ideal for drivers.

A Synchronar 2100 solar-powered watch with LED readout, with stainless steel bracelet.

This watch was designed by Roger Riehl, a pioneer of LED wristwatches development.

1973   *Face 1.5in (4cm) wide*

$1,200-1,800   **SEVW**

FIND OUT MORE...

'History of the Modern Wristwatch', *by Pieter Doensens, published by Snoeck-Ducaju & Zoon 1994.*

COLLECTORS' NOTES

■ One of the most collectible objects in this sector of the market is the corkscrew. There are 'straight pull' or 'mechanical' examples, where either the strength of the user or the ingenuity of the invented mechanism takes the strain. The 19th century is the most prolific period of production with many variations due to the large number of patents issued during the period. However, many innovative and eminently more affordable examples can be found from the early decades of the 20th century.

■ Look for early examples, fine materials and good levels of decoration, particularly with straight pull examples. Consider the shape, material, and decoration as these often hold clues to when the piece was made. The value of complex, innovative mechanisms such as the Thomason type is also enhanced by these factors. Notable names can make a considerable difference to value, so examine pieces closely for maker's marks.

■ As with corkscrews, many wine and drinking accessories can still be used, and thus a sense of fun is important with whimsical items often fetching comparatively high values due to their appeal – providing they are in appealing condition. Popularity of pieces from the 1930s and 1950s in particular continues to grow, with amusing or novelty designs more important than quality.

A German nickel silver base pocket-sized corkscrew, in the form of ladies' legs, with mother-of-pearl thighs and striped stockings, stamped "Germany".

A large number of variations of these screws, based on the 'CanCan' Girls of the Moulin Rouge and similar establishments, were produced in Germany during the 1890s. The use of mother-of-pearl is relatively unusual – others have stripy celluloid stockings and some have two-color celluloid stocking panels. As well as acting as a pulling handle, the 'legs' fold down to protect the worm.

c1900   2.5in (6.5cm) long

$150-200   **CSA**

An English silver corkscrew, by Joseph Taylor of Birmingham, with a green-stained two-fingered ivory grip and engraved stem.

This is the standard for many 18thC and early 19thC silver corkscrews, which are often Dutch in origin and include pipe tampers or nutmeg graters. The use of ivory for the handle of this example, particularly stained bright green, is unusual.

c1790   3in (8cm) long

$320-380   **CSA**

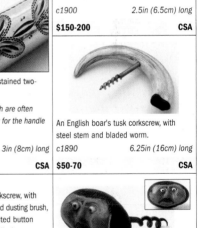

An English boar's tusk corkscrew, with steel stem and bladed worm.

c1890   6.25in (16cm) long

$50-70   **CSA**

An English turned corkscrew, with turned bone handle and dusting brush, fine baluster stem, fluted button cork-stopper, plain helical worm.

c1840   5.5in (14cm) long

$100-150   **CSA**

A late 19thC Corozo nut corkscrew, with carved grotesque face, droopy mustache and glass eyes.

This amusing corkscrew was carved from a Corozo or tagua nut, the fruit of a tropical palm and popular during the late 19thC. It is very dense and hard, making it ideal for carving and as it ages, it takes on an yellowy-amber color. Here the darker outer layer has been used to represent hair and a beard.

An English straight-pull corkscrew, with turned bone handle and dusting brush, tapered stem, helical worm.
c1850   5.5in (14cm) long

$60-90   **CSA**

A 1920s steel corkscrew, with bottle opener.

4.5in (11.5cm) long

$50-70   **BS**

3.5in (9cm) wide

$100-150   **CSA**

An English silver-plated four-pillar rack-and-pinion 'King's Screw' corkscrew, with turned bone handle, dusting brush and side wind handle.

The 'King's' type can be recognized by the side handle. This operates a rack and pinion mechanism to draw the cork upward. It came in both 'open' styles as here, and 'closed' styles, where a cylinder covered the mechanism.

c1820   7.75in (20cm) long

$600-900   CSA

A 19thC Thomason-type corkscrew, with bone handle and side brush above a rack and brass drum applied with a gilt Royal Coat of Arms.

A 'Thomason' type uses a special mechanism, patented in 1802 by Sir Edward Thomason. It enables the worm to be forced into the cork and the cork extracted by constant turning of the handle. Look out for decorated barrels, such as those molded with gothic windows. These tend to be more valuable than this more common banded version with a coat of arms.

7.25in (18cm) long

$320-380   GORL

An English faceted bow pocket corkscrew, in cut steel with a button hook for perforating perfume and ink bottles.

c1800   1.5in (3.5cm) long

$40-60   CSA

A CLOSER LOOK AT A BOW CORKSCREW

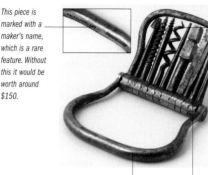

This piece is marked with a maker's name, which is a rare feature. Without this it would be worth around $150.

As well as a corkscrew, this piece also includes a gimlet, buttonhook, and screw. Each tool folds out and the protecting bow can be used as a grip.

The maker, Holtzapffel & Co., were founded in 1792 in London. They were renowned for their lathes and important, complex tool benches and sets which fetch very high values.

The more tools included and the larger the piece the higher the value will usually be.

A rare English steel 11-tool folding bow, stamped with maker's name "Holtzapffel & Co. 53 Haymarket".

c1840   3.25in (8.5cm) long

$800-1,200   CSA

An English silver-plated pocket roundlet folding corkscrew, inscribed "Drew & Sons, Piccadilly Circus, London".

'Roundlet' corkscrews typically contain other tools in the tapering cylindrical sheath. Drew & Sons were a notable central London retailer of accessories, including picnic sets and gentlemen's and ladies' luggage and prerequisites.

c1880   3.25in (8.5cm) long

$25-35   CSA

An unusual left-handed screwed steel pocket corkscrew, with ciphered (or sharpened) worm.

Few of these screws have survived complete, as the cross bar is removable and was often lost.

c1850   4.5in (11.5cm) long

$100-150   CSA

A 1920s cast brass corkscrew, in the form of a kilted Scotsman holding a bottle of Scotch and leaning on a walking stick, with registration number.

4.5in (11.5cm) high

$15-25   CSA

A Heeley 'King's Screw' mechanical corkscrew, with turned bone handle and brush, steel side handle, the brass barrel with applied Royal Coat of Arms, signed "Heeley".

8in (20cm) long

$400-600   GORL

A silver hipflask, with engine-turned decoration and an engraved crest, Birmingham hallmarks.

1873

$150-200   CSA

A clear glass hipflask, covered with silver and crocodile skin, with armorial motif, motto and initials, hallmark for JD&S, Sheffield.

1907   *5.5in (14cm) high*

$320-380   GS

A cocktail shaker, in the form of a dumb-bell.

11in (28cm) wide

$280-320   DETC

A 1930s silver and leather hip flask, makers mark for "J.D. & Sons", London hallmarks.

$70-100   CSA

A 1930s silver fully overlaid clear glass hipflask, with plain finish, hallmarks rubbed.

5.25in (13.5cm) high

$80-120   GS

A slim silver hipflask, with fine barley decoration, hallmark for JD&S, Sheffield.

An 'Abyssinian' champagne tap, with original box.

c1880   *5.75in (14.5cm) long*

$50-70   CSA

An English silver-plate champagne tap, with Prince of Wales feather design and inscription "Maw & Son".

c1890   *4in (10cm) long*

$50-80   CSA

An English steel champagne wire clipper, handle for opening wooden crates with dusting brush.

c1880   *7in (18cm) long*

$40-60   CSA

An early 20thC faceted clear glass hip flask, with silver sleeve, hallmarks indistinct.

5.25in (13.5cm) high

$300-500   GS

A slim silver hipflask, with fine barley decoration, hallmark for JD&S, Sheffield.

1936   *5.5in (14cm) high*

$600-900   GS

A Stelton Cylinda-Line stainless steel cocktail shaker, designed by Arne Jacobsen, with original box.

Famed Danish architect and designer Arne Jacobsen is well known for his 'Ant' chair designs. The idea for his starkly modernist, functional cylinder shape 'Cylinda-Line' range of accessories, was reputedly first sketched on a napkin! The range was produced by the company of his foster son, Peter Holmblad.

1968   9in (23cm) high

$80-120   **L**

A cocktail shaker in the form of a man, wearing a medal inscribed "Gin" hanging from his waistcoat and a female figure on his forehead, the stopper in the form of a top hat, paper label "Japan", original sticker "Yona original by Shafford Japan", inscribed "8001-Y".

We wonder what this 'gentleman' is preoccupied with!

$120-180   **DETC**

An unusual faceted soda siphon, with bird's head spout, mid-blue glass, faceted body, good condition.

12in (30.5cm) high

$18-22   **BBR**

An acid-etched glass cocktail shaker, with two of seven matching stem glasses.

10.5in (26.5cm) high

$120-180 set   **DETC**

A Robj pottery spirit flask, in the form of a stylized image of Napoleon Bonapart wearing a gray greatcoat with black buttons and a medal, his distinctive black hat for a stopper, signed "Robj Paris" and "Made in France".

10in (25.5cm) high

$220-280   **DN**

An English silver-plate wine bottle-holder, with shepherd's crook grip, the base with gadroon border and adjustable stem.

c1860   12in (30cm) high

$120-180   **CSA**

A CLOSER LOOK AT A BAR SET

The 1950s saw a return to glamor and fun after WWII and a large number of whimsical, novelty bar designs were produced - look for those that are in great condition, are complete and have an appealing sense of fun with a period feel.

The plastic stirrers are shaped like gentleman's walking canes, continuing the theme of the upper class lounge lizard or 'boulevardier'.

Transfer-decorated glassware was popular during the 1950s - here the top hat motif is followed through in the design of the lid of the cocktail shaker.

A pair of decanters within a case, in the form of an armored torso, marked

"Bourbon" and "Scotch", with helmet stoppers, together with six shot glasses.

12.5in (32cm) wide

$280-320   **DETC**

The tray is designed to resemble a city park, complete with street lamps and handles modeled as benches.

A bar set, comprising a shaker and six glasses with cane-shaped stirrers, depicting gentlemen wearing top hats.

c1955   16in (40.5cm) wide

$400-600   **DETC**

COLLECTORS' NOTES

■ The manufacture of contemporary glass spheres is one of the most dynamic and rapidly developing areas of the American contemporary studio glass movement. Many glassmakers have worked extensively in the field and have experience in related areas such as marbles or paperweights.

■ Available at a wide range of prices and easy to display due to their size, look out for key names and complex designs displaying the glassmaker's art. It is anticipated that they will increase in value as the field becomes more popular.

An American 'Joe Cool' contemporary glass sphere, by Harry Besett of the Vermont Glass Workshop, painted by artist Ken Leslie.

2001 2in (5cm) d

$400-600   **BGL**

An American 'Temari' contemporary glass sphere, by Dinah Hulet Tulet, inscribed very faintly with "Hulet 2002".

Hulet has worked with glass for over 30 years and is probably the best known studio glass artist producing spheres. She is a board member of the Glass Art Society and on the board of directors of the American Crafts Council.

2002   *1.5in (4cm) diam*

$300-500   **BGL**

A CLOSER LOOK AT A CONTEMPORARY SPHERE

The sphere is composed of four layers of colored glass representing the sea, landmasses, and clouds, plus clear layers.

The landmasses are marked out in 'dichroic' glass, a speciality of Beetem's. They change color as the sphere is moved.

The cloud forms correctly represent the gulf/jet streams and peak at the pole.

The size of the sphere, and the fact that the design covers it entirely, creates a tactile effect.

An American 'World Marble' contemporary glass sphere, by Geoffrey Beetem, signed and numbered "GD Beetem 2003 C 1618".

Beetem studied glassmaking at Ohio State University and at the Pilchuk School. He worked with Lino Tagliapietra, before establishing his own shop in 1987.

2003   *3.5in (9cm) diam*

$800-1,200   **BGL**

An American 'School of Fish' contemporary glass sphere, by Cathy Richardson, with three layers of glass and signed "C Richardson 03".

Richardson is also known for her paperweights.

2003   *2in (5cm) diam*

$150-200   **BGL**

An American contemporary glass sphere, by Douglas Sweet, with densely packed millefiori, signed "Sweet".

Sweet is a prolific and well-known American contemporary studio glass maker and is also known for his paperweights.

2003   *2in (5cm) diam*

$150-200   **BGL**

An American 'Hummingbird with flowers' contemporary glass sphere, by Jesse Taj, signed "Taj 03".

2003   *1.25in (3cm) diam*

$150-200   **BGL**

An American 'Cat In The Hat' contemporary glass sphere, by Jesse Taj, made from murrine canes worked with a hot torch, signed "Taj 03".

2003   *1.5in (4cm) diam*

$220-280   **BGL**

COLLECTORS' NOTES

■ Modern crafts, particularly in the medium of ceramics and glass, have become increasingly rated as works of art over the past few decades. This is partly due to the influence and growing importance of the studio movement of the mid-20th century. The market for contemporary and studio glass is led by the US and parts of Europe. The works of many designers seem set to become the collectibles of the future.

■ Always look for fine workmanship and an understanding of design, often twinned with ancient techniques, as very little in this aspect of glass is new. Long-standing masters and innovators of new movements are likely to remain popular. Spotting talented new artists early can be exciting and rewarding, but developing an eye for quality and design is important.

■ As each work is unique, they are usually one-offs, but some are released in limited editions. Unique pieces are more valuable and may remain so in the future, but do not underestimate limited editions. They appeal to a wider number of collectors, particularly if they embody the artist's typical style.

■ Only a single price is given as this reflects the retail price of that individual contemporary piece.

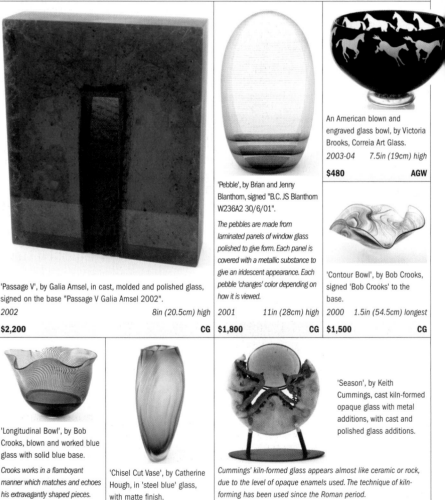

An American blown and engraved glass bowl, by Victoria Brooks, Correia Art Glass.

2003-04   7.5in (19cm) high

$480   AGW

'Passage V', by Galia Amsel, in cast, molded and polished glass, signed on the base "Passage V Galia Amsel 2002".

2002   8in (20.5cm) high

$2,200   CG

'Pebble', by Brian and Jenny Blanthom, signed "B.C. JS Blanthom W236A2 30/6/01".

The pebbles are made from laminated panels of window glass polished to give form. Each panel is covered with a metallic substance to give an iridescent appearance. Each pebble 'changes' color depending on how it is viewed.

2001   11in (28cm) high

$1,800   CG

'Contour Bowl', by Bob Crooks, signed 'Bob Crooks' to the base.

2000   1.5in (54.5cm) longest

$1,500   CG

'Longitudinal Bowl', by Bob Crooks, blown and worked blue glass with solid blue base.

Crooks works in a flamboyant manner which matches and echoes his extravagantly shaped pieces.

2003   8.5in (21.5cm) highest

$550   CG

'Chisel Cut Vase', by Catherine Hough, in 'steel blue' glass, with matte finish.

2002   13in (33cm) high

$600   CG

'Season', by Keith Cummings, cast kiln-formed opaque glass with metal additions, with cast and polished glass additions.

Cummings' kiln-formed glass appears almost like ceramic or rock, due to the level of opaque enamels used. The technique of kiln-forming has been used since the Roman period.

2003   5in (13cm) wide

$1,800   CG

'Windfall', by Keith Cummings, kiln-formed opaque glass with metal and applied colored glass 'cabochons'.

2000   *8.25in (21cm) long*

$1,400   **CG**

An American blown glass mantle vase, by Paul Cunningham.

2003-04   *4in (10cm) high*

$520   **AGW**

An iridescent blue and orange 'rose' murrine vase, designed and made by Vittorio Ferro, signed to the base "VITTORIO FERRO".

2000   *7.5in (19cm) high*

$1,200   **VET**

An American blown glass mantle vase by Paul Cunningham.

Cunningham has worked alongside legendary studio glass artists such as Dale Chihuly, Richard Marquis, and Lino Tagliapietra. He has exhibited in Italy and across the US, including at the American Craft Museum, New York.

2003-04   *11.5in (29cm) high*

$2,900   **AGW**

A yellow and red murrine vase, designed and made by Vittorio Ferro from the 'Autumn Impression' series, with iridescent areas between the murrines, signed to the base "VITTORIO FERRO".

2002   *8in (20cm) high*

$800   **VET**

A gray and orange 'rose' murrine vase, designed and made by Vittorio Ferro, signed to the base "Vittorio Ferro V&A Murano 2000".

2000   *8in (20cm) high*

$1,200   **VET**

A green and red murrine cased vase, designed and made by Vittorio Ferro at Fratelli Pagnin, Murano, with iridescent areas around the murrines and a black foot, signed to the base "VITTORIO FERRO".

2004   *9.5in (24cm) high*

$1,400   **VET**

A glass chicken, by Vittorio Ferro.

One of Murano's leading glass artists, Ferro worked at Fratelli Toso and De Majo. His passion is for murrine work, and he has won many prestigious prizes in Italy.

2004   *9in (22.5cm) high*

$2,500   **VET**

An American yellow and purple clear glass plate stand, by David Garcia, Yacult, Washington.

2003-04 10.5in (26.5cm) high

$420　　　　　　　　　**AGW**

'Floral with vines' American scent bottle, by Richard Gillian, iridescent finish to sides, front and back facets, using flamework painting, signed "R. Gillian 2002".

5in (12.5cm) high

$300　　　　　　　　　**BGL**

'Aesculus', by Kate Jones and Stephen Gillies, in cased colored glass, signed on the base "Gillies Jones Aesculus 2004/01 Rosedale".

Designer and glass artist Kate Jones works with Stephen Gillies, her husband, who is the glass blower.

2004　　　　　　　　10in (25.5cm) diam

$3,000　　　　　　　　　**CG**

An American hand-blown glass mantle vase, by Dale Heffernan, San Raphael, California.

2003-04　　23in (57.5cm) high

$250　　　　　　　　　**AGW**

An Aerial 'stone form' cased vase, by Peter Layton.

Layton (b.1937) is one of Britain's most prominent glass artists and co-founded the 'Glasshouse' in London in 1969. This piece shows his current interest in the optical effects of casing – the clear outer layer reflects the design of the colored core.

2004　　8in (20.5cm) high

$2,200　　　　　　　　　**PL**

An Aurora cased 'stone form' vase, by Peter Layton.

2004　　　　　　　9.25in (23.5cm) high

$800　　　　　　　　　**PL**

A large Mirage bowl, by Peter Layton.

2004　　13.5in (34cm) wide

$1,800　　　　　　　　　**PL**

A unique Skyline 'pebble form', by Peter Layton.

This piece is from a new and experimental range. Its delicate yet varied and vibrant coloration is highly appealing.

2004　　　　　　　　11.5in (29cm) wide

$2,200　　　　　　　　　**PL**

A tall vase, by Annette Meech, from the 'Les Fauves' series, signed "Annette Meech Glasshouse de Savignon".

2002　　19in (48cm) high

$200　　　　　　　　　**CG**

A tall vase, by Annette Meech, from the 'Les Fauves' series, orange blown glass vase with red zig-zagging red trails, signed "Annette Meech Glasshouse de Savignon".

2002   16.25in (41cm) high

$200   CG

A Simon Moore blue jug, with fins along the back.

1986   13.5in (34cm) high

$1,000   JH

'Face Two Face' bowl, by Stephen Newell, blown and cased, with silver leaf inside, signed "Newell".

American born and trained Newell often tells stories or portrays emotions though his complex works. Examples can be found in public collections in Japan, Britain, and the US.

2003   6in (15cm) high

$3,800   CG

An American glass scent bottle, by Michael Nourot.

2003-04   6in (15cm) high

$180   AGW

An American glass scent bottle, by Michael Nourot.

Michael Nourot (b.1949) has studied with glassblowers on the island of Murano, Italy and also with studio glass artist Marvin Lipofsky. He works with his wife, also a glass artist, in the US.

2003-04   6in (15cm) high

$180   AGW

'Por do Sol em Bozios' sommerso glass block, signed and dated by Bruno Pedrosa and bearing his cruciform monogram.

Multi-talented Brazilian artist Bruno Pedrosa (b.1950) began working in glass in 1995. He designs his pieces and then guides the glass master's hand, using it as a brush, to execute his designs. His work can be found in Museum of Modern Art, Rio de Janeiro, and the Corning Museum of Glass, New York.

2003   11.25in (28.5cm) high

$2,800   VET

An American hand-blown glass jug, by Janusz Pozniak, with cast clear glass handle.

2003-04   12in (30.5cm) high

$820   AGW

'Greek Head VIII', by David Reekie, kiln-formed opaque glass, signed "Greek Head VIII David Reekie Norwich July94".

David Reekie (b.1947) trained at the Stourbridge College of Art. He is known for his often humorous and surreal depiction of the human form and its many feelings and attitudes. In this series, Reekie aimed to add more life and excitement to Ancient Greek head designs.

1994   16.75in (42.5cm) high

$5,500   CG

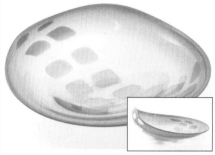

'Drifter Bowl', by Karlin Rushbrooke, orange glass with internal opaque white rounded rectangles, signed "Karlin Rushbrooke" on the base.

Well known for bottle forms, his glass has a fluid, flowing property as he works with very hot glass. He was one of the first people to have a hot glass studio of his own in the UK.

2003   12.75in (32.5cm) widest

$120   **CG**

An American 'Angelfish' scent bottle, by David Salazar, ground glass aquarium scene, with clear stopper signed "D P Salazar 5/02".

Salazar is a leading practitioner of 'painting with glass' technique where the artist heats the glass rod and 'draws' a design onto hot glass, using the cane as colored pencil.

2002   4in (10cm) high

$500   **BGL**

An American 'New Mexico Blue Bowl with Red Lip', by Josh Simpson, signed "Simpson 8-4-01".

Known for his 'planet' spheres, Simpson was inspired by the color of the night sky in Summer to create this color and range of bowls. Each is unique and uses metallic silver on cobalt blue glass. Each one is created in controlled conditions to create the right color and pattern.

2001

$300   **BGL**

'Marine Light III', by Pauline Solven, blown and cased colored glass, signed 'Pauline Solven 2003'.

The abstract patterns are created with powdered colored enamels and inspired by marine light, as the title suggests.

2003   6in (15cm) high

$1,000   **CG**

'Paintwork XIV', by Pauline Solven, signed on the base "Pauline Solven 2004".

This is part of a series of 15 'vessels' inspired by the distressed state of painted boats in a dry dock.

2004   6.5in (16.5cm) high

$1,000   **CG**

'Emerging Sun', by Pauline Solven, constructed from blown and cased elements, with sandblasted finish giving a matte texture, the individual segments adhered with ultraviolet bonding.

Solven is unusual in that she works alone in her studio, without assistants. She trained at the Royal College of Art in London, and worked at the Glasshouse with Sam Herman, before co-founding Cowdy Glass. Her finely colored, painterly work is often inspired by nature and light.

2000   14in (35.5cm) high

$2,800   **CG**

A 'Mirrored Vase', signed and made by Anthony Stern, made using blown mirrored glass

2004   19.75in (50cm) high

$400   **ASG**

A large blown 'Seascape' bowl, by Anthony Stern.

Stern's expressive 'Seascape' pieces work with light to bring the design, which incorporates impressions of sea, sky, and landscape, alive.

2003   8.75in (22cm) high

$2,200   **ASG**

A 'Rolling Stone Vase', by Anthony Stern, using images from original photographs taken by Stern when he was a photographer during the 1960s.

The photographic images of the 'Rolling Stones' seen here were captured by Stern in one of his early roles as a photographer during the 1960s. Using an innovative process, they are suspended between two clear layers of glass, over a core of opaque white glass.

2004   8.5in (21.5cm) high

$1,400   **ASG**

An American blown glass bowl, by Valerie Surjan, decorated with leaf and cherry motifs.

Surjan's highly detailed sandblasted cameo work on handblown vessels is influenced by the world of nature, with exotic animals, fruits, vines, and leaves being typical subjects. She has studied in Italy and has won a number of awards for her designs, many of which can be found in limited editions.

2003-04   5in (13cm) high

$950   **AGW**

A River Trout shaped stem goblet, by Milon Townsend, with lampwork fish stem and blown foot and bowl, signed "C Milon Townsend".

2000   8in (20cm) high

$280   **BGL**

'Quilt Platter 7', by David Traub, cased colored glass dish comprising layers of colored glass strips and clear glass.

American born and trained Traub now lives and works in Wanganui, New Zealand. His works, such as this, focus on pure form and resonant, vibrant color.

2003   17.25in (44cm) square

$3,200   **CG**

'Waterfall Bowl', by Fleur Tookey, blown bowl with blue striations created by applying powdered color to the glass gather, signed on the base "Fleur Tookey".

2003   7.25in (18.5cm) wide

$220   **CG**

An American blown glass mantle vase, by Lucy Vergamini.

2003-04   12in (30.5cm) high

$720   **AGW**

An American molded and blown glass sculpture by Nikolas Weinstein.

2003-04   14.5in (37cm) high

$445   **AGW**

'String Ball', by Christopher Williams, free engraved with a fine wheel, signed on the base, "Christopher Williams Savignon".

2002   14.25in (36.5cm) high

$1,400   **CG**

An American molded and blown glass sculpture, by Nikolas Weinstein.

2003-04   6in (15cm) high

$290   **AGW**

FIND OUT MORE...

'DK Collectors Guide: 20th Century Glass', by Judith Miller, published by Dorling Kindersley, 2004.

'Glass Art', by Peter Layton, published by A & C Black Ltd, 1996.

GLOSSARY

A

Acid etching A technique using acid to decorate glass to produce a matt or frosted appearance.

Albumen print Photographic paper is treated with egg white (albumen) to enable it to hold more light-sensitive chemicals. After being exposed to a negative, the resulting image is richer with more tonal variation.

Applied Refers to a separate part that has been attached to an object, such as a handle.

B

Baluster A curved form with a bulbous base and a slender neck.

Base metal A term describing common metals such as copper, tin and lead, or metal alloys, that were usually plated in gold or silver to imitate more expensive and luxurious metals. In the US, the term 'pot metal' is more commonly used.

Bisque A type of unglazed porcelain used for making dolls from c1860 to c1925.

Boards The hard covers of a book.

Brassing On plated items, where the plating has worn off to reveal the underlying base metal.

C

Cabochon A large, protruding, polished, but not faceted, stone.

Cameo Hardstone, coral or shell that has been carved in relief to show a design in a contrasting color.

Cameo glass Decorative glass made from two or more layers of differently colored glass, which are then carved or etched to reveal the color beneath.

Cartouche A framed panel, often in the shape of a shield or paper scroll, which can be inscribed.

Cased Where a piece of glass is covered with a further layer of glass, often of a contrasting color, or else clear and colorless. In some cases the casing will be further worked with cutting or etching to reveal the layer beneath.

Charger A large plate or platter, often for display, but also for serving.

Chromolithography A later development of 'lithography', where a number of printing stones are used in succession, each with a different color, to build up a multi-colored image.

Composition A mixture including wood pulp, plaster and glue used as a cheap alternative to bisque in the production of dolls' heads and bodies.

Compote A dish, usually on a stem or foot, to hold fruit for the dessert course.

Craze/Crazed/Crazing A network of fine cracks in the glaze caused by uneven shrinking during firing. It also describes plastic that is slowly degrading and has the same surface patterning.

Cuenca A technique used for decorating tiles where molded ridges separate the colored glazes, like the 'cloisonné' enameling technique.

Cultured pearl A pearl formed when an irritant is artificially introduced to the mollusc.

D

Damascened Metal ornamented with inlaid gold or silver, often in wavy lines. Commonly found on weapons or armor.

Dichroic Glass treated with chemicals or metals that cause it to appear differently colored depending on how it is viewed in the light.

Diecast Objects made by pouring molten metal into a closed metal die or mold.

Ding A very small dent in metal.

E

Earthenware A type of porous pottery that requires a glaze to make it waterproof.

Ebonized Wood that has been blackened with dye to resemble ebony.

E.P.N.S. Found on metal objects and standing for 'electroplated nickel silver', meaning the object is made from nickel which is then electroplated with silver.

F

Faïence Earthenware that is treated with an impervious tin glaze. Popular in France from the 16th century and reaching its peak during the 18th century.

Faceted A form of decoration where a number of flat surfaces are cut into the surface of an object such as a gem or glass.

Faux A French word for 'false'. The intention is not to deceive fraudulently but to imitate a more costly material.

Finial A decorative knob at the end of a terminal, or on a lid.

Foliate Leaf and vine motifs.

G

Guilloché An engraved pattern of interlaced lines or other decorative motifs, sometimes enameled over with translucent enamels.

H

Hallmark The series of small stamps found on gold or silver that can identify the maker, the standard of the metal and the city and year of manufacture. Hallmarks differ for each country and can consist only of a maker's or a city mark. All English silver made after 1544 was required to be fully marked.

IJKL

Incised Applied to surface decoration or a maker's mark that has been scratched into the surface of an object with a sharp instrument.

Inclusions Used to describe all types of small particles of decorative materials embedded in glass.

Iridescent A lustrous finish that subtly changes color depending on how light hits it. Often used to describe the finish on ceramics and glass.

Lithography A printing technique developed in 1798 and employing the use of a stone upon which a pattern or picture has been drawn with a grease crayon. The ink adheres to the grease and is transfered to the paper when pressed against it.

MNO

Millefiori An Italian term meaning 'thousand flowers' and used to describe cut, multi-colored glass canes which are arranged and cased in clear glass. When arranged with the cut side facing the exterior, each circular disc (or short cane) resembles a small flower.

Mint A term used to describe an object in unused condition with no signs of wear and derived from coinage. Truly 'mint' objects will command a premium.

Mount A metal part applied to an object made of ceramic, glass or another material, with a decorative or functional use.

Nappy A shallow dish or bowl with a handle used for drinking.

Opalescent An opal-like, milky glass with subtle gradations of color between thinner more translucent areas and thicker, more opaque areas.

P

Paisley A stylized design based on pinecones and foliage, often with added intricate decoration. It originated in India and is most often found on fabrics, such as shawls.

Paste (jewelry) A hard, bright glass cut the same way as a diamond and made and set to resemble them.

Patera An oval or circular decorative motif often with a fluted or floral centre. The plural is 'paterae'.

Piqué A decorative technique where small strips or studs of gold are inlaid onto ivory or tortoiseshell on a pattern and secured in place by heating.

Pontil A metal rod to which a glass vessel is attached when it is being worked. When it is removed it leaves a raised disc-shaped 'pontil mark'.

Pot metal Please see 'Base metal'.

Pounce pot A small pot made of wood (treen), silver or ceramic. Found on inkwells or designed to stand alone, it held a gum dust that was sprinkled over parchment to prevent ink from spreading. Used until the late 18th century.

Pressed (Press molded) Ceramics formed by pressing clay into a mold. Pressed glass is made by pouring molten glass into a mold and pressing it with a plunger.

R

Reeded A type of decoration with thin raised, convex vertical lines. Derived from the decoration of classical columns.

Relief A form of molded, pressed or carved decoration that protrudes above the surface of an object. Usually in the form of figures of foliate and foliage designs, it ranges in height from 'low' to 'high'.

Repoussé A French term for the raised, 'embossed' decoration on metals such as silver. The metal is forced into a form from one side causing it to bulge.

S

Sgraffito An Italian word for 'little scratch' and used to describe a decorative technique where the outer surface of an object, usually in glazed or colored ceramic, is scratched away in a pattern to reveal the contrasting colored underlying surface.

Sommerso Technique developed in Murano in the 1930s. Translates as 'submerged' and involves casing one or more layers of transparent colored glass within a layer of thick, clear, colorless glass.

Stoneware A type of ceramic similar to earthenware and made of high-fired clay mixed with stone, such as feldspar, which makes it non-porous.

T

Tazza A shallow cup with a wide bowl, which is raised up on a single pedestal foot.

Tooled Collective description for a number of decorative techniques applied to a surface. Includes engraving, stamping, punching and incising.

V

Vermeil Gold-plated silver.

Vesta case A small case or box, usually made from silver, for carrying matches.

W

White metal Precious metal that is possibly silver, but not officially marked as such.

Y

Yellow metal Precious metal that is possibly gold, but not officially marked as such.

INDEX TO ADVERTISERS

KEY TO ILLUSTRATIONS

Every collectible illustrated in DK Collectibles Price Guide 2005 by Judith Miller has a letter code identifying the dealer or auction house that sold it. The list below is a key to these codes. In the list, auction houses are shown by the letter A and dealers by the letter D. Some items may have come from a private collection, in which case the code is accompanied by the letter P. Inclusion in this book in no way constitutes or implies a contract or a binding offer on the part of any of our contributors to supply or sell the goods illustrated, or similar items, at the prices stated.

AAC (A)
Alderfer Auction Company
501 Fairgrounds Road,
Hatfield, PA 19440
Tel: 215 393 3000
info@alderferauction.com
www.alderferauction.com

AAG (D)
Animation Art Gallery
13-14 Great Castle Street,
London W1W 8LS UK
Tel: +44 (0)20 7255 1456
gallery@animaart.com
www.animaart.com

AB (A) (D)
Auction Blocks
The Auction Blocks, 10 Twarog
Place, P.O. Box 2321,
Shelton, CT 06484
Tel: 203 924 2802
auctionblocks@aol.com
www.auctionblocks.com

BIJ (D)
Aurora Bijoux
525 Perkiomen Avenue,
Lansdale PA 19446
Tel: 215 855 1921
aurora@aurorabijoux.com
www.aurorabijoux.com

ADE (D)
Art Deco Etc
73 Upper Gloucester Road,
Brighton, Sussex BN1 3LQ UK
Tel: +44 (0)1273 329 268
Mob: +44 (0)7971 268 302
johnclark@artdecoetc.co.uk

AG (D)
Antique Glass
at Frank Dux Antiques
33 Belvedere,
Bath, BA1 5HR UK
Tel: +44 (0)1225 312 367
m.hopkins@antique-glass.co.uk
www.antique-glass.co.uk

AGO (D)
Anona Gabriel
Otford Antiques Centre,
26-28 High Street, Otford,
Kent TN15 9DF UK
Tel: +44 (0)1959 522 025
info@otfordantiques.co.uk
www.otfordantiques.co.uk

AGW (D)
American Art Glass Works Inc
41 Wooster Street, 1st floor,

New York, NY 10013
Tel: 212 625 0783
www.americanartglassgallery.com

AHL (D)
Andrea Hall Levy
P.O. Box 1243,
Riverdale, NY 10471
Tel: 718 601 4239
barangrill@aol.com

AL (D)
Andrew Lineham Fine Glass
The Mall Antiques Arcade, 359
Upper Street, London N1 UK
Tel: +44 (0)20 7704 0195
andrew@andrewlineham.co.uk
www.antiquecolouredglass.co.uk

ALL (A)
Allard Auctions
P.O. Box 1030, 419 Flathead
St. 4, St. Ignatius, MT 59865
Tel: 460 745 0500
Fax: 460 745 0502
www.allardauctions.com

ANAA (D)
Anastacia's Antiques
617 Bainbridge Street,
Philadelphia, PA 19147
Tel: 215 928 0256

ASG (D)
Anthony Stern Glass
Unit 205, Avro House, Havelock
Terrace, London SW8 4AL UK
Tel: +44 (0)20 7622 9463
www.anthonysternglass.com

ATA (D)
Atomic Age
318 East Virginia Road,
Fullerton, CA 92831
Tel: 714 446 0736
atomage100@aol.com

ATK (D)
Auction Team Köln
Postfach 50 11 19, Bonner Str.
528-530, D-50971 Köln, Germany
Tel: +49 (0) 221 38 70 49
auction@breker.com
www.breker.com

ATM (D)
At the Movies
17 Fouberts Place, London
W1F 7QD UK
Tel: +44 (0)20 7439 6336
info@atthemovies.co.uk
www.atthemovies.co.uk

B&H (A)
Burstow & Hewett
Lower Lake, Battle,
East Sussex TN33 0AT UK
Tel: +44 (0)1424 772 374
auctions@burstowandhewett.co.uk
www.burstowandhewett.co.uk

BA (D)
Branksome Antiques
370 Poole Road, Branksome,
Poole, Dorset BH12 1AW UK
Tel: +44 (0)1202 763 324

BAD (D)
Beth Adams
Unit GO43/4,
Alfies Antique Market,
13 Church Street, Marylebone,
London NW8 8DT UK
Tel: +44 (0)20 7723 5613
badams@alfies.clara.net

BAR (A)
Dreweatt Neate (Bristol)
St John's Place, Apsley Road,
Clifton, Bristol BS8 2ST UK
Tel: +44 (0)117 973 7201
bristol@dnfa.com
www.dnfa.com

BB (D)
Barbara Blau
South Street Antiques Center,
615 South 6th Street,
Philadelphia, PA 19147-2128
Tel: 215 739 4995

BBR (A)
BBR Auctions
Elsecar Heritage Centre,
Nr Barnsley, South Yorkshire
S74 8AA UK
Tel: +44 (0)1226 745156
www.bbrauctions.co.uk

BCAC (D)
Bucks County Antique Center
Route 202, Lahaska PA 18931
Tel: 215 794 9180

BEJ (D)
Bébés & Jouets
c/o Post Office,
165 Restalrig Road, Edinburgh
EH7 6HW Scotland
Tel: +44 (0)131 332 5650
bebesetjouets@u.genie.co.uk

BEV (D)
Beverley
30 Church Street,
London NW8 8EP UK
Tel: +44 (0)20 7262 1576

BG (A)
Bob Gowland International
Golf Auctions
The Stables, Claim Farm,
Manley Road, Frodsham,
Cheshire WA6 6HT UK
Tel: +44 (0)1928 740 668
bob@internationalgolfauctions.com
www.internationalgolfauctions.com

BGL (D)
Block Glass Ltd.
60 Ridgeview Avenue,
Trumbull, CT 06611
Tel: 203 556 0905
blockglss@aol.com
www.blockglass.com

BIB (D)
Biblion
1/7 Davies Mews,
London W1K 5AB UK
Tel: +44 (0)20 7629 1374
info@biblion.com
www.biblion.com

BMA (D)
Bill & Myrtle Aquilino
P.O. Box 9, Chalfont, PA 18914
Tel: 215 822 6867

BMN (A)
Auktionhaus Bergmann
Möhrendorferstraße 4,
D-91056 Erlangen Germany
Tel: 00 49 (0) 9131 45 06 66
kontact@auction-bergmann.de
www.auction-bergmann.de

BONM (A)
Bonhams, Knowle
The Old House, Station Road,
Knowle, Solihull, B93 0HT UK
Tel: +44 (0)1564 776 151
info@bonhams.com
www.bonhams.com

BONS, BONBAY, BONC (A)
Bonhams, Bond Street
101 New Bond Street,
London W1S 1SR UK
Tel: +44 (0)1732 740 310
info@bonhams.com
www.bonhams.com

BP (D)
The Blue Pump
178 Davenport Road,
Toronto,
Canada M5R 1J2
Tel: 416 944 1673

BR (D)
Beyond Retro
110-112 Cheshire Street,
London E2 6EJ UK
Tel: +44 (0)20 7613 3636
sales@beyondretro.com
www.beyondretro.com

BRB (D)
Bauman Rare Books
535 Madison Avenue,
New York, NY 10022
Tel: 212 751 1011
brb@baumanrarebooks.com
www.baumanrarebooks.com

BRU (A)
Brunk Auctions
P.O. Box 2135,
Ashville, NC 28802
Tel: 828 254 6846
keith@brunkauctions.com
www.brunkauctions.com

BS (D)
Below Stairs of Hungerford
103 High Street,
Hungerford,
Berkshire RG17 0NB UK
Tel: +44 (0)1488 682 317
hofgartner@belowstairs.co.uk
www.belowstairs.co.uk

BY (D)
Bonny Yankauer
Tel: 201 825 7697
bonnyy@aol.com

CAA (D)
Contemporary Applied Arts
2 Percy Street,
London W1T 1DD UK
Tel: +44 (0)20 7436 2344
www.caa.org.uk

CAC (D)
Charles A. Cohn
P.O. Box 8835,
Elkins Park, PA 19027
Tel: 215 840 6112
cacint@comcast.net

CAMA (D)
Camelot Antiques
7872 Ocean Gateway,
Easton, MD 21601
Tel: 410 820 4396
camelot@goeaston.net
www.about-
antiques.com/CamelotAntique

CANT (D)
Carlton Antiques
43 Worcester Road, Malvern,
Worcestershire WR14 4RB UK
Tel: +44 (0)1684 573 092
dave@carlton-antiques.com
www.carlton-antiques.com

CARS (D)
Classic Automobilia & Regalia Specialists
4-4a Chapel Terrace Mews,
Kemp Town, Brighton BN2 1HU
Tel: +44 (0)1273 601 960

CAT (D)
Catalin Radios
5443 Schultz Drive,
Sylvania, OH 43560
Tel: 419 824 2469
Mob: 419 283 8203
steve@catalinradio.com
www.catalinradio.com

CBE (P)
Christina Bertrand
tineke@rcn.com

CBU (D)
Chéz Burnette
South Street Antiques Center,
615 South 6th Street,
Philadelphia, PA 19147-2128
Tel: 215 592 0256

CCL (D)
Cloud Cuckoo Land
6 Charlton Place, Camden
Passage, London N1 8EA UK
Tel: +44 (0)20 7354 3141

CG (D)
Cowdy Gallery
31 Culver Street, Newent,
Gloucestershire GL18 1DB UK
Tel: +44 (0)1531 821 173
info@cowdygallery.co.uk
www.cowdygallery.co.uk

CGC (P)
Cheryl Grandfield Collection

CHAA (A)
Cowan's Historic Americana Auctions
673 Wilmer Avenue,
Cincinnati, OH 45226
Tel: 513 871 1670
info@historicamericana.com
www.historicamericana.com

CHEF (A)
Cheffins
The Cambridge Salerooms,
1&2 Clifton Road,
Cambridge CB1 7EA UK
Tel: +44 (0)1223 213 343
fine.art@cheffins.co.uk
www.cheffins.co.uk

CHS (D)
China Search
P.O. Box 1202, Kenilworth,
Warwickshire CV8 2WW UK
Tel: +44 (0)1926 512 402
helen@chinasearch.uk.com
www.chinasearch.uk.com

CL (D)
Chisholm Larsson
145 8th Avenue,
New York, NY 10011
Tel: 212 741 1703
www.chisholm-poster.com

CLV (A)
Clevedon Salerooms
The Auction Centre,
Kenn Road, Clevedon,
Bristol BS21 6TT UK
Tel: +44 (0)1934 830 111
info@clevedonsalerooms.co.uk
www.clevedon-salerooms.com

CO (A)
Cooper Owen
10 Denmark Street,
London WC2H 8LS UK
Tel: +44 (0)20 7240 4132
info@cooperowen.com
www.cooperowen.com

COB (D)
Cobwebs
78 Old Northam Road,
Southampton SO14 0PB UK
Tel: +44 (0)2380 227 458
www.cobwebs.uk.com

CR (A)
Craftsman Auctions
333 North Main Street,
Lambertville, NJ 08530
Tel: 609 397 9374
info@ragoarts.com
www.ragoarts.com

CRIS (D)
Cristobal
26 Church Street, Marylebone,
London NW8 8EP UK
Tel: +44 (0)20 7724 7230
steven@cristobal.co.uk
www.cristobal.co.uk

CSA (D)
Christopher Sykes Antiques
The Old Parsonage, Woburn,
Milton Keynes MK17 9QL UK
Tel: +44 (0)1525 290 259
sykes.corkscrews@sykes-
corkscrews.co.uk
www.sykes-corkscrews.co.uk

CVS (D)
Cad Van Swankster at The Girl Can't Help It
G115, Alfies Antique Market,
13 Church Street, Marylebone,
London NW8 8DT UK
Tel: +44 (0)20 7724 8984

CW (P)
Christine Wildman Collection
wild123@allstream.net

DAC (D)
Dynamite Antiques & Collectibles
Tel: 301 652 1140
bercovici@erols.com

DAW (A)
Dawson's Auctioneers & Appraisers,
now trading as Dawson & Nye
128 American Road, Morris
Plains, NJ 07950
Tel: 973 984 6900
info@dawsonandnye.com
www.dawsonandnye.com

DE (D)
The Doll Express
Ceased trading.

DETC (D)
Deco Etc
122 West 25th Street
(between 6th & 7th Aves),
New York, NY 10001
Tel: 212 675 3326
deco_etc@msn.com
www.decoetc.net

DG (D)
Donay Games
34 Gower Road,
Haywards Heath,
West Sussex RH16 4PN UK
Tel: +44 (0)1444 416 412
donaygames@btconnect.com
www.donaygames.com

DH (D)
Huxtins
11 & 12 The Lipka Arcade,
288 Westbourne Grove,
London W11 UK
Mob: +44 (0)7710 132 200
david@huxtins.com
www.huxtins.com

DN (A)
Dreweatt Neate
Donnington Priory Salerooms,
Donnington, Newbury,
Berkshire RG14 2JE UK
Tel: +44 (0)1635 553 553
auctions@dnfa.com
www.dnfa.com

DRA (A)
David Rago Modern Auctions
333 North Main Street,
Lambertville, NJ 08530
Tel: 609 397 9374
info@ragoarts.com
www.ragoarts.com

DTC (D)
Design20c
Tel: +44 (0)794 609 2138 /
+44 (0)776 013 5203
sales@design20c.com
www.design20c.com

EAB (D)
Anne Barrett
Otford Antiques & Collectables
Centre, 26-28 High Street,
Otford, Kent TN15 9DF UK
Tel: +44 (0)1959 522 025
info@otfordantiques.co.uk
www.otfordantiques.co.uk

ECLEC (D)
Eclectica
2 Charlton Place, Islington,
London N1 UK
Tel: +44 (0)20 7226 5625
eclecticaliz@yahoo.co.uk

EOH (D)
The End of History
548 1/2 Hudson Street,
New York, NY 10014
Tel: 212 647 7598

EPO (D)
Elaine Perkins
Otford Antiques & Collectables
Centre, 26-28 High Street,
Otford, Kent TN15 9DF UK
Tel: +44 (0)1959 522 025
info@otfordantiques.co.uk
www.otfordantiques.co.uk

ET (D)
Early Technology
Monkton House, Old Craighall,
Musselburgh, Midlothian
EH21 8SF Scotland
Tel: +44 (0)131 665 5753
michael.bennett-levy@virgin.net
www.earlytech.com

F (A)
Fellows & Sons
Augusta House,
19 Augusta Street, Hockley,
Birmingham B18 6JA UK
Tel: +44 (0)121 212 2131
info@fellows.co.uk
www.fellows.co.uk

FAN (D)
Fantiques
30 Hastings Road, Ealing,
London W13 8QH UK
Tel: +44 (0)20 8840 4761
Mob: 07956 242 450
paulajraven@aol.com

FFM (D)
Festival
136 South Ealing Road,
London W5 4QJ UK
Tel: +44 (0)20 8840 9333
info@festival1951.co.uk

FIS (A)
Auktionhaus Dr Fischer
Trappensee-Schößchen, D-74074 Heilbronn Germany
Tel: +49 (0)71 31 15 55 70
kunstauktionendr.fischer@t-online.de
www.auctions-fischer.de

FM (D)
Francesca Martire
F131-137,
Alfies Antique Market,
13 Church Street, Marylebone,
London NW8 8DT UK
Tel: +44 (0)20 7724 4802
martire@alfies.clara.net

FRE (A)
Freeman's
1808 Chestnut Street,
Philadelphia, PA 19103
Tel: 215 563 9275
info@freemansauction.com
www.freemansauction.com

G (A)
Guernsey's Auctions
108 East 73rd Street,
New York, NY 10021
Tel: 212 794 2280
guernsey@guernseys.com
www.guernseys.com

GAZE (A)
Thos. Wm. Gaze & Son
Diss Auction Rooms,
Roydon Road, Diss,
Norfolk IP22 4LN UK
Tel: +44 (0)1379 650 306
sales@dissauctionrooms.co.uk
www.twgaze.com

GC (P)
Graham Cooley Collection
Mob: +44 (0)7968 722 269
graham.cooley@metalysis.com

GCA (D)
Griffin & Cooper Antiques
South Street Antiques Center,
615 South 6th Street,
Philadelphia, PA 19147-2128
Tel: 215 582 0418 / 3594

GCL (D)
Claude Lee
The Ginnel Antiques Centre, off
Parliament Street, Harrogate,
North Yorkshire HG1 2RB UK
Tel: +44 (0)1423 508 857
info@theginnel.com
www.redhouseyork.co.uk

GGRT (D)
Gary Grant
18 Arlington Way,
London EC1R 1UY UK
Tel: +44 (0)20 7713 1122

GHA (D)
Hawkswood Antiques
The Ginnel Antiques Centre, off
Parliament Street, Harrogate,
North Yorkshire HG1 2RB UK
Tel: +44 (0)1423 508 857
info@theginnel.com
www.redhouseyork.co.uk

GKA (D)
Kismet Antiques
The Ginnel Antiques Centre, off
Parliament Street, Harrogate,
North Yorkshire HG1 2RB UK
Tel: +44 (0)1423 508 857
info@theginnel.com
www.redhouseyork.co.uk

GMC (D)
Mary Cooper
The Ginnel Antiques Centre, off
Parliament Street, Harrogate,
North Yorkshire, HG1 2RB UK
Tel: +44 (0)1423 508 857
info@theginnel.com
www.redhouseyork.co.uk

GMW (D)
Geoffrey and Millicent
Woolworth
Otford Antiques & Collectables
Centre, 26-28 High Street,
Otford, Kent TN15 9DF UK
Tel: +44 (0)1959 522 025
info@otfordantiques.co.uk
www.otfordantiques.co.uk

GORL (A)
Gorringes, Lewes
15 North Street, Lewes,
East Sussex BN7 2PD UK
Tel: +44 (0)1273 472 503
clientservices@gorringes.co.uk
www.gorringes.co.uk

GROB (D)
Geoffrey Robinson
Stand GO77-78 & GO91-92,
Alfies Antiques Market,
13-25 Church Street,
London NW8 8DT UK
Tel: +44 (0)20 7723 0449

H&G (D)
Hope and Glory
131A Kensington Church
Street, London W8 7LP UK
Tel: +44 (0)20 7727 8424

HA (A)
Hunt Auctions
75 East Uwchlan Avenue,
Suite 130, Exton, PA 19341
Tel: 610 524 0822
info@huntauctions.com
www.huntauctions.com

HB (D)
Victoriana Dolls
101 Portobello Rd,
London W11 2BQ UK
Tel: +44 (0)1737 249 525
heather.bond@totalserve.co.uk

HD (D)
Halcyon Days
14 Brook Street,
London W1S 1BD UK
Tel: +44 (0)20 7629 8811
info@halcyondays.co.uk
www.halcyondays.co.uk

HGS (D)
Harper General Store
10482 Jonestown Road,
Annville, PA 17003
Tel: 717 865 3456
lauver5@comcast.com
www.harpergeneralstore.com

HLJ (D)
Hugo Lee-Jones
Tel: +44 (0)1227 375 375

Mob: +44 (0)7941 187 2027
electroniccollectables@hotmail.com

HP (D)
Hilary Proctor
Vintage Modes, Grays Antiques
Market, 1-7 Davies Mews,
London W1Y 2PL UK
Tel: +44 (0)20 7409 0400
Mob: +44 (0)7956 876 428
hproctor@antiquehandbags.fsne
t.co.uk
www.vintagemodes.co.uk

INT (D)
Intercol
43 Templar's Crescent, Finchley,
London N3 3QR UK
Tel: +44 (0)20 8349 2207
yasha@intercol.co.uk
www.intercol.co.uk

JBC (D)
James Bridges Collection
james@jbridges.fsnet.co.uk

JDJ (A)
James D Julia Inc
P.O. Box 830, Fairfield,
Maine 04937
Tel: 207 453 7125
jjulia@juliaauctions.com
www.juliaauctions.com

JF (D)
Jill Fenichell
305 East 61st Street,
New York, NY 10021
Tel: 212 980 9346
jfenichell@yahoo.com

JH (D)
Jeanette Hayhurst Fine Glass
32A Kensington Church Street,
London W8 4HA UK
Tel: +44 (0)20 7938 1539

JJ (D)
Junkyard Jeweler
937 West Beech Street,
Suite 49,
Long Beach, NY 11561
spignerc@aol.com
www.junkyardjeweler.com

JL (D)
Eastgate Antiques
S007/009, Alfies Antique
Market, 13 Church Street,
Marylebone,
London NW8 8DT UK
Tel: +44 (0)20 7258 0312

JSC (D)
Jean Scott Collection
jean@stanhopes.info
www.stanhopes.info

JV (D)
June Victor
Vintage Modes,
Grays Antiques Market,
1-7 Davies Mews,
London W1Y 2PL UK
Tel: +44 (0)20 7409 0400
info@vintagemodes.co.uk
www.vintagemodes.co.uk

K&R (D)
Keller & Ross
P.O. Box 783,
Melrose, MA 02176
Tel: 978 988 2070
kellerross@aol.com

http://members.aol.com/kellerross

KF (D)
Karl Flaherty Collectables
Tel: +44 (0)2476 445 627
kfckarl@aol.com
www.kfcollectables.co.uk

KK (D)
Kathy's Korner
Tel: 516 624 9494

KNK (D)
Kitsch-N-Kaboodle
South Street Antiques Center,
615 South 6th Street,
Philadelphia, PA 19147-2128
Tel: 215 382 1354
kitschnkaboodle@yahoo.com

L (D)
Luna
23 George Street,
Nottingham NG1 3BH
Tel: +44 (0)115 924 3267
info@luna-online.co.uk
www.luna-online.com

L&T (A)
Lyon and Turnbull Ltd.
33 Broughton Place, Edinburgh
EH1 3RR Scotland
Tel: +44 (0)131 557 8844
info@lyonandturnbull.com
www.lyonandturnbull.com

LAN (A)
Lankes
Triftfeldstrasse 1, 95182
Döhlau Germany
Tel: +49 (0)928 69 50 50
www.lankes-auktionen.de

LB (D)
Linda Bee
Stand L18-21, Grays Mews
Antique Market, 58 Davies
Street, London W1Y 2LP UK
Tel: +44 (0)20 7629 5921
Mob: +44 (0)7956 276384
www.graysantiques.com

LC (A)
Lawrence's Fine Art
Auctioneers
The Linen Yard, South Street,
Crewkerne,
Somerset TA18 8AB UK
Tel: +44 (0)1460 73041
enquiries@lawrences.co.uk
www.lawrences.co.uk

LCA (D)
Lights, Camera, Action
6 Western Gardens,
Western Boulevard, Aspley,
Nottingham HG8 5GP UK
Tel: +44 (0)115 913 1116
nickstraw@ntlbusiness.com
www.lca-autographs.co.uk

LDE (D)
Larry & Dianna Elman
P.O. Box 415,
Woodland Hills, CA 91365

LFA (D)
Law Fine Art Ltd.
The Long Gallery,
Littlecote House, Hungerford,
Berkshire RG17 0SS UK
Tel: +44 (0)1635 860 033
www.lawfineart.co.uk

LG (D)
Legacy
G50/51, Alfies Antique Market,
13 Church Street, Marylebone,
London NW8 8DT UK
Tel: +44 (0)20 7723 0449
legacy@alfies.clara.net

LHS (A) (D)
L.H. Selman Ltd.
123 Locust Street,
Santa Cruz, CA 950600
www.selman.com/pwauction/

LOB (D)
Louis O'Brien
Tel: +44 (0)1276 32907

LW (D)
Linda Warren
Otford Antiques Centre,
26-28 High Street, Otford,
Kent TN15 9DF UK
Tel: +44 (0)1959 522 025
info@otfordantiques.co.uk
www.otfordantiques.co.uk

MA (D)
Manic Attic
Stand S011, Alfies Antiques
Market, 13 Church Street,
London NW8 8DT UK
Tel: +44 (0)20 7723 6105
manicattic@alfies.clara.net

MAC (D)
Mary Ann's Collectibles
South Street Antiques Center,
615 South 6th Street,
Philadelphia, PA 19147-2128
Tel: 215 923 3247

MC (D)
Metropolis Collectibles, Inc.
873 Broadway, Suite 201,
New York, NY 10003
Tel: 212 260 4147
orders@metropoliscomics.com
www.metropoliscomics.com

MEM (D)
Memory Lane
45-40 Bell Blvd, Suite 109,
Bayside, NY 11361
Tel: 718 428 8181
memlnny@aol.com
www.tias.com/stores/memlnny

MHC (P)
Mark Hill Collection
Mob: +44 (0)7798 915 474
stylophile@btopenworld.com

MHT (D)
Mum Had That
Tel: +44 (0)1442 412 360
info@mumhadthat.com
www.mumhadthat.com

MILLB (D)
Million Dollar Babies
47 Hyde Boulevard,
Ballston Spa,
NY 12020
Tel: 518 885 7397

ML (D)
Mark Laino
South Street Antiques Center,
615 South 6th Street,
Philadelphia, PA 19147-2128

MM (A)
Mullock Madeley
The Old Shippon, Wall-under-
Heywood, Church Stretton,
Shropshire SY6 7DS UK
Tel: +44 (0)1694 771 771
info@mullockmadeley.co.uk
www.mullock-madeley.co.uk

MSC (P)
Mark Slavinsky Collection

MTS (D)
The Multicoloured Time Slip
Unit S002, Alfies Antiques
Market, 13-25 Church Street,
London NW8 8DT UK
Mob: +44 (0)7971 410 563
d_a_cameron@hotmail.com

MUW (D)
MuseumWorks
525 East Cooper Avenue,
Aspen CO 81611
www.mwhgalleries.com

NB (A)
Noel Barrett Antiques &
Auctions Ltd
P.O. Box 300,
Carversville, PA 18913
Tel: 215 297 5109
toys@noelbarrett.com
www.noelbarrett.com

NBEN (D)
Nigel Benson
20th Century Glass, 58-60
Kensington Church Street,
London W8 4DB UK
Tel: +44 (0)20 7938 1137
Mob: +44 (0)7971 859 848
nigelbenson@20thcentury-
glass.com
www.20thcentury-glass.com

NF (D)
Nifty Fifties
Tel: 734 782 3974

NOR (D)
Neet-O-Rama
93 West Main Street,
Somerville, NJ 08876
Tel: 908 722 4800
www.neetstuff.com

NWC (P)
Nigel Wright Collection
xab@dircon.co.uk

ON (A)
Onslows
The Coach House,
Manor Road,
Stourpaine,
Dorset DT11 8TQ UK
Tel: +44 (0)1258 488 838
enquiries@onslows.co.uk
www.onslows.co.uk

P (D)
Posteritati
239 Centre Street,
New York, NY 10013
Tel: 212 226 2207
mail@posteritati.com
www.posteritati.com

P&I (D)
Paola & Iaia
Unit SO57-58,
Alfies Antiques Market,
13-25 Church Street,

London NW8 8DT UK
Tel: +44 (0)7751 084 135
paolaeiaialondon@hotmail.com

PA (D)
Senator Phil Arthurhultz
P.O. Box 12336,
Lansing, MI 48901
Tel: 517 334 5000
Mob: 517 930 3000

PAC (D)
Port Antiques Center
289 Main Street, Port
Washington, NY 11050
Tel: 516 767 3313
visualedge2@aol.com

PC (P)
Private Collection

PKA (D)
Phil & Karol Atkinson
May-Oct:
713 Sarsi Tr, Mercer, PA 16137
Tel: 724 475 2490
Nov-Apr:
7188 Drewry's Bluff Road,
Bradenton, FL 34203
Tel: 941 755 1733

PL (D)
London Glass Blowing
7 The Leather Market, Weston
Street, London SE1 3ER UK
Tel: +44 (0)20 7403 2800
inf@londonglassblowing.co.uk
www.londonglassblowing.co.uk

POOK (A)
Pook and Pook
P.O. Box 268,
Downington, PA 19335 /
463 East Lancaster Avenue,
Downingtown, PA 19335
Tel: 610 269 4040 /
610 269 0695
info@pookandpook.com
www.pookandpook.com

PSA (A)
Potteries Specialist Auctions
271 Waterloo Road, Cobridge,
Stoke-on-Trent ST6 3HR UK
Tel: +44 (0)1782 286 622
enquiries@potteriesauctions.com
www.potteriesauctions.com

PSL (D)
The Propstore, London
Great House Farm, Chenies,
Rickmansworth, Herts WD3 6EP
Tel: +44 (0)1494 766 485
steve.lane@propstore.co.uk
www.propstore.co.uk

PST (D)
Patricia Stauble Antiques
180 Main Street, P.O. Box 265,
Wiscasset, ME 04578
Tel: 207 882 6341

QU (A)
Quittenbaum
Hohenstaufenstraße 1, D-
80801, München Germany
Tel: +49 859 33 00 75 6
dialog@quittenbaum.de
www.quittenbaum.de

REN (D)
Rennies
13 Rugby Street, London WC1
3QT UK

Tel: +44 (0)20 7405 0220
info@rennart.co.uk
www.rennart.co.uk

RG (D)
Richard Gibbon
34/34a Islington Green,
London N1 8DU UK
Tel: +44 (0)20 7354 2852
neljeweluk@aol.com

ROS (A)
Rosebery's
74-76 Knight's Hill,
West Norwood,
London SE27 0JD UK
Tel: +44 (0)20 8761 2522
Fax: +44 (0)20 8761 2524
enquiries@roseberys.co.uk
http://www.roseberys.co.uk/

ROX (D)
Roxanne Stuart
Tel: 888 750 8869 /
215 750 8868
gemfairy@aol.com

RP (D)
Rosie Palmer
Otford Antiques & Collectable
Centre, 26-28 High Street,
Otford, Kent TN15 9DF UK
Tel: +44 (0)1959 522 025
Fax: +44 (0)1959 525 858
info@otfordantiques.co.uk
www.otfordantiques.co.uk

RR (D)
Red Roses
Vintage Modes, Grays Antiques
Market, 1-7 Davies Mews,
London W1Y 2PL UK
Tel: +44 (0)20 7409 0400
Mob: +44 (0)7778 803 876
sallie_ead@lycos.com
www.vintagemodes.co.uk

RSJ (D)
Roger & Susan Johnson
1701 Venture Farms Road, Pilot
Point, TX 76258
Tel: 940 365 9149
Fax: 940 365 4401
czarmann@aol.com

RTZ (D)
Ritzy
7 The Mall Antiques Arcade,
359 Upper Street,
London N1 0PD UK
Tel: +44 (0)20 7351 5353
Fax: +44 (0)20 7351 5350

RWA (D)
Richard Wallis Antiks
Tel: +44 (0)20 8529 1749
Fax: +44 (0)870 051 5740
Mob: +44 (0)7721 583 306
info@richardwallisantiks.co.uk
www.richardwallisantiks.co.uk

S&K (A)
Sloans & Kenyon
4605 Bradley Boulevard,
Bethesda, MD 20815
Tel: 301 634 2330
Fax: 301 656 7074
info@sloansandkenyon.com
www.sloansandkenyon.com

SAS (A)
Special Auction Services
Kennetholme, Midgham,
Nr. Reading, Berkshire

APPENDICES

Tel: +44 (0)118 971 2949
commemorative@aol.com
www.invaluable.com/sas

SCG (D)
Gallery 1930 Susie Cooper
18 Church Street,
Marylebone,
London NW8 8EP UK
Tel: +44 (0)20 7723 1555
gallery1930@aol.com
www.susiecooperceramics.com

SEG (D)
Galerie Segas
34, Passage Jouffroy, 75009
Paris France
Tel: +33 (0)1 47 70 89 65

SEVW (D)
70s Watches
graham@gettya.freeserve.co.uk
www.70s-watches.com

SK (A)
Skinner, Inc.
The Heritage on the Garden
63 Park Plaza,
Boston, MA 02116
Tel: 617 350 5400
www.skinnerinc.com

SL (A)
Sloans
Ceased trading.

SM (D)
**Sparkle Moore at The Girl
Can't Help It**
G100 & G116,
Alfies Antique Market,
13 Church Street, Marylebone,
London NW8 8DT UK
Tel: +44 (0)20 7724 8984
Mob: +44 (0)7958 515 614
sparkle.moore@virgin.net
www.sparklemoore.com

SOTT (D)
Sign of the Tymes
Mill Antiques Center,
12 Morris Farm Road,
Lafayette, NJ 07848
Tel: 973 383 6028
jhap@nac.net
www.millantiques.com

SSC (P)
Sue Scrivens Collection

STC (D)
Seaside Toy Center
Joseph Soucy
179 Main St,
Westerly, RI 02891
Tel: 401 596 0962

SUM (D)
Sue Mautner
Stand A18-19,
Antiquarius,
135 King's Road,
London SW3 4PW UK
Tel: +44 (0)20 7376 4419

SWA (A)
Swann Galleries Image Library
104 East 25th Street,
New York, NY 10010,
Tel: 212-254-4710
Fax: 212-979-1017
www.swanngalleries.com.

TA (A)
333 Auctions LLC
333 North Main Street,
Lambertville, NJ 08530
Tel: 609 397 9374
www.333auctions.com

TAB (D)
Take-A-Boo Emporium
1927 Avenue Road, Toronto,
Ontario M5M 4A2 Canada
Tel: 416 785 4555
swinton@takeaboo.com
www.takeaboo.com

TAG (D)
Tagore Ltd
302, Grays Antique Market, 58
Davies Street, London W1Y 2LP
Tel: +44 (0)20 7499 0158
tagore@grays.clara.net

TAM (D)
Antiques & Militaria
Toronto Antiques Centre,
276 King Street West, Toronto,
Ontario M5V 1J2 Canada
Tel: 416 345 9941
sales@antiquesandmilitaria.com
www.antiquesandmilitaria.com

TCF (D)
Cynthia Findlay
Toronto Antiques Centre,
276 King Street West, Toronto,
Ontario, M5V 1J2 Canada
Tel: 416 260 9057
call@cynthiafindlay.com
www.cynthiafindlay.com/

TCS (D)
The Country Seat
Huntercombe Manor Barn,
Nr Henley on Thames,
Oxon RG9 5RY UK
Tel: +44 (0)1491 641 349
info@whitefriarsglass.com
www.whitefriarsglass.com

TCT (D)
The Calico Teddy
Tel: 410 433 9202
calicteddy@aol.com
ww.calicoteddy.com

TDG (D)
The Design Gallery
5 The Green,
Westerham,
Kent TN16 1AS UK
Tel: +44 (0)1959 561 234
sales@thedesigngallery.uk.com
www.thedesigngallery.uk.com

TEN (D)
Tennants
The Auction Centre, Leyburn,
North Yorkshire DL8 5SG UK
Tel: +44 (0)1969 623 780
enquiry@tennants-ltd.co.uk
www.tennants.co.uk

TH (D)
Toy Heroes
42 Westway, Caterham-on-the-
Hill, Surrey CR3 5TP UK
Tel: +44 (0)188 334 8
andydroon@aol.com
www.toyheroes.co.uk

TM (D)
Tony Moran
South Street Antiques Center,
615 South 6th Street,

Philadelphia, PA 19147-2128
Tel: 215 592 0256

TOG (D)
A Touch of Glass
Tel: 973 857 2617
deold@antiqueconnection.com
www.antiqueconnection.com

TP (D)
Tenth Planet
Unit 36, Vicarage Field
Shopping Centre, Ripple Road,
Barking, Essex IG11 8DQ UK
Tel: +44 (0)20 8591 5357
sales@tenthplanet.co.uk
www.tenthplanet.co.uk

TR (D)
Terry Rodgers & Melody LLC
30 & 31 Manhattan Art &
Antique Center, 1050 2nd
Avenue, New York, NY 10022
Tel: 212 758 3164
melodyjewelnyc@aol.com

TRA (D)
Toy Road Antiques
200 Highland Street, Canal
Winchester, OH 43110
Tel: 614 834 1786
toyroad@aol.com
www.goantiques.com/members
/toyroadantiques

TSG (D)
Shand Galleries
Toronto Antiques Centre, 276
King Street West, Toronto,
Ontario, M5V 1J2 Canada
Tel: 416 260 9056
kenshand@attcanada.ca

TSIS (D)
Three Sisters
South Street Antiques Center,
615 South 6th Street,
Philadelphia, PA
Tel: 215 739 4995 /
215 592 0256

TWC (A)
T.W. Conroy
36 Oswego St, Baldwinsville, NY
13027
Tel: 315 638 6434
www.twconroy.com

TYA (D)
Yank Azman
Toronto Antiques Centre, 276
King Street West, Toronto,
Ontario, M5V 1J2 Canada
Tel: 416 260 5662
yank@yank.ca
www.antiquesformen.com

VE (D)
Vintage Eyeware of New York
Tel: 646 319 9222
www.vintage-eyeware.com

VEC (A)
Vectis Auctions Ltd.
Fleck Way, Thornaby, Stockton
on Tees TS17 9JZ UK
Tel: +44 (0)1642 750 616
enquiries@vectis.co.uk
www.vectis.co.uk

VET (D)
Vetro & Arte Gallery
Calle del Capeler 3212,
Dorsoduro, Venice 30123 Italy

Tel: +39 041 522 8525
alvise@venicewebgallery.com
www.venicewebgallery.com

VGA (D)
Village Green Antiques
Port Antiques Center, 289 Main
Street, Port Washington, NY
11050
Tel: 516 625 2946
amysdish@optonline.net

VM (D)
VinMagCo
39/43 Brewer Street, London
W1R 9UD UK
Tel: +44 (0)20 7439 8525
sales@vinmag.com
www.vinmag.com

VSC (D)
Vintage Sports Collector
3920 Via Solano, Palos Verdes
Estates, CA 90274
Tel: 310 375 1723

VV (D)
Vintage to Vogue
28 Milsom Street, Bath BA1
1DG UK
Tel: +44 (0)1225 337 323
www.vintagetovoguebath.com

W&W (D)
Wallis & Wallis
West Street Auction Galleries,
Lewes, East Sussex BN7 2NJ
UK
Tel: +44 (0)1273 480 208
auctions@wallisandwallis.co.uk
www.wallisandwallis.co.uk

WAC (D)
What A Character!
hughk@aol.com /
bazuin32@aol.com
www.whatacharacter.com

WAD (D)
Waddington's
111 Bathurst Street, Toronto,
Ontario M5V 2R1 Canada
Tel: 416 504 9100
info@waddingtonsauctions.com
www.waddingtons.ca

WHA (D)
Willis Henry Auctions Inc
22 Main Street, Marshfield, MA
02050
Tel: 781 834 7774
wha@willishenry.com
www.willishenry.com

WKA (D)
**Wiener Kunst Auktionen -
Palais Kinsky**
Freyung 4, A-1010 Wien Austria
Tel: +43 15 32 42 00
office@palais-kinsky.com
www.palais-kinsky.com

WW (D)
Woolley & Wallis
51-61 Castle Street, Salisbury,
Wiltshire SP1 3SU UK
Tel: +44 (0)1722 424 500
enquiries@woolleyandwallis.co.uk
www.woolleyandwallis.co.uk

DIRECTORY OF SPECIALISTS

If you wish to have any item valued, it is advisable to contact the dealer or specialist in advance to check that they will carry out this service and whether there is a charge. While most dealers will be happy to help you with an enquiry, do remember that they are busy people. Telephone valuations are not possible. Please mention the DK Collectibles Price Guide 2005 by Judith Miller when making an enquiry.

ADVERTISING

Senator Phil Arthurhultz
P.O. Box 12336,
Lansing, MI 48901
Tel: 517 334 5000
Mob: 517 930 3000

Phil & Karol Atkinson
May-Oct:
713 Sarsi Tr, Mercer, PA 16137
Tel: 724 475 2490
Nov-Apr:
7188 Drewry's Bluff Road,
Bradenton, FL 34203
Tel: 941 755 1733

The Nostalgia Factory
51 North Margin St,
Boston, MA 02113
Tel: 617 720 2211
posters@nostalgia.com
www.nostalgia.com

Toy Road Antiques
200 Highland St., Canal
Winchester, OH 43110
Tel: 614 834 1786

AMERICANA

Bill & Myrtle Aquilino
P.O. Box 9, Chalfont,
PA 18914
Tel: 215 822 6867

Richard Axtell Antiques
1 River St, Deposit, NY 13754
Tel: 607 467 2353
Fax: 607 467 4316
raxtell@msn.com
www.axtellantiques.com

Buck County Antique Center
Route 202, Lahaksa, PA 18931
Tel: 215 794 9180

Larry & Dianna Elman
P.O. Box 415,
Woodland Hills, CA 91365

Fields of Glory
55 York St, Gettysburg,
PA 17325
Tel: 717 337 2837
foglory@cvn.net
www.fieldsofglory.com

Olde Hope Antiques
P.O. Box 718, New Hope,
PA 18938
Tel: 215 297 0200
Fax: 215 297 0300
info@oldhopeantiques.com
www.oldhopeantiques.com

The Splendid Peasant
Route 23 & Sheffield Rd,
P.O. Box 536,
South Egremont, MA 01258
Tel: 413 528 5755
folkart@splendidpeasant.com
www.splendidpeasant.com

Patricia Stauble Antiques
180 Main Street, P.O. Box 265,
Wiscasset, ME 04578
Tel: 207 882 6341

AUTOGRAPHS

Autographs of America
P.O. Box 461, Provo,
UT 84603-0461
tanders3@autographsofamerica
.com
www.autographsofamerica.com

Nate's Autograph Hound
10020 Raynor Road,
Silver Spring, MD 20901
autohnd@access.digex.net

Platt Autographs
1040 Bayview Dr #428,
Fort Lauderdale, FL 33306
Tel: 954 564 2002
ctplatt@ctplatt.com
www.ctplatt.com

AUTOMOBILIA

Dunbar's Gallery
76 Haven St, Milford,
MA 01757-3821
Tel: 508 634 8697
Fax: 508 634 8698

BOOKS

Abebooks
www.abebooks.com

Aleph-Bet Books
218 Waters Edge,
Valley Cottage,
NY 10989
Tel: 914 268 7410
Fax: 914 268 5942
helen@alephbet.com
www.alephbet.com

Bauman Rare Books
4535 Madison Ave, between
54th & 55th Streets,
New York, NY 100022
Tel: 212 751 0011
brb@baumanrarebooks.com
www.baumanrarebooks.com

Deer Park Books
609 Kent Rd, Route 7,
Gaylordsville, CT 06755
Tel/Fax: 860 350 4140
deerparkbk@aol.com
www.abebooks.com/home

CANADIANA

Yank Azman
Toronto Antiques Centre, 276
King Street West, Toronto,
Ontario, M5V 1J2 Canada
Tel: 416 260 5662
yank@yank.ca
www.antiquesformen.com

The Blue Pump
178 Davenport Road,
Toronto, Canada M5R 1J2
Tel: 416 944 1673

CANES

**Tradewinds Antiques
& Auctions**
24 Magnolia Ave, P.O. Box 249,
Manchester, MA 01944
Tel: 978 768 3327
Fax: 978 526 4085
taron@tiac.com
www.tradewindsantiques.com

CERAMICS

The Perrault-Rago Gallery
65 Ferry Street,
Lambertville, NJ 08530
Tel: 609 397 1802
www.ragoarts.com

Pair Antiques
12797 Hillcrest Dr, Longmont,
CO 80501-1162
Tel: 303 772 2760

The World of Ceramics
208 Hemlock Dr, Neptune,
NJ 07753
antique208@msn.com
(Cups & Saucers)

Greg Walsh
32 River View Lane, P.O. Box
747, Potsdam, NY 13676-0747
Tel: 315 265 9111
gwalsh@northnet.org
(Stoneware)

Happy Pastime
P.O. Box 1225, Ellicott City,
MD 21041-1225
Tel: 410 203 1101
hpastime@bellatlantic.net
www.happypastime.com
(Figurines)

Keller & Ross
P.O. Box 783, Melrose, MA
02716, Tel: 978 988 2070
kellerross@aol.com
http://members.aol.com/kellerross

Ken Forster
5501 Seminary Road,
Ste 1311, South Falls Church,
VA 22041
Tel: 703 379 1142
(Art Pottery)

Mellin's Antiques
P.O. Box 1115, Redding,
CT 06875
Tel: 203 938 9538
remellin@aol.com

Mark & Marjorie Allen
6 Highland Dr, Amherst,
NH 03031
mandmallen@antiquedelft.com
www.antiquedelft.com

Charles & Barbara Adams
289 Old Main St, South
Yarmouth, MA 02664
Tel: 508 760 3290
adams_2430@msn.com

Stephanie Hull Winters
Classic Treasures, 3232 Morgan
Rd, Temple, GA 30179
Tel: 770 562 1332
swinters@bellsouth.net

CHARACTER COLLECTIBLES

What A Character!
hughk@aol.com /
bazuin32@aol.com
www.whatacharacter.com

COMICS

Carl Bonasera
A1-American Comic Shops,
3514 W. 95th St,
Evergreen Park, IL 60642
Tel: 708 425 7555

Metropolis Collectibles Inc.
873 Broadway, Suite 201,
New York, NY 10003
Tel: 212 260 4147
Fax: 212 260 4304
orders@metropoliscomics.com
www.metropoliscomics.com

The Comic Gallery
4224 Balboa Ave, San Diego,
CA 92117
Tel: 619 483 4853

COSTUME & ACCESSORIES

Andrea Hall Levy
P.O. Box 1243,
Riverdale, NY 10471
Tel: 718 601 4239
barangrill@aol.com

Fayne Landes Antiques
593 Hansell Road,
Wynnewood, PA 19096
Tel: 610 658 0566
fayne@comcast.net

Vintage Clothing Company
P.O. Box 20504, Keizer, OR
97307-0504
retrothreads@aol.com

Yesterday's Threads
206 Meadow St, Branford,
CT 06405-3634
Tel: 203 481 6452

Lucy's Hats
South Street Antiques Center,
615 South 6th Street,
Philadelphia, PA 19147
Tel: 215 592 0256
shak06@aol.com

Vintage Eyeware
Tel: 917 721 6546

COSTUME JEWELRY

Aurora Bijoux
Tel: 215 855 1921
aurora@aurorabijoux.com
www.aurorabijoux.com

Barbara Blau
South Street Antiques Center,
615 South 6th Street,
Philadelphia, PA 19147
Tel: 215 592 0256
Tel: 215 739 4995

The Junkyard Jeweler
937 West Beach Street, Suite
49,Long Beach, NY 11561
spigner@aol.com
www.tias.com/stores/thejunkya
rdjeweler

Mod-Girl
South Street Antiques Center,
615 South 6th Street,
Philadelphia, PA 19147
Tel: 215 592 0256

Roxanne Stuart
Tel: 215 750 8868
gemfairy@aol.com

Terry Rodgers & Melody LLC
30 & 31 Manhattan Art and
Antiques Center, 1050 2nd
Avenue, New York, NY 10022
Tel: 212 758 3164
melodyjewelry@aol.com

Bonny Yankauer
Tel: 201 825 7697
bonnyy@aol.com

DISNEYANA

MuseumWorks
525 East Cooper Avenue,
Aspen CO 81611
www.mwhgalleries.com

DOLLS

Memory Lane
45-40 Bell Blvd, Suite 109,
Bayside, NY 11361
Tel: 718 428 8181
memlnny@aol.com
www.tias.com/stores/memlnny

Treasure & Dolls
518 Indian Rocks Rd, N.
Belleair Bluffs, FL 33770
Tel: 727 584 7277
dolls@antiquedoll.com
www.antiquedoll.com

FIFTIES & SIXTIES

Deco Etc
122 West 25th Street,
between 6th & 7th Aves.,
New York, NY 10010
Tel: 212 675 3327
deco_etc@msn.com

Kathy's Korner
Tel: 516 624 9494

Lois' Collectibles
Market III, 413 W Main St,
Saint Charles, IL 60174-1815
Tel: 630 377 5599

Nifty Fifties
Tel: 734 782 3974

Neet-O-Rama
93 West Main Street,
Somerville, NJ 08876
Tel: 908 722 4800
www.neetstuff.com

Steve Colby
Off The Deep End, 712 East St,
Frederick, MD 21701-5239
Tel: 301 698 9006
chilimon@offthedeepend.com
www.offthedeepend.com

FILM MEMORABILIA

STARticles
58 Stewart St, Studio 301,
Toronto, Ontario,
M5V 1H6 Canada
Tel: 416 504 8286
info@starticles.com

Norma's Jeans
3511 Turner Lane, Chevy
Chase, MD 20815-2313
Tel: 301 652 4644
Fax: 301 907 0216

George Baker
CollectorsMart, P.O. Box
580466, Modesto, CA 95358
Tel; 290 537 5221
Fax: 209 531 0233
georgeb1@thevision.net
www.collectorsmart.com

GENERAL

Anastacia's Antiques
617 Bainbridge Street,
Philadelphia, PA 19147

Antiques of Cape May
Tel: 800 224 1687

Bucks County Antique Center
Route 202, Lahaska, PA 18931
Tel: 215 794 9180

Burlwood Antique Center
Route 3, Meredith, NH 03523
Tel: 603 279 6387

Camelot Antiques
7872 Ocean Gateway,
Easton, MD 21601
Tel: 410 820 4396
camelot@goeaston.net
www.about-
antiques.com/CamelotAntiques

Manhattan Art & Antiques Center
1050 Second Avenue (between
55th & 56th Street) New York,
NY, 10022 Tel: 212-355-4400
Fax: 212-355-4403
info@the-maac.com

The Lafayette Mill Antiques
12 Morris Farm Road (Just off
Rte 15), Lafayette NJ 07848
Tel: 973 383 0065
millpartners@inpro.net
www.millantiques.com

South Street Antiques Center
615 South 6th Street,
Philadelphia, PA 19147
Tel: 215 592 0256.

Toronto Antiques Centre
276 King Street West, Toronto,
Ontario M5V 1J2 Canada
Tel: 416 345 9941

GLASS

American Art Glass Works Inc
41 Wooster Street, 1st floor,
New York, NY 10013
Tel: 212 625 0783
Fax: 212 625 0217
www.americanartglassgallery.com

The End of History
548 1/2 Hudson Street,
New York, NY 10014
Tel: 212 647 7598
Fax: 212 647 7634

Past-Tyme Antiques
Tel: 703 777 8555
pasttymeantiques@aol.com

Jeff E. Purtell
P.O. Box 28, Amherst,
NH 03031-0028
Tel: 603 673 4331
Fax: 603 673 1525
(Steuben)

Paul Reichwein
2321 Hershey Ave, East
Petersburg, PA 17520
Tel: 717 569 7637
paulrdg@aol.com

Paul Stamati Gallery
1050 2nd Ave, New York,
NY 10022
Tel: 212 754 4533
Fax: 718 271 6958
mail@rene-lalique.com
www.rene-lalique.com

Suzman's Antiques
P.O. Box 301, Rehoboth,
MA 02769
Tel: 508 252 5729
suzmanf@ride.ri.net

HOLIDAY MEMORABILIA

Chris & Eddie's Collectibles
South Street Antiques Center,
615 South 6th Street,
Philadelphia, PA 19147
Tel: 215 592 0256

Sign of the Tymes
2 Morris Farm Rd, Lafayette,
NJ 07848
Tel: 973 383 6028
jhap@nac.net
www.millantiques.com

KITCHENALIA

Dynamite Antiques & Collectibles
Tel: 301 652 1140
bercovici@erols.com

Village Green Antiques
Port Antiques Center, 289 Main
Street, Port Washington, NY
11050
Tel: 516 625 2946
amysdish@optonline.net

LUNCH BOXES

Seaside Toy Center
Joseph Soucy
179 Main St,
Westerly, RI 02891
Tel: 401 596 0962

MARBLES

Auction Blocks
P.O. Box 2321, Huntington
Station, CT 06484
Tel: 203 924 2802
auctionblocks@aol.com
www.auctionblocks.com

MECHANICAL MUSIC

The Music Box Shop
7236 E 1st Ave, Scottsdale,
AZ 85251
Tel: 602 945 0428
musicboxshop@home.com
www.themusicboxshop.com

Mechantiques
The Crescent Hotel,
75 Prospect St,
Eureka Springs, AR 72632
Tel: 501 253 9766
mroenigk@aol.com
www.mechantiques.com

MILITARIA

Articles of War
358 Boulevard,
Middletown, RI 02842
Tel: 401 846 8503
dutch5@ids.com

PENS & WRITING EQUIPMENT

Fountain Pen Hospital
10 Warren Street,
New York, NY 10007
Tel: 212 964 0580
info@fountainpenhospital.com
www.fountainpenhospital.com

Gary & Myrna Lehrer
16 Mulberry Rd, Woodbridge,
CT 06525-1717
Tel: 203 389 5295
Fax: 203 389 4515
garylehrer@aol.com
www.gopens.com

David Nishimura
Vintage Pens, P.O. Box 41452
Providence, RI 02940-1452
Tel: 401 351 7607
Fax: 401 351 1168
www.vintagepens.com

Sandra & L. 'Buck' van Tine
Lora's Memory Lane, 13133
North Caroline St, Chillicothe, IL
61523-9115
Tel: 309 579 3040
Fax: 309 579 2696
lorasink@aol.com

Pendemonium
15231 Larkspur Lane,
Dumfries, VA 22026-2075
Tel: 703 670 8549
Fax: 703 670 3875
www.pendemonium.com

PLASTICS

Dee Battle
9 Orange Blossom Trail,
Yalaha, FL 34797
Tel: 352 324 3023

Malabar Enterprises
172 Bush Lane, Ithaca,
NY 14850
Tel: 607 255 2905
Fax: 607 255 4179
asn6@cornell.edu

POSTERS

Posteritati
239 Center St, New York,
NY 10013
Tel: 212 226 2207
Fax: 212 226 2102
mail@posteritati.com
www.posteritati.com

Chisholm Larsson
145 8th Avenue,
New York, NY 10011
Tel: 212 741 1703
Fax: 212 645 6691
www.chisholm-poster.com

Vintage Poster Works
P.O. Box 88, Pittford, NY 14534
Tel: 716 218 9483
Fax: 716 218 9035
debra@vintageposterworks.com
www.vintageposterworks.com

La Belle Epoque
11661 San Vincente, 3304 Los
Angeles, CA 90049-5110
Tel: 310 442 0054
Fax: 310 826 6934
ktscicon@ix.netcom.com

RADIOS

Catalin Radios
5443 Schultz Drive,
Sylvania, OH 43560
Tel: 419 824 2469
steve@catalinradio.com
www.catalinradio.com

ROCK & POP

Heinz's Rare Collectibles
P.O. Box 179, Little Silver,
NJ 07739-0179
Tel: 732 219 1988
Fax: 732 219 5940
(The Beatles)

Tod Hutchinson
P.O. Box 915, Griffith,
IN 46319-0915
Tel: 219 923 8334
toddtcb@aol.com
(Elvis Presley)

SCENT BOTTLES

Oldies But Goldies
P.O. Box 217, Hankins,
NY 12741-0217
Tel: 914 887 5272
oldgood@catskill.net
www.catskill.net/oldgood

Monsen & Baer Inc
P.O. Box 529, Vienna, VA
22183-0529
Tel: 703 938 2129
monsenbaer@erols.com

SCIENTIFIC & TECHNICAL, INCLUDING OFFICE & OPTICAL

George Glazer
28 East 2nd St,
New York, NY 10021
Tel: 212 535 5706
Fax: 212 988 3992
worldglobe@aol.com
www.georgeglazer.com

Tesseract
Box 15, Hastings-on-Hudson,
NY 10706
Tel: 914 478 2594
Fax: 914 478 5473
e-mail: coffeen@aol.com
www.etesseract.com

The Olde Office
68-845 Perez Rd, Ste 30,
Cathedral City, CA 92234
Tel: 760 346 8653
Fax: 760 346 6479
info@thisoldeoffice.com
www.thisoldeoffice.com

Jane Hertz
6731 Ashley Ct, Sarasota, FL
34241-9696
Tel: 941 925 0385
Fax: 941 925 0487
auction@breker.com
www.breker.com
(Cameras, Office & Technical
Equipment)

SMOKING

Richard Weinstein
International Vintage Lighter
Exchange, 30 W. 57th St,
New York, NY 10019
vinlighter@aol.com
www.vintagelighters.com

Ira Pilossof
Vintage Lighters Inc., P.O. Box
1325, Fairlawn,
NJ 07410-8325
Tel: 201 797 6595
vintageltr@aol.com

Mike Cassidy
1070 Bannock #400,
Denver, CO 80204
Tel: 303 446 2726

Chuck Haley
Sherlock's, 13926 Double Girth
Ct., Matthews, NC 28105-4068
Tel: 704 847 5480

SPORTING MEMORABILIA

Classic Rods & Tackle
P.O. Box 288, Ashley Falls, MA
01222
Tel: 413 229 7988

Larry Fritsch Cards Inc
735 Old Wassau Rd, P.O. Box
863, Stevens Point, WI 54481
Tel: 715 344 8687
Fax: 715 344 1778
larry@fritschcards.com
www.fritschcards.com
(Baseball Cards)

George Lewis
Golfiana, P.O. Box 291,
Mamaroneck, NY 10543
Tel: 914 835 5100
Fax: 914 835 1715
george@golfiana.com
www.golfiana.com

Golf Collectibles
P.O. Box 165892,
Irving, YX 75016
Tel: 972 594 7802
furjanic@directlink.net
www.folfforallages.com

The Hager Group
P.O. Box 952974, Lake Mary,
FL 32795
Tel: 407 788 3865
(Trading Cards)

Hall's Nostalgia
21-25 Mystic St, P.O. Box 408,
Arlington, MA 02174
Tel: 781 646 7757

Tom & Jill Kaczor
1550 Franklin Rd, Langhorne,
PA 19047
Tel: 215 968 5776
Fax: 215 946 6056

Vintage Sports Collector
3920 Via Solano, Palos Verdes
Estates, CA 90274
Tel: 310 375 1723

TEDDY BEARS & SOFT TOYS

Harper General Store
10482 Jonestown Rd, Annville,
PA 17003
Tel: 717 865 3456
Fax: 717 865 3813
www.harpergeneralstore.com

Marion Weis
Division St Antiques, P.O. Box
374, Buffalo, MN 55313-0374
Tel: 612 682 6453

TOYS & GAMES

Atomic Age
318 East Virginia Road,
Fullerton, CA 92831
Tel: 714 446 0736
Fax: 714 446 0436
atomage100@aol.com

Barry Carter
Knightstown Antiques Mall, 136
W. Carey St, Knightstown,
IN 46148-1111
Tel: 765 345 5665
bcarter@spitfire.net

France Antique Toys
Tel: 631 754 1399

Roger & Susan Johnson
1701 Venture Farms Road, Pilot
Point, TX 76258
Tel: 940 365 9149
Fax: 940 365 4401
czarmann@aol.com

Kitsch-N-Kaboodle
South Street Antiques Center,
615 South 6th Street,
Philadelphia, PA 19147-2128
Tel: 215 382 1354
kitschnkaboodle@yahoo.com

Litwin Antiques
P.O. Box 5865, Trenton,
NJ 08638-0865
Tel/Fax: 609 275 1427
(Chess)

Harry R. McKeon, Jr.
18 Rose Lane, Flourtown,
PA 19031-1910
Tel: 215 233 4094
toyspost@aol.com
(Tin Toys)

Jessica Pack Antiques
Chapel Hill, NC
Tel: 919 408 0406
jpants1@aol.com

The Old Toy Soldier Home
977 S. Santa Fe, Ste 11
Vista, CA 92083
Tel: 760 758 5481
Fax: 760 758 5481
info@oldtoysoldierhome.com
www.oldtoysoldierhome.com

Trains & Things
106 East Front St, Traverse City,
MI 49684
Tel: 616 947 1353
Fax: 616 947 1411
tctrains@traverse.net
www.tctrains.com

WATCHES

Mark Laino
South Street Antiques Center,
615 South 6th Street,
Philadelphia, PA 19147
Tel: 215 592 0256

Texas Time
3076 Waunuta St, Newbury
Park, CA 1320
Tel: 805 498 5644
Fax: 805 480 9514
paul@dock.net
www.texastime.com

WINE & DRINKING

Derek White
The Corkscrew Pages, 769
Sumter Dr, Morrisville,
PA 19067
Tel: 215 493 4143
Fax: 609 860 5380
dswhite@marketsource.com
www.taponline.com

Donald A. Bull
P.O. Box 596, Wirtz, VA 24184
Tel: 540 721 1128
Fax: 540 721 5468
corkscrue@aol.com

Steve Visakay Cocktail Shakers
P.O. Box 1517 West Caldwell,
NJ 07007-1517
Tel: 914 352 5640
svisakay@aol.com

DIRECTORY OF AUCTIONEERS

This is a list of auctioneers that conduct regular sales. Auctioneers who wish to be listed in this directory for our next edition, space permitting, are requested to email info@thepriceguidecompany.com by February 2005.

ALABAMA

Flomaton Antique Auctions
P.O. Box 1017, 320 Palafox Street, Flomaton, AL 36441
Tel: 334 296 3059
Fax: 334 296 3710

ARIZONA

Dan May & Associates
4110 N. Scottsdale Road, Scottsdale, AZ 85251
Tel: 602 941 4200

ARKANSAS

Ponders Auctions
1504 South Leslie, Stuttgart, AR 72160
Tel: 501 673 6551

CALIFORNIA

Aurora Galleries International
30 Hackamore Lane, Ste 2, Bell Canyon, CA 91307
Tel: 818 884 6468
Fax: 818 227 2941
vjc@auroragalleriesonline.com
www.auroragalleriesonline.com

Butterfield & Butterfield
7601 Sunset Blvd, Los Angeles, CA 90046
Tel: 323 850 7500
Fax: 323 850 5843
info@butterfields.com
www.butterfields.com

Butterfield & Butterfield
220 San Bruno Ave, San Francisco, CA 94103
Tel: 415 861 7500
Fax: 415 861 8951
info@butterfields.com
www.butterfields.com

Clark Cierlak Fine Arts
14452 Ventura Blvd, Sherman Oaks, CA 91423
Tel: 818 783 3052
Fax: 818 783 3162
clark@estateauctionservice.com
www.estateauctionservice.com

I.M. Chait Gallery
9330 Civic Center Dr, Beverly Hills, CA 90210
Tel: 310 285 0182
Fax: 310 285 9740
imchait@aol.com
www.chait.com

Cuschieri's Auctioneers & Appraisers
863 Main Street, Redwood City, CA 94063
Tel: 650 556 1793
Fax: 650 556 9805
www.cuschieris.com

eBay, Inc
2005 Hamilton Ave, Ste 350, San Jose, CA 95125
Tel: 408 369 4839
www.ebay.com

L.H. Selman
123 Locust St, Santa Cruz, CA 95060
Tel: 800 538 0766
Fax: 408 427 0111
leselman@got.net

Malter Galleries
17003 Ventura Blvd, Encino, CA 91316
Tel: 818 784 7772
Fax: 818 784 4726
www.maltergalleries.com

Poster Connection Inc
43 Regency Dr, Clayton, CA 94517
Tel: 925 673 3343
Fax: 925 673 3355
sales@posterconnection.com
www.posterconnection.com

Profiles in History
110 North Doheny Dr, Beverly Hills, CA 90211
Tel: 310 859 7701
Fax: 310 859 3842
www.profilesinhistory.com

San Rafael Auction Gallery
634 Fifth Avenue, San Rafael, CA 9490
Tel: 415 457 4488
Fax: 415 457 4899
www.sanrafael-auction.com

Slawinski Auction Co.
6221 Graham Hill Road, Ste C, Felton, CA 95018
Tel: 831 335 9000
Fax: 831 335 6933
www.slawinski.com

CONNECTICUT

Alexander Autographs
100 Melrose Ave, Greenwich, CT 06830
Tel: 203 622 8444
Fax: 203 622 8765
peter@alexautographs.com
www.alexautographs.com

Norman C. Heckler & Co.
79 Bradford Corner Road, Woodstock Valley, CT 0682
Tel: 860 974 1634
Fax: 860 974 2003
www.hecklerauction.com

Lloyd Ralston Gallery
250 Long Beach Blvd, Stratford, CT 016615
Tel: 203 386 9399
Fax: 203 386 9519
lrgallery@aol.com
www.lloydralstontoys.com

DELAWARE

Remember When Auctions Inc.
42 Sea Gull Rd, Swann Estates, Selbyville, DE 19975
Tel: 302 436 8869
Fax: 302-436-6144
sales@history-attic.com
www.history-attic.com

FLORIDA

Auctions Neapolitan
995 Central Avenue, Naples, FL 34102
Tel: 941 262 7333
kathleen@auctionsneapolitan.com
www.auctionsneapolitan.com

Burchard Galleries
2528 30th Ave N, St Petersburg, FL 33713
Tel: 727 821 11667
www.burchardgalleries.com

Dawson's
P.O. Box 646, Palm Beach, FL 33480
Tel: 561 835 6930
Fax: 561 835 8464
info@dawsons.org
www.dawsons.org

Arthur James Galleries
615 E. Atlantic Ave, Delray Beach, FL 33483
Tel: 561 278 2373
Fax: 561 278 7633
www.arthurjames.com

Kincaid Auction Company
3214 E Hwy 92, Lakeland, FL 3381
Tel: 800 970 1977
www.kincaid.com

Sloan's Auction Galleries
8861 NW 19th Terace, Ste 100, Miami, FL 33172
Tel: 305 751 4770
sloans@sloansauction.com
www.sloansauction.com

GEORGIA

Great Gatsby's
5070 Peachtree Industrial Blvd, Atlanta, GA
Tel: 770 457 1905
Fax: 770-457-7250
www.gatsbys.com

My Hart Auctions Inc
P.O. Box 2511, Cumming, GA 30028
Tel: 770 888 9006
www.myhart.net

IDAHO

The Coeur D'Alene Art Auction
P.O. Box 310, Hayden, ID 83835
Tel: 208 772 9009
Fax: 208 772 8294
cdaartauction@cdaartauction.com
www.cdaartauction.com

ILLINOIS

Leslie Hindman Inc.
122 North Aberdeen Street, Chicago, IL 60607
Tel: 312 280 1212
Fax: 312 280 1211
www.lesliehindman.com

Joy Luke
300 East Grove Street, Bloomington, IL 61701
Tel: 309 828 5533
Fax: 309 829 2266
robert@joyluke.com
www.joyluke.com

Mastronet Inc
10S 660 Kingery Highway, Willobrook, IL 60527
Tel: 630 471 1200
info@mastronet.com
www.mastronet.com

INDIANA

Curran Miller Auction & Realty Inc
4424 Vogel Rd, Ste 400, Evansville, IN 47715
Tel: 812 474 6100
Fax: (812) 474-6110
cmar@curranmiller.com
www.curranmiller.com

Kruse International
5540 County Rd 11A, Auburn, IN 46706
Tel: 800 968 4444
info@kruseinternational.com
www.kruse.com

Lawson Auction Service
923 Fourth Street, Columbus, IN 47265
Tel: 812 372 2571
dlawson@lawson-auction.com
www.lawson-auction.com

Slater's Americana
5335 N. Tacoma Ave, Ste 24, Indianapolis, IN 46220
Tel: 317 257 0863

Stout Auctions
529 State Road 28 East, Willamsport, IN 47993
Tel: 765 764 6901
Fax: 765-764-1516
www.stoutauctions.com

IOWA

Gene Harris Auctions
2035 18th Ave, Marshalltown, IA 50158
Tel: 641 752 0600
ghaac@geneharrisauctions.com
www.geneharrisauctions.com

Jackson's Auctioneers & Appraisers
2229 Lincoln St, Cedar Falls, IA 50613
Tel: 319 277 2256
sandim@jacksonsauction.com
www.jacksonsauction.com

Tubaugh Auctions
1702 8th Ave, Belle Plaine, IA 52208
Tel: 319 444 2413
www.tubaughauctions.com

KANSAS

Manions International Auction House
P.O. Box 12214, Kansas City, KS, 66112
Tel: 913 299 6692
Fax: 913 299 6792
collecting@manions.com
www.manions.com

CC Auctions
416 Court St, Clay Center, KS 67432
Tel: 785 632 6021
dhamilton@cc-auctions.com
www.cc-auctions.com

Spielman Auctions
2259 Homestead Rd, Lebo, KS 66856
Tel: 316 256 6558

KENTUCKY

Hays & Associates Inc
120 South Spring Street, Louisville, KY 40206
kenhays@haysauction.com
www.haysauction.com

Steffens Historical Militaria
P.O. Box 280, Newport, KY 41072
Tel: 859 431 4499
Fax: 859 431 3113
www.steffensmilitaria.com

LOUSIANA

Morton M. Goldberg Auction Galleries
547 Baronne Street
New Orleans, LA 70113
Tel: 504 592 2300
Fax: 504 592 2311

New Orleans Auction Galleries
801 Magazine Street, New Orleans, LA 70130
Tel: 504 566 1849
Fax: 504 566 1851
info@neworleansauction.com
www.neworleansauction.com

MAINE

Guyette & Schmidt
P.O. Box 522, West Farmington, ME 04992
Tel: 207 778 6256
Fax: 207 778 6501
decoys@guyetteandschmidt.com

James D. Julia Auctioneers Inc.
P.O. Box 830, Fairfield ME 04937
Tel: 207 453 7125
Fax: 207 453 2502
jjulia@juliaauctions.com
www.juliaauctions.com

Thomaston Place Auction Galleries
P.O. Box 300, 51 Atlantic Highway, US Rt 1 Thomaston ME 04861
Tel: 207 354 8141
Fax: 207 354 9523
barbara@kajav.com
www.thomastonauction.com

MARYLAND

DeCaro Auction Sales Inc.
117A Bay Street, Ste D, Easton, MD 21601
Tel: 410 820 4000
Fax: 410 820 4332
info@decaroauctions.com
www.decaroauctions.com

Hantman's Auctioneers & Appraisers
P.O. Box 59366, Potomac, MD 20859
Tel: 301 770 3720
Fax: 301 770 4135
hantman@hantmans.com
www.hantmans.com

Isennock Auctions & Appraisals
4106B Norrisville Road, White Hall, MD 21161
Tel: 410-557-8052
Fax 410-692-6449
info@isennockauction.com
www.isennockauction.com

Sloans & Kenyon
4605 Bradley Boulevard, Bethesda, Maryland 20815
Tel: 301 634-2330
Fax: 301 656-7074
info@sloansandkenyon.com
www.sloansandkenyon.com

MASSACHUSETTS

Eldred's
P.O. Box 796, 1483 Route 6A East Dennis, MA 02641
Tel: 508 385 3116
Fax: 508 385 7201
info@eldreds.com
www.eldreds.com

Grogan & Company
22 Harris St, Dedham, MA 02026
Tel: 800-823 1020
grogans@groganco.com
www.groganco.com

Simon D. Hill & Associates
420 Boston Turnpike, Shrewsbury, MA 01545
Tel: 508 845 2400
Fax: 978 928 4129
www.simondhillauctions.com

Skinner Inc
The Heritage on the Garden, 63 Park Plaza, Boston, MA 02116
Tel: 617-350-5400
Fax: 617-350-5429
info@skinnerinc.com
www.skinnerinc.com

Willis Henry Auctions
22 Main St, Marshfield, MA 02050
Tel: 781 834 7774
wha@willishenry.com
www.willishenry.com

MICHIGAN

DuMouchelles
408 East Jefferson Ave, Detroit, MI 48226
Tel: 313 963 6255
Fax: 313 963 8199
info@dumouchelles.com
www.dumouchelles.com

MINNESOTA

Buffalo Bay Auction Co
5244 Quam Circle, Rogers, MN 55374
Tel: 612 428 8480
buffalobayauction@hotmail.com
www.buffalobayauction.com

Rose Auction Galleries
2717 Lincoln Dr, Roseville, MN 55113
Tel: 651 484 1415
Fax: 651 636 3431
auctions@rosegalleries.com
www.rosegalleries.com

MISSOURI

Ivey-Selkirk
7447 Forsyth Blvd, Saint Louis, MO 63105
Tel: 314 726 5515
Fax: 314 726 9908
www.iveyselkirk.com

MONTANA

Allard Auctions Inc
P.O. Box 460 St Ignatius, MT 59865
Tel: 406 745 0500
Fax: 406 745 0502
www.allardauctions.com

NEW HAMPSHIRE

Northeast Auctions
93 Pleasant St, Portsmouth, NH 03801-4504
Tel: 603 433 8400
Fax: 603 433 0415
www.northeastauctions.com

NEW JERSEY

Bertoia Auctions
2141 Demarco Dr, Vineland, NJ 08360
Tel: 856 692 1881
Fax: 856 692 8697
www.bertoiaauctions.com

Craftsman Auctions
333 North Main St, Lambertville, NJ 08530
Tel: 609 397 9374
Fax: 609 397 9377
www.ragoarts.com

Dawson & Nye
128 American Road, Morris Plains, NJ 07950
Tel: 973 984 6900
Fax: 973 984 6956
info@dawsonandnye.com
www.dawsonandnye.com

Greg Manning Auctions Inc
775 Passaic Ave, West Caldwell, NJ 07006
Tel: 973 883 0004
Fax: 973 882 3499
www.gregmanning.com

Rago Modern Auctions LLP
333 North Main St, Lambertville, NJ 08530
Tel: 609 397 9374
Fax: 609 397 9377
info@ragoarts.com
www.ragoarts.com

NEW MEXICO

Parker-Braden Auctions
P.O. Box 1897, 4303 National Parks Highway, Carlsbad, NM 88220
Tel: 505 885 4874
Fax: 505 885 4622
www.parkerbraden.com

NEW YORK

Christie's
20 Rockefeller Plaza, New York, NY 10020
Tel: 212 636 2000
Fax: 212 636 2399
www.christies.com

TW Conroy
36 Oswego St, Baldwinsville, NY 13027
Tel: 315 638 6434
Fax: 315 638 7039
brad@twconroy.com
www.conroy.com

Samuel Cottone Auctions
15 Genesee St, Mount Morris, NY 14510
Tel: 585 658 3119
Fax: 585 658 3152
scottone@rochester.rr.com
www.cottoneauctions.com

William Doyle Galleries
175 E. 87th St, New York, NY 10128
Tel: 212 427 2730
Fax: 212 369 0892
www.doylenewyork.com

Guernsey's Auctions
108 East 73rd St, New York, NY 10021
Tel: 212 794 2280
Fax: 212 744 3638
auctions@guernseys.com
www.guernseys.com

Phillips, De Pury & Luxembourg
450 West 15 Street, New York NY 10011
Tel: 212 940 1200
Fax: 212 688 1647
inquiry.desk@phillips-dpl.com
www.phillips-dpl.com

Sotheby's
1334 York Ave at 72nd St, New York, NY 10021
Tel: 212 606 7000
Fax: 212 606 7107
info@sothebys.com
www.sothebys.com

Swann Galleries Inc
104 E. 25th St, New York, NY 10010
Tel: 212 254 4710
Fax: 212 979 1017
swann@swanngalleries.com
www.swanngalleries.com

NORTH CAROLINA

Robert S. Brunk
P.O. Box 2135, Asheville, NC 28802
Tel: 828 254 6846
Fax: 828 254 6545
www.brunkauctions.com

Historical Collectible Auctions
P.O. Box 975 Burlington,
NC 27215
Tel: 336 570 2803
bids4hca@aol.com
www.hcaauctions.com

NORTH DAKOTA

**Curt D Johnson Auction
Company**
P.O. Box 135, Grand Forks,
SC 58201
Tel: 701 746 1378
merfeld@rrv.net
www.curtdjohnson.com

OHIO

Cowans Historic Americana
673 Wilmer Avenue, Cincinnati,
OH 45226
Tel: 513 871 1670
Fax: 513 871 8670
www.historicamericana.com

DeFina Auctions
1591 State Route 45 Sth,
Austinburg, OH 44010
Tel: 440 275 6674
info@definaauctions.com
www.definaauctions.com

Garth's Auctions
2690 Stratford Rd, Box 369,
Delaware, OH 43015
Tel: 740 362 4771
Fax: 740 363 0164
info@garths.com
www.garths.com

Metropolitan Galleries
3910 Lorain Ave, Cleveland, OH
44113
Tel: 216 631 2222
Fax: 216 529 9021
www.metropoliangalleries.com

PENNSYLVANIA

Alderfer Auction Gallery
501 Fairgrounds Rd, Hatfield,
PA 19440
Tel: 215 393 3000
info@alderferauction.com
www.alderferauction.com

Noel Barrett
P.O. Box 300, Carversville,
PA 18913
Tel: 215 297 5109
toys@noelbarrett.com
www.noelbarrett.com

Dargate Auction Galleries
214 North Lexington,
Pittsburgh, PA 15208
Tel: 412 362 3558
info@dargate.com
www.dargate.com

Freeman's
1808 Chestnut Ave,
Philadelphia, PA 19103
Tel: 610 563 9275
info@freemansauction.com
www.freemansauction.com

Hunt Auctions
75 E. Uwchlan Ave, Ste 1, 30
Exton, PA 19341
Tel: 610 524 0822
Fax: 610 524 0826
www.huntauctions.com

Morphy Auctions
2000 North Reading St,
Denver PA
Tel: 717 335 3435
morphy@morphyauctions.com
www.morphyauctions.com

Pook & Pook Inc
463 East Lancaster Ave,
Downington, PA 19335
Tel: 610 269 4040
Fax: 610 269 9274
info@pookandpook.com
www.pookandpook.com

Skinner's Auction Co.
170 Northampton St,
Easton, PA 18042
Tel: 610 330 6933
skinnauct@aol.com
www.skinnerauct.baweb.com

Stephenson's Auctions
1005 Industrial Blvd,
Southampton, PA 18966
www.stephensonsauction.com

RHODE ISLAND

WebWilson
P.O. Box 506, Portsmouth,
RI 02871
Tel: 800 508 0022
hww@webwilson.com
www.webwilson.com

SOUTH CAROLINA

Charlton Hall Galleries
912 Gervais St Columbia,
SC 29201
Tel: 803 799 5678
info@charltonhallgalleries.com
www.hcharltonhallgalleries.com

TENNESSEE

Berenice Denton Estates
4403 Murphy Road,
Nashville, TN 37209
Tel: 615 292 5765
lnichols66@home.com

Kimball M. Sterling Inc
125 W. Market St, Johnson City,
TN 37604
Tel: 423 928 1471
www.sterlingsold.com

TEXAS

Austin Auctions
8414 Anderson Mill Rd,
Austin, TX 78729-4702
Tel: 512 258 5479
Fax: 512 219 7372
austinauction@cs.com
www.austinauction.com

Dallas Auction Gallery
1518 Socum St, Dallas,
TX 75207
Tel: 213 653 3900
Fax: 213 653 3912
info@dallasauctiongallery.com
www.dallasauctiongallery.com

Heritage Galleries
Heritage Plaza, 100 Highland
Park Village, 2nd Floor, Dallas,
TX 75205-2788
Tel: 214 528 3500
Fax: 214 520 6968
www.heritagegalleries.com

UTAH

America West Archives
P.O. Box 100, Cedar City,
UT 84721
Tel: 435 586 9497
awa@utah.net
www.americawestarchives.com

VERMONT

Eaton Auction Service
RR1 Box 333, Fairlee,
VT 05045
Tel: 802 333 9717

VIRGINIA

Ken Farmer Auctions & Estates
105A Harrison St, Radford,
VA 24141
Tel: 540 639 0939
Fax: 540 639 1759
info@kfauctions.com
www.kfauctions.com

Phoebus Auction Gallery
14-16 E. Mellen St, Hampton,
VA 23663
Tel: 757 722 9210
Fax: 757 723 2280
bwelch@phoebusauction.com
www.phoebusauction.com

Signature House
407 Liberty Ave, Bridgeport,
WV 25330
Tel: 304 842 3386
Fax: 304 842 3001
www.signaturehouse.net

WASHINGTON DC

Weschlers
909 E St, NW Washington,
DC 20004
Tel: 202 628 1281
Fax: 202 628 2366
fineart@weschlers.com

WISCONSIN

Krueger Auctions
P.O. Box 275, Iola,
WI 54945-0275
Tel: 715 445 3845

Schrager Auction Galleries
2915 North Sherman Blvd,
P.O. Box 100043,
Milwaukee, WI 53210
Tel: 414 873 3738
Fax: 414 873 5229
askus@schragerauction.com
www.schragerauction.com

WYOMING

**Cody Old West Show
& Auction**
1215 Sheridan Ave,
Cody, WY 82414
Tel: 317 587 9014
Fax: 307 587 3979
oldwest@codyoldwest.com
www.codyoldwest.com

Manitou Gallery
1715 Carey Ave, Cheyenne,
WY 82001
Tel: 307 635 7670
Fax: 307 778 3926
ptassi@aol.com

CLUBS, SOCIETIES & ORGANISATIONS

ADVERTISING

Antique Advertising Association of America
P.O. Box 1121, Morton Grove,
IL 60053
Tel: 708 446 0904
www.pastimes.org

Coca Cola Collectors' Club International
P.O. Box 49166, Atlanta,
GA 30359-1166

Tin Container Collectors' Association
P.O. Box 440101 Aurora,
CO 80044

AMERICANA

Folk Art Society of America
P.O. Box 17041, Richmond, VA
23226-70

American Political Items Collectors
P.O. Box 340339 San Antonio,
TX 8234-0339
www.collectors.org/apic

AUTOGRAPHS

International Autograph Collectors' Club & Dealers' Alliance
4575 Sheridan St, Ste 111,
Hollywood, FL 33021-3515
Tel: 561 736 8409
www.iacc-da.com

Universal Autograph Collectors' Club
P.O. Box 6181, Washington,
DC 20044
Tel: 202 332-7388
www.uacc.com

AUTOMOBILIA

Automobile Objets d'Art Club
252 N. 7th St. Allentown,
PA 18102-4204
Tel: 610 432 3355
oldtoy@aol.com

BOOKS

Antiquarian Bookseller's Association of America
20 West 44th St, 4th Floor,
New York, NY 10036
Tel: 212 944 8291

CERAMICS

American Art Pottery Association
P.O. Box 834, Westport, MA
02790-0697
www.amartpot.com

American Ceramics Circle
520 16th St, Brooklyn,
NY 11215
Tel: 718 832 5446
nlester@earthlink.net

American Cookie Jar Association
1600 Navajo Rd, Norman,
OK 73026
davismj@ionet.net

Style 1900
David Rago, 9 Main St,
Lambertville, NJ 08530

U.S. Chintz Collectors' Club
P.O. Box 50888, Pasadena,
CA 91115
Tel: 626 441-4708
Fax: 626 441-4122
www.chintznet.com

Goebel Networkers
P.O. Box 396, Lemoyne, PA
17043

Homer Laughlin China Collectors' Association
P.O. Box 1093
Corbin KY 40702-1093
www.hlcca.org
(Fiesta ware)

Hummel Collectors Club
1261 University Dr, Yardley,
PA 19067-2857
Tel: 888 548 6635
Fax: 215 321 7367
www.hummels.com

Roseville of The Past Pottery Club
P.O. Box 656 Clarcona,
FL 32710-0656
Tel: 407 294 3980
Fax: 407 294 7836
rosepast@bellsouth.net

Royal Doulton International Collectors' Club
700 Cottontail Lane,
Somerset, NJ 08873
Tel: 800 682-4462
Fax: 732 764-4974

Stangl & Fulper Club
P.O. Box 538, Flemington,
NJ 08822
Tel: 908 995 2696
kenlove508@aol.com

American Stoneware Collectors' Society
P.O. Box 281, Bay Head,
NJ 08742
Tel: 732 899 8707

COSTUME JEWELRY

Leaping Frog Antique Jewelry & Collectible Club
4841 Martin Luther King Blvd,
Sacramento, CA 95820-4932
Tel: 916 452 6728
pandora@cwia.com

Vintage Fashion & Costume Jewelry Club
P.O. Box 265, Glen Oaks,
NY 11004-0265
Tel: 718 939 3095
vfcj@aol.com

DISNEYANA

National Fantasy Club For

Disneyana Collectors & Enthusiasts
P.O. Box 106, Irvine,
CA 92713-9212
Tel: 714 731 4705
info@nffc.org
www.nffc.org

Walt Disney Collectors' Society
500 South Buena Vista St,
Burbank, CA 91521-8028
Tel: 800 932 5749

FIFTIES & SIXTIES

Head Hunters Newsletters
P.O. Box 83H, Scarsdale,
NY 10583.
Tel: 914 472 0200

FILM & TV MEMORABILIA

The Animation Art Guild
330 W. 45th St, Ste 9D, New
York, NY 10036-3864
Tel: 212 765 3030
theaagltd@aol.com

Lone Ranger Fan Club
19205 Seneca Ridge Court,
Gaithersburg, MD 20879-3135

GLASS

American Carnival Glass Association
9621 Springwater Lane,
Miamisburg, OH 45342

Land of Sunshine Depression Glass Club
P.O. Box 560275, Orlando,
FL 32856-0275
Tel: 407 298 3355

HATPINS

American Hatpin Society
20 Montecillo Dr, Rolling Hills
Estates, CA 90274-4249
Tel: 310 326 2196
hatpnginia@aol.com
www.collectorsonline.com/AHS

KITCHENALIA

Kitchen Antiques & Collectibles News
4645 Laurel Ridge Dr,
Harrisburg, PA 17119

MARBLES

Marble Collectors Unlimited
P.O. Box 206, Northborough,
MA 01532-0206 USA
marblesbev@aol.com

MECHANICAL MUSIC

Musical Box Society International
700 Walnut Hill Rd,
Hockessin DE 19707
Tel: 302 239 5658
cotps@aol.com
www.mbsi.org

MILITARIA

Civil War Collectors & The American Militaria Exchange
5970 Toylor Ridge Dr,
West Chester, OH 45069
Tel: 513 874 0483
rwmorgan@aol.com
www.civiwar-collectors.com

OPTICAL, MEDICAL, SCIENTIFIC & TECHNICAL

International Association of Calculator Collectors
P.O. Box 345, Tustin,
CA 92781-0345
Tel: 714 730 6140
Fax: 714 730 6140
mrcalc@usa.net
www.geocities.com/siliconvalley
/park/7227/

PENS & WRITING

The Society of Inkwell Collectors
P.O. Box 324, Mossville,
IL 61552
Tel: 309 579 3040
director@soic.com
www.soic.com

Pen Collectors of America
P.O. Box 80, Redding Ridge,
CT 06876
www.pencollectors.com

PEZ

Pez Collectors News
P.O. Box 14956, Surfside
Beach, SC 29587
info@pezcollectorsnews.com
www.pezcollectorsnews.com

ROCK N ROLL

Elvis Forever TCB Fan Club
P.O. Box 1066, Miami, FL
33780-1066

Working Class Hero Beatles Club
3311 Niagara St, Pittsburgh,
PA 1213-4223

SCENT BOTTLES

International Perfume Bottle Association
396 Croton Rd,
Wayne, PA 19087
Tel: 610-995-9051
jcabbott@bellatlantic.net
www.perfumebottles.org

SMOKING

Cigarette Lighter Collectors' Club
SPARK International
intSpark@aol.com
http://members.aol.com/intspark

Pocket Lighter Preservation Guild & Historical Society, Inc.
P.O. Box 1054, Addison,
IL 60101-8054
Tel: 708 543 9120

SNOWDOMES

Snowdome Collectors' Club
P.O. Box 53262, Washington,
DC 20009-9262

SPORTING MEMORABILIA

Boxing & Pugilistica Collectors International
P.O. Box 83135, Portland,
OR 97283-0135
Tel: 502 286 3597

Golf Collectors' Society
P.O. Box 24102, Cleveland,
OH 44124
Tel: 216 861 1615
www.golfcollectors.com

National Fishing Lure Collectors' Club
H.C. 33, Box 4012, Reeds
Spring, MO 65737
spurr@kingfisher.com

Society for American Baseball Research
812 Huron Rd, E. 719,
Cleveland, OH 441155
info@sabr.org
www.sabr.org

TEXTILES & COSTUME

The Costume Society of America
55 Edgwater Dr, P.O. Box 73,
Earleville, MD 21919-0073
Tel: 410 275 1619
www.costumesocietyamerica.com

American Fan Collectors' Association
P.O. Box 5473, Sarasota, FL
34277-5473
Tel: 817 267 9851
Fax: 817 267 0387

International Old Lacers
P.O. Box 554, Flanders,
NJ 07836
iolinc@aol.com

TOYS & GAMES

Annalee Doll Society
P.O.Box 1137, Meredith,
NH 03253
Tel: 800 433-6557
Fax: 603 279-6659

The Antique Toy Collectors' of America, Inc
C/o Carter, Ledyard & Milburn,
Two Wall St (13th Floor),
New York, NY 10005

Chess Collectors' International
P.O. Box 166, Commack,
NY 11725-0166
Tel: 516 543 1330
lichness@aol.com

National Model Railroad Association
4121 Cromwell Rd,
Chattanooga, TN 37421
Tel: 423 892 2846
nmra@tttrains.com

Toy Soldier Collectors of America
5340 40th Ave N, Saint
Petersburg, FL 33709
Tel: 727 527 1430

United Federation of Doll Clubs
10920 N. Ambassador Dr,
Kansas City, MO 64153
Tel: 816-891-7040
ufdc@aol.com

WATCHES

Early American Watch Club
P.O. Box 81555, Wellesley Hills,
MA 02481-1333

National Association of Watch & Clock Collectors
514 Poplar St, Columbia,
PA 17512-2130
Tel: 717 684 8261
www.nawacc.org

WINE & DRINKING

International Correspondence of Corkscrew Addicts
670 Meadow Wood Road
Mississauga Ontario,
L5J 2S6 Canada
dugohuzo@aol.com
www.corkscrewnet.com/icca

COLLECTING ON THE INTERNET

■ The internet has revolutionised the trading of collectibles. Compared to a piece of furniture, most collectibles are easily defined, described and photographed. Shipping is also comparatively easy, due to average size and weight. Prices are also generally more affordable and accessible than for antiques and the Internet has provided a cost effective way of buying and selling, away from the overheads of shops and auction rooms. Many millions of collectibles are offered for sale and traded daily, with sites varying from global online marketplaces, such as eBay, to specialist dealers' websites.

■ When searching online, remember that some people may not know how to accurately describe their item. General category searches, even though more time consuming, and even purposefully misspelling a name, can yield results. Also, if something looks too good to be true, it probably is. Using this book to get to know your market visually, so that you can tell the difference between a real bargain and something that sounds like one, is a good start.

■ As you will understand from buying this book, color photography is vital – look for online listings that include as many images as possible and check them carefully. Beware that colors can appear differently, even between computer screens.

■ Always ask the vendor questions about the object, particularly regarding condition. If there is no image, or you want to see another aspect of the object – ask. Most sellers (private or trade) will want to realise the best price for their items so will be more than happy to help – if approached politely and sensibly.

■ As well as the 'e-hammer' price, you will probably have to pay additional transactional fees such as packing, shipping and possibly regional or national taxes. It is always best to ask for an estimate for these additional costs before leaving a bid. This will also help you tailor your bid as you will have an idea of the maximum price the item will cost if you are successful.

■ As well as the well-known online auction sites, such as eBay, there is a host of other online resources for buying and selling, for example fair and auction date listings.

INTERNET RESOURCES

Live Auctioneers
www.liveauctioneers.com
info@liveauctioneers.com
A free service which allows users to search catalogs from selected auction houses in Europe, the USA and the United Kingdom. Through its connection with eBay, users can bid live via the Internet into salerooms as auctions happen. Registered users can also search through an archive of past catalogs and receive a free newsletter by email.

invaluable.com
www.invaluable.com
sales@invaluable.com
A subscription service which allows users to search selected auction house catalogs from the United Kingdom and Europe. Also offers an extensive archive for appraisal uses.

The Antiques Trade Gazette
www.atg-online.com
The online version of the UK trade newspaper, comprising British auction and fair listings, news and events.

Maine Antiques Digest
www.maineantiquesdigest.com
The online version of America's trade newspaper including news, articles, fair and auction listings and more.

La Gazette du Drouot
www.drouot.com
The online home of the magazine listing all auctions to be held in France at the Hotel de Drouot in Paris and beyond. An online subscription enables you to download the magazine online.

Auctionnet.com
www.auctionnet.com
Simple online resource listing over 500 websites related to auctions online.

AuctionBytes
www.auctionbytes.com
Auction resource with community forum, news, events, tips and a weekly newsletter.

Auctiontalk
www.auctiontalk.com
Auction news, online and offline auction search engines and live chat forums.

Go Antiques/Antiqnet
www.goantiques.com
www.antiqnet.com
An online global aggregator for art, antiques and collectibles dealers who showcase their stock online, allowing users to browse and buy.

eBay
www.ebay.com
Undoubtedly the largest and most diverse of the online auction sites, allowing users to buy and sell in an online marketplace with over 52 million registered users. Collectors should also view eBay Live Auctions (www.ebayliveauctions.com) where traditional auctions are combined with realtime, online bidding allowing users to interact with the saleroom as the auction takes place.

Tias
www.tias.com
An online global aggregator for art, antiques and collectibles dealers who showcase their stock online, allowing users to browse and buy.

Collectors Online
www.collectorsonline.com
An online global aggregator for art, antiques and collectibles dealers who showcase their stock online, allowing users to browse and buy.

INDEX

A